41: *Afro-American Poets Since 1955*, edited by Trudier Harris and Thadious M. Davis (1985)

42: *American Writers for Children Before 1900*, edited by Glenn E. Estes (1985)

43: *American Newspaper Journalists, 1690-1872*, edited by Perry J. Ashley (1986)

44: *American Screenwriters*, Second Series, edited by Randall Clark, Robert E. Morsberger, and Stephen O. Lesser (1986)

45: *American Poets, 1880-1945*, First Series, edited by Peter Quartermain (1986)

46: *American Literary Publishing Houses, 1900-1980: Trade and Paperback*, edited by Peter Dzwonkoski (1986)

47: *American Historians, 1866-1912*, edited by Clyde N. Wilson (1986)

48: *American Poets, 1880-1945*, Second Series, edited by Peter Quartermain (1986)

49: *American Literary Publishing Houses, 1638-1899*, 2 parts, edited by Peter Dzwonkoski (1986)

50: *Afro-American Writers Before the Harlem Renaissance*, edited by Trudier Harris (1986)

51: *Afro-American Writers from the Harlem Renaissance to 1940*, edited by Trudier Harris (19ᶜ

52: *American Writers for Children Since 1960: Fiction*, edited by Glenn E. Estes (1986)

53: *Canadian Writers Since 1960*, First Series, edited by W. H. New (1986)

54: *American Poets, 1880-1945*, Third Series, 2 parts, edited by Peter Quartermain (1987)

55: *Victorian Prose Writers Before 1867*, edited by William B. Thesing (1987)

56: *German Fiction Writers, 1914-1945*, edited by James Hardin (1987)

57: *Victorian Prose Writers After 1867*, edited by William B. Thesing (1987)

58: *Jacobean and Caroline Dramatists*, edited by Fredson Bowers (1987)

59: *American Literary Critics and Scholars, 1800-1850*, edited by John W. Rathbun and Monica M. Grecu (1987)

60: *Canadian Writers Since 1960*, Second Series, edited by W. H. New (1987)

61: *American Writers for Children Since 1960: Poets, Illustrators, and Nonfiction Authors*, edited by Glenn E. Estes (1987)

62: *Elizabethan Dramatists*, edited by Fredson Bowers (1987)

63: *Modern American Critics, 1920-1955*, edited by Gregory S. Jay (1988)

64: *American Literary Critics and Scholars, 1850-1880*, edited by John W. Rathbun and Monica M. Grecu (1988)

65: *French Novelists, 1900-1930*, edited by Catharine Savage Brosman (1988)

66: *German Fiction Writers, 1885-1913*, 2 parts, edited by James Hardin (1988)

67: *Modern American Critics Since 1955*, edited by Gregory S. Jay (1988)

68: *Canadian Writers, 1920-1959*, First Series, edited by W. H. New (1988)

69: *Contemporary German Fiction Writers*, First Series, edited by Wolfgang D. Elfe and James Hardin (1988)

70: *British Mystery Writers, 1860-1919*, edited by Bernard Benstock and Thomas F. Staley (1988)

71: *American Literary Critics and Scholars, 1880-1900*, edited by John W. Rathbun and Monica M. Grecu (1988)

72: *French Novelists, 1930-1960*, edited by Catharine Savage Brosman (1988)

73: *American Magazine Journalists, 1741-1850*, edited by Sam G. Riley (1988)

74: *American Short-Story Writers Before 1880*, edited by Bobby Ellen Kimbel, with the assistance of William E. Grant (1988)

75: *Contemporary German Fiction Writers*, Second Series, edited by Wolfgang D. Elfe and James Hardin (1988)

76: *Afro-American Writers, 1940-1955*, edited by Trudier Harris (1988)

77: *British Mystery Writers, 1920-1939*, edited by Bernard Benstock and Thomas F. Staley (1988)

78: *American Short-Story Writers, 1880-1910*, edited by Bobby Ellen Kimbel, with the assistance of William E. Grant (1988)

79: *American Magazine Journalists, 1850-1900*, edited by Sam G. Riley (1988)

(Continued on back endsheets)

Nineteenth-Century French Fiction Writers: Romanticism and Realism, 1800-1860

Nineteenth-Century French Fiction Writers: Romanticism and Realism, 1800-1860

Edited by
Catharine Savage Brosman
Tulane University

A Bruccoli Clark Layman Book
Gale Research Inc.
Detroit, London

For Paul and Kate

Contents

Plan of the Series.....................................ix

Introduction..xi

Acknowledgments......................................xix

Honoré de Balzac (1799-1850) 3
  Allan H. Pasco

Jules-Amédée Barbey d'Aurevilly
  (1808-1889)......................................33
  Will L. McLendon

Pétrus Borel (1809-1859) 49
  Norman Araujo

Champfleury (Jules-François-Félix Husson)
  (1821-1889)......................................62
  K. G. McWatters

François-René de Chateaubriand
  (1768-1848)......................................72
  John R. Williams

Benjamin Constant (1767-1830) 90
  Dennis Wood

Alexandre Dumas *père* (1802-1870)....................98
  Barbara T. Cooper

Gustave Flaubert (1821-1880)........................120
  Stirling Haig

Théophile Gautier (1811-1872) 151
  Albert B. Smith

Victor Hugo (1802-1885) 164
  Timothy Raser

Prosper Mérimée (1803-1870) 193
  Scott D. Carpenter

Henry Murger (1822-1861) 206
  Harry Redman, Jr.

Charles Nodier (1780-1844)...........................215
  Grant Crichfield

George Sand (Amantine-Aurore-Lucile
  Dupin) (1804-1876).............................238
  David A. Powell

Etienne de Senancour (1770-1846) 255
  Martha Noel Evans

Germaine de Staël (Anne-Louise Germaine
  de Staël-Holstein) (1766-1817) 262
  Madelyn Gutwirth

Stendhal (Marie-Henri Beyle) (1783-1842) 282
  James T. Day

Eugène Sue (Marie-Joseph Sue)
  (1804-1857)....................................300
  Ian Pickup

Alfred de Vigny (1797-1863).........................312
  Robert T. Denommé

Checklist of Further Readings 334

Contributors..337

Cumulative Index....................................339

Plan of the Series

. . . Almost the most prodigious asset of a country, and perhaps its most precious possession, is its native literary product—when that product is fine and noble and enduring.

Mark Twain*

The advisory board, the editors, and the publisher of the *Dictionary of Literary Biography* are joined in endorsing Mark Twain's declaration. The literature of a nation provides an inexhaustible resource of permanent worth. We intend to make literature and its creators better understood and more accessible to students and the reading public, while satisfying the standards of teachers and scholars.

To meet these requirements, *literary biography* has been construed in terms of the author's achievement. The most important thing about a writer is his writing. Accordingly, the entries in *DLB* are career biographies, tracing the development of the author's canon and the evolution of his reputation.

The purpose of *DLB* is not only to provide reliable information in a convenient format but also to place the figures in the larger perspective of literary history and to offer appraisals of their accomplishments by qualified scholars.

The publication plan for *DLB* resulted from two years of preparation. The project was proposed to Bruccoli Clark by Frederick C. Ruffner, president of the Gale Research Company, in November 1975. After specimen entries were prepared and typeset, an advisory board was formed to refine the entry format and develop the series rationale. In meetings held during 1976, the publisher, series editors, and advisory board approved the scheme for a comprehensive biographical dictionary of persons who contributed to North American literature. Editorial work on the first volume began in January 1977, and it was published in 1978. In order to make *DLB* more than a reference tool and to compile volumes

that individually have claim to status as literary history, it was decided to organize volumes by topic, period, or genre. Each of these freestanding volumes provides a biographical-bibliographical guide and overview for a particular area of literature. We are convinced that this organization—as opposed to a single alphabet method—constitutes a valuable innovation in the presentation of reference material. The volume plan necessarily requires many decisions for the placement and treatment of authors who might properly be included in two or three volumes. In some instances a major figure will be included in separate volumes, but with different entries emphasizing the aspect of his career appropriate to each volume. Ernest Hemingway, for example, is represented in *American Writers in Paris, 1920-1939* by an entry focusing on his expatriate apprenticeship; he is also in *American Novelists, 1910-1945* with an entry surveying his entire career. Each volume includes a cumulative index of the subject authors and articles. Comprehensive indexes to the entire series are planned.

With volume ten in 1982 it was decided to enlarge the scope of *DLB*. By the end of 1986 twenty-one volumes treating British literature had been published, and volumes for Commonwealth and Modern European literature were in progress. The series has been further augmented by the *DLB Yearbooks* (since 1981) which update published entries and add new entries to keep the *DLB* current with contemporary activity. There have also been *DLB Documentary Series* volumes which provide biographical and critical source materials for figures whose work is judged to have particular interest for students. One of these companion volumes is entirely devoted to Tennessee Williams.

We define literature as the *intellectual commerce of a nation:* not merely as belles lettres but as that ample and complex process by which ideas are generated, shaped, and transmitted. *DLB* entries are not limited to "creative writers" but extend to other figures who in their time and in their way influenced the mind of a people. Thus the series encompasses historians, journalists, publishers, and screenwriters. By this means

*From an unpublished section of Mark Twain's autobiography, copyright © by the Mark Twain Company

readers of *DLB* may be aided to perceive literature not as cult scripture in the keeping of intellectual high priests but firmly positioned at the center of a nation's life.

DLB includes the major writers appropriate to each volume and those standing in the ranks immediately behind them. Scholarly and critical counsel has been sought in deciding which minor figures to include and how full their entries should be. Wherever possible, useful references are made to figures who do not warrant separate entries.

Each *DLB* volume has a volume editor responsible for planning the volume, selecting the figures for inclusion, and assigning the entries. Volume editors are also responsible for preparing, where appropriate, appendices surveying the major periodicals and literary and intellectual movements for their volumes, as well as lists of further readings. Work on the series as a whole is coordinated at the Bruccoli Clark Layman editorial center in Columbia, South Carolina, where the editorial staff is responsible for accuracy of the published volumes.

One feature that distinguishes *DLB* is the illustration policy—its concern with the iconography of literature. Just as an author is influenced by his surroundings, so is the reader's understanding of the author enhanced by a knowledge of his environment. Therefore *DLB* volumes include not only drawings, paintings, and photographs of authors, often depicting them at various stages in their careers, but also illustrations of their families and places where they lived. Title pages are regularly reproduced in facsimile along with dust jackets for modern authors. The dust jackets are a special feature of *DLB* because they often document better than anything else the way in which an author's work was perceived in its own time. Specimens of the writers' manuscripts are included when feasible.

Samuel Johnson rightly decreed that "The chief glory of every people arises from its authors." The purpose of the *Dictionary of Literary Biography* is to compile literary history in the surest way available to us—by accurate and comprehensive treatment of the lives and work of those who contributed to it.

The *DLB* Advisory Board

Introduction

To many readers of literature in both French- and English-speaking countries, the nineteenth century in France is preeminently the age of the novel. Although commentators have often proclaimed drama to be the dominant genre in France, chiefly because of the brilliant achievements of the great classical dramatists of the seventeenth century, the two centuries of writing that followed the Revolution of 1789 were most prominently marked by fiction. It is sometimes assumed even that French fiction is chiefly a creation of the nineteenth century. To be sure, in some ways, the Romantic and realistic novels that flourished in the 1800s represent a break from eighteenth-century models, in both content and style. But it was the prerevolutionary authors—l'abbé Antoine-François Prévost, Denis Diderot, Pierre Carlet de Chamblain de Marivaux, Jean-Jacques Rousseau, and Choderlos de Laclos—who, through their craftsmanship and their use of the form to express individual emotions and evoke the social reality of their time, developed the novel into a major genre.

Jean-Paul Sartre observed in *Qu'est-ce que la littérature?* (1947; translated as *What is Literature?*, 1949) that the eighteenth century was the first period in France in which writers were not subservient to a conservative institution—throne, aristocracy, church; rather, they acted as spokesmen for a developing, and literate, middle class with its concerns, to whom self-expression and self-examination, in both writing and politics, were becoming increasingly important. In *The Rise of the Novel* (1960), Ian Watt connected the appearance of the form in eighteenth-century England with the rise to prominence of the middle classes. Similarly, in France in the period of cultural transition between the death of Louis XIV in 1715—which brought to a tardy end the cultural hegemony of the previous century—and 1800, the novel flourished as literacy and readership expanded greatly among the bourgeoisie; it is estimated by Hadyn Mason in *French Writers and Their Society, 1715-1800* (1982) that in the eighteenth century there were 250,000 people in France who could read. The middle class furnished not only readers but writers; with the exception of Charles-Louis de Secondat, Baron de Montesquieu, the major literary figures were self-made men from the middle classes. Doubtless the freedom offered by the novel and the story—a freedom deriving from the fact that there were no classical models—contributed to the popularity of these genres among writers and readers.

It can be argued, then, that the novel was a plausible choice for those who were to create a new literature after the fall of the ancien régime. In nineteenth-century France nearly all the important literary figures chose the form as at least one of their genres, usually the major one. (The chief exceptions are the pre-Symbolist and Symbolist giants: Charles Baudelaire, Stéphane Mallarmé, and Arthur Rimbaud.) The literary landscape after 1800 is marked by monumental achievements in fiction by writers some of whom themselves are monumental. Honoré de Balzac's title *La Comédie humaine* (The Human Comedy, 1842-1855; translated, 1895-1900), with its suggestion of universality, fits well its creator's vast ambitions, energies, and visions, both artistic and social. Victor Hugo's first great novel, *Notre-Dame de Paris* (1831; translated, 1832), dominates Romantic fiction the way the cathedral dominates the city in his masterful reconstruction, and the way he himself dominated the 1800s in France, by his genius, his energies, and his massive literary production. Gustave Flaubert, the great mid-century realist who rejected romanticism, produced two weighty novels considered masterpieces—*Madame Bovary* (1857; translated, 1881) and *L'Education sentimentale* (1869; translated as *Sentimental Education*, 1898)—plus outstanding long stories. He also set the example of the writer so devoted to his art that all other considerations became secondary, and so obsessed with craft that he rewrote not just sentences and pages but entire works. As a master of fictional style and a technical innovator, he occupies a crucial position in French fiction, a position recognized by such figures as Henry James and Sartre, who paid him oblique homage by a massive psychobiography. Emile Zola, whose work will be treated in a companion volume to this one, stands out in the second half of the century not only as the author of a massive series of novels, *Les Rougon-Macquart* (1871-1893; translated as *The Rougon-Macquarts*, 1896-1900), whose aim was to chronicle an entire society, but also as a theoretician of naturalism and a heroic figure whose political convictions led him to leap into the battle that raged around the 1894 court-martial and ensuing conviction of Capt. Alfred Dreyfus for espionage.

To these towering figures, who created fictional worlds that, in the readers' minds, often rival or stand for the actual historical worlds in which they are set, one can add the name of Stendhal (Marie-Henri Beyle), the author of *Le Rouge et le noir* (1830; translated as *The Red and the Black*, 1913), underrated by readers and critics in his own time—Balzac being a striking exception—but considered since the late 1880s as the premier psychologist among nineteenth-century novelists and one of the most acute students of social dynamics that France has produced. Prosper Mérimée, while not a literary giant, left a body of stories known throughout the world; Flaubert's pupil, Guy de Maupassant, less appreciated perhaps in his own country than abroad, stands out as a peerless practitioner of the short story. If one adds to this list such novelists as Edmond and Jules de Goncourt, George Sand, Alexandre Dumas *père*, and Anatole France, as well as a score of additional well-recognized fiction writers of the century, and if one considers the massive output of many on the list, one sees how dominant fiction was during the period in France and with what impressive results it was cultivated.

Throughout the later nineteenth century and part of the twentieth, the popularity of French fiction was demonstrated by many editions of collected works by major Romantic and realist authors—often dozens of volumes in each—in both the original language and translation. Toward the mid twentieth century, after the upheaval of one world war, then another, and with a deep cultural crisis reaching to the heart of literature, it might have appeared that, except for Stendhal, the giants of the previous century would lose their standing, to be replaced by the avant-garde artists of modernism, or the committed writers of the 1930s and 1940s, or, after 1950, those who cultivated the New Novel and the literature of the absurd. The novel itself was attacked by the poet Paul Valéry, for instance, and the Surrealists, then the New Novelists, such as Alain Robbe-

Grillet, who, while publishing books called novels, undermined methodically the aesthetic of representation on which the novel had rested since the eighteenth century. But recent decades have shown that to readers and critics alike nineteenth-century fiction retains great literary vitality. New editions of Stendhal, Balzac, Flaubert, and Zola find buyers among the general reading public in France. Similarly, both historical scholarship and critical inquiry on major figures and some lesser ones have flourished; indeed, renowned critics such as Roland Barthes, in *S/Z* (1970), and respected university scholars have shown the fecundity of postmodern critical positions with respect to authors so apparently tied to their age as Balzac and Flaubert.

The reasons for this ongoing interest in nineteenth-century fiction and the new critical approaches that have been taken toward it will be suggested by the essays that follow. It will be useful here to survey briefly the development of fiction in France and especially of the eighteenth-century background against which Romantic and realist fiction developed. The term *roman* (translated first as *romance*, then as *novel*), which comes from Old French *romanz*, initially signified the vernacular tongue, then, from the twelfth century, a work, in prose or verse, in that tongue. Such examples as *Le Roman d'Alexandre* (twelfth century), Chrétien de Troye's *Yvain, ou Le Chevalier au lion* (twelfth century; called a *roman courtois* or courtly romance), the anonymous *Roman de Renart* (late twelfth century), and, somewhat later, the *Roman de la Rose* (thirteenth century), by Guillaume de Lorris and Jean de Meung, which Geoffrey Chaucer helped translate as the *Romaunt of the Rose* (fourteenth century), illustrate the wide variance in uses of the term, from narratives of adventures in the pseudoantique mode and stories of chivalric quests, intended for a courtly audience, through a collection of satiric tales of animals, to the elaborate allegory spun around the image of the rose, which caught up the medieval imagination in the webs of love and jealousy.

With the replacement in the sixteenth century of nearly all medieval genres by ancient ones, when the Renaissance humanists gained wide access to and deliberately cultivated the forms of antiquity, the courtly romance nearly disappeared; but vestiges remained in the pastoral novel and the novel of adventures, which flourished in France in the seventeenth century following models by Italian and Spanish writers. Similarly, the popular tales that had appeared in the

Roman de Renart, in the shorter medieval verse narratives called *fabliaux*, and in the *Cent nouvelles nouvelles* (fifteenth century; translated as *One Hundred Merrie and Delightsome Stories*, 1899) are not without connection to the *Heptaméron* (1558; translated, 1654) of Marguerite de Navarre (the sister of Francis I), who also borrowed from Italian models. While often mixed with fantasy or farce, the mimetic, or imitative, impulse so important to the modern novel of representation is found in many of these forms, whether in their concern for human psychology or the depiction of manners.

Until the latter part of the seventeenth century, however, there is little on the French literary landscape that can be called a novel in the modern sense, in which the marvelous and the artificial are replaced by a close and extensive study of the human heart or mores, or both. Samuel Richardson wrote that seventeenth-century French narratives "dealt so much in the marvelous and improbable, or were so unnaturally inflaming to the passions and so full of love and intrigue, that most of them seem calculated to fire the imagination rather than inform the judgment." With *La Princesse de Clèves* (1678; translated, 1679) by Marie-Madeleine, Comtesse de La Fayette, the French psychological novel was born. Its judicious analysis of conflicting sentiments and motivations is not the only mode of the French novel—far from it—and especially not during the nineteenth century, but for many readers the type remains a major strain, and such novels as Benjamin Constant's *Adolphe* (1816; translated, 1816) and Eugène Fromentin's *Dominique* (1863; translated, 1948) are close in spirit to Mme de La Fayette's masterpiece.

Georges May is one of several critics who has stressed the importance, for the development of fiction, of the claim to *truth* that began to characterize novels from the late 1600s on—a claim that provides some of the foundation for nineteenth-century realism. As Pierre Daniel Huet noted in *De l'origine des romans* (On the Origin of Novels, 1670): "Novels are fictions of things that might have existed but did not." The eighteenth century, during which some three thousand novels were published in France, produced a wide variety of styles. Such types as the epistolary novel and the novel in the form of memoirs, which had as a model the *Mémoires du Sieur de Pontis* (1676), by Louis de Pontis, laid claim, by their first-person voice and other features, to reality. "The word memoir," wrote Richard Steele, "is French for a novel." Dozens of writers, both

men and women, exploited these forms, and undeterred by what seems to modern taste the excessive length of the works, eighteenth-century readers devoured them.

At the same time, Voltaire (François-Marie Arouet le jeune) developed the philosophical tale, with *Zadig* (1747; translated, 1749) and *Candide* (1759; translated, 1864), and Diderot used, in addition to such types as the Oriental tale and the memoir-novel, his own creation, the dialogue form, as illustrated in *Le Neveu de Rameau* (1823; translated as *Rameau's Nephew*, 1897), *Jacques le Fataliste et son maître* (1796; translated as *James the Fatalist and His Master*, 1797), and "Ceci n'est pas un conte," whose title ("This Is Not a Story") and whose form—a dialogue with a reader-character—call into question in a modern way its own form and raison d'être.

This development of the novel, which would be followed by an immense production in the next century (although Diderot's inventive forms would have few parallels until André Gide and other twentieth-century figures produced their own type of metafiction—a fiction that takes itself as its topic, investigating the ontology and epistemology of imaginative writing), took place against an intellectual and social background that deserves examination. Whereas philosophical and political thought in the eighteenth century—the first cultural period in France to give itself a name (l'Age des Lumières, or Age of Enlightenment)—was chiefly rationalistic, the arts were marked by two somewhat contradictory strains, reason and feeling. In the previous century, Cartesian rationalism had given rise to or favored the scientific thought of the early modern period, but had not generally penetrated the area of political thought, where institutionalized authoritarianism in the form of absolute monarchy and church provided its own rationalism based on the authority of Scripture and tradition. After the death of Louis XIV and the ensuing Regency (1715-1723)—and despite the continued dominance of a nearly monolithic church and state—Cartesian reason was turned increasingly toward criticism of the principles of revealed religion and arbitrary royal power and their philosophical underpinnings. By their commanding intellects, Montesquieu, Voltaire, Diderot, and Rousseau all used critical reason to attack, in varying degrees, political and religious tyranny, ultimately with the implication that, since reason is universal, it alone should be the basis for society, in which all have an equal claim to authority.

Traceable through Montesquieu's *Lettres persanes* (1721; translated as *Persian Letters*, 1722) and *De l'esprit des lois* (1748; translated as *The Spirit of Laws*, 1750), Voltaire's *Lettres philosophiques* (1734; originally published in English as *Letters Concerning the English Nation*, 1733) and countless other texts, as well as Rousseau's *Contract social* (1762; translated as *The Social Contract*, 1893), surely one of the most influential political tracts of all time, the critical spirit found its culmination in the monumental *Encyclopédie* (1750-1780), assembled by Diderot, Jean Lerond d'Alembert, and others. While none of the philosophes just mentioned called for violent overthrow of the monarchy, the cumulative effect of their works, together with the example of the American Revolution, was to channel widespread social unrest and economic frustration into an uprising that resulted in the overthrow of the absolute monarchy and, eventually, regicide, and the establishment of government by popular assembly—a government that, tragically, produced not a stable constitutional republic but the Terror.

The sentimental strain in eighteenth-century literature and thought is not unrelated to the political developments just sketched. Sentimentalism was partly an import from England, through the fiction of Richardson, whose *Pamela* (1740-1741) and *Clarissa* (1747-1748) as translated by Pierre Letourneur were immensely popular. Richardson's focus on the virtue of ordinary men and women was paralleled in the novels of l'abbé Prévost and Marivaux and the fiction and plays of Diderot, among others. This appeal to the feeling of the common man and woman may well reflect readers' reaction against a long-dominant monarchy and oligarchy, whose splendid court life did not conceal the immense cost of recurrent warfare and much popular misery. The sentimental strain was also a response to the literary tyranny of a neoclassical literature that reflected the authority and concerns of the monarchy and followed too closely, for popular taste, the models of antiquity. One should not be surprised to see authors such as Diderot and Rousseau displaying in some areas a commanding critical reason, yet cultivating feeling and insisting that personal virtue, which comes from the heart, was superior—in practice and in principle—to nobility conveyed merely by birth and to morality imposed by authority. Sentimentalism was bolstered by critical reason inasmuch as the latter insisted on its own universality and a corresponding freedom of conscience. Both are the prerogative of the common man, as he was seen by poets and philosophers alike, and whose apotheosis in the Declaration of the Rights of Man (1789) was a political and philosophical revolution of major proportions.

In the artistic domain, sentimentalism produced scores of novels and a whole school of painting (genre painting, in which domestic subjects replaced the heroic ones appreciated by the aristocracy). An associated inspiration, which emphasized meditation in nature, led to a substantial, though now neglected, body of verse, such as that of Jean-François, Marquis de Saint-Lambert, inspired in part by the English poets Edward Young (*Night Thoughts*, translated 1769), and James Thomson (*The Seasons*, translated 1769). Rousseau's oeuvre provides the outstanding examples of these veins. His lengthy novel *Julie ou La Nouvelle Héloïse* (1761; translated as *Julia, or the New Eloisa*, 1773) and his treatise on education, *Emile* (1762; translated, 1911), have domestic subjects, stress the value of the natural, and propose as the guiding principle of life a virtue based on individual conscience. Even more instructive than these fictional works are his *Confessions* (1781 and 1788; translated, 1880) and *Rêveries du promeneur solitaire* (1782; translated as *Reveries of a Solitary*), both of which emphasize the uniqueness and importance of the self, the role of nature, the value of solitude, and natural religion.

Defined sometimes as "freedom in art"—more precisely the throwing off of formal and rationalistic shackles and the proclamation of the individual, especially individual feeling—French romanticism, the last major Romantic movement in Europe, can be divided into two phases: preromanticism, lasting until about 1820, when the publication of Alphonse de Lamartine's *Méditations poétiques* signaled to the reading public at large that the new wave in literature had triumphed; and romanticism proper, when Romantic features triumphed in all major genres, the last being the drama, with the premiere of Victor Hugo's play *Hernani* (1830). One can add perhaps a third phase, the decline of the movement in the 1840s, a decline marked by the failure of Hugo's last Romantic drama, *Les Burgraves*, in 1843, five years before the Orléans monarchy, which had replaced the Bourbons after the "Trois Glorieuses" (three glorious days) of the July Revolution in 1830, itself was replaced by the Second Republic.

Romanticism arose from several historical and literary circumstances: the rejection of classicism and eighteenth-century rationalism; the failure of the Revolution and subsequent cataclysmic social disorder, and the replacement of a popular government by the Napoleonic consulat (1799-1804) and empire (1804-1814), then by the restored Bourbon monarchy until 1830; the influence of sentimentalism, a literature of self-expression, and nature meditations; and various foreign influences.

The traumatic events of the French Revolution and its failure to establish a stable government on the basis of popular sovereignty and to maintain the rational principles of the philosophes—a failure underlined by Napoleon's centralization of authority, creation of a new nobility, and concordat with the church of Rome—were doubtless responsible in great part for the loss of confidence in critical reason that marked the Romantic period. While it had done much to bring about the new structures of the nineteenth century, rationalism was associated with the ancien régime, which had produced it; the example of Voltaire, who was the apostle of reason and a firm enemy of church and monarchy, but had nevertheless written dozens of five-act classical tragedies, is pertinent. In the minds of many who were young around 1800 or later, the eighteenth century became connected with the undermining of stability and faith and the invitation to anarchy. The poet Alfred de Musset, in his *Confession d'un enfant du siècle* (1836; translated as *Confession of a Child of the Century*, 1892), was not the first to assail the Age of Enlightenment for having deprived his generation of religious belief and a reassuring social order; François-René de Chateaubriand had already converted to the Christian faith shortly after 1800, explaining that feeling had triumphed over skepticism: "J'ai pleuré et j'ai cru" (I wept and I believed).

Moreover, somewhat paradoxically, the advent of the new century was seen by many—Chateaubriand is one example, Constant and Alfred de Vigny are others—as constituting not a new age of opportunity but rather the closure of a world that left them little other than disorder or the pragmatic, authoritarian order of Napoleon. The effect of this deception and the sense of betrayal was a malaise that came to be known as the *mal du siècle*—the sickness of the century. This malaise, fostered by the influence of Rousseau, the quintessential maladjusted introvert,

was a central ingredient in early French romanticism.

Other major influences on preromanticism and early romanticism came from abroad. The poems of James Macpherson, the Scotsman who published in 1762 and 1763 poems purporting to be translations from Ossian (a legendary Gaelic bard of the third century A.D.), had a tremendous following in France after Letourneur translated them in 1777; even when it was revealed that the poems bearing Ossian's name were mostly forgeries, many admirers remained under his spell. William Wordsworth and Samuel Taylor Coleridge's *Lyrical Ballads* (1798-1805) attracted less attention in France than one might expect, but there was immense enthusiasm for George Gordon, Lord Byron, and the Byronic hero turns up in fiction as well as poetry and drama. The historical novels of Sir Walter Scott, translated by Auguste Jean Baptiste Defauconpret in the 1820s and widely read, exercised an enormous influence on such figures as Hugo and Vigny. *Die Alpen* (The Alps, 1732), by the Swiss poet Albrecht von Haller, translated in 1750, also was influential, as were the plays of Gotthold Ephraim Lessing and his treatise *Laokoon* (1766; translated as *Laocoon*, 1836), which appeared in French in 1802.

Johann Wolfgang von Goethe's *Die Leiden des jungen Werthers* (1774; translated as *The Sorrows of Werther*, 1779), the story of a romantic suicide, was translated into French fifteen times by 1797, and produced a large literary posterity. The brothers August Wilhelm and Friedrich von Schlegel and Johann Christoph von Schiller were less well known than Goethe, but their influence was important, the former two in the area of aesthetics, the latter as a playwright, whose dramas, such as *Wallenstein* (1799) and *Maria Stuart* (1800), furnished models by which the French could throw off the sway of their own classical structures. The chief influence in the drama was, however, William Shakespeare, partially translated by Pierre-Antoine de la Place (1745-1748), then retranslated by Letourneur (1776-1783), and, by the early 1800s, admired by all the rising Romantic figures. Stendhal's *Racine et Shakespeare* (1823) and Hugo's preface to *Cromwell* (1827) are the best known of the tracts that compared French classical tragedies unfavorably to those of the English writer and called for a new style of writing in French, to which Stendhal gave the name *romanticisme* (the form *romantisme* not yet having been standardized).

The first wave of Romantic authors—Chateaubriand, Germaine de Staël, Etienne de Senancour—display in their novels and other prose a strong emphasis on the individual and feeling, fascination with the primitive and skepticism concerning social institutions and structures (a vogue that owed much to Rousseau), sometimes a taste for the medieval, and dithyrambic enthusiasm for nature. While their works frequently retain the expansiveness that marks most novels of the previous century, these authors show little concern for the forms and techniques of fiction as developed by their predecessors; their novels and tales are often more like meditations than stories. Following this first wave are others who may give similar importance to individual experience but whose romanticism, developed under the influence of Scott, turns toward historical re-creation or at least a striking local color—the sort that marks the fiction of Mérimée as much as the painting of Eugène Delacroix. Violence in action and extremes of emotion; striking contrasts in setting, characters, and images; melodramatic turns of plot; and a dynamic, emphatic prose mark the fiction of such writers as Vigny, Hugo, Charles Nodier, and Mérimée. Some of these authors and others, including Théophile Gautier and Pétrus Borel, were also influenced by the English Gothic novel and the fantastic tales of E. T. A. Hoffmann, Novalis (Friedrich Leopold von Hardenberg), and Joseph von Eichendorff.

By some aspects of their works, Stendhal and Balzac belong to this second group of Romantic novelists who emphasize the violent and the colorful. Balzac's *Le Dernier Chouan* (1829; translated as *The Chouans*, 1889), set in the revolutionary period, includes highly picturesque characters and a melodramatic plot built on contrasts; Stendhal's *Chroniques italiennes* (1855) includes tales of violence and passion. But these two masters may more properly be called Romantic realists. Stendhal's work, even at its most dramatic, is characterized by social criticism, directed at the France of the Restoration and the Orléans monarchy—ruling classes, church, and government. Moreover, like the later realists, he was interested in causality and relied partly on documentation. His great novels are marked also by a psychological incisiveness that is rivaled by few works, and that made Friedrich Nietzsche consider the author of *Le Rouge et le noir* as one of his masters. Balzac, who similarly drew heavily on his observations and documentation, turned his genius to a fictional reconstruction and critique of his own

period—a critique in which the Romantic impulses of the characters and melodramatic turns of plot are counterbalanced by thorough, probing studies of contemporary institutions, classes, and mores.

Except in the theater, there was no clear rupture between French romanticism and its sequels. Indeed, in poetry and in aesthetics generally, the movements that followed—beginning with the Parnassian poets, such as Gautier, Théodore de Banville, and Charles-Marie-René Leconte de Lisle, and the Symbolists, through the early modernism of Marcel Proust and Gide and the surrealism of the 1920s and thereafter—can be considered direct developments of romanticism, the Parnassians and realists similarly emphasizing the concern for the exterior world that differentiated romanticism from classicism, the Symbolists and surrealists, as well as many other modern authors, developing romanticism's concern with the irrational or suprarational. Indeed, to some degree modern French literature as a whole remains Romantic, prizing emotion above reason, the individual above society, spontaneity above reserve, nature above human constructs, and free forms above strict ones. One can nevertheless speak of the demise of the French Romantic movement as such, shortly before the middle of the century, and the rise of major literary reactions, which, in one way or another, all deserve the term *realist*.

A realist, said Gautier, is a man for whom the external world exists. As a literary movement, realism developed, parallel to a similar movement in painting, as the Industrial Revolution finally replaced, on a wide scale, the artisanry of the eighteenth century, opening the way for the making of large fortunes by many in the middle classes, increased prosperity for many more, and the development of urban labor, which would gradually lead to the creation of a French proletariat where, before, there had been only a peasantry and a class of artisans and shopkeepers. This increase in wealth and power for the bourgeoisie was favored by the Revolution of 1830, in which popular uprisings first played a crucial role—the insurgents expected to overturn the monarchy completely and found a new republic—until conservative bourgeois elements intervened to place on the throne Louis-Philippe of the branch of Orléans (1830-1848). Sometimes called the "roi-parapluie" (the umbrella king), he was the first king to wear "bourgeois" dress (a frock coat and trousers).

The disappointments of those who favored a radical revolution color some of the literature of the 1830s and 1840s, in which popular misery appears as a theme and the alienation of the artist from society, which earlier took the form of the *mal du siècle*, becomes violent hatred. The Second Republic, which was proclaimed in February 1848, again with the participation of popular and radical elements, gave encouragement to both liberal-minded thinkers and the radically alienated; but, after an auspicious beginning, it turned violent in the famous "journées de juin" (June days), leading to another conservative reaction. Following the coup d'état of its president, Louis-Napoleon (Napoleon III), in December 1851, the Second Republic became the Second Empire (1852-1870) and ushered in a period of prudery, conservatism, and repression of freedom of the press.

The powerful middle classes, with money to buy books and attend plays, were far more pragmatic than the literary generation that had preceded them, and less interested in reverie than in the issues of the day. Even for the literati, by the 1840s and 1850s romanticism had lost much of its luster. Major figures of the movement were either dead (Chateaubriand and Balzac died about mid century, and Stendhal died even earlier) or had changed their styles and taken up new causes. Hugo had gone through great personal grief and then, after the coup d'état of Napoleon III, went into exile. In the preface to *Mademoiselle de Maupin* (1835), Gautier had adopted the position of "l'art pour l'art" (art for art's sake), although the tale itself is Romantic, as suggested by the subtitle of an 1889 English translation, *A Romance of Love and Passion*. In 1848 Lamartine attempted to carry out in the political arena the social liberalism favored by him and Hugo, another defender of liberty, but failed. Vigny's poem "La Maison du berger" (The Shepherd's Hut, 1844) symbolizes one of the changes of the age by contrasting its pastoral setting with the railroad, which threatens the Romantic spirit. It is true that lurid romanticism, especially in the form of rebellion against society, persisted long, notably in clusters of authors who participated in what Henry Murger identified in his novel by that name as *la vie de bohème* (the bohemian life) and whose slogan was "Epater le bourgeois!" (Amaze the bourgeois!). But a new generation had come to maturity, that of Flaubert and Baudelaire, both born in 1821, who would either deny romanticism or use its own premises to go beyond it.

To many, Flaubert is the supreme figure of realism. Others preceded him by taking the social reality of their own time as their subject: the transitional place of Stendhal and Balzac as Romantic realists has been noted, but their work was bound up in crucial ways with Romantic conventions, including the cult of the individual and belief in passion as the supreme justification and end of life. Still others, such as Jules Husson (Champfleury) and Murger, encouraged by the doctrines of the painter Gustave Courbet, had begun to insist that fiction must render only observable reality, and to portray elements of the lower classes. In 1857, the same year that Flaubert's *Madame Bovary* appeared, Champfleury even published articles collectively titled *Le Réalisme*, which served as a manifesto for the new aesthetic.

But, while he did not accept the label of realist, Flaubert is the first major name to *deny* romanticism as part of an artistic platform, to set as a goal the depiction of the most banal reality imaginable, and to develop a method of composition and a style for rendering this reality that would envelop it, paradoxically, in artistic beauty. His denial of romanticism was almost certainly a type of self-punishment; one way to interpret the famous phrase "Madame Bovary, c'est moi" (I am Madame Bovary) is to see it as a confession of Romantic impulses that would be visible throughout his career, as witness his flamboyant historical novel *Salammbô* (1862; translated, 1885)—impulses that were paralleled by an intense dislike for everything that was mean, ordinary, dull, and venal: in a word, everything that was bourgeois. Flaubert thus is preeminently, with Baudelaire, the writer opposed to his society, spiting and transcending it by making art from its evils and platitudes.

By 1860, the date chosen as the terminus ad quem for this volume, romanticism, with its emphasis on feeling and the irrational, on solitary experience, on nature, passion, and the exotic, was a closed chapter in French literary history, and the real, in the sense of the quotidian, was firmly entrenched as the subject for fiction. The consolidation of realism took place against the political background of the Second Empire, which had charged Flaubert with offense to public morals for publishing *Madame Bovary* but was to be somewhat less repressive in its last decade, and against the ideological background of positivism as illustrated by Auguste Comte, a pragmatic philosophy that holds that only material reality is knowable and implies belief in the progressive amelioration of life through application of a materialist outlook and the scientific method to social problems. The assumption that literature also could be scientific—the underlying assumption of Zola's work—was soon to be made explicit. And the novel, already a widely popular genre in the previous 150 years, had acquired credentials not only as the form most suited to the main literary impulse of mid century—the imitation of everyday life—but as an artistic form as well. The following decades would show how these two roles, the mimetic and the aesthetic, could be developed even further.

—*Catharine Savage Brosman*

Acknowledgments

This book was produced by Bruccoli Clark Layman, Inc. Karen L. Rood is senior editor for the *Dictionary of Literary Biography* series. David Marshall James was the in-house editor.

Production coordinator is James W. Hipp. Projects manager is Charles D. Brower. Photography editors are Edward Scott and Timothy C. Lundy. Layout and graphics supervisor is Penney L. Haughton. Copyediting supervisor is Bill Adams. Typesetting supervisor is Kathleen M. Flanagan. Systems manager is George F. Dodge. The production staff includes Rowena Betts, Steve Borsanyi, Teresa Chaney, Patricia Coate, Rebecca Crawford, Henry Cuningham, Margaret McGinty Cureton, Bonita Dingle, Mary Scott Dye, Denise Edwards, Sarah A. Estes, Robert Fowler, Mary Lee Goodwin, Avril E. Gregory, Ellen McCracken, Kathy Lawler Merlette, John Myrick, Pamela D. Norton, Thomas J. Pickett, Maxine K. Smalls, and Jennifer C. J. Turley.

Walter W. Ross and Dennis Lynch did library research. They were assisted by the following librarians at the Thomas Cooper Library of the University of South Carolina: Jens Holley and the interlibrary-loan staff; reference librarians Gwen Baxter, Daniel Boice, Faye Chadwell, Jo Cottingham, Cathy Eckman, Rhonda Felder, Gary Geer, Jackie Kinder, Laurie Preston, Jean Rhyne, Carol Tobin, Virginia Weathers, and Connie Widney; circulation-department head Thomas Marcil; and acquisitions-searching supervisor David Haggard.

Nineteenth-Century French Fiction Writers: Romanticism and Realism, 1800-1860

Dictionary of Literary Biography

Honoré de Balzac
(Honoré Balzac)
(20 May 1799 - 18 August 1850)

Allan H. Pasco
University of Kansas

BOOKS: *L'Héritière de Birague*, as Lord R'Hoone, with others, 4 volumes (Paris: Hubert, 1822);

Jean-Louis, ou la Fille trouvée, as Lord R'Hoone, with others, 4 volumes (Paris: Hubert, 1822);

Clotilde de Lusignan, ou le Beau Juif, as Lord R'Hoone, 4 volumes (Paris: Hubert, 1822);

Le Centenaire, ou les Deux Béringheld, as Horace de Saint-Aubin, 4 volumes (Paris: Pollet, 1822);

Le Vicaire des Ardennes, as Horace de Saint-Aubin, 4 volumes (Paris: Pollet, 1822);

La Dernière Fée, ou la Nouvelle Lampe merveilleuse, as Horace de Saint-Aubin, 2 volumes (Paris: Barba, Hubert Mondor, Bobée, 1823; enlarged edition, 3 volumes, Paris: Delongchamps, 1824);

Annette et le criminel, as Horace de Saint-Aubin, 4 volumes (Paris: Emile Buissot, 1824);

Du droit d'ainesse, anonymous (Paris: Delongchamps, 1824);

Histoire impartiale des Jésuites, anonymous (Paris: Delongchamps, Maze, 1824);

Wann-Chlore, anonymous, 4 volumes (Paris: Canel et Delongchamps, 1825);

Code des gens honnêtes, ou l'Art de ne pas être dupe des fripons, anonymous (Paris: J. - N. Barba, 1825);

Physiologie du mariage, ou Méditations de philosophie éclectique sur le bonheur et le malheur conjugal, anonymous (Paris: Balzac, 1826; revised and augmented edition, Paris: Levavasseur et Urbain Canel, 1829; revised and

Honoré de Balzac, 1829 (portrait by Louis Boulanger; Musée de Versailles)

augmented edition, Paris: Ollivier, 1834); revised in *La Comédie humaine* (Paris: Furne, 1846); translated as *Physiology of Marriage*

3

(Philadelphia, 1899);

Le Dernier Chouan, ou la Bretagne en 1800, 4 volumes (Paris: Urbain Canel, 1829); revised as *Les Chouans, ou la Bretagne en 1799*, 2 volumes (Paris: Charles Vimont, 1834); revised in *La Comédie humaine* (1845); translated by George Saintsbury as *The Chouans* (London: Nimmo, 1889);

Les Dangers de l'inconduite, in *Scènes de la vie privée*, volume 1 (Paris: Mame et Delaunay-Vallée, 1830); revised as *Le Papa Gobseck* in *Scènes de la vie parisienne, Etudes de mœurs au XIXᵉ siècle*, volume 9 (Paris: Mme Charles Béchet, 1835); republished as *Gobseck* in *La Comédie humaine* (1842); translated by Katherine Prescott Wormeley in *Gobseck and Other Stories* (Boston: Roberts Brothers, 1896);

Gloire et malheur, in *Scènes de la vie privée*, volume 2 (Paris: Mame et Delaunay-Vallée, 1830; revised edition, Paris: Mme Charles Béchet, 1835); revised as *La Maison du chat-qui-pelote* in *La Comédie humaine* (1842); translated by Philip Kent as *The Cat and Battledore, and Other Tales* (Chicago: Belfords, Clark, 1879);

La Peau de chagrin, 2 volumes (Paris: Gosselin et Canel, 1831); revised in *Romans et contes philosophiques*, volumes 1-2 (Paris: Gosselin, 1831; revised, 1833); republished in *Etudes philosophiques*, volumes 1-4 (Paris: Werdet, 1835); republished in *La Comédie humaine* (1845); translated as *Luck and Leather. A Parisian Romance* (Boston: Brainard, 1843);

Les Deux Rêves, in *Romans et contes philosophiques*, volume 3 (Paris: Gosselin, 1831); republished with *Le Secret des Ruggieri* in *Etudes philosophiques*, volume 13 (Paris: Werdet, 1837); collected with *Le Secret des Ruggieri* and *Le Martyr calviniste* in *Catherine de Médicis expliquée*, 3 volumes (Paris: Souverain, 1842-1843); this work revised as *Sur Catherine de Médicis* in *La Comédie humaine* (1846); translated by Wormeley as *Catharine de'Medici* (Boston: Roberts Brothers, 1894);

Le Chef-d'œuvre inconnu, in *Romans et contes philosophiques*, volume 3 (Paris: Gosselin, 1831); republished in *Contes philosophiques* (Paris: Gosselin, 1832); revised and enlarged in *Etudes philosophiques*, volume 17 (Paris: Delloye et Lecou, 1837); republished in *La Comédie humaine* (1846); revised in *Le Provincial à Paris*, volume 2 (Paris: Gabriel Roux et Cassanet, 1847); translated as "The

Hidden Masterpiece" in *Stories by Foreign Authors*, volume 3 (New York: 1898);

Les Célibataires, in *Scènes de la vie privée*, volume 3 (Paris: Mame et Delaunay, 1832); revised in *Scènes de la vie de province, Etudes de mœurs au XIXᵉ siècle* (Paris: Mme Charles Béchet, 1834); republished in *Scènes de la vie de province* (Paris: Charpentier, 1839); revised as *Le Curé de Tours* under collective title of *Les Célibataires* in *La Comédie humaine* (1843); translated by Clara Bell as *The Celibates and Other Stories* (Philadelphia: Gebbie, 1898);

La Grande Bretèche, in *Scènes de la vie privée*, volume 3 (Paris: Mame et Delaunay, 1832); republished as *La Grande Bretèche ou les trois vengeances*, in *Scènes de la vie de province, Etudes de mœurs au XIXᵉ siècle*, volume 7 (Paris: Werdet, 1837); republished in *Scènes de la vie de province*, volume 2 (Paris: Charpentier, 1839); republished as "La Grande Bretèche, Fin d'*Autre étude de femme*" in *La Comédie humaine* (1845);

Les Cent Contes drolatiques: Premier dixain (Paris: Gosselin, 1832); *Secund dixain* (Paris: Gosselin, 1833); *Troisième dixain* (Paris: Werdet, 1837); translated by George Robert Sims as *Balzac's Contes drolatiques; Droll Stories Collected from the Abbays of Touraine* (London: Chatto & Windus, 1874);

Le Rendez-vous, La Femme de trente ans, Le Doigt de Dieu, Les Deux Rencontres, and *L'Expiation*, in *Scènes de la vie privée*, volume 4 (Paris: Mame et Delaunay, 1832); collected, revised, and enlarged as *Même histoire* (Paris: Mme Charles Béchet, 1834); revised, without a general title, in *Etudes de mœurs au XIXᵉ siècle*, volumes 7-8 (Paris: Werdet, 1837); revised as *Même histoire* in *Scènes de la vie privée*, volume 2 (Paris: Charpentier, 1839); revised as *La Femme de trente ans* in *La Comédie humaine* (1842); translated by Ellen Marriage as *A Woman of Thirty* (New York: Macmillan, 1901);

Notice biographique sur Louis Lambert, in *Nouveaux contes philosophiques* (Paris: Gosselin, 1832); revised and augmented as *Histoire intellectuelle de Louis Lambert* (Paris: Gosselin, 1833); revised and augmented in *Le Livre mystique*, volume 1 (Paris: Werdet, 1835); and in *Etudes philosophiques*, volumes 23-24 (Paris: Werdet, 1836); revised in *Louis Lambert suivi de Séraphîta* (Paris: Charpentier, 1842); republished in *La Comédie humaine* (1846); translated by Wormeley as *Louis Lambert* (Boston: Roberts Brothers, 1889);

Le Médecin de campagne, 2 volumes (Paris: Mame-Delaunay, 1833; revised edition, Paris: Werdet, 1834; revised, 1836; revised edition, Paris: Charpentier, 1839); republished in *La Comédie humaine* (1846); translated by Wormeley as *The Country Doctor* (Boston: Roberts Brothers, 1887);

Eugénie Grandet, in *Scènes de la vie de province, Etudes de mœurs au XIXᵉ siècle*, volume 1 (Paris: Mme Charles Béchet, 1834; revised edition, Paris: Charpentier, 1839); republished in *La Comédie humaine* (1843); translated by Edward S. Gould as *Eugenia Grandet* (New York: J. Winchester, 1843);

Ferragus, chef des dévorants, in *Scènes de la vie parisienne, Etudes de mœurs au XIXᵉ siècle*, volume 10 (Paris: Mme Charles Béchet, 1834); republished in *Histoire des Treize* (1839);

Ne touchez pas la hache, in *Scènes de la vie parisienne, Etudes de mœurs au XIXᵉ siècle*, volume 11 (Paris: Mme Charles Béchet, 1834); revised as *La Duchesse de Langeais* in *Histoire des Treize*;

La Fille aux yeux d'or, in *Scènes de la vie parisienne, Etudes de mœurs au XIXᵉ siècle*, volumes 11-12 (Paris: Mme Charles Béchet, 1834); revised in *Histoire des Treize*;

La Recherche de l'absolu, in *Scènes de la vie privée, Etudes de mœurs au XIXᵉ siècle*, volume 3 (Paris: Mme Charles Béchet, 1834; revised edition, Paris: Charpentier, 1839); revised in *La Comédie humaine* (1846); translated as *The Philosopher's Stone* (New York: J. Winchester, 1844);

Le Père Goriot, histoire parisienne, 2 volumes (Paris: Werdet et Spachmann, 1835; 4 volumes, Paris: Figaro, 1837; revised edition, Paris: Charpentier, 1839); republished in *La Comédie humaine* (1845); translated as *Daddy Goriot; or Unrequited Affection* (London: Ward & Lock, 1860);

Le Contrat de mariage, in *Etudes de mœurs au XIXᵉ siècle*, volume 2 (Paris: Mme Charles Béchet, 1835); revised in *Scènes de la vie privée*, volume 1 (Paris: Charpentier, 1839); republished in *La Comédie humaine* (1842);

Séraphîta, in *Le Livre mystique*, volume 2 (Paris: Werdet, 1835); republished in *Etudes philosophiques*, volumes 28-29 (Paris: Souverain, 1840); revised in *Louis Lambert suivi de Séraphîta* (Paris: Charpentier, 1842); revised

in *La Comédie humaine* (1846); translated by Wormeley as *Seraphita* (Boston: Roberts Brothers, 1889);

La Comtesse à deux maris, in *Scènes de la vie parisienne, Etudes de mœurs au XIXᵉ siècle*, volume 12 (Paris: Mme Charles Béchet, 1835); republished in *Scènes de la vie parisienne* (Paris: Charpentier, 1839); revised as *Le Colonel Chabert* in *La Comédie humaine* (1844);

Le Lys dans la vallée, 2 volumes (Paris: Werdet, 1836; revised edition, Paris: Charpentier, 1838); revised in *La Comédie humaine* (1844); translated by Wormeley as *The Lily of the Valley* (Boston: Roberts Brothers, 1891);

L'Interdiction, in *Etudes philosophiques*, volumes 24-25 (Paris: Werdet, 1836); republished in *Scènes de la vie parisienne* (Paris: Charpentier, 1839); republished in *La Comédie humaine* (1845);

La Vieille Fille, in *Scènes de la vie de province, Etudes de mœurs au XIXᵉ siècle*, volume 7 (Paris: Werdet, 1837); republished in *Scènes de la vie de province*, volume 2 (Paris: Charpentier, 1839); revised in *La Comédie humaine* (1844);

Histoire de la grandeur et de la décadence de César Birotteau, 2 volumes (Paris: Boulé, 1837; revised edition, Paris: Musée littéraire du Siècle, 1847); republished in *La Comédie humaine* (1844); translated by J. H. Simpson as *History of the Grandeur and Downfall of Cesar Birotteau* (London: Saunders, Otley, 1860);

Illusions perdues, in *Scènes de la vie de province, Etudes de mœurs au XIXᵉ siècle*, volume 4 (Paris: Werdet, 1837); revised and expanded in *La Comédie humaine* (1843); translated by Wormeley as *Lost Illusions* (Boston: Roberts Brothers, 1892);

La Femme supérieure, 2 volumes (Paris: Werdet, 1838)—contains *La Maison Nucingen* and *La Torpille*; *La Femme supérieure* revised and expanded as *Les Employés, ou la Femme supérieure* in *La Comédie humaine* (1844); translated by Wormeley as *Bureaucracy; or, A Civil Service Reformer* (Boston: Roberts Brothers, 1889);

La Femme comme il faut, in *Les Français peints par eux-mêmes* (Paris: L. Curmer, 1839); revised and republished with *La Grande Bretèche* and five untitled fragments from *Les Contes bruns* (Paris: U. Canel, 1832) as *Autre étude de femme* in *La Comédie humaine* (1842);

Histoire des Treize (Paris: Charpentier, 1839); republished in *La Comédie humaine* (1843);

translated by William Walton as *History of the Thirteen* (Philadelphia: G. Barrie and Sons, 1896);

Le Cabinet des antiques; Gambara, 2 volumes (Paris: Souverain, 1839); revised in *La Comédie humaine* (1844); translated by Wormeley as *The Gallery of Antiques* (Boston: Hardy, Pratt, 1899);

Gambara, in *Le Cabinet des antiques; Gambara*, volume 2 (Paris: Souverain, 1839); republished in *Le Livre des douleurs*, volume 1 (Paris: Souverain, 1840); republished in *La Comédie humaine* (1846); translated by G. Burnham Ives and Thomas H. Walls in *Gambara. Massimilla Doni. The Accursed Child* (Philadelphia: G. Barrie, 1899);

Une Fille d'Eve, 2 volumes (Paris: Souverain, 1839); revised in *La Comédie humaine* (1842);

Massimilla Doni, in *Une Fille d'Eve*, 2 volumes (Paris: Souverain, 1839); republished in *Le Livre des douleurs* (Paris: Souverain, 1840); republished in *La Comédie humaine* (1846);

Béatrix, ou les Amours forcés, 2 volumes (Paris: Souverain, 1839); republished as *Béatrix* in *La Comédie humaine* (1842); translated by Wormeley as *Béatrix* (Boston: Roberts Brothers, 1895);

Pierrette, 2 volumes (Paris: Souverain, 1840); republished in *La Comédie humaine* (1843);

Vautrin (Paris: Delloye et Tresse, 1840; revised, 1840);

Le Curé de village: Scène de la vie de campagne (Paris: Souverain, 1841); republished in *La Comédie humaine* (1845); translated by Wormeley as *The Village Rector* (Boston: Roberts Brothers, 1893);

Une Ténébreuse Affaire, 3 volumes (Paris: Souverain, 1842); revised in *La Comédie humaine* (1846); translated by Wormeley as *An Historical Mystery* (Boston: Roberts Brothers, 1891);

Ursule Mirouët, 2 volumes (Paris: Souverain, 1842); revised in *La Comédie humaine* (1843); translated by Wormeley as *Ursula* (Boston: Roberts Brothers, 1891);

Albert Savarus, in *La Comédie humaine*, volume 1 (1842); revised as *Rosalie* in *Les Mystères de province*, volumes 3-4 (Paris: Souverain, 1843); translated by H. H. Walker in *The Purse, and Albert Savarus* (New York: G. Munro, 1883);

Les Deux Frères, 2 volumes (Paris: Souverain, 1842); revised as *Un Ménage de garçon en province* in *La Comédie humaine* (1843); retitled *La Rabouilleuse* in *Œuvres complètes de H. de*

Evelina Hanska in 1835, fifteen years before she married Balzac (miniature by Moritz Daffinger; from André Maurois, Prometheus: The Life of Balzac, *1965)*

Balzac. Edition définitive, 26 volumes (Paris: Calmann-Lévy, 1869-1876, 1899, 1906); translated by Wormeley as *The Two Brothers* (Boston: Roberts Brothers, 1887);

La Comédie humaine, 16 volumes (Paris: Furne, 1842-1846); volume 17 (Paris: Furne [Houssiaux], 1848); volumes 18-20 (Paris: Houssiaux, 1855)—contains *Scènes de la vie privée, Scènes de la vie de province, Scènes de la vie parisienne, Scènes de la vie politique, Scènes de la vie militaire, Scènes de la vie de campagne,* and *Etudes analytiques*; translated by Clara Bell, Ellen Marriage, R. C. Scott, and James Waring as *La Comédie humaine*, 40 volumes, edited by George Saintsbury (London: J. M. Dent, 1895-1900);

Les Ressources de Quinola (Paris: Souverain, 1842);

La Muse du département, in *La Comédie humaine*, volume 6 (Paris: Furne, 1843); revised in *Les Mystères de province*, volumes 1-3 (Paris: Souverain, 1843);

Un Début dans la vie, 2 volumes (Paris: Dumont, 1844); revised in *La Comédie humaine* (1845); translated by Wormeley as *A Start in Life* (Boston: Little, Brown, 1901);

Splendeurs et misères des courtisanes. Esther, 3 volumes (Paris: Potter, 1844); revised and expanded in *La Comédie humaine* (1846); translated by Ellery Sedgwick as *Splendors and Miseries of Courtisans* (Philadelphia: G. Barrie, 1895);

Honorine, 2 volumes (Paris: Potter, 1844); republished in *La Comédie humaine* (1845);

Modeste Mignon, 4 volumes (Paris: Chlendowski, 1844); republished in *La Comédie humaine* (1845); translated by Wormeley as *Modeste Mignon* (Boston: Roberts Brothers, 1888);

La Lune de miel, 2 volumes (Paris: Chlendowski, 1845); republished as *Béatrix, Dernière partie* in *La Comédie humaine* (1845);

L'Envers de l'histoire contemporaine / Premier épisode, in *La Comédie humaine*, volume 12 (Paris: Furne, 1846); republished as *La Femme de soixante ans*, 3 volumes (Paris: Roux et Cassanet, 1847); republished as *Madame de La Chanterie* [part 1] (Paris: Potter, 1854); part 2 published as *L'Initié*, 2 volumes (Paris: Potter, 1854); republished as *L'Envers de l'histoire contemporaine / Deuxième partie / L'Initié* in *La Comédie humaine*, volume 18 (Paris: Houssiaux, 1855); translated by Wormeley as *The Brotherhood of Consolation* (Boston: Roberts Brothers, 1893);

Un Drame dans les prisons [part 3 of *Splendeurs et misères des courtisanes*], 2 volumes (Paris: Souverain, 1847);

La Cousine Bette: Où la passion va-t-elle se nicher?, in *Les Parents pauvres*, volumes 1-7 (Paris: Chlendowski-Pétion, 1847); republished as *La Cousine Bette: Le Père prodigue* in *Les Parents pauvres* (Paris: Musée littéraire du Siècle, 1847); republished in *La Comédie humaine* (1848); translated by Wormeley as *Cousin Bette* (Boston: Roberts Brothers, 1888);

Le Cousin Pons, in *Les Parents pauvres*, volumes 7-12 (Paris: Pétion, 1847); republished as *Le Cousin Pons: Les Deux Musiciens* in *Les Parents pauvres* (Paris: Musée littéraire du Siècle, 1847); republished in *La Comédie humaine* (1848); translated by Philip Kent as *Cousin Pons* (London: Simpkin, Marshall, 1880);

La Dernière Incarnation de Vautrin [part 4 of *Splendeurs et misères des courtisanes*], 3 volumes (Paris: Chlendowski, 1847); republished in *La Comédie humaine* (1855);

La Marâtre (Paris: Michel Lévy, 1848); translated as *The Stepmother* (Philadelphia, 1901).

Collections: *Scènes de la vie privée*, 2 volumes (Paris: Mame et Delaunay-Vallée, 1830; revised edition, 4 volumes, Mame et Delaunay, 1832);

Romans et contes philosophiques, 3 volumes (Paris: Gosselin, 1831); revised as *Contes philosophiques* (Paris: Gosselin, 1832);

Nouveaux contes philosophiques (Paris: Gosselin, 1832);

Romans et contes philosophiques (Paris: Gosselin, 1833);

Etudes de mœurs au XIX' siècle, 12 volumes (Paris: Mme Charles Béchet, Werdet, 1834-1837)—contains *Scènes de la vie privée*, *Scènes de la vie de province*, and *Scènes de la vie parisienne*;

Etudes philosophiques, 20 volumes [volumes numbered incorrectly] (Paris: Werdet, Delloye et Lecou, Souverain, 1835-1840);

Scènes de la vie de province, 2 volumes (Paris: Charpentier, 1839);

Scènes de la vie parisienne (Paris: Charpentier, 1839);

Scènes de la vie privée (Paris: Charpentier, 1839);

Œuvres complètes de H. de Balzac. Edition définitive, 26 volumes (Paris: Calmann-Lévy, 1869-1876, 1899, 1906);

[*Romans de jeunesse:*] *Annette et le criminel, Le Centenaire, Clotilde de Lusignan, La Dernière Fée, L'Héritière de Birague, Jean-Louis, Le Vicaire des Ardennes, Wann-Chlore*, 15 volumes, edited by Jean A. Ducourneau (Paris: Les Bibliophiles de l'Originale, 1961-1963)—facsimiles of pseudonymous or anonymous texts dating from the early 1820s and generally believed by Balzac;

Œuvres complètes illustrées, 30 volumes, edited by Ducourneau (Paris: Les Bibliophiles de l'Originale, 1965-1976)—facsimiles of the Furne *corrigé*: Balzac's corrected copy of the first 16 volumes of *La Comédie humaine* in the Furne edition (1842-1846), followed by volume 17 (1848) of the Furne edition, of which Balzac's copy has not been found; volumes 18-19 contain works considered part of *La Comédie humaine* but not included in the Furne edition; volume 20, edited by Roland Chollet, contains *Les Contes drolatiques*; volumes 21-23, edited by René Guise, contain Balzac's theatrical works; volumes 24-25, edited by Ducourneau, contain texts of fictional works not in *La Comédie humaine*, including *Code pénal des honnêtes gens*; volume 26, edited by Ducourneau, contains *Les Français peints par eux-mêmes* and *Le Diable à*

Paris; the last four [unnumbered] volumes include *Lettres à Mme Hanska*, edited by Roger Pierrot;

La Comédie humaine, 12 volumes, edited by Pierre-Georges Castex (Paris: Gallimard, Bibliothèque de la Pléiade, 1976-1981);

Œuvres diverses, 3 volumes, edited by Pierre-Georges Castex (Paris: Gallimard, Bibliothèque de la Pléiade, 1990-   ).

Had Balzac been a less masterful novelist, the disreputably profligate fraud in him might have overwhelmed his artistry. Still, the other Balzac, the artist, is tainted by his well-earned reputation for what has been called artistic license or dishonesty. And though, like a cowbird, he left at least one and possibly three children in the nests of others, he took away with him knowledge, insights, images, and stories that later took their places in *La Comédie humaine* (1842-1846, 1848, 1855; translated as *La Comédie humaine* [The Human Comedy], 1895-1900). Balzac's life regularly fertilized his fiction; however, his literary reputation would benefit if he lacked a biography. The view of his masterpiece, *La Comédie humaine*, has been seriously undermined by his irresponsibility, his casual attitude toward debts and contracts, his crass *arrivisme*, his naiveté about his purchases and investments, and perhaps even by his ridiculous appearance. On the one hand, he was a born sucker, the answer to many an antique dealer's dreams, the solution to some shaky business deals. On the other he was the nemesis of mistresses and relatives with money. He was indiscriminate in those he exploited. His first mistress, Mme Laure de Berny, loved him tenderly; his mother preferred her adulterous offspring to him; and Balzac impoverished the first and significantly reduced the fortune of the other. At his death he left his wife of five months with mountains of debts. The thought of what he could have done with credit cards defies the imagination.

Like many great artists he made changes in the genres in which he worked, and evaluations of his success depend on whether or not one understands what he was doing. Those who seek traditional short stories and novels will often be disappointed. While the eighteenth-century novel was dominated by narration, one must look beyond that level in the works of many period writers and, certainly, in *La Comédie humaine*. Authors of Balzac's day were turning away from the commitment to Aristotelian structuring of plot and char-

acter. Stendhal's revolutionary essay *Racine et Shakespeare* (1823-1825) was an aesthetic symptom of the age. Though Balzac was more than willing to please his popular audience and provide enough in the way of melodramatic plots to sell his books, he was a narrational minimalist and was thoroughly committed to his oft-repeated desire to be the secretary of his age, the portrait painter of the July Monarchy. While his books contain many wonderful tales, the stories are always subordinate to the overriding vision of the whole of his society. Unlike the normal plot-based novel—which may begin with birth and end with death, begin with a crisis and end with its resolution, or begin with an event and end with its cause and result—Balzac's novels conclude with an understanding of a character, such as Eugénie Grandet, or a type of person, such as a thirty-year-old woman, or the cause of a significant social phenomenon, such as the lust for gold and pleasure that informs *La Fille aux yeux d'or* (The Girl with Golden Eyes, 1834).

Another major cause for the misreadings of Balzac's oeuvre comes from a seemingly compulsive quest for Balzac's stylistic infelicities. Reviewers early on complained about his style. In two long catalogues of Balzac's supposed problems, Emile Faguet raised such complaints to an apogee of critical punctiliousness notable for its obtuseness. Although Faguet admitted the novelist's ability as an observer and creator, it is difficult in the context of his criticism to believe his sincerity. Likewise, although Percy Lubbock's and Henry James's admiration is incontrovertible, they are unable to resist prissy complaints about Balzac's style. In this regard it seems wiser to follow Pierre Larthomas, who insists that if one finds that Balzac writes poorly, the criteria one is using to judge his style are inadequate. Larthomas points to the intrinsically imagistic nature of the novelist's style and to the importance of understanding his comparisons in the context of the whole text. Context is king. Those images that are most susceptible to ridicule when taken out of their intended place most often seem masterful when considered where they were meant to occur.

The way Balzac worked encouraged these prejudices. As he wrote to Zulma Carraud in 1833, his normal workday was grueling. He would go to bed at six or seven in the evening, rise at one in the morning, and work until eight or so, then he would go back to bed for an hour or an hour and a half. On rising he would eat sub-

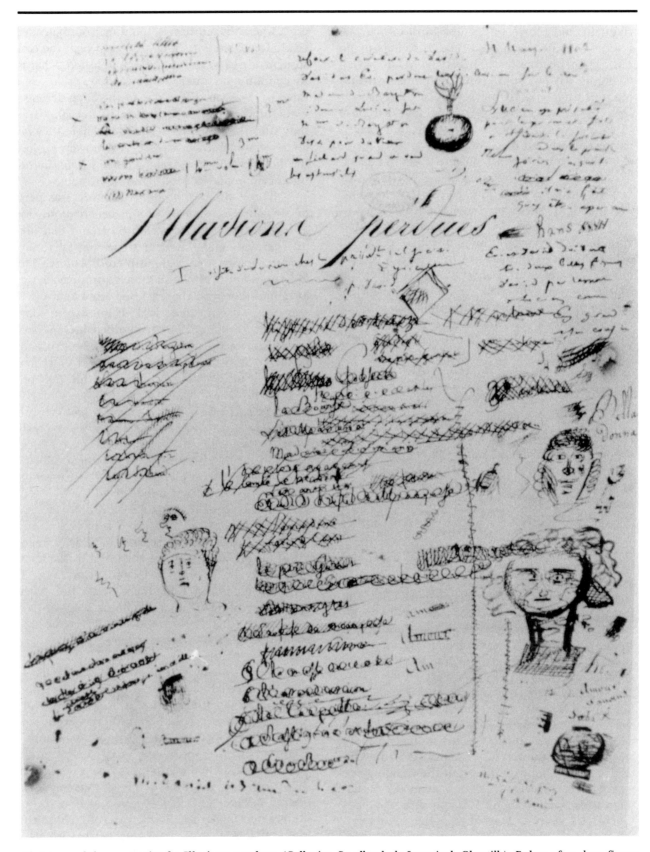

First page of the manuscript for Illusions perdues *(Collection Spoelberch de Lovenjoul, Chantilly). Balzac often drew figures when he was trying to envision his characters.*

stantially and return to his desk until four in the afternoon, when he would receive friends or go out. Then he was back in bed at six or seven. The only way he could keep this up was by drinking cup after cup of extraordinarily strong coffee. He believed, probably rightly, that the abuse of coffee was an important factor in the sickness that eventually led to his death.

Balzac's conception of context was of considerably wider scope than that of most of his readers. It includes the entire *La Comédie humaine*, which should be accepted and if possible read in the order he intended. The number of times that specific texts changed position within the cycle does not indicate Balzac's lack of interest in the sequence his novels and short stories finally took. To the contrary, there can be no doubt of his efforts to place each work exactly right. Since scholars generally accept the Furne edition of *La Comédie humaine* that Balzac corrected (normally called the Furne *corrigé*) as the definitive edition of his individual creations, the reader should do likewise in examining the organization of Balzac's oeuvre.

In a 26 March 1836 letter to Mme Evelina Hanska, Balzac remarked, pathetically: "Le mois de mai 36 approche, et j'aurai 37 ans; je ne suis rien encore, je n'ai rien fait de complet ni de grand, je n'ai que des pierres amassées" (The month of May '36 approaches, and I will be 37; I am still a nobody, I have finished nothing, and not done anything grand, I have only amassed stones). He was to use this image again. Earlier, he explained the fact that his works had appeared in seemingly random order as a result of changing fashion, or of his desire to fill out a volume, or to satisfy his need for variation to renew his inspiration during the gargantuan labors, and so on. Nonetheless, he said through the character Félix Davin, in the introduction to *Etudes philosophiques* (Philosophic Studies, 1835-1840), "L'auteur ne s'inquiétait pas plus de ces transpositions qu'un architecte ne s'enquiert de la place où sont apportées dans le chantier les pierres dont il doit faire un monument" (The author no more worried about these transpositions than an architect inquires about the place on the building site where the stones with which he is to make a monument have been brought). It is only after the monument has been completed that the position of the materials matters. During the building process, each beam, door, window, and gargoyle can be appreciated in itself and compared with similar items, but total appreciation can be achieved only when the edifice is standing complete and ready for habitation. The order in which the constituent works were created or published—that is, to continue his image, the way the rocks were piled—makes no difference to the final arrangement of the monumental *Comédie humaine*. It is only after the stones have been put where they belong, wherever that may be and however often the builder/author may have changed his mind, that position and context matter.

Balzac always thought of his works as parts of a whole. Occasionally he put his creations into an explicit, skillfully constructed frame that limits, defines, and intensifies. He usually succeeded, however, in making them do more. The incorporating fiction usually sets up a parallel or an opposition with the enclosed story that operates rather like a tuning fork, beginning at some point to reverberate. The reader becomes increasingly conscious of the resonances as he proceeds through the fiction. Balzac understood every single one of his works as belonging within the context of its *Scène*, its *Etude*, and indeed of the whole of *La Comédie humaine*. One might call this frame its context, whether that means the entire cycle or the reality that served Balzac as a backdrop. In the "Avant-propos" (Introduction) to *La Comédie humaine*, he mentions that the enormous number of "lives" included in his work "exigeaient des cadres et, qu'on me pardonne cette expression, des galeries" (required frames and, if I may be excused this expression, galleries). Readers of his prefaces might be surprised by the apology, since the analogy is by no means new. It picks up an image Félix Davin uses. It is even more interesting to discover Balzac's spokesperson saying that "les grandes salles" (the big rooms) of this particular gallery "s'étendent à l'infini" (are infinitely extended). For Balzac there were no empty spaces. He merely chose what he wanted to share with his reader, and then he framed it and hung it in a carefully arranged gallery show. Although there were activities occurring between the various "paintings," events at which one can only guess, Balzac could have inserted something in every one of the interstices. For him the lives of his characters in *La Comédie humaine* were continuous and flowed into the reality of his day. Balzac carefully chose the most suitable gallery, arranging each work with its own lighting and context. In addition, the gallery was in his world, with doors opening onto the street. Balzac's frames enclose, but they also open to give additional definition, intensity, and meaning.

Of course, Balzac is not just his *Comédie humaine*. He was also a person. His Gascon father, Bernard-François Balzac, was the eldest of eleven children. A successful bureaucrat, he managed to stay alive during the Revolution and to rise under Napoleon. Although he had no fortune, his salary and promising future warranted a pretty Parisian wife, Anne Laure Sallambier, the daughter of wealthy drapers, who brought a substantial dowry to the marriage. That she was thirty-two years his junior did not seem to bother him. Neither Bernard-François nor the rest of the family dwelt on their peasant origins. Instead, they liked to pretend that they were related to the Marquis d'Entragues and that they had the right to the aristocratic particle "de," which Bernard-François occasionally—and Honoré regularly—added to the family name. Honoré was sent to a wet nurse immediately after his birth in Tours on 20 May 1799. There was reason for doing so: not only was it common practice among families of their class, but Mme Balzac's first child had died when she tried to nurse it herself. One might question the necessity of "abandoning" Honoré for four years, however. Certainly he never forgot or forgave his mother, and when he was packed off to an Oratorian boarding school several years after returning home, he was convinced that he was unloved. In fact, Mme Balzac was about to have a child by one of the local gentlemen, Jean de Margonne, and there seems little doubt that she preferred the love child.

Honoré's time with the Oratorian fathers was unhappy. He was a poor student, regularly criticized for daydreaming. The conditions at the school were Spartan, and his mother left him without the pocket money that provided others with a few treats. His father had nurtured the boy's love of Laurence Sterne and François Rabelais. Thanks to an indulgent priest he was able to escape into books, the beginning of indiscriminate reading that provided the base of an extraordinary background so obvious in his creations. But after seven years of regular punishments, rejection, and long hours attempting to read the entire library, his health broke. He was sent home, for he was a very sick boy. Bernard-François, a man of the world and health enthusiast, decided that he needed to spend time in the out-of-doors and sent him to Mme Balzac's lover, Jean de Margonne, at Saché. There Honoré had his first

Balzac's monogrammed coffeepot (Maison de Balzac, Paris). Perhaps the most celebrated coffee drinker in literary history, he relied on caffeine for his nightly writing routine.

taste of freedom. M. de Margonne seems to have enjoyed being with him more than with his own son. As the future novelist regained his strength, he developed an abiding love of the Touraine countryside that radiates from such novels as *Le Lys dans la vallée* (1836; translated as *The Lily of the Valley*, 1891).

In 1814, because of Bernard-François's disastrous investments, the family had to sell their house in Tours and move back to Paris, near the maternal grandparents in the Marais quarter. Honoré lived in a boardinghouse and studied at the Lycée Charlemagne. Though the Marais was a colorful, interesting part of the city, life was once again difficult for the boy. As a matter of discipline, Mme Balzac made certain that he had little freedom, and she refused to give him an allowance. He managed to wheedle some money from his doting grandmother, Sophie Sallambier, however, and contracted his first debt, to the boardinghouse porter, so that he could satisfy his newly developed taste for coffee and sugar. Though a thoroughly mediocre student, he managed to finish his course work in 1816. The family arranged for him to study law in what seems to have been a very literary firm, since Augustin-Eugène Scribe had recently passed through and Jules-Gabriel Janin was the errand boy. Although there is no doubt that Honoré's experience with the law was important to his future oeuvre, he was more interested in listening to his grandmother's stories. She and others, such as Mlle de Rougemont, told him about Pierre-Augustin Caron de Beaumarchais and life under the monarchy, at least when Honoré was not attending lectures on science, philosophy, and the occult, or voraciously reading anything that came his way: Victor Cousin, Johann Kaspar Lavater, Jean-Baptiste Nacquart, André-Marie de Chénier, Georges Cuvier, Etienne Geoffroy Saint-Hilaire, Beaumarchais, the *Arabian Nights*, and Abel-François Villemain.

His formation continued pell-mell with whatever happened to excite his unending curiosity and hunger for knowledge. Laure, his favorite sister and confidante, says his amorous adventures began in this period. And with all that activity, he still managed in early 1819 to pass his baccalaureate in law. Honoré's future, the family agreed, was assured. They found a law office where, after a period of practical training, he would be able to purchase the practice (with the dowry from one of the young ladies who would doubtless make themselves available to the budding lawyer). Then, about the time M. Balzac was forced to retire, at seventy-three, on a small pension and the family moved to less expensive quarters in Villeparisis, Honoré announced that he was not going to follow the nice, safe path mapped out for him. He would not be a lawyer. He would be a famous writer. He would have not just wealth but glory as well.

Although the resulting storm was impassioned, the family finally weakened. Honoré would be supported for two years in a garret while he tried writing. The young dreamer lived on the sixth floor of a filthy old building and had to make do on very little. It was nonetheless a grand adventure. He describes some of the difficulties, and especially the thrill of working to fulfill a grandiose design, in *La Peau de chagrin* (1831; translated as *Luck and Leather. A Parisian Romance*, 1843). One of his amusements was to follow people around the quarter and let his imagination run as he vicariously lived their lives, an activity he described in "Facino Cane" (in *Etudes philosophiques*, 1837). While there is no doubt that he worked hard and that the period was benefi-

cial, there were moments when the grind began to lose its piquancy. Then, he could renew himself by a quick trip home for a few days of middle-class comfort.

By September 1819 he had settled on a project: he would storm the theater with a verse tragedy on Oliver Cromwell. A few months later he was ready to submit the play to the judgment of the family. While everyone was excited that a member of their family had managed to write a whole play in verse, the reading was performed by the enthusiastic author to an increasingly negative audience of family and neighbors. It was abominable. To give Honoré every opportunity, the work was also submitted to François-Guillaume Andrieux, a playwright of some small success, and to an actor, but everyone agreed: "The author should do anything he wishes, except write." Somewhat daunted perhaps, but unsubdued, Balzac dismissed the actor, Pierre Rapenouille, known as Lafon, as a fool. Honoré was not about to give up the dream. He did give up the garret, however, and moved back home. Although he continued from time to time to try the theater, he succeeded only with *Mercadet* (1851), and that only when another author, Adolphe Philippe, known as Dennery, had significantly revised it after Honoré's death. The novel was to be his genre.

He started a couple of prose works, "Falthurne" and "Sténie ou les erreurs philosophiques" (Sténie or Philosophic Errors), but by 1821 he had still not published anything. Then, August Lepoitevin introduced him to the potboiler trade. For Lepoitevin, it was by no means art, rather a business with tricks and formulas where he and his acquaintances rolled out whatever kind of work the public demanded. Either in collaboration with others or under his own pseudonyms of Lord R'Hoone (an anagram of Honoré), Viellerglé, or Horace de Saint-Aubin, Balzac produced a whole string of works inspired by the period's penchant for *codes*, or laws; for quasi-scientific studies of social types, or *physiologies*; for Sir Walter Scott's historical novels; and for the English gothic novels by Ann Radcliffe, Charles Robert Maturin, and Monk Lewis. Scholars have apparently sorted out those for which Balzac was more or less responsible; one, *Annette et le criminel* (Annette and the Criminal, 1824), has been republished in paperback. Although scholars traditionally find evidence of Balzac's genius in these appalling novels, it takes a fair amount of goodwill to do so. Balzac himself termed *L'Héritière de Birague* (The Heiress of Birague, 1822) "veritable literary pig swill." The young man was making some money, however, which gave his middle-class parents hope and allowed him to resist the legal vocation, and he was learning the trade, which he discusses in uncomplimentary terms in *Illusions perdues* (1837; translated as *Lost Illusions*, 1892) and *La Muse du département* (The Muse of the Department, 1843). Most important, he was writing. As much by opposition and contrast to what he felt to be acceptable as by anything else, he was mastering the craft of fiction. Some of the drafts begun and set aside during this period would become mature works of art. In 1826, for example, Balzac himself printed at least one and perhaps more copies of an early version of *Physiologie du mariage* (1826; translated as *Physiology of Marriage*, 1899), in which marriage is treated as a sickness—a work that would become an ironic masterpiece included in *La Comédie humaine*. Although few worthwhile crops were harvested during this period, everything was serving as seed in the tremendously fertile bed of his mind.

At least as important as his writing was the relationship he was establishing with Mme Laure de Berny, who lived near his parents in Villeparisis. Honoré's father had long been acquainted with her husband, M. Gabriel de Berny, who had been a counselor at the royal court, then later at the imperial court. Most interesting for the starry-eyed Honoré, however, was the fact that Mme de Berny was born in 1777 and raised at Versailles under the monarchy. Not only had she retained the courtly graciousness of her youth, but also she had many amusing stories about the court. Perhaps best of all, Louis XVI and Marie Antoinette had been her godparents. Balzac found her irresistible. Her marriage had not been a happy one, since M. de Berny was both sickly and sour-tempered. When Balzac set his cap for her, she was forty-five years old and admitted to being the mother of nine children (one of whom resulted from an affair) and a grandmother. The age disparity between M. and Mme Balzac was reversed in Honoré and Mme de Berny. The result was a long-lived affair that was essential to the novelist's development. Much of Balzac's vaunted insight into women came from Mme de Berny's frankness. She even managed to smooth out some of the young man's rough edges, while giving him his first experience of true elegance. Despite Balzac's many intervening affairs and his shameless habit of extracting

money from her, his *"pauvre maman"* (poor mama), as he called her, remained committed to him and his reputation until her death.

Mme de Berny did not occupy all of Balzac's time. By 1824 he had set himself up again in Paris (his mother disapproved, since she felt it was only to allow him total freedom with his middle-aged mistress). He continued to write and had some small, critical success with *Wann-Chlore* (1825). He also had another middle-aged conquest in an impoverished Napoleonic duchess, Mme Laure Permon d'Abrantès. Though she flattered his ego and provided him with many wonderful tales from the days of the empire, Mme de Berny pulled his chain, issued an ultimatum, and brought him back to order. Financial success eluded him. Encouraged by his family, several friends, and his mistress, he decided to become a businessman. This affair set a pattern that would be repeated with few variations over and over through the course of his life. He heard that Urbain Canel was thinking of publishing major, classical French authors in inexpensive editions, and he recognized the idea's potential. He borrowed 9,000 francs from a friend of his family, 9,250 francs from Mme de Berny, and became a partner. An edition of Jean de La Fontaine was to begin the series, with Balzac writing the prefaces. Unfortunately, when the edition of three thousand copies began to appear in fascicles, sales were few and far between. Balzac's partners sold him their shares, and the aborning businessman had to borrow more money to finish printing the book. By this time his investment totaled 16,741 francs, and he was broke. He sold out to Alexandre and Hippolyte Baudouin, bookdealers, for 24,000 francs, which, though it sounds like a successful coup, was in fact disastrous. Baudouin paid him with notes drawn on bankrupt businesses worth only 30 percent of the face value.

The family friend who had lent him the original 9,000 francs encouraged him to try again, this time with a printing business that could be had for 60,000 francs. Another family friend lent the first 30,000 francs (Honoré's parents co-signed the loan), and Mme de Berny, the divine *Dilecta*, filled in the gaps once more. Although there is no reason to question the young man's effort, or indeed his correct understanding of the business's basic promise, he was undercapitalized; worse, he had difficulty keeping his personal expenses at the tailor's and bootmaker's separate from those of the press. Despite more borrowed

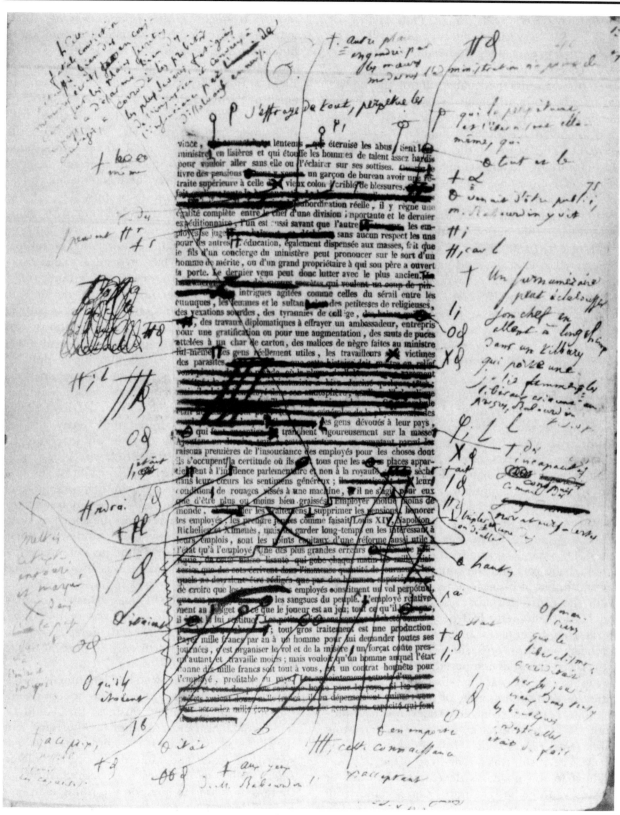

Page from Balzac's corrected proof for La Femme supérieure *(Bibliothèque Nationale). Such extensive revisions at this stage are unusual, as they result in considerable reduction of the author's fee.*

money, desperate strategies of one sort or another—such as going deeper into debt and purchasing a type-foundry—there was eventually no way to avoid selling out at a terrible loss. To avoid the shame of bankruptcy for their eldest son, Balzac's family picked up the bills, but the no longer young Honoré owed them 45,000 francs, an enormous sum in those days. Nonetheless, as André Maurois points out in *Prométhée ou la vie de Balzac* (1956; translated as *Prometheus: The Life of Balzac*, 1965), he came away with experience of inestimable value for a novelist. He had learned about money, credit, debtors, and a failing business. No one can fault the accuracy of his account of going broke in *Histoire de la grandeur et de la décadence de César Birotteau* (1837; translated as *History of the Grandeur and Downfall of Cesar Birotteau*, 1860) or *Illusions perdues*. Though the lessons would enrich *La Comédie humaine*, sadly they had no effect on his fundamental inability to run a real business. He was and would remain a writer, not a businessman.

Of course his debts were not uniquely in the family ledgers. He owed others as well; V. S. Pritchett notes in *Balzac* (1973) that it was as much as 100,000 francs. So when his brother-in-law offered to stake him in a hideout on the rue Cassini near the Observatoire, which at the time was at the far edge of Paris, practically in the country, Balzac agreed without hesitation. He needed to recoup his losses. While he was tired of rolling out half-baked novels for little money and no luster, he was by no means willing to give up his desire for glory. He wanted to write, though he did not know precisely what would be appropriate, and he wanted for once to write something he could sign with his own name. Scott's *Waverley* (1814) had long attracted him. He began to think of a fictionalized history of France that would illuminate the characteristics and customs of his own society. It would be different from Scott, of course, since the long, drawn-out conversations did not appeal to him. He would start with a portrayal of the 1799 Royalist uprising against the Revolution, which he had heard about as a boy.

Many of the elements of what would later become *La Comédie humaine* are apparent in the resultant novel, *Le Dernier Chouan, ou la Bretagne en 1800* (1829; translated as *The Chouans*, 1889). Though he had not yet moved into the present, the Romantic "local color" (realistic details that give a semblance of verisimilitude) had already been turned into an all-encompassing system. To make certain that he had a true sense of Brittany,

where *Le Dernier Chouan* is set, he wangled an invitation to the château of General Gilbert de Pommereul, whose father he had known in Tours. The general had retired and lived in the heart of the *chouannerie* (Breton royalist country). The novel is held together by the love affair between a handsome royalist rebel and a beautiful revolutionary spy who are allowed only their wedding night before being killed. The melodrama catered to the public's taste, but, as he was to do throughout his career, Balzac rose above the popular elements with an artistic portrayal of his society. Christopher Prendergast has pointed to Balzac's ability to take the conventions of contemporary popular fiction and adapt them to the aims of his art. Balzac saw the love story as the focus for the larger vision of the excruciating pain and torment caused by civil war.

It is difficult to overemphasize the importance of *Le Dernier Chouan*, for Balzac was started on his major endeavor of presenting and evaluating the life and times of contemporary France. It was an awesome task, one that would have immediately discouraged anyone less enthusiastically energetic, observant, and imaginative. It was a task fit for the genius he sensed within him. Unfortunately this novel sold no better than his other anonymous or pseudonymous ones, although it drew a more discriminating audience. Balzac had come into his own; he was right to sign the work. *Physiologie du mariage* appeared the same year in a revised edition. Although published anonymously, it was an open secret that the author was Balzac. The work, which takes the side of young women and wives in the war of the sexes, is most important in that it established Balzac's reputation as someone who understood the rapidly growing feminine contingent of his readers.

From 1829 until 1846, Balzac was to work at a high, productive pitch, often publishing five or six works a year, with as many others at various stages of completion. When critics mention that the novelist's works would regularly double in length as he forged through the successive sets of proofs, they talk about Romantic exuberance or frenzy, implying a manic logorrhea out of control, but it was rather his way of achieving perfection. If one studies the changes, there is no question that he was improving, perfecting, and intensifying his texts, that he was an artist in firm control of the creative process. That he generally received less for his creations than Eugène Sue or Alexandre Dumas *père* had less to do with his popularity or his considerable negotiating skills than with his revisions on printers' expensive page proofs. For the most part he paid a stiff price, deducted from his payments, for the five to seven or more sets of proofs that he insisted on for almost every one of his novels and short stories. He frequently called himself a *galérien* (galley slave), punning on the galley proofs that consumed so much of his life. This costly and time-consuming method worked magnificently for Balzac.

Even after a work had appeared, he would frequently return to it for a capital development—for example, *Gobseck*, a novella that first appeared as *Les Dangers de l'inconduite* (The Perils of Misconduct) in the 1830 collection of six stories titled *Scènes de la vie privée* (Scenes of Private Life), a title he would retain in *La Comédie humaine*. The first version focuses on the usurer Gobseck, an incarnation of the malignant power of money created by the vices of a corrupt society. The narrator displays palpable horror at the way the miser's sway extends to the great, noble families of the realm, and at his ability to determine the marriage of the Grandlieus' daughter with the Restauds' son. For Balzac, such great families were essential for the preservation of civilization. They joined the institutions of church and state to maintain the traditions and the structures that resist anarchy and chaos. If a Gobseck can reach into the home of a Grandlieu, if a usurer can decide whether a Grandlieu can marry a Restaud, conditions are in dire need of correction.

In 1835, however, Balzac returned to the work and added a coda in which he takes the reader beyond the portrait of a society committed to cold cash and shows how Gobseck's cult of money has deteriorated into a religion of things. The miser attributes the permanence of gold to merchandise he has received, whether silverware or food. Overcome by greed, he quibbles about the price he is offered for the merchandise, refuses to sell, and dies surrounded by the vile, asphyxiating odors of spoiled garbage. Perhaps the best image of Gobseck's false religion appears in the heap of gold beneath the ashes before which his cold body is found. The gold remains, but Gobseck's spiritual values are reduced to ashes. In the midst of realistic details informing the reader of the period's interest rates, the dress of the day, and the objects decorating the rooms of the poor and the rich, Balzac creates a timeless figure who represents the all-pervading and heartless power of gold. While remaining true in detail and atmosphere, Balzac's best works present a world of essences that illuminates the values of society. He is a moralist in the best French tradition.

Another masterwork, *La Peau de chagrin*, also appeared in 1831. Here Balzac opens with an impoverished young man, Raphaël de Valentin, living in a garret and struggling to complete a seminal work on the human will. Balzac's novel is often used to illustrate his belief that human thought in its guise as will, passion, and idea can become a powerful force to serve good or ill. The capacity to concentrate the power of the will raises one above the norm, but it also exhausts the individual who commits himself so intensely. The title presents the central image. At the moment when Raphaël has been reduced by poverty and failure to suicide, he is given a magic skin, symbolic of life, and asked to choose between self-sacrifice on the one hand and egotistic self-gratification on the other. He can do as he will with his life by focusing his will, but as he wills, and receives his wish, the skin shrinks, thus reducing his life. Earlier, he has dreamed of a life accompanied by the virtuous Pauline and devoted to significant service to humankind. Instead, he turns at first to Fœdora and debauchery, then to the passive egotism he saw in the antique dealer, which was supposed to keep him from the desires that would use up the skin and bring death. Raphaël's choice is the choice of his world, the novel suggests, a blatantly self-indulgent society that will inevitably disintegrate.

Balzac took up again with Mme d'Abrantès, who introduced him to the gathering around Mme Jeanne Récamier, and thus to Benjamin Constant, Alphonse de Lamartine, and François-Auguste-René de Chateaubriand. Little by little, Balzac was received by aristocratic socialites, an experience that would enrich his books, though his naive hunger for acceptance by the blue bloods would never allow him to see the ridiculousness of these still-pretentious but now useless aristocrats, whether of the pre-revolutionary monarchy, Napoleonic, or Restoration variety. For that, it would take Marcel Proust. In an increasingly middle-class society based not on land but on capital, the power had shifted. But Balzac, suspecting he was merely tolerated by the nobles, made every effort to find acceptance. With the purchase of appropriate gloves, boots, and clothing, his debts grew without doing much for his social status. He was always somewhat out of step, too flashy, or simply overdressed. Although his sparkling black eyes, his amazing ability as a racon-

Photogravure of Balzac, from a daguerreotype by Nadar

teur, and his quick wit made him welcome, his short legs, pudgy body, big head, and missing teeth always left him feeling inferior to the handsome young men who surrounded the highborn beauties. Balzac resembled nothing so much as a child in a candy store where everything was prominently marked *noli me tangere*.

Balzac's experience with older women was put to good effect with a series of studies that considered the thirty-year-old woman. His point of departure, for example, in *La Maison du chat-qui-pelote* (1842; first published as *Gloire et malheur*, 1830; translated as *The Cat and Battledore, and Other Tales*, 1879), was that the lack of preparation, experience, and understanding in girls and young women, which often resulted in mismatches, would encourage disabused older women into more or less disastrous affairs. But the history of one series of texts that eventually resulted in the 1842 novel *La Femme de trente ans* (translated as *A Woman of Thirty*, 1901) has more importance for understanding his novelistic practices. The works he wrote in 1831 and 1832 and gathered together as *Même histoire* (Same Story) in 1834 have in common a stern thematic warning against adultery. He said that the sketches were tableaux or pictures unified by a thought and

that other transitions were unnecessary, since the reader could provide them. There is no indication that he shared Félix Davin's regrets that the tableaux lacked a common character and other standard links of novels. Works such as *Histoire des Treize* (1839; translated as *History of the Thirteen*, 1896) make his lack of allegiance to the transitions of traditional narration clear. When in *La Femme de trente ans* he joined the sketches of *Même histoire* by turning the series of women involved in adultery into one woman, Julie d'Aiglemont, his motivation seems to have been less a desire to make a novel than to emphasize, and thus strengthen, the theme of destructive adultery and filial disobedience by showing how an entire family can be destroyed through the errant behavior of one woman.

Adultery was to be an important theme in Balzac's works. Not only had he seen its effects from the standpoint of an unloved child, from the trouble occasioned by Bernard-François's fathering an illegitimate child in his dotage, and from the misery of his sister Laure in her marriage to a scoundrel, he was able to study it as he pursued his own affair with the still-married Mme de Berny, whom he was betraying with the duchess d'Abrantès. It is difficult to know whether he was insisting on a morality he accepted but was for one reason or other unable to put into practice, or whether he was simply telling his middle-class audience what it wanted to hear.

In the midst of all this, Balzac was also writing articles for various reviews and newspapers. He was already the harbinger of the literature of the future, and his cynical articles were welcomed by publishers such as Emile de Girardin, who was representative of the wave of businessmen who came after the Romantic book publishers and who were to find wealth in the growing number of avid readers. The book publishers of the 1820s followed in the footsteps of the *Bibliothèque bleue* (Blue Library), cheap editions of almanacs, saints' lives, and simple tales that peddlers had sold for the preceding three centuries. By the late teens and early twenties, however, publishers wanted interesting new writings that would attract readers for their inexpensive products. Reading rooms, which rented books by the volume (the more volumes per novel the better), made it possible to produce more expensive books, but at most there were only around five hundred such places in Paris. Balzac unquestionably benefited from the book-publishing business of the day, but it was especially the newspaper-men such as Girardin who really made fortunes possible for popular novelists in the 1830s and 1840s. Because of modern printing methods and machinery, high-volume, low-cost periodicals became possible. The addictive "continued in the next installment" provided a faithful readership, and "art" became a business with a seemingly insatiable need for articles, essays, stories, and serialized novels. Editors and publishers solicited Balzac's work. Reading room patrons waited impatiently for the next installments.

Literary success arrived in 1831. With the acclaim of his novels, financial independence should have followed. As Maurois details, Balzac received 1,125 francs for *La Peau de chagrin*, 3,750 francs for the stories included in *Scènes de la vie privée*, 5,250 francs for *Romans et contes philosophiques* (Philosophic Novels and Stories) and *Les Cent Contes drolatiques: Premier dixain* (1832; translated as *Balzac's Contes drolatiques; Droll Stories Collected from the Abbays of Touraine*, 1874), and 4,166 francs for his contributions to various reviews and newspapers. He should have been able to live very, very well indeed on the resulting 14,291 francs. By the end of the year, however, excluding the 45,000 francs he still owed his mother, his debts had increased by 15,000 francs. His bills for his tailor, for wine, bookbinding, gloves, entertaining, and finally for a tilbury with a smartly turned out tiger to hold the whip were staggering. But since neither thrift nor moderation were a part of his character, he was forced to develop extraordinarily clever stratagems to avoid his creditors.

In 1832 he published what he would retitle *Le Curé de Tours* in 1843 (first titled *Les Célibataires* [translated as *The Celibates and Other Stories*, 1898]), a novella that shows the new financial forces working in a small provincial setting. A selfish old maid and an ambitious priest bring provincial scheming and Parisian power together to crush a pathetic village curé. This tempest in a teacup provides an excellent example of Balzac's genius. In the hands of Molière, the story would have made good comedy. Father Birotteau's palpable greed and ingenuous enjoyment in the midst of the furniture he inherits would have served as the center for burlesquing powerful capitalistic currents brought to bear on an insignificant country priest. In the end, rather like Sganarelle in *Dom Juan* (1665) whimpering, "My wages! My wages!" Birotteau would have been left the butt of a laughing audience as he cried pathetically,

"My furniture! my furniture!" But in Balzac's hands the devices of the mock-heroic make the reader aware of the awesome, destructive power wielded in modern society by occult forces, power that can frighten traditional institutions into silent acquiescence and thus destroy helpless innocents such as Birotteau.

Le Colonel Chabert (1844; first titled *La Comtesse à deux maris* [The Countess with Two Husbands], 1835) chronicles the return of a Napoleonic hero who, left for dead on the battlefield of Eylau, regains his memory and returns to Paris to find his wife busily engaged in spending his fortune with a new husband. Although Balzac makes the pathos of this relic of former glory come alive as he confronts and bows to the greedy selfishness of his wife, modern readers have seen it as a commentary on the July Monarchy's greedy *arrivisme* and desire to sweep embarrassing comparisons to Napoleonic glories beneath the carpet.

Balzac's ego and amorous desires once again focused on a potential conquest. Mme la marquise de Castries (originally Claire-Clémence-Henriette de Maillé) joined his many correspondents, invited him to her salon (to which she regularly invited writers), and began to pursue him energetically. Balzac was delighted to join her late in the evening and hoped that her flirtatiousness went beyond what one could reasonably expect from a hostess—though he suspected she might be making a fool of him. When she invited him to accompany her to Aix and perhaps later to Italy, his doubts dissipated. At least one of the signs in the candy shop had been taken away. What would have been a minor episode became a major catastrophe, however, since his mountain of debts did not allow such trips without enormous effort both to arrange his writing commitments and to find the necessary money. But he succeeded. While on the trip he would work most of the day, composing a new novel and several short stories, and correcting proofs for *Notice biographique sur Louis Lambert* (1832; translated as *Louis Lambert*, 1889). During the evening he pursued the "angelic" Mme de Castries. Finally she made it clear that though she found his attentions flattering and enjoyed his wonderful mind, she had no intention of going to bed with him. He was mortally offended and left in a huff. Still, while he could not carve a notch in one of his extravagant canes, he had accomplished quite a lot of work, and he had the material to describe a tease in *La Duchesse de Langeais* (The Duchess of Langeais, 1839).

Louis Lambert appeared shortly after his contretemps with Mme de Castries. It offers a description of Balzac's bookish youth, begins to lay out his strange theology (continued in *Séraphîta*, 1835), and insists on the dangerous power of human thought. The critics excoriated the work; Balzac felt his explanations should have been more complete. Although his novels increasingly insisted on the importance of the institutional church, his private beliefs were a bizarre stew of spotty, often secondhand readings in Louis-Claude Saint-Martin, Emanuel Swedenborg, the Cabalists, Friedrich Anton Mesmer, and Franz Joseph Gall. The occult practices and supernatural events that appear in such works as *Ursule Mirouët* (1842; translated as *Ursula*, 1891) did not strike him as unrealistic, however anomalous they may seem to modern readers.

The young novelist was also receiving letters from female fans who recognized themselves in his characters. No one knows how many adventures these occasioned, but there were certainly several. In fact Balzac was looking for more than just an affair. If he could just find a young, aristocratic, beautiful, and wealthy woman without a husband, he could offer his genius (and, of course, his debts). The most important letter arrived in 1832, signed *L'Etrangère* (the Foreigner, or Stranger). She was to be the love of his life. A fabulously wealthy Russian countess, married to a man twenty-two years her senior, and bored in the midst of vast estates, Mme Evelina Hanska began an affair that was to last, more or less, until Balzac's death. Only a few of her letters remain, since she forced him to destroy them, but his correspondence has been carefully preserved and provides valuable information about the years in question. The two did not meet until 1833, but despite Balzac's intervening love affairs and the divine "Eve's" autocratic capriciousness and well-justified jealousy, the novelist was from then on her faithful epistler and, when he could spare the time or find the money for a visit, her lover. She became the center of his dreams.

Eugénie Grandet (translated as *Eugenia Grandet*, 1843), one of Balzac's most widely acclaimed masterpieces, appeared in 1834. Even the establishment critic Sainte-Beuve greeted it with exaggerated praise, by implication holding it up as a classical exception to the rest of Balzac's ungainly production—praise that Maurice Bardèche terms "perfide," since it congratulates Balzac for

all the qualities that he does not have: delicacy, measure, sobriety, gracefulness. Bardèche echoes Balzac's own discomfort. Both realized that readers who like *Eugénie Grandet* often do so for the wrong reasons. Still, while fervent Balzacians may see it lacking the magnificently pulsating details that give other of the novelist's works depth of meaning and passionate life, there can be no question of its enduring popularity. It tells of a sweet, young provincial maiden, the daughter of a brutish miser, who because of her inexperience in worldly matters falls in love with her weak and unworthy cousin, Charles. Still, at the end of her gray life, the few years of fruitless love remain the only spark of color. Grandet finally dies, but his household continues to operate as it always has: Eugénie, an excellent steward of her enormous fortune, lives pretty much as she did when her father was alive. She lights the fire only on those days when it was permitted in her youth; she dresses as her mother did; and she remains in the dark, cold, melancholy house where she was raised. Balzac picks up the images of the novel's introduction and repeats them in the end, thus insisting on a continuation of the cycle of provincial behavior. Seemingly, though there has been some small turbulence in the placid pond of Saumur, it has passed, and equilibrium has returned.

Eugénie Grandet differs from much of Balzac's work in that the economy of language he always sought was achieved with less apparent prolixity. At base, his stories are usually quite simple and straightforward. The descriptive complexity arose from his desire to fit his characters and their lives into a physical and metaphysical world that would satisfactorily highlight the point he wanted to make. The seeming simplicity of *Eugénie Grandet* comes from Balzac's decision to use uneventfulness to emphasize the few things that matter to the heroine. In spite of being surrounded by gross materialism, she is quite successful at establishing and pursuing the spiritual values implied by her love of Charles and of the church.

La Recherche de l'absolu (1834; translated as *The Philosopher's Stone*, 1844) brings some already established themes and images together in a novel of considerable power. The monomania that marks so many of Balzac's characters recurs in Balthazar Claës, who focuses not on money but on the attempt to find the essential force underlying reality, the hypostasis. From faithful husband and father, he becomes an insane scientist, pouring the family fortune into the purchase of chemicals, laboratory equipment, furnaces, and machines. For Balzac such concentrated thought could scarcely fail. Add to that his belief in some sort of elemental power at the base of all things (outlined in *Louis Lambert* and *Séraphîta*), and it was difficult for the novelist to leave Balthazar's twenty years of efforts and seven-million-franc investment without any results. On his deathbed the now-paralyzed maniac has a sudden idea that will doubtless lead to success—"Eurêka!" he cries before falling back, lifeless. The discovery comes too late, however. He no longer has the strength even to speak, much less to pursue his quest. His dull eyes express his regret at his inability to leave behind the enigmatic key to the hypostasis he has sought his life long.

Balzac's most important publication of 1834 was *Scènes de la vie parisienne* (Scenes of Parisian Life), since, by adding to *Scènes de la vie privée* and *Scènes de la vie de province* (Scenes of Provincial Life, 1834-1837), it continued laying out the structural armature for what would become *La Comédie humaine*. The centerpiece of the collection (which also republished several of the best stories of 1832) was *Histoire des Treize*, which followed the pattern indicated in *Même histoire* and brought together three seemingly disparate stories. By their very lack of obvious links to each other, they reflect the fragmented reality of the society that permits the secret league of the Thirteen to operate, but they are integrated in some ways, first of all by the occult power of the group acting in each of the three stories. There are other unifying elements. Paris, a setting of enormous importance to each of the three episodes, is a monster, and it produces monstrous people who prey on the innocent. Comparisons to demons and the devil; references to the Orient and "Asiatic pleasures"; themes of revenge, wasted youth, and useless aristocrats; and images of fire, branding, masks, and veils are notable in all three. After explicitly referring to Caligula and Nero in the first two novellas, the author introduces us to a world of comparable depravity in the third. With each rereading the common elements multiply. The volume includes a veritable plethora of orphans, either real (M. Jules, Auguste de Maulincour, Armand de Montriveau) or functional (Mme Jules, Henri de Marsay, and his sister, Margarita de San-Réal).

On the most accessible level the three stories are joined by reappearing characters, the most important of whom are members of this terri-

Caricature of Balzac and his wife, depicting him as a member of a fictitious holy order of a debtors' prison

fying and secret league of "treize hommes qui recommencèrent la Société de Jésus au profit du diable" (thirteen men who started the Society of Jesus over again for the benefit of the devil). As a group they are very gifted, completely amoral, and intensely loyal to each other. Balzac knew his audience and was delighted to give them the melodramatic tales of intense emotion and violence they wanted, and it would be wrong to neglect the popular side of his plots and characters. But it would be equally wrong to limit his fictions to such traits. If the reader follows well-established narrative practice and views the characters as empty of individual significance in their roles of master, victim, or violator—and, as John R. O'Connor notes, the plots as penetrations—other comments seem appropriate.

Every one of the three stories is a tale of seduction. In each the destructive power penetrates further, killing the object of desire, while only in the last does the penetration result in the physical act of love. The masters are divine and human, both male and female. The victims come from each of the classes: proletariat (slave), bourgeoisie, and aristocracy. And the violators are in every case young and aristocratic. They have no legitimate right to intrude, but, when frustrated, each feels justified in seeking revenge, becoming not just judge but executioner as well. When viewed abstractly, the progression in the stories cannot be mistaken. The seducer, in all cases an intruder, is unwelcome in the first story. While increasingly welcome in succeeding accounts, he is always illegitimate. Balzac's methods of linking through analogous character types and plot structures in *Histoire des Treize* were to be exploited more fully as he continued to erect the monumental *Comédie humaine*.

Scholars cite *Le Père Goriot, histoire parisienne* (1835; translated as *Daddy Goriot*, 1860) as the work in which Balzac first systematically made use of the device of reappearing characters. His sister, Laure, reported that around 1833 he burst into her apartment and announced that he had just become a genius. He was talking of his idea to use his characters to link various works. The idea doubtless resulted from the enormous pressure under which he regularly worked. On needing a character, it was probably easier to use one he had already developed, and, while other novelists would have stopped there, Balzac went on and recognized that it could through multiplication become a device of considerable power in creating a warp and woof that would bind all his novels into one enormous tapestry. In addition, it had the tremendous advantage of realism. Human beings commonly meet people and later may lose track of them. On coming into contact again, the latter have usually changed considerably because of activity about which the other party knows, learns, or remains ignorant. In *Le Père Goriot*, Balzac took Gobseck and Mme de Restaud from *Les Dangers de l'inconduite*. From "La Femme abandonnée" (The Forsaken Woman, included in *Scènes de la vie de province*, 1834) he took Mme de Beauséant. He also employed Mme de Langeais from *La Duchesse de Langeais* and Rastignac from *La Peau de chagrin*. And as he had been doing regularly, he mixed in the names of historic personages and added new creations.

The size of Balzac's project and its ultimate shape were becoming clearer to him. On 16 October 1834 he detailed the project in a letter to Mme Hanska. Balzac meant his cycle to be broken into three parts or *études* (studies). *Etudes de mœurs* (Studies of Manners) would consider particular social "effects," with a view to universals and types. Then *Etudes philosophiques* would focus on the causes. Finally *Etudes analytiques* (Analytic Studies) would present the principles. As he explained to Mme Hanska, "A mesure que l'œuvre gagne en spirale les hauteurs de la pensée, elle se resserre et se condense. S'il faut 24 volumes pour les *Etudes de mœurs*, il n'en faudra que 15 pour les *Et*[udes] *phil*[osophiques]; il n'en faut que 9 pour les *Etudes analytiques*" (as the work spirals up to the heights of thought, it grows close together and is condensed. If 24 volumes are necessary for the *Etudes de mœurs*, only 15 will be necessary for the *Et*[udes] *phil*[osophiques]; only 9 are necessary for the *Etudes analytiques*).

Etudes de mœurs was to be broken into six *scènes* (in the 1842 "Avant-propos" to *La Comédie humaine* he calls them "six books"). He saw the first section on private life as representing infancy and adolescence, where he would consider emotions, sensations, and sins resulting from inexperience and ignorance of the world's ways. These episodes are not limited geographically; they come from the countryside, from the provinces, and from Paris. The following *Scènes de la vie de province* is limited in setting and subject matter to the phase of human life where passions, calculations, and ideas take the place of sensations and thoughtless impulses. Though not neglecting the unavoidable relationships to Paris, it is centered on provincial life and on the changes taking place in the moral and financial arenas.

Scènes de la vie parisienne is of course set in the capital city and in what Félix Davin termed the age approaching decrepitude. These scenes demonstrate Balzac's belief that in Paris true feelings seldom exist but are rather crushed by the coldhearted forces of a society where virtue is maligned, innocence is for sale, and passions become ruinous vices. Everything and everyone has a price. *Scènes de la vie politique* (Scenes of Political Life; first published in *La Comédie humaine*, 1846) takes up the interests of groups, as does *Scènes de la vie militaire* (Scenes of Military Life; first published in *La Comédie humaine*, 1845). In *Scènes de la vie de campagne* (Scenes of Country Life; first published in *La Comédie humaine*, 1846), however, the forces of society begin to wind down, and in *Etudes philosophiques*, the author claims to paint Life struggling with Desire. He leaves the terminal *Etudes analytiques* (first published in *La Comédie humaine*, 1846) with little comment, since the latter was, as he says, largely incomplete. In short, Balzac discussed the outline of *La Comédie humaine* at length, making quite certain the contour, if not the detail, of the whole.

The novelist's direction was clear by the time he published *Le Père Goriot*. The novel has importance beyond its reappearing characters and its position as a sort of crossroads for some of his themes. Because it chronicles the story of a charming rascal from the provinces who comes to Paris to make his fortune, it has long seemed quintessential Balzac, but it is also a widely acclaimed masterpiece. Its dual plots of a dying father and of a young man determined to rise in society on his mistress's back are subordinated to a vision of Paris in the early years of the Industrial Revolution. Both plots exemplify that tableau, as do the novel's images, relationships, and events. The picture Balzac draws is not a pretty one: a society that views money as virtue, a degraded society where familial love has no more value than it will bring in cold cash. Goriot should be understood as the incarnation of a society where the values have gone awry, where a debauched, profligate people have perverted the family, one of the basic institutions of civilization. Rastignac merely illustrates the implied theme, while Goriot is the only character who has manifested all three of "les trois grandes expressions de la société: l'Obéissance, la Lutte et la Révolte; la Famille, le Monde et Vautrin" (the three great manifestations of society: Obedience, Struggle, and Revolt; the Family, the World, and Vautrin). Like the recurring character Vautrin, Goriot has been a rebel; he even served as president of his section during the Revolution. This involvement gave birth to his fortune, since he sold grain to the revolutionaries, but it was his "struggle" that solidified his position. He not only knew grains, he was a genius at predicting the future market. When he tries to buy his daughters' love, he merely takes the "struggle" of a merchant to an extreme. Finally, he gives flesh to the concepts of Family and Obedience. "[P]our Eugène," and for the reader, Goriot "représentait la Paternité" ([F]or Eugène, [Goriot], represented Paternity).

This is a society where women prostitute themselves and feel perfectly justified in exploiting their families to satisfy their greed, where the war of the sexes does not stop with marriage. Its tainted love is best exemplified by Père Goriot. His excessive passion vividly sets it off when he actively encourages the irregular relationships that Paris has accepted in the stead of family and fatherhood. Moreover, he has taken part in all aspects of the society. He has been a rebel, he has struggled, and he has obediently submitted to the whims of his daughters. The price he pays for the latter failing is awesome. Fatherhood as represented by Goriot has worth in this world only to

the degree that it has financial value, the one value that has subsumed all others. Familial, fatherly love has indeed been corrupted. One might even say it is diseased, for it has been polluted by the all-consuming desire for luxurious self-gratification. Paternity has become a boardinghouse, a tailor, adulterous relationships, a venal bargain. Le Père Goriot was a tremendous success. Balzac's fame spread across Europe, as he was to discover to his pleasure when he made a quick trip to Vienna in 1835 to see Mme Hanska.

Balzac remained preoccupied with the sexual tensions of older women. In Le Lys dans la vallée, Henriette (Mme de Castries's given name) de Mortsauf refuses to take Félix de Vendenesse as a lover and dies of starvation and stomach cancer. On her deathbed she explicitly reveals the frustration and regret that the narrator has previously expressed symbolically. She suffers from her failure to "gather rosebuds." Sainte-Beuve claimed that Balzac was rewriting his own novel, Volupté (Voluptuous Pleasure, 1834), and thus getting even for the establishment critic's having panned La Recherche de l'absolu. Certainly Balzac both detested Sainte-Beuve and had read the latter's novel, but the theme of the ménage à trois with a platonic love affair on the distaff side had provided a well-worked model for dozens of variations since Jean-Jacques Rousseau's Julie, ou la Nouvelle Héloïse (1761; translated as Julia, or the New Eloisa, 1773). Still, there is little doubt that Balzac wanted to show what could be done with a theme that was patently beyond the likes of a Sainte-Beuve. He told Mme Hanska that he wanted to show the terrible struggle of a woman trying to remain faithful to her unlovable husband while being desperately in love with another man. While contemporary critics panned Le Lys dans la vallée, Balzac began working on La Vieille Fille (The Spinster, 1837), which is superficially in the same general line—an aging woman of wealth finally settles on a healthy-looking local suitor who turns out to be impotent. Georges Laffly, Fredric Jameson, and others see this as a wide-ranging critique of Restoration politics, where sterile middle-class values come up against a still potent but wasting monarchy.

Another string to Balzac's bow was his knowledge of the law. It resonates throughout La Comédie humaine—in the contract, for example, that deprived Father Birotteau of his apartment and furniture, and in Grandet's machinations to save his nephew Charles from bankruptcy—and occasionally provides the dominant key. In Le

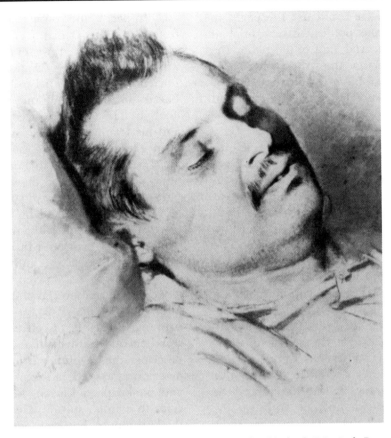

Drawing by Eugène Giraud of Balzac, several hours after his death (Musée de Besançon)

Contrat de mariage (The Marriage Contract, 1835), Paul de Mannerville, the weak-willed pretty boy of *La Fille aux yeux d'or*, has become enamored of Nathalie Evangélista, the assiduous disciple of her rapacious mother, who has wasted much of Nathalie's inheritance and has decided to use her to extort another fortune from Paul. The besotted young Mannerville is protected, however, by his shrewd attorney, Maître Mathias, in a key episode where Mme Evangélista tries through her legal representative to use the marriage contract and open the Mannerville estates to her depredations. Frustrated before the law, Nathalie is more successful. She convinces her new husband to distance the faithful Mathias and to allow himself little by little to be despoiled. In the end the bankrupted husband goes off to the Indies to attempt to repair his fortunes, while his wife continues her affair with the no longer chaste Félix de Vandenesse.

Where in *Le Contrat de mariage* the law was incapable of protecting a fool despite the best efforts of a shrewd lawyer, in *L'Interdiction* (The Prohibition, 1836) the law proves incapable before the collusions of society. Mme d'Espard has de-

cided to despoil her husband of his fortune. Although she claims M. d'Espard has become mentally incompetent, the poor man's only sin is perhaps exaggerated honesty and the refusal to follow his wife's wishes. The magnificently competent Judge Popinot, however, quickly sees through the wife's weak case, but before he is able to render a suitable judgment, Mme d'Espard pulls strings and succeeds in having the case removed from his authority. Justice can be easily perverted in a corrupt society.

In 1836 Balzac was under unstinting attack by writers working for the publisher François Buloz, with whom he had broken. He owed stories and novels to several publishers, who had already paid him. And his debts continued to mushroom. In short, he needed to make a lot of money very fast. On Christmas Eve of 1835, he had joined several others and bought a review, the *Chronique de Paris*. From Balzac's point of view, it was a tremendous coup. He could take his revenge on Buloz and such writers as Jules Janin and Sainte-Beuve who had been less than generous in their reviews of his work. He could call on the best writers of the day, who were, after all, his friends. He could use the pages to set himself up for the political career he had dreamed of for years. And, best of all, Balzac the publisher could pay Balzac the writer generously.

Every Saturday, Balzac had dinners for "his" writers and artists. The wonderful food and wines were, of course, on the cuff. The guests—Gustave Planche, Alphonse Karr, Théophile Gautier, Victor Hugo, Charles de Bernard, Henri Monnier, Honoré Daumier, and others—were amusing, and everyone had a good time. Unfortunately, Balzac did not receive as much material as he had expected from his friends. In fact, stimulated by the excitement of the new venture to increase his already unbelievable production, he wrote most of the copy himself. Operating funds were limited, and the bankers had not proven as ready to lend money as the eternal optimist had expected. Given that he lacked the deep pockets that would have permitted extensive publicity and continued publication despite a difficult beginning—when new subscribers were not only slow to come but actually decreased from month to month—by mid May, Balzac announced to Mme Hanska that there was no hope. By July nothing remained but more debts and, on the credit side, an even more thorough understanding of the publishing scene, knowledge that would join with what he had learned through his printing business and his experience as an author trying to make a living in Paris. It would serve as the base for one of his best novels, *Illusions perdues*.

This first part of *Illusions perdues* was written at top speed. Mme Charles Béchet, finally at the end of her patience, took Balzac to court. He owed her two volumes, and she wanted them within twenty-four hours. That was impossible, even for Balzac, so he fled Paris for Saché, where he set to work and, he told Mme Hanska, produced two volumes in twenty days. Part 1 tells the tale of "two poets": Lucien Chardon and his brother-in-law David Séchard. David's father manages to convince his son to accept a fool's bargain for the barely viable printing business he has built. As the third part of the novel makes clear, David and his wife, Eve, would have been successful had Lucien not burdened them with debt. Lucien, who takes his mother's maiden name to become M. de Rubempré, is handsome and prefers adventure to effort. He runs off to Paris with Mme de Bargeton. He plans on becoming a famous poet, but the much older Mme de Bargeton soon has second thoughts, and Lucien is left to his own devices.

In part 2, the young man's options are manifested first in Daniel d'Arthez and the small group of dedicated writers committed to hard work and excellence. Daniel makes it clear that Lucien has the potential to be a fine poet, but as Balzac insisted over and over, talent is not enough. The long patience displayed by d'Arthez and his friends, required of outstanding writers, soon exposes Lucien's basic weakness of character. Lucien succumbs to Lousteau and the facile journalism that Balzac describes at length. Even here, however, in a world that Balzac paints as lacking in aesthetic and moral standards, Lucien is exceptional in his willingness to shift with the wind of every proffered franc, and he soon loses his credibility, even as a journalist.

In part 3, Lucien returns home to Angoulême. Despite David's invention of an inexpensive, new kind of paper that permits modern printing, Lucien is forced to watch the Séchards sink beneath the debts that he contracted. Balzac describes the revolutionary changes taking place in printing as well as the process of credit, debt, and bankruptcy. Lucien, filled with shame, decides to commit suicide. He changes his mind at the last minute, however, and purchases his salvation by agreeing to become the "creature" of the homosexual criminal Vautrin. After Angoulême's competing printers steal David's invention, he is left penniless—until he receives a miraculous inheritance. His father has managed to invest cleverly and leaves the Séchards reasonably well fixed.

No one could maintain Balzac's pace. In the midst of long hours with pen, manuscripts, and proofs, he had a stroke. It did not slow him for long, however. Soon he began an affair with Contessa Fanny Guidoboni-Visconti; took a trip to Italy with Caroline Marbouty, who was dressed like a man (or like George Sand); continued his abundant correspondence with Mme Hanska, claiming undying fidelity; and of course wrote more novels and short stories: "Facino Cane," "La Messe de l'athée" (The Atheist's Mass, 1836), *La Femme supérieure* (1838; translated as *Bureaucracy; or, a Civil Service Reformer*, 1889), *Gambara* (1839), and *Massimilla Doni* (1839; both translated in *Gambara. Massimilla Doni. The Accursed Child*, 1899). But the increasingly determined creditors were making life impossible. His tilbury was seized; bailiffs battered on the doors of both his addresses; and publisher William Duckett was determined to have him thrown in jail for debts. Using an errand for the Guidoboni-Viscontis as an excuse, he fled again for Italy, and for three months he had a wonderful time basking in the adulation of an international audience. When he returned to Paris, the problems had not gone away. As Maurois points out, it was not merely that he owed something like 162,000 francs, but that his opportunities for minting new money were limited. Editors had already paid for a goodly number of novels and short stories that remained stored in Balzac's mind, and the point had come where they resisted paying more advances. As Maurois concludes, one of the most astonishing characteristics of Balzac's creation was that regardless of the pressures forcing him to produce another work, each new addition was not only artistically satisfying but fit in the growing edifice of *La Comédie humaine*. Nothing interfered with Balzac's sure sense of aesthetic integrity. As for his debts, clearly what he needed was a new hideout. He moved in with the Guidoboni-Viscontis, thanks to the eccentric but understanding contessa.

Of course, the bailiffs were not far behind, and Balzac was soon forced to flee to Saché, which could only be a temporary solution. He could not live without Paris, and he needed to be in touch with his editors. The only solution was to buy land on the outskirts of Paris and build a house that would be convenient for him but difficult for creditors (one with several exits). The project would cost something like 40,000 francs, of which he lacked the first sou. But he found some land and a builder who would begin work for a small down payment, and Les Jardies was under way.

Balzac set to work on *Histoire de la grandeur et de la décadence de César Birotteau* (1837), which tells the story of one of the many thousands who came to Paris to make their fortunes. Unlike most, César does very well, so much so that as the novel opens, he prepares to celebrate his success by luxuriously redecorating his house, by throwing a grand ball, and by capping his already significant fortune with an investment in some undeveloped property. Just as the wife of Julius Caesar had a premonitory dream, so does César's wife in Balzac's novel, and César, like his eponym, refuses to listen. When his notary Roguin embezzles his money and flees, the Birotteau world collapses with the perfumer's bankruptcy.

The novel allowed Balzac to investigate the world of the small shopkeeper and the demon of speculation. Certainly the novelist knew all there

was to know about borrowing money, about the way bankers and usurers made money from others' misfortunes, about the legal ramifications of debt. Perhaps the most interesting aspect of the novel is the portrait of Birotteau as he rebuilds his fortune. Though he and his family work together, scrimping and saving, to pay the debt, the final rehabilitation comes because of Anselme Popinot, who goes against the advice of his uncle, Judge Popinot, for the love of Birotteau's daughter Césarine. He turns César's idea for regenerative hair oil into a raging success.

Modern-day advertising was making significant strides in the nineteenth century. Not only do the perfumer and his future son-in-law develop several products, they manage to make them salable, and they exploit every means at their disposal for making people aware and desirous of the products. Birotteau is the quintessential shopkeeper in a nation of shopkeepers. His mistake, for which he pays dearly, is to turn from his talent as an entrepreneur to the greedy world of speculation. He thus falls victim to the villainous du Tillet. After many years of poverty, he is finally able to pay his debts and thus shake off the opprobrium of the bankrupt, but the effort kills him. At the ball given to celebrate Anselme's marriage to Césarine, Birotteau's joy is unbearable. He collapses and dies. In the midst of a touching love story, a family tragedy, and a knowing consideration of the financial world, Balzac thus issues a stern warning that speculation was undermining France.

The companion piece to *César Birotteau, La Maison Nucingen* (The Nucingen House, 1838), has been called an intersection of *La Comédie humaine*, since it mentions so many characters and touches on so many events. It is, as well, a masterpiece of indirection and subtlety. The anonymous narrator happens to overhear the malicious, verbal-pyrotechnician Bixiou explain the source of the banker Nucingen's fabulous fortune and Rastignac's comfortable wealth. Just as the narrator hears the story through the thin partition, so Bixiou slowly tears down all the veils and baffles with which Nucingen has hidden his fraud, and the reader is allowed behind the scenes in both the Nucingen Bank and family. Birotteau the sheep is opposed to Nucingen the lynx.

Soon Balzac had a new scheme for making an enormous amount of money. He had heard about some Sardinian slag heaps, left by Romans, from which modern methods could extract a fortune in silver. For once the affair was apparently legitimate, but by the time Balzac left Paris to investigate the matter it was too late, and he was out the expenses of his trip. While traveling, he sketched *La Torpille* (The Torpedo, 1838), which was to become the first part of another of his enormous frescoes, *Splendeurs et misères des courtisanes* (written 1838-1846; translated as *Splendors and Miseries of Courtisans*, 1895). It would take many years to complete; indeed, part 4 was not joined to the other three parts, as a note in the Furne *corrigé* directed, until long after his death. In its final incarnation (1869, in *Œuvres complètes de H. de Balzac. Edition définitive*) the novel paints the picture of Paris as a sycophant or prostitute. Rotten with greed and a frenetic desire for pleasure, the city has sold its soul to Vautrin. The novel illustrates the theme with Lucien de Rubempré and Esther van Gobseck—a courtesan previously known as "La Torpille" (The Torpedo)—who, despite their love for each other, are committed to obey Vautrin.

Esther attracts the wealthy banker Nucingen, who pays Vautrin a handsome price to sleep with her. Tragically, the now elegant young woman cannot bear to sink back to her previous state, so she commits suicide. Lucien, however, has fewer scruples, and he conducts a series of compromising affairs with wealthy and socially powerful women, all to bring power and wealth to Vautrin. Finally Lucien's weakness, which was so thoroughly demonstrated in *Illusions perdues*, brings about Vautrin's arrest. In despair, Lucien commits suicide as well. And Vautrin decides to "compromise" with the society against which he has long been at war. He uses letters that Lucien's conquests had written to blackmail representatives of the government into appointing him Chief of Police. The lesson is clear. Vautrin has not really changed. It is simply that society has become so debased that the criminal can easily find acceptance as an equal.

When Balzac returned from Italy, he moved into his new hideaway, Les Jardies, and settled down to finish *Le Cabinet des antiques* (1839; translated as *The Gallery of Antiquities*, 1899). This novel is once again set in Alençon, where *La Vieille Fille* takes place. For some reason Balzac never did integrate the two novels, and characters who are patently the same bear different names. Nonetheless *Le Cabinet des antiques*, like *La Vieille Fille*, continues to fill in Balzac's vision of the provinces, where an impotent aristocracy is

not only incapable of controlling a rapacious and burgeoning middle class but falls prey to it.

In *Béatrix, ou les Amours forcés* (1839; translated as *Béatrix*, 1895), he tells the thinly veiled story of Franz Liszt and Marie d'Agoult, if not of George Sand and Jules Sandeau. Of course he changed the names and shifted Sand's Nohant from Berry to Brittany, but his Félicité des Touches, who uses the authorial pseudonym Camille Maupin, can write as well as any man—the male chauvinist Balzac felt that the cigar-smoking Sand, whom he admired, was an androgyne. The book begins with the idea of a dying love that has become a burden, but it soon turns to the rivalry between Camille Maupin and Béatrix de Rochefide over Calyste du Guénic. Camille virtually throws the young man into Béatrix's arms, thus causing the young, naive Calyste to leave his wife for the quickly bored Béatrix, who takes delight in letting Calyste's wife know of her husband's affair. Camille herself decides that she loves him to desperation, gives away her money, repudiates her books, and withdraws to a convent. Balzac used the novel to explore the personalities of two women who feel themselves sufficiently above the law to ignore conventions. The one, Camille, truly is superior, the other merely rebellious.

Balzac's debts had become staggering (Maurois calculates that in June 1840, the novelist owed something like 262,000 francs), and his creditors had discovered Les Jardies. Clearly, Balzac needed to do something decisive. He would write a play. He found a director who was anxious to have something of his to produce. Unfortunately, Balzac had other obligations—novels to write—so he was not able to devote himself to the script of *Vautrin* (1840) until the night before he was scheduled to read it to Félix Harel. He called together several of his friends: Auguste de Belloy, Edouard Ourliac, Alphonse-Jean Laurent, known as Laurent-Jan, and Gautier (who told the story later). They thought he was going to use them for a sounding board before attempting the theater itself. Balzac quickly disabused them: they were going to help him. If each of them wrote an act, the play would be ready in the morning. At first, the friends seemed willing. Could Balzac give them some idea of what was supposed to happen? That, however, would not do. Balzac was well aware of his marathon habits as a raconteur, and he simply lacked the time for such niceties. Of course, when morning came, though they had had a good time, Balzac lacked a draft, and the reading was postponed. Finally, with help from Laurent-Jan, the play was finished and performed on 14 March 1840. It closed the next day. Many journalists, who resented the way Balzac had portrayed them in *Illusions perdues*, were hostile, as was King Louis-Philippe, who learned that a thoroughly ridiculous character resembled him rather too much.

Apparently undismayed, Balzac finished *Le Curé de village: Scène de la vie de campagne* (1841; translated as *The Village Rector*, 1893), in which he used a good deal of what he had learned in his unsuccessful attempt to save the life of the murderer Peytel. Certain realities in the author's life were difficult to ignore. Betrayed by the theater, lacking money, and constantly harassed by his creditors (even his now impoverished mother was beginning to press for help), he borrowed 10,000 francs from his lover Hélène de Valette and started *La Revue Parisienne* (July-September, 1840). As always, Balzac turned to such enterprises with great enthusiasm. He wrote a devastating review of Sainte-Beuve's *Histoire de Port-Royal* (History of Port-Royal, 1840-1848); a brilliantly insightful piece about the unknown Stendhal and his *La Chartreuse de Parme* (1839; translated as *The Charterhouse of Parma*, 1925); a masterpiece in "Z. Marcas," which insisted that the gerontocracy of the July Monarchy left the youth with no future whatsoever. Again, he wrote virtually all the copy himself. When creditors made him especially miserable, he offered to placate some of them by allowing them to auction off Les Jardies. It only brought 17,500 francs (from Balzac himself, who secretly bought it back before fleeing to another hideaway in the village of Passy).

The "Avant-propos" to the Furne edition of *La Comédie humaine* in 1842 proclaims in no uncertain terms that Balzac's novels and short stories fit into a carefully constructed whole. Indeed, by the late 1830s and early 1840s, the grand design of Balzac's cycle was filling in. The study of "causes" and, especially, of the human will in *Etudes philosophiques* and the passionate dramas of *Scènes de la vie privée* had been pretty much fixed since the early 1830s. Now *Scènes de la vie de province* was almost complete. In the first half of the section, he describes the traits that make the provinces distinctive. In general, the provinces are defined primarily by what they are not, which is Paris. The main difference is that, while provincials usually work together, especially against outsiders, Parisians are solitary creatures. Their primary allegiance is almost always to themselves,

and those who cannot stand alone are destroyed. One needs to be particularly strong to succeed in France's capital, where weak provincials such as Savinien de Portenduère or Victurnien d'Esgrigon are quickly stripped of their assets and weighted down with debts.

The first portion of *Scènes de la vie de province*, from *Ursule Mirouët* through *La Muse du département*, is organized around the repulsion of outsiders, usually from Paris, in order to maintain provincial monopolies. Without exception, the novels portray rival groups of provincials that band together at some point to repel the foreigner, all for the purpose of retaining any wealth or advantage within the community. Although the provincials do not always succeed— Ursule Mirouët (the diaeresis marks her as an outsider) and the Parisian Joseph Bridau, for example, eventually gain inheritances—the efforts of the locals constitute the basic activity of these novels, forming an armature around which there is considerable room for variation.

In *Eugénie Grandet*, the Cruchotins and the Grassinistes forget their rivalry in order to expel Grandet's nephew, Charles. Although the constituent elements change in *Pierrette* (1840), the pattern remains the same. Like Denis Minoret of *Ursule Mirouët*, who returns home after making something of a fortune in Paris, the Rogrons of *Pierrette* come back to the provinces where they were born. Also like Dr. Minoret, though for different reasons, they have problems with the local powers, and they begin slowly to build their own group. Minoret brings his ward, Ursule, with him, and tries to protect her from his preying relatives, while the Rogrons do not import their cousin, Pierrette, until long after their arrival. Despite their promises to allow the girl to inherit their wealth, the Rogrons abuse and eventually kill her. In *Le Curé de Tours*, Troubert uses the Congregation's (an influential organization of Catholic laymen) power from Paris to impose his will on the natives who, while never accepting him, are obliged to allow Father Birotteau's destitution. Birotteau had a group of provincial friends, but the little priest has been so entranced with his self-centered pleasures that he acts on his own, ignores the warnings, is isolated from his protectors, and loses everything.

La Rabouilleuse, first published as *Les Deux Frères* (1842; translated as *The Two Brothers*, 1887), incorporates other variations. Here the inheritance has long been in the provinces. Because Agathe left at an early age for Paris, however, her half brother who stayed in the provinces found it simple to disinherit her. From then on, the novel recounts the story of several outsiders who attempt to build an indigenous support group that will allow them to seize the fortune successfully if not always legitimately. Philippe Bridau is able to overcome Max Gilet because he can gain acceptance by the local powers and discredit Max's group. And so it goes. The last three works of this section, *La Vieille Fille, Le Cabinet des antiques,* and *Illusions perdues,* describe the stultifying provinces, which have become demonstratively less capable of defending themselves against Parisians and modern financial forces.

The year 1842 was important for Balzac. Most important, without any doubt, was the publication of the first volume of his monumental cycle, *La Comédie humaine.* The collective title was a stroke of genius. Not only did *Comédie* suggest the personal dramas that would satisfy the hungers of a nineteenth-century audience, it promised something with the significance and beauty of Dante's *Divine Comedy.* In the "Avant-propos" Balzac announced that he was a naturalist who would study the varieties of human beings—whether soldiers, shopkeepers, or criminals—in the same way that scientists investigate plants and animals. The thought was daunting, since humankind had far more such "species" than other natural kingdoms. A miser, for example, changed depending on his situation. If one thinks of the misers that have been portrayed in French literature, there can be no doubt that the type can include notably differing traits and qualities. Some misers are thieves; some are stupid, some brilliant, some married; some live in small towns, some in the country, some in Paris. Balzac even introduced a charitable miser in *Ursule Mirouët.* The novelist felt that each variety deserved to be recorded and set off appropriately. Of course, not even Balzac could complete the task. Spoelberch de Lovenjoul has published a list of more than fifty projected but uncompleted titles. The novelist's letters and notes contain many other ideas.

It was also in 1842 that Balzac learned that Mme Hanska's husband had passed away. Finally, he thought, the dream could be realized. He would throw himself at his dear Eve's feet, as soon as he could gather the necessary funds to make the trip (he busily wrote another play, *Les Ressources de Quinola* [Quinola's Resources, 1842], which held out a little longer than *Vautrin,* but

nonetheless failed miserably). Mme Hanska's response was slow in coming, and when it came, she was decidedly unenthusiastic. She had her daughter to educate; there were problems with the inheritance; her family would not approve of a marriage to a man like Balzac. In such an extremity, there was only one thing to do. The indefatigable creator wrote a novel—*Albert Savarus* (1842; translated in *The Purse, and Albert Savarus* 1883)—in which the hero loses the love of his life and joins the Carthusians, dedicating the rest of his days to silence and meditation. Mme Hanska neither appreciated the novel nor took the hint. She remained cool to her ardent suitor.

Although Balzac maintained that he was uniquely in a state of waiting, his production continued unabated. *Honorine* (1844) tells of the title heroine's leaving her husband for an unworthy lover, who quickly abandons her. Though she tries to support herself by making artificial flowers, she escapes starvation only because her husband secretly buys her product. *La Muse du département* was, the author claimed, like a more realistic version of Benjamin Constant's *Adolphe* (1816), relentlessly following a love affair killed by poverty and betrayal.

To Balzac's terror, Franz Liszt visited the still attractive Evelina Hanska. Clearly, Balzac needed to make a trip to Russia. Unfortunately, there were debts, promised manuscripts, and the never-ending proofs for his collected works. Part 3 of *Illusions perdues, Les Souffrances de l'inventeur* (The Inventor's Sufferings, 1843), continues the touching love story of David Séchard and his Eve, as he falls victim to unscrupulous villains and loses his invention. Finally, however, the novelist was able to break away and travel to St. Petersburg and his much loved Eve. There seems little doubt that Balzac reconquered Mme Hanska and that they spent one of their happiest times together. Both he and Eve remembered the interlude with joy.

Back in Paris, Balzac was once again denied entrance to the French Academy. The immortals did not view debts with the same equanimity as the creator of *La Comédie humaine.* Despite his exhaustion and his increasingly worrisome health, his extraordinary output continued. The fashion in novels was changing, however. Eugène Sue's *Les Mystères de Paris* (1842-1843; translated as *The Mysteries of Paris,* 1844) had been especially successful, and newspaper readers waited breathlessly for the next installment of Alexandre Dumas, *père*'s serialized novels. Balzac's long introductions and tales marked by a paucity of romantic episodes were difficult to serialize, and the master found it frustrating to satisfy the new exigencies. He tried with *Modeste Mignon* (1844; translated as *Modeste Mignon*, 1888), a novel Mme Hanska had inspired. It tells the story of a young woman who becomes enamored of Balzac's fictional poet, Canalis. The latter, surfeited with such attention, passes off the girl's letters to his secretary, Ernest de La Brière, for answers, and a prolonged correspondence grows into love on both sides. Unfortunately the girl continues to believe that her correspondent is Canalis, and, on being disabused, it takes a long time for her to recognize the real love that unites her with Ernest. Herbert J. Hunt appropriately summarizes the way the novel ends: "The fairy-tale conclusion which benefits this story—*they lived happily ever afterwards*—is translated by Balzac into terms of estates, incomes and titles."

Balzac remembered *Splendeurs et misères des courtisanes*, left unfinished. This event-filled narration was perfect for the new expectations: full of mystery, masks, pseudonyms, criminals, villains of the first water, purified prostitutes, murders, and suicides; in short, everything that melodrama demanded. He wrote part 2, which he called *Esther, ou les Amours d'un vieux banquier* (Esther, or The Loves of an Old Banker, 1844). *Les Paysans* began serialization in *La Presse* in December 1844, but it simply could not stand up to the competition. The newspaper unceremoniously dumped it in midstream, switching to Dumas's *La Reine Margot* (1845; translated as *Marguerite de Valois*, 1846). *Les Paysans* was still unfinished at his death. Critics gleefully announced that Balzac's time had passed. Headaches, jaundice, and terrible stomach pains continued, but he worked nonetheless. If only he could go see Eve in Dresden. However, his beloved countess was in the midst of arranging her daughter Anna's marriage. If there was anything she did not want, it was the help of her French lover. Balzac was firmly told to remain where he was. Finally, in April 1845, he was allowed to come. He left immediately and began four months of play, traveling with Eve, Anna, and her new fiancé.

On arriving in Paris, Mme Hanska was displeased with Balzac's housekeeper, Mme Louise de Brugnol (Balzac baptized her with the particle), suspecting correctly that there was more to this keeping house than met the eye. The novelist was ordered to get rid of her, a process that turned out to be painful and expensive, since

Mme de Brugnol stole Eve's letters and began to blackmail Balzac with them. While Evelina and the others went on toward Italy, the novelist needed to remain and meet obligations. The Parisian side of his affairs was less than absorbing, however, and he soon threw it all up to rejoin the travelers. Finally he returned to Paris with a hundred thousand of Mme Hanska's francs, which were supposed to pay for the couple's Parisian house, but his creditors came running. In addition, he "invested" some of it, and he began to buy antiques (without exception "genuine" originals with passionately interesting histories, guaranteed of course by the merchants). He had no fear of the growing hole in the funds entrusted to him. The stock he bought in the Northern Railroad would refill the coffers. He tried to work, but the results were disappointing. The only thing that slowed his unreasoning spending was a call from his beloved to join her in Rome.

On returning to Paris, while the Hanska group continued on to Germany, Balzac was frantically busy, paying debts and searching for a house. Delighted with the news that his dear Eve would have their child, he was so excited that he seemingly did not notice his mistress's growing hesitation about marriage. There were many reasons for Mme Hanska's second thoughts, but the most obvious was simple. Balzac as lover was a wonderful lark; the thought of him as a husband with his hands in the purse was considerably less amusing. Although Mme Hanska now explicitly forbade him to purchase a house, he found a wonderful buy and could not resist. To seal the bargain, he deposited fifty shares of the Northern Railroad (which were dropping in value). And he began a whirlwind of activity, arranging for repairs, restoring, redecorating, buying furniture. Although few of Mme Hanska's letters remain, her trepidation at the irrepressible spendthrift is tangible in Balzac's letters as he tried to placate her. As for his writing, he continued to be stumped with *Les Paysans*, and when he learned not only that the baby had died but that Eve did not wish to see him, he went into what sounds like serious depression. It seemed impossible to rekindle his creative hearth.

However much one may know that Balzac was himself responsible for his problems, one cannot but feel enormous sympathy for him. In his late forties, as he approached the end of his life, he had no peace. Creditors continually harassed him; his investments in the Northern Railroad soured; Louise de Brugnol threatened all kinds of difficulties; the French Academy preferred mediocrities to him; jealous journalists pilloried him; and, worst of all, his lifetime dream of marriage into aristocracy and wealth was crumbling around him.

Balzac lived everything in excess. He abused coffee and rich food in order to work excessively. The mythomania that so richly infused his creations spilled over into his life, and women such as Mme de Brugnol can scarcely be blamed for believing his promises. Even when antique dealers and investment counselors did not advance an absurdly extravagant story, Balzac would concoct and apparently believe one of his own. His profligate spending seemed to respond to some deep-seated pathological need. Today, he would belong to Gamblers Anonymous, to Overeaters Anonymous, and have enough compulsive tendencies left over for a dozen psychoanalysts. But he was nonetheless a master artist—Auguste Rodin was right to portray him as a monument. When his health began to fail and marriage to Mme Hanska seemed improbable, few would not pity him in the depths of his despair.

His depression lifted and his fire was reignited when Mme Hanska suddenly announced a visit to Paris. He found the energy to complete *La Dernière Incarnation de Vautrin* (The Last Incarnation of Vautrin, 1847—part 4 of *Splendeurs et misères des courtisanes*), and more important, since they represent two stars in his crown, he finished *Les Parents pauvres* (The Poor Parents, 1847), that is, *La Cousine Bette* (1847; translated as *Cousin Bette*, 1888) and *Le Cousin Pons* (1847; translated as *Cousin Pons*, 1880). The account of cousin Bette uses an everyday story of jealousy and weakness to show how France can be destroyed by its own demons, by the self-indulgence of the idle haves, which was feeding the envious hatred of the have-nots. Adeline Fischer, a Cinderella figure, is swept off her feet by the Napoleonic war-hero Baron Hulot d'Ervy. Hulot seems a development of the character Victor d'Aiglemont, whom the duc de Chastillonnest in *Une Femme de trente ans* describes as "un de ces hommes que le ciel a créés pour prendre et digérer quatre repas par jour, dormir, aimer la première venue et se battre" (one of these men whom heaven created to eat and digest four meals a day, to sleep, to love the first woman he crosses, and to fight). Although Hulot is as ignorant and as egotistical as Victor, he goes further in that one of his weaknesses is out of control. He is a satyr, and his satyriasis dishonors him personally, impoverishes his

family, and reduces his wife to prostitution. The family is saved from the besotted Hulot (who takes on the name of Vyder—*vider* means *to empty*) because of the son's financial astuteness and his cold-blooded willingness to accept one of Vautrin's murderous solutions. *La Cousin Bette* paints a France where family, church, and state are so weakened that the depredations of self-centered greed and lust can be controlled only by an evil genius like Vautrin.

Mme Hanska finally arrived in Paris, and although Balzac abandoned his work to show her his city, the visit was not a happy one. She hated the barnlike structure he had bought and saw little to recommend the furnishings, even though each one had a story and was especially chosen by her lover. She was regularly reminded of his many affairs and of his outrageously spendthrift ways. When she left in early 1847, he moved into the unappreciated house and tried to resist the marvelous investments offered by various antique dealers. He continued negotiations in an attempt to extract Eve's letters from Mme de Brugnol, and he calculated and recalculated how many new novels were needed to pay his debts. Though the great novelist seemed frenetically busy with such activities, he was incapable of serious work. He begged to visit his love in Russia, but the wary Evelina long refused him permission. When she finally relented, he extracted the necessary money from the publisher Souverain and joyously flew to join her on her estates in the Ukraine. The excitement and pleasure stimulated him, and he managed to work on several projects, though only *L'Envers de l'histoire contemporaine* (1846-1854; translated as *The Brotherhood of Consolation*, 1893) was ever completed. This novel would eventually close *Scènes de la vie parisienne*, and it serves as a mirror image of *Histoire des Treize*, which opens *Scènes de la vie parisienne*. Rather than thirteen men devoted to imposing their self-centered will on society, Mme de La Chantrie's equally secret group is committed to doing good and opposing the destructive ways of Paris.

By February, Balzac was back in Paris, once again trying to meet his obligations. Because his books were not selling in the quantities to satisfy his gargantuan needs, he turned again to the theater. This time he succeeded with *La Marâtre* (1848; translated as *The Stepmother*, 1901), which opened in May to undeviating praise but sparse audiences. The civil unrest surrounding the revolution of 1848 made people afraid to leave their homes, and the play quickly closed. However, he was not discouraged (he could ill afford to be), and he immediately began work on *Mercadet*. Here again, though, he had no success, at least not while he was alive. His health had definitely turned for the worse. His eyes were weak, he frequently had trouble getting his breath, and his heart was not functioning properly. With it all he suffered from depression and growing lassitude. He wanted nothing so much as to flee Paris and marry his dream.

Once he did arrive again at Mme Hanska's estates in the Ukraine, things did not go as smoothly as he would have liked. Whether because of his sickness or because he was far away from the stimulus of demanding creditors, he could summon little energy and was unable to concentrate. That he was seriously ill became increasingly evident. After a second heart attack the doctor forbade him to work and put him on various bizarre diets. Mme Hanska's fear of being shackled to Balzac's debts weakened, though the czar obliged her to transfer the family property to her daughter before marrying the foreigner. She finally received the czar's permission for the marriage. On 14 March 1850, the two ill people (Mme Hanska suffered increasingly from gout) made the long trip to the church in Berdichev and were married. Everyone must have known that Balzac was dying. The trip back to Paris was incredibly difficult. Balzac was almost blind, he had trouble breathing, and the pain in his chest scarcely let up. They had to stop and rest in Dresden. Though he perked up on arriving in Paris, he was soon bedridden. He would die just a few months later, on 18 August 1850. "La peau de chagrin," the magic skin, had shrunk to nothing.

Maurois tells that, at his funeral, the Minister of the Interior leaned over to Victor Hugo and said, "He was a distinguished man." Hugo replied, "He was a genius." It is an appropriate epitaph. Though Balzac's personal life was distressing, he was indeed a genius, and he left the work of a genius. *La Comédie humaine* stands strong among the great works of the Western world. His masterworks were sufficiently numerous to have made a half dozen writers famous; indeed, it is far from certain that a half dozen writers would have had the energy to produce his life's work. He was to have a profound impact on the novel, not just of France, Italy, Germany, Spain, Russia, and England, but of the Americas as well. Looking at the matter more than a century later, it seems that of French writers with international

reputations, perhaps Rabelais and Proust rival him in impact. For reasons having little to do with art, only Rousseau and Voltaire have had more impressive international influence. Only Baudelaire's aesthetic importance has been more profound. Truly, Balzac was a giant, and *La Comédie humaine* an extraordinary achievement.

Letters:
Correspondance, 5 volumes, edited by Roger Pierrot (Paris: Garnier, 1960-1968).

Bibliographies:
William Hobart Royce, *A Balzac Bibliography*, 2 volumes (Chicago: University of Chicago Press, 1929-1930);

"Revue bibliographique," *L'Année Balzacienne* (1961-);

Annie Lucienne Cosson, "Vingt ans de bibliographie balzacienne: 1948-67," Ph.D. dissertation, Columbia University, November 1970;

David Bellos, *Balzac Criticism in France 1850-1900* (New York: Oxford University Press, 1976);

Allan H. Pasco, with Anthony R. Pugh, "Balzac," in *Cabeen Critical Bibliography of French Literature: The Nineteenth Century*, 2 volumes (Syracuse: Syracuse University Press, 1992).

Biographies:
André Maurois, *Prométhée ou la vie de Balzac* (Paris: Hachette, 1956); translated by Norman Denny as *Prometheus: The Life of Balzac* (London: Bodley Head / New York: Harper & Row, 1965);

V. S. Pritchett, *Balzac* (London: Chatto & Windus / New York: Knopf, 1973).

References:
Erich Auerbach, "In the Hôtel de la Mole," in *Mimesis*, translated by W. R. Trask (Princeton: Princeton University Press, 1953), pp. 468-482;

Balzac: Génies et réalites (Paris: Hachette, 1959);

Balzac: L'Invention du roman, edited by Claude Duchet and Jacques Neefs (Paris: Belfond, 1982);

Balzac: Le Livre du centenaire (Paris: Flammarion, 1952);

Pierre Barbéris, *Balzac et le mal du siècle 1799-1833*, 2 volumes (Paris: Gallimard, 1970);

Maurice Bardèche, *Balzac, romancier* (Paris: Plon, 1940);

David F. Bell, "Balzac S.A.R.L.," *French Forum*, 14 (1989): 43-53;

David Bellos, "Varieties of Myth in Balzac's *La Cousine Bette*," in *Myth and Legend in French Literature*, edited by Keith Aspley (London: Modern Humanities Research Assn., 1982), pp. 137-154;

Victor Brombert, "Nathalie, or Balzac's Hidden Reader," in *The Hidden Reader: Stendhal, Balzac, Hugo, Baudelaire, Flaubert* (Cambridge, Mass.: Harvard University Press, 1988), pp. 23-36;

Peter Brooks, *Reading for the Plot: Design and Intention in Narrative* (New York: Knopf, 1984);

Michel Butor, "Balzac et la réalité," in *Répertoire I* (Paris: Editions de Minuit, 1960), pp. 79-93;

Ross Chambers, "Seduction Denied: *Sarrasine* and the Impact of Art," in *Story and Situation: Narrative Seduction and the Power of Fiction* (Minneapolis: University of Minnesota Press, 1984), pp. 72-96;

Pierre Citron, *Dans Balzac* (Paris: Seuil, 1986);

Priscilla P. Clark, "The Metamorphoses of Mentor: Fénelon to Balzac," *Romanic Review*, 75 (1984): 200-215;

Ernst Robert Curtius, *Balzac*, translated by H. Jourdan (Paris: Grasset, 1933);

Emile Faguet, *Balzac*, in *Etudes littéraires sur le dix-neuvième siècle* (Paris: Lecène et Dudin, 1887), pp. 413-453;

Faguet, *Les Grands Ecrivains français. Balzac* (Paris: Hachette, 1913);

Diana Festa, "Linguistic Intricacies in Balzac's *La Maison du chat-qui-pelote*," *Nineteenth-Century French Studies*, 17 (1988-1989): 30-43;

Alexander Fischler, "Rastignac-Télémaque: The Epic Scale in *Le Père Goriot*," *Modern Language Review*, 63 (1968): 840-848;

Lucienne Frappier-Mazur, *L'Expression métaphorique dans la "Comédie humaine": Domaine social et physiologique* (Paris: Klincksieck, 1976);

Eric Gans, "Balzac's Unknowable Masterpiece and the Limits of the Classical Esthetic," *MLN*, 90 (1975): 504-516;

F. W. J. Hemmings, *Balzac: An Interpretation of "La Comédie humaine"* (New York: Random House, 1967);

Léon-François Hoffmann and the Princeton Balzac Seminar, 1974, "Thèmes religieux dans *Eugénie Grandet*," *L'Année Balzacienne* (1976): 201-229;

Hommage à Balzac (Paris: Mercure de France, 1950);

Herbert J. Hunt, *Balzac's "Comédie humaine"* (London: Athlone, 1959);

Henry James, "The Lesson of Balzac," in *The Future of the Novel* (New York: Vintage Books, 1956), pp. 97-124;

Fredric Jameson, *The Political Unconscious: Narrative as a Socially Symbolic Act* (Ithaca, N.Y.: Cornell University Press, 1981);

Martin Kanes, *Balzac's Comedy of Words* (Princeton: Princeton University Press, 1975);

Georges Laffly, "La Politique dans *La Vieille Fille*," *Ecrits de Paris* (November 1970): 66-75;

Pierre Larthomas, "Sur le style de Balzac," *L'Année Balzacienne* (1987): 311-327;

Roland Le Huenen and Paul Perron, eds., *Le Roman de Balzac: Recherches critiques, méthodes, lectures* (Montreal: Didier, 1980);

Percy Lubbock, *The Craft of Fiction* (London: Cape, 1921), pp. 203-212, 220-235;

Georg Lukács, *Balzac et le réalisme français*, translated by Paul Laveau (Paris: Maspero, 1967);

Henri Mitterand, "Le Lieu et le sens: L'Espace parisien dans *Ferragus*, de Balzac," in *Le Discours du roman* (Paris: P.U.F., 1980), pp. 189-212; translated by Denise Mercer as "Place and Meaning: Parisian Space in *Ferragus*, by Balzac," *Sociocriticism*, 4-5 (1986-1987): 13-34;

Armine Kotin [Mortimer], "La Maison Nucingen ou le récit financier," *Romanic Review*, 69 (1978): 60-71;

Mortimer, "La Sémiotique de la clôture," *La Clôture narrative* (Paris: Corti, 1985), pp. 142-163;

John R. O'Connor, *Balzac's Soluble Fish* (Madrid: Turanzas, 1977);

Allan H. Pasco, *Balzacian Montage: Configuring "La Comédie humaine"* (Toronto: University of Toronto Press, 1991);

Pasco, "Ursule Through the Glass Lightly," *French Review*, 64 (October 1991): 36-45;

Pasco, ed., *Reading Balzac*, special issue of *L'Esprit Créateur*, 31 (1991);

William R. Paulson, "Balzac," in *Enlightenment, Romanticism and the Blind in France* (Princeton: Princeton University Press, 1987), pp. 134-166;

Sandy Petrey, "Castration, Speech Acts, and the Realist Difference: *S/Z* versus *Sarrasine*," *PMLA*, 102 (1987): 153-165;

Gaëtan Picon, *Balzac par lui-même* (Paris: Editions du Seuil, 1956);

Christopher Prendergast, *Balzac: Fiction and Melodrama* (London: Arnold, 1978);

Prendergast, *The Order of Mimesis: Balzac, Stendhal, Nerval, Flaubert* (Cambridge: Cambridge University Press, 1986), pp. 83-118;

Anthony R. Pugh, *Balzac's Recurring Characters* (Toronto: University of Toronto Press, 1974);

Michael Riffaterre, "Production du récit (I): *La Paix du ménage* de Balzac," *La Production du texte* (Paris: Seuil, 1979), pp. 153-162;

Charles A. Sainte-Beuve, "Monsieur de Balzac. *La Recherche de l'absolu*," in *Portraits contemporains I* (Paris: Didier, 1846), pp. 443-465;

Lawrence R. Schehr, "Fool's Gold: The Beginning of Balzac's *Illusions perdues*," *Symposium*, 36 (1982): 149-165;

Emile J. Talbot, "Pleasure/Time or Egoism/Love: Rereading *La Peau de chagrin*," *Nineteenth-Century French Studies*, 11 (1982-1983): 72-82.

Papers:
Balzac's manuscripts, proofs, letters, and miscellaneous papers are found, for the most part, in the Institut de France: Bibliothèque Spoelberch de Lovenjoul in Chantilly.

Jules-Amédée Barbey d'Aurevilly

(2 November 1808 - 23 April 1889)

Will L. McLendon
University of Houston

BOOKS: *L'Amour impossible* (Paris: Delanchy, 1841);

La Bague d'Annibal (Paris: Duprey, 1843);

Du dandysme et de George Brummell (Caen: Mancel, 1845); translated by D. B. Wyndham Lewis as *The Anatomy of Dandyism, with Some Observations on Beau Brummell* (London: Davies, 1928);

Une Vieille Maîtresse, 3 volumes (Paris: Cadot, 1851);

Les Prophètes du passé (Paris: Hervé, 1851);

Poésies (Caen: Hardel, 1854);

L'Ensorcelée, 2 volumes (Paris: Lemerre, 1854)—contains *Le Dessous de cartes d'une partie de whist*;

Memorandum (Caen: A. Hardel, 1856);

Les Œuvres et les hommes, 14 volumes (Paris: Amyot, Palmé, Frinzine, Quantin, Lemerre, 1860-1895);

Le Chevalier des Touches (Paris: Michel-Lévy, 1864);

Les Quarante Médaillons de l'Académie (Paris: E. Dentu, 1864);

Memorandum, Pour l'A. . . B. . . (n.d.) [1864];

Un Prêtre marié, 2 volumes (Paris: A. Faure, 1865);

Poésies (Brussels: Briard, 1870);

Les Diaboliques (Paris: E. Dentu, 1874)—contains *Le Rideau cramoisi, Le Plus Bel Amour de Don Juan, Le Bonheur dans le crime, Le Dessous de cartes d'une partie de whist, A un dîner d'athées,* and *La Venegeance d'une femme*; translated by Ernest Boyd as *The Diaboliques* (New York: Knopf, 1925); translated by Jean Kimber as *The She-Devils* (London & New York: Oxford University Press, 1964); translated by Ernest Boyd as *The She-Devils* (London: Dedalus, 1986);

Goethe et Diderot (Paris: E. Dentu, 1880);

Une Histoire sans nom (Paris: Lemerre, 1882); translated by Edgar Saltus as *The Story Without a Name* (New York: Belford, 1891);

Une Page d'histoire [with *Une Histoire sans nom*] (Paris: A. Lemerre, 1882);

Memoranda (Paris: Rouveyre et Blond, 1883);

Les Ridicules du temps (Paris: Rouveyre et Blond, 1883);

Ce qui ne meurt pas (Paris: Dubuisson, 1883); translated by Sebastian Melmoth [Oscar Wilde] as *What Never Dies* (Paris: Privately printed, 1902);

Les Vieilles Actrices; Le Musée des antiques (Paris: Librairie des auteurs modernes, 1884);

Une Page d'histoire, (1603) (Paris: Lemerre, 1886);

Le Théâtre contemporain (Paris: L. Frinzine, 1887-1889);

Pensées détachées; Fragments sur les femmes (Paris: A. Lemerre, 1888);

Polémiques d'hier (Paris: Savine, 1889);

Amaïdée (Paris: A. Lemerre, 1890).

Editions and Collections: *Dernières polémiques* (Paris: Savine, 1891);

Nouvelle série: Théâtre contemporain, 1870-1883 (Paris: Tresse & Stock, 1892);

Dernière série: Théâtre contemporain, 1881-1883 (Paris: P.-V. Stock, 1896);

Poussières (Paris: Lemerre, 1897);

Premier memorandum, 1836-1838 (Paris: A. Lemerre, 1900);

Deuxième memorandum, 1838 (Paris: Stock, 1906);

Léa (Paris: La Société normande du livre illustré, 1907);

Poussières; Rhythmes oubliés; Amaïdée (Paris: A. Lemerre, 1909);

Le Cachet d'onyx. Léa (1831-1833) (Paris: La Connaissance, 1919);

Victor Hugo (Paris: Crès, 1922);

Œuvres complètes, 17 volumes (Paris: Bernouard, 1926-1927);

Œuvres romanesques complètes, 2 volumes, edited by Jacques Petit (Paris: Gallimard, Bibliothèque de la Pléiade, 1964-1966);

Les Œuvres et les hommes, 26 volumes (Geneva: Slatkine Reprints, 1968).

OTHER: *Aux héros des Thermopyles*, edited by Barbey d'Aurevilly (Paris: Sanson, 1825);

Laocoon, translated by H. M. Carey, edited by Barbey d'Aurevilly (Caen: Mancel, 1857);

Deux rhythmes oubliés, edited by Barbey d'Aurevilly (Caen: Buhour, 1857);

Articles justificatifs pour Charles Baudelaire, auteur des "Fleurs du Mal," by Barbey d'Aurevilly, Edouard Thierry, Frédéric Duulamon, and Charles Asselineau (Paris: Vve Dondey-Dupré, 1857);

"Les Misérables" de M. V. Hugo, edited by Barbey d'Aurevilly (Paris: Chez tous les libraires, 1862);

Histoire des inhumations chez les peuples anciens et modernes, edited by Barbey d'Aurevilly (Paris: Poupart-Davyl, 1869);

Barbey d'Aurevilly (photograph by Nadar)

La Généreuse Jeunesse, edited by Barbey d'Aurevilly (Paris: Cassigneul, 1872);

Rhythmes oubliés, edited by Barbey d'Aurevilly (Paris: Lemerre, 1897);

Disjecta membra, Les Textes, 2 volumes (Paris: La Connaissance, 1925);

Articles inédits (1852-1884) (Paris: Les Belles Lettres, 1972);

Premiers articles (1834-1852), edited by Andrée Hirschi and Jacques Petit (Paris: Les Belles Lettres, 1973).

As one of the most outrageous and outraged novelists and critics of nineteenth-century France, Jules-Amédée Barbey d'Aurevilly weathered nearly all the major literary storms from romanticism to symbolism. In playing out his role as a *dandy* and literary eccentric par excellence, Barbey ran the gamut of poses and sartorial refinements that leads from George Brummell, Stendhal and Charles Baudelaire to such latter-day avatars as Joséphin Péladan, Joris-Karl Huysmans, Rachilde, and Jean Lorrain. Barbey's extravagant literary manners and merciless pen, which earned him the nickname *le Connétable des Lettres Françaises* (High Constable of French Letters), are perhaps best exemplified graphically in his florid manuscripts copied in brilliant purple, orange, and green inks. His personal image is doubtless fixed for all time in the haughty, corseted figure, the frock coat, the dyed hair and mustache, the scarlet and black-braided robes. The lonely and somewhat wretched circumstances in which Barbey d'Aurevilly's long and pretentious career came to a close in Paris have been noted in many a literary memoir, the account in Edmond de Goncourt's *Journal* (1851-1896) being probably the best known.

Jules Barbey d'Aurevilly was born 2 November 1808 in Saint-Sauveur-le-Vicomte, the son of Théophile and Ernestine Ango Barbey. He endured a childhood and early upbringing characterized by lack of parental affection and by the knowledge that he was the younger son born into a family of obscure and financially strapped, if not impoverished, Norman nobility. His grandfather, Vincent Barbey, had secured the family's claim to nobility through purchase of the purely honorary title of royal secretary to a court in Clermont-Ferrand in 1756. Louis Ango, the maternal grandfather, was a model of action, resolve, and somber devotion to the royalist cause. According to Barbey's *Memorandum* (1864), "*Jamais* [on ne l'avait] vu rire *après la mort du Roi, et il a vécu encore des années*" (he was never seen to laugh again after the king's death, and he lived on for years). This much admired ancestor, who had been born at Versailles, was rumored to be a son of Louis XV.

The only bright spots in the morose period of Barbey's boyhood would seem to have been his identification with the local lore of the Cotentin peninsula of Normandy and the understanding, care, and guidance of an uncle, Jean-Louis Pontas-Duméril, who was mayor of Valognes and a gentleman of liberal political persuasions. He saw to Barbey's education in Latin, giving him as tutor the abbé de Percy, who inspired the boy to read Virgil and entertained his young imagination with his recollections of several eighteenth-century salons. While still under the parental roof, Barbey delved into the works of François-René de Chateaubriand, Vittorio Alfieri, Sir Walter Scott, and especially George Gordon, Lord Byron, committing to memory long passages from *Childe Harold* (1812). The lad's first serious romantic encounter, reputedly with a woman twice his age, left him with misgivings and mixed impressions. After studies at the Collège Stanislas in Paris, where he became the close friend of Maurice de Guérin, Barbey's plans to seek a military career were vehemently opposed by his father. The ensuing rift embittered the young man, who nevertheless submitted to parental authority and left to study law in Caen.

By 1833, after a first unhappy love affair and the beginning of his long friendship with the erudite publisher Guillaume Trébutien, Barbey was in Paris, thanks to a small inheritance. His efforts there at vying with the most eccentric of the *dandys* and the most impassioned Romantics of these years soon led to monumental frustrations and serious financial straits. In the Paris of the 1830s the *dandys* were pretentious, often wealthy (if not always aristocratic) young men bent on shocking the bourgeois through arrogant defiance of established dress codes, moral attitudes, and political philosophies. Their particular abhorrence of utilitarianism was manifested in whimsical sartorial additions and refinements; their scorn for efforts to eradicate social inequalities was evident in their refusal to pursue "productive" and "meaningful" careers, their determination to disassociate themselves from what they perceived as a trivial and insipid society. An ideal of useless beauty, elegance, and capriciousness dominated their every public appearance or endeavor, since for the *dandy*, as for women, Barbey noted, "*paraître, c'est être*" (appearance is being). Preeminent among this elite was Alfred de Grimaud, Comte d'Orsay, otherwise known as "le beau d'Orsay" (handsome d'Orsay); his peers were such Anglophiles—Brummell being their mentor—as Alfred de Maussion, Count Guy de La Tour du Pin, the Viscount d'Arlincourt, and Charles de Mornay. On a very different, more bohemian level, that of literature and the arts, such aspiring *dandys* as Théophile Gautier, Gérard de Nerval, Alfred de Musset, Paul Gavarni, Alphonse Karr, Roger de Beauvoir, and Eugène Sue attracted perhaps more general attention and certainly achieved more enduring fame.

As for Barbey, despite his dwindling inheritance and overt contempt for financial matters, he managed at least to adhere closely to one of the prime tenets of the *dandy*, that of constantly seeking to astound the plebeians without ever letting them astound him. Disillusioned by the new idols emerging on every hand from the industrial and scientific revolutions, Barbey, by age forty, had haughtily turned his back on the "modernist" ideologies and resolutely set his sights on a bygone social and political order, indeed on an aesthetic that had been swept aside by the Revolution and the Napoleonic era. The eradication of the old order and aesthetic had not, however, been thorough in his native Normandy, so that the young Barbey's attitudes and sensitivities were shaped by many a vestige of the ancien régime. His choice of a violently reactionary Catholicism can be attributed as much to nostalgia as to any prospect of "saving" what he considered to be endangered traditional values. One must always keep in mind his irresistible urge to go against the grain, to play the Mousquetaire in defense of lost causes.

Never one to shun a potentially disastrous encounter, Barbey, were he alive today, might well be expected to enter into the artistic fray, vociferously defending such causes as Robert Mapplethorpe's photography, for example, not so much in the name of individual artistic freedom as in that of a kind of reverse "morality." Barbey maintained that any vice, if truly and convincingly portrayed, implicitly contained condemnation of that very vice. So ran his argument in his preface to *Les Diaboliques* (1874; translated as *The Diaboliques*, 1925), defending the excesses that some of his contemporaries found in these stories. As a forerunner of *décadence* he instinctively championed an artistic stance that contained in its basic tenets the implication of its own demise.

The quaint, often depressing details of Barbey's personal predicaments as he stubbornly pursued a course against the mainstream of French society and letters are regularly reflected in the isolation and ostracism that beset his fictional heroes and heroines. They consistently adopt poses as extreme for their milieus as those Barbey successively adopted in his own struggle to maintain his precarious position in French letters. Yet the equivocation and lack of widespread acclaim for his works during his lifetime did not stem from a dearth of creativity on his part. In his long career as a journalist and novelist, Barbey produced an impressive array of novels and stories, as well as a veritable monument of critical articles that have been reprinted in twenty-six volumes, *Les Œuvres et les hommes* (Works and Men, 1860-1895).

Whether it be taken on first consideration as a prerequisite for the dramas of violent passion that form the core of his novels and stories,

or simply as a coincidental state, physical isolation was manifestly of absorbing interest to Barbey d'Aurevilly. But the insistence with which this state is treated in his works suggests the possibility of an interest transcending mere coincidence; indeed, Barbey's predilection for depicting geographically isolated localities and morally and physically isolated human beings points to an obsession of the strongest sort. Since ostracism is, after all, one of this author's major themes, what could be more natural to his often highly "unnatural" heroes and heroines than a setting that outwardly reflects their negatively oriented passions and introverted desires? Frequently his creatures succumb, usually in some violent manner, to an idée fixe, thus dramatically underlining the dangers inherent in the ardent temperaments that for a time lie dormant but, once excited, fester and perish in their isolated world.

Geographical isolation is particularly easy to pinpoint in the productions of an author so regionally oriented as Barbey. The forbidding Norman manor house Le Quesnay, occupied by the renegade priest Sombreval and his daughter Calixte in *Un Prêtre marié* (A Married Priest, 1865), and the village in the Forez region where Mme de Ferjol, the heroine of *Une Histoire sans nom* (1882; translated as *The Story Without a Name*, 1891), and her unfortunate offspring, Lasthénie, act out their drama of mutual incomprehension are hundreds of miles apart. But one readily senses that the setting of each novel is essentially the same: that special plot of earth, not exempt from original sin, as Jean Giraudoux's Holophernes would have it in his play *Judith* (1931), but a spot charged with all the tyrannies of the flesh. Barbey's brief, somber prelude to *Une Histoire sans nom* suggests that life in this remote community is comparable to that of "ces anciens captifs des cloîtres . . . engloutis dans de ténébreuses oubliettes" (those ancient captives of the cloisters . . . swallowed up in dismal secret dungeons). The villagers are repeatedly referred to with such labels as "isolated souls," and in this setting it is small wonder that Mme de Ferjol and Lasthénie should fall victims to a peculiar kind of promiscuous solitude from which there is no escape. They are indeed in a trap, what Mme de Ferjol dubs a "trou de formica-leo" (a formica-leo's [ant's] hole). Located in a deep trough in the mountains of the Forez, this village, through Barbey's symbolic description, undergoes strange metamorphoses, evolving from the formica-leo's cone into an "abyss," then a "funnel," and finally into a bottle that encloses its inhabitants. The neck of the bottle, or circular patch of sky above their heads, is rarely blue; on gray days "la bouteille avait son bouchon" (the bottle had its stopper).

The physical and geographical vacuum so essential to the incubation of the violent passions of his creatures is obtained by Barbey with monotonous regularity through the use of two elements of decor, the quiet provincial town and the isolated house or château. "The little town of ***" is the trite, almost insufferable device he exploits to designate some obscure locale, usually in the Cotentin peninsula of his native Normandy. It seems as if giving the true name of a town would be an act of daring comparable only to total disrobing in public. The striptease, however, is another matter. Nothing delights him more in his description of locale than to carry suggestion almost, but not quite, to the point of certain identity. Thus, in his view of Valognes, which serves as a setting for *Le Dessous de cartes d'une partie de whist* (Behind the Scenes at a Whist Game, 1854), Barbey paints a town that he tells us shall remain nameless (properly draped); but he at once adds that, after a certain detail he is about to supply, the reader will have no trouble recognizing the spot (read: "seeing through the flimsy clothes"). Similarly the little village in the Forez of *Une Histoire sans nom* elicits the comment: "A ce détail original, on l'aura peut-être reconnue" (From this curious detail, the reader will probably have recognized it). And what matter if the reader should recognize the village as Bourg-Argental, or mistake it perhaps for Lamastre? The prudishness of Barbey's attitude in regularly withholding place names is, paradoxically enough, quite revealing of his psychological problems. His penchant for voyeurism is echoed by many a turn of phrase in which he expresses his admiration for "les plaisirs de l'observateur, que j'ai toujours mis au-dessus de tous les autres" (the pleasures of the observer, which I have always considered superior to all others).

Most often the town or village in Barbey's tale seems to be suspended in time and space, despite such superficial contacts with the outside world as the stagecoach route in *Le Rideau cramoisi* (The Crimson Curtain, 1874) or the visiting English gentry in *Le Dessous de cartes*. The particularly forbidding terrain of moors and marshes in *L'Ensorcelée* (A Woman Bewitched, 1854) breeds superstition as well as physical and moral stagnation, all of which are grotesquely com-

Caricature by Félicien Rops, depicting Barbey d'Aurevilly as a dandy. The caption reads, "Il n'a pour page que son ombre" (He has only his shadow for a page boy).

bined in the highly symbolic climax of Jeanne Le Hardouey's drowning in the village pond. In *Un Prêtre marié* barriers and buffers of taboo cut off the abbé Sombreval's manor house from the nearby village more effectively than a dozen moats. Haut-Mesnil, the château of debauchery frequented by the young abbé de la Croix-Jugan in *L'Ensorcelée*, is a den of iniquity held in such horror by the villagers that even the passing of the years after its destruction cannot efface the blight on the reputations of those who flocked to it, namely la Croix-Jugan and la Clotte.

Through his sentimental and artistic return to his native province of Normandy, the Parisian dandy, quite overtly it would seem, sought a nostalgic course of consolation and compensation for the constant disappointments and frustrations that were his lot as a journalist in the cruel capital. Yet, despite his recourse to the device of the intermediary or second narrator in his storytelling, one readily suspects Barbey of portraying personal solitude not from the point of view of the detached observer and connoisseur, but from that of a man all too intimately aware of its perspectives of moral desolation. Long before Georges Bernanos was to paint in his novels the awesome spectacle of the degradation resulting from ennui, Barbey d'Aurevilly created a host of sensational but essentially lonely sinners whose natures and fates offer striking parallels with those of the inveterate *dandy* that Barbey was.

In *L'Ensorcelée* one such haughty and indomitable character, Clotilde Mauduit, called la Clotte, is ostracized because the villagers judge her guilty of a double betrayal of standards. As a young woman, before the present action of the story begins, not only had she given herself over to debauchery at the infamous château de Haut-Mesnil, but she, a commoner, had done so by selling herself out to the ancien régime—by consorting with dissolute young noblemen of the region. After suffering the public humiliation of having her head shaved by the outraged villagers, she had been excluded from their society while still quite young. Many years later, in the narrative present, the aged la Clotte makes a heroic attempt to break down the barriers that have for so long relegated her to a pariah's existence in a hovel outside the town: she hobbles along, then drags her decrepit body, and finally crawls the remaining distance to the church where the "bewitched" Jeanne Le Hardouey's funeral is in progress. But la Clotte's courage in daring at last to challenge the forces of isolation, to appear in public out of respect for the one local personage to have befriended her, is rewarded only with the anger of the village mob, who lynch her almost on the spot.

In *Un Prêtre marié*, the anathema pronounced against Sombreval, the married priest, is visited on all those who are closely related to him, by bonds of blood or otherwise. The fruit of his "unholy" marriage, his hapless daughter Calixte, lives in almost total isolation at Le Quesnay with her father. Néel de Néhou, the superb young swaggerer who falls in love with Calixte, is inevitably forced to break with his family, fiancée, and friends once he is drawn into Sombreval's proscribed sphere. And the curiously ambivalent Calixte, with only one foot in the real world—since she is afflicted with somnambulism and subject to prolonged trances that amount to living death—has further compounded her isolation and solitude by secretly taking the Carmelite vows. By special permission she has been allowed to keep these vows secret and remain at home, since to find some way to bring her father to true repentance is her only hope and goal in life.

Calixte's physical and moral barriers to love prove too much even for so vigorous and deter-mined a young swain as Néel de Néhou; his great love engenders equally powerful frustration. And, in view of the extreme, almost inhuman rigor of the obstacles that fate and Calixte have erected (somnambulism, fainting fits, ostracism, Carmelite vows), it is almost understandable that Néel's prolonged attempts to break through to her should lead to the desperate, atrocious cauterization scene near the end of the novel. But the real heat that Néel applies to the dead girl's feet in a frantic effort to determine whether this is just another trance can no more burn through the absolute barrier now separating them than could the flame of his passion consume the obstructive taboos that isolated their lives.

Another lonely soul in *Un Prêtre marié*, and one of the most memorable of all Barbey's creatures, is the solitary la Malgaigne, who lives apart from everyone in an isolated shack. Though reformed and repentant, she is still suspected of having engaged in sorcery and other unsavory practices in her younger days. A distant satellite of Sombreval's sphere for having been a sort of mother to him in his youth, la Malgaigne is now an ancient hag who strides through the desolate countryside uttering prophecies and imprecations, like some Norman hybrid of Cassandra and Mad Maggie.

And so physical and geographical remoteness engenders or at least goes hand in hand with ostracism. But the separateness of Barbey's heroes transcends mere estrangement of those who dare flout local customs; it often stems from hereditary dispositions or transgressions of deeper (national or universal) significance. Examples of all three isolating factors, and combinations of them, can be observed in the following: Hauteclaire Stassin, heroine of *Le Bonheur dans le crime* (Happiness in Crime, 1874), whose unconventional upbringing sets her apart from other young women and doubtless fosters her inclinations to defy traditions; Jeanne Le Hardouey (*L'Ensorcelée*), the comte de Savigny (*Le Bonheur dans le crime*), and Ryno de Marigny (*Une Vieille Maîtresse* [An Old Mistress, 1851]), persons of aristocratic birth who marry or choose partners beneath their stations, but who do so precisely out of an overbearing desire to assert their sense of ancestral superiority (other complex psychological factors being of course involved in their poses); la Croix-Jugan (*L'Ensorcelée*) and the abbé Sombreval (*Un Prêtre marié*), both of whom—before returning home to transgress local customs—divorce themselves from mainstream society, la Croix-Jugan by espousing the cause of the Chouans (Breton royalists), Sombreval by embracing atheism.

Many of these characters, along with a host of others, are isolated also by virtue of their imposing physical characteristics. They are most often endowed with a sinister majesty or beauty that immediately puts them head and shoulders above their fellows. And it is not difficult to see that Barbey himself, usually through the artifice of a narrator's comments, has considerable admiration for the traits or eccentricities that distinguish such creatures, making them the poles of attraction in magnetic fields whose lines are the reactions of lesser characters, the narrators, and the listener-reader. Jeanne Le Hardouey and Hauteclaire Stassin are women whose bearing and beauty inspire both admiration and awe; the same can be said of Mme de Ferjol, whose charm, at age forty, is still disturbing: "une espèce de majesté rigide dont sa fille et le monde subissaient également l'empire" (a kind of rigid majesty that exerted its sway over both her daughter and society). The itinerant monk Riculf, author of Lasthénie de Ferjol's woes—the poor girl, another Aurevillian somnambulist, becomes pregnant, she knows not how—looks like a combination of Adonis and Mephistopheles in Capuchin garb. His sandaled feet are like those of a marble statue, and his powerful neck and sensual features, set off by bronze beard and mustache, lead his hostess, Mme de Ferjol, to say: "Quand on vous regarde, mon Père, on est presque tenté de se demander ce que vous auriez été si vous n'aviez été un saint homme" (When one looks at you, Father, one is almost tempted to wonder what you would have been if you hadn't been a man of God).

The physique of another priest, la Croix-Jugan, also has an almost hypnotic power that even his hideously disfigured face cannot diminish. And Barbey dwells at length on the admiration aroused by the appearance of Marmor de Karkoüel, the English hero of Le Dessous de cartes d'une partie de whist, who, though described as being not at all handsome, nevertheless intrigues the ladies and gentlemen alike, the old as well as the young, by the mysterious authority of his bearing and gestures. A complete listing of those who have such physical magnetism would involve practically all Barbey's principal characters. In A un dîner d'athées (A Dinner Party of Atheists, 1874) Menilgrand, a Napoleonic army officer, "se distinguait—impérialement—de tous les autres

... n'était pas de la même espèce" (stood out—imperially—from all the others . . . was not of the same species). Ryno de Marigny, the hero of Une Vieille Maîtresse, has a reputation whose devastating effect on young girls Barbey compares to the opiate powers of the manchineel tree!

Other aspects of Barbey's characters' solitude affect their physical attractiveness. They are invariably haughty souls, overly sensitive to the real or imagined scorn of their fellow humans. They find the security that solitude offers their easily wounded pride preferable to the risk of subjecting themselves to a rebuff. Despite her husband's Cévanol name, Mme de Ferjol is of Norman origin. However, after her husband's untimely death, she cannot bear the thought of returning to her native province because there she might encounter a certain coolness on the part of the local aristocrats, who would remember her elopement with de Ferjol: "Son âme altière avait horreur du mépris" (Her haughty soul could not bear the idea of scorn). This very trait of her character, as suggested earlier, soon gains the upper hand, transforming the widow's physical appearance from opulent beauty into cruel, even despotic, matronly distinction. The disdain for the rank and file so fiercely cultivated by Barbey's heroes and heroines in general may be a result of their milieu and upbringing, most often aristocratic, or a defense mechanism of the most flagrant sort. A thorough study of this problem would doubtless tend to converge on yet another definition of Barbey's dandysme.

In Le Bonheur dans le crime, Hauteclaire Stassin, from her early childhood, is a young lady apart. Her father, an ex-army officer, brings her up to be an expert fencer, and she is soon skillful enough to give instruction in the noble art to the local gentry. Upon her father's death, she takes over the management of his fencing school. Thus Hauteclaire's isolation from other females in the town is almost total, a fact the author dramatizes through the young amazon's insistence on covering her face with a dark veil whenever she goes riding with her father. The veil, which shields her from the gazes of the townswomen who watch from behind closed shutters as she rides by, is the worldly counterpart of the protective mask that Hauteclaire normally wears when giving fencing lessons. And, at a deeper level of interpretation, both riding veil and fencing mask are symbols of the human mask that this iron-willed female adopts once she takes up residence in the Savigny château as chambermaid to the

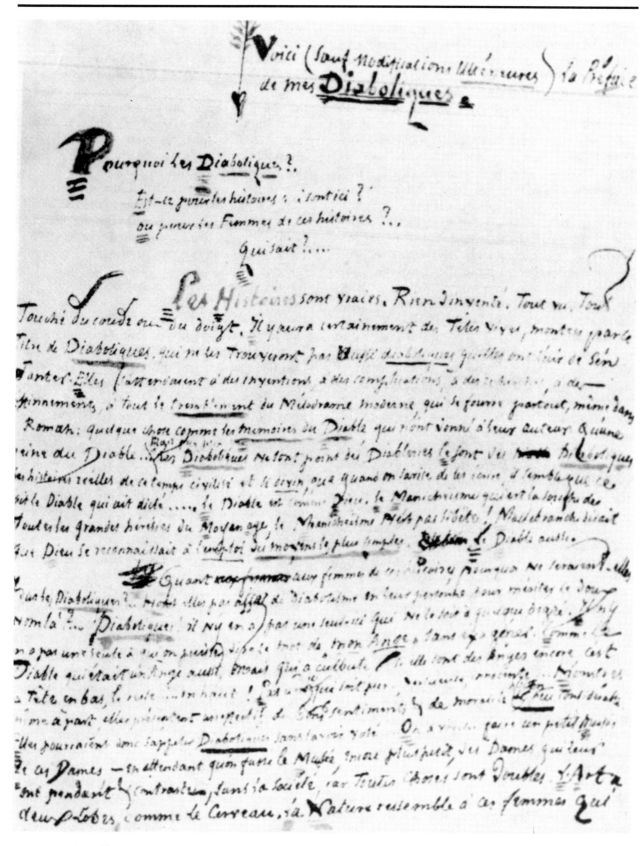

Page from the December 1870 manuscript for the preface to Les Diaboliques *(from Catherine Boschian-Campaner,*
Barbey d'Aurevilly, 1989)

countess. Hauteclaire's disappearance from the town is thus a natural transition; it is simply an intensification of an already isolated existence.

Barbey d'Aurevilly's predilection for the mask in general betrays a certain deficiency of a talent that many authors have developed to a high degree, that for establishing perspective between themselves and their heroes. Like Giraudoux's evaluation of Pierre Choderlos de Laclos's writing in *Les Liaisons dangereuses* (*Dangerous Acquaintances*, 1782), Barbey's interest in the mask can be likened to a weakness for posing before the mirror to admire himself disguised now as iconoclast, next as atheist, then as seducer, and so forth. And the result is that the more masks the artist adopts, the clearer his self-portrait becomes. Surely Barbey the artist must have been acutely aware of this possibility in his own case, for the critic in him recognizes such subterfuges precisely for what they are in connection with another author, Stendhal, whom, as he says, he cannot help admiring.

A most significant distinction between Hauteclaire and other solitary Aurevillian heroines is that her separateness—so far from being imposed on her by outside social forces, as in the case of la Clotte or la Malgaigne—is freely chosen. And it is to this basic difference in the origin and direction of forces that one may attribute the exceptional (for Barbey d'Aurevilly) tone and theme of this story: calm and happiness. If most of his heroes and heroines are bored and wretched, often to the point of tragedy, it is precisely because they are victims of forces outside themselves. But Hauteclaire and her consort Savigny, quite to the contrary, stand out like the regal couple that they are because, through victimizing others—namely the comtesse de Savigny, whom the two lovers slowly poison—they find *le bonheur dans le crime*. It is as if through their carefully planned, self-imposed, and highly successful ostracism—since their crime remains undiscovered—they avenge the sorry plight of so many other Aurevillian creatures weaker than they.

Although the magnificently stigmatized and isolated hero of *L'Ensorcelée*, the abbé de la Croix-Jugan, is the first major character to be introduced, his entry is delayed until the closing pages of the second chapter. Indeed, the reader may experience boredom and annoyance in these opening chapters, which involve the swamps and moors of the Cotentin peninsula as detailed by two narrators. Just as in *Un Prêtre marié, Le*

Rideau cramoisi, and many other stories, the additional precaution of a second narrator seems to give Barbey the feeling of security and immunity he requires for relating what he considers to be risqué situations and shocking events. This narrative device alone, presenting yet another aspect of the mask mania, would make a rich subject as well for stylistic analysis. But it must also be conceded that, despite such weaknesses, the leisurely introduction in *L'Ensorcelée* is on the whole well conceived, the progression of details most effectively contrived to reproduce the atmosphere of the lonely setting in which la Croix-Jugan's unrequited spirit can interpose itself. This intrusion of the fantastic in the humdrum world has considerable artistic merit in the example under consideration here, for Barbey forgoes the direct apparition that one might expect under the lugubrious circumstances (midnight, a desolate moor, two lonely travelers) in favor of a remote apparition suggested musically through the unwonted pealing of distant church bells. These eerie sounds would seem to indicate that a midnight Mass is being celebrated in a lonely chapel, according to local legend, and the officiating clergyman is presumed to be the late abbé de la Croix-Jugan. Maître Tainnebouy assures his traveling companion, the first first-person narrator, that no one has ever dared enter the chapel on such occasions, but that several people have peeped through a hole in the door and have seen la Croix-Jugan's ghost celebrating Mass in the brightly lighted but completely empty sanctuary. Thus at the outset Barbey presents his hero as one who remains ostracized even in death, just as in real life he had been isolated from his fellowmen through his uncommon physique and personality as well as through his extravagant conduct.

Finding oneself set apart from the mob, whether through choice or the cruelty of fate, is a state the Aurevillian *dandy* must manipulate and intensify if he is to achieve the illusion that he is master of his own destiny, hence the exacerbation of his attitude. This isolated hero or heroine often is clinging to life by the tenuous thread of pride alone. The duchesse de Sierra-Leone in *La Vengeance d'une femme* (*A Woman's Revenge*, 1874) pursues of necessity an extravagant course, that is to say one that leaves the beaten path and allows her to delight in her uniqueness and alienation. Having been caught with her lover in flagrante delicto she is forced to watch as her husband cuts out the lover's heart and feeds it to the dogs. Her unwavering determination to achieve

Illustrations by Félicien Rops for the 1882 edition of Les Diaboliques: *"Le Bonheur dans le crime" and "Le Rideau cramoisi"*

an even more humiliating revenge eventually leads the duchess to conceive the idea of degrading herself through frenzied prostitution in order to debase the ancient and glorious name of her detested husband. Her courage and perseverance are, to be sure, well-nigh heroic. At the conclusion of each new encounter she delights in revealing her identity to her temporary companion. She stipulates in her will that her tombstone bear the following legend: "Ci-gît Sanzia-Florinda-Concepcion de Turre-Cremata, Duchesse d'Arcos de Sierra-Leone, Fille Repentie, Morte à la Salpêtrière, le . . . Requiescat in Pace" (Here lies Sanzia-Florinda-Concepcion de Turre-Cremata, Duchess of Arcos de Sierra-Leone, a Repentant Whore, who died in the Salpêtrière [hospital] on . . . Rest in Peace). But the bravura element in this great lady's scheme of vindictive retaliation betrays the *dandy* in her; and in the final analysis the sensational character of her revenge seems calculated almost as much to shock her unsuspecting clients as it is to humiliate the duc de Sierra-Leone by debasing his illustrious name.

And so the examination of separateness, isolation, and ostracism in Barbey's works leads inevitably back to his own *dandysme*, and that in turn, when thoroughly analyzed, to a fuller understanding of the proliferation of masochistic and sadistic acts, all the potpourri of criminal attitudes and gory deeds that impart to his novels and stories an aura of the Grand Guignol. Several critics, and particularly Philippe Berthier, have studied in considerable detail various elements that link Barbey to a certain erotic tradition associated not only with the Gothic novel and the French fantastic narrative in general, but also with the lucubrations of the marquis de Sade. It is particularly in Barbey's delight in the transgression of taboos for the sake of transgression that he comes closest to Sade. From the early *Léa* (*Revue de Caen*, 30 October 1832), to *Une Page d'histoire* (A Page of History, 1882), and all in between with the excesses rampant in the major novels and the tales of *Les Diaboliques*, Barbey's works underline his conviction that sexual pleasure is heightened by the knowledge that the dangerous, the sinful, or the criminal is involved.

Nor is there any dearth of elements many readers would consider, if not criminal or sinful, quite simply distasteful or repulsive. Necrophilia and vampirism are frequent themes, as in *Léa, Une Histoire sans nom,* or *Une Vieille Maîtresse.* As B. G. Rogers has noted, a kind of parodic reversal of the Sleeping Beauty theme is at the core of *Léa,* since the kiss of the lover brings death rather than life. La Vellini, the old mistress in *Une Vieille Maîtresse,* insists on a rather barbarous blood pact between herself and the lover whom she has enslaved, Ryno de Marigny, and who will feel her "liquid fire" in his veins. Their love will amount to nothing less than a prolonged and much savored mutual feeding, and mutual destruction in the end. Sombreval's desperation upon learning of the death and burial of his daughter Calixte pushes him to the outrageous display of passion recorded in the cemetery scene near the end of *Un Prêtre marié.* Having disinterred the corpse in the dead of night as Néel de Néhou looks on aghast, Sombreval prances about with the remains of Calixte in his arms in a display of frenzy that A. E. Carter calls "incestuous necrophilia." Other examples of what Barbey appears to consider an appealing perversion can be found in *Ce qui ne meurt pas* (1883; translated as *What Never Dies,* 1902) and in *Le Rideau cramoisi:* making love to a corpse, or at least holding in one's arms the body that has expired during the act. The Liebestod (Love-death) as conceived by Richard Wagner is a different matter entirely.

In the late nineteenth century, when religious fervor was on the wane and it was becoming fashionable not to believe in God but rather in occultism, Barbey d'Aurevilly took pride in affirming his belief in Satan. His quip about hell's being nothing more than "le ciel en creux" (the concave side of heaven) was another way of expressing his conviction that the devil must exist, since God does. Barbey's concept of the devil is essentially a modern one, not far removed from what many today prefer simply to call *evil*—any of a multitude of things, concepts, or actions that take on the most surprising names: liberal, reactionary, communist, capitalist, racist, integrationist, and so forth. One must bear in mind that Barbey's was a dual personality or nature. He was the visionary who indeed wanted to believe in the devil; but he was also the dogmatist who realized that the devil could not be positioned at the heart of some system as the creature with horns, a hairy body, a forked tail, and other tradi-

tional attributes. The message is rather that Satan exists on every hand within us, or at least within those who have been possessed of this nonexistent devil. It is not in the sudden display of violent passion that Barbey's devil manifests himself but rather in cold-blooded acts that have been lovingly and carefully premeditated. The most satanic deeds are those in which the individual's cunning and lucidity are fully brought to bear. This approach is of the kind that gives the reader a sudden chill or thrill, as in the case of Mme de Stasseville, that imperturbable whist player; or Hauteclaire Stassin, who calmly thrusts her hand into the panther's cage at the zoo; or Alberte in *Le Rideau cramoisi,* who brazenly but secretly leads the young man on under the very eyes of her unsuspecting parents. Situations and calculations such as these open up troubling vistas of the aptitude that certain creatures possess for living out crime or violence within the apparently calm confines of their consciences. As Ernest Seillière noted: "Il [Barbey] a cru discerner autour de lui le règne du Démon" (He thought that he discerned the Demon's sway on every hand).

To the degree that he espouses the early nineteenth century's preoccupation with Byronic attitudes, Barbey is certainly a Romantic and, in the opinion of Richard Griffiths, a "Romantic Catholic" along with Villiers de L'Isle-Adam. Barbey finds undeniable charm in the hero who enters into a pact with the devil, or at least with some demonic power. Yet the originality of Barbey's romanticism lies in his very personal way of maintaining a marked sympathy for such a hero while expressing a tantalizing remorse for having portrayed such damnable acts. He skillfully plays the two forces against one another, portraying Satan's triumphs and conquests while abstaining from giving them his unqualified approval. The basic paradox of such an attitude is even more evident in that he pretends to cater to the prudish sensitivities of many of his contemporaries, often through interposing the opinions of a second narrator. Which of his two narrators represents his real convictions is not always easy to determine.

Barbey's plots and characters point up the ambivalence of an author who both admires and deplores the attitudes and actions of the creatures who animate the pages of his novels and tales. Sombreval, the married priest, is perhaps the most striking example. But there is also the title character of *Le Chevalier des Touches* (The Knight of Touches, 1864). His is an ambiguous attractiveness, for this dashing figure is also insensitive, cruel, and heartless. Father Riculf in *Une Histoire sans nom* is of the same breed. In *Les Diaboliques*, Barbey further engages himself in the portrayal of what might be called infernal mysticism, and in so doing—and in spite of the precaution of a second narrator—he clearly identifies with several of the heroes of these tales. The aging vicomte de Brassard in *Le Rideau cramoisi* is obviously an alter ego, an idealization of the *dandy* that Barbey strove so hard to remain. *Le Plus Bel Amour de Don Juan* (Don Juan's Finest Affair, 1874) offers an even more direct portrait of the author, since the fictional hero's name is Jules-Amédée, Barbey's own! And this Don Juan's surname is more than an atrocious pun: Ravila de Ravilès (*ravis-la, ravis-les* [rape her, rape them]); it expresses an important aspect of the personal myth that Barbey so long cultivated. When one is beloved of God (Amédée), the sky, or the depths, would appear to be the limit.

On occasion Barbey remarked that "moralement comme esthétiquement, c'est intéressant, un démon" (both morally and aesthetically a demon is an interesting creature). Toward the end of his life he took to signing his letters "Le Prince des Ténèbres" (The Prince of Darkness). He readily acknowledged the attraction of what he dubbed "le ragoût du sacrilège" (the sacrilegious stew), noting with the usual caveat that an attitude or action can be sacrilegious only if one believes in what he is profaning. This of course explains why Barbey, seeking an authorial alibi, takes special pains to put the more daring remarks or more offensive actions on the account of some fictional character who is an atheist or an outcast. Hence there are many such creatures in the ranks of Barbey's second narrators. One of the most brilliant examples of this technique is Dr. Torty (*Le Bonheur dans le crime*), who, when talking about his various deathbed experiences, quips: "Il fallait . . . qu'ils choisissent entre moi et l'Extrême-Onction" (They [his patients] had to choose either me or extreme unction). The distinction Barbey makes between his first narrator and the responsibilities of Dr. Torty as a fictional character is made even clearer further on: "Il me regarda malicieusement, car il connaissait mon respect et mon amour pour les choses du catholicisme, dont il était l'ennemi" (He [Torty] looked at me with a malicious glance, knowing full well my respect and my love for things Catholic, since he was their enemy).

Profanatory acts in Barbey's works easily become bravado of the most flagrant sort. A defrocked priest, a member of the stag party in *A un dîner d'athées*, delights in relating a story about clandestine Masses during the Revolution, a time when loyal priests had to hide the consecrated hosts wherever and however they could. One such cache was the bosom of a pious but buxom peasant woman. When these hosts were discovered during a military raid on the farmhouse, the defrocked priest (second narrator at this point) took diabolical pleasure in retrieving the wafers and throwing them into the nearest pigsty. Such a gesture is what Barbey calls "une crânerie à tenter un crâne aussi crâne" (pluck most tempting to so plucky a skull). A certain logic is apparent in this orientation of an author who thus carries the pose of the *dandy* that he always aspired to be to its literary realization. The preoccupation with pose raises the question of its possible extension to ruse in general. Did Barbey's unflagging efforts to lead, at least in public, the life of the consummate *dandy* have as their real thrust the dissimulation of his most private inclinations? Various critics, among them Eric Bentley, Michel Philip, and Pierre Tranouez, have wondered whether Barbey's "secret" was not homosexuality, or at least impotence. An incisive comment by the principal narrator in *Le Dessous de cartes* lends credence to such speculation: "Je suis convaincu que, pour certaines âmes, il y a le bonheur de l'imposture. Il y a une effroyable, mais enivrante félicité dans l'idée qu'on ment et qu'on trompe; dans la pensée qu'on se sait seul soi-même, et qu'on joue à la société une comédie dont elle est la dupe, et dont on se rembourse les frais de mise en scène par toutes les voluptés du mépris" (I am convinced that, for certain souls, there is happiness in imposture. There is a frightening but heady felicity in the notion that one is lying and deceiving others; in the thought that one is the only person aware of one's real self, that one is a sham and that society is the dupe in this comedy for whose production expenses one will be reimbursed with all the pleasure that scorn affords).

This somewhat Romantic pronouncement may well be read as an astonishing if indirect confession on Barbey's part. It is, in any case, at the very heart of the drama of imposture that Georges Bernanos created for the young lesbian who impersonates the murdered priest in *Un Crime* (A Crime, 1934). His heroine, like Barbey, is singularly attracted by examples of passions that

Portrait of Barbey d'Aurevilly in 1881 by Emile Lévy
(Musée de Versailles)

feed on difficulties to be overcome and taboos to be violated. Or, as Dr. Torty, a great connoisseur of human nature, puts it: "Mais, si c'était l'imprudence même qui fît la situation? . . . Il est des passions que l'imprudence allume, et qui, sans le danger qu'elles provoquent, n'existeraient pas" (But what if it were rashness itself that created the situation? . . . There are passions that are aroused by rashness and that would not even exist without the dangers that they entail).

The reader may indeed wonder whether Alberte, the young heroine of *Le Rideau cramoisi*, would have been irresistibly drawn to the young Brassard if he had not been a boarder in her parents' house and, consequently, too intimately involved in the logistics of the family's daily life for their liaison to be easily concealed. The passion of this extraordinary young woman is clearly kindled by the need to make incredibly rash advances to the young soldier, under the very eyes of her parents. She grasps the fellow's hand under the dinner table as they sit facing her mother and father; she later in the dead of night tiptoes—on numerous occasions—through her parents' bedroom as they sleep in order to reach the hallway and then slips upstairs to Brassard's

room. Without these rather formidable, if not altogether insurmountable, obstacles to her passion, would Alberte really have been interested in seducing Brassard? One may have doubts. In her own way Alberte is a *dandy* of the first order.

Michel Philip has shown that the link between *dandysme* and androgyny so evident in *Les Diaboliques* was first made by Barbey himself in his 1845 essay *Du dandysme et de George Brummell* (translated as *The Anatomy of Dandyism, with Some Observations on Beau Brummell*, 1928). After showing that *dandysme* and androgyny are synonymous with seductiveness, Philip studies what he calls the coefficient of femininity in each of the *dandy* heroes of *Les Diaboliques*, then juxtaposes these effeminate heroes and the virile heroines and suggests that Barbey probably dreamed of a Third Sex that would include two superior types of humans, the Androgyne and the Amazon. His basic thesis is that the tales of *Les Diaboliques* are built on a triangular relationship in which the woman is but a kind of relay device in the concealed desire of one man for another.

Barbey's boldness or recklessness in treating the taboo themes of androgyny and reversal of sexual roles blazed the trail for several younger French writers, acquaintances and disciples of his who were to put these themes at the very center of many of their works. During the years 1884-1892 Joséphin Péladan would publish in his cycle called *La Décadence latine* (Latin Decadence) such novels as *Le Vice suprême* (The Supreme Vice, 1884), with a preface by Barbey, *Curieuse* (Curious, 1885), and *L'Androgyne* (The Androgyne, 1891). Jean Lorrain, who, on first contact, had found the elderly Barbey's entourage repulsive but later became one of Barbey's most ardent admirers, repeatedly treated the subject of vacillating or indeterminate sex in such volumes of short stories as *Sensations et souvenirs* (Sensations and Souvenirs, 1895) and *Histoires de masques* (Stories of Masks, 1900) and his novels *Monsieur de Phocas* (1901), and *Le Vice errant* (Vice Errant, 1902). Barbey's tale of blood and incest, *Une Page d'histoire*, was dedicated to Lorrain and a gift copy thus inscribed: "A Jean Lorrain, ce qui n'est pas une monstruosité pour lui" (To Jean Lorrain, what, for him, is not a monstrosity). Both men were inordinately proud of their Norman heritage and delighted in their shared hatred of Emile Zola and his clique at the *Revue des Deux Mondes*. And what Robert Ziegler has recently called Lorrain's marked tendency to use narrative distancing (second, third narrators) as a means to reshape his identity was surely influenced by Barbey's literary example. Rachilde, who was introduced to Barbey during his last years, made her scandalous debut in the world of Parisian letters with *Monsieur Vénus* (1884) and kept up the pace with such books as *La Marquise de Sade* (The Marquise de Sade, 1887) and *Les Hors-nature* (The Unnatural Ones, 1897). These and other authors of the younger generation were doubtless influenced by what is perhaps Barbey's most effective model of the androgyne, or more properly put the *amazone*, la Vellini, heroine of *Une Vieille Maîtresse*, the seductive though unbeautiful female with an abrasive, mannish personality. Her enslavement of the dashing, excessively handsome womanizer Ryno de Marigny reduces him in many a scene to the physical and emotional attitudes of an odalisque and so provides the basic relationship and models for Rachilde's *Monsieur Vénus*.

Although Barbey expended more and more of his energies in literary criticism after 1852, his creativity did not suffer in this more restricted medium, for he dared inject subjectivity into what in French letters had tended to be a rather polite and gentlemanly endeavor. He made it quite clear in his preface to the first volume of his critical essays, *Les Œuvres et les hommes*, that he believed in speaking the truth about any author, living or dead, and that he would not shy away from stepping on the most sacred of toes. Gradually leaving aside the areas of history, philosophy, and politics, Barbey soon became one of the dominant voices in judgment of the contemporary novel. His harsh, often petty and vitriolic pronouncements were nonetheless tempered with remarkable discernment. He did much soon after Honoré de Balzac's death in 1850 to establish this novelist's reputation as a giant among giants; in fact Barbey could find almost nothing to denigrate in Balzac's genius and reasoned that the latter's choice of the novel, that vastly superior modern genre, was in great part responsible for promoting him to even greater heights than William Shakespeare.

Barbey deserves to be more widely recognized for having proclaimed the greatness of Stendhal long before this author emerged from the literary purgatory that he had indeed prophesied. Although he somewhat grudgingly praised the strength of the atheist Stendhal's character and style, Barbey, as early as 1853, heaped almost unlimited praise on the head of this brilliant nonconformist and essentially noble soul whom, he said,

he could not help admiring. The intensely personal approach in the critic's judgment is apparent in the explanation he offers for Stendhal's strange magnetism: "Ainsi que tous les tartuffes qui possèdent l'esprit de leur vice, et la majorité des hommes doublés d'une idée qu'ils ne disent pas, mais qui chatoie dans leur silence, comme le jais brille malgré sa noirceur, Stendhal inspire un intérêt dont on ne saurait se défendre.... Il a l'attrait du mystère et du mensonge, l'attrait d'un grand esprit masqué" (Like all Tartuffes who possess the spirit of their vice and the majority of men preoccupied with an idea that they do not talk about, but which glistens in their silence, just as black onyx shines despite its blackness, Stendhal arouses an interest that one really cannot ward off.... His is the attraction of mystery and falsehood, that of a great masked spirit).

The limitations imposed on Barbey's critical acumen by his uncompromising political, religious, and aesthetic attitudes can best be observed in his almost childishly foolish deprecations of Victor Hugo, or in his vicious, male-chauvinist dismissal of certain women writers—among them George Sand and Sophie Gay—whom he dubbed "bas-bleus" (bluestockings). Spurred to violent reaction after witnessing the well-orchestrated 1862 publicity campaign for Hugo's *Les Misérables*, Barbey tauntingly pointed up the "ridiculous" appearance of such efforts as a "boursouflure d'omelette démocratique" (puffiness of the democratic omelet). Besides—as he had long since remarked—the press, and newspapers in particular, were nothing more than "les chemins de fer du mensonge" (the railways of untruth). Such essays as these indeed exemplify one of Barbey's enduring aphorisms: "J'ai toujours mis mes passions au-dessus de mes principes" (I have always put my passions above my principles). Yet this prejudiced and "most diabolical of Catholics," as Lorrain once opined, had the courage and critical foresight to plead Baudelaire's cause when *Les Fleurs du mal* (1857; translated as *Flowers of Evil*, 1909) was being impugned in the courts. Barbey's friendship with Baudelaire and numerous published defenses of the latter's genius do much to offset the weaknesses and injustices rampant in other essays, such as those on Hugo and Gustave Flaubert.

Perhaps no body of French nineteenth-century literary criticism other than that of Charles-Augustin Sainte-Beuve can surpass Barbey's contribution for sheer volume of material and breadth of scope. No love was ever lost between these two contemporaries, whose paths and interests frequently and necessarily crossed. After having for a while heaped compliments on Barbey, Sainte-Beuve soon stooped to insinuation and character assassination, blaming Barbey for having exerted a pernicious influence over Maurice de Guérin. As Arnould de Liederkerke notes in *Talon rouge: Barbey d'Aurevilly, le dandy absolu* (Red Heel: Barbey d'Aurevilly, the Absolute Dandy, 1986) Barbey had, after all, invited such an attack for having remarked rather publicly that Sainte-Beuve, in his acclaim of established talents, was "un baise-cul du fait accompli" (an ass-kisser of the fait accompli). Such skirmishes in no way detract from the overall accomplishments of either critic, but they probably contributed to reducing recognition of Barbey's seriousness of purpose during his own time.

However biased his critical essays may at times be, the range of authors treated in *Les Œuvres et les hommes* is impressive, extending from the luminaries Stendhal, Prosper Mérimée, Théophile Gautier, Flaubert, Hugo, Alfred de Vigny, Baudelaire, and Zola to lesser stars, such as Eugène Sue, Jules Sandeau, Edmond About, Ernest Feydeau, Jules Janin, Edmond and Jules de Goncourt, Emile Erckmann, and Louis Chatrian. Dozens of even slighter figures abound in Barbey's extraordinary catalogue: Hector Malot, Maurice Cousen de Courchamps, Henri Murger, Philarète Chasles, Louis Bouilhet, to say nothing of foreign genius, as represented by the likes of Shakespeare, Edgar Allan Poe, Nikolay Vasilyerich Gogol, Thomas Carlyle, and William Hickling Prescott. Few if any nineteenth-century women writing in French escape his scorn, for Barbey, despite his title, devotes an entire volume of *Les Œuvres et les hommes* to those he relegates to the category "les bas bleus." The extensive survey includes Mme de Staël, Sophie Gay, Mme Emile de Girardin (Delphine Gay), Mme Edgar Quinet, Eugénie de Guérin, Marceline Desbordes-Valmore, Mme Marie-Alexandre Dumas, Mme Swetchine, Louise Colet, and on and on. The full scope of the word *œuvres* is covered by Barbey's thorough consideration of works in other fields than literature, namely in music, politics and diplomacy, and the plastic arts. Pierre-Paul Prudhon, Jean Courbet, Théodore Géricault, Emmanuel Frémiet, and Gavarni have their niches alongside Jules II, Elizabeth I, Catherine II, Napoleon, Wolfgang Amadeus Mozart, Hector Berlioz, Cardinal de Retz, Louis XI, and events such as the Saint Bartholomew Massacre.

Jacques Petit, in his monumental study of the critical writings, *Barbey d'Aurevilly critique* (1963), has documented every nuance of the attitudes and principles so haughtily proclaimed by Barbey. The polemic generated by differences of approach and opinion between him and colleagues such as Nettement, Janin, and Sainte-Beuve clearly shows that Barbey at times pushed authoritarianism and dogmatism beyond all reasonable limits. He was even capable, in a paroxysm of critical brutality, of actually affirming what he basically did not believe, out of spite, a taste for scandal, or for no good reason at all—"just for the hell of it," as he might well have said had English been his tongue. In just such a spirit Barbey maintained in 1853 that the aesthetic aspect of a work of literature was of far less concern to him than its moral import, something that he quite obviously did not believe. This is just one of many indications that even this early in his career, writing was fast becoming the insurrectional act par excellence.

That Barbey d'Aurevilly has gained in stature and readership since the mid twentieth century is generally recognized as one impressive offshoot of the pioneering scholarship of the late Jacques Petit, whose Pléiade edition of the novels and tales (1964-1966) has most contributed to making Barbey more contemporary. Both quantity and quality of critical studies have made impressive gains over the past twenty years. An ongoing monograph series devoted to Barbey, in the *Revue des Lettres Modernes* collection, was inaugurated by Petit in 1966 and has become a barometer of this academic interest. Many reprints of the major works in inexpensive editions attest to and feed this renewed appeal as do the ever more frequent papers on Barbey's works presented before gatherings of learned societies. An international colloquium held in Paris in April 1989 commemorated the centennial of the author's death and culminated in a volume that covers most aspects of the Aurevillian corpus, convincingly underscoring the contemporary appeal of the major novels as well as the unwavering popularity of *Les Diaboliques*.

Letters:
Lettres à Trébutien, extraits, 1843-1851 (Caen: Valin, 1899);
Lettres à Léon Bloy (Paris: Mercure de France, 1903);

Lettres à une amie (Paris: Mercure de France, 1907);

Lettres intimes (Paris: Edouard-Joseph, 1921);

Lettres à Trébutien, 4 volumes (Paris: Bernouard, 1927);

Lettres et fragments (Paris: Aubier, 1958).

Biographies:

René-Louis Doyon, *Barbey d'Aurevilly, amoureux et dupe* (Paris: Corrêa, 1934);

Jean Canu, *Barbey d'Aurevilly* (Paris: Laffont, 1965);

Catherine Boschian-Campaner, *Barbey d'Aurevilly* (Paris: Librarie Séguier, 1989).

References:

Philippe Berthier, *Barbey d'Aurevilly et l'imagination* (Geneva: Droz, 1978);

Berthier, "La Question du père dans les romans de Barbey d'Aurevilly," *Revue des Lettres Modernes*, 600-604 (1981): 7-47;

Berthier, ed., *Barbey d'Aurevilly cent ans après (1889-1989)* (Geneva: Droz, 1990);

J.-H. Bornecque, *Paysages extérieurs et monde intérieur dans l'œuvre de Barbey d'Aurevilly* (Caen: Publications de la Faculté des Lettres de Caen, 1967);

Jean-Pierre Boucher, *Les Diaboliques de Barbey d'Aurevilly: Une Esthétique de la dissimulation et de la provocation* (Montreal: Presses de l'Université de Québec, 1976);

Emilien Carassus, *Le Mythe du dandy* (Paris: Colin, 1971);

A. E. Carter, *The Idea of Decadence in French Literature, 1830-1900* (Toronto: University of Toronto Press, 1958);

Armand B. Chartier, *Barbey d'Aurevilly* (Boston: Twayne, 1977);

Françoise Coblence, *Le Dandysme, obligation d'incertitude* (Paris: Presses Universitaires de France, 1988);

Pierre Colla, *L'Univers tragique de Barbey d'Aurevilly* (Brussels: Renaissance du Livre, 1965);

Gisèle Corbières-Gille, *Barbey d'Aurevilly, critique littéraire* (Geneva: Droz, 1962);

Norbert Dodille, "L'Amateur de noms: essai sur l'onomastique aurevillienne," in *La Chose capitale*, edited by Alain Buisine and Philippe Bonnefils (Lille: Université de Lille 3, 1981);

Anne Giard, "Le Récit lacunaire dans *Les Diaboliques*," *Poétique*, 11 (February 1980): 39-50;

Julien Gracq, *Préférences* (Paris: Corti, 1961);

Elisabeth de Gramont, *Barbey d'Aurevilly* (Paris: Grasset, 1946);

Eugène Grelé, *Barbey d'Aurevilly, sa vie, son œuvre*, 2 volumes (Caen: Jouan, 1902-1904);

Richard Griffiths, *The Reactionary Revolution: The Catholic Revival in French Literature, 1870-1914* (New York: Frederick Ungar, 1965);

Peter C. Hoy, ed., *Carnets bibliographiques de la Revue des Lettres Modernes: Barbey d'Aurevilly* (Paris: Minard, 1985);

Arnould de Liederkerke, *Talon rouge: Barbey d'Aurevilly, le dandy absolu* (Paris: Orban, 1986);

Aristide Marie, *Le Connétable des Lettres, Barbey d'Aurevilly* (Paris: Mercure de France, 1939);

Françoise C. Mugnier, "Dissimulation des classes sociales, de l'économie et de l'histoire dans la fiction de Barbey d'Aurevilly," *Nineteenth-Century French Studies*, 19 (Winter 1991): 279-289;

Jacques Petit, *Barbey d'Aurevilly critique* (Paris: Belles-Lettres, 1963);

Michel Philip, "Dandysme et androgynie dans *Les Diaboliques* de Barbey d'Aurevilly," *Nouvelle Revue Française*, 342-343 (July-August 1981): 141-149;

Revue des Lettres Modernes: Barbey d'Aurevilly (Paris: Minard, 1966-   );

Jacques Reynaud [pseudonym of Gabrielle Pouillöue-de-Saint-Mars], *Portraits Contemporains* (Paris: Amyot, 1859);

B. G. Rogers, *The Novels and Stories of Barbey d'Aurevilly* (Geneva: Droz, 1967);

Ernest Seillière, *Barbey d'Aurevilly, ses idées et son œuvre* (Paris: Bloud, 1910);

Pierre Tranouez, "L'Efficacité narrative: Etude du 'Rideau cramoisi'," *Poétique*, 11 (February 1980): 51-59;

Philip J. Yarrow, *La Pensée politique et religieuse de Barbey d'Aurevilly* (Geneva: Droz / Paris: Minard, 1961);

Robert Ziegler, "Through the Eyes of Astarte: Vision and Reception in Lorrain's *Monsieur de Phocas*," *Essays in French Literature*, 27 (November 1990): 28-39.

Papers:

Manuscripts and letters by Barbey d'Aurevilly are at the Bibliothèque Nationale; the Archives of the Musée Barbey d'Aurevilly in Saint-Sauveur; the Archives of the Musée Guérin, au Cayla; and the Museum Calvet in Avignon.

Pétrus Borel
(29 June 1809 - 17 July 1859)

Norman Araujo
Boston College

SELECTED BOOKS: *Rhapsodies* (Paris: Levavasseur, 1832);

Champavert: Contes immoraux (Paris: Renduel, 1833); translated by Tom Moran as *Champavert: Seven Bitter Tales* (Chicago: Indigo Press, 1959);

Madame Putiphar, 2 volumes (Paris: Ollivier, 1839);

Le Voyageur qui raccommode ses souliers, edited by Jean-Luc Steinmetz, with a preface by Alain Borer (La Chaux-de-Cossonay, Switzerland: Parisod, 1978).

Collections: *Œuvres complètes de Pétrus Borel, Le Lycanthrope*, 3 volumes, edited, with an introduction, by Aristide Marie (Paris: La Force Française, 1922);

Œuvres complètes de Pétrus Borel, Le Lycanthrope, 5 volumes (Geneva: Slatkine Reprints, 1967);

Opera polemica: Préfaces, pamphlets, satires, articles e bibliografia, edited by Bruno Pompili (Bari, Italy: Adriatica Editrice, 1979).

OTHER: "Les Pressentimens, medianoche," in *Album de la mode, chronique du monde fashionable, ou choix de morceaux de littérature contemporaine* (Paris: Janet, 1833), pp. 313-342; published simultaneously in *Scènes du beau monde* (Paris: Magen, 1833), pp. 313-342;

Daniel Defoe, *Robinson Crusoe*, translated by Borel (Paris: Francisque Borel et Alexandre Varennes, 1836);

J.-B. Pérès, *Comme quoi Napoléon n'a jamais existé*, preface by Borel (Paris: Francisque Borel et Alexandre Varennes, 1838);

"Le Croque-mort," in *Les Français peints par eux-mêmes, encyclopédie morale du dix-neuvième siècle*, volume 2 (Paris: Curmer, 1840), pp. 121-133;

"Le Gniaffe," in *Les Français peints par eux-mêmes, encyclopédie morale du dix-neuvième siècle*, volume 4 (Paris: Curmer, 1841), pp. 373-385.

Pétrus Borel (lithograph by Célestin Nanteuil from a portrait by Louis Boulanger)

SELECTED PERIODICAL PUBLICATIONS—UNCOLLECTED: "Jérôme Chassebœuf," *Artiste*, first series 7 (1834): 102-106, 114-117;

"Vendrapedrou," *Journal des Demoiselles*, second series, no. 5 (15 June 1834): 145-147;

"Le Maréchal de Gié," *Journal des Demoiselles*, second series, no. 8 (15 September 1834): 238-243; revised as "Anne de Bretagne," in *Le Livre de beauté, souvenirs historiques* (Paris: Janet, 1834), pp. 149-163;

"Jeanniquette," *Presse*, 23-24 July 1839;

49

"Le Capitaine François de Civile," *Commerce*, 8-9 June 1841;

"Miss Hazel," *Artiste*, third series 1 (January-June 1842): 201-204; republished in *Revue Pittoresque*, first series 2 (1844): 171-180;

"La Nonne de Peñaranda," *Revue de Paris*, 6 (June 1842): 242-258; republished in *Plein Chant*, no. 1 (1981): 51-56;

"Gottfried Wolfgang," *Revue Parisienne: La Sylphide*, fourth series 8 (1843): 331-334;

"Le Trésor de la caverne d'Arcueil," *Revue de Paris*, 16 (April 1843): 221-251, 301-329; republished separately (Paris: Editions de la Connaissance, 1927);

"Daphné," *Le Messager*, 19-22 November 1843;

"La Famille Wakefield," *Revue Parisienne: La Sylphide*, fourth series 9 (1844): 257-262;

"Le Vert-Galant," *Artiste*, fourth series 2 (6 October 1844): 82-86;

"De la chaussure chez les anciens et chez les modernes," *Artiste*, fourth series 2 (15 December 1844): 241-243; (29 December 1844): 273-275;

"Mab Ivin de Roscof," *Pandore*, 1 (15 April 1845); republished in *Annales de Bretagne et des Pays de l'Ouest*, 81, no. 2 (April 1974): 415-446;

"Sur l'amour," *Artiste*, fourth series 3 (11 May 1845): 29-30;

"De la pantoufle," *Artiste*, fourth series 3 (29 June 1845): 141-142;

"Philologie humoristique," *Artiste*, fourth series 4 (27 July 1845); 40-42;

"Alger et son avenir littéraire," *Artiste*, fourth series 5 (23 November 1845): 57-59;

"Le Fou du roi de Suède," *Commerce*, 30-31 December 1845; 1-3 January 1846; republished separately (Lille: L'Homme du sable, 1980);

"Mon Ami Panturier," *Commerce*, 8-9 January 1846; republished in *Nouveau Commerce*, no. 38 (1977): 92-112;

"Quelques mois chez les Amazoulous: Chasse au lion et à l'éléphant," *Journal des Chasseurs*, 10 (8 January 1846): 69-84;

"Sur l'art," *Artiste*, fourth series 5 (11 January 1846): 73;

"Du jugement publicque," *Artiste*, fourth series 11 (9 January 1848): 145-147.

Identified early on by literary historians as one of the *petits romantiques*, or minor French Romantic writers of the first half of the nineteenth century, and acknowledged for his leadership in the Petit Cénacle—a smaller version of Charles Nodier's and then Victor Hugo's literary group of the same name (Cénacle), recalling the room where Christ and his disciples had the Last Supper—Pétrus Borel has rarely escaped, in the eyes of his critics, the negative connotations of a persistently diminutive designation. Yet no less a judge of artistic excellence than Charles Baudelaire—whose work owes much to Borel—recognized his importance: "Sans Pétrus Borel, il y aurait une lacune dans le Romantisme" (Without Pétrus Borel, there would be a gap in romanticism). The author of *Les Fleurs du mal* (1857; translated as *Flowers of Evil*, 1909) admired Borel's uncompromising opposition to bourgeois vulgarity and materialism, his adamant refusal to sell his soul for monetary gain. At a deeper level, however, Baudelaire perceived in Borel not only an acute sensitivity to the principle of negativity at work in the universe, a kindred willingness to confront directly the literary implications of evil and death, but also an arresting illustration of the *malheur*, or adversity—artistic or social—that can afflict the writer in a world hostile to his art, an adversity reflected in the word that was to become the title of a famous poem by Baudelaire (and later that of a famous poem by Stéphane Mallarmé): *le guignon*, or bad luck.

But more a prose writer than a poet, Borel could have been seen as a *prosateur maudit*—the prosaic counterpart of the *poètes maudits*, the "accursed poets" later treated by Paul Verlaine in his celebrated essays, "Les Poétes maudits" (1884-1886). In any event, a more direct and dramatic recognition of Borel's significance would come from twentieth-century movements in art and literature: dada and surrealism. André Breton, Tristan Tzara, and Paul Eluard would evoke with unbridled admiration Borel's thirst for total liberty—Breton noting, in the process, his gallows humor; Tzara, his advocacy of an activistic and not conventionally sentimental literary expression; and Eluard, his rightful place between the marquis de Sade and Isidore Ducasse, called Lautréamont.

Between the extreme positions—almost complete disregard for the value of his contribution on the one hand and overly exuberant praise for his iconoclasm on the other—perhaps there lies a median area in which Borel can be more fairly viewed. Although he carried to outrageous lengths the Romantic rebellion against social and artistic tradition without the literary genius to justify or impose his extremism, he nevertheless articulated, however imperfectly, a "modern" outlook on society, art, and the human experience. More gifted writers would express this outlook in language at once more temperate, more polished, and more persuasive than his.

Joseph-Pétrus Borel was born 29 June 1809 in Lyons, the son of André Borel, a hardware merchant, and Magdeleine-Victoire Borel, née Garnaud. The latinized Christian name appears to have been the result of two converging influences: Saint Peter's birthday and the onomastic fashions of the Revolution and its Directory stage. Only much later, during the final phase of his life given over to colonial administration, did Borel adopt the aristocratic *particule* (the *de* in his name) and become Borel d'Hauterive. Yet no evidence has been adduced to show that there was any blood link between the noble Hauterive family of Dauphiné and the Borels of Lyons despite the claims to the contrary of a brother, André, after his self-styled genealogical research.

His father determined that a move to Paris might enhance his son's educational opportunities, so Pétrus's early schooling occurred principally in the capital, at the Petit Séminaire de Sainte-Elisabeth and the Petit Séminaire de Saint-Roch, where he seems to have studied literature extensively and to have acquired a solid grounding in Greek, Latin, and English. But Borel's formal education was interrupted when he was fourteen, the initiative coming again from his father, who decided to make an architect out of him, placing him as an apprentice with Antoine Garnaud, whose architectural style was still, to Pétrus's profound dismay, firmly wedded to the classical mode. Borel would harbor deep resentment toward his father for having created this period of thralldom in his life: "Je suivis mon père, et il me vendit pour deux ans" (I followed my father, and he sold me into slavery for two years).

He trained for a total of five years before striking out on his own. It would be a cruel misstatement to say that Borel achieved success as an architect: he received few commissions and lived in abject poverty, often seeking shelter, it appears, in the basements of the very houses that he was building. His unorthodox sense of design flew so much in the face of established practices as to cause those few people who commissioned his constructions to question their structural soundness, and, in at least one instance, he felt obliged under such questioning to tear down what he had built.

Borel's turning away from architecture was to a considerable degree the consequence of his meeting, in 1829, the painter Eugène Devéria, with whom he then proceeded to study and in whose studio he made the acquaintance of key figures in the Romantic movement. Soon Borel was assuming a leadership role in the Petit Cénacle, which gravitated around the sculptor Jehan Duseigneur and included, among others, Devéria, Célestin Nanteuil, Aloysius Bertrand, Auguste Maquet, Philothée O'Neddy (anagram of Théophile Dondey), Joseph Bouchardy, and two writers later to achieve particular distinction, Théophile Gautier and Gérard de Nerval. The members of the Petit Cénacle were united in their aversion to classical convention and to the bourgeoisie.

This aversion took in part the form of an unconventional physical appearance, as witness Borel's imperial beard and *gilet à la Robespierre*, or Robespierre-style vest. It also took the shape of collective and vociferous championing of Romantic ideals, as when Borel commanded a contingent of literary shock troops whose mission was to guarantee the triumph of the premiere of Hugo's play *Hernani* on 25 February 1830 at the Comédie-Française. Borel was subsequently willing, in his republican ardor, to play an active role in the Revolution of 1830; but his father locked him in his room, thus preventing his involvement in *les trois glorieuses*, the three glorious days of 27, 28, and 29 July, which led to the enthronement of the "bourgeois king," Louis-Philippe. The failure of revolutionary republicanism did little, initially, to discourage the rebelliousness of Borel and his cohorts, although it would be partially responsible for the deep pessimism that would permeate Borel's literary productions.

In 1831 the Petit Cénacle group, whose members were also then known as the Jeune-France (they fancied themselves the proud and adventurous young men of the nation, dedicated to the struggle against philistinism and stultifying aesthetic conformity), left its haunts in the Latin Quarter to settle on the heights of Rochechouart, later to become Boulevard Rochechouart. The settlement's name, Le Camp des Tartares, or The Camp of the Tartars, bespoke the group's "barbaric" defiance of society. In fact, its intolerable behavior eventually compelled its removal from the neighborhood.

The Tartars' hostility to prevailing social customs, and much more, was reflected in Borel's bitter book of poetry, *Rhapsodies* (1832). The author himself was featured in the frontispiece wearing a Phrygian cap and staring intently at a dagger

Title page, designed and engraved by Célestin Nanteuil, for Borel's first book, a collection of poetry

ironic source, since in *Rhapsodies* Borel proudly refused to let himself fall under Byron's spell.

The poems of *Rhapsodies* are, unfortunately, inadequate to the intrepid promise of the preface, at least where craftsmanship is concerned. But their real interest lies elsewhere, in their irreverent attitude—startling in the case of a so-called *petit romantique*—toward the conventions of Romantic lyricism, and therein they foreshadow Baudelaire. There is no evocation of a consoling nature, as in Alphonse de Lamartine's poetry, no contemplative rapture in the presence of a resplendent landscape à la Hugo: Borel seeks refuge not in the countryside but in that ill-defined zone between the city and the country, the "outskirts," where lurk the true pariahs. There is also no great love theme, neither in the form of the poet's broad compassion for humanity nor as homage to the theme of the *souvenir amoureux*, or amorous remembrance. There is, finally, no exaltation of death as the great liberator; on the contrary, Borel expresses his horror of death, which is not at all surprising for one who sees the deity, in "Rêveries," as "un ogre appelé Dieu" (an ogre called God).

What dominates *Rhapsodies*—and at once attests its fidelity to the confessional tradition of Romantic literature, whatever the poet's unconventional treatment of certain Romantic clichés—is the bleak revelation of Borel's quite physical, or physiological, misery. He reveals forthrightly in the last verse of the last poem, "Misère" (Misery), that he is simply *hungry*. Yet this raw acknowledgment of hunger, this admission of desperate poverty, goes hand in hand, paradoxically, with the assertion that adversity is in truth the wellspring of poetic creation, that the poet actually develops and matures only when he is "enivré de besoin" (intoxicated by his need). So Borel has not completely rejected the Romantic linkage between suffering and creativity; but he has given it a particularly somber resonance, especially when, again in "Misère," he evokes his *guignon*, his inability to realize his poetic ideal: "Je sentais ma puissance, et je sentais des fers!" (I felt my power, and I felt the grip of chains!).

Rhapsodies did not set the literary world on fire. Yet for a while still Borel—who in the meantime had founded a newspaper, *Liberté, Journal des Arts*, designed to attack established conservative institutions such as the university and the academies—continued to enjoy considerable prestige among the Jeune-France. The activities of this group took on a richer political significance,

in his hand, as if wanting to plunge it into the heart of some tyrant in order to reverse the disillusionment engendered by the sorry fate of the ideals of the Revolution. But the real shocker was the preface, in which, seeming at once to be looking back at Jean-Jacques Rousseau and ahead to Baudelaire, by his insistence on absolute sincerity and the narcissistic distinction between himself and an inferior society (whose crassness, he observed impertinently, left only the consolations of adultery, Maryland tobacco, and Spanish paper for cigarettes), Borel vaunted his independence: "Je n'ai jamais été le paillasse d'aucun" (I have never been anyone's buffoon). And he defined his brand of republicanism as lycanthropy: the social philosophy of a wolf-man yearning for unrestricted liberty. The lycanthrope is technically one who is under the delusion that he or she is a wolf; and the image came perhaps from George Gordon, Lord Byron's *Don Juan* (1819-1824), an with its members now calling themselves the Camaraderie du Bousingo, *bousin* (noise) suggesting their unruly public conduct. *Bousingo*, or *bousingot*, was the name of the leather cap worn by the volunteers from Le Havre who came to Paris, albeit too late, to fight for the triumph of the republic at the time of the Revolution of 1830. The Camaraderie du Bousingo actually planned to organize a collection of short stories called "Contes du Bousingo" (Tales of the Bousingo), only one of which, Nerval's "La Main de gloire" (The Hand of Glory, 1832), was ever written.

In 1833, after barely a few months of existence, *Liberté, Journal des Arts* failed, but Borel was not in the least discouraged. He was now banking on the success of a different literary endeavor, a collection of his short stories called *Champavert: Contes immoraux* (1833; translated as *Champavert: Seven Bitter Tales*, 1959). Its cover, as striking as the frontispiece of *Rhapsodies*, spotlights a bluebeard dragging a woman by the hair, reenacting a scene from a one of the stories, "Don Andréa Vésalius, l'anatomiste" (Don Andréa Vésalius, the Anatomist). Similar to *Rhapsodies* in yet another respect, this work begins with a *notice*, or kind of preface, more extensively autobiographical than that of the earlier book of poetry. In the *notice* the author announced, among other things, that because the newspapers had persisted in calling the verses of *Rhapsodies* lycanthropic, and their creator a lycanthrope, he was gladly assuming that name (the book itself was even presented as being authored by Pétrus Borel, *Le Lycanthrope*).

But this was perhaps the most innocuous of Borel's onomastic surprises. Almost literally taking an autobiographical leaf from the book of the Romantic critic Charles-Augustin Sainte-Beuve—who in 1829 had published a collection of poems and prose selections, *Vie, poésies et pensées de Joseph Delorme* (The Life, Poetry and Thought of Joseph Delorme), claiming that they were the product of a certain recently departed Joseph Delorme, who would have committed suicide had he not simply died—Borel maintained that the short stories were actually the work of Champavert, who had in fact, he assured the reader, committed suicide, and had previously published a book of poetry called *Rhapsodies*, using the pseudonym Pétrus Borel. The "identity crisis" implications of such a beginning were enormous: before Arthur Rimbaud's "Je est un autre" ("I" is someone else) and Mallarmé's fascination with the "disappearance" of the authorial voice,

Medallion of Borel designed by Jehan Duseigneur in 1832, originally displayed in the salon of the Jeune-France (Musée Carnavalet)

Borel was not only pointing to the awesome complexity of the self but also characterizing his real name, in so many words, as fictional. Beyond that, he was bizarrely, and very symbolically, disclosing his own double suicide in a literary sense—in light of the fact that Champavert, alias Pétrus Borel, was said to have committed suicide, as if no more literature were to be expected to flow from his pen.

The stories—one of which, "Champavert, le lycanthrope," does recount its hero's suicidal demise—are not "immoral" in the traditional sense but rather intended to expose the immorality of society itself as highlighted in tales of rape, drowning, infanticide, and decapitation. For the most part these horrors are shown to occur not on center stage, where all is hypocritically proper, but in the "corridors" of society, in remote, secluded, sometimes strictly private areas far removed from the public gaze and condemnation. Indeed, the stories underscore dismally the immunity from punishment of those in power and the intimidating impact of authority and prestige. In "Monsieur de l'Argentière, l'accusateur" (Mr. de l'Argentière, the Accuser), for example, a public prosecutor deceives a helpless young woman and later shows her no mercy in his courtroom when she is accused of having killed the child born of their intercourse. In "Don Andréa Vésalius, l'anatomiste," an anatomist, too old to consummate his marriage, murders his wife's lovers with absolute impunity and dissects their bodies in his laboratory.

Dominated by suffering, death, and destruction, the stories of *Champavert* pay no more tribute to the Romantic conventions of love and nature than does *Rhapsodies*. Passereau, the hero of a story by the same name, believes at first religiously—faithful to the highest Romantic tradition—in love, and the object of that love is a woman whose name, Philogène, means "engendering love." He soon discovers, however, that she has betrayed him, and, answering betrayal with death, he murders her. In "Champavert, le lycanthrope," the protagonist, similarly disenchanted, defines love in terms of hatred and groans of pain. Champavert's remarks on the subject of nature (his name can be broken down into *champ pas vert*, or "a field that is not green") are equally damning: he decries the tiresome monotony of the cyclic patterns of sun and rain, spring and autumn; in particular, he deplores the eternal recurrence of *green* trees.

The godless universe of these stories, where violence and bloodshed are so prevalent and so lavishly described as to suggest that the author himself takes a perverse pleasure in their depiction, admits of none of the escapist or fanciful diversions associated with narratives that focus on travel or adventure. While exoticism and primitivism are characteristic of two tales, "Jacquez Barraou, le charpentier" (Jacquez Barraou, the Carpenter) and "Three Fingered Jack, l'obi" (Three Fingered Jack, the Witch Doctor), set in Havana and Jamaica respectively, their atmosphere is no less brutal than that of the other stories. Whatever true relief can be found from the negativity and cruelty of life as depicted in all these tales—and it is not to be sought in the refinements of style, given Borel's frequently pedantic writing (in "Three Fingered Jack" he translates excerpts from an English treatise on sugar)—comes from the author's gallows humor, what Breton would call his *humour noir*, the most celebrated example of which occurs in "Passereau, l'écolier" (Passereau, the Schoolboy). Full of disillusionment and despair, Passereau pays a visit to the public executioner and makes a polite request of him, a request remarkable both because of its preposterousness and because of its consummate grammatical propriety: "Je désirerais ardemment

que vous me guillotinassiez!" (I should be ever so pleased if you would guillotine me!).

Less diverting, but perhaps more revealing in the final analysis than such occasional examples of *humour noir* in *Champavert*, are the two definitions of the lycanthrope that emerge from the work. One definition concerns Three Fingered Jack, the Jamaican witch doctor, described as an example of those sturdy characters born to rule but placed in a cage by fate and society, which is bent on reducing everyone to its own mediocre standards of measurement. But if Borel calls Three Fingered Jack—who is helpful to others and has never harmed a woman or a child—a lycanthrope, he employs the same term to characterize another protagonist, Champavert, whose life ends in suicide after he has killed his mistress Flava. Her murder is the first phase of a suicide pact, the consequence of Champavert's rage against society, which he blames for the death of his illegitimate son, murdered at birth by Flava, the child's mother.

It is significant that Champavert takes his own life at Montfaucon, the infamous site of past hangings, used as a graveyard for horses in the nineteenth century. But Champavert's association with the animalistic in this sense is not the worst of it: killing himself by plunging a knife into his heart, he recalls the legend of the vampire and how one destroys it with a stake. Thus the image of Borel's lycanthrope as it emerges from a reading of the stories of *Champavert* is, at the very least, a disturbingly ambiguous one.

Champavert received its fair share of critical praise. Writing in the *Revue des Deux Mondes* (1 March 1833), Sainte-Beuve singled out "Passereau" in laudatory terms. Nevertheless, like other favorably disposed critics, he took exception to the eccentricities of Borel's style, objecting in particular to the author's abundant use of epigraphs in several different languages, a practice that, according to Sainte-Beuve, made comprehension difficult. It was rather in financial terms that the work turned out to be a colossal failure, heralding the commencement of a new period in Borel's life that would be marked by even greater indigence than he had known before, coupled with literary as well as social isolation.

The isolation stemmed from the gradual desertion of important members of the Bousingo group, such as Gautier and Nerval. They became more and more convinced that *la littérature frénétique* (the extreme cultivation of certain Romantic tendencies, such as the exaltation of the individual and fascination with the horrible and the macabre) was no longer the answer to social or artistic ills, especially when the growing, if gray, stability of Louis-Philippe's government quashed hopes of a republican revival. Gautier's aesthetic reflections were moving in the direction of *l'art pour l'art*, or art for art's sake, and the publication of his *Les Jeunes-France* (1833), a collection of humorous tales, was already a gentle rebuke to the excesses of Borel's coterie. The preface to Gautier's novel *Mademoiselle de Maupin* (1836) contained the essentials of the art for art's sake credo.

Meanwhile Borel was trying his hand both at the writing of less bleak short stories and at translation. In the rags-to-riches tale "Jérôme Chasseboeuf," which appeared in *Artiste* in 1834, a gifted young composer of modest means and background passes himself off as an aristocrat and marries the noble heiress to a large fortune. She loves him so much that she forgives him when he confesses his deceit. Far more aesthetically successful was Borel's 1836 translation of Daniel Defoe's *Robinson Crusoe* (1719), a rendition worthy of note not only because of Borel's fidelity to the original but also, once again, because of the unique flavor of the translator's preface, in which he spoke of his poetic achievement with regard to the handling of Defoe's text. Borel appeared to be saying that his translation of *Robinson Crusoe* was more a process of identification with the English writer than a translation in the ordinary sense of the word—more along the lines of that aesthetic fusion that occurred when Baudelaire translated Edgar Allan Poe. In light of Borel's ever-increasing solitude, it was not astonishing that he should identify so intimately with the semisolitary destiny of the shipwrecked hero of Defoe's novel.

The spiritual satisfactions of translation did nothing to arrest the continued deterioration of Borel's financial situation, and in November 1836 he left Paris with his mistress Marie-Antoinette Claye (who had borne him a son, Justus, two years earlier) in order to settle in Le Baizil, a village in Champagne. There he tried desperately to eke out a living from the soil, sheltered in a shack with a leaky roof and subsisting on the meager vegetables that he was able to cultivate. The author of *Rhapsodies*, who had spoken unabashedly of his hunger and poverty, was now perhaps more destitute than he had ever been. It was in these harsh material circumstances that Borel composed his novel *Madame Putiphar*, and they were

to color indelibly the tragic episodes of this sprawling work. *Madame Putiphar* appeared in 1839, introduced this time not by a preface, nor by a *notice*, but by a poem of Baudelairean texture featuring three knights—the first representing the world; the second, solitude; and the third, death or nothingness—who fight for the author's soul, and he wonders out loud which one will claim him.

The fate of the lovers in *Madame Putiphar* suggests that Borel opted for the last of the three knights, or indeed felt claimed by him. More unrelieved in the degree of its adversity and pessimism than any of the writer's previous works, the novel chronicles the frightful destiny of Deborah Cockermouth and Patrick Fitz-Whyte, natives of Ireland whose love is thwarted from one end of the novel to the other. The first obstacle to their passion is Deborah's father, Lord Cockermouth, whose heartless opposition to Patrick simply because he is poor and of the peasant class forces the lovers to flee to Paris, where Patrick, after enlisting in the French army, runs afoul of Madame Putiphar (intended to represent Madame de Pompadour) by resisting her advances. This resistance lands him in prison, a fate shared by his friend Fitz-Harris (who has satirized Madame Putiphar in his writings) and by Deborah herself, who is kidnapped through the agency of the jealous Madame Putiphar in order to be "trained" for Pharaon's (Louis XV's) sexual satisfaction but who courageously repulses him.

In prison, Deborah gives birth to Patrick's son, whom she appropriately names Vengeance in anticipation of the day when he will avenge his father, the false report of whose death she has received. Eventually, Deborah escapes from prison and is able to raise Vengeance in the sole thought of this revenge. But her plans go awry when Vengeance is killed in a duel with Patrick's commanding officer, the marquis de Gave de Villepastour, who, coveting Deborah, had sought to damn her lover. When, many years later, the Bastille falls, an insane prisoner is found there: Patrick. Deborah is informed and comes to the prison to reclaim him, only to discover that in his madness he no longer recognizes her. This ironic form of rejection is more than she can bear, and she falls dead.

On the social and political levels at least, Borel's thematic objectives in *Madame Putiphar* are clear enough: consonant with the author's republicanism, and inspired in part, like so many other novels of the period, by Silvio Pellico's *My*

Un festin de Jeunes France

Principes: Un maintien d'homme, debout devant une table brute, pour plat, assiette et verre le crâne d'une maîtresse, le tibia d'un ami pour couvert, un poignard pour couteau, puis des alimens communs et la tristesse au cœur.

Borel, Gérard de Nerval, and Jehan Duseigneur pictured at a feast of the Jeune-France.
Drinking from human skulls was one of the group's many bizarre activities.

Prisons (1832), the novel denounces the tyranny and corruption of the monarchical regime, contrasting them with the principles of a medieval, chivalric code of honor characteristic of Patrick and Deborah. But on the philosophical and religious levels, the novelist's intentions are far less clear. The first chapter of *Madame Putiphar* formulates a belief in *destinées fatales* (fatal destinies), the idea that certain people are pursued by unrelenting bad luck or misfortune, caught in a particularly devastating form of the Baudelairean *guignon*. The metaphysical corollary of this belief is that, if God indeed exists, he is indifferent to their tribulations and may well delight in them. *Madame Putiphar* is thus offered as a persuasive, if horrifying, illustration of this

truth, its lesson all the more disturbing in that, like *Rhapsodies* and *Champavert* before it, it ascribes no mitigating role to the splendors of nature.

Yet, close to the end of his novel, Borel reverses his field. Possibly influenced by the thinking of Joseph de Maistre and Pierre Ballanche, he now advances a theory of expiation, according to which those innocents who suffer on this earth are either not so just as they seem, or are instruments of divine retribution in that they are atoning for the sins of others. Whatever the case, Borel assures the reader, the guilty do not go unpunished. The author invites his reader to see, in a reexamination of the novel's meaning, God's punishment visited on the monarchy by the people acting as his instrument. But as he develops this Old Testament vision of divine vengeance, Borel does not clarify, to the reader's satisfaction, in what precise manner the tragic fate that befalls his principal "good" characters is just, nor does he explain how, in these circumstances, a *new* monarchy is allowed to emerge after the Revolution.

The thematic inconsistency of *Madame Putiphar* is not rendered any more palatable on the stylistic plane by the sometimes haphazard convergence of elements drawn from different novelistic traditions. The work is in part a historical novel, set in a realistic chronological framework and evocative of authentic fashions and trends of the period, such as the rococo. The prisons are real, the details of prison life gleaned from reliable sources, such as the memoirs of Henri Masers de Latude. Real too are the prisoners and their *hunger* (one is reminded once again of the Borel of *Rhapsodies*), Patrick Whyte having existed and having been imprisoned in the Bastille. Borel's admiration for the novel's most illustrious prisoner, the marquis de Sade, would infuriate at least one literary critic of the period, Jules Janin.

At the same time, however, *Madame Putiphar* is obviously indebted to the tradition of the *roman noir*, or Gothic novel. There is, at the outset, the sinister atmosphere of the Irish castle of Lord Cockermouth, architecturally not Gothic to be sure, but unsettling nonetheless, especially with its mysterious East Tower. There are the dark, dank, labyrinthine prisons themselves, where the inmates, often unjustly accused and condemned, languish without hope of release. There is the typically oversimplified portrayal of the villains, Louis XV and Madame de Pompadour being completely reduced to their mean and sensual components as Pharaon and Putiphar.

At once historical and Gothic, *Madame Putiphar* is also epic in the grand biblical sense, as is already implicit in the notion of a divinely ordained expiation, the carrying out of God's will. The novel's very title has an Old Testament resonance, since Potiphar is, in Genesis 39, Pharaoh's Egyptian officer whose wife tries to seduce Joseph and is instrumental in having him put into prison when her attempt at seduction fails, much as Madame Putiphar herself, rebuffed, has Patrick confined. Born in a manger, Patrick is inseparably attached to his crucifix and traverses his own Passion. The name Deborah is relatively com-

mon in the Old Testament, being in one instance (Book of Judges) that of a prophetess.

As if this richness of levels were not enough, there is even an autobiographical strain in *Madame Putiphar*. Reflected in its multiple prisons and sustained horror is the measure of Borel's own despair, "imprisoned" as he was in his wretched existence in Le Baizil, no longer the respected leader of his literary group and deserted by most of its members. The hope of some sort of revenge against destiny, mirrored in the fictional choice of the name Vengeance, recalls that Borel, with a comparable hope, had named his first son Justus. Moreover, the motif of the tyrannical father, incarnated in the novel's Lord Cockermouth, reminds the reader of Borel's unhappy relationship with his own father, who, in forcing his son to become an architect, displayed nothing but scorn for Pétrus's personal preferences. A final, unmistakable autobiographical note is to be seen, alas, in the narrator's pedantry. Much as the narrator of "Three Fingered Jack, l'obi" translated a generous excerpt from a treatise on sugar, the narrator of *Madame Putiphar*—beyond exhibiting a bizarre penchant for archaic words in no less archaic spellings—discourses at length on the innumerable varieties of ebony and pridefully observes, in the novel's final chapter, that any misprints in the work should not be attributed to his ignorance or carelessness.

Madame Putiphar was savagely attacked by the ruling Prince de la Critique (Prince of Criticism), Janin, who in the *Journal des Débats* (3 June 1839) alluded to the novel's obscene premise and bloody conclusions, comparing the author to the marquis de Sade. Years later, Baudelaire and Breton would have more complimentary things to say about the novel and the novelist. Though disappointed by the unevenness of the style (he appreciated the description of the nocturnal ride of Vengeance's dead body, attached to his horse and sent back to his mother by his slayer), Baudelaire was struck by Borel's honest portrayal of sin, punishment, and the void of life, while Breton was taken with the depth and insight of the poetic prologue.

After the largely indifferent critical reception accorded his novel—Janin's violent reaction notwithstanding—Borel decided to pursue other avenues of approach to literary and financial success, writing satirical sketches as a kind of freelance journalist and continuing to contribute short stories to different reviews and newspapers.

Among the most noteworthy of his attempts at satire were "Le Croque-mort" (The Undertaker's Assistant, 1840) and "Le Gniaffe" (The Cobbler, 1841), which appeared in *Les Français peints par eux-mêmes* (The French Portrayed by Themselves). These satirical pieces gave vent more effectively to the *humour noir* that had been for the most part overshadowed in previous works by the grave themes of violence and tragedy. They also revealed another modernist aspect of Borel's thought: his concern that the bourgeois obsession with administrative bureaucracy had made of the undertaker—a contemporary "type" whose physiology could be studied—no more than a stuffy formalist excessively preoccupied with the purely procedural facet of funerals; or that the restoration of old shoes mirrored the modern technological society's manic determination to rescue and recycle the old and the worn.

In the specific case of shoes, Borel's curiosity ran deep, embracing the absurd symbolism of man's vainglorious concern with the lower, the "base" region of his being. Several works attested to this curiosity—and the relish with which Borel availed himself of the opportunity to treat a "low" subject in a dignified style—among them a piece in the *Artiste*, "De la chaussure chez les anciens et chez les modernes" (On Shoes among the Ancients and the Moderns, 1844). Five years later Borel would return to the subject with a long poem, *Le Voyageur qui raccommode ses souliers* (The Traveler Who Repairs His Shoes), which was not published until 1978.

It was also in 1844 that, having lived for four years in Asnières on the outskirts of Paris after his return from Le Baizil, Borel took up residence again in the capital itself and assumed the editorship of a newspaper called *Satan*, the name signifying—in the Romantic era of a "rehabilitated" Satan—not a teller of lies, but a fearless teller of disturbing social truths. The publication had been run by Borel's brother Francisque, but he had been fined and imprisoned for writing editorials attacking government officials. In addition to serving as editor of *Satan*, Borel also wrote articles on art and literature for the newspaper, as well as book reviews. But the venture was not successful, and another newspaper, the *Corsaire*, absorbed *Satan* after a few months. Undaunted, Borel created that same year the *Revue Pittoresque*, and, with Nerval, established a publishing house and a collection, *L'Ane d'or* (The Golden Ass), designed to present works by the modern-day disciples of Desiderius Erasmus,

Giovanni Boccaccio, and other Renaissance writers. These ambitious enterprises also failed, as Borel's characteristic bad luck persisted. Around this time Champfleury, who used to see Borel in the offices of the *Artiste*, seeking to have this or that piece published, observed how old and worn the lycanthrope was for his thirty-five years. It was around this time, too, that Baudelaire, who would also have some of his work published by the *Artiste*, might well have met Borel personally.

In 1845 Gautier suggested to the perpetually impecunious Borel that he should consider applying for a position in Algeria as inspector of colonization. Borel took his advice and, thanks in part to Gautier's connections, was appointed to a post in Algiers in December of that year. He left for Algeria the following January and began his administrative career during the last phase of Marshal Thomas Bugeaud's stint as governor-general. At first Borel's performance was favorably graded by his superiors, although the style of his official reports was judged to be somewhat too literary. After Bugeaud's departure in 1847, Borel served in Mostaganem, where he built a Gothic home airily called Castel de Haute Pensée (Castle of High Thought) for himself and his nineteen-year-old bride, Gabrielle Claye (the daughter of his former mistress Marie-Antoinette and Augustin Claye), whom he had married on 2 September 1847 in Algiers. Although he wrote a clever pastiche of Michel de Montaigne that was published in the *Artiste* (9 January 1848), Borel's activities at this time were almost exclusively administrative and political.

In 1852 he became mayor of the village Blad-Touaria and won the gratitude and affection of the local population for his devoted service during a cholera epidemic. But by now Borel, who had had his difficulties both with the officials of the Republic—this lycanthropic republican, like so many others, had been disillusioned by the revolution of 1848—and with those of Napoleon III, was under fire for the increasingly desultory style of his reports and for his accusations of corruption in the colonial administration. These factors led to two dismissals, the second of which, coming in 1855, was to be definitive.

During this interval Borel composed one of the rare poems of his Algerian period, "Léthargie de la muse" (Lethargy of the Muse), only fragments of which have survived. In them he expresses despair at not having been able to motivate his indifferent muse. His despondency notwithstanding, Borel, as firmly convinced as ever

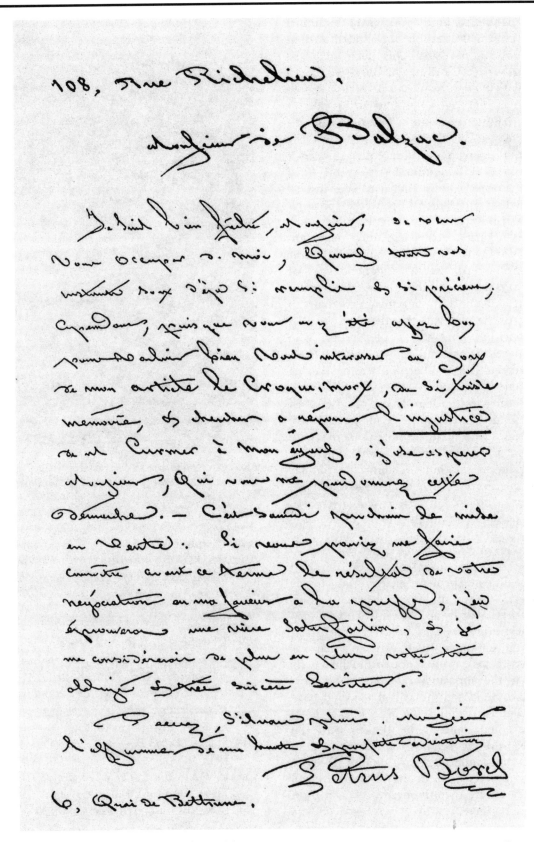

Undated letter from Borel to Honoré de Balzac, in which Borel discusses his story "Le Croque-mort"
(Collection Spoelberch de Lovenjoul)

of his independence, points with pride to the fact that he has never utilized his poetic talent to flatter the powerful nor stolen his poetic material from others. After his dismissal Borel continued to work his fields around Castel de Haute Pensée as a simple farmer, aged well beyond his not yet fifty years, bald and unkempt. He stubbornly refused to wear a hat for protection against the sun, maintaining, with a residual touch of *humour noir*, that if God had intended that his head should be covered, he would not have lost so much of his hair. Borel died 17 July 1859, presumably of sunstroke.

By his Algerian experience Borel might appear finally to have joined the ranks—whatever his pretensions to artistic independence—of those literary figures of the nineteenth century who began as iconoclasts but then ended up in the employ of the very state that they had so vehemently criticized. One thinks of Nodier, who openly opposed Napoleon I yet was named librarian of L'Arsenal prior to becoming a member of the Académie Française in 1833; or of Gautier, Borel's literary comrade-in-arms of the Petit Cénacle, Jeune-France, and Camaraderie du Bousingo days, who forsook *la littérature frénétique* for the art for art's sake movement and then became Princess Mathilde's librarian. Similar thoughts must have governed the reaction of Albert Camus, who, in *L'Homme révolté* (*The Rebel*, 1951), recalled disparagingly Borel's career as a civil servant.

Yet, in leaving for Algeria, Borel was exercising his sole option to avoid utter destitution. It may not be too much of an exaggeration to say that it was a matter of life or death. Furthermore, Borel was hardly a conformist and submissive administrator. Even as he served the state, he continued, paradoxically, to fight it. What was unfortunate in his case was not so much that he went over to the opposition but that, in his literary rebellion, he lacked the gifts that would have permitted him to ascend to the highest level of artistic achievement, and to be ranked with the Baudelaires and the Bretons (one is tempted to add "and the Lautréamonts," though Ducasse never formally recognized any debt to Borel), whom he so manifestly influenced.

Letters:

J. Richer, "Lettres de la vie littéraire de Pétrus Borel," *Revue des Sciences Humaines*, nos. 98-99 (April-September 1960): 249-255.

Frontispiece engraving for Pétrus Borel, Le Lycanthrope *(1865), the first biography of the author*

Bibliography:

Antoine Laporte, *Pétrus Borel, Le Lycanthrope-Bonnaffé-Bonnardot: Etude bibliographique* (Paris: St.-Amand, 1884).

Biographies:

Jules Claretie, *Pétrus Borel, Le Lycanthrope: Sa vie—ses écrits—sa correspondance; poésies et documents inédits* (Paris: Pincebourde, 1865);

Aristide Marie, *Pétrus Borel, Le Lycanthrope: Sa vie et son œuvre, suivi d'une bibliographie* (Paris: La Force Française, 1922);

Enid Starkie, *Pétrus Borel en Algérie* (Oxford: Blackwell, 1950);

Starkie, *Pétrus Borel, The Lycanthrope: His Life and Times* (London: Faber & Faber, 1953; Norfolk, Conn.: New Directions, 1954).

References:

Eugène Asse, *Les Petits Romantiques* (Paris: Leclerc, 1900);

Charles Asselineau, *Mélanges tirés d'une petite bibliothèque romantique* (Paris: Pincebourde, 1866);

Jean-Louis Audin (pseudonym of Jean Rousselot), "Pétrus Borel l'Algérien," in *Les Petits Romantiques français* (Marseilles: Editions des Cahiers du Sud, 1949), pp. 74-80; revised in *Rencontres sur les chemins de la poésie* (Paris: Nouvelles Editions Debresse, 1958), pp. 61-69;

Paul Bénichou, "Jeune-France et Bousingos: Essai de mise au point," *Revue d'Histoire Littéraire de la France*, 71 (1971): 439-462;

René Bourgeois, "Pétrus Borel," in his *L'Ironie romantique: Spectacle et jeu de Mme de Staël à Gérard de Nerval* (Grenoble: Presses Universitaires de Grenoble, 1974), pp. 65-83;

André Breton, "Pétrus Borel," in his *Anthologie de l'humour noir* (Paris: Pauvert, 1966), pp. 137-149;

Victor Brombert, "Borel, Prison Horrors and the Gothic Tradition," *Novel*, 2 (Winter 1969): 143-152; republished in his *La Prison romantique: Essai sur l'imaginaire* (Paris: Corti, 1975), pp. 53-66;

Champfleury, "Croquis romantiques: Pétrus Borel," *Livre*, 3 (April 1882): 105-109; republished in his *Vignettes romantiques: Histoire de la littérature et de l'art, 1825-1840* (Paris: Dentu, 1883), pp. 146-155;

Béatrice Didier, "*Madame Putiphar*, roman sadien?," introduction to Borel's *Madame Putiphar* (Paris: Deforges, 1972), pp. viii-xx;

Francis Dumont, *Naissance du romantisme* (Paris: Editions Calmann-Lévy, 1942);

Dumont, *Nerval et les Bousingots* (Paris: La Table Ronde, 1958);

Théophile Gautier, *Histoire du romantisme, suivie de notices romantiques, et d'une étude sur la poésie française (1830-1868); avec un index alphabétique* (Paris: Charpentier et Fasquelle, 1895);

Henri Lardanchet, *Les Enfants perdus du romantisme* (Paris: Perrin et Cie, 1905);

Bruno Pompili, "Il Segno del licantropo," in his edition of Borel's *Opera polemica* (Bari, Italy: Adriatica Editrice, 1979), pp. 9-78;

F. P. Smith, "Un Conte fantastique chez Irving, Borel et Dumas," *Revue de Littérature Comparée*, no. 2 (1958): 331-346;

Jean-Luc Steinmetz, "L'Acte manqué du romantisme," in his *La France frénétique de 1830: Choix de textes* (Paris: Editions Phébus, 1978), pp. 9-45;

Steinmetz, "Du poète infortuné au poète maudit," *Œuvres et Critiques*, no. 7 (1982): 75-86;

Steinmetz, "L'Ecriture homicide," in his edition of Borel's *Champavert: Contes immoraux* (Paris: Editions Le Chemin Vert, 1985), pp. vii-xxv;

Steinmetz, "Le Fil des Parques," in his edition of Borel's *Madame Putiphar* (Paris: Editions Le Chemin Vert, 1987), pp. vii-xxii;

Steinmetz, "Les Malheurs du récit," postface to Borel's *Madame Putiphar* (Paris: Deforges, 1972), pp. 379-441;

Steinmetz, "L'Ouïe du nom," *Littérature*, no. 33 (February 1979): 86-99; republished in his *Le Champ d'écoute: Essais critiques* (Neuchâtel: Les Editions de la Baconnière, 1985), pp. 79-103;

Steinmetz, *Pétrus Borel: Un auteur provisoire* (Lille: Presses Universitaires de Lille, 1986);

Arthur Symons, "Pétrus Borel," *Forum*, no. 53 (1915): 763-765.

Papers:

Borel's papers are at the Archives Nationales; the Bibliothèque Nationale, Fonds Nadard; Fonds Borel d'Outre-Mer; the Bibliothèque de l'Académie Française at Chantilly; and the Etat-Civil of Lyons, Algiers, and Mostaganem.

Champfleury
(Jules-François-Félix Husson)
(17 September 1821 - 6 December 1889)

K. G. McWatters
University of Liverpool

BOOKS: *Chien-Caillou, fantaisies d'hiver* (Paris: Martinon, 1847);

Feu Miette, fantaisies d'été (Paris: Martinon, 1847);

Pauvre Trompette, fantaisies de printemps (Paris: F. Sartorius, 1847);

Essai sur la vie et l'œuvre des Le Nain, peintres laonnois (Laon: Imprimerie E. Fleury and A. Chevergny, 1850);

Les Excentriques (Paris: Michel Lévy, 1852);

Contes vieux et nouveaux (Paris: M. Lévy frères, 1852)—contains *Les Confessions de Sylvius* and *Van Schaendal*;

Les Oies de Noël (Paris: Hachette, 1853);

Contes de printemps: les Aventures de Mademoiselle Mariette (Paris: Lecou, 1853);

Contes d'été: Souffrances du professeur Delteil; Les Trios des chenizelles; Les Ragotins (Paris: Lecou, 1853);

Les Bourgeois de Molinchart (Paris: Librairie Nouvelle, 1855);

Les Grands Hommes du ruisseau (Paris: Michel Lévy, 1855);

Les Peintres de Laon et de Saint-Quentin-De La Tour (Paris: Didron, 1855);

La Gazette de Champfleury, 1er novembre 1856 - 1er decembre 1856 (Paris: Blanchard, 1856);

Monsieur de Boisdhyver (Paris: A. Cadot, 1857);

Le Réalisme (Paris: Michel Lévy frères, 1857);

La Succession Le Camus, misères de la vie domestique (Paris: A. Cadot, 1858);

L'Usurier Blaizot (Paris: Michel Lévy frères, 1859);

Les Amis de la nature (Paris: Poulet-Malassis et De Broise, 1859);

Les Amoureux de Sainte-Périne (Paris: A. Bourdilliat, 1859);

Les Sensations de Josquin (Paris: Michel Lévy, 1859);

La Mascarade de la vie parisienne (Paris: Dubuisson, 1859);

Grandes Figures d'hier et d'aujourd'hui—Balzac, Gérard de Nerval, Wagner, Courbet (Paris: Poulet-Malassis et De Broise, 1861);

Champfleury, circa 1865 (photograph by Nadar)

Recherches sur les origines et les variations de la légende du bonhomme Misère (Paris: Poulet-Malassis et De Broise, 1861);

Les Peintres de la réalité sous Louis XIII—Les Frères Le Nain (Paris: Renouard, 1862);

Le Violon de faïence; L'Avocat qui trompe son client; Les Amis de la nature; Les Enfants du Professeur Turck (Paris: Hertzel, 1862);

Les Bons Contes font les bons amis (Paris, 1863);

Les Demoiselles Tourangeu (Paris: Michel Lévy frères, 1864);

Histoire de la caricature antique (Paris: Dentu, 1865);

Histoire de la caricature moderne (Paris: Dentu, 1865);

Monsieur Tringle (Paris: Dentu, 1866);

Ma Tante Péronne (Paris: A. Faure, 1867);

La Comédie académique; La Belle Paule (Paris: Dubuisson, 1867);

Histoire des faïences patriotiques sous la Révolution (Paris: Dentu, 1867);

L'Hôtel des commissaires-priseurs (Paris: Dentu, 1867);

Les Chats, histoire, mœurs, observations, anecdotes (Paris: J. Rothchild, 1869);

Histoire de l'imagerie populaire (Paris: Dentu, 1869);

L'Avocat Trouble-ménage (Paris: E. Dentu, 1870);

Histoire de la caricature au moyen âge (Paris: Dentu, 1870);

Souvenirs et portraits de jeunesse (Paris: Dentu, 1872);

Les Enfants, éducation, instruction (Paris: J. Rothchild, 1872);

Madame Eugénio (Paris: Charpentier, 1874)—contains *La Sonnette de M. Berloquin*; *Les Bras de la Vénus de Milo*; and *L'Histoire du Lieutenant Valentin*;

Le Secret de M. Ladureau (Paris: Dentu, 1875);

Documents pour servir à la biographie de Balzac (Paris: A. Patay, 1875-1878);

La Pasquette (Paris: Charpentier, 1876);

La Petite Rose (Paris: Dentu, 1877);

Henry Monnier, sa vie, son œuvre (Paris: Dentu, 1879);

Histoire de la caricature sous la Réforme et la Ligue—Louis XIII à Louis XVI (Paris: Dentu, 1880);

Surtout n'oublie pas ton parapluie (Paris: Dentu, 1881);

Bibliographie céramique. Nomenclature analytique de toutes les publications faites en Europe ou en Orient sur l'art et l'industrie céramiques depuis le XVIᵉ siècle jusqu'à nos jours (Paris: A. Quantin, 1882);

Fanny Minoret (Paris: Dentu, 1882);

Vignettes romantiques, histoire de la littérature et de l'art, 1825-1840 (Paris: Dentu, 1883);

Les Artistes célèbres—La Tour (Paris: J. Rouan, 1886);

Nouvelles études sur l'art et la littérature romantiques: le drame amoureux de Célestin Nanteuil d'après des lettres inédites adressées à Marie Dorval (Paris: Dentu, 1887);

Le Musée secret de la caricature (Paris: Dentu, 1888).

Editions and Collections: *Le Violon de faïence, Les Enfants du Professeur Turck, La Sonnette de M.*

Berloquin, edited by Michael Weatherilt (Geneva: Droz, 1985);

Champfleury, son regard et celui de Baudelaire, edited by Geneviève and Jean Lacambre, with *L'Amitié de Baudelaire et de Champfleury,* edited by Claude Pichois (Paris: Collection Savoir, Hermann, 1990).

Champfleury was a central figure in the mid-nineteenth-century controversy over realism in literature and in the fine arts. He was at once a theoretician, a regional novelist, an art critic, an art historian, a remarkable collector, and much else besides. His friends included Gustave Courbet, Charles Baudelaire, Honoré Daumier, and Henri Monnier, and his own origins were in *la bohème* (the bohemian world).

Jules-François-Félix Husson, born in Laon on 17 September 1821, was the son of a minor civil servant whose wife was in the grocery business. A difficult schoolboy, he removed himself to Paris at the age of seventeen to work for a bookseller, taking his first step in the direction of Parisian bohemia. He there encountered the painter Antoine Chintreuil, like himself *un commis-libraire* (bookseller's clerk); the brothers Joseph and Leopold Desbrosses, who founded the Société des Buveurs d'eau (Society of Water Drinkers); and Henri Murger. His family obliged him to return to Laon in 1840, where he remained for three years, leading a life of dissipation, according to the citizenry. There is no doubt that his unhappiness as a schoolboy at the Collège de Laon, as well as this period at home between 1840 and 1843, gave his more successful novels their specific coloring.

His father provided a link between bohemian son and respectable family. In 1840 the father bought a printery and founded the *Journal de l'Aisne,* which was edited by another son, Edouard Fleury (the Hussons adopted *Fleury* as a nom de plume). Although he returned to Paris in 1844, Jules continued to write for his father's newspaper, and in 1849 he contributed to the *Journal de l'Aisne* his first investigations into the Le Nain brothers (Antoine, Louis, and Mathieu), seventeenth-century artists from Laon whom he rediscovered and repopularized. Such pieces demonstrate the author's taste for research along with his local piety.

His entry into *la bohème* led to a change of name. As he wrote to his mother, he was much less likely to achieve a breakthrough with the family name, and besides there was already another

Jules Fleury, a journalist who wrote for the *Démocratie Pacifique*. With perhaps an unconscious middle-class bias in an age of accumulation of capital, he assured his mother that he both kept the family name and added to it.

Writing for Champfleury meant journalism of at least two kinds. One was concerned with the bohemian writing about *la bohème*, the other with art history and contemporary production in the visual arts. The two occupations were interdependent, at least initially. Champfleury—along with Théophile Gautier, Gérard de Nerval, and Pétrus Borel—wrote for *L'Artiste*, edited by his compatriot Arsène Houssaye, and contributed to the *petits journaux* (ephemeral satirical newspapers), notably the *Corsaire-Satan*, for which Baudelaire wrote, but also to the *Silhouette*, the *Tam-Tam*, and the *Pamphlet*. He also wrote successful pantomimes, but his literary career was initiated in the *petits journaux*, in which those living close to *la bohème* invented budding artists and recounted their struggles with the bourgeoisie.

These bohemian writers attempted to make a name as *feuilletonistes* (columnists) and devised portraits of eccentrics and oddities whose attraction lay in their being self-marginalized or marginal members of society. Champfleury's story *Van Schaendal* (1852) tells of an artist who insists upon total harmony between himself and the subject he paints. To him, a still life means a period of vegetarianism. *Feu Miette* (The Late Miette, 1847) is the story of a tumbler and showman who seeks above all else to meet the painter Horace Vernet, whose father had painted his portrait. *Les Souvenirs du doyen des croque-morts* (Memories of the Dean of Undertakers, in *Les Excentriques* [1852]) involves a mute undertaker who writes verse to captivate a child audience. He can no longer appreciate nature, for trees after all are made into coffins.

Champfleury collected this copious literary journalism and published it in volume form, adding dedications to Victor Hugo, Eugène Delacroix, and Honoré de Balzac. *Chien-Caillou, fantaisies d'hiver* (Chien-Caillou: Winter Fantasies), *Feu Miette, fantaisies d'été* (The Late Miette: Summer Fantasies), and *Pauvre Trompette, fantaisies de printemps* (Poor Trumpet: Spring Fantasies) appeared in 1847. *Les Confessions de Sylvius* (The Confessions of Sylvius) and *Les Excentriques* (The Eccentrics) followed in 1852, and *Les Grands Hommes du ruisseau* (Great Men from the Gutter) in 1855. This last publication marked his final exploitation of such material. Champfleury

changed direction, particularly after a visit to Balzac on 27 February 1848 brought with it the counsel to write no more than three short stories a year, and an implicit encouragement to write novels.

Any summing up of Champfleury's bohemian work involves the idea and situation of the artist as well as that of his polar opposite, the bourgeois, whom the more hardened reader of nineteenth-century French fiction will dismally recognize as having problems enough. The exemplar of the artist is Chien-Caillou, an engraver modeled on Rodolphe Bresdin, who was at once highly original and recognized as a marginal being. Indeed he is the exemplar of the artist in a commercial world, where dealers buy his works for derisory sums and sell them off as productions of Flemish masters. Chien-Caillou reminds one of Gustave Flaubert's *L'Education sentimentale* (1869; translated as *Sentimental Education*, 1898) and of the world of *l'art industriel*, the world of counterfeits. In both instances the artist is dispossessed; the trade value of his work depends upon his not being perceived as himself. *Chien-Caillou* is thus a radical and prophetic text, and was praised as such by Baudelaire. As for the name "Chien-Caillou," legend has it that Bresdin, who resembled an American Indian, was called "Chingachgook," after a character in James Fenimore Cooper's *The Last of the Mohicans* (1826). This name was soon corrupted to "Chien-Caillou." To twentieth-century readers this is proof of further marginalization. "Caillou" is also nineteenth-century slang for a bald head.

Champfleury's presentation of eccentrics takes the reader further into nineteenth-century views of the creative artist. Alfred de Vigny produced the *paria* (outcast); Baudelaire, the artist subject to *la guigne* (bad luck); Champfleury perhaps looks forward to Stéphane Mallarmé and his sonnet on the artist as a clown who receives punishment, merited or not: *le pitre châtié* (the punished clown), to use Mallarmé's expression. In the preface to *Les Excentriques*, dedicated to Daumier, Champfleury presents poets as sad exhibitionists who "marchent dans la vie les pieds dans l'air, la tête en bas … et reçoivent déjà assez de coups de pied des ânes qui les entourent" (walk through life with their feet up in the air, their head down … and already get enough kicks from the asses who surround them). One should not seek to expose them publicly, "en compagnie des presque fous, aux risées d'une foule ignorante" (in the company of the nearly-insane, to the ridicule of an ignorant crowd).

Champfleury became an art critic as well, writing most notably in *L'Artiste*, whose proprietor, Arsène Houssaye, was much struck by the extent of his knowledge. The refurbishment of part of the Louvre and a further opening up of the Cabinet des dessins gave Champfleury the opportunity to study eighteenth-century art in particular. He preferred Jean-Baptiste Chardin and the pastel-painter Maurice Quentin de la Tour to Antoine Watteau, François Boucher, and Jean-Baptiste Greuze. He preferred truth and naturalness to the mannered, whether virtuous (Greuze) or licentious (Boucher). In 1846 Champfleury served as critic for the *Corsaire* at the annual Salon, where he dismissed everyone save Delacroix, whom he praised in a magnificent tautology: "Il peint" (He paints), that is to say, appears to be little preoccupied with values—the poetic, the picturesque, the classical, the sentimental, the historical, which Champfleury felt to be extrapictorial. He thus adumbrated one of the cardinal tenets of realism.

One of the nineteenth century's great watersheds was 1848, the year of revolutions. It was to prove a watershed for Champfleury himself. He welcomed the February revolution and with Baudelaire founded a Republican newspaper, *Le Salut Public*, which extended to two numbers, the painter Courbet providing a vignette for the front page of the second number. By June, Champfleury's views had changed to lofty and resigned conservatism, and he wrote for the *Bonhomme Richard*, founded by another son of Laon, Jean Wallon. This newspaper lasted for three numbers, being overtaken by the working-class insurrection of 22 June 1848. It is to Champfleury's credit that unlike, for example, George Sand, he did not wait until the June Days to recoil from the revolution. One consequence of the violent confrontation for Champfleury was that in the emerging school of realism, he would eschew politics in art. This did not, however, inhibit him from publishing *Les Excentriques* in Pierre Proudhon's radical *Voix du Peuple*, along with a dedication to Daumier.

In 1848, too, Champfleury ceased to write for the *Corsaire-Satan*, and this may be taken as symbolic of his rejection of *la bohème* one year later. Offered the title "roi de la Bohème," he announced that "ce mot de bohème, accepté et reçu dans la nouvelle langue, est forgé de paresse, d'ignorance et de mœurs douteuses" (this word

bohème, accepted and received into recent language, is made from sluggishness, ignorance and doubtful morals) (*Le Messager des Théâtres*, 12 April 1849). In *Souvenirs et portaits de jeunesse* (Souvenirs and Portraits from Youthful Days, 1872), Champfleury digs up and cuts off any roots his later work and the realist movement may have in *la bohème*. Indeed, he appears to congratulate himself in that the disciples of realism are free from any of the stigmata of bohemianism, through which most of them had lived.

According to Claude Pichois, "le jeune Champfleury alla vers la bohème, puis vers la bourgeoisie. Le jeune Baudelaire vers le dandysme, la dilapidation etc" (Young Champfleury turned toward Bohemia, then the middle class. Young Baudelaire toward dandyism, dissipation, etc.). One may ask whether this turn represented self-mutilation or self-fulfillment in Champfleury's case. It is noteworthy that the one artist Champfleury encountered and knew throughout the bohemian period was Chintreuil, whom he praised precisely for his tenacity, for "la volonté persistante" (tenacious willpower). Like other self-made men, such as Emile Zola, Champfleury praised willpower and routine.

In 1848 Champfleury first encountered works by Courbet, at the Salon of that year, renamed *Salon libre* (Open Exhibition), and greeted them enthusiastically. And thus *le réalisme* as a school was born, even though Champfleury had used the word the previous year in *Chien-Caillou*, and use of the term appears as early as 1837. Courbet laid hands upon the disciple Champfleury. Symbolically enough, the meeting place of the realists taken as a group, la Brasserie Andler, 32 rue Hautefeuille, was next door to Courbet's studio. The need to defend Courbet's *L'Enterrement à Ornans* (Burial at Ornans, Salon of 1850) produced some of Champfleury's best writing as a defender of realism, as did his earlier defense of *L'Après-dinée à Ornans* (Evening at Ornans, Salon of 1849).

In 1856 the quarrel surrounding realism led to the foundation of the review *Réalisme*, which lasted from 10 July 1856 to April 1857, with Edmond Duranty and Jules Assezat as adjutants, both "plus royaliste que le roi" (out-Heroding Herod). Deviations, false doctrine, and fallings-off led to Champfleury's decision in 1857 to collect and republish in volume form his principal articles concerning realism. *Le Réalisme* (1857) is a disconcerting text, all the more so in that it is much referred to in manuals of literary history and little read. It begins with a preface that is no preface and ends with a "letter" to Louis Veuillot concerning Jules-Amédée Barbey d'Aurevilly's novel *Une Vieille Maîtresse* (An Old Mistress, 1851), which provokes the reflection that 150 years later, Barbey d'Aurevilly's novels will be read, but not those of Champfleury.

Le Réalisme also paradoxically denies the sort of exclusiveness claimed by theoreticians for realism in art while developing an idiosyncratic and often muddled sort of purism of its own. Thus in his preface he assures the reader that he uses the term *réalisme* under provocation, in a "moment d'emportement, abasourdi par les cris de la critique qui s'obstinait à voir en moi un être systématique" (moment of rage, dumbfounded by the cries of critics who stubbornly kept seeing me as a systematic creature). The preface ends with an organicist metaphor—artist as apple tree, in itself highly reactionary—that makes nonsense of all attempts to regulate literary productions. Champfleury's friend the exiled poet Max Buchon used the same metaphor, which makes nonsense too of the counterclaim that realism is a form of ascesis, requiring much time of the artist to rid himself of memories, imitations, and the pressure of his own milieu.

Notwithstanding these contradictions, *Le Réalisme* does transmit an artistic credo. The artist is free in his choice of subject matter. Champfleury quotes Proudhon with approval: "Toute figure belle ou laide peut remplir le but de l'art" (Any beautiful or ugly form can fulfill the aim of art). There is, of course, a restriction: "Il faut être de son temps" (One must fit one's time). Champfleury appears to suggest that the temptation to go outside one's historical situation means charlatanism in the end. His exemplar is Robert Challes, a seventeenth-century author of tales entitled *Les Illustres françoises* (Renowned Ladies of France, 1712) who remained decidedly within his period. His choice of subjects made him the first to depict *la réalité absolue* (absolute reality), which relies upon a commonsense epistemology: "Tous ses personnages sont des petits nobles et des bourgeois du temps; ils parlent le langage de leur époque, *ils portent des noms de la fin du XVIIᵉ siècle*" (All his characters are petty aristocrats and bourgeois of the period; they speak the language of their time, *they bear seventeenth-century names* [emphasis added]). Such an attitude implies a rejection of tradition, and indeed Champfleury asserts that for all his being well-read, Challes was ignorant, in a state of grace.

"Cette précieuse ignorance" (this invaluable ignorance), in Champfleury's phrase, is what some nineteenth-century writers have to struggle toward at great cost.

The state of ignorance, native or self-willed, has as its corollary a relationship between writer and reader ideally characterized, to use a twentieth-century expression, by transparency. The teller of stories, illustrated by Challes, is perhaps a special case now complicated by the rise of the novel; nonetheless, each narrator has as his mission "d'exprimer clairement sa pensée, d'essayer de se faire comprendre des petits et des grands, et de ne pas froisser les esprits simples et d'une éducation médiocre" (to express his thought clearly, to try to be understood by great and small, and not to wound innocent minds simply educated). Transparency implies a mixed public, whose unity is not problematic, and this is the outstanding characteristic of Champfleury's thought.

It underpins the preface to *Le Réalisme*, that strange medley of quotation and expostulation. Blaise Pascal is quoted to advantage: "Les meilleurs livres sont ceux que chaque lecteur croit qu'il aurait pu faire" (The best books are those that each reader thinks he could have written); but Champfleury moves quickly to occupy the higher ground of style, where the traditionally influenced reader can be opposed to the populist one. Thus, according to his most transgressive utterance, the *Marseillaise* is to be preferred to a justly famed line from Jean Racine's *Phèdre* (1677), "La fille de Minos et de Pasiphaé" (The daughter of Minos and Pasiphaë), which later was to become the battle cry of theoreticians of *la poésie pure* (pure poetry), such as Henri Bremond, and of Anglo-Saxon aesthetes, such as Lytton Strachey. The populist approach complicates in fact what was a plea for a "styleless style," or the denial of style. Challes serves once more as an exemplar, for he will be accused of *le style gris* (gray style) and *le style plat* (flat style). Champfleury looks forward to a bonfire of critical terms, which in his view lead to self-doubt and to an overvaluation of the critical function.

Such purism ultimately condemns Courbet (this is one of the surprises of *Le Réalisme*), for his painting of the artist's studio, in which Champfleury himself appears, is called *Allégorie réelle* (Allegory from the Real). *Allégorie* is a doubtful term, suggesting at once conventional pictorial elements and conventional moral values. Champfleury much preferred *L'Enterrement à*

Ornans to *L'Atelier du peintre* (The Artist's Studio), doubtless because the former work offered no easy interpretation. Yet in preferring it, Champfleury seems to be driven toward a populist stylization of the painting. In spite of the yawning grave, there is a circumambient peacefulness, which is shared by the gravedigger: "type grandiose et philosophique que le peintre a su reproduire dans toute sa beauté d'homme du peuple" (a grandiose and philosophical type that the painter succeeded in reproducing in all his beauty as a man of the people). The underlying populism here expressed is, however, far from dictating the frontiers of realism, or of Champfleury's own taste. Such would seem to be the lesson to be derived from his praise of an allegorical painting by Daumier, entered in a competition organized in 1848 by the provisional government of the Republic with an aim to producing pictorial representation of the Republic itself. Daumier presents a hefty woman, enthroned and suckling two children, while two others are seated at her feet reading. For Champfleury there are no conventional pictorial elements here. Daumier's painting is "une toile, simple, sérieuse, modeste" (a simple, serious, modest canvas). *Domestique* is perhaps the missing term. Five heroes of style mentioned at the end of the study of Challes are Oliver Goldsmith, Franz Joseph Haydn, and the brothers Le Nain. Such a list tends to indicate that realism and idealized domesticity are not incompatible.

The final dimension of Champfleury's view of realism is erudition. *Le Réalisme* contains a letter to J. J. Ampère on French folk songs and popular music, Ampère having been appointed chairman of a commission given the task of producing a national collection of such music. What Champfleury writes about is the bowdlerization of a particular song, "La Femme du roulier," along with reflections on Hindu, Chinese, and Iowa Indian music. He had the good sense and the political sense to send his piece, which first appeared in the *Revue de Paris* (15 November 1853), to George Sand, including some further reflections on the realist battle, thus linking the two strands of thought. In her reply of 18 January 1854, Sand writes fascinatingly about music, while recommending abstention in the literary battle. Her advice did not of course dictate Champfleury's future behavior. But this exchange can stand as a symbol of a further bifurcation in Champfleury's career: after 1860 much less is said of realism and of the novel, and

Champfleury's works of scholarly research begin to appear.

Le Réalisme is marvelously contradictory: the artist is both an apple tree and highly disciplined; realism itself is "*une insurrection,*" but many of its heroes of style are the least insurrectional possible: Challes, Goldsmith, Haydn, and the brothers Le Nain. Realism is "sincerity in art," but Courbet's changes of direction are anathema. Realism as a school is doubtless critical, but critics are a tribe to be shunned. And above all, Champfleury refuses to be a leader, even if all others seem lost. In fact, the best leader is dead, and he is no less a person than Denis Diderot, who figures in *Le Réalisme* in a letter to a secretary of state protesting the failure of the Comédie Française to allow a performance of Diderot's play: Est-il bon? Est-il méchant?" (Is he good? Is he wicked?). To include Diderot is a remarkable sign of prescience; to harbor, as Champfleury perhaps did, the desire to be a Diderot is something else.

The decade in which Champfleury carried on the battle for realism as an unwilling leader was also that in which his principal novels appeared. Both realism and Champfleury's literary production belong to the first years, that is to say the authoritarian years, of the Second Empire. Baudelaire and Flaubert, whom Champfleury supported, were victims of the criminal law. Champfleury himself had to endure both the censor's red pencil and the refusal to publish. *Les Souffrances du professeur Delteil* (Professor Delteil's Sufferings, 1853), a record of school days in Laon, brought all the wrath of the local prefect down upon the head of Champfleury's brother Edouard. The 1856 edition of *Les Aventures de Mademoiselle Mariette* (The Adventures of Miss Mariette, 1853) was pulped. *La Succession Le Camus* (The Le Camus Inheritance) was first published in Belgium in 1857 and its export to France forbidden. *La Mascarade de la vie parisienne* (The Masquerade of Parisian Life, 1859) and *Les Amoureux de Sainte-Périne* (The Lovers of Sainte-Périne, 1859) greatly troubled the minister of the interior.

The earlier novels have been read as autobiographical works and romans à clef. Baudelaire provides the key to *Les Aventures de Mademoiselle Mariette*, which is a re-creation of Henri Murger's bohemian world, but seen through different eyes and proposing a different moral: the artist achieves his aim through the exercise of strict self-discipline and willpower. *Les Souffrances du*

L'Atelier du peintre (1855), by Gustave Courbet (Musée du Louvre). The artist called his painting "an allegory from the real"; Courbet (seated center) depicts the world of trivialities on the left, while on the right are such acquaintances as Champfleury (seated, middle right) and Charles Baudelaire (seated, reading).

professeur Delteil, again recognized as a roman à clef, describes what the modern reader would see as an unregulated private educational system, which throws up many of Champfleury's villains and villainesses. *Les Amoureux de Sainte-Périne* is a supposedly close observation of people living in an old folks' home, or hospice.

But the best of Champfleury's production lies in two novels: *Les Bourgeois de Molinchart* (The Molinchart Bourgeois, 1855) and *La Succession Le Camus*. The first of these suffers somewhat, for literary historians see it as a forerunner to *Madame Bovary* (1857), a view to which Flaubert himself gave some weight, since it is clear that he read Champfleury's novel very carefully as it appeared in the *Presse*, and he feared it would forestall *Madame Bovary*. Indeed, the theme of the two novels is the same—adultery in a provincial setting—and the seducer of Champfleury's bourgeois heroine is of higher social standing than she, employing quite effortlessly the platitudes of Romantic lovemaking. In addition, a burlesque speech day with a kind of symphonic mingling of voices—those of headmistress, guest speaker, local savants, musicians, and indignant parents—can be related to the "Comices agricoles" scene in *Madame Bovary*, with its many voices intended, to quote Flaubert, to "hurler d'ensemble" (howl together). But above all, Champfleury creates a char-

acter who prefigures Flaubert's Homais: M. Creton du Coche, the husband of the adulterous wife.

Champfleury anticipates the higher fatuousness of Emile Faguet (of the French Academy, as he signed himself), who saw an answer to Emma Bovary's problems in a marriage with Homais. M. Creton du Coche is, like Homais, a statistician, his aim being to create a temperature grid for the whole of France at all times and in all seasons. He wears proudly in his buttonhole a miniature thermometer given him by a charlatan, and he is ultimately the victim of the employees at the Paris Observatory. His peers include M. Bonneau, an archaeologist who measures the historical monuments of France in umbrella-lengths, a reflection perhaps of disputes over medieval lengths and measures; and also M. Vole, the president of a learned society that celebrates the works of Jean Racine. There is also an epigrammatist called Prudhommeau.

These characters—representatives of *la bêtise* (stupidity)—constitute a revenge of Champfleury, the autodidact who knows his own worth. But more important, they are mere caricatures and stereotypes, and have nothing of the menace of a Homais. They may be traced to Champfleury's bohemian journalism, and to Henri Monnier and his character Joseph

Prudhomme, who represent a considerable influence. Joseph Prudhomme exemplifies bourgeois complacency and stupidity, which are not redeemed by any degree of dynamism. This want of dynamism fatally limits the scope of Champfleury's characters. The author also seems to have been incapable of making a plan for his novels, which of course is not an overwhelming defect. As he put it in *Le Réalisme*, a novel is only "un conte développé" (a developed story), though he meant extendable. The development is episodic and proceeds always in the direction of the *saynète* (dramatic skit), of comic dialogue, of the vignette, of caricature and farce. Champfleury, alas, had no feeling for structure.

To this catalogue of defects may be added the treatment of passion in its widest sense. "Combien il est difficile de faire un livre où la passion est développée, longuement, avec réalité" (How difficult it is to write a book in which passion is developed at length, realistically), wrote Champfleury in his notebooks. As for the passion of love, *Les Bourgeois de Molinchart* shows a sort of short-windedness, equivalent to the way in which Champfleury structurally extends his narrative. The man falls in love; uses in his lovemaking the vocabulary of romanticism, which amounts to a form of emotional blackmail; and falls out of love quite unseasonably and apparently unreasonably. Male fickleness is the only clue to these actions, but one that at least provides an ending.

La Succession Le Camus is set in Laon and turns upon the testamentary decisions of the near-bedridden wife, then widow, of a successful professional cum landowner who is also a usurer and miser. The family members attendant upon her represent different facets of the middle classes, dominated in this instance by an icy housekeeper (with an illegitimate child) who, one feels in Champfleury's world, should have been a schoolteacher. The outcome is happy, in that the widow's will turns out to be totally conformist. However, the novel is striking for Champfleury's failure to seize upon the interpretative or symbolic value of what he relates.

Thus the usurer-miser Le Camus keeps in his attics a decaying collection of objects from the earliest times of French history as a kind of industrial archaeology. Undervalued, this hoard is set upon by children, who use it to dress up and to create a denigrating version of history, and in so doing not only affront but frighten a local judge. The news of this escapade spreads throughout

the town; the hoard is then wildly overvalued and acquires a legendary worth. As a derisory fable of the middle classes as history's heirs, this episode could have been savage. In Champfleury's hands it remains a mere anecdote and is diluted by whimsy, by too arch a sense of humor, and by the facile sentimentality that characterizes his work. The frequent cheap reissues of his works in the 1870s and 1880s suggest a successful strategy toward a new reading public.

Champfleury also wrote short stories, and critics, beginning with Charles-Augustin Sainte-Beuve, have valued them higher than the novels, timorously perhaps, since in them defects of composition, tone, and style are less obvious. Viewed as a group, the short stories are heterogeneous, but one might single out their psychological strain: After reading Balzac's *Les Paysans* (*The Peasants*, 1855) and then *Madame Bovary*, Champfleury apparently concluded that the *roman d'observation* (novel of middle-class manners) was dead: "*Madame Bovary* sera le dernier roman bourgeois" (*Madame Bovary* will be the last bourgeois novel). "Madame Eugenio" (1874) relates the seduction of the wife of an entrepreneurial Portuguese Jew by a friend of an art student, who himself becomes the lover of the wife of a masochistic businessman. "L'Histoire du Lieutenant Valentin" (The Story of Lieutenant Valentin, 1874) presents the insipid amorous longings of a young neurasthenic officer for the nun who is his nurse.

Prior to the appearance of *Madame Bovary*, Champfleury essayed the *roman d'observation* vein in "Madame d'Aigrizelles" (1854), in which the central problem is how to prosecute the son and demand his head for the guillotine after having been the lover of the mother. His most praised story, "Le Violon de faïence" (The Earthenware Violin, 1862), has impeccable realist credentials, since it is largely a true story, a study of the mentality of art collectors. Its fictional ending—the provincial art collector destroys his collection and sagely marries—reflects perhaps the strains within Champfleury's own personality, for he too was a collector, and at the age of forty-six he married a goddaughter of Delacroix. Other stories are responses to topical events, such as "Les Deux Amis" (The Two Friends, 1871), which relates the adventures of two elderly Alsatian musicians in Paris during the street fighting of the Commune. One of the insurgents' last stands takes place under their windows. The story ends with the two friends tranquilly playing chamber music by Haydn amid the ruins. Champfleury spent the period of the Commune in Bordeaux.

The most successful of these stories lead one back to the themes of *la bohème* and the bourgeois. This is paradoxical, since an examination of *Les Bourgeois de Molinchart* and *La Succession Le Camus* shows that recourse to the stereotypes and caricatures of bohemian writing makes of Champfleury's realist novels a sort of *temps mort* (dead period) between the dynamic, power-oriented worlds of Balzac and Zola. Champfleury never quite escapes this handicap. The whimsical story "Les Enfants du professeur Turck" (Professor Turck's Children, 1862) tells of a middle-class professor of anthropology who is so overwhelmed by new proof of the spontaneous generation of life that he forgets about the begetting of his own children. Professor Turck and the meteorological M. Creton du Coche from *Les Bourgeois de Molinchart*, with their ambition of universal knowledge, go in the direction of Flaubert's *Bouvard et Pécuchet* (1881), but do not really go very far.

More effective, original, and inspired are two tales of middle-class expropriation of life and art. The first is *La Sonnette de M. Berloquin* (Mr. Berloquin's Doorbell, 1874), which to English-speaking readers may appear as a pessimistic Gallic gloss on Charles Dickens's *A Christmas Carol* (1843), for both take as their theme the expansiveness of Christmas and the narrowness of employees' rights. M. Berloquin's doorbell is efficiently sabotaged each Christmas after midnight Mass, an obvious violation of property rights. The saboteur turns out to be none other than the trusted servant Véronique, who has been frustrated in her hopes of marrying her master. Her employer considers her more or less a millstone about his neck, but her tyranny over him is possible only because of her master's flight from human society, as is the case with Dickens's Scrooge. She is both called into being by her master's limited sympathies and a victim of them. This short story is quite remarkable as a bourgeois nightmare, without any reconciling features à la Dickens. The bourgeois desire for independence and sovereignty is denied by the creature it has summoned up.

Equally impressive is *Les Bras de la Vénus de Milo* (The Arms of Venus de Milo, 1874), which is Champfleury's one authentic *conte fantastique* (fantastic story), and a reminder that he experienced the attraction of E. T. A. Hoffmann. The story, which has strong anti-German overtones,

Caricature of Champfleury by Nadar

tells of a German professor who has a perfect intuition of the shape and attitude of the missing arms of the Venus de Milo and dreams of the reconstruction of the incomplete statue. He appears, Hoffmannesque, the victim of the statue, which totally dominates him and apparently invades his physical being, for he constantly poses as the statue. In reality, the opposite is taking place: each pose represents a further expropriation of the statue, its further reduction to the dimensions of an arrogant scholar's mind. The situation is saved by a sort of quintessential *rapin* (painter's apprentice), who casts the German in plaster and keeps him prisoner for a time to allow him to repent. The story can be read as belated revenge of *la bohème* against official art and criticism, as the professor has been well received by all the academies of France. Although in 1848 Champfleury had attacked official art in the *Pamphlet*, by 1873 he had established himself as a scholar.

After 1860 Champfleury devoted himself more and more to works of scholarship. Various reasons have been adduced for this. Albert

Thibaudet indulgently expressed the view that, having for literary purposes extracted the last drop of juice from his provincial boyhood, adolescence, and early manhood, Champfleury had to turn elsewhere his acquired habits of investigation—to French earthenware, cats, and the history of caricature—signifying a want of inspiration and talent. Champfleury believed he had been discouraged by the imperial censorship; in both 1858 and 1859 the publication of two of his novels in serial form had been curtailed.

He viewed his scholarly works as a sort of masked commitment, or obligation. And thus they have been taken, but narrowly labeled as concerned with the "minor arts," under the general rubric "art for the people." Such a view is at best a half-truth. Champfleury wrote a pioneering study of the Le Nain brothers (1850), and he published the documentation upon which it was based, along with details of the reception of their work. His idea of a history of caricature in the ancient world (*Histoire de la caricature antique* [History of Ancient Caricature, 1865]) represents a creative leap of the imagination. Its continuation, *Histoire de la caricature moderne* (History of Modern Caricature, 1865), a trifle too committed perhaps, gives pride of place to Monnier, Charles-Joseph Traviès de Villers, and especially Daumier.

Champfleury also had some idea of a history of popular imagination. He collected folk songs and studied too all the ramifications of popular symbolism in the printing trade and in other arts. In this line he produced *Histoire des faïences patriotiques sous la Révolution* (History of Patriotic Earthenware During the Revolution, 1867). In 1872 he became principal keeper of the collections of the national porcelain factory at Sèvres, of which he was later to head the administration. He did not fare as well in his personal life. His daughter's clothing was set on fire by his son, and the girl died. Two years later Champfleury was a widower. On his death his various private collections were sold to provide for the maintenance of his son in a mental asylum.

At the end of the century, Michel Tourneux, author of the favorable entry on Champfleury in *La Grande Encyclopédie*, was already a little hesitant concerning the survival of Champfleury's literary reputation. In 1864 Flaubert announced that Champfleury was *enfoncé* (a has-been), flattering Edmond and Jules Goncourt, whose *Germinie Lacerteux* (1864) had just appeared. Edmond was happy to record in his *Jour-* *nal* (3 February 1891) that were it not for his artistic collections, Champfleury would be dead as a dodo. Indeed, for all his friendship with Baudelaire, Champfleury had little feeling for the modern and can easily be classified as a fossil, yet the modern reprint industry has begun to save him. The struggle for critical approval will be difficult. Inevitably studies are of the sort "Champfleury and . . . ," with Baudelaire, Courbet, Daumier, or Monnier in the title, for he was often overshadowed. A revaluation of his earlier career and *la bohème* has begun with an anthology of his writings on art. Nevertheless, it is somewhat predictably titled *Champfleury, son regard et celui de Baudelaire* (Champfleury: His Views and Baudelaire's, 1990).

Letters:
"Lettres à Max Buchon," *Revue Mondiale*, 1 December 1919, pp. 531-545;
"Champfleury, Duranty et Camille Lemonnier," *Revue d'Histoire Littéraire de la France*, 58 (June-September 1958): 365-391;
"Six Letters from Champfleury to Zola," *Romanic Review*, 55 (1964): 274-277;
Lettres à Charles Baudelaire (Neuchâtel, 1973);
Correspondance avec Madame Hanska (1851-1855), edited by Lorin Uffenbeck and E. Fudakowska (Geneva: Slatkine, 1989).

Bibliography:
Maurice Clouard, *L'Œuvre de Champfleury dressée d'après ses propres notes* (Paris: Sapin, 1891).

References:
Luce Abélès and Geneviève Lacambre, eds., *Champfleury, l'art pour le peuple* (Paris: Dossiers du Musée d'Orsay, 1990);
Joseph-Marc Bailbé, "Champfleury et la musique de chambre," in *Motifs et figures* (Rouen: Publications de l'Université de Rouen, 1974), pp. 65-83;
Bailbé, "Stendhal et Champfleury: du réalisme à l'intimité," *Revue d'Histoire Littéraire de la France* (March-April 1984): 231-244;
Charles Baudelaire, "Les Contes de Champfleury," in *Œuvres complètes*, volume 2 (Paris: Gallimard, Bibliothèque de la Pléiade, 1975), pp. 21-23;
Emile Bouvier, *La Bataille réaliste* (Paris: René Debresse, 1927);
David A. Flanary, *Champfleury: The Realist Writer as Art Critic* (Ann Arbor: UMI Research Press, 1980);

F. J. W. Hemmings, "Champfleury and Duranty," in *The Age of Realism* (Harmondsworth, U.K.: Penguin, 1975), pp. 162-166;

Marie-Eve Payen-Faucher, ed., *Champfleury à Sèvres* (Paris: Bibliothèque Denis Diderot de Sèvres, 1989);

Pier-Luigi Pinelli, "Une Emma Bovary à Laon: Louise Creton du Coche," *Letteratura*, 10 (1987): 63-100;

Albert Thibaudet, *Histoire de la littérature française de 1789 à nos jours* (Paris: Stock, 1936), pp. 362-369;

Jules Troubat, *Souvenirs sur Champfleury et le réalisme* (Paris: Librairie de la Province, 1905);

Michael Weatherilt, "Les Cahiers inédits de Champfleury: quelques considérations sur l'époque réaliste et naturaliste," *Cahiers Naturalistes*, 55 (1981): 117-128;

Weatherilt, "Les Romans et contes de Champfleury," Ph.D. dissertation, University of Liverpool, 1977.

Papers:
Champfleury's notebooks for the years 1853 to 1880 are at the Butler Library, Columbia University, New York.

François-René de Chateaubriand
(4 September 1768 - 4 July 1848)

John R. Williams
University of New Orleans

SELECTED BOOKS: *Essai historique, politique et moral sur les révolutions anciennes et modernes, considérées dans leurs rapports avec la Révolution française* (London: J. Deboffe, 1797); translated anonymously as *An Historical, Political, and Moral Essay on Revolutions, Ancient and Modern* (London: H. Colburn, 1815);

Atala, ou les amours de deux sauvages dans le désert (Paris: Migneret, 1801; revised edition, Paris: Le Normant, 1805)—revised edition contains *René ou les effets de la passion*; translated by Caleb Bingham as *Atala, or The Love and Constancy of Two Savages in the Desert* (Boston: Caleb Bingham, 1802);

Génie du christianisme, ou beautés de la religion chrétienne, 5 volumes (Paris: Migneret, 1802; revised edition, Paris: Le Normant, 1816); translated by Charles I. White as *The Genius of Christianity, or The Spirit and Beauty of the Christian Religion* (Boston, 1802);

René ou les effets de la passion (Paris: Le Normant, 1805)—contains *Atala, ou les amours de deux sauvages dans le désert*; translated anonymously as *René* (London: T. Hamilton, 1813);

Les Martyrs, ou le triomphe de la religion chrétienne, 2 volumes (Paris: Le Normant, 1809); translated anonymously as *The Martyrs, or The Triumph of the Christian Religion* (New York: Whiting & Watson, 1812);

Itinéraire de Paris à Jérusalem et de Jérusalem à Paris, 3 volumes (Paris: Le Normant, 1811); translated by Frederic Shoberl as *Travels in Greece, Palestine, Egypt and Barbary . . .* (London: H. Colburn, 1811; New York: Van Winkle & Wiley, 1814);

De Buonaparte, des Bourbons, et de la nécessité de se rallier à nos princes légitimes pour le bonheur de la France et celui de l'Europe (Paris: Mame frères, 1814);

De la monarchie selon la charte (Paris: Le Normant, 1816);

Les Aventures du dernier Abencérage, in *Œuvres complètes*, volume 16 (Paris: Ladvocat, 1826); translated by Isabel Hill as *The Last of the Abencerages* in Washington Irving, *Tales of the Alhambra* (London: R. Bentley, 1850);

Les Natchez, in *Œuvres complètes*, volumes 19-20 (Paris: Ladvocat, 1826); translated anonymously as *The Natchez: An Indian Tale* (Lon-

François-René de Chateaubriand, circa 1787 (portrait attributed to Charles-Joseph de La Celle de Châteaubourg; Musée de Saint-Malo)

don: H. Colburn, 1827); revised French edition (Paris: Lefèvre & Ladvocat, 1829);

Voyages en Amérique et en Italie, in *Œuvres complètes*, volumes 6-7 (Paris: Ladvocat, 1827); translated anonymously as *Travels in America and Italy* (London: Henry Colburn, 1828); revised French edition (Paris: Lefèvre, 1829);

Moïse, in *Œuvres complètes*, volume 22 (Paris: Ladvocat, 1831);

Etudes ou discours historiques, in *Œuvres complètes*, volumes 4-5 (Paris: Ladvocat, 1831); revised as *Etudes ou discours historiques sur la chute de l'empire romain, la naissance et les progrès du christianisme et l'invasion des barbares*, 4 volumes (Paris: Lefèvre, 1831);

Essai sur la littérature anglaise et Considérations sur le génie des hommes, des temps et des révolutions, 2 volumes (Paris: Charles Gosselin et Furne, 1836); translated anonymously as *Sketches of English Literature, with Considerations on the Spirit of the Times, Men and Revolutions* (London: Henry Colburn, 1836);

Vie de Rancé (Paris: H.-L. Delloye, 1844; revised and enlarged, 1844);

Mémoires d'outre-tombe, 12 volumes (Paris: Eugène et Victor Penaud frères, 1849-1850); translated by Alexander Teixeira de Mattos as *The Memoirs* (London: Freemantle, 1902).

Editions and Collections: *Œuvres complètes*, 28 volumes (Paris: Ladvocat, 1826-1831);

Œuvres complètes, 36 volumes (Paris: Pourrat frères, 1836-1839);

Mémoires d'outre-tombe, 4 volumes (Paris: Flammarion, 1948);

Œuvres romanesques et voyages, 2 volumes, edited by Maurice Regard (Paris: Gallimard, Bibliothèque de la Pléiade, 1969).

François-René de Chateaubriand was the outstanding French literary figure of the early nineteenth century. He can only loosely be attached to the history of the novel, but he did produce two famous romances, *Atala, ou les amours de deux sauvages dans le desert* (1801; translated as *Atala, or The Love and Constancy of Two Savages in the Desert*, 1802) and *René ou les effets de la passion* (1805; translated as *René*, 1813). Often called novels, they are in reality short tales or novellas. A third, less well known romance, *Les Aventures du dernier Abencérage* (1826; translated as *The Last of the Abencerages*, 1850), may also be termed a novel, as may *Les Natchez* (1826; translated as *The Natchez: An Indian Tale*, 1827), which is part historical prose epic and part novel.

Whether Chateaubriand possessed something of the transcendent ability that one associates with genius is a matter for debate, but he was a born writer. During his life he was a towering presence over the literary scene in France, and his prose style has exercised a profound and lasting influence on French literature. His oeuvre—which includes poetry, fiction, literary theory, journalism, biography, history, prose epics, Christian apologetics, travel sketches, political pamphlets, and autobiography—reflects an existence that was bound up with the most turbulent period of France's history. He knew the Old Regime, the Revolution, the Empire, and the Restoration. A disciple of Jean-Jacques Rousseau, Chateaubriand was nevertheless imbued with a certain amount of eighteenth-century skepticism, and he carried the spirit of the old order into an age of transition.

All the characteristics associated with French romanticism can be found in him: his projection of himself into his works, his religious sentimentality, his contribution to the medieval vogue, and his exotic feeling for nature. Much of his work has not lasted. The uninitiated reader is likely to find him too sentimental, too self-indulgent, or too anchored in archaic values.

Yet he is held in high esteem. Despite his shortcomings, he had a perfectly tuned ear for the evocative possibilities of the French language. Readers were swept away by his rhythmic, flowing prose, which had the power to dissolve visual impressions into sumptuous, musical sound. He spoke directly to the emotions, and, by his shrewd ability to sense what the public wanted, he was able to emerge as the one writer who more than any other imposed his way of thinking and feeling on a whole generation. He made possible the final break with the eighteenth century and is revered today as one of the great precursors of French romanticism, as well as some of the linguistic experiments of the symbolists.

Chateaubriand's influence upon French literature cannot be overestimated. During the nineteenth century he was held as a model of French prose writing. The effect of his lyrical style made the young Victor Hugo cry, "Je veux être Chateaubriand ou rien!" (I want to be Chateaubriand or nothing!). Later, a dismayed Emile Zola reported that Gustave Flaubert, the author of *Madame Bovary* (1857), once told him that it was so much "dung," that he would willingly trade it for a single sentence by Chateaubriand. And Remy de Gourmont, a renowned symbolist critic of the late nineteenth century, stated unequivocally that "Chateaubriand plane invisible sur toute notre littérature" (Chateaubriand hovers invisible over all our literature).

By all accounts Chateaubriand could be given to histrionics, insufferable vanity, and ridiculous posturing. He saw the world reflected in and through himself, and, indirectly, became the subject of all his works. When he set about to write his memoirs (*Mémoires d'outre-tombe* [1849-1850; translated as *The Memoirs*, 1902]), he described his life in theatrical terms, likening it to a drama in three acts: the Traveler and Soldier (until 1800), the Man of Letters (1800-1814), and the Man of Action (1814-1833). There was a fourth period until his death in 1848, years of retirement, which he appears to have viewed as unworthy of dramatization, but during which time he did some of his finest writing.

Chateaubriand was born on 4 September 1768 in the Breton town of Saint-Malo, the tenth child of a noble but not wealthy family. He had only intermittent formal education: four years at the nearby Collège de Dol (1777-1781), where he acquired a sound classical background; a little more than a year with the Jesuits at Rennes (October 1781 - December 1782), where his father had decided he should study for his naval certificate (he never got it); and slightly more than a year at the Collège de Dinan (1784-1785), where he prepared for the priesthood. All his teachers judged him a remarkably gifted student. He possessed a quick intelligence, a phenomenal memory, and a concise mind. Yet he had difficulty discovering a mission in life or choosing a profession. His cantankerous father, René Auguste, appeared willing enough to help him but at heart attached little importance to this younger son.

The boy's interest in studying for the priesthood proved short-lived. He frequently interrupted his courses at Dinan to vacation at the family château in Combourg, and these sojourns led to permanent residence there. Inaction brought on mental instability, as he recalled in *Mémoires*: "Ingénieux à me forger des souffrances, je m'étais placé entre deux désespoirs; quelquefois je ne me croyais qu'un être nul, incapable de s'élever au-dessus du vulgaire; quelquefois il me semblait sentir en moi des qualités qui ne seraient jamais appréciées. Un secret instinct m'avertissait qu'en avançant dans le monde, je ne trouverais rien de ce que je cherchais" (Adept in the art of suffering, I found myself torn between two extremes; sometimes I seemed of no worth to myself, a being incapable of rising above the ordinary; at other times I sensed that I had qualities that no one could ever appreciate. My instincts told me that, as I went through life, I would never find what I was looking for). The bitterness became so intense that one day he attempted to shoot himself, but the gun misfired.

His father decided that it was time to put an end to a way of life that appeared to be going nowhere. When Chateaubriand was almost eighteen, Réne Auguste determined his career for him: he would join the French army. A commission as second lieutenant in the Navarre regiment was obtained for him by his older brother, and he was stationed at Cambrai in 1786. He got his first look at Paris in 1787, was eventually presented at court, and—most important of all—made many literary friends, notably Louis de Fontanes, a statesman and man of letters who greatly encouraged the young man. The decadence of the court did not appeal to him, and he found his faith foundering under the influence of the freethinkers he met in Paris. The atmosphere of Combourg had prepared him to be a disciple of Rousseau, and he dreamed of a new world based on the Rousseauist concept of nature's laws.

The Revolution was just about to erupt, and when it did, most of Chateaubriand's fellow officers joined counterrevolutionary forces, either at home or abroad. For Chateaubriand, it was a lost cause. He quit the army and decided to satisfy a longing for travel and adventure. In 1791 he set sail for America to see the forests and the free, natural savages about whom he had read. For almost five months—from July to December—he wandered and explored North America. By his own highly imaginative, uncorroborated account, he interviewed George Washington in Philadelphia, visited Boston, saw Niagara Falls, crossed Pennsylvania to Pittsburgh, sailed down the Ohio and Mississippi rivers to Natchez, Mississippi, and made a side trip to Florida. What is known is that he disembarked in Baltimore, journeyed to Philadelphia, probably made the trip to Niagara and back, and may have penetrated as far west as Ohio. It makes little difference what he actually saw; the important thing is that exile widened his horizon. He used his powers of observation to introduce into French literature color and imagery that no writer before him had captured.

The news of the flight and arrest of Louis XVI brought him quickly back to France to fight on the royalist side. Desperately in need of money (the Revolution had impoverished his family), he married Céleste Buisson de la Vigne—a girl of recent nobility with a reputation for wealth. It was a loveless marriage on his part; worse, her fortune turned out to be less than expected. Céleste was intelligent and witty, but she could also be stubborn, jealous, and disparaging. Over the years they were frequently apart, and Chateaubriand took on a succession of mistresses. Céleste apparently loved her husband and simply resigned herself to enduring his many infidelities.

After four months of marriage, Chateaubriand joined the army of the émigrés in 1792, was wounded during the siege of Thionville, and fled alone to England in 1793. He lived in London for seven years (except for a short stay at Bungay in Suffolk), much of the time in abject poverty. He managed to support his miserable existence by tutoring and translating; at the same time he succeeded in composing a theoretical, anti-Catholic work on revolutions, *Essai sur les*

Juliette Récamier, whose salon influenced much of Chateaubriand's writing (portrait, circa 1799, by Eulalie Morin; Musée de Versailles)

révolutions (1797; translated as *An Historical, Political, and Moral Essay on Revolutions, Ancient and Modern*, 1815).

The project was ambitious, but he hoped that it might bring him out of poverty and obscurity. In it he suggests parallels between the revolutions in Greece and Rome and the French Revolution. It was an attempt not only to use the past to explain the present, but also to forecast the political future of France. Rereading the work some thirty years later, he admitted to having created something of a hodgepodge and was severe on the bombastic style he had employed. But two characteristics of his effort are noteworthy: first, his love of tackling vast subjects, reading widely in known and unknown authors, and embroidering his knowledge with ideas from his experience; second, his impartiality and sense of relative values, especially in a period of political chaos and violent partisanship where he found himself one of revolution's victims.

During this time Chateaubriand also worked on the first versions of a prose epic, *Les Natchez*, which had probably begun to take shape in his mind during his visit to America. Not published until 1826 (by which time such things were out of fashion), it contains an epic section in deliberate imitation of the traditional form and a section that might more properly be called a novel. The epic part (twelve books), from which *Atala* was drawn, is a sophisticated example of aspects of the genre: epic similes and epithets, actions of supernatural agents, and large-scale setting. To this part is joined the amusing voyage of Chactas to France, where natural man judges civilization. The second part, from which *René* was drawn, is without divisions and written in a much simpler style. It tells of the hero's adventures in America, his death and that of Chactas, and the fate of the Natchez. The work was conceived to depict the conflict between nature and civilization, before Chateaubriand's return to Christianity. *Atala* and *René* were extracted and reworked to fit into the *Génie du christianisme* (1802; translated as *The Genius of Christianity*, 1802) and established the author's reputation.

The year after the publication of *Essai sur les révolutions*, Chateaubriand learned of the deaths of one of his sisters and of his mother, Apolline. If one can believe his account in *Génie du christianisme*, the emotional stress caused him suddenly to rediscover his faith and return to Christianity: "Ces deux voix sorties du tombeau . . . m'ont frappé. Je suis devenu chrétien. Je n'ai pas cédé, j'en conviens, à de grandes lumières surnaturelles; ma conviction est sortie du cœur: j'ai pleuré et j'ai cru" (These two voices coming from the tomb . . . struck me. I became a Christian. I was not overcome, I confess, by any great supernatural revelation; my conversion came from the heart: I wept and I believed). The exact nature and sincerity of this conversion have been much debated. There had always been something of a struggle between faith and doubt in Chateaubriand's mind, and the deaths in all likelihood predisposed him once again to believe. On the other hand, there is little doubt that the Christian tradition of the French was a powerful counterrevolutionary force, even among skeptics, and that Christianity was slowly making a return around 1800. Whether out of deep religious conviction or other circumstances, Chateaubriand was inspired by a great subject suited to his talents, and he seized the opportunity to become the poet of the new trend. His *Génie du christianisme* is a defense of Catholicism, chiefly on aesthetic and emotional grounds.

But France's fortunes—and Chateaubriand's—were suddenly to change. On 9 November 1799 the Directory fell. Gen. Napoleon Bonaparte was made first consul of France. It was not a restoration, but émigrés began flowing back. Chateaubriand's old friend Fontanes became an important figure and called upon him to return. Chateaubriand interrupted publication of an edition of *Génie du christianisme* in London and was back in Paris by May 1800. He immediately set to readying for publication the manuscripts he had brought back in his luggage.

There were indications that the time was right for a return to organized religion. Bonaparte sought order and knew that France was still Christian and Catholic at heart. Religion would provide a moral and disciplinary foundation needed in the state. Chateaubriand, eager for fame, began exploring the possibilities of publishing *Génie du christianisme*. Unfortunately, in 1801 philosophers were strong on the counterattack against religion, and many ex-revolutionaries, such as Joseph Fouché, then minister of police, were opposed to any restoration. Publication of the work might mean professional suicide. In a letter to the *Journal des Débats*, Chateaubriand shrewdly gave advance publicity: "Citoyen, dans mon ouvrage sur le *Génie du Christianisme* . . . il se trouve une section entière consacrée à la *poétique du Christianisme*. . . . Cette partie est terminée par une anecdote extraite de mes voyages en Amérique, et écrite sous les huttes mêmes des Sauvages. Elle est intitulée: *Atala*" (Citizen, in my work on the *Genius of Christianity* . . . an entire section is devoted exclusively to the poetics of Christianity. . . . This section is terminated by a story taken from my travels in America, and written beneath the very huts of the savages. It is entitled *Atala*). The story was intended to illustrate the power of Christianity to subdue the wildest passions of man. Chateaubriand's friends advised him to extract the tale and publish it separately to test public reaction. The short novel had emotional appeal and was politically neutral; it might also make readers yearn for more. On 2 April 1801 *Atala* was published, making its author famous overnight. The work was read, discussed, and reprinted twelve times between 1801 and 1805 (the date of the definitive edition).

Atala is the extravagant, tragic tale of two lovers set in the American wilderness and told by an old Natchez Indian, Chactas, to a fascinated young Frenchman, René, around the year 1725. As a young Indian brave, Chactas had fallen in love with an Indian maiden, Atala, who as a Chris-

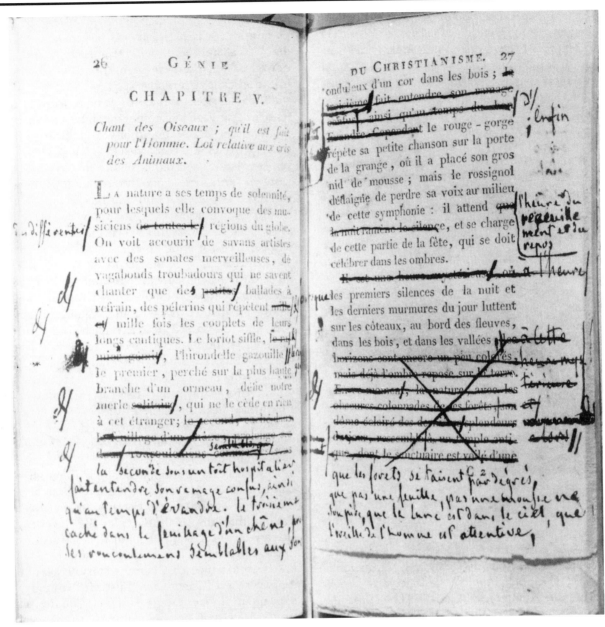

Copy of the fourth edition (1804) of Génie du christianisme, *volume 2, with revisions by Chateaubriand*
(Bibliothèque Victor Cousin-Sorbonne, Paris)

tian had taken a vow of chastity by her mother's deathbed. Later, when she finds herself consumed with love for Chactas, she obeys what she believes to be a higher law and takes poison. The tale is filled with obstacles and melodramatic rescues: the lovers' tribes are in conflict, and Chactas is taken prisoner by her tribe; she helps him escape, and together they roam through pathless forests surrounded by luxuriant nature. Images of productive life among converted savages abound; the lovers lose their way amid a storm of lightning and rain and are sheltered in a cave

by a pious missionary, Father Aubry, whose Christianity is perhaps closer to a natural religion than it is to orthodoxy.

Atala finally tells Father Aubry of her vow and of her temptation. His advice that she could be released from her vow comes too late; she has already taken poison to end her torment, and he spends her last hours consoling her. His words shocked some readers: he emphasizes that the world is a wicked place, that one's life is worth little, even to one's friends, and that she should give thanks to God for sparing her a long and painful earthly existence. (Victor Giraud, in *Maîtres d'autrefois et d'aujourd'hui* [Masters of Yesterday and Today, 1912], suggested that *Atala* is the precursor of a long line of anticlerical novels.) Atala nevertheless dies reconciled and at peace. A distraught Chactas carries her in his arms to a grave prepared by the missionary. The wind blows her hair in his face, and together Chactas and the missionary leave her to rest in the wilderness.

The novel is highly structured. A prologue and an epilogue frame the first-person account itself. The story consists of four episodes: "Les chasseurs" (the hunters), "Les laboureurs" (the laborers), "Le drame" (the tragic event), and "Les funérailles" (the funeral). The narrative unfolds and progresses toward the fatal denouement like a classical tragedy.

The prologue opens with a celebrated description of the *Meschacebé* (Mississippi), in which Chateaubriand uses form, color, and sound to create a tone poem of nature: "Les deux rives du Meschacebé présentent le tableau le plus extraordinaire. Sur le bord occidental, des savanes se déroulent à perte de vue; leurs flots de verdure, en s'éloignant, semblent monter dans l'azur du ciel où ils s'évanouissent. On voit dans ces prairies sans bornes errer à l'aventure des troupeaux de trois ou quatre mille buffles sauvages.... Telle est la scène sur le bord occidental; mais elle change sur le bord opposé, et forme avec la première un admirable contraste. Suspendus sur le cours des eaux, groupés sur les rochers et sur les montagnes, dispersés dans les vallées, des arbres de toutes les formes, de toutes les couleurs, de tous les parfums, se mêlent, croissent ensemble, montent dans les airs à des hauteurs qui fatiguent les regards" (The banks of the Mississippi present the most extraordinary picture. On the western shore, savannahs stretch out as far as the eye can see; their surging waves of greenery, receding in the distance, seem to rise into the blue of the sky where they disappear. Herds of three or four thousand buffalo wander about aimlessly on the endless plains.... Such is the scene on the western shore; but it changes on the opposite side, and forms with the first an admirable contrast. Suspended over the flowing water, grouped together on rocks and mountains and in the valleys, trees of every shape, every color, and every odor intermingle and grow to heights in the sky that tire the eye).

Hostile critics have been quick to deny the accuracy of the details, but that misses the point. Dennis J. Spininger has pointed out that the landscape details are shaped by a governing principle: the setting is intended as an approximate paradise. Chateaubriand calls the New World "le nouvel Eden" (the new Eden), but the features of his landscape ironically suggest dualities in a state of tension. While the whole forms "une tendre et sauvage harmonie" (a tender and harmonious wilderness), the author's river has two contrasting banks: the western side is a lush subtropical grassland where all is silence and repose; the eastern side is a rugged, mountainous terrain where all is muted sound and movement. There is no real synthesis, and the ambivalence creates a symbolic locale against which the reader is subtly prepared for another Fall.

In the epilogue the author imagines that he meets near Niagara an Indian woman, the granddaughter of René. Along with her husband she is nearly all that remains of the Natchez Indians, who were massacred by the French in an Indian uprising. René also perished. The author learns too that Father Aubry was brutally murdered by the Cherokee Indians and that Chactas returned to his tribe to be near Atala's grave, located on what had been a lush plain but was now a swamp, where he grew old and died—but not before being baptized (in *Les Natchez* he dies without being baptized).

While Chateaubriand attempts to emphasize that in all these deaths there is the religious reconciliation of opposites and the attainment of celestial paradise, the final images of the novel translate a pessimistic state of mind that has its origin in the Christian notion of original sin. René, who has been listening to Chactas's story, cries out in despair when Chactas has finished: "Homme, tu n'es qu'un songe rapide, un rêve douloureux; tu n'existes que par le malheur; tu n'es quelque chose que par la tristesse de ton âme et l'éternelle mélancolie de ta pensée!" (Man, you are but a fleeting image, a sorrowful dream; you exist only through misery; your essence is in the sadness of your soul and the eternal melancholy of your thought!). Despondent, he yields to self-pity: "Indiens infortunés que j'ai vus errer dans les déserts du Nouveau-Monde avec les cendres de vos aïeux, vous qui m'aviez donné l'hospitalité malgré votre misère, je ne pourrais vous la rendre aujourd'hui, car j'erre, ainsi que vous, à la merci des hommes; et moins heureux dans mon exil, je n'ai point emporté les os de mes pères" (Unfortunate Indians whom I have seen wandering in the wildernesses of the New World with the ashes of your ancestors, you who gave me hospitality in spite of your misery, today I am not able to return it, for I wander, like you, at the mercy of men; and less fortunate than you in my exile, I have not brought the remains of my ancestors with me).

Thematically, *Atala* can be linked to the eighteenth-century idea of the noble savage. However, the happy innocence of the Indians is not compatible with the Christian concept of the duality of man and the tragic consequences it engenders. If religion has the power to console Atala, and perhaps even Chactas in the end, a blind and mistaken enthusiasm for it is responsible for Atala's suicide (a sin in the eyes of the Church) and Chactas's misery. The judgment of the reader is left in the balance.

With *Atala* a popular success, Chateaubriand felt confident that the public was ready to applaud his *Génie du christianisme*, and he launched the larger work opportunely on 14 April 1802—four days before official ratification of a concordat by which Bonaparte reached agreement with the papacy and reestablished Roman Catholicism as the religion of the majority of Frenchmen. The work not only won widespread approval for its author, but also earned him the goodwill of Napoleon, who subsequently assigned him to various diplomatic posts.

When one is considering *Génie du christianisme*, its subtitle should not be forgotten: *beautés de la religion chrétienne* (Beauty of the Christian Religion). The essential aim of the author was to extol Christianity as a great force capable of developing the soul of man and of inspiring an art, a poetry, and an architecture that are superior to pagan art; and to show how its doctrine and ceremony ennoble and beautify life. To his consideration of the poetry of Christianity, Chateaubriand added a section on dogma and doctrine, generally thought to be the weakest part of the work. Chateaubriand was neither a theologian nor a systematic thinker. He was rather a painter of inner passions and external nature. The truth of religion for him was to be found in the beauty of the Catholic ritual, in the great works of art inspired by Christianity, and in the harmonies he discovered in nature. The book did not appeal to cold reason but rather was designed to make Christianity attractive by making it morally and politically desirable. Chateaubriand struck the right chord: public taste was gratified. Today the work seems little more than a diffuse marshaling of arguments in favor of sen-

timental apologetics—poetically strong and philosophically shallow.

Much of the success of *Génie du christianisme* rested on a brief tale interpolated into it, *René*, an intriguing study of high-strung adolescent angst. If *Atala* had been intended to illustrate the power of Christianity to subdue the wildest passions of man, *René* served to illustrate a chapter on a new state of spiritual frustration that would shortly be called the *mal du siècle* (sickness of the century). Johann Wolfgang von Goethe's *Die Leiden des jungen Werthers* (1774; translated as *The Sorrows of Young Werther*, 1902) had already revealed the malady to a certain class of readers in Europe, and Etienne Sénancour's *Obermann* (1804) also described it, but *René* was the first authentic portrait of this mood of moral isolation to reach a wide audience in France. The heroes and heroines are morbidly introspective; they long for a vague but infinite ideal; they are afflicted with despair and melancholy; they are defeated by life before they experience it.

The attitude probably originated in the pervasive malaise that afflicted an entire generation shaken to its very depths by the cataclysmic years just past: ideals and the value of universals had been questioned; models for government and religion had proven impermanent. It became the fashion for young people to react with contempt and an inability to meet the demands of life. Being depressed made the right statement. Chateaubriand adapted *René* to his purposes in *Génie du christianisme* in order to show the evils of this condition, and to suggest that the remedy lay in accepting responsibility toward one's fellowmen by engaging in useful, social action.

Like *Atala*, *René* is also the fruit of Chateaubriand's American travels and was originally intended to be a part of the prose epic *Les Natchez*. It is in the form of a monologue spoken by a Frenchman of that name who has fled Europe to take refuge in the solitude of the New World. Listening to his melancholy tale are the aged Indian Chactas (his adoptive father) and the French missionary Father Souël. Clearly patterned on certain aspects of the author himself, René is a gifted, intensely emotional young man who feels alienated. Seated under a sassafras tree, he tells his listeners the story of his boyhood and his wanderings from land to land in search of mental peace.

A terrible "secret" weighs upon his mind. He is conscious of his superiority but is prey to a self-indulgent brooding that is both despairing

Il y a bien longtems que je vous cherche.

Pag. 104.

Engraving from the 1805 edition of Atala

who still does not satisfy his yearning, and finally perishes in an Indian uprising against the French.

The plot is almost as implausible as that of *Atala*, but that is not what matters. The real subject of the book is the self-absorption, the guilt, the anxiety, and the unsatisfied longing of a hero who never comes to terms with his state of mind. Chateaubriand is especially good as a novelist who invests the symbols of René's life with a sense of loss and impending doom. René's confession is framed by a setting of majestic proportions where color, light, and shadow are used to describe states of mind. "Vers l'Orient, au fond de la perspective, le soleil commençait à paraître entre les sommets brisés des Apalaches, qui se dessinaient comme des caractères d'azur, dans les hauteurs dorées du ciel; à l'occident, le Meschacebé roulait ses ondes dans un silence magnifique, et formait la bordure du tableau avec une inconcevable grandeur" (Toward the east, in the background, the sun was beginning to appear behind the rugged peaks of the Appalachians, which stood out like azure objects in the golden hues of the sky; in the west, the Mississippi rolled its waves in majestic silence, framing the scene with a border of indescribable grandeur).

Blue and gold dominate the landscape— blue with its traditional connotations of religious feeling and innocence, and gold with its suggestion of divine intelligence and illumination of all that is superior. These colors contrast throughout the work with the dark hues of shadowy tombs bathed in pale moonlight, implying neutralization, depression, and inertia. Red and black capture René's violent moods. In an early scene, before leaving for America, he finds himself seated at the edge of Mount Etna. In front of him is the sea disappearing into the horizon; on his other side is the burning interior of the volcano with its billowing black smoke. He observes: "Un jeune homme plein de passions, assis sur la bouche d'un volcan, et pleurant sur les mortels dont à peine il voyait à ses pieds les demeures, n'est sans doute, ô vieillards, qu'un objet digne de votre pitié; mais, quoi que vous puissiez penser de René, ce tableau vous offre l'image de son caractère et de son existence: c'est ainsi que toute ma vie j'ai eu devant les yeux une création à la fois immense et imperceptible, et un abîme ouvert à mes côtés" (A young man full of passions, seated on the mouth of a volcano, and weeping over mortals whose dwellings he could barely

and violent. This unhappiness began early: his mother died giving birth to him, and his father favored his older brother. He found happiness only in the company of his sister Amélie, whose temperament was similar to his own. An unsatisfied yearning drives him from home, and to his sorrow his beloved sister seems happy to see him go. He travels but finds no solace in any of the monuments humanity has erected to itself, past or present. Civilization corrupts; nothing endures. Suicidal, he is briefly rescued by Amélie, who tries to guide his mind back to life, only to decide to seclude herself forever in a convent. As she is about to take her final vows, she confesses a secret shame to God, which her brother overhears: her affection for him has been incestuous. Shocked and more miserable than ever, René goes to America, joins an Indian tribe in search of an impossible ideal, marries an Indian maiden see below his feet, is without doubt, oh elders, an object worthy only of your pity; whatever you may think of René, this picture offers you an image of his character and his life: as now, all my life, I have had before my eyes an immense and barely discernible creation, and, around me, an open abyss at my sides).

René is extraordinarily sensitive to his surroundings in a perverse sort of way. Experiences and associations that are normally pleasurable are turned on end. Viewing a calm landscape, for example, plunges him into despair and melancholy. This state of mind is, as he himself acknowledges, not without "quelques charmes" (a certain charm). A kind of willful psychic masochism pervades his account of his life. He enjoys wallowing in self-pity. But—and herein lies the importance of his account—his suffering is turned into creative energy. He becomes the lyric poet of his own soul: "Notre cœur est un instrument incomplet, une lyre où il manque des cordes, et où nous sommes forcés de rendre les accents de la joie sur le ton consacré aux soupirs" (Our heart is an incomplete instrument, a lyre with missing strings, on which we are forced to express joy with tones reserved for sighing). Narrative discourse dissolves into lyrical effusiveness as René lays bare his soul to his astonished listeners on such subjects as the innocence of childhood, the beauty of religious ceremonies, and the pleasure in contemplating ruins.

To guarantee reader interest Chateaubriand adds an element of suspense. There is the "criminelle passion" (criminal passion) of Amélie for her brother, which is revealed only toward the end of the story. Since there is much of Chateaubriand himself in René (including his name), readers have wondered whether Lucile de Chateaubriand had a deviant attachment to her brother, but there is no evidence to support such an allegation. Rather, Chateaubriand appears simply to have made use of a then-prevalent theme in romances to spice up his story. Structurally, the theme of incest reinforces the system of reversals set up in the work: civilization is fatal, beautiful landscapes engender sadness, love is accursed, sexual passion culminates in death—all exquisitely felt by the narrator through the consciousness of original sin: "Qui ne se trouve quelquefois accablé du fardeau de sa propre corruption . . . ?" (Who has not sometimes felt overwhelmed by the burden of his own depravity. . . ?).

In a way, the thrill of incestuous love is indirectly suggested in *Atala*. The lovers live like brother and sister in the wilderness and, at the height of their passion, discover that Atala's father, a Spaniard named Lopez, was also Chactas's adoptive father. Their passion is made all the more intense by this sudden revelation of an "amitié fraternelle" (fraternal friendship) that unites them and by the hint now of a forbidden love.

The weakness of these works for readers today lies in their obvious extravagance and bathos. Dated too is the frequent use of periphrasis—elegant circumlocution to avoid commonplace terms—a characteristic of much eighteenth-century poetic diction. But Chateaubriand's language has the power to obliterate clear thinking. For the reader willing to suspend belief, the musicality of Chateaubriand's prose can still be a deeply moving experience. Readers of the time were only too willing to identify with guilt, longing, and despair, and to experience secret pleasure in it. Years later Chateaubriand expressed regret for the vogue he had created: "Si *René* n'existait pas, je ne l'écrirais plus; s'il m'était possible de le détruire, je le détruirais. Une famille de René poètes et de René prosateurs a pullulé: on n'a plus entendu que des phrases lamentables et décousues; il n'a plus été question que de vents et d'orages, que de maux inconnus livrés aux nuages et à la nuit. Il n'y a pas de grimaud sortant du collège qui n'ait rêvé d'être le plus malheureux des hommes; de bambin qui à seize ans n'ait épuisé la vie, qui ne se soit cru tourmenté par son génie; qui, dans l'abîme de ses pensées, ne se soit livré au *vague de ses passions*; qui n'ait frappé son front pâle et échevelé, et n'ait étonné les hommes stupéfaits d'un malheur dont il ne savait pas le nom, ni eux non plus" (If *René* did not exist, I would no longer write it; if I could destroy it, I would. A family of René poets and René prose writers has multiplied quickly: we hear now only pathetic and disconnected phrases; writers describe only winds and storms, and unknown ills are shouted to clouds and to the night. There is not an ignoramus just out of school who has not dreamed of being the unhappiest of men; not an urchin who has not been exhausted by life at sixteen, who has not thought himself a tormented genius; who, in the depths of his thoughts, has not given in to the *unsettled state of his passions*; who has not struck his pale and disheveled brow, and astonished men with an unhappiness that neither he nor they could name).

Nevertheless, the larger work in which *René* was first published, *Génie du christianisme*, served the purposes of both Chateaubriand and Napoleon well. His name was removed from the proscribed list of émigrés, and on 4 May 1803 he was appointed to the French Embassy in Rome. His tenure was marked by growing boredom and various diplomatic blunders (for example, a visit to a king the French had deposed). In 1804 he found a pretext to resign: Bonaparte, afraid of a royalist plot against his life, had Louis-Antoine-Henri, Duc D'Enghien, a Bourbon prince, kidnapped and executed. Chateaubriand, disgusted by the arrest and trial, refused to serve any longer under Napoleon; thenceforth, he proclaimed the legitimist principle.

Between 1806 and 1807 he traveled in Greece, the Near East, and Spain. On his return he bought a small property near Paris—La Vallée-aux-Loups (The Valley of Wolves)—which was quiet and conducive to work. (Later he was obliged to sell it.) It was there that he finished *Les Martyrs, ou le triomphe de la religion chrétienne* (1809; translated as *The Martyrs, or The Triumph of the Christian Religion*, 1812), wrote *Itinéraire de Paris à Jérusalem* (1811; translated as *Travels in Greece, Palestine, Egypt and Barbary . . .*, 1811), *Moïse* (Moses, 1831), and *Les Aventures du dernier Abencérage*, and began *Mémoires d'outre-tombe* and *Etudes ou discours historiques* (Historical Studies, 1831).

Les Martyrs is a sequel, in the form of a prose epic in twenty-four cantos, to *Génie du christianisme*. It served to illustrate the thesis that the Christian religion is better suited than paganism to the development of character in the epic, and that the Bible is superior to Homer as a source of inspiration. The work depicts the persecution and triumphs of the early Christians in the third century under the emperor Diocletian. The opening is nearly a paraphrase of Homer, and the many parallels with classical mythology caused Charles-Augustin Sainte-Beuve (in *Chateaubriand et son groupe littéraire* [Chateaubriand and His Literary Group, 1861]) to call it "le phénix de l'épopée systématique" (the phoenix of the systematic epic). Chateaubriand himself later admitted that there were too many descriptions of Heaven and Hell, and that he had used too much traditional epic machinery. There is a curious irony in the fact that the structure of the classical epic, with its invocation to the Muses, its epi-

sodes, voyages, storms, and unhappy love affairs, serves to frame the victory of early Christianity over dying paganism. The work abounds in anachronisms. But it sold well, and the public of the empire read it with enjoyment.

Victor Giraud, in *Le Christianisme de Chateaubriand* (Chateaubriand's Christianity, 1925), insisted that it was less an epic poem than a novel, and the first in a long line of historical novels that includes Lewis Wallace's *Ben Hur* (1880) and Henryk Sienkiewicz's *Quo Vadis?* (1896). The story line centers on the thwarted love between the Christian Eudore and the pagan Cymodocée. The two marry but are separated by events. Eventually they are reunited in Rome only to suffer common martyrdom in the arena. Their martyrdom ends in triumph, however, for in the same arena where they have died the emperor Constantine proclaims Christianity as the official religion of the Roman Empire. In addition to the vogue of historical novels the work may have inspired, it also provided a model of historical reconstruction for young historians such as Augustin Thierry, François Guizot, and Jules Michelet.

Les Aventures du dernier Abencérage was probably written in late 1809, but for reasons of propriety not published until 1826. The heroine, Blanca, is a thinly veiled portrait of Natalie de Noailles, an apparently irresistible woman who had many lovers and who had captured Chateaubriand's affections in 1805. Despite her reputation for breaking hearts, she had promised to oblige him if he came to join her in Granada. Not much is known about their encounter, but it became the source of one of the author's most inspired pieces of writing.

More of a novella than a novel, the work is a model of the *genre troubadour*, much in vogue at the end of the eighteenth century. It is tightly constructed, and the style is less encumbered by excessive ornamentation than *Atala* and *René*. The central theme—like that of *Atala* and *René*—is the love of two beings who must remain forever separated by insurmountable barriers. Once again religion is pitted against nature and comes between a young Muslim and a young Christian. The characters are all of an equally lofty nature but preserve the natural passions, manners, and even prejudices of their country.

Set in sixteenth-century Spain after the Spaniards have driven out the Moors, the tale has as its hero the noble Aben-Hamet, the last descendant of the house of the Abencerages, which had previously ruled Granada and which had been

Chateaubriand in 1809 (portrait by Louis Girodet; Musée de Saint-Malo)

driven into exile in Tunis. He decides to visit the land of his forefathers, where he falls in love and is loved in return by Blanca, a daughter of the Spanish governor of Granada and a Christian of the lineage of the Cid. Symmetrical pronouncements set forth the problem—Blanca: "Qu'Aben-Hamet soit chrétien, qu'il m'aime, et je le suis au bout de la terre" (If Aben-Hamet becomes a Christian and loves me, I will follow him to the ends of the earth); Aben-Hamet: "Que Blanca soit musulmane, qu'elle m'aime et je la sers jusqu'à mon dernier soupir" (If Blanca becomes a Muslim and loves me, I will serve her until my dying breath).

The artistic high point of the tale is a moment of spellbound rapture and delirium in which the two visit the Alhambra together: "La lune, en se levant, répandit sa clarté douteuse dans les sanctuaires abandonnés et dans les parvis déserts de l'Alhambra. Ses blancs rayons dessinaient sur le gazon des parterres, sur les murs des salles, la dentelle d'une architecture aérienne, les cintres des cloîtres, l'ombre mobile des eaux jaillissantes, et celle des arbustes balancés par le zéphyr. Le rossignol chantait dans un cyprès qui perçait les dômes d'une mosquée

en ruine, et les échos répétaient ses plaintes. Aben-Hamet écrivit, au clair de la lune, le nom de Blanca sur le marbre de la salle des Deux Sœurs: il traça ce nom en caractères arabes, afin que le voyageur eût un mystère de plus à deviner dans ce palais des mystères" (The moon, as it was rising, spread its uncertain light through the abandoned sanctuaries and the deserted courts of the Alhambra. Its pale rays, reflecting off the grassy flower beds and the walls of the great halls, cast patterns created by the lacy, airy architecture, the arches of the cloisters, the moving shadows of gushing water, and the shrubs swaying in the breeze. A nightingale sang from a cypress tree that pierced the domes of a ruined mosque, and the echoes repeated its lamentation. In the moonlight, Aben-Hamet wrote the name of Blanca on the marble in the Hall of the Two Sisters: he traced her name in Arab characters, so that the traveler might come upon one more mystery in this palace of mysteries).

Aben-Hamet returns twice more to Granada. Blanca introduces him to her brother, Carlos, and a French knight, Lautrec, who is in love with her. Carlos challenges Aben-Hamet to a duel. The latter is victorious but cannot bring himself to take Carlos's life. Blanca obtains a momentary reconciliation among them, and at a great feast given by Lautrec they all sit around and sing ballads to each other. So strong is Aben-Hamet's love for Blanca that he finds himself on the verge of converting but is held back by loyalty to his heritage. Distraught, he begs Blanca to tell him how else he may become worthy of her love. In a sublime gesture of renunciation, she cries: "Retourne au désert!" (Return to the desert!), and she faints. Honor and faith come between the lovers and force them apart forever. Blanca will spend the remainder of her days wandering amid the ruins of the Alhambra; Lautrec goes away; Carlos will eventually be killed in a duel; Aben-Hamet's fate is never known.

Atala, René, and *Les Aventures du dernier Abencérage* share a common character type of male hero: Chactas, René, and Aben-Hamet (to whom may be added Eudore in *Les Martyrs*) are all outsiders incapable of achieving happiness in this world. More than one critic has pointed out how they reflect their creator and his experiences in exile, his sense of alienation, and his basic restlessness. Love and marriage, moreover, appear incompatible, as was the case in the author's own unfortunate marriage. The plots of the stories turn on a passionate love that proves fatal. Lovers are separated by religious and cultural imperatives, sometimes by death. A profound sense of melancholy pervades the tales.

Itinéraire de Paris à Jérusalem et de Jérusalem à Paris was published in three volumes in 1811. Chateaubriand describes his trip through the Near East from 1806 to 1807 in order to gather material for *Les Martyrs*. Historical reconstruction is coordinated with long quotations from the Bible. Critics have pointed out that Chateaubriand's personal recollections and impressions tend to get buried under masses of documentation, but his masterly descriptions and the semilegendary character he gives to his account could very nearly qualify the work as fiction.

During these years Chateaubriand became more and more critical of the Empire and Napoleon. In 1811 he was elected to the Académie française, and his reception speech was so openly hostile that he was not permitted to read it. In the last days of the emperor's political career, Chateaubriand wrote *De Buonaparte et des Bourbons* (Of Bonaparte and the Bourbons, 1814), an anti-Napoleonic tract in which he expresses his sympathies for the legitimate monarchy. Louis XVIII is reported to have said that it was worth an army to him. After Waterloo and with the restoration of the Bourbons, Louis XVIII made Chateaubriand a peer.

His political career began again. He was successively minister to Berlin (1821), ambassador in London (1822), minister of foreign affairs (1823-1824), and ambassador to Rome (1828). But he increasingly found himself in opposition to the ministers of the Restoration, who, he felt, had betrayed the principles of the legitimate monarchy. He had expressed his beliefs in a pamphlet, *De la monarchie selon la charte* (Principles of Constitutional Monarchy, 1816). Briefly put, he was a royalist who believed in a parliamentary monarchy and freedom of the press. He also believed that important government appointments should be held by supporters of the legitimate monarchy, whereas the king contended that he could find competent administrators only from among those who had been trained by Bonaparte. Finally, in 1830, refusing to accept the monarchy of Louis Philippe, Chateaubriand retired once again from public service.

After 1830 he lived in Paris, mostly editing his autobiography, *Mémoires d'outre-tombe*, and enjoying a reputation as the grand old man of literature. His poverty, however, drove him to publish a few things of relatively little interest today.

Moïse, a tragedy written in 1809, was published in 1831. It had a disastrous reading in the salon of Madame Juliette Récamier in 1829 and proves to be little more than a static pastiche of Jean Racine's *Esther* (1689) and *Athalie* (1691).

Etudes historiques, begun years earlier at La Vallée-aux-Loups, was hastily made ready for publication in 1831. The original plan had called for six essays on the origins of Western civilization to introduce a monumental history of France. Only the essays had been completed; the history became a short "analyse raisonnée" (reasoned analysis). Chateaubriand added a preface explaining that, as he had begun his career with an examination of Christianity in the light of poetry and morals, he now wished to consider it in its historical aspects. Among other things, his intention was to reconcile religion and progress. He held that Christianity and the monarchy had been corrupted by absolutism but were about to benefit from liberty and freedom. It is a curious synthesis, but the work contains many keen insights and is eloquent testimony to the encyclopedic range of the author's interests.

Essai sur la littérature anglaise (1836; translated as *Sketches of English Literature*, 1836) seems to have been largely a misguided effort, full of errors, digressions, and secondhand information, and never free from the canons of French neoclassicism. Moreover, at the height of the Romantic triumph in France, Chateaubriand occasionally alludes disparagingly to some of his contemporaries. His remarks on John Milton and George Gordon, Lord Byron, however, are substantive and sympathetic. Milton was closest in spirit to him, and the *Essai* served to introduce a complete prose translation of *Paradise Lost* (1674), which was done with great care.

Mémoires d'outre-tombe, on the other hand, is Chateaubriand's masterpiece and one of the monuments of French literature. A volume of personal reminiscences begun about 1811 at La Vallée-aux-Loups and worked on in both Berlin and London, it purports to be the story of what he was and what he did. Yet it is much more. After the chapters on his youth, he broadens out to embrace history, and the story of his own life is linked to that of his country and to the age in which he lived. Autobiography is transformed into epic with the author as hero. Descriptions of personal experiences and emotions commingle with current events and memorable portraits of contemporaries. From 1830 to 1834 he wrote, corrected, and revised in Geneva (1831), in Coppet

(1832), and in Prague and Venice (1833). In 1834 he went back over the period from 1800 to 1828 and discussed his literary career. *Mémoires* was finally finished in 1841, although he continued to make revisions until the end of his life (1848). All told, the work occupied him for a period of nearly forty years.

He was determined that it not be published until after his death: "J'ai toujours supposé que j'écrivais assis dans mon cercueil. L'ouvrage a pris de là un certain caractère religieux que je ne lui pourrais ôter sans préjudice; il m'en coûterait d'étouffer cette voix lointaine qui sort de la tombe et que l'on entend dans tout le cours du récit" (I have always written, in my mind, as though from my grave. The work has thus taken on a certain religious character, which I could not suppress without ruining it; it would cost me dearly to stifle that distant voice from the tomb, which is heard throughout the whole course of the narrative). However, to ensure the work's success and arouse public interest, he read passages in Madame Récamier's salon in 1834 and had the press begging for fragments to publish. A few writers, such as Sainte-Beuve, were permitted to consult the manuscript, and laudatory articles ensued. They were collected and published as a volume late in 1834, with a preface by Désiré Nisard. As a result, the author, in financial straits as usual, was able to negotiate an advance on future sales, which permitted him to live comfortably in his last years. The work came out in truncated installments from 1849 to 1850. The first complete text was not published until 1948.

The work is in four sections, each divided into books (forty-four in all), with the books subdivided into chapters. Thematically, at the heart of *Mémoires* is the overwhelming sense of the fragility of human life and the poignant but destructive drama of time. Implied is the notion that remembrance through art alone can preserve the traces of a life lived and become a kind of victory over death.

As the author of a confession, Chateaubriand has no pretense of being a Rousseau and detailing his weaknesses: "Je ne dirai de moi que ce qui est convenable à ma dignité d'homme" (I will tell only what is suitable to my dignity as a man). There is much on which he is silent, and much that he invents. There are errors in dates and facts in order to heighten dramatic effect. He constructs his own image and, in the process, turns himself into a legendary, mythical figure. Likewise, as history, *Mémoires* is far from being reli-

able, for Chateaubriand is at once actor, witness, and victim. Considerable distance separates him from the events recounted, but the distance varies. Over the years, upon meditative reflection and the reworking of the text, different perspectives are superimposed. Chateaubriand becomes both narrator of events and commentator of his own text. The presence of an unstable narrator, whose age, social situation, and point of view shift constantly, reinforces the underlying theme of instability and change in *Mémoires*. The process of shaping his experiences into a literary work of art becomes, in a sense, the real subject of the work. Past and present memories come together and are invariably colored by the author's emotions and personal sensations.

The style is at once historical, epic, lyrical, descriptive, satiric, polemical, and humorous. It is a search for the true meaning of past experience through simultaneous existence in the past and present; the essence common to both reveals a transcendental reality independent of time. "Ma jeunesse pénétrant dans ma vieillesse, la gravité de mes années d'expérience attristant mes années légères, les rayons de mon soleil, depuis son aurore jusqu'à son couchant, se croisant et se confondant, ont produit dans mes récits une sorte de confusion, ou, si l'on veut, une sorte d'unité indéfinissable; mon berceau a de ma tombe, ma tombe a de mon berceau: mes souffrances deviennent des plaisirs, mes plaisirs des douleurs, et je ne sais plus, en achevant de lire ces *Mémoires*, s'ils sont d'une tête brune ou chenue" (My youth thrusting itself into my old age, the seriousness of my mature years casting a sorrowful look over my youthful years, the rays of my sun, from dawn to dusk, meeting and intermingling, have resulted in a kind of confusion, or, if one wishes, have given a kind of indefinable unity to my work; there is something of my grave in my cradle, something of my cradle in my grave: my sufferings become my pleasures, my pleasures my sufferings, and I no longer know, in finishing these *Mémoires*, whether they are the work of a youthful or old gray head). Chateaubriand's methods prefigure those of Marcel Proust.

The work concludes its consideration of historical facts in 1833, but nothing could be more arresting than Chateaubriand's insight into the future of society. He talks about the distribution of wealth, socialism, private property, internationalism, the power of the press, the progress of science, unemployment, leisure, and the education

Chateaubriand in 1820 (sketch by Hilaire Ledru)

of the masses. The visionary quality of the writing is eerily prophetic and disquieting. But the future, he adds, is no longer of any concern to him. In his last days he will settle for salvation through Christianity. The final words of *Mémoires*—a closure in which the author seems to wish to leave the reader with the impression that he has found ultimate composure—were penned 16 November 1841: "Ma fenêtre, qui donne à l'ouest sur les jardins des Missions étrangères, est ouverte: il est six heures du matin; j'aperçois la lune pâle et élargie; elle s'abaisse sur la flèche des Invalides à peine révélée par le premier rayon doré de l'Orient: on dirait que l'ancien monde finit, et que le nouveau commence. Je vois les reflets d'une aurore dont je ne verrai pas se lever le soleil. Il ne me reste qu'à m'asseoir au bord de ma fosse; après quoi je descendrai hardiment, le crucifix à la main, dans l'éternité" (My window, which opens onto the gardens of the Foreign Missions, is open: it is six in the morning; I catch a glimpse of the large, pale moon; it is descending over the spire of the Invalides, which is faintly outlined by the first golden rays from the East: one might say that the old order is coming

to an end, and that the new is beginning. I see glints of a dawn but will not see the sun rise. There remains for me only to sit on the edge of my grave; after which I will boldly descend, my crucifix in my hand, into eternity).

Chateaubriand's discourse in *Mémoires* always reflects the structures of his consciousness. His tendency to portray himself in fictionalized terms suggests that he cannot be trusted with the truth whatever he says, and the troubling question of his sincerity has been raised by more than one critic. Biographical honesty, however, has nothing to do with critical evaluation of the work as art; honesty and literary sincerity are different matters. The latter involves a writer's faithfulness to his artistic vision, and here Chateaubriand cast a spell that is one of the great achievements of French letters.

After *Mémoires*, Chateaubriand had time on his hands, and his confessor, Abbé Seguin, suggested that he write a biography of Abbé de Rancé, the famous seventeenth-century abbot who reformed La Trappe monastery. *Vie de Rancé* (Life of Rancé, 1844) is the story of a man who—having been blessed with superior intelligence, money, and social position—withdraws from worldly life because of the death of his lover, undergoes a conversion, and does repentance in the abbey of La Trappe, where he introduces a rule of great austerity. It is Chateaubriand's last work and, written at the age of seventy-five, his most daring and innovative. It has appealed especially to twentieth-century writers and critics, who find its strange art singularly modern.

The work may seem simple enough in summary, but it is structured around a complex, double-voiced discourse. Although Chateaubriand was writing the life of another, and although material provided by earlier documents and biographies imposed a certain structure on him, his treatment is full of mute reference to himself. Rancé's life emerges by means of a third-person narrator whose lean, unadorned discourse continually prompts a dialogue with the narrator responsible for the narration. The originality of Chateaubriand's biography lies in its unexpected digressions, imagery, and details, which the facts of the abbot's life call into being. The overall impression is one of disconnectedness (Sainte-Beuve, in *Chroniques parisiennes* [Parisian Chronicles, 1844], called it "un véritable bric-à-brac" [a real collection of odds and ends]), but the apparent incoherence suited Chateaubriand's purpose.

He is able to stand above and beyond Rancé's world and meditate on the themes of penance and death.

For example, in an often-quoted passage where Rancé's youth and La Fronde (a series of seventeenth-century revolts against royal absolutism, exemplified by the unpopular Cardinal Mazarin) are discussed, he suddenly interrupts, with no transition, to observe: "Sociétés depuis long-temps évanouies, combien d'autres vous ont succédé! Les danses s'établissent sur la poussière des morts, et les tombeaux poussent sous les pas de la joie. Nous rions et nous chantons sur les lieux arrosés du sang de nos amis. Où sont aujourd'hui les maux d'hier? Où seront demain les félicités d'aujourd'hui? Quelle importance pourrions-nous attacher aux choses de ce monde? L'amitié? elle disparaît quand celui qui est aimé tombe dans le malheur, ou quand celui qui aime devient puissant. L'amour? il est trompé, fugitif ou coupable. La renommée? vous la partagez avec la médiocrité ou le crime. La fortune? pourrait-on compter comme un bien cette frivolité? Restent ces jours dits heureux qui coulent ignorés dans l'obscurité des soins domestiques, et qui ne laissent à l'homme ni l'envie de perdre ni de recommencer la vie" (Societies long ago vanished, how many have succeeded you! Dancing takes place over the dust of the dead, and tombs spring up under the joyous steps of the living. We laugh and we sing in places watered by the blood of our friends. Where are the pains of yesterday today? Where will our bliss of today be tomorrow? What importance can be attached to things of this world? Friendship? It disappears when the one loved falls into misfortune, or when the one who loves rises to power. Love? It is betrayed, fleeting, or guilty. Renown? One shares it with the mediocre and criminals. Fortune? Can one count this frivolity as a blessing? There remain only the so-called happy days, which flow by unnoticed in the obscurity of domestic cares, and which leave to man neither the wish to lose life nor begin it again). Biography is transformed into autobiography.

Chateaubriand died on 4 July 1848, semi-paralyzed, unable to walk, melancholic, and incapable of sustained thought (according to Sainte-Beuve). He had written in *Vie de Rancé*, on the subject of Jacques Bossuet and his love of visiting La Trappe, "Les hommes éclatants ont un penchant pour les lieux obscurs" (Famous men have a penchant for obscure places), and, accordingly, he asked to be buried on the tiny island of Grand-

Bé off the port of Saint-Malo in Brittany. There he lies today, high on a rocky promontory, overlooking the sea.

Chateaubriand is remembered as one of the great French writers of all time. His contemporaries tended to see him not so much as an innovator, but as the master of an inherited tradition. He borrowed unashamedly and could be insufferably vain, yet his style transformed whatever it touched. His exquisitely measured rhythms and system of sounds are often described as distinctively musical. Certain ways of speaking about music—the impression of a continuous melodic line, the use of unresolved harmonies, the varied tone colors—can metaphorically be applied to Chateaubriand. The ebb and flow of his prose, its mounting tensions and sublime releases, were calculated for maximum impact on the reader, and they earned him the epithet "l'Enchanteur" (the Enchanter).

Chateaubriand was most appreciated by his contemporaries for the vibrancy of his prose, his exotic nature descriptions, his paintings of religious life, his essays on politics, his portraits of souls in distress, and his observations on notable people of his age. Yet his work quickly became dated and went out of fashion, for Chateaubriand's view of life, the meaning he attached to it, and what he had to say about it do not always speak to later ages. But his importance has been solidly affirmed today—both historically and aesthetically—by scholars and critics the world over. Chateaubriand continues to invite study on a wide range of subjects: his life as an individual, his personality, his career as a statesman, his art as the focus of recent critical theory, his place in the history of ideas, his relation to the arts, his treatment of single themes, his style, and his influence. His stylistic innovations have been the subject of meaningful observations in recent Chateaubriand criticism.

Above all, his style is personal. It incorporates and reflects every aspect of what he saw and did, as well as the vast reading he enjoyed throughout his life. The use of unexpected similes, daring wordplays, deliberate suppression of transitions, abruptness of contrasts, interplay of various styles, and stunning poetic cadences reflects his disconnected and contradictory public and private lives. Today he can be viewed as a precursor to twentieth-century notions of structured disorder in art. One can discern in Chateaubriand the *mémoire involontaire* (involuntary memory) that Proust utilized later, find models for prose

Marble sculpture of Chateaubriand made in 1853 by François-Joseph Duret and exhibited at the Exposition universelle of 1855 (Institut de France, Paris)

poems before the genre had been defined, and discover techniques of association and suggestion that the late-nineteenth-century poets practiced. Such an art appeals to the active participation of the reader's imagination.

Chateaubriand cannot be considered a novelist in the usual sense of the word. *Atala* and *René* may have been turning points in the history of French literature, but they are essentially vehicles for displaying striking attitudes and a pretext for verbal performances that celebrate authorial power. Language and style triumph at the expense of plot and characterization. It is for his aesthetic brilliance that Chateaubriand has been remembered and will continue to be studied.

Letters:
Correspondance générale, 5 volumes, edited by

Louis Thomas (Paris: Champion, 1912-1924);
Lettres à Madame Récamier, edited by Maurice Levaillant and E. Beau de Loménie (Paris: Flammarion, 1951).

Bibliography:
Pierre and Ann Dubé, *Bibliographie de la critique sur François-René de Chateaubriand, 1801-1986* (Paris: Nizet, 1988).

Biographies:
H. Le Savoureux, *Chateaubriand* (Paris: Rieder, 1930);
André Maurois, *René, ou la vie de Chateaubriand* (Paris: Grasset, 1938); translated by Vera Fraser as *Chateaubriand: Poet, Statesman, Lover* (New York & London: Harper, 1938);
Louis Martin-Chauffier, *Chateaubriand ou l'obsession de la pureté* (Paris: N.R.F., 1943);
Pierre Moreau, *Chateaubriand: L'homme et l'œuvre* (Paris: Hatier-Boivin, 1956);
Henri Guillemin, *L'Homme des "Mémoires d'outre-tombe"* (Paris: Gallimard, 1965).

References:
Pierre Barbéris, *A la recherche d'une écriture: Chateaubriand* (Paris: Delarge, 1976);
Barbéris, *Chateaubriand: Une réaction au monde moderne* (Paris: Larousse, 1976);
Barbéris, *"René" de Chateaubriand: Un nouveau roman* (Paris: Larousse, 1973);
Christian Bazin, *Chateaubriand en Amérique* (Paris: Table Ronde, 1969);
Jon Becker, "Archetype and Myth in Chateaubriand's *Atala,*" *Symposium,* 31 (1977): 93-106;
Edmond Biré, *Les Dernières Années de Chateaubriand, 1830-1848* (Paris: Garnier, 1902);
Jean Boorsch, "Motion and Rest in *René,*" *Yale French Studies,* 13 (Spring-Summer 1954): 76-82;
José Cabanis, *Chateaubriand* (Lyons: Manufacture, 1988);
Michall J. Call, *Back to the Garden: Chateaubriand, Sénancour and Constant* (Saratoga, Cal.: Anma Libri, 1988);
Albert Cassagne, *La Vie politique de François Chateaubriand* (Paris: Plon, 1911);
D. G. Charlton, "The Ambiguity of Chateaubriand's *René,*" *French Studies,* 23 (July 1969): 229-243;

Gilbert Chinard, *L'Exotisme américain dans l'œuvre de Chateaubriand* (Paris: Hachette, 1918);

Piette Clarac, *A la recherche de Chateaubriand* (Paris: Nizet, 1975);

Jean Cohen, *Structure du langage poétique* (Paris: Flammarion, 1966);

Albert Dollinger, *Les Etudes historiques de Chateaubriand* (Paris: Les Belles Lettres, 1932);

Pierre Dubé, "*Les Aventures du dernier Abencérage*: A Mirror of Time and Civilization," *Revue de l'Université d'Ottawa*, 46 (1976): 407-414;

Marie-Jeanne Durry, *La Vieillesse de Chateaubriand, 1830-1848* (Paris: Le Divan, 1933);

Eric Gans, "*René* and the Romantic Model of Self-Centralization," *Studies in Romanticism*, 22 (Fall 1983): 421-435;

Jean-Maurice Gautier, *Le Style des "Mémoires d'outre-tombe" de Chateaubriand* (Geneva: Droz, 1959);

Victor Giraud, *Le Christianisme de Chateaubriand* (Paris: Hachette, 1925);

Giraud, *Maîtres d'autrefois et d'aujourd'hui* (Paris: Hachette, 1912);

Merete Grevlund, *Paysage intérieur et paysage extérieur dans les "Mémoires d'outre-tombe"* (Paris: Nizet, 1968);

James F. Hamilton, "The Anxious Hero in Chateaubriand's *René*," *Romance Quarterly*, 34 (November 1987): 415-424;

Hamilton, "The Ideology of Exoticism in Chateaubriand's *Atala*: An Eighteenth-Century Perspective," *French Literature Series*, 13 (1986): 28-37;

Diana Knight, "The Readability of René's Secret," *French Studies*, 37 (January 1983): 35-46;

Raymond Lebègue, *Aspects de Chateaubriand: Vie, voyage en Amérique, œuvres* (Paris: Nizet, 1979);

Maija Lehtonen, "L'Evolution du langage imagé de Chateaubriand," *Société Chateaubriand Bulletin*, 9 (1965-1966): 20-24;

Maurice Levaillant, *Chateaubriand, prince des songes* (Paris: Hachette, 1960);

Levaillant, *Splendeurs et misères de Monsieur de Chateaubriand* (Paris: Albin-Michel, 1948);

E. Beau de Loménie, *La Carrière politique de Chateaubriand de 1814 à 1830* (Paris: Plon, 1929);

Joyce O. Lowrie, "Motifs of Kingdom and Exile in *Atala*," *French Review*, 43 (April 1970): 755-764;

Carlos Lynes, Jr., *Chateaubriand as a Critic of French Literature* (Baltimore: Johns Hopkins University Press, 1946);

Pierre Moreau, *Chateaubriand devant Dieu* (Paris: Desclée de Brouwer, 1965);

Jean Mourot, *Chateaubriand, rythme et sonorité dans les "Mémoires d'outre-tombe"* (Paris: Armand Colin, 1969);

Mourot, "Chateaubriand satirique: Quelques aspects de son style," *Cahiers de l'Association internationale des études françaises*, 21 (May 1969): 167-191;

Mourot, *Etudes sur les premières œuvres de Chateaubriand: Tableaux de la nature; Essai sur les révolutions* (Paris: Nizet, 1962);

Charles A. Porter, *Chateaubriand: Composition, Imagination, and Poetry* (Saratoga, Cal.: Anma Libri, 1978);

Laurence M. Porter, "Chateaubriand's Revenge on History in the *Mémoires d'outre-tombe*," *Symposium*, 35 (Fall 1981): 267-280;

Porter, "Writing Romantic Epiphany: *Atala, Séraphîta, Aurélia, Dieu*," *Romance Quarterly*, 34 (November 1987): 435-442;

Michèle Respaut, "*René*: Confession, répétition, révélation," *French Review*, 57 (October 1983): 14-19;

Jean-Pierre Richard, *Paysage de Chateaubriand* (Paris: Seuil, 1967);

Charles-Augustin Sainte-Beuve, *Chateaubriand et son groupe littéraire sous l'Empire*, edited by Maurice Allem (Paris: Garnier, 1948);

Société Chateaubriand. Bulletin, nos. 1-6 (1930-1937);

Société Chateaubriand. Bulletin, new series 1- (1954-);

Société Chateaubriand. Petit Bulletin, nos. 1-6 (1947-1954);

Dennis J. Spininger, "The Paradise Setting of Chateaubriand's *Atala*," *PMLA*, 89 (May 1974): 530-536;

Richard Switzer, ed., *Chateaubriand Today* (Madison, Milwaukee & London: University of Wisconsin Press, 1970);

Victor-L. Tapié, *Chateaubriand par lui-même* (Paris: Seuil, 1967);

André Vial, *Chateaubriand et le temps perdu* (Paris: Julliard, 1963).

Papers:
There is no principal collection of Chateaubriand's manuscripts, which are widely scattered in small private collections and libraries.

Benjamin Constant
(Henri-Benjamin de Constant de Rebecque)

(25 October 1767 - 8 December 1830)

Dennis Wood
University of Birmingham, England

SELECTED BOOKS: *De l'esprit de conquête et de l'usurpation, dans leurs rapports avec la civilisation européenne* (Hanover: Hahn, 1814); translated and edited by Helen Byrne Lippmann as *Prophecy from the Past. Benjamin Constant on Conquest and Usurpation* (New York: Reynal & Hitchcock, 1941);

Principes de politique, applicables à tous les gouvernemens représentatifs et particulièrement à la constitution actuelle de la France (Paris: Alexis Eymery, 1815);

Adolphe; anecdote trouvée dans les papiers d'un inconnu (London: Colburn / Paris: Tröttel et Wurtz, 1816); translated by Alexander Walker as *Adolphe: An Anecdote Found among the Papers of an Unknown Person* (London: H. Colburn, 1816); translated by Carl Wildman in *Adolphe and The Red Note-Book* (London: Hamish Hamilton, 1948);

De la religion, considérée dans sa source, ses formes et ses développements, volume 1 (Paris: Bossange père, Bossange frères, Treuttel et Wurtz, Rey et Gravier, Renouard, Ponthieu, 1824); volumes 2 and 3 (Paris: Béchet aîné, 1825, 1827); volumes 4 and 5 (Paris: Pichon et Didier, 1831);

Mélanges de littérature et de politique (Paris: Pichon et Didier, 1829);

Du polythéisme romain, considéré dans ses rapports avec la philosophie grecque et la religion chrétienne, 2 volumes (Paris: Béchet aîné, 1833);

Journal intime de Benjamin Constant et lettres à sa famille et à ses amis, introduction by D. Melegari (Paris: Paul Ollendorff, 1895);

Le "Cahier rouge" de Benjamin Constant (Paris: Calmann-Lévy, 1907); translated by Norman Cameron in *Adolphe and The Red Note-Book* (London: Hamish Hamilton, 1948);

Cécile, edited by Alfred Roulin (Paris: Gallimard, 1951); translated by Cameron as *Cécile* (London: J. Lehmann, 1952).

Editions and Collections: *Benjamin Constant. Œuvres*, edited by Alfred Roulin and Charles Roth (Paris: Gallimard, Bibliothèque de la Pléiade, 1957);

De la liberté chez les modernes. Ecrits politiques, edited by Marcel Gauchet (Paris: Livre de poche, 1980);

Political Writings—Benjamin Constant, translated and edited by Biancamaria Fontana (Cambridge: Cambridge University Press, 1988)—contains *De l'esprit de conquête*, *Principes de politique*, and *De la liberté des anciens comparée à celle des modernes;*

Ma Vie (Le Cahier rouge), edited by C. P. Courtney (Cambridge: Daemon, 1991).

TRANSLATION: *Wallstein, tragédie en cinq actes et en vers, précédée de quelques réflexions sur le théâtre allemand, et suivie de notes historiques*, translated and adapted from Friedrich von Schiller's *Wallenstein* (Paris & Geneva: J. J. Paschoud, 1809).

Critical interest in Benjamin Constant has in recent decades tended to focus on three principal areas: his life, including his dilemmas and personal difficulties with women; his novel *Adolphe* (1816; translated as *Adolphe*, 1816), which continues to fascinate the general reading public and to attract and perplex literary critics of very different persuasions; and his views on politics and religion. The bicentennial of his birth (1967) and the sesquicentennial of his death (1980) were the occasions for important publications and exhibitions, the latter anniversary giving the impetus to the founding of the Institut Benjamin Constant in Lausanne, Switzerland, and of the journal *Annales Benjamin Constant*. No edition yet exists of Constant's complete works, but an editorial board was set up in 1980 with the aim of publishing Constant's full œuvre and correspondence.

Constant's life is intriguing to biographers, and though much is known about it, a great deal remains mysterious and open to speculation. He was born in Lausanne on 25 October 1767, the son of Louis-Arnold-Juste de Constant de Rebecque, a Swiss aristocrat and military officer in the service of the Netherlands. His mother, Henriette-Pauline de Chandieu, died sixteen days after his birth. His father, an unpredictable, domineering, and irascible man, later entrusted his son to the care of a woman whom Benjamin hated, Marianne Magnin, who, unbeknown to him, was his father's mistress and later became his stepmother. Thereafter Benjamin was put in the care of a series of tutors, each of whom was morally unsuitable in some major respect, if one is to believe the account in his autobiographical *Le Cahier rouge* (1907; translated as *The Red Note-Book*, 1948), now known as *Ma Vie* (My Life).

Juste finally took personal charge of his son's education. Benjamin proved extraordinarily precocious and gifted, being particularly able in both ancient and modern languages. In 1782 Juste sent him to study at the University of Erlangen in Germany, where all instruction was in Latin. There, according to *Ma Vie*, Benjamin became involved in a characteristically harebrained way (as he was so often to be in years to come) with a young woman at court, earned official disapproval, and was obliged to rejoin his father.

More serious and fruitful studies began in 1783 when his father sent him to the University of Edinburgh. He studied Greek and history, and became proficient enough in English to address meetings of the Speculative Society, whose debates he regularly attended. It was during his time at Edinburgh, a period to which he would later refer as the most enjoyable year of his life, that Constant appears to have acquired a passionate interest in the religions of antiquity. This provided the point of departure for a lifetime spent in the study of religious sentiment, culminating in *De la religion* (On Religion, 1824-1831) and *Du polythéisme romain* (On Roman Polytheism, 1833). While at Edinburgh he made several friends, the most important of whom were John Wilde, later professor of civil law; the historian Malcolm Laing; and James (later Sir James) Mackintosh, whom he would see again in the middle and later years of his life. At the same time Constant developed another lifelong passion—gambling—and left Scotland having amassed debts that he could not meet. He continued to gamble during stays in Paris (1785 and 1786-1787), where he fre-

Benjamin Constant (portrait by Hercule de Roches; Musée Carnavalet, Paris)

quented literary and political salons and stayed with Jean-Baptiste Suard and his family.

During the winter of 1786-1787 he met a woman who was to exercise an important influence on him for many years, the novelist Isabelle de Charrière. She combined a skeptical intellect with human warmth of a kind that had hitherto been conspicuously lacking in Constant's life. Although he later believed that she had exerted a pernicious influence on him during his formative years by encouraging wild behavior (such as his fleeing to England in the summer of 1787 to be out of reach of his father's influence), Mme de Charrière's correspondence with Constant leaves no doubt about the motherly, unselfish concern she had for his welfare. Indeed, she may have encouraged him at this time to collaborate with her on an unfinished epistolary novel, *Lettres de d'Arsillé fils* (Letters of d'Arsillé junior).

Constant's father secured for him the post of gentleman of the bedchamber to Karl Wilhelm Ferdinand, Duke of Brunswick, an appointment that began a bleak period in Benjamin's life (1788-1794), one of depression and boredom, during which he made a disastrous and short-lived marriage (1789-1795) to a lady-in-waiting, Wilhelmina von Cramm. His meeting in Switzerland on 18 September 1794 with Germaine de Staël and their subsequent liaison marked an unmistakable turning point in his life. They embarked on political activity in favor of the moderate republican cause and opened a salon in Paris. With Mme de Staël's encouragement Constant secured political office, first as a councillor at Luzarches and later as a member of Napoleon Bonaparte's *Tribunat*.

A recurring theme in Constant's life and work is fear and resentment of domination by others. While it fueled his staunch resistance to Bonaparte's dictatorship, it made Mme de Staël's increasing possessiveness profoundly irksome to him, leading to years of violent arguments and reconciliations until their final separation in 1811. During the same stormy years, Constant was involved in a passionate affair with the Irishwoman Anna Lindsay. The affair was intense from 1800 to 1801 and flared up sporadically in later years. In 1806 he began a liaison with Charlotte Dutertre, née von Hardenberg, whom he secretly married on 5 June 1808. Constant's experiences of these years found their way, in transmuted form, into *Adolphe* and *Cécile* (1951; translated as *Cécile*, 1952). Both novels may have been begun in October 1806, although there is considerable debate about this. Constant's earlier critics argued over which of the women in his life at the time—Mme de Staël, Anna Lindsay, or Charlotte von Hardenberg—was the inspiration for Ellénore in *Adolphe*. Critics now tend to avoid such simple equations, though there do seem to be traits in Ellénore borrowed from all three women.

After his marriage to Charlotte, Constant settled down to a few years of study (1811-1813), spent largely in Germany, devoted to the history of religion in preparation for his *Du polythéisme romain*. He resumed his political career, with disastrous results, during Napoleon's brief return to power in 1815, when he agreed to act as an adviser to the emperor. During the period of semi-exile that followed this ill-judged change of allegiance, Constant gave readings of *Adolphe* in literary salons, and the novel was published simultaneously in London and Paris in the summer of 1816. After his return to France in 1816, he was eventually elected to the Chamber of Deputies and became a leader of the liberal opposition and a writer of memorable speeches and political essays and pamphlets. He lived to see the July Revolution of 1830 and was active in subsequent months in support of the new government. He died in Paris on 8 December 1830 and after a

state funeral was buried in the Père-Lachaise cemetery on 12 December 1830.

"Tout se tient dans la nature" (all things are interconnected in nature), Constant wrote in the "Préface de la seconde édition" (Preface to the Second Edition) of *Adolphe*. The statement can very well be applied to Constant himself. There are strong links between his personality, his autobiographical and fictional writings, his political preferences, and his views on the historical development of religion. In the preface to *Mélanges de littérature et de politique* (Literary and Political Miscellany, 1829), he pointed to a common thread in his life and work: "J'ai défendu quarante ans le même principe, liberté en tout, en religion, en philosophie, en littérature, en industrie, en politique: et par liberté, j'entends le triomphe de l'individualité, tant sur l'autorité qui voudrait gouverner par le despotisme, que sur les masses qui réclament le droit d'asservir la minorité à la majorité." (For forty years I have defended the same principle: freedom in everything, in religion, in philosophy, in literature, in industry, in politics, and by freedom I mean the triumph of individuality, both over an authority that seeks to govern by despotism, and over the masses who demand the right to enslave the minority to the majority.)

Constant's fierce desire for personal independence had perhaps been exacerbated by his father's unpredictable manner of loosening and tightening the reins of his authority over him. It reemerged in every relationship that he formed with a woman, most notably with Mme de Charrière, Mme de Staël, Anna Lindsay, and Charlotte von Hardenberg, but also in less well known relationships. On a wider stage, this intense desire to be free drew from Constant a spirited, courageous response of hostility to tyranny, political or religious, wherever he found it, whether in the structures of the ancien régime or in the organized military despotism of Napoleon's France with its informers and secret police. His vocal opposition to Napoleon brought about his expulsion from the *Tribunat* in 1802 and for many rendered inexplicable his rallying to him again during the Hundred Days in 1815. Constant explained that he believed that Napoleon had finally been won over to the cause of constitutional democracy.

Adolphe, Cécile, Ma Vie, and the *Journaux intimes* (Diaries; first *Journal intime* published in 1895) each touch on the issue of individual freedom in a relationship. *Adolphe*, a retrospective first-

Charlotte de Constant, née von Hardenberg (portrait by an unknown artist; from Harold Nicolson, Benjamin Constant, *1949). She was twice divorced when she married Constant in 1808.*

person narrative, is the story of a highly intelligent young man brought up with a degree of indulgence by a father who maintains an ironic distance from him and who has encouraged him to consider that love affairs can be ended as easily as they are begun. Out of boredom Adolphe sets about seducing an older woman, Ellénore, the mistress of the comte de P***. For a brief moment he finds happiness in the affair and believes himself to be in love but soon discovers, to his dismay, that Ellénore is herself passionately in love with him.

The major part of the novel then explores in minute detail the inward deliberations and hesitations of Adolphe as he attempts to free himself from a relationship that has grown burdensome. His dilemma is that although he no longer loves Ellénore with the passion that he once briefly felt, he nevertheless does not wish her to suffer. The result is an unhappy stalemate: affection, loyalty, and a sense of responsibility for Ellénore lead him to postpone ending their liaison, yet the more it is prolonged, the more painful any sepa-

ration will be for both of them. Ellénore's possessiveness in the meantime leads to arguments and recriminations that cause them both great suffering. The novel's denouement results from the intervention of a third party, the baron de T***, who sends Ellénore a letter he has received from Adolphe, promising that he will break off the affair with her. The news proves fatal to Ellénore's health, and the novel ends with her death and Adolphe's feelings of utter desolation.

Adolphe's need to be free of all *liens* (bonds) is made clear in the first chapter of the novel. Once he becomes involved with Ellénore, his quest for freedom provides the momentum for the rest of the novel and becomes the focus for observations and self-analysis of extraordinary depth and insight on the part of the narrator, the older Adolphe. Out of these reflections grow many aphoristic statements comparable in their power and concision to François, Duc de La Rochefoucauld's *Réflexions ou sentences et maximes morales* (1665; translated as *Maxims and Moral Reflections*, 1694). The novel hangs on a series of paradoxes, the most obvious being that a man who proclaims his dislike of all *liens* is unable to break the ties that bind him to Ellénore. He thereby causes both of them to suffer so much longer than they otherwise might have.

As well as appreciating the quality of thought in the novel, critics have seen in *Adolphe* a model of French prose—elegant, precise, and direct—with great intensity of feeling behind it. Among recent commentators on the novel, Han Verhoeff, in *"Adolphe" et Constant: une étude psychocritique*, has advanced the theory that Adolphe's behavior toward Ellénore reflects Constant's own ambivalent feelings toward women, which resulted from the early loss of his mother. Verhoeff argues that Constant's feelings of abandonment resulted in reactions toward women that were always characterized by attraction and a desperate need for affection on the one hand, and by aggression on the other. This would account for the emotional paralysis of Adolphe, wishing to be rid of Ellénore but unable to go through with the separation. Another potentially fruitful line of inquiry has been to link *Adolphe* to Constant's political and moral concerns, an approach suggested by Norman King's article "Romantisme et opposition" in the journal *Romantisme* (1986). Written against the background of political oppression and moral corruption that characterized the Napoleonic regime, *Adolphe* presents a society and a set of values based on ruthless self-interest (particularly in the person of the baron de T***), to which Adolphe, a man with a *cœur naturel* (natural heart), ultimately falls victim. Seen in this light, *Adolphe* can be viewed as representing the spirit of opposition and resistance to Napoleon emanating from Mme de Staël's Coppet and the group of liberal thinkers whom she gathered around her there.

Indecision and hesitation are also characteristic of the central protagonist of *Cécile*, an unfinished novel whose manuscript was lost for more than a century and published in 1951. *Cécile* is based on the long period of Constant's life when he was unable to commit himself unequivocally to either Germaine de Staël or Charlotte von Hardenberg, but instead moved indecisively between the two women. If, as Paul Delbouille has noted in "Benjamin Constant romancier" in *Annales Benjamin Constant* (1986), Constant's personal writings occupy a spectrum running from the pure fiction of *Adolphe* to the arranged historical fact of *Ma Vie*, then *Cécile* seems to occupy a place halfway along that spectrum. There are similarities between Cécile de Walterbourg and Charlotte as there are between Mme de Malbée and Mme de Staël, but there are also significant differences between them, as Simone Balayé has emphasized in an article in *Benjamin Constant, Madame de Staël et le groupe de Coppet* (1982). Between *Adolphe* and *Cécile*, there is the essential difference that *Cécile* lacks an ending. The style is more relaxed, less tightly controlled than in *Adolphe*; the theme of *Cécile* is also less bleak and for that reason more appealing to some readers. The exact relationship in time between the two texts is unclear; *Cécile* may have been begun in 1806, at the same time as *Adolphe*, or it may, as its style suggests, have been written later, at a time of less tension in the author's life, perhaps in or around 1810.

In about 1810 Constant also wrote the last of the three texts based on his life for which he is usually remembered, *Ma Vie* (formerly known as *Le Cahier rouge* from the color of the notebook in which it was written), an account of the first twenty years of his life composed in the often humorous manner of an eighteenth-century memoir. The narrative takes the reader from Constant's birth through his experiences with various tutors to his early encounters with women, which are often described in comic terms. As *Ma Vie* unfolds, it develops away from a fairly bald statement, year by year in the manner of a diary, of what happened to the young Constant and into something different. Longer sections reconstruct

dialogue and concentrate on perhaps only a day or two in Constant's adolescence that were of great significance.

The climax of *Ma Vie* is Constant's meeting with Mme de Charrière in Paris during the winter of 1786-1787. An immediate rapport springs up between them and is presented as having led to Constant's madcap expedition to England and Scotland during the summer of 1787 to escape from his father and to find old friends. Rather like *Cécile*, the text appears to have been abandoned, in this case at the point where Benjamin Constant is about to fight a duel. Commentators have offered differing explanations for the unfinished state of *Ma Vie*, suggesting for example that its frequently comic and ironic tone would not have suited the more serious events that were shortly to follow in his life, such as his father's court-martial in the Netherlands. Another possible reason is that much of *Ma Vie* can be read as a veiled indictment of Juste's incompetence as a father and a hymn to the freedom Benjamin briefly rediscovered in England. After 1788 Benjamin could no longer be presented as a minor who was dependent on Juste. *Ma Vie* has been extensively explored from the point of view of its fidelity to ascertainable historical facts by C. P. Courtney, Dennis Wood, and others who draw comparisons with Constant's correspondence with Mme de Charrière during the 1780s. The text's status as a work of literature still remains to be analyzed. Its cyclical pattern of minor disasters followed by the intervention of Juste recalls the Abbé Prévost's *Manon Lescaut* (1731), and its tone is akin to that of English picaresque novels by Henry Fielding and Tobias Smollett, especially in the section dealing with the *escapade d'Angleterre* (English escapade).

In addition to texts based closely or loosely on Constant's experience, modern readers also have his diaries, the *Journaux intimes*, the most convenient and reliable edition of which can be found in the *Œuvres* edited by Alfred Roulin and Charles Roth (1957). The first section of the *Journaux intimes* is known as *Amélie et Germaine 6 janvier - 10 avril 1803* (Amélie and Germaine 6 January - 10 April 1803) and is a meditation on the problem of choosing a wife, and whether that wife is to be Amélie Fabri or Germaine de Staël. Later sections provide candid insights into Constant's character, revealing the pain his relationships with many women cause both him and them, and information on the progress of his writ-

Silhouette of Constant by Mlle Moula (from Elizabeth W. Schermerhorn, Benjamin Constant: His Private Life and His Contribution to the Cause of Liberal Government in France, 1767-1830, *1924)*

ing on religion, often a release from the emotional tension he frequently felt.

Constant's status as an introspective writer belonging to a line that stretches back through Jean-Jacques Rousseau to Michel Eyquem de Montaigne and beyond, and his authorship of an acknowledged masterpiece of psychological analysis, *Adolphe*, have occasionally led to the neglect of other aspects of his intellectual activity. This situation has been redressed in recent decades as the result of a considerable amount of research on his political writings and works on religion, as well as on his translation/adaptation (*Wallstein*, 1809) of Friedrich von Schiller's *Wallenstein* (1800). Constant's political thought was deeply informed by a variety of sources, including Charles-Louis de Montesquieu and Emmanuel-Joseph Sieyès, and his experience of the parliamentary system of Great Britain during his studies in Scotland had a lasting influence on him. During the 1780s he was a *démocrate*, perhaps as a result of the Whig radicalism of his Edinburgh friend

John Wilde and others. While in Brunswick he was a supporter of the French Revolution and for a time sought to justify the Terror to Mme de Charrière, much to her dismay. From 1794, working closely with Mme de Staël, Constant supported the establishment of a moderate republican administration in France, one that would maintain a distance from both the Catholic church and the Jacobins. Such an objective was thwarted by the rise of Bonaparte, against whose cult of personal power Constant firmly set himself.

Of his many polemical writings, perhaps the most successful is *De l'esprit de conquête et de l'usurpation* (1814; translated as *Prophecy from the Past. Benjamin Constant on Conquest and Usurpation*, 1941), a forceful indictment of military tyranny intended to hasten the downfall of Napoleon and ensure his replacement by a constitutional monarchy under Jean Bernadotte, Crown Prince of Sweden. As Ephraïm Harpaz, the editor of a 1986 edition of the work, has said, although the context in which *De l'esprit de conquête* was written has been largely forgotten, it has become "un classique contre l'arbitraire de tous les âges, aussi applicable aux totalitarismes de droite que de gauche" (a classic work against the arbitrary exercise of power in any age, as applicable to totalitarianism of the right as of the left), and its relevance to twentieth-century history hardly needs underlining.

In Constant's eyes a regime such as Napoleon's was anachronistic, out of tune with modern aspirations to individual freedom and privacy. This theme was further developed in *Principes de politique* (Political Principles, 1815), in which Constant defends the modern world against what he sees as Rousseau's pernicious adulation of the democracy of ancient Greece in *Du contrat social* (1762; translated as *The Social Contract*, 1764). Privacy; the right to own property; and freedom of religion, education, and the press are the prerogatives of modern societies. There must be no turning back of the clock to societies where there is no privacy in matters of opinions and beliefs. Here again Constant's words have proved prophetic, as modern societies have developed ever more effective secret-police apparatuses, systems of surveillance, and propaganda to force the individual to support their programs. In parliament Constant was as forceful an orator as he was a polemical writer. His speeches— polished, confident, persuasive, and reminiscent in style of such classical models as Tacitus and

Cicero—are characterized by stinging irony. In his later years Constant put his eloquence at the service of a French democracy increasingly threatened by a repressive monarchy, and all his skill as a polemicist was mobilized in campaigns favoring freedom of opinion and of the press, Greek independence, and the abolition of the slave trade.

Despite his early interest in ancient religions, Constant's development into a writer on religion would have seemed unlikely in the 1780s, given his fierce anticlerical and anti-Christian bias at that time. Only gradually—probably under the influence of his Brunswick friend, the polymath Jakob Mauvillon—did the intrinsic importance of religious feeling become apparent to him. Underlying the tireless studies that led to *De la religion* and *Du polythéisme romain* was Constant's conviction that the urge to believe is a permanent feature of human nature, though the expression of that religious feeling may take on different forms in different geographical and historical contexts.

Constant's belief in human perfectibility, so characteristic of the late Enlightenment, led him to see in recorded history a recurrent movement away from the prison of dogma and from religions dominated by a priestly caste toward a pure religion of the heart. Although in every age there is likely to be an attempt to impose a doctrinal straitjacket and a sacerdotal hierarchy on believers, sooner or later *le sentiment religieux* (religious sentiment) will break away from what has become rigid and static and find new forms more appropriate to its current state of development. For Constant, early Christianity and its modern Protestant form represent the highest expression that this religious sentiment has yet reached. What characterizes this feeling is the spirit of self-sacrifice and self-denial, a willingness to postpone immediate pleasure in tribute to a higher ideal. The freedoms of belief and worship are social necessities in Constant's view. Because change and development are permanent features of human existence, nothing must be allowed to impede growth and movement in belief or its expression.

These opinions on religion echo the recurring themes of Constant's thought—freedom to choose and to change, hatred of oppressive fixity and stasis, and an awareness of the conflict between egotism and the spirit of self-sacrifice—on which the author works such elaborate and moving variations in *Adolphe* and *Cécile*. Constant's search for self-understanding through autobiography and fiction produced works of literature that anticipate later novelists and introspectives such as Eugène Fromentin and André Gide. Constant's writings on society are of great relevance to the ongoing debate on the future of liberalism, as Sir Isaiah Berlin, Stephen Holmes, and others have shown, while his works on religion continue to provide cogent reasons for treating religious belief in its many forms with sympathy and respect.

Letters:

L'Inconnue d'Adolphe. Correspondance de Benjamin Constant et d'Anna Lindsay, edited by Baronne Constant de Rebecque (Paris: Plon, 1933);

Benjamin et Rosalie de Constant. Correspondance, 1786-1830, edited, with an introduction, by Alfred and Suzanne Roulin (Paris: Gallimard, 1955);

Benjamin Constant. Cent lettres, edited by Pierre Cordey (Lausanne: Bibliothèque romande, 1974);

Isabelle de Charrière / Belle de Zuylen, *Œuvres complètes*, 10 volumes, edited by Jean-Daniel Candaux and others (Amsterdam: G. A. van Oorschot / Geneva: Editions Slatkine, 1979-1984)—correspondence with Constant in volumes 3-6;

Correspondance générale I (1774-1792), edited by C. P. Courtney and Dennis Wood (Tübingen: Max Niemeyer Verlag, 1992).

Bibliographies:

C. P. Courtney, *A Bibliography of Editions of the Writings of Benjamin Constant to 1833* (London: Modern Humanities Research Association, 1981);

Courtney, *A Guide to the Published Works of Benjamin Constant* (Oxford: Voltaire Foundation, 1985).

Biographies:

Gustave Rudler, *La Jeunesse de Benjamin Constant, 1767-1794* (Paris: Armand Colin, 1909);

Elizabeth W. Schermerhorn, *Benjamin Constant: His Private Life and His Contribution to the Cause of Liberal Government in France, 1767-1830* (Boston & New York: Houghton Mifflin, 1924);

Harold Nicolson, *Benjamin Constant* (London: Constable, 1949);

Kurt Kloocke, *Benjamin Constant. Une biographie intellectuelle* (Geneva: Droz, 1984);

Dennis Wood, *Benjamin Constant. A Biography* (London: Routledge, 1993).

References:

Annales Benjamin Constant (Lausanne: Institut Benjamin Constant, 1980-);

Simone Balayé, "Les Degrés de l'autobiographie chez Benjamin Constant: une écriture de la crise," in *Benjamin Constant, Madame de Staël et le groupe de Coppet. Actes du deuxième congrès de Lausanne,* edited by Etienne Hofmann (Oxford: Voltaire Foundation, 1982);

Paul Bastid, *Benjamin Constant et sa doctrine* (Paris: Armand Colin, 1966);

Benjamin Constant, special issue of *Europe,* no. 467 (March 1968);

Sir Isaiah Berlin, *Four Essays on Liberty* (London: Oxford University Press, 1969);

Pierre Cordey and Jean-Luc Seylaz, eds., *Benjamin Constant. Actes du congrès de Lausanne (Octobre 1967)* (Geneva: Droz: 1968);

John Cruickshank, *Benjamin Constant* (New York: Twayne, 1974);

Pierre Deguise, *Benjamin Constant méconnu. Le livre "De la religion"* (Geneva: Droz, 1966);

Paul Delbouille, "Benjamin Constant romancier," *Annales Benjamin Constant,* 6 (1986): 1-10;

Delbouille, *Genèse, structure et destin d' "Adolphe"* (Paris: Les Belles Lettres, 1971);

Alison Fairlie, *Imagination and Language: Collected Essays on Constant, Baudelaire and Flaubert* (Cambridge: Cambridge University Press, 1981);

Eve Gonin, *Le Point de vue d'Ellénore. Une réécriture d' "Adolphe"* (Paris: José Corti, 1981);

Henri Gouhier, *Benjamin Constant* (Bruges: Desclée De Brouwer, 1967);

William W. Holdheim, *Benjamin Constant* (London: Bowes & Bowes, 1961);

Stephen Holmes, *Benjamin Constant and the Making of Modern Liberalism* (New Haven: Yale University Press, 1984);

Norman King, "Romantisme et opposition," *Romantisme,* 51 (1986): 63-71;

Georges Poulet, *Benjamin Constant par lui-même* (Paris: Editions du Seuil, 1968);

Timothy Unwin, *Constant: "Adolphe"* (London: Grant & Cutler, 1986);

Han Verhoeff, *"Adolphe" et Constant: une étude psychocritique* (Paris: Klincksieck, 1976);

Dominique Verrey, *Chronologie de la vie et de l'œuvre de Benjamin Constant,* volume 1 (1767-1805) (Geneva: Slatkine, 1992);

Dennis Wood, *Benjamin Constant: "Adolphe"* (Cambridge: Cambridge University Press, 1987).

Papers:

The Bibliothèque publique et universitaire, Neuchâtel, Switzerland, and the Bibliothèque publique et universitaire, Geneva, have important collections of Constant's correspondence. Collections of correspondence and manuscripts are located at the Bibliothèque cantonale et universitaire, Lausanne, and at the Bibliothèque Nationale, Paris.

Alexandre Dumas *père*

(24 July 1802 - 5 December 1870)

Barbara T. Cooper
University of New Hampshire

SELECTED BOOKS: *La Chasse et l'amour*, as
Davy, with Pierre-Joseph Rousseau [James
Rousseau] and Adolphe [Adolphe de
Leuven] (Paris: Duvernois, 1825);
La Noce et l'enterrement, as Davy, with [Hippolyte]
Lassagne and Gustave [Alphonse Vulpian]
(Paris: Bezou, 1826);
Nouvelles contemporaines (Paris: Sanson, 1826);
Henri III et sa cour (Paris: Vezard et Cie., 1829);
translated by Lord F. L. Gower as *Catherine
of Cleves* (London: J. Andrews, 1831);
Christine, ou Stockholm, Fontainebleau et Rome (Paris:
Barba, 1830);
*Napoléon Bonaparte, ou Trente ans de l'histoire de
France* (Paris: Tournachon-Molin, 1831);
Antony (Paris: Auguste Auffray, 1831); translated by Frederick Schwab (New York: F.
Rullman, 1880);
Charles VII chez ses grands vassaux (Paris: Lemesle
et la Veuve Béchet, 1831); translated by
Dorothy Trench-Bonnet as *Charles VII at the
Homes of His Great Vassals* (Chicago: Noble
Press, 1991);
Teresa (Paris: Charles Lemesle, Barba, Veuve
Charles Béchet, 1832);
La Tour de Nesle, by Dumas and Frédéric
Gaillardet (Paris: Barba, 1832); translated
by George Almar as *The Tower of Nesle; or,
The Chamber of Death* (London: J. Cumberland, 1832); translated by Adam L. Gowans
as *The Tower of Nesle* (London & Glasgow:
Gowans & Gray Ltd. / New York: Frederick
A. Stokes, 1906);
Gaule et France (Paris: U. Canel and Guyot,
1833); translated as *The Progress of Democracy; Illustrated in the History of Gaul and
France* (New York: J. & H. G. Langley,
1841);
Impressions de voyage: En Suisse, volume 1 (Paris:
Guyot, 1834); volume 2 (Paris: Charpentier,
1835); volumes 3-5 (Paris: Dumont, 1837);
translated by Mrs. W. R. Wilde as *The Glacier Land* (Belfast: Simms & McIntyre / London: J. W. S. Orr, 1852);

Alexandre Dumas père, *circa 1857 (photograph by Nadar)*

Chroniques de France. Isabel de Bavière, 2 volumes
(Paris: Dumont, 1835); translated by William Barrow as *Isabel of Bavaria; or, The Chronicles of France for the Reign of Charles VI* (London: Bruce & Wild, 1846);
Kean, ou Désordre et génie (Paris: Barba, 1836);
translated as *Edmund Kean, or The Genius
and the Libertine* (London: Vickers, 1847);
Le Capitaine Paul, 2 volumes (Brussels: J. Jamar /
Paris: Dumont, 1838); translated by Thomas Williams as *Captain Paul* (New York & Boston: E. P. Williams, 1846); drama entitled
Paul Jones (Paris: Marchant, 1838); translated by William Berger (Philadelphia:
T. K. & P. G. Collins, 1839);
La Comtesse de Salisbury, 6 volumes (Paris:
Dumont, 1839); translated as *The Countess of*

98

Salisbury; A Chronicle of the Order of the Garter (New York: Stringer & Townsend, 1851);

Mademoiselle de Belle-Isle (Paris: Dumont, 1839); translated by Raphael Felix (New York: Darcie & Corbyn, 1855);

L'Alchimiste (Paris: Dumont, 1839); translated by Henry Bertram Lister as *The Alchemist* (San Francisco: La Bohème Club, 1940);

Crimes célèbres, 8 volumes (Paris: Administration de librairie, 1839-1840); translated as *Celebrated Crimes* (London: Chapman & Hall, 1843);

Un Mariage sous Louis XV (Paris: Marchant, Ch. Tresse, 1841); translated by Sydney Grundy as *A Marriage of Convenience* (London: Mrs. Marshall's Type-Writing Office, 1896);

Impressions de voyage: Le Midi de la France, 3 volumes (Paris: Dumont, 1841); translated as *Pictures of Travel in the South of France* (London: Offices of the National Illustrated Library, n.d.);

Une Année à Florence, 2 volumes (Paris: Dumont, 1841);

Excursions sur les bords du Rhin, 3 volumes (Paris: Dumont, 1841);

Le Chevalier d'Harmental, 4 volumes (Paris: Dumont, 1842); translated by P. F. Christin and Eugene Lies as *The Chevalier d'Harmental; or, Love and Conspiracy* (New York: Harper, 1846); original adapted as a drama (Paris: Cadot, 1849);

Le Speronare, 4 volumes (Paris: Dumont, 1842); translated by Katharine Prescott Wormeley as *Journeys with Dumas; The Speronara* (Boston: Little, Brown & Co., 1902);

Le Capitaine Aréna, 2 volumes (Paris: Dolin, 1842);

Georges, 3 volumes (Paris: Dumont, 1843); translated by G. J. Knox as *George; or The Planter of the Isle of France* (Belfast: Simms & McIntyre / London: J. W. S. Orr, 1846);

Les Demoiselles de Saint-Cyr (Paris: Marchant, 1843); translated as *The Ladies of Saint-Cyr. Or, The Runaway Husbands* (London: Thos. Hailes Lacy, 1870);

Le Corricolo, 4 volumes (Paris: Dolin, 1843); translated by A. Roland as *Sketches of Naples* (Philadelphia: E. Ferrett, 1845);

Sylvandire, 3 volumes (Paris: Dumont, 1844); translated as *Sylvandire; or, The Disputed Inheritance* (New York: Harper, 1846);

Cécile, 2 volumes (Paris: Dumont, 1844); also published as *La Robe de noces* (Brussels: Méline Cans et Cie., 1844); translated by Eug.

Plunkette as *Cecilia; or, Woman's Love* (New York: Jarrett, 1846);

Le Château d'Eppstein, 3 volumes (Paris: L. de Potter, 1844); translated as *The Spectre-Mother; or, Love after Death* (London: C. H. Clarke, 1864); translated by Alfred Allinson as *The Castle of Eppstein* (London: Methuen, 1903);

Fernande, 3 volumes (Paris: Dumont, 1844); translated as *Fernande; or, The Fallen Angel. A Story of Life in Paris* (New York: Stringer & Townsend, 1849);

Les Trois Mousquetaires, 8 volumes (Paris: Baudry, 1844); translated as *The Three Musketeers* (London: G. Vickers, 1846); translated by William Barrow as *The Three Musketeers; or, The Feats and Fortunes of a Gascon Adventurer* (London: Bruce & Wyld, 1846); translated by Park Benjamin as *The Three Guardsmen* (Baltimore: Taylor, Wilde, 1846);

Une Fille du régent, 3 volumes (Brussels: Méline Cans et Cie., 1844); 4 volumes (Paris: Cadot, 1845); translated by Charles H. Town as *The Regent's Daughter* (New York: Harper, 1845); original adapted as a drama (Paris: Marchant, 1846);

Le Comte de Monte-Cristo, 18 volumes (Paris: Pétion, 1844-1845); translated as *The Count of Monte-Cristo* (London: Chapman & Hall, 1846); original adapted as a drama (Paris: Tresse, 1848);

La Bouillie de la comtesse Berthe (Paris: J. Hetzel, 1845); translated as *Good Lady Bertha's Honey Broth* (London: Chapman & Hall, 1846); translated by Mrs. Cooke Taylor as *The Honey Stew of Lady Bertha* (London: Jeremiah How, 1846);

Les Frères corses, 2 volumes (Paris: Souverain, 1845); translated by a pupil of Mons. G. J. Sanders as *The Corsican Brothers* (Philadelphia: G. B. Zieber, 1845);

La Reine Margot, 6 volumes (Paris: Garnier frères, 1845); translated as *Marguerite de Valois* (London: David Bogue, 1846); translated by Frederick Gilbert as *Queen Margot; or, Marguerite de Valois* (London: John Dicks, 1885); original adapted as a drama by Dumas and Auguste Maquet (Paris: Michel Lévy, 1847);

Vingt ans après, 10 volumes (Paris: Baudry, 1845); translated by William Barrow as *Twenty Years After; or, The Further Feats and Fortunes of a Gascon Adventurer* (London: Bruce & Wyld, 1846);

La Guerre des femmes, 8 volumes (Paris: L. de Potter, 1845-1846); translated by Samuel

Springer as *The War of Women; or, Rivalry in Love* (New York: Stringer & Townsend, 1850); original adapted as a drama (Paris: Cadot, 1849);

Le Chevalier de Maison-Rouge, 6 volumes (Paris: Cadot, 1845-1846); translated as *Marie Antoinette; or, The Chevalier of the Red House* (London: G. Peirce, 1846); translated by Henry Wm. Herbert as *Genevieve; or, The Chevalier of Maison Rouge* (New York: Williams, 1846); original adapted as a drama, *Le Chevalier de Maison-Rouge, épisode du temps des Girondins* (Paris: M. Lévy, 1847); translated by Colin Hazlewood as *The Chevalier of the Maison Rouge; or, The Days of Terror!* (London: Thos. Hailes Lacy, 1859);

La Dame de Monsoreau, 8 volumes (Paris: Pétion, 1846); translated as *Diana of Meridor; or, The Lady of Monsoreau* (New York: Williams Bros., 1846); translated as *Chicot, the Jester* (London: Thos. Hodgson, 1857); original adapted as a drama (Paris: M. Lévy frères, 1860);

Les Deux Diane, 10 volumes (Paris: Cadot, 1846-1847); translated by Eug. Plunkett as *The Two Dianas: or, The Son of a Count and the Daughter of a King* (New York: Williams Bros., 1848); original adapted as a drama (Paris: Librairie internationale, 1865);

Le Bâtard de Mauléon, 9 volumes (Paris: Cadot, 1846-1847); translated as *The Bastard of Mauléon* (London: E. Appleyard, 1848); translated by L. Lawford as *The Half Brothers, or The Head and the Hand* (London: G. Routledge, 1858);

Mémoires d'un médecin: Joseph Balsamo, 19 volumes (Paris: Cadot, 1846-1848); translated as *The Memoirs of a Physician* (London: Thos. Hodgson, 1848);

De Paris à Cadix, 5 volumes (Paris: Garnier frères, 1847-1848);

Les Quarante-Cinq, 10 volumes (Paris: Cadot, 1847-1848); translated as *The Forty-Five Guardsmen* (London: E. Appleyard, 1848);

Le Vicomte de Bragelonne, ou Dix ans plus tard, 26 volumes (Paris: Michel Lévy frères, 1848-1850); translated as *The Vicomte de Bragelonne; or, Ten Years Later* (London: G. Routledge, 1857);

Le Véloce, ou Tanger, Alger et Tunis, 4 volumes (Paris: Cadot, 1848-1851); translated by Richard Meade Bache as *Tales of Algeria, or Life Among the Arabs* (Philadelphia: Claxton, Remsen & Heffelfinger, 1868);

Le Collier de la reine, 11 volumes (Paris: Cadot, 1849-1850); translated as *The Queen's Necklace; or The Secret History of the Court of Louis XVI* (New York: W. F. Burgess, 1850; Philadelphia: T. B. Peterson & Bros., 1853);

Les mille et un fantômes, une journée à Fontenay-aux-Roses, 2 volumes (Paris: Cadot, 1849); translated by Alfred Allinson as *Tales of the Supernatural* (London: Methuen, 1907);

La Femme au collier de velours, 2 volumes (Paris: Cadot, 1850); translated by Mary Stuart Smith as *The Woman with the Velvet Necklace* (New York: Geo. Munro's Sons, 1897);

La Tulipe noire, 3 volumes (Paris: Baudry, 1850); translated by Fayette Robinson as *The Black Tulip* (New York: W. F. Burgess, 1850);

Ange Pitou, 8 volumes (Paris: Cadot, 1851); translated by Thomas Williams as *Six Years Later; or, The Taking of the Bastille* (Philadelphia: T. B. Peterson, 1851); translated as *Ange Pitou, or The Taking of the Bastille* (New York: President & MacIntyre, 1859);

Olympe de Clèves, 9 volumes (Brussels: A. Lebègue, 1851-1852; Paris: Cadot, 1852); translated in two parts by H. L. Williams, Jr., as *Olympia of Cleves; or, The Loves of a King of France* and *The Count of Mailly* (Philadelphia: F. A. Brady, 1864);

Mes Mémoires. Souvenirs de 1830 à 1842, 22 volumes (Paris: Cadot, 1852-1854); translated by E. M. Waller as *My Memoirs* (London: Methuen, 1907-1909);

La Comtesse de Charny, 19 volumes (Paris: Cadot, 1852-1855); translated as *The Countess de Charny; or, The Fall of the French Monarchy* (Philadelphia: T. B. Peterson, 1853);

Isaac Laquedem, 2 volumes (Paris: Marchant, 1853); translated (New York: Bunnell & Price, 1853);

Ingénue, 7 volumes (Paris: Cadot, 1853-1855); translated by Julie de Marguerittes as *Ingénue; or, The First Days of Blood* (Philadelphia: Lippincott, Grambo, 1855);

Les Mohicans de Paris, 19 volumes (Paris: Cadot, 1854-1855); translated as *The Mohicans of Paris* (Philadelphia: T. B. Peterson & Bros., 1859); original adapted as a drama (Paris: Michel Lévy, 1864);

Le Meneur de loups, 3 volumes (Paris: Cadot, 1857); translated by Allinson as *The Wolf-Leader* (London: Methuen, 1904);

Les Compagnons de Jéhu, 7 volumes (Paris: Cadot, 1857-1858); translated in two parts as *Royalists and Republicans; or, the Companions of Jehu* and *The Guillotine: or, the Death of Morgan* (London: E. D. Long, 1861); original adapted as a drama (Paris: Beck, 1857);

Le Capitaine Richard, 3 volumes (Paris: Cadot, 1858); translated as *The Twin Captains* (London: C. H. Clarke, 1861); translated by H. L. Williams as *The Twin Lieutenants; or, The Soldier's Bride* (Philadelphia: T. B. Peterson & Bros., 1862);

Black, 4 volumes (Paris: Cadot, 1858); translated by Alma Blakeman Jones as *Black, The Story of a Dog* (New York: Croscup / London: Dent & Sons, 1895);

Contes pour les grands et les petits enfants, 2 volumes (Brussels: Méline Cans et Cie., 1859);

Les Louves de Machecoul, épisodes de la guerre de Vendée en 1832, by Dumas and G. de Cherville, 10 volumes (Paris: Cadot, 1859); translated in two parts by Henry L. Williams as *The Royalist Daughters* and *The Castle of Souday* (New York: Dick & Fitzgerald, 1862); translated as *The She-Wolves of Machecoul* and *The Last Vendée* (New York: Geo. Munro's Sons, 1894);

Le Caucase (Paris: Librairie Théâtrale, 1859);

La Route de Varennes (Paris: Michel Lévy frères, 1860);

De Paris à Astrakan, 3 volumes (Paris: A. Bourdillart, 1860); revised as *Impressions de voyage: En Russie*, 4 volumes (Paris: Lévy frères, 1865); extracts translated as *Celebrated Crimes of the Russian Court* (London: Hurst & Blackett, 1906);

Causeries, 2 volumes (Paris: Lévy frères, 1860; enlarged edition, Paris: Calmann Lévy, 1885);

Bric-à-brac, 2 volumes (Paris: Michel Lévy frères, 1861);

Les Garibaldiens, révolution de Sicile et de Naples (Paris: Michel Lévy frères, 1861); translated by Edmund Routledge as *The Garibaldians in Sicily* (London: Routledge, Warne, Routledge, 1861);

I Borboni di Napoli, 10 volumes (Naples: 1862-1864);

Le Volontaire de '92, in *Le Monte-Cristo*, second series (25 April 1862 - 3 October 1862) and *Le Mousquetaire*, second series (23 February 1867 - 11 March 1867); translated as *Love and Liberty; or, A Man of the People* (Philadelphia: T. B. Peterson & Bros., 1874); republished as *Les Mémoires de René Besson, témoin de la Révolution* (Paris: Editions Champflour, 1989);

Portrait of Dumas as a young man

Le Comte de Moret (New York: Mareil, 1866); translated by H. L. Williams, Jr., as *The Count of Moret; or, Richelieu and His Rivals* (Philadelphia: Peterson Bros., 1868);

Histoire de mes bêtes (Paris: Michel Lévy frères, 1867); translated by Allinson as *My Pets* (London: Methuen & Co., 1909);

Une Aventure d'amour (Paris: Michel Lévy, 1867);

Les Blancs et les bleus, 3 volumes (Paris: Lévy, 1867-1868); translated by Wormeley as *The First Republic; or, The Whites and the Blues* (London: Sampson Low, Marston & Co., 1895); original adapted as a drama (Paris: Michel Lévy, 1874);

La Terreur prussienne, 2 volumes (Paris: Michel Lévy frères, 1868); translated by R. S. Garnett as *The Prussian Terror* (London: Stanley Paul, 1915);

Souvenirs dramatiques, 2 volumes (Paris: Michel Lévy frères, 1868); republished as *Souvenirs dramatiques et littéraires* (Paris: Tallandier, 1928);

Création et rédemption, 4 volumes (Paris: Michel Lévy frères, 1872)—contains *Le Docteur mystérieux* and *La Fille du marquis*;

Grand Dictionnaire de cuisine (Paris: Lemerre, 1873); translated by A. & J. Davidson as *Dumas on Food. Selections from "Le Grand Dictionnaire de cuisine"* (Charlottesville: University of Virginia Press, 1982; New York & London: Oxford University Press, 1987);

Propos d'art et de cuisine (Paris: Michel Lévy frères, 1877).

Collections: *Œuvres complètes d'Alexandre Dumas. Théâtre*, 6 volumes (Paris: Charpentier, 1834-1836; revised edition, Paris: C. Gosselin, 1841);

Théâtre d'Alexandre Dumas. Œuvres nouvelles, 3 volumes (Paris: Passard, 1846);

Œuvres complètes d'Alexandre Dumas, 17 volumes (Paris: Bureau du Siècle, 1850-1857);

Œuvres complètes d'Alexandre Dumas, 225 volumes (Paris: Michel Lévy frères, 1860-1865);

Théâtre complet d'Alexandre Dumas, 15 volumes (Paris: Michel Lévy, 1863-1874);

Œuvres complètes (Paris: C. Lévy, 1869-1889);

Œuvres complètes, 38 volumes, edited by Gilbert Sigaux (Lausanne: Editions Rencontre, 1962-1967);

Théâtre complet, edited by Fernande Bassan (Paris: Lettres Modernes-Minard, 1974-   );

Préludes poétiques, edited by Claude Schopp (Paris: Editions Champflour, 1989).

PLAY PRODUCTIONS: *Henri III et sa cour*, Paris, Théâtre-Français, 10 February 1829;

Antony, Paris, Théâtre de la Porte-Saint-Martin, 3 May 1831;

La Tour de Nesle, by Dumas and Frédéric Gaillardet, Paris, Théâtre de la Porte-Saint-Martin, 29 May 1832;

Kean, Paris, Théâtre des Variétés, 31 August 1836;

Paul Jones, Paris, Théâtre du Panthéon, 8 October 1838;

Mademoiselle de Belle-Isle, Paris, Théâtre-Français, 2 April 1839;

Un Mariage sous Louis XV, Paris, Théâtre-Français, 1 June 1841;

Les Demoiselles de Saint-Cyr, Paris, Théâtre-Français, 25 July 1843;

La Reine Margot, by Dumas and Auguste Maquet, Paris, Théâtre-Historique, 20 February 1847.

OTHER: Marceline Desbordes-Valmore, *Les Pleurs*, preface by Dumas (Paris: Charpentier, 1833);

William Shakespeare, *Hamlet, prince de Danemark*, translated by Dumas and Paul Meurice (Paris: M. Lévy, 1847);

Mémoires de J.-F. Talma, edited and compiled by Dumas (Paris: Souverain, 1849-1850);

Mémoires de Garibaldi, translated by Dumas (Paris: Michel Lévy, 1860); translated by William Robson as *Garibaldi, An Autobiography*, edited by Dumas (London: Routledge, Warne, Routledge, 1860).

SELECTED PERIODICAL PUBLICATIONS: *La Psyché*, March 1826 - January 1830;

Le Mois, March 1848 - February 1850;

Le Mousquetaire, November 1853 - February 1857; November 1866 - April 1867;

Le Monte-Cristo, April 1857 - May 1860; January 1862 - October 1862;

L'Indépendant/L'Indipendente, October 1860 - May 1861; May 1862 - March 1864;

Le D'Artagnan, February 1868 - July 1868;

Théâtre-Journal, July 1868 - March 1869.

Despite their unflagging worldwide popularity, their perennial availability, and their innumerable cinematographic adaptations, the works of Alexandre Dumas *père* have been largely unappreciated by critics. There has been, for some time now, a specialized journal devoted to Dumas studies, and articles on Dumas have regularly appeared in other scholarly publications. Still, a rapid comparison between the immense bibliography generated by the writings of Charles Baudelaire—whose total literary output, when measured in quantitative terms, is utterly dwarfed by that of Dumas—and the paucity of critical literature devoted to Dumas's writings affords a reasonably accurate means to gauge the place Dumas occupies in today's literary pantheon. Equally telling is the fact that Dumas's novels and plays receive scant attention in the standard histories of nineteenth-century French literature and are rarely found on lists of required reading at French or American universities. There appear to be several reasons for this gap between Dumas's mass appeal and his lack of scholarly or institutional status.

First, as is the case for many of his contemporaries, most notably Honoré de Balzac and George Sand, the enormous size of Dumas's opus and a fascination with his personal life have, from the very beginning, proved a handicap to Dumas's prestige in intellectual circles. To be sure, much of the early preoccupation with Dumas's debts and mistresses has given way to serious biographical and literary-historical research and a few broadly interpretative analyses. To date, however, critical commentary on Dumas's works has tended to focus on a limited number of texts, and scholars have yet to come to terms with Dumas's astonishing productivity.

Throughout his long career, Dumas wrote works in virtually every literary genre, sometimes publishing two or more novels simultaneously in serial form. From the nineteenth century to the present, critics have tended to be suspicious of *la démesure* (excessiveness), and they will often dismiss as facile and unworthy of respect any author who writes a great deal. That attitude is quite apparent in the imaginary conversation Delphine de Girardin included in one of her *Lettres parisiennes* (Parisian Letters, 5 May 1845) to explain why Dumas, like Balzac, failed to get elected to the French Academy: "MM. de Balzac et Alexandre Dumas écrivent quinze à dix-huit volumes par an, on ne peut pas leur pardonner ça.—Mais ces romans sont excellents.—Ce n'est pas une excuse, ils sont trop nombreux.—Mais ils ont un succès fou.—C'est un tort de plus: qu'ils en écrivent un seul tout petit, médiocre, que personne ne le lise, et on verra. Un trop fort bagage est un empêchement à l'Académie, la consigne est la même qu'au jardin des Tuileries; on ne laisse point passer ceux qui ont de trop gros paquets" (Messrs. Balzac and Alexandre Dumas write fifteen to eighteen volumes a year, one can't forgive them for that.—But they are excellent novels.—That's no excuse, there are too many of them.—But they are wildly successful.—That's one more thing to hold against them: let them write a single, slim, mediocre volume, let no one read it, and then we'll see. Too much baggage is an impediment to admission to the Academy, where the orders are the same as at the Tuileries Garden; those who carry oversize packages are not allowed inside).

Of course, even working twelve to fourteen hours a day as he did, Dumas alone could not have produced the more than three hundred titles that he published during his lifetime. This accounts for the second factor that appears to have detracted from Dumas's critical stature: namely, his use of collaborators. "Dumas n'a pas l'imagination inventive, mais combinatoire" (Dumas does not have the kind of imagination that invents things, but one that puts things together), writes one of his more recent biographers, Claude Schopp. Schopp goes on to suggest that,

with the possible exception of Auguste Maquet, most of the author's collaborators contributed little more than the initial idea for a work, which Dumas then developed and wrote by himself. Still, at least since the time when the Romantics redefined literary genius in terms of originality and individuality, literary critics have been reluctant to accord a place of prominence to authors who, like Dumas, rely on collaborators to help them research and develop their texts.

In Dumas's case the matter is further complicated by the fact that his collaborators' contributions were not always publicly acknowledged and that their names were not always printed on the theater bill or the title page of a text. This occasionally led to confusion in matters of attribution and at times prompted legal disputes over matters of literary property. As a result—and even though Dumas's collaborators, when writing on their own, almost never achieved the success they were to know when working with him—critics have generally balked at assigning Dumas a central place in French letters. Close study of Dumas's opus and of letters to and from his collaborators might have set this issue to rest were it not for a third factor that is often cited to explain his exclusion from the canon: his "nonliterariness."

There are those who, like Michel Picard, would argue that while Dumas's writings are engaging and even seductive, they do not display the characteristics of serious literature. A Dumas text reads so easily, contends Picard, that one is not even conscious of reading it; it operates "comme une véritable machine à décerveler" (in such a way as to deprive the reader of the capacity to think). Behind this and other attempts to denigrate the "pleasures of the text" (the phrase is Roland Barthes's) lies the belief that "real" literature is defined by its complexities. There are, no doubt, works that are more aesthetically self-conscious than Dumas's. It would, however, be a mistake to conclude that texts which reinvent and recount four centuries of French history are artlessly composed and innocent of meaning or that characters whose passions and ambitions have so enthralled generations of readers are psychologically flat.

Dumas expressed his own simultaneously boastful and modest view of his place in nineteenth-century French letters when he wrote to Napoleon III in August 1864 that he, along with Victor Hugo and Alphonse de Lamartine, were the preeminent French writers of the day, just as they had been in 1830. "Quoi que je sois le moins digne des trois," he observed, "ils [mes douze cents volumes] m'ont fait, dans les cinq parties du monde, le plus populaire des trois, peut-être parce que l'un est un penseur, l'autre un rêveur, et que je ne suis, moi, qu'un vulgarisateur" (Although I am the least worthy of the three, [my twelve hundred volumes] have made me the most popular of the three on all five continents, perhaps because one is a thinker, the other a dreamer, and I am only a popularizer).

Popularizer though he may have been, Dumas was not and should not be regarded as merely the author of entertaining adventure novels for adolescents. He considered himself a historian, and he believed that his works, with their reappearing characters and their broad chronological scope, might accurately be compared to those of Balzac. Thus he wrote in *Les Compagnons de Jéhu* (1857-1858; translated in two parts as *Royalists and Republicans; or, the Companions of Jehu* and *The Guillotine: or, the Death of Morgan*, 1861) that "Balzac a fait une grande et belle œuvre à cent faces, intitulée *La Comédie humaine*. Notre œuvre à nous, commencée en même temps que la sienne, mais que nous ne qualifions pas, bien entendu, peut s'intituler *Le Drame de la France*" (Balzac wrote a vast and beautiful work with a hundred sides to it entitled *The Human Comedy*. Begun at the same time as his, our work, which we shall of course refrain from characterizing in any way, might be called *The Drama of France*). In the end, though, no collective title ever became attached to Dumas's works, perhaps because his writings could not be subsumed under any single heading, however broadly defined. The author of novels and plays, short stories and fantastic tales, travel writings and memoirs, newspaper articles and recipes, Dumas chronicled the political experiences and personal adventures of innumerable real and imagined characters across the ages.

The view of Dumas as the "French Walter Scott," based as it is on a series of novels written from the mid 1840s to the mid 1850s, is likewise reductionist in nature. Although Dumas may be particularly remembered as the author of historical romances, when those works began appearing, he was already famous for such plays as *Henri III et sa cour* (1829; translated as *Catherine of Cleves*, 1831), *Antony* (1831; translated, 1880), *La Tour de Nesle* (1832; translated as *The Tower of Nesle; or, The Chamber of Death*, 1832), *Kean, ou Désordre et génie* (1836; translated as *Edmund*

Mlle Mars (Anne Boutet) in costume as the duchesse de Guise in Dumas's Henri III et sa cour

Kean, or The Genius and the Libertine, 1847), and *Mademoiselle de Belle-Isle* (1839; translated, 1855). It is important to remember, too, that Dumas never abandoned his career as a playwright, although once his success as a novelist was confirmed, he came increasingly to adapt his novels for the stage rather than to write original pieces for the theater.

Dumas's journalistic activity, whether as a contributor or as a publisher, likewise spanned his entire career. An inveterate traveler throughout his adult life, Dumas, like so many other nineteenth-century French writers, regularly turned his journeys to profit, often publishing his impressions of the people and places he had visited in the press before collecting them in a volume. And, again like many of his contemporaries, in works such as *Mes Mémoires* (1852-1854; translated as *My Memoirs*, 1907-1909) and the utterly charming if less consequential *Histoire de mes bêtes* (1867; translated as *My Pets*, 1909), Dumas transformed his life into autobiographical fictions more or less faithful to fact.

Alexandre Dumas was born on 24 July 1802 at 46, rue de Lormet (today rue Alexandre-Dumas) in Villers-Cotterêts (Aisne). His father, Thomas-Alexandre Dumas Davy de la Pailleterie—born in Haiti (then known as Saint-Domingue) to the Marquis Antoine-Alexandre Davy de la Pailleterie, a minor Norman nobleman, and to Marie-Céssette Dumas, a black slavewoman—had risen to the rank of general in the revolutionary army. His mother, Marie-Louise-Elisabeth Labouret, was the daughter of Claude Labouret, an innkeeper and the head of the local militia unit in Villers-Cotterêts, where he and his wife, née Marie-Josephe Prévost, had both been born. Dumas's parents met when Thomas-Alexandre, a young dragoon who had dropped the *Davy de la Pailleterie* from his name when he entered the service, was billeted at the Labouret family inn in August 1789. The couple was married in Villers-Cotterêts on 28 November 1792 and subsequently had three children: Alexandrine-Aimée (called Aimée), born in September 1793; Louise-Alexandrine, who lived for only one year following her birth in February 1796; and Alexandre, born a few months prior to his father's involuntary retirement from active duty. The infant Alexandre was baptized in the local church on 12 August 1802 with his maternal grandfather and his sister Aimée serving as godparents.

Unsuccessful in his attempts to collect either back pay for the time he spent as a prisoner of war in Naples (1799-1801) or retirement benefits, General Dumas and his family lived in straitened circumstances. The general's health, which had declined during his detention in Italy, continued to fail, and he died on 26 February 1806 at the Hôtel de l'Epée in Villers-Cotterêts. In his *Mémoires*, published more than forty years later, Dumas would recall his deep affection and admiration for this gentle, Herculean father whose image remained vivid in his mind. It is likely, however, that this image is only slightly more real than that of the many father figures in Dumas's fictional works.

Despite her growing economic difficulties, from 1811 to 1813 Mme Dumas sent her son to study at the elementary school that the abbé Louis-Chrisostome Grégoire had opened in Villers-Cotterêts in 1810. An indifferent student, Dumas learned Latin, penmanship (at which he excelled), and reading from the abbé. He showed little talent for the mathematics lessons dispensed by Jean-Baptiste Oblet and the violin lessons of Antoine-Nicolas Hiraux. Dumas would later come to realize how poorly educated he was and would work to fill in the gaps in his studies. He would also transform his boyhood experience as a student in Villers-Cotterêts into the stuff of fiction, using it as the basis for his description of the titular character's education in the novel *Ange Pitou* (1851; translated as *Six Years Later; or, The Taking of the Bastille*, 1851).

In November 1814 Mme Dumas, whose repeated and increasingly desperate requests for payment of her husband's military pension had fallen on deaf ears, was granted instead a license to open a tobacconist's shop. From 1814 to 1822 she lived with her son above her shop on the Place de la Fontaine in Villers-Cotterêts and earned only a meager income. It seems reasonable to assume that the ingratitude and indifference with which his father's (and later also his own) services were rewarded by the government colored Dumas's views of most political regimes. What is certain is that the rich and powerful characters who people Dumas's novels and plays only belatedly and begrudgingly recompense those who have served them, if at all.

In 1816 Mme Dumas decided that since her son was no longer in school, it was time for him to find a job. Thus, in August of that year Alexandre began working as an errand boy in the office of *Maître* Mennesson, a family friend and the local notary. Hired to run legal documents out to area farmers unable to come to town to sign them, Dumas often took time out to go hunting rather than attend promptly to his duties. His lifelong passion for hunting and his intimate knowledge of the forest would later provide the raw materials for masterful descriptions of animals, woods, and sporting scenes in works as different as *La Reine Margot* (1845; translated as *Marguerite de Valois*, 1846) and *Le Meneur de loups* (1857; translated as *The Wolf-Leader*, 1904), to name only those two. Likewise, the game that the adolescent Dumas used to supplement the family's income and diet would become the object of many of the recipes in *Histoire de mes bêtes* and the posthumously published *Grand*

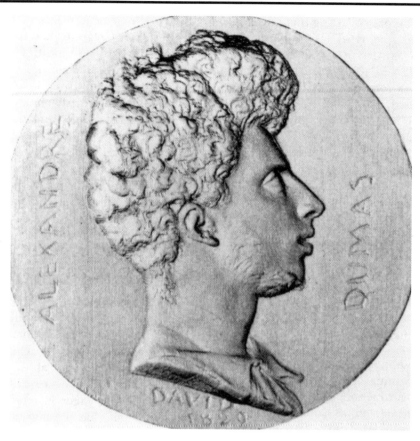

Medallion of Dumas at age twenty-seven, by David d'Angers (Musée Carnavalet)

Dictionnaire de cuisine (1873; translated as *Dumas on Food*, 1982).

The year 1819 was marked by several significant events. On 27 June, Dumas met Adolphe Ribbing de Leuven, a young Swedish nobleman who spent part of his time in Villers-Cotterêts and the rest in Paris. Destined to become a lifelong friend and occasional literary collaborator, Leuven stimulated Dumas's love of the theater. Through Leuven, Dumas would meet others who helped determine his career. In September, after months of secret meetings, the nineteen-year-old Aglaé Tellier became the first of Dumas's many mistresses. Their liaison would last three years. In October, Dumas attended a performance of Jean-François Ducis's 1769 adaptation of *Hamlet* in Soissons and was so overwhelmed by the experience that he purchased a copy of the text and learned the lead role by heart. When Leuven returned from a five-month stay in Paris in March 1820, he and Dumas collaborated on two vaudevilles and a drama: "Le Major de Strasbourg" (The Major from Strasbourg), "Un dîner d'amis" (A Dinner with Friends), and "Les Abencérages" (The Abencérages). No trace remains of any of

these early pieces, which the authors tried, unsuccessfully, to have produced in Paris.

From August to November 1822 Dumas lived in Crépy-en-Valois, where he had a job as a second clerk in the office of the notary *Maître* Lefèvre. A brief trip to Paris in early November, made without his employer's consent, not only afforded Dumas the opportunity to meet François-Joseph Talma, the great French tragedian whose *Mémoires* he would edit in 1849 and 1850, but also resulted in his dismissal from his post.

The family's financial circumstances were such that Dumas could not long remain without work. Thus, during the last days of March 1823, the young man once again left for Paris, where he contacted some of his father's former comrades-in-arms in the hope that they would help him to find a job. After he had been rebuffed, it was only thanks to Gen. Maximilien Foy's last-minute discovery of Dumas's fine penmanship that the youth obtained a position on Louis-Philippe, Duc d'Orléans's secretarial staff. Following a brief trip home to collect some possessions, Dumas returned to Paris on 8 April and rented a room in a building at 1, place des

Italiens (today Place Boïeldieu), where he lived until 20 February 1824.

On 10 April 1823 Dumas began working in offices in the Palais-Royal for an annual salary of twelve hundred francs. There, under the supervision of Jacques-Parfait Oudard, the young man copied correspondence to be sent out under official signature. Oudard's assistant, Hippolyte Lassagne, soon befriended Dumas and undertook his literary education. He furnished him with a list of readings including works by classical and modern dramatists and poets as well as the writings of novelists and memorialists. A chance meeting with Charles Nodier at an 1823 performance of Nodier's play *Le Vampire* led Dumas to become a regular at the Arsenal librarian's literary salon. Dumas grew extremely fond of Nodier and eventually used the older man's boyhood experiences during the French Revolution in books such as *Les Blancs et les bleus* (1867-1868; translated as *The First Republic; or, The Whites and the Blues*, 1895).

In August 1823 Dumas moved in with a seamstress named Marie-Catherine-Laure Labay, whose lodgings were across the hall from his. In February 1824 Mme Dumas arrived in Paris, where she shared an apartment with her son at 53, rue du Faubourg-Saint-Denis. Dumas continued seeing Laure, however, and on 27 July 1824 she gave birth, out of wedlock, to an infant she named Alexandre after his father. Dumas did not legally recognize the child until March 1831, when he and Laure were engaged in a battle over the custody of the boy.

In March 1825 Dumas, Leuven, and James Rousseau wrote a one-act vaudeville, *La Chasse et l'amour* (Hunting and Love), which was performed at the Théâtre de l'Ambigu-Comique on 22 September 1825 and was published the same year under the names Davy (Dumas), Pierre-Joseph Rousseau, and Adolphe (de Leuven). Dumas was reprimanded by Oudard, who insisted that the young man stop wasting his time writing literature and attend to his office duties, but he paid no attention to this advice, and in February 1826 he, Leuven, and the printer L.-P. Sétier founded and managed a poetry review named the *Psyché*, which appeared from March 1826 until January 1830. Dumas published many of his own poems in this review, the first of several newspaper ventures he would undertake during his lifetime. A second vaudeville, *La Noce et l'enterrement* (The Wedding and the Burial), written in collaboration with Lassagne and Alphonse

Vulpian, opened at the Théâtre de la Porte-Saint-Martin on 21 November 1826 and was published the same year.

On 3 June 1827 Dumas met Mélanie Waldor, a minor poetess who presided over her father's literary salon. The wife of François-Joseph Waldor, a military officer stationed in Thionville, Mélanie became Dumas's mistress on 22 September. Ambitious for her lover, she encouraged Dumas to try his hand at more noble dramatic genres. Their relationship, which lasted until February 1831, would later become the basis for Dumas's play *Antony*.

On 11 September 1827 Dumas attended a performance of *Hamlet* by a visiting troupe of English actors (including Fanny Kemble, Edmund Kean, William Charles Macready, and Harriet Smithson); deeply moved by the experience, he began studying the play-writing techniques of William Shakespeare, Johann Wolfgang von Goethe, Friedrich von Schiller, Pierre Corneille, Molière, and Pedro Calderón de la Barca. These dramatic studies began to bear fruit once Dumas was transferred to the duc d'Orléans's forestry office in February 1828 and was allowed to work on a five-act verse tragedy, *Christine à Fontainebleau*, after he had completed his regular assignments. The play was accepted at the Théâtre-Français on 4 August 1828. Rehearsed, it was never performed, despite the *tour de faveur* (priority status) the play was granted on 12 September.

In the meantime, in the space of two months, Dumas had written a five-act historical drama in prose, *Henri III et sa cour*. This second play was accepted for performance at the Théâtre-Français on 17 October. The *tour de faveur* for *Christine* passed to *Henri III* on 25 October, and rehearsals for the play began immediately. Because Dumas neglected his work to attend rehearsals, he was forced to choose between his job and his play. He chose the latter. The piece opened on 10 February 1829 with the duc d'Orléans and his dinner guests in attendance. With François Firmin in the role of Saint-Mégrin and Mlle Mars (Anne Boutet) as the duchesse de Guise, the play was a triumph; it was published two weeks later.

The success of *Henri III et sa cour* marked not only the true beginning of Dumas's literary career but also a turning point in the history of French drama. With this play, the decorous, language-centered representations of events typical of French neoclassical tragedy began to give way to the dynamic, action-centered re-creations of events characteristic of Romantic drama. Dumas's piece, which was warmly praised by the partisans of romanticism and roundly condemned by the defenders of neoclassicism, made ample use of local color and spectacle. In the preface to his text, Dumas claimed that he was not interested in illustrating any dramatic theory. He would later reiterate his distaste for theory in the preface to the 1863 edition of another play, *Charles VII chez ses grands vassaux* (Charles VII amid His Principal Vassals, 1831), where he wrote: "Le théâtre est, avant tout, chose de fantaisie; je ne comprends donc pas qu'on l'emprisonne dans un système" (Theater is, above all, a thing of the imagination; I cannot therefore understand [why] people imprison it in a system).

Inspired by passages from Louis-Pierre d'Anquetil's *L'Esprit de la Ligue* (The Spirit of the League, 1767) and Pierre de L'Estoile's *Mémoires pour servir à l'histoire de France* (Memoirs Intended to Serve as a Basis for the History of France, 1719), *Henri III et sa cour* is set in July 1578, at a time when Henri III's royal powers were being challenged from several quarters. The Queen Mother, Catherine de Médicis, who feels her influence over her son and over matters of state to be threatened as much by the political ambitions of the duc de Guise as by the affection Henri bears the handsome and noble courtier Saint-Mégrin, strives to weaken or destroy both men. Using the duchesse de Guise (née Catherine de Clèves) as a pawn, she adroitly provokes a series of confrontations between the duke and the king's favorite that exacerbates the sentimental and political rivalry that exists between them. In the end, after Saint-Mégrin is assassinated and Guise loses control over the Holy League, Henri's rule and his mother's power are (temporarily) set on firm ground.

This play includes many elements Dumas would use again in other dramas and novels: a compelling if broadly sketched picture of a society in the midst of a political conflict; real people and places used as a backdrop for an invented tale of passion and ambition; masterful dialogues coupled with powerfully dramatic conclusions; unhappy lovers, at least one of whom dies a spectacular death; a practitioner of some (pseudo-) scientific profession; characters who jump out of windows or use secret passages; women who are portrayed either as angels or devils, and men whose friendships are at least as powerful as love, if not more so. Written without the help of

a collaborator, *Henri III et sa cour* marks the first real flowering of Dumas's artistic talent and unmistakably sets in place many of the most readily identifiable characteristics of his aesthetic.

With the money he earned from *Henri III*, Dumas moved to 25, rue de l'Université, where he lived from 1829 to 1831. Though suddenly a successful playwright, he nonetheless resumed working for the duc d'Orléans, and on 20 June 1829 he was assigned a position as assistant librarian at the Palais-Royal. On 30 March 1830 a revised version of *Christine* opened at the Odéon, where it met with only limited success. In July, Dumas participated in the Revolution of 1830. He describes this tumultuous period in his *Mémoires*, highlighting in particular his seizure of an arsenal in Soisson. In mid October Dumas resigned his librarian's position after a quarrel with the duc d'Orléans (now King Louis-Philippe) over a report on the state of political sentiment in the Vendée. The knowledge he acquired during his extended journey through western France would later find a place in the novel *Les Louves de Machecoul, épisodes de la guerre de Vendée en 1832* (1859; translated as *The Royalist Daughters* and *The Castle of Souday*, 1862), 1894), written in collaboration with Gaspard-Georges de Pescow, Marquis de Cherville.

In June 1830 Dumas had begun a liaison with actress Belle Krelsamer, known in the theater as Mélanie Serre. Soon pregnant with his child, she forced Dumas to break with Mélanie Waldor. Belle gave birth to a daughter, Marie-Alexandrine, on 5 March 1831, and on 7 March Dumas legally recognized the baby as his. From mid September 1831 to December 1833, Dumas lived with Belle at 40, rue St-Lazare. During this period he wrote more plays, including *Antony* and *La Tour de Nesle*, and had several other love affairs.

Although originally destined for the Comédie-Française, *Antony* premiered on 3 May 1831 at the Théâtre de la Porte-Saint-Martin, where it was performed by Marie Dorval and Pierre-Martinien Tousez, known as Bocage. The most personal of Dumas's plays, this five-act prose drama is loosely based on the playwright's relationship with Mélanie Waldor, and some of the dialogue is borrowed directly from their correspondence. This piece, which, by virtue of its setting and its subject, marked another milestone in the history of French Romantic drama, was an even greater triumph than *Henri III*. Dumas ordered that brief intermissions be used to sustain the work's heightened emotions, and the audience, moved to a fever pitch of excitement by the performance of the leads, was delirious after the final scene, where Antony, having murdered his mistress at her own request, tells her husband: "Elle me résistait, je l'ai assassinée!" (She resisted me, [so] I assassinated her!). The text of the play was published at Dumas's expense later that year.

A modern drama of adultery set in the faubourg Saint-Honoré, *Antony* highlights the conflicts between the individual and society in contemporary Paris. The central figures in the play are Adèle d'Hervey, a wife and mother who, when forced to choose between her lover and her reputation, bows to social pressures; and Antony, a man of exceptional merit whose illegitimate birth and unjust ostracism have brought him to despair and then to revolt. Dumas would use illegitimacy again in many of his works: *Le Capitaine Paul* (1838; translated as *Captain Paul*, 1846), *Le Vicomte de Bragelonne, ou Dix ans plus tard* (1848-1850; translated as *The Vicomte de Bragelonne; or, Ten Years Later*, 1857), *Les Deux Diane* (1846-1847; translated as *The Two Dianas*, 1848), and *Une Fille du régent* (1844; translated as *The Regent's Daughter*, 1845). The alienated hero whose superior intelligence, pride, and frustrated passion render him an outsider would also reappear in such works as *Kean, Georges* (1843; translated as *George*, 1846), and *Le Comte de Monte-Cristo* (1844-1845; translated as *The Count of Monte-Cristo*, 1846), while the theme of adultery would figure prominently in *La Tour de Nesle* and *La Dame de Monsoreau* (1846; translated as *Diana of Meridor*, 1846) as well as *Les Trois Mousquetaires* (1844; translated as *The Three Musketeers*, 1846) and *Le Collier de la reine* (1849-1850; translated as *The Queen's Necklace*, 1850), among others.

On 29 May 1832 *La Tour de Nesle*, a five-act historical drama based on legends about Marguerite de Bourgogne's nightly orgies in the Nesle Tower, opened at the Théâtre de la Porte-Saint-Martin with Frédérick Lemaître as Buridan and Mlle George (Marguerite Weimer) as Marguerite. The piece was first performed and published as the work of Frédéric Gaillardet, a novice writer whose manuscript Charles-Jean Harel, then manager of the Porte-Saint-Martin, had asked Dumas to revise. Dumas added a new opening tavern scene, a prison scene in act 3, and several dramatic twists of fortune. In the end only the core of Gaillardet's plot remained. Although Dumas requested that his name not be mentioned, Harel quickly leaked word of his collaboration and, reversing the order of the names on the original playbill, announced *La Tour de Nesle* as the work of "MM. *** and F. Gaillardet." This led to a quarrel between Dumas and Gaillardet that would result in exchanges in the press, repeated lawsuits, and even a duel. Although Dumas chose on several occasions to publish the text among his theatrical works, it was not until 1861 that Gaillardet finally gave formal consent for Dumas's name to appear on the play that had an incredible eight hundred consecutive performances in 1832.

Set in Paris in 1314, the darkly dramatic events of this tale of love and ambition, crime and punishment turn on the secrets that the mysterious captain Buridan shares with the queen. Will his knowledge of her past and present transgressions make his fortune or result in his death? By turns each seems to triumph over the other, but in the end, after each has unwittingly sent one of their illegitimate twin sons to his death, they die together, victims of their lust for power and of the moral conventions of melodrama. This piece also includes several characteristics found in Dumas's subsequent works. Many other Dumas novels and plays feature critical confrontations set in prisons and taverns. Twins appear in several stories, including *Les Frères corses* (1845; translated as *The Corsican Brothers*, 1845), *Black* (1858; translated as *Black, The Story of a Dog*, 1895) and *Le Capitaine Richard* (1858; translated as *The Twin Captains*, 1861). Likewise, here as in many other Dumas texts, secrets weigh heavily not only on an individual's destiny but also on parent-child relationships: thus, in works such as *Vingt ans après* (1845; translated as *Twenty Years After*, 1846), and *Les Deux Diane*, a child's fate is either identical to its parent's or is decided by a parent's actions.

From 21 July to 20 October 1832, while audiences continued to flock to *La Tour de Nesle*, Dumas traveled in Switzerland with Belle. His *Impressions de voyage: En Suisse* (1834-1837; translated as *The Glacier Land*, 1852) initially appeared in serial form in the *Revue des Deux Mondes* (15 February 1833 - 15 August 1834). The first of Dumas's many published travelogues, his personal, impressionistic account of the landscape and people of Switzerland was accompanied by information on Swiss history and food. Like the rest of Dumas's travels, this journey would provide an opportunity to collect stories and descriptions that would later be used in his fiction. As Dumas himself would later observe: "Il y a une chose que je ne sais pas faire: c'est un livre ou un drame sur des localités que je n'ai pas vues" (There is one thing I don't know how to do and that is a book or a play about a place I haven't seen).

From November to December 1834 Dumas traveled to the south of France on what was to be the beginning of a trip around the Mediterranean, but in January he was forced to return to Paris to raise money for the rest of the journey. From mid May 1835 to late December 1835, Dumas toured Italy with Ida Ferrier and the painter Louis-Godefroy Jadin. His *Impressions de voyage: Le Midi de la France* (1841; translated as *Pictures of Travel in the South of France*) first appeared in the *Siècle* (28 April 1840 - 27 May 1840). The trip was also the source of several other texts, including *Le Speronare* (1842; translated as *Journeys with Dumas; The Speronara*, 1902), *Le Capitaine Aréna*, (1842), and *Le Corricolo* (1843; translated as *Sketches of Naples*, 1845), each of which first appeared in serial form. But when Dumas and Ida returned to Paris at Christmas 1835, they were penniless. They moved into an apartment at 30, rue Bleu that Dumas had rented in December 1833, and they lived there with his daughter Maric (whom Ida loved) and his son Alexandre (whom she hated and who hated her) until May 1837.

In July 1836 Dumas became drama critic for the *Presse*. He held that job until 1838 while continuing to write other texts. *Kean* premiered at the Théâtre des Variétés on 31 August 1836. The play, a revised and expanded version of a work written by Marie-Emmanuel Théaulon de Lambert and Frédéric de Courcy, was published under Dumas's name alone. The title role was composed for Lemaître, whose outstanding performance in the part contributed greatly to the work's success. Like Alfred de Vigny's *Chatterton* (1835; translated, 1847), the play depicts an artist's sufferings and alienation from society, but unlike Vigny's chaste and sober poet, Dumas's drunken, womanizing actor lives an extravagant life. When urged to exercise some self-control, Kean replies: "Avoir de l'ordre, c'est cela, et le génie, qu'est-ce qu'il deviendra pendant que j'aurai de l'ordre?" (Lead an orderly existence, indeed, and what will become of [my] genius when I do that?). When Jean-Paul Sartre adapted *Kean* in 1954, Dumas's view of the artist as a social outcast gave way to existentialist concerns about the "essence" behind the theatrical mask.

On 1 August 1838 Dumas's beloved mother died. Grief-stricken, he traveled with Ida to Bel-

Title page for the first illustrated edition (1846) of Dumas's perennially popular adventure romance involving Louis XIII and Cardinal Richelieu

gium and then along the Rhine from 8 August to 2 October. Gérard de Nerval joined them in Frankfurt on 15 August, and the two men set to work on *L'Alchimiste* (1839, performed and published under Dumas's name) and *Léo Burckart* (1839, performed and published as Nerval's). The trip would also lead to the publication of *Excursions sur les bords du Rhin* (Excursions along the Banks of the Rhine, 1841), which initially appeared in serial form in the *Siècle* (13 August 1840 - 25 December 1840).

On 8 October 1838 Dumas's five-act drama *Paul Jones* was performed at the Théâtre du Panthéon. Although written first, he later claimed that it was the first play he adapted from one of his novels. That novel, *Le Capitaine Paul*, had been serialized in the *Siècle* from 30 May 1838 to 23 June 1838. In his preface to an 1856 edition of the novel, Dumas states that *Le Capitaine Paul* had been inspired by James Fenimore Cooper's *The Pilot* (1823), a work that left him wondering about John Paul Jones's origins and early life. Dumas also claims to have predicted, when his novel first appeared, that "il y aura une époque où les libraires ne voudront éditer que des livres déjà publiés dans les journaux, et où les directeurs ne voudront jouer que des drames tirés du roman" (there will come a time when book dealers will want to publish only books that have already appeared in serial form, and when theater directors will want to perform only plays derived from novels). It is impossible to say whether this is foresight or hindsight. What is clear is that the John Paul Jones who arrives at the marquise d'Auray's estate in Brittany in time to prevent a young woman from being married against her wishes and in time to learn the secret of his own mysterious birth owes more to Dumas's imagination than to the historical record.

In 1839 Dumas became a regular contributor to the *Siècle*, and on 2 April 1839 his five-act drama (later labeled a comedy) *Mademoiselle de Belle-Isle* opened at the Théâtre-Français. Based on a text by Brunswick (pseudonym of Léon Lhéri) that was completely revised by Dumas, the action takes place at the marquise de Prie's castle in Chantilly in 1726. The title role was written for Mlle Mars, who persisted at age sixty in playing ingenues and whose talent contributed to the considerable success of the drama. Firmin played the duc de Richelieu, a grandnephew of the great Cardinal Richelieu and a man who enjoys a considerable reputation as a lover.

The story turns on Richelieu's boastful wager that he will spend the night with the first woman he sees. Chance designates Gabrielle de Belle-Isle as his victim. Richelieu is later tricked by Prie, who takes Gabrielle's place in bed after sending the young woman, via a secret door, to meet with her father in prison. Because Gabrielle has sworn not to reveal to anyone where she was that night, her fiancé, Raoul d'Aubigny, and Richelieu are both deceived. Later, when Prie and her current lover, the prime minister, are disgraced, Gabrielle is free to tell the truth and to marry Raoul. It is interesting to note that, in *Les Trois Mousquetaires*, d'Artagnan plays the same trick on Milady as Prie does here on Richelieu.

On 5 February 1840, to the surprise of almost everyone and the displeasure of Alexandre *fils*, Dumas married Ida Ferrier in Paris. Deeply in debt, they left the city in late May for Florence, where, except for occasional trips back to Paris, the couple lived from June 1840 to March 1841. On 1 June 1841 *Un Mariage sous Louis XV*

(translated as *A Marriage of Convenience*, 1896), a five-act comedy, opened at the Théâtre-Français to mixed reviews. Yet another comedy in the same style, *Les Demoiselles de Saint-Cyr* (1843; translated as *The Ladies of Saint-Cyr*, 1870), would premiere at the Théâtre-Français two years later.

From 28 June 1841 to 14 January 1842, the *Siècle* published *Le Chevalier d'Harmental* (1842; translated as *The Chevalier d'Harmental*, 1846), the first of many novels Dumas was to write based on a preliminary draft by Maquet. Introduced by Nerval, the two had met on 30 November 1838 and had already collaborated on Maquet's play *Bathilde*, performed at the Théâtre de la Renaissance on 14 January 1839 without mention of Dumas's name. In 1849 Dumas and Maquet transformed *Le Chevalier d'Harmental* into a play that opened on 26 July at the Théâtre-Historique. Set in Paris from 1718 to 1719, the novel tells the story of a failed conspiracy against the regent (Philippe II d'Orléans) planned by the duchesse de Maine. The plot is complicated when conspirator Raoul d'Harmental falls in love with his beautiful young neighbor, Bathilde du Rocher, whose father gave his life to save the regent. Her guardian, Jean Buvat, a copyist in the regent's employ, learns about the conspiracy and reveals what he knows to the regent's prime minister, abbé Dubois. Raoul, imprisoned and abandoned by his coconspirators, is saved from death by Bathilde (the regent honors his debt to her father).

Le Chevalier d'Harmental was neither Dumas's first historical novel nor his first excursion into French history, but it was the first of a long series of novels set at moments in French history marked by political discord. Using a pattern that would be common to virtually all of their subsequent books, Dumas and Maquet establish the date and place of the action in the initial sentences of *Le Chevalier* and then quickly move on to show the main character—a young man arriving from the provinces who hopes to satisfy his ambitions—get into a conflict (such as a duel) and meet others (friends, mentors, enemies) who will later play a determining role in his future. He soon falls in love and faces challenges both to his ambition and to his love that often lead to his imprisonment and / or execution. Dumas later described his technique in the following terms: "... commencer par l'intérêt, au lieu de commencer par l'ennui; commencer par l'action, au lieu de commencer par la préparation; parler des personnages après les avoir fait paraître, au lieu de les faire paraître après avoir parlé d'eux" (. . .

begin with something interesting rather than beginning with something boring; begin with action rather than beginning with background information; speak about the characters after they have appeared [on scene, in action] rather than having them appear after having spoken about them).

If *Harmental* marks the beginning of one series of novels, *Georges* (1843) is clearly part of another set of works stretching from *Antony* to *Le Comte de Monte-Cristo* and beyond, works that present a superior being who is rejected by society. Written in collaboration with Félicien Mallefille, who in all likelihood contributed details of local color, the first draft of this novel was completely revised by Dumas in late 1842 during a third stay in Florence. Serialized in the *Siècle* before publication as a book, *Georges* presents a portrait of racial prejudice against the backdrop of the exotic colonial setting of the île de France (now known as île Maurice/Mauritius).

Upon returning to the île de France after fourteen years of study and several celebrated adventures abroad, Georges, the younger son of wealthy mulatto plantation owner Pierre Munier, falls in love with Sara de Malmédie. The cousin and fiancée of Henri de Malmédie, who is the scion of the most powerful French family on the island, Sara scandalizes her social class after she dances with Georges at the English governor's ball. When his request for Sara's hand in marriage and his challenge to Henri are both rejected because he is a mulatto, Georges decides to lead a slave revolt, the only means he sees open to him to strike at that society which has humiliated him, and his father before him. The rebellion fails, and Georges is imprisoned and sentenced to die. A dramatic, last-minute rescue, organized by his slave-trading older brother, allows the book to end with Georges and Sara (whom he has married on his way to the gallows) leaving the island.

A brilliant example of the French Romantic novel, far too infrequently read and too often discussed in biographical terms, *Georges* must be examined not only in the context of Dumas's writing but also within the lineage of Jacques Bernardin de Saint-Pierre's *Paul et Virginie* (1788), Mme Claire de Duras's *Ourika (1824)*, and Hugo's *Bug-Jargal* (1826; translated as *The Slave-King*, 1833) to be properly understood. Often overshadowed by *Les Trois Mousquetaires* and *Le Comte de Monte-Cristo*, published close on their heels, *Le Chevalier d'Harmental* and *Georges* are nonetheless important works deserving of a broader audience.

The year 1844 marks the beginning of one of the most productive periods in Dumas's life. Almost all of the books composed during the next fifteen years first appeared in serial form. Dumas certainly profited from this arrangement but so, too, did the newspaper owners who saw their readership increase whenever they printed a Dumas text. While Dumas and his collaborators continued throughout this time to write what might be called "stand alone" novels, they also developed several series of novels that are now among Dumas's best-known works. Thus, in 1844 Dumas published, among other titles, *Les Trois Mousquetaires* (*Siècle*, 14 March - 11 July), destined to become part of a trilogy of works set in the seventeenth century; *Une Fille du régent* (*Commerce*, 25 April - 13 July), a chronological sequel to *Le Chevalier d'Harmental*; *Le Comte de Monte-Cristo* (*Journal des Débats*, 28 August 1844 - 15 January 1846), a "stand alone" novel set in the nineteenth century; and *La Reine Margot* (*Presse*, 25 December 1844 - 5 April 1845), the inaugural work in a sixteenth-century trilogy. In 1845 he published several volumes, including *Vingt ans après* (*Siècle*, 21 January - 28 June), the sequel to *Les Trois Mousquetaires*; *Le Chevalier de Maison-Rouge* (*Démocratie Pacifique*, 21 May 1845 - 12 January 1846), the first of a series of novels set at the time of the French Revolution; and *La Dame de Monsoreau* (*Constitutionnel*, 27 August 1845 - 12 February 1846), the sequel to *La Reine Margot*. Dumas and his associates almost always adapted their novels for the theater, where they were also very well received.

Not surprisingly, Dumas's success during this period produced resentment among some of his contemporaries. In late February 1845 Eugène de Mirecourt published a pamphlet entitled *Fabrique de romans: Alexandre Dumas & Compagnie* (The Novel Factory: Alexandre Dumas & Company). Notorious for its virulent, racist attack on the author, Mirecourt's brochure also denounced Dumas for using collaborators and for unfairly monopolizing publishing opportunities in the newspapers. Dumas sued Mirecourt for slander and won his case on 15 March 1845. On 26 March he signed five-year exclusive contracts the *Presse* and the *Constitutionnel* to furnish multivolume works for serial publication. In early 1847 the *Presse* and the *Constitutionnel* would have to sue Dumas to compel him to live up to his agreement. Thus his *Mémoires d'un médecin: Joseph Balsamo* (1846-1848; translated as *The Memoirs of a Physician*, 1848), which began appearing in the

Presse from 31 May 1846 to 6 June 1846, resumed appearing in that paper from 3 September 1847 to 22 January 1848. The final volume of the *Reine Margot* trilogy, *Les Quarante-Cinq* (1847-1848; translated as *The Forty-Five Guardsmen*, 1848), was not published in the *Constitutionnel* until 13 May 1847 - 20 October 1847. No sooner was that commitment met, however, than *Le Vicomte de Bragelonne*, the last installment in the *Mousquetaire* trilogy, began appearing in the *Siècle* (20 October 1847 - 12 January 1850).

During this period of intense literary production from 1844 to 1850, Dumas's personal life was also marked by significant events. On 15 October 1844 he separated from Ida on amiable terms, but his failure to provide the agreed-upon support payments led her to the courts, which in February 1848 decreed a formal *séparation des biens* (division of property). In May 1845 Dumas moved to the Villa Médicis in Saint-Germain-en-Laye, where he lived until the completion of work on the Château de Monte-Cristo he was having built in Port-Marly. On 25 July 1847 he would invite six hundred guests to a housewarming party at the lavishly decorated and landscaped château. In August 1846 he began a liaison with Béatrix Person, a young actress whom he engaged to perform in the translation of *Hamlet* he had written with Paul Meurice. The play premiered on 14 September 1846 at the Théâtre de Saint-Germain and would open again at the Théâtre-Historique in Paris on 15 December 1847. Person, who would star in an array of roles at the Théâtre-Historique, would remain Dumas's mistress until 1850.

From October 1846 to January 1847, accompanied by Alexandre *fils* and several collaborators, Dumas traveled first to Spain for the marriage of Antoine-Marie, Duc de Montpensier, with the Infanta Luisa Fernanda, and then to North Africa, where, under the terms of a government commission, he was to negotiate the release of some prisoners of war and to prepare a work that would glorify the French colonial presence in the region. Two books originated from this journey. The first, *De Paris à Cadix* (From Paris to Cadix, 1847-1848), appeared in serial form in the *Presse* from 12 March 1847 to 27 March 1847. When the second, *Le Véloce, ou Tanger, Alger et Tunis* (1848-1851; translated as *Tales of Algeria*, 1868), was published, some questioned Dumas's expenses.

Château de Monte-Cristo, the lavish residence Dumas had built in Port-Marly during the mid 1840s

Dumas returned to Paris in time for the successful opening, on 20 February 1847, of his and Maquet's adaptation of *La Reine Margot* at the Théâtre-Historique. Dumas had obtained the patent for this theater, dedicated to the performance of his own works, thanks to the influence of his friend the duc de Montpensier, fifth son of Louis-Philippe. This was not Dumas's first experience with theater proprietorship—a decade earlier he and Hugo had briefly held the patent for the Théâtre de la Renaissance. The success of several of his pieces notwithstanding, the poor management practices of those he hired to run the theater and other circumstances soon brought Dumas to the brink of ruin.

From February to June 1848, while Dumas and others participated in the events of the revolution, box-office receipts at his theater dropped off dramatically. Dumas spent much of the year in an unsuccessful attempt to get elected to the Constituent Assembly. From 1 March 1848 to 1 February 1850, he published the *Mois*, a newspa-

Photograph of Dumas in late middle age

per devoted to politics. Dumas did not entirely neglect his literary career, though. During this time he and Maquet wrote two sequels to *Joseph Balsamo*, first *Le Collier de la reine* (*Presse*, 29 December 1848 - 28 January 1849) and then *Ange Pitou* (17 December 1850 - 26 June 1851). The income earned from those projects was not enough to stem the tide of Dumas's ever-mounting debts, however, and on 22 March 1849 he was obliged to sell Monte-Cristo. Then the Théâtre-Historique folded on 16 October 1850, and Dumas was forced into bankruptcy in December of that year.

In August 1850, when he had still had some hopes of saving his theater, Dumas had auditioned fifteen-year-old Isabelle Constant, a drama student of Mlle George, for a role in his play *Le Capitaine La Jonquière*, a retitled version of the drama he had earlier adapted from *Une Fille du régent*. She not only got the part, but she also became Dumas's mistress, replacing Béatrix Person in both functions. Isabelle and Dumas lived together at 96, boulevard Beaumarchais from Au-

gust 1850 to December 1851, at which time their possessions were seized to pay some of Dumas's debts.

Under pressure from creditors who threatened him with jail, Dumas left for exile in Brussels on 10 December 1851. From December 1851 to December 1852, while the novel *Olympe de Clèves* (16 October 1851 - 19 February 1852) was being published in the *Siècle*, Dumas resided at the Hôtel de l'Europe on the place Royale. Then from January 1852 to November 1853 he lived at 73, boulevard Waterloo with his daughter Marie (who arrived 1 May 1852) and his secretary Noël Parfait. Although not a political exile himself, Dumas did frequent those of his compatriots who, like Hugo, had fled to Belgium because of their opposition to the regime of Napoleon III. Dumas traveled extensively during this period. He also began publishing *Mes Mémoires* in the *Presse* (16 December 1851 - 26 October 1853), wrote a version of the story of the Wandering Jew, *Isaac Laquedem*, for the *Constitutionnel* (10 December 1852 - 11 March 1853), and began work on the last volume of his *Balsamo* series, *La Comtesse de Charny* (1852-1855; translated as *The Countess de Charny*, 1853). Finally, after reaching an agreement with his creditors regarding payment of his outstanding debt, Dumas returned to Paris, where from 29 November 1853 to September 1854 he lived at 1, rue Laffitte.

In November 1853 Dumas founded the newspaper the *Mousquetaire* so as to continue publication of his *Mémoires*, which Girardin had been forced to suspend. After his principal collaborators resigned en masse in October 1854 to protest the nonpayment of their wages, Dumas continued the paper on his own until February 1857. During 1854 Dumas began to write *Les Mohicans de Paris* (1854-1855; translated as *The Mohicans of Paris*, 1859) with Bocage; he also traveled to eastern France to do research for *La Route de Varennes* (The Road to Varennes, 1860) and *Les Compagnons de Jéhu*, first published in the *Journal Pour Tous* (20 December 1856 - 4 April 1857) and set against the backdrop of the coup d'état of the 18th of Brumaire. In 1857 Maquet sued Dumas for back wages and royalties but lost; the relationship between the two men had been strained since 1848, and this suit permanently ended their collaborative efforts, which had already all but ceased by the time of Dumas's exile in Belgium. On 23 April 1857 Dumas founded the *Monte-Cristo*, a newspaper devoted exclusively to the publication of his own works; this new venture would fold in May 1860 and then be briefly reborn from January 1862 to October 1862. In the *Monte-Cristo*, Dumas would publish *Histoire de mes bêtes* (12 November 1857 - 9 November 1857) and children's stories, among other works. Together with his new collaborator, Gaspard de Cherville, with whom he worked on *Histoire de mes bêtes*, Dumas would also publish the fantastic tale of *Le Meneur de loups* (*Siècle*, 2 October 1857 - 30 October 1857) and his novel on the Vendée in 1832, *Les Louves de Machecoul* (*Journal Pour Tous*, 27 February 1858 - 21 August 1858). From 15 June 1858 to 10 March 1859, Dumas traveled in Russia, eventually publishing two new episodes of his *Impressions de voyage*, *Le Caucase* (Travels in Caucasia, 1859) and *En Russie* (Travels in Russia, 1865).

When Ida Ferrier died in Genoa on 11 March 1859, Dumas shed no tears. In April the aspiring young actress Emilie Cordier became Dumas's mistress and moved in with him at 77, rue d'Amsterdam, where he had been living since September 1854. Together they traveled the Mediterranean aboard the *Emma*. In July,

Emilie, already pregnant, returned to Paris, where on 26 December 1859 she gave birth to Dumas's daughter, baptized Micaëlla-Josepha in honor of Giuseppe Garibaldi, whom Dumas admired and hoped to join. Dumas did not immediately recognize the child as his, though there is no doubt that she was; when he finally offered to do so in 1863, it was under conditions that Emilie did not find acceptable, and the matter was dropped. On 20 December 1859 Dumas signed a 120,000-franc contract with Michel Lévy for publication of all of his past and future works until December 1870. This agreement, which would later be extended to 1880, ended a long-standing legal battle between the two men.

During 1860 Dumas participated in Garibaldi's campaign to unify Italy. He also translated Garibaldi's memoirs as *Mémoires de Garibaldi*, which was published first in the *Siècle* (30 May 1860 - 5 September 1860) and then as a book (1860; translated as *Garibaldi, An Autobiography*, 1860). Later that same year he founded *L'Indépendant/L'Indipendente*, a Franco-Italian journal published from October 1860 to May 1861 and then from May 1862 to March 1864 at the Chiatamone Palace in Naples, where Dumas, in continued support of Garibaldi's work, lived from September 1860 to March 1864. With the exception of *Le Volontaire de '92* (translated as *Love and Liberty*, 1874), parts of which were published in 1862 in the *Monte-Cristo* and in 1867 in the *Mousquetaire*, Dumas's new works during this period generally relate to Italy.

When Dumas returned to Paris, he had with him his latest mistress, singer Fanny Gordosa; the relationship, begun in Italy in 1863, did not last beyond March 1865. On 1 March of that year, Dumas embarked on what would become a long series of lectures in Paris, the provinces, and abroad with a talk on Eugène Delacroix; these later were published in the press and in a volume entitled *Causeries* (Chats, 1885). From November 1865 to January 1866, Dumas traveled to Vienna and Budapest. Back in Paris, on 10 November 1866 he founded the second *Mousquetaire*, which he published until April 1867. The most important of his works to appear in this paper was undoubtedly *Les Blancs et les bleus* (13 January 1867 - 22 February 1867), a chronological sequel to *Les Compagnons de Jéhu*. Later that year, sensing the impending invasion of France by Prussian troops, he wrote *La Terreur prussienne* (1868; translated as *The Prussian Terror*, 1915), a novel that went virtually unnoticed.

Already tired and ill, Dumas nonetheless began a new liaison in 1867, this time with the American actress Adah Isaacs Menken; scantily dressed (for those times), Adah had herself photographed with Dumas. The photographer, to whom Dumas owed money, sold the picture, without permission, in order to recover some of what was due him. The image caused a scandal, and Dumas had to go to court to stop its sale. His relationship with Adah ended when she left for a theater engagement in Vienna. In February 1868 Dumas founded yet another paper, the *D'Artagnan*, which lasted only until 4 July 1868; then, from 5 July 1868 to March 1869, he published a weekly paper, the *Théâtre-Journal*. Dumas's dramatic adaptation of *Les Blancs et les bleus*, which opened at the Théâtre du Châtelet on 19 March 1869, was his last work to be staged during his lifetime. In September 1870, as the Prussians were moving into France, Dumas went to Dieppe to live with Alexandre *fils* and his family; they were soon joined by Marie. Dumas died at his son's home on 5 December; his body was transferred to its final resting place in the cemetery at Villers-Cotterêts in 1872.

The works for which Dumas is best remembered today are the *Reine Margot* trilogy (*La Reine Margot, La Dame de Monsoreau, Les Quarante-Cinq*); the *Mousquetaire* trilogy (*Les Trois Mousquetaires, Vingt ans après, Le Vicomte de Bragelonne*); the *Balsamo* tetralogy (*Joseph Balsamo, Le Collier de la reine, Ange Pitou, La Comtesse de Charny*); and *Le Comte de Monte-Cristo*. Although each novel is set at a different moment in the history of France (from the sixteenth to the nineteenth centuries), they all have much in common. Each work recounts the story of an individual's personal struggles against the backdrop of the larger national-historical tensions of an era. In every instance political considerations and events play a role in determining the character's chances for success in finding happiness (love) and/or a place in the world. Thus Dumas strives at all times to create a sense of the forces at play and of the atmosphere and the manners of a period while avoiding the extremes of archaeological reconstruction and superficial local color.

The real historical figures he uses in his fictions exercise their power in the background while his invented characters (including those based on existing persons) are foregrounded. The real figures, at times feigning illness or weakness so as better to deceive their opponents, often rely on treachery (poison, ambush) or the de-

Monument to Dumas by Gustave Doré, in the Place Malesherbes, Paris. It depicts the Mousquetaire d'Artagnan.

liberate miscarriage of justice (imprisonment, execution) to achieve their aims, while the fictional figures, although strong of body and heart, fail to realize their objectives and often are as much victims of their own integrity and passions as they are of the forces they oppose. Occasionally one of Dumas's "noble" characters will succeed, however. In that event, as Schopp has noted, the character must first undergo a symbolic death and then return to life purged of all desires and material goals extraneous to his or her mission.

This resurrected character becomes the instrument of a divine plan, a tool in what Schopp describes as Dumas's providential view of history. If one considers exile a form of symbolic death, then John Paul Jones and Georges belong as much to this class of characters as Dantès/comte de Monte-Cristo or Balsamo/comte de Foenix, whose names so directly point to their life after death, or Diane de Méridor, Dame de Monsoreau. The Bonaparte/Napoléon of Dumas's drama *Napoléon Bonaparte, ou Trente ans de l'histoire de France* (1831) is likewise a Christ figure of sorts.

Another character type, the healer or seer, also appears in each of Dumas's most celebrated series and in many of his individual works. These savants, at once scientists and students of the human condition, are often surrounded by mystery and are generally the object of respect. They possess powers that are frequently essential to the principal protagonist's continued existence or success, and thus they, too, seem tied to a providential view of history. What is more, their presence allows Dumas to engage in philosophical and metaphysical speculation about the fate of France and its leaders.

A third character type common to each of the multivolume series is the "giant" whose physical prowess and appetites are nothing short of prodigious. Porthos in the *Mousquetaire* trilogy, Chicot in the *Reine Margot* trilogy, and Ange Pitou in the *Balsamo* tetralogy, while of varying degrees of intelligence and narrative importance, all accomplish material feats beyond the power of most ordinary men. Yet, tied to the earth in life, they rarely transcend the limits of human existence or point the way forward. Thus, although Pitou, who effortlessly traverses great distances on foot and just as easily devours great quantities of food, survives the cataclysm of the Revolution and returns home to farm his beloved Catherine's land, it is for her son and not for him that the future seems to hold the brightest promise. Likewise Porthos, although able to satisfy his gargantuan appetites and to become a major property owner, nonetheless dies buried under tons of rock.

It is tempting to suggest that Dumas, whose size, appetites, and capacity for work so closely match those of these giants, has, like them, been buried under an enormous weight—not only the weight of the hundreds of volumes he produced, but also the weight of scholarly disdain. A few courageous critics have begun to dig beneath the surface in order to resurrect both the man and his works. The task before them is monumental, and one can only hope that many others will come to their aid.

Letters:
Lettres d'Alexandre Dumas à Mélanie Waldor, edited by Claude Schopp (Paris: Presses Universitaires de France, 1982).

Bibliographies:
Frank Wilde Reed, *A Bibliography of Alexandre Dumas père* (London: J. A. Neuhuys, 1933);

Douglas Munro, *Alexandre Dumas père: A Bibliography of Works Translated into English to 1910* (New York & London: Garland, 1978);

Munro, *Alexandre Dumas père: A Bibliography of Works Published in French, 1825-1900* (New York & London: Garland, 1981);

Munro, *Alexandre Dumas père: A Secondary Bibliography of French and English Sources to 1983, with Appendices* (New York & London: Garland, 1985).

Biographies:
A. Craig Bell, *Alexandre Dumas: A Biography and a Study* (London: Cassell, 1950);

Henri Clouard, *Alexandre Dumas* (Paris: Albin Michel, 1955);

André Maurois, *Les Trois Dumas* (Paris: Hachette, 1957); translated by Gerard Hopkins as *The Titans: A Three-Generation Biography of the Dumas* (New York: Harper, 1957); also published as *The Three Musketeers: A Study of the Dumas Family* (London: Jonathan Cape, 1957);

Jean de Lamaze, *Alexandre Dumas père* (Paris: Pierre Charron, 1972);

Richard S. Stowe, *Alexandre Dumas père* (Boston: Twayne, 1976);

F. W. J. Hemmings, *The King of Romance: A Portrait of Alexandre Dumas* (London: H. Hamilton, 1979);

Michael Ross, *Alexandre Dumas* (London: David & Charles, 1981);

Jean Thibaudeau, *Alexandre Dumas, le prince des Mousquetaires* (Paris: Hachette, 1983);

Claude Schopp, *Alexandre Dumas: Le Génie de la vie* (Paris: Editions Mazarine, 1985); translated by A. J. Koch as *Alexandre Dumas: Genius of Life* (New York & Toronto: Franklin Watts, 1988);

Christian Biet, Jean-Paul Brighelli, and Jean-Luc Rispail, *Alexandre Dumas, ou les Aventures d'un romancier* (Paris: Gallimard, 1986).

References:
L'Arc, issue on Dumas, no. 71 (1978);

Michel Autrand, "Le Roman d'Alexandre Dumas à l'épreuve de la Révolution," *Revue d'Histoire Littéraire de la France*, 90, nos. 4-5 (July-October 1990): 679-691;

Ora Avni, "Ils courent, ils courent les ferrets: Mauss, Lacan et *Les Trois Mousquetaires*," *Poétique*, 16, no. 62 (April 1985): 215-235;

Avni and John Rosenthal, "The Semiotics of Transactions: Mauss, Lacan and *The Three*

Musketeers," *MLN*, 100, no. 4 (September 1985): 728-757;

Fernande Bassan, "Le Cycle des *Trois Mousquetaires*—du roman au théâtre," *Studia Neophilologica*, 57 (1985): 243-249;

Bassan, "Dumas père et l'histoire: A propos du drame *La Reine Margot*," *Revue d'Histoire du Théâtre*, 39, no. 4 (1987): 384-392;

Bassan, "Histoire de *La Tour de Nesle* de Dumas père et Gaillardet," *Nineteenth-Century French Studies*, 3, nos. 1-2 (Fall-Winter 1974-1975): 40-57;

Bassan and Sylvie Chevalley, *Alexandre Dumas et la Comédie-Française* (Paris: Lettres Modernes-Minard, 1972);

Jacques Baudou, "Catacombs-Cristo et le marionnettiste," *Europe*, nos. 626-627 (June-July 1981): 127-131;

Raymond Bellour, *Mademoiselle Guillotine. Cagliostro, Dumas, Œdipe et la Révolution française* (Paris: Editions La Différence, 1989);

Jeanne Bem, "D'Artagnan et après. Lecture symbolique et historique de la 'trilogie' de Dumas," *Littérature*, 22 (1976): 13-29;

Simone Bertière, "Le Coadjuteur et son double: Retz inspirateur d'Alexandre Dumas," *Travaux de Littérature*, 3 (1990): 169-177;

Maurice Bouvier-Ajam, *Alexandre Dumas, ou Cent ans après* (Paris: Les Editeurs Français Réunis, 1972);

Patrick Brady, "L'Epée, la lettre et la robe: Symbolisme dramatique et thématique des *Trois Mousquetaires*," *Acta Litteraria Academiae Scientiarum Hungaricae*, 23, nos. 3-4 (1981): 215-225;

Bulletin de l'Association des Amis d'Alexandre Dumas (1971-1977);

Bulletin de la Société des Amis d'Alexandre Dumas (1978-1982);

Cahiers Alexandre Dumas (1983-);

Edith Covensky, "Les Débuts d'Alexandre Dumas père au théâtre: *Henri III, Antony* et *La Tour de Nesle*," *Revue d'Histoire du Théâtre*, 35, no. 3 (1983): 329-337;

The Dumasian, nos. 1-11 (1956-1960);

Europe, issue on Dumas, 48, nos. 490-491 (February-March 1970;

François Germain, "Dumas et *La Tour de Nesle*," in *D'Eschyle à Genet. Hommage à Francis Prunier* (Dijon: Université de Dijon, 1986), pp. 175-181;

Marcel Graner, "Un Roman tombe dans l'histoire: Dumas adaptateur de Michelet dans *Ange Pitou* et *La Comtesse de Charny*," in

Récit et histoire, edited by Jean Bessière (Paris: Presses Universitaires de France, 1984), pp. 61-74;

Charles Grivel, "Alexandre Dumas: le bas-narrer littéraire," in *Richesses du roman populaire*, edited by René Guise and H.-J. Neuschäfer (Nancy: Presses Universitaires de Nancy, 1986), pp. 293-314;

Réginald Hamel, *Dumas insolite* (Montreal: Editions Guérin, 1988);

Hamel and Pierrette Méthé, *Dictionnaire Dumas* (Montreal: Editions Guérin, 1990);

Livien d'Hulst, "Le Voyage allemand de Nerval et Dumas en 1838," *Etudes Nervaliennes et Romantiques*, 3 (1981): 53-57;

G. Infusino, *Alessandro Dumas giornalista a Napoli* (Naples: Editions del Delfino, 1972);

Isabelle Jan, *Alexandre Dumas romancier* (Paris: Editions Ouvrières, 1973);

Serge Jongué, "Histoire et fiction chez Alexandre Dumas," *Europe*, 52, no. 542 (June 1974): 94-101;

Odile Krakovitch, "Manuscrits des pièces d'Alexandre Dumas et procès-verbaux de censure de ces pièces . . . ," *Revue d'Histoire Littéraire de la France*, 82, no. 4 (July-August 1982): 638-646;

Anne Léoni, Geneviève Mouillaud, and Roger Ripoll, "Feuilleton et révolution: *Ange Pitou*," *Europe*, 52, no. 542 (June 1974): 101-118;

Louise Fiber Luce, "Alexandre Dumas' *Kean*: An Adaptation by Jean-Paul Sartre," *Modern Drama*, 28, no. 3 (September 1985): 355-361;

Magazine Littéraire, issue on Dumas, no. 72 (1973);

Emily A. McDermott, "Classical Allusion in *The Count of Monte Cristo*," *Classical and Modern Literature*, 8, no. 2 (Winter 1988): 93-103;

Michel Picard, "Pouvoirs du feuilleton, ou d'Artagnan anonyme," *Littérature*, 50 (May 1983): 55-76;

Lise Queffélec, "Figuration de la violence dans le roman de l'avant à l'après 1789: Sade, Rétif, Dumas," *Revue d'Histoire Littéraire de la France*, 90, nos. 4-5 (July-October 1990): 663-678;

Queffélec, "Inscription romanesque de la femme au XIXᵉ siècle: le cas du roman-feuilleton sous la Monarchie de Juillet," *Revue d'Histoire Littéraire de la France*, 86, no. 2 (March-April 1986): 189-206;

Claude Schopp, "Dumas critique dramatique," *Nineteenth-Century French Studies*, 18, nos. 3-4 (Spring-Summer 1990): 348-362;

Schopp, "Dumas, les romans de la Révolution dans le 'Drame de France,'" *Littérature Populaire*, 11 (Summer-Autumn 1989): 47-55;

Schopp, "Les Excursions de Dumas sur les bords du Rhin," *Etudes Nervaliennes et Romantiques*, 3 (1981): 59-71;

Schopp, "Hugo et Dumas, les chocs d'une amitié," *Historia*, 466 (October 1985): 74-81;

Schopp, "Journal de campagnes. A. Dumas candidat dans l'Yonne [1848], révolutions et mutations au XIXe siècle," *Bulletin de la Société d'Histoire de la Révolution de 1848 et des Révolutions du XIXe siècle* (1987): 51-66;

Jean-Yves Tadié, "Dumas," in *Le Roman d'aventures* (Paris: Presses Universitaires de France, 1982), pp. 29-68;

Jean-Jacques Thomas, "Image d'Epinal ou les périls de la struction," *Poétique*, 18, no. 70 (April 1987): 209-217;

Pierre Tranouez, "*Cave Filium!* Etude du cycle des *Mousquetaires*," *Poétique*, 18, no. 71 (September 1987): 321-331;

Tranouez, "Relecture. L'Air des bijoux dans *Les Trois Mousquetaires*," *L'Ecole des Lettres*, 13-14 (June 1989): 49-57;

Anne Ubersfeld, "Dumas père et le drame bourgeois," *Cahiers de l'Association Internationale des Etudes Françaises*, 35 (1983): 121-139;

André Vial, "Ce qui restera de Dumas père," *Revue d'Histoire Littéraire de la France*, 74, no. 6 (November-December 1974): 1015-1031.

Papers:
Some of Dumas's manuscripts can be found at the Bibliothèque Nationale and the Archives Nationales in Paris.

Gustave Flaubert

(12 December 1821 - 8 May 1880)

Stirling Haig
University of North Carolina at Chapel Hill

BOOKS: *Madame Bovary, mœurs de province,* 2 volumes (Paris: Michel Lévy frères, 1857); translated by John Sterling as *Madame Bovary. A Tale of Provincial Life* (Philadelphia: T. B. Peterson & Bros., 1881); translated by Eleanor Marx-Aveling as *Madame Bovary. Provincial Manners* (London: Vizetelly, 1886; Chicago: Laird & Lee, 1891);

Salammbô (Paris: Michel Lévy frères, 1862); translated by M. French Sheldon (New York: Lovell, Coryell, 1885; London: Saxon, 1886);

L'Education sentimentale, histoire d'un jeune homme, 2 volumes (Paris: Michel Lévy frères, 1869); translated by D. F. Hannigan as *Sentimental Education: A Young Man's History* (London: H. S. Nichols, 1898; Chicago: Magee, 1904);

Lettre à la municipalité de Rouen (Paris: Michel Lévy frères, 1872);

Préface aux Dernières chansons de Louis Bouilhet (Paris: Michel Lévy frères, 1872);

Le Candidat, comédie en 4 actes (Paris: Charpentier, 1874); translated as *The Candidate: A Humorous Political Drama in Four Acts* (Chicago: S. P. Magee / New York: W. Walter Dunne, 1904);

La Tentation de Saint Antoine (Paris: Charpentier, 1874); translated by Hannigan as *The Temptation of Saint Anthony* (London: H. S. Nichols, 1895; Akron: St. Dunstan Society / Chicago: Magee, 1904);

Trois contes (Paris: G. Charpentier, 1877)— contains "Un Cœur simple," "La Légende de Saint Julien l'hospitalier," and "Hérodias"; translated by Arthur McDowall as *Three Tales* (London: Chatto & Windus, 1923; New York: Knopf, 1924);

Bouvard et Pécuchet (Paris: Alphonse Lemerre, 1881); translated by Hannigan (London: H. S. Nichols, 1896; Akron: St. Dunstan Society / Chicago: Magee / New York: M. Walter Dunne, 1904);

Par les champs et par les grèves (voyage en Bretagne), in volume 6 of *Œuvres complètes* (Paris: A. Quantin, 1885); translated as *Over Strand*

Gustave Flaubert (photograph by Nadar)

and Field: A Record of Travel through Brittany (Akron: St. Dunstan Society / New York & London: M. Walter Dunne, 1904);

A bord de la cange, in volume 6 of *Œuvres complètes* (Paris: A. Quantin, 1885);

Novembre, in volume 6 of *Œuvres complètes* (Paris: A. Quantin, 1885); translated by Frank Jellinek as *November* (London: John Lane, 1934);

Mémoires d'un fou (Paris: H. Floury, 1901);

La Première Tentation de Saint Antoine, edited by Louis Bertrand (Paris: Charpentier, 1908); translated by René Francis as *The First Temptation of Saint Anthony* (London: Duckworth, 1910);

120

Notes de voyage (Paris: L. Conard, 1910; Tours: J. Allard, 1912);

Notes inédites de Flaubert (Paris: L. Conard, 1910);

Œuvres de jeunesse inédites (Paris: L. Conard, 1910);

La Première Education sentimentale (Paris: L. Conard, 1910);

Théâtre: Le Candidat, Le Château des cœurs, Le Sexe faible (Paris: L. Conard, 1910);

Dictionnaire des idées reçues, edited by E. L. Ferrère (Paris: L. Conard, 1913); translated by Jacques Barzun as *Flaubert's Dictionary of Accepted Ideas* (London: Max Reinhardt / Norfolk, Conn., 1954); translated by Edward J. Fluck as *A Dictionary of Platitudes* (London: Rodale Press / Emmaus, Pa.: Rodale Books, 1954);

Madame Bovary, ébauches et fragments inédits, 2 volumes, edited by Gabrielle Leleu (Paris: Conard, 1936);

Voyages, 2 volumes (Paris: Collection des Universités de France, 1948);

Madame Bovary, nouvelle version, edited by Jean Pommier and Leleu (Paris: José Corti, 1949);

Carnets de travail, edited by Pierre-Marc de Biasi (Paris: Balland, 1988).

Collections: *Œuvres complètes*, 8 volumes (Paris: A. Quantin, 1885);

Œuvres complètes de Gustave Flaubert, 18 volumes (Paris: L. Conard, 1910; republished, 21 volumes, 1923; republished, 28 volumes, 1954);

Œuvres complètes de Gustave Flaubert, 10 volumes, edited by René Dumesnil (Paris: Les Belles Lettres, 1945-1948);

Œuvres complètes, 2 volumes, edited by Bernard Masson (Paris: Editions du Seuil, 1964).

Editions: *Madame Bovary*, edited by Claudine Gothot-Mersch (Paris: Editions Garnier, 1971);

Bouvard et Pécuchet, edited by Gothot-Mersch (Paris: Gallimard, 1979);

L'Education sentimentale, edited by P. M. Wetherill (Paris: Editions Garnier, 1984);

Trois contes, edited by Wetherill (Paris: Editions Garnier, 1988).

The enduring literary fame of Gustave Flaubert was established all at one go, in the course of a famous trial that simultaneously brought him success and scandal. In 1857, when *Madame Bovary* (translated 1881) was appearing in serial form, the imperial prosecutor accused Flaubert of publishing a novel offensive to public morality and religion. *Madame Bovary* was nothing less than the glorification of the "poésie de l'adultère" (poetry of adultery), and in the course of his indictment, the prosecutor repeatedly accused the author of painting "tableaux" of lascivity. Such charges may seem absurdly overblown to the modern reader, who will find little to object to in Flaubert's measured and sympathetic portrait of Emma Bovary's discontents and dalliances.

The France of the Second Empire (1852-1870), however, was the result of a coup d'état against the short-lived Second Republic, and the republican form of government in the 1850s was still associated in bourgeois minds with dangerous left-wing revolutionary causes. The government of Emperor Louis-Napoléon Bonaparte (whom the exiled Victor Hugo ridiculed as "Napoléon le petit," which could be construed either as "the petty Napoleon" or "the small Napoleon") intended to set a moral tone. Thus it sought to assert its legitimacy as the regime of Moral Order and treated perceived affronts to tradition and social stability as challenges to be pursued and repressed. Art, still intended to serve a moral function in the conservative mind, should condemn adulterous conduct such as Emma Bovary's, yet nowhere did this novel condemn it— "pas une larme, pas un soupir de Madeleine sur son crime d'incrédulité, sur son suicide, sur ses adultères" (not a tear, not one sigh of a repentant Magdalene for her crime of incredulity, for her suicide, for her adulteries).

Poor Emma was no better than a whorish "Messalina." And all was Flaubert's fault, for having indulged in *realism*. Here was the artistic shibboleth of the age! Even though Flaubert was eventually acquitted of all charges—more fortunate he than the great poet of *Les Fleurs du Mal* (1857; translated as *Flowers of Evil*, 1909), Charles Baudelaire, who was found guilty of similar charges later in the same year—the judge felt it his duty not to discharge Flaubert without a stern lecture on the excesses of *realism*, a realism that he deplored as both "vulgaire et souvent choquant" (vulgar and often shocking).

Flaubert's name has indeed been long associated with realism, and *Madame Bovary* figures often as its canonical, liturgical text. It is heroic in a sense, especially because of its long and arduous composition, which lasted from 1851 to 1855. (The composition of the novel through its manuscript stages has been magisterially presented by Claudine Gothot-Mersch in *La Genèse de "Madame Bovary"* [The Genesis of *Madame Bovary*, 1966].) Flaubert constantly wrote and rewrote his masterpiece, spending hours and often entire days on the redaction of a single page, the polishing of a single phrase. The well-documented history of its writing has turned it into a legendary book—and its author into an apostle of objective art, of single-minded devotion, of the chill and impartial hypostatized artist who was summed up in a contemporary caricature of Flaubert as a surgeon: "Flaubert dissecting Emma Bovary." In the left background of the caricature is a dissection table bearing a female form (wearing boots and fully clothed!). Flaubert stands before the table in surgeon's garb. His handlebar mustache is long and waxed. His eyelids seem to veil his outlook, which may be imagined to be pensive or pitiless. From his apron, cutting instruments protrude: a saw, a pair of scissors. In his uplifted left hand, at the end of a scalpel, he displays the heart of Emma Bovary, whose blood, drop by drop, is gathered in an inkwell at his feet. And in his right hand he holds a mirror, the time-honored emblem of verisimilitude or mimesis (the exact representation of reality). Virtually all of Flaubert's contemporaries concurred that his treatment of his characters was detached and often cold: in a word, clinical. He himself acknowledged that he had a *coup d'œil médical* (a medical outlook).

Lemot's caricature is a manifestation of the positivistic spirit of the age, for positivism was an epistemology relying heavily on relations of cause and effect. This concept of causality resulted in theories of literature that one would today term "genetic." Books were biographical extensions of their authors. (And thus a "bad" book connoted a bad person, one who could be brought to bar.) Charles-Augustin Sainte-Beuve, the leading literary critic of the day, summed up the biographical approach to literature, in his work on François-René de Chateaubriand, with the proverbial expression "tel arbre, tel fruit" (the fruit does not fall far from the tree). So Flaubert, as the son of a doctor, could be presumed to have absorbed his *coup d'œil médical* in childhood.

There was much to justify these beliefs. Achille-Cléophas, Flaubert's father, was the son of a veterinarian, and was to become chief surgeon and head of the Hôpital Dieu in Rouen. Flaubert's elder brother, Achille, would succeed him in this post. The family lived in a wing of the hospital, and so Flaubert could be said to

"Flaubert dissecting Emma Bovary," an 1857 caricature by Lemot (Bibliothèque Nationale)

have grown up in pathological surroundings. "L'amphithéâtre de l'Hôtel-Dieu donnait sur notre jardin; que de fois avec ma sœur n'avons-nous pas grimpé au treillage et, suspendus entre la vigne, regardé curieusement les cadavres étalés; le soleil donnait dessus, les mêmes mouches qui voltigeaient sur nous et sur les fleurs allaient s'abattre là, revenaient, bourdonnaient" (The lecture hall of the hospital had windows on our garden; how many times did my sister and I not climb the trellis and, hanging amid the vines, look with curiosity upon the laid-out cadavers; the sun beat down upon them, the same flies that flitted around us and the flowers alit upon them, returned, buzzed). There is more than a lingering romantic taste for the macabre in such memories, for a child who is raised in a hospital will be exposed to real suffering and pain, and may be expected to acquire a gloomy perspective on life and death.

The Flaubert family, with the father's flourishing medical career, led a life of considerable ease and even wealth. Three children survived: Achille, born in 1813; Gustave; and his beloved sister Caroline, "le bon rat" (the good rat), born in 1824. Flaubert adored his mother, née Anne-Justine-Caroline Fleuriot. A close boyhood friend somewhat older than he, Ernest Chevalier, lived nearby and is said to have taught Gustave to read in an illustrated edition of *Don Quixote*.

The Flauberts formed an affectionate family, and despite Flaubert's obvious "pathologies," there is little hard evidence to support the Oedipal drama creatively constructed by Jean-Paul Sartre in his lengthy three-volume study of Flaubert, *L'Idiot de la famille* (1971-1972; translated as *The Family Idiot*, 1981-1991). Pace family anecdote and the existentialist philosopher, Flaubert learned to read at a normal age (thus he was hardly the "idiot" of Sartre's title), and his earliest extant letters (from 1829 to 1830) even show him in command of a certain style (if not spelling). By 1832 he had become an author, as a family friend reproduced two very different texts of his: an *Eloge de Corneille* (Tribute to Corneille; the great seventeenth-century playwright was a Rouen native) and a bit of schoolboy naughtiness, *La Belle Explication de la fameuse constipation* (The Fine Explanation of the Famous Constipation).

This was the year he entered secondary school, the Collège Royal de Rouen. Following the custom of the day, young Gustave was a boarder. He was not particularly happy there, but he did well in his studies, carrying off several end-of-year prizes, including one for best all-around in his class. During this time he read voraciously in the classics and began mounting home theatrical productions (works by Hugo, Alexandre Dumas *père*, and Molière) with his sister and friends. These included Ernest Chevalier and the Le Poittevin children: Alfred, whom Flaubert admired perhaps to excess; and his sister Laure, who was to be the mother of Guy de Maupassant.

At school he was assigned "narrations to compose." These resulted in historical narratives and dramas, such as *La Mort du duc de Guise* (Death of the Duke de Guise) and *Loys XI*; "philosophical" tales in the manner of Honoré de Balzac, such as *Passion et vertu* (Passion and Virtue); and muddled "mysteries," such as *Smarh*. The juvenilia, about two dozen texts written between 1835 and 1840, foreshadow many a scene of the mature novels and establish important psychological oppositions (such as that of the insider and the outsider) that Flaubert would incorporate into his later fictional portraits. The dualistic opposition between Homais on the one hand and Emma and the Blind Man on the other is an example of the Flaubertian paradigm of inclusion and exclusion.

Soon came the early novels *Mémoires d'un fou* (Memoirs of a Madman, 1901) and *Novembre* (1885; translated as *November*, 1934). *Mémoires* is the record of the strong adolescent love Flaubert conceived for a married woman whom he met, with her young daughter and companion, in 1836 at the seaside in Trouville. (Dr. Flaubert was an early proponent of sea bathing and had extensive property holdings in the Deauville-Trouville area.) Flaubert was fourteen, and Elisa Foucault Schlesinger was twenty-six. She had dark eyes, dark hair worn in bandeaux, brownish skin, and the full figure of a mature woman. She seemed beautiful and inaccessible. "Elle me regarda. Je baissai les yeux et rougis. Quel regard, en effet! comme elle était belle, cette femme!" (She looked at me. I lowered my eyes and blushed. What a look indeed! how beautiful that woman was!).

A psychological imprinting took place that was to mark Flaubert's fiction permanently: Elisa Schlesinger, the great love of his life, is the sensual model for Maria of *Mémoires*, Madame Renaud of *La Première Education sentimentale* (The First Sentimental Education, composed 1845, published 1910), and particularly Madame Arnoux, the heroine of the Fra Angelico-like "apparition" in the definitive version of *L'Education sentimentale* (1869; translated as *Sentimental Education*, 1898). She became the incarnation and projection of male passion in all its complexities and contradictions: virginal, maternal, erotic. At summer's end, Flaubert returned to school.

Flaubert's readings continued apace, often to be discussed with Alfred Le Poittevin. They included William Shakespeare; Johann Wolfgang von Goethe; George Gordon, Lord Byron; François Rabelais; Michel de Montaigne; and Jean-Jacques Rousseau. Flaubert's works during this period deal with grand metaphysical questions of death and God, of evil and freedom. An incident at school led to the rebellious adolescent's expulsion in 1839, but he nevertheless passed his baccalaureate exams the next year and was rewarded with a trip to southern France. Led by Dr.

Cloquet, a disciple of his father, Flaubert and a small group visited Bordeaux, Bayonne, and the Pyrenees. Next they traveled eastward to Provence, to Marseilles, and finally to Corsica. Returning through Marseilles, Flaubert had an unexpected physical encounter with the proprietress of the hotel in which they stayed. Thus to the romantic component of love furnished by Elisa Schlesinger was added the "flambée des sens" (the conflagration of the senses).

This trip was a revelation of the exotic and the "Oriental" for Flaubert. It was an introduction to the sun-drenched lands of the Mediterranean with which he would so strongly identify. It was a prelude of sorts to his conviction that he, with his native gloom and pessimism, had led a mystical series of what Baudelaire would soon term "anterior existences." Flaubert expresses this very well in a letter (13 August 1846) to his mistress Louise Colet: "J'ai au fond de l'âme le brouillard du Nord que j'ai respiré à ma naissance. Je porte en moi la mélancolie des races barbares, avec ses instincts de migrations et ses dégoûts innés de la vie, qui leur faisait quitter leur pays comme pour se quitter eux-mêmes. Ils ont aimé le soleil tous les barbares qui sont venus mourir en Italie, ils avaient une aspiration frénétique vers la lumière, vers le ciel bleu, vers quelque existence chaude et sonore, ils rêvaient des jours heureux pleins d'amour, juteux pour leurs cœurs comme la treille mûre que l'on presse avec les mains. J'ai toujours eu pour eux une sympathie tendre comme pour des ancêtres" (Deep in my soul I have the fog of the North that I breathed at my birth. Within me I bear the melancholy of the barbarian races, with their instincts for migration and their innate disgust for life, which made them leave their lands as if to flee themselves. They loved the sun, all those barbarians who came to Italy to die, they had a frenzied yearning toward light, toward the blue sky, toward some warm and resonant existence, they dreamt of days filled with love, as succulent for their hearts as the ripe grape that one presses with one's hands. I have always had a tender sympathy for them, as for ancestors).

The year 1841 was mostly one of study for Flaubert, but in November, yielding to his father's wishes, he enrolled in law school in Paris. Before moving there in July 1842, he met an English family in Trouville, the Colliers. Flaubert kept up sporadic contact for many years with the two Collier daughters, Gertrude and Harriet. During this time he was at work on *Novembre*, an auto-

Flaubert at age ten (portrait by Ernest Langlois; Bibliothèque Nationale)

biographical rumination in the Romantic vein. The work owes much to Rousseau, to Alfred de Musset, and to Chateaubriand; it evokes the narrator's childhood, school days, and discovery of sexual love in the arms of a warmhearted prostitute named Marie.

Marie, inspired by Elisa Schlesinger but also by the less ethereal Eulalie Foucauld de Langlade of Marseilles, adumbrates Emma Bovary in her mixing of sensual and spiritual love: "A l'église, je regardais l'Homme nu étalé sur la croix . . . je le détachais de la croix et je le faisais descendre vers moi, sur l'autel; l'encens l'entourait, il s'avançait dans la fumée, et de sensuels frémissements me couraient sur la peau" (At church, I used to gaze at the naked Man spread on the cross . . . I used to detach him from the cross and bring him down toward me, on the altar; incense surrounded him, he would advance in the smoke, and sensual shudderings would run over my skin). Flaubert later dismissed this text as an "amorous and sentimental ratatouille," noting that the action was "nil."

A similarly sensual liaison takes place between a schoolboy and his headmaster's wife in the first *Education sentimentale*. The title is unfortunate, for this early work, though fascinating, bears scant resemblance to the 1869 masterpiece of the same name. A better title would have simply been "The Story of Two Young Men," since the work contrasts the adolescences of two friends who evolve in very different ways. Henry becomes the lover of Emilie, who is older than he, and comes to lead a successful worldly existence. Meanwhile his friend Jules, an aspiring playwright, is unhappy in love and withdraws progressively from life to embrace an austere artistic creed. Jules's cult of style and impersonal expression presage the aesthetic principles that Flaubert would enunciate in his letters to Louise Colet during the "Bovary" years. The two characters represent twin aspirations of Flaubert's temperament: the socially successful lion and (as he would later be termed) the "hermit of Croisset," living in his ivory tower. As Jean Bruneau has noted, this is the work that marks the end of Flaubert's youth and the beginning of his artistic maturity. Yet before this long novella was finished, one important event produced a break in Flaubert's life and career.

Flaubert was unhappily enrolled in law school. At the end of 1842 he passed his first-year exams. During the next year he began writing the first *Education sentimentale*, visited the Schlesingers, frequented the studio of the sculptor James Pradier (where he met Hugo), and made friends with Maxime Du Camp, whom he would accompany a few years later to Egypt and who left important if suspect impressions of Flaubert in his *Souvenirs littéraires* (Literary Memories, 1882-1883). But in August he failed his second-year exams and returned to his family. While riding in a carriage with his brother in January 1844, he suddenly fell over, stricken by an epileptic seizure in which he felt "carried away in a sea of flame." His brother thought he was dead.

Flaubert eventually recovered, despite secondary attacks (he was probably suffering from venereal disease as well), but his law career was at an end; henceforth, his father would accept his son's destiny as a writer. He was at last free to become the "Homme-plume" (Pen-Man) he had always wished to be. The seizure, which may have been psychosomatic if not actually self-induced, was a turning point in his life. Soon he was installed at the new family property at Croisset (just downstream from Rouen), and here all his

masterpieces were to be written. Today, all that remains of the house is its pavilion, which houses a small Flaubert museum.

In March 1845 Caroline married Emile Hamard, a young lawyer. Astonishingly, the bride's mother, father, and brother decided to accompany them on their honeymoon trip to Italy. When they reached Marseilles, Flaubert tried to look up Eulalie, but there was no trace of her. In Genoa, Pieter Brueghel's painting *Temptation of Saint Anthony* made a strong impression on him. His decision to adapt the subject of the hermitic saint's temptations for the theater was to become a lifelong obsession. Modern editions of Flaubert recognize at least three versions of the text.

At home in Croisset, Flaubert's research on Saint Anthony was interrupted by his father's illness. Then, in a terrible series of events, Dr. Flaubert died from an abscessed thigh (operated on by Achille), and Caroline, after giving birth to a little girl also named Caroline, died of puerperal fever two months later. The mother and brothers were devastated. Hamard entrusted the upbringing of little Caroline to Mme Flaubert, who was then fifty-three years old. (Mme Flaubert's own mother had died in childbirth. Many years later, Flaubert's niece would become the owner and executor of his papers.) Achille would follow in his father's footsteps and live at the hospital in Rouen, and so at Croisset a new little household was formed: Flaubert, his mother, baby Caroline, and the faithful servant Julie.

About this time Flaubert became close friends with a former classmate, Louis Bouilhet. A minor poet and playwright, Bouilhet shared Flaubert's ideal of artistic rigor and became something like his literary conscience. And on a visit to Paris, Flaubert met Louise Colet in Pradier's studio.

Louise Colet was a beautiful poet of meager talent who was living apart from her husband but enjoying the protection of the philosopher Victor Cousin. Her affair with Flaubert would be long and stormy, lasting from 1846 to 1848 (when there was a break) and then from 1851 to 1855 (the final break). Its literary significance is enormous, for Colet preserved the letters Flaubert wrote her during the crucial Bovary years. Although there are some love letters (yet he told her that love could never be the main course in his life, only the "relish"), most of the correspondence deals with fascinating aesthetic reflections by Flaubert, which allow the reader to follow the composition of *Madame Bovary*. There are a lot of letters, for Flaubert refused to live with Louise in Paris and did not want her to visit Croisset. (She was roundly humiliated on the one occasion when she arrived unannounced, hoping to force her way into the household to meet his mother.) As a result, he would write to her two and sometimes three times a week.

Of course Flaubert had numerous other correspondents, and today the *Correspondance* is considered a great literary monument in itself. The tone of the letters may vary according to their audience, but many are written in a vigorous, often vehement style that makes them most appealing. To express his contempt for his own age (a sentiment soon to inform his writing on the Saint Anthony theme), he wrote to Bouilhet (30 September 1855): "Je sens contre la bêtise de mon époque des flots de haine qui m'étouffent. Il me monte de la merde à la bouche.... Mais je veux la garder, la figer, la durcir. J'en veux faire une pâte dont je barbouillerais le XIXᵉ siècle, comme on dore de bougée de vache les pagodes indiennes; et qui sait? cela durera peut-être?" (Against the stupidity of my age I feel waves of hatred that suffocate me. The taste of shit comes to my mouth.... But I want to keep it there, congeal it, harden it, make it into a paste to daub all over the nineteenth century, as Indian pagodas are gilded with cow dung; and who knows, maybe it will endure?).

Despite his nervous crises, Flaubert decided to undertake a walking tour of Brittany with Du Camp. The two friends left Paris with their backpacks on 1 May 1847, going through Anjou and Touraine and returning to Normandy in August. They resolved to write up their trip, with Flaubert doing the odd-numbered chapters and Du Camp the even ones. This travel narrative is entitled *Par les champs et par les grèves* (1885; translated as *Over Strand and Field*, 1904).

Shortly after this, in February 1848, he and Bouilhet traveled to Paris to observe the uprising that marked the fall of the July Monarchy. In the company of Du Camp, the friends "attended" the revolution of 1848 as if it were a spectacle or a theatrical performance. They witnessed street fighting near the Palais Royal and later the pillaging of the palace. (A fictional transposition of these events is found in part 3 of the 1869 *Education sentimentale*.) Hardly had he returned to Croisset than his great friend Alfred Le Poittevin ("lost" to him already through marriage) died. Flaubert wrote Du Camp a moving account of his friend's death (7 April 1848).

Then he began writing his account of Saint Anthony, for which he had long been preparing. Earlier (21-22 August 1846) he had explained to Colet that the subject appealed to the charm that the "grotesque triste" (sad grotesque) held for his comically bitter nature. *La Tentation de Saint Antoine* (1874; translated as *The Temptation of Saint Anthony*, 1895), which he called his "vieille toquade" (old infatuation), is a difficult work to describe. It could be called a philosophical prose poem or a dramatic narration and dialogue. It opens with Anthony, a fourth-century Christian hermit, alone on his mountain in Egypt (North Africa as the crossroads of religions), overlooking the desert and the Nile. He recalls his childhood and his decision to become a hermit. The ascetic reflects on other lives he might have led and feels discouragement. His Bible is little consolation to him, and, weak from fasting, he becomes prey to hallucinations. Dreams and visions of temptation ensue.

He is attracted by rich food, participates in an orgy, and is visited and tempted by the Queen of Sheba. But it is the temptation of knowledge that proves most dangerous to Anthony. His former pupil Hilarion assumes the role of Science and summons before Anthony's eyes a long succession of sages and heresiarchs, magicians and prophets. The world's religions appear to present their claims as Hilarion notes how similar they are: they flow in and out of one another in an endless metamorphosis. The Devil-Hilarion takes Anthony through space and shows him countless other worlds. Upon his return to Earth he is tempted by two women, one young, one old, who turn out to be incarnations of Lust and Death. Taking each other by the waist, they sing:

—Je hâte la dissolution de la matière!
—Je facilite l'éparpillement des germes!
—Tu détruis, pour mes renouvellements!
—Tu engendres, pour mes destructions!
—Active ma puissance!
—Féconde ma pourriture!

(—I hasten the dissolution of matter!
—I expedite the scattering of germs!
—You destroy, for my renewals!
—You beget, for my destructions!
—Activate my power!
—Fecundate my decay!)

This typically Flaubertian obsession with the reciprocity of destruction and creation is followed by the impossible attempt at coupling of

Flaubert in early adulthood (sketch by Jules Delaunay; Bibliothèque Municipale de Rouen)

the Chimaera and the Sphinx, emblematic of the irreconcilability of fantasy and matter. A proliferation of life in all its forms confronts him, and the saint would like to be absorbed in the amalgam of animal, vegetable, and mineral—he aspires to "être la matière!" (be matter!). Daybreak finally comes; the face of Jesus Christ appears in the disk of the sun; and Anthony returns to his prayers.

Flaubert's identification with Anthony is at the heart of this strange work. There can be little doubt that this is a portrait of the artist himself, of an obstinate artist who resisted all self-doubt and every temptation in order to remain faithful to his self-imposed mission, to his text. As Victor Brombert has shown, it also reflects the fear of decadence that haunted the nineteenth century. This was the legacy of the historical relativism of the Enlightenment married to the comparative study of religions in Flaubert's day. The Wagnerian "Twilight of the Gods" and Oswald Spengler's *Decline of the West* (1918-1922) are adumbrated in Flaubert's treatment of Saint Anthony.

Meanwhile, Du Camp had been pushing Flaubert to undertake together another, more ambitious trip, this time to Egypt and the Levant. Flaubert would not leave before finishing *Saint Antoine.* When at last the work was finished,

Bouilhet and Du Camp, who knew only the book's title, were summoned to Croisset for a reading of the text. Over four days Flaubert read for thirty-two hours, at the end of which the hitherto silent friends were called upon to give their opinions. "Nous pensons qu'il faut jeter cela au feu et n'en jamais reparler" (We think you should throw it in the fire and never mention it again). Flaubert was horrified and disappointed, but in the end he bowed to their arguments. Yet he was to return to his dear *Saint Antoine* after finishing *Madame Bovary,* and yet again five years before his death, when a "definitive" version was published. Thus there are three versions, progressively shorter, of 1849, 1856, and 1874.

Then it was off for a trip of almost two years to the Orient. Du Camp was charged with a semiscientific mission by the French government that provided the travelers with some official introductions. He took along cumbersome camera equipment and produced the first photographically illustrated book on the Near East. Flaubert's mission was ostensibly to assess commercial potential, but he was chiefly intent upon satisfying an ancient thirst for the land of Saint Anthony, for that East where he had long thought he was born to live.

The travelers sailed from Marseilles on 4 November 1849, and after stops in Malta and Alexandria, they reached Cairo on the twenty-sixth. They visited the Pyramids and the Sphinx, and eventually sailed up the Nile on a two-masted *cangia,* past Karnak and the Valley of the Kings to Luxor. At Esna they stopped to visit the *almehs,* or singing dancers (that is to say, prostitutes), who had been exiled from Cairo to Upper Egypt. Flaubert left a famous account of his night with Kuchuk-Hanem, who performed the Dance of the Bee for him.

It is certain that Flaubert's self-confidence had been shaken and that he was still brooding over the reception of *Saint Antoine.* In his memoirs, Du Camp claims that his friend was passive and even bored throughout their trip. One day, though, on the second cataract of the Nile, he came to life. Shouting "Eureka! Eureka!," Flaubert proclaimed, "Je l'appellerai Emma Bovary" (I'll call her Emma Bovary). But there is no reference to the character or the novel in Flaubert's own letters or travel notes from this time, and such anecdotes cause one to treat Du Camp's recollections with caution.

Returning to Cairo and Alexandria, they took a ship to Beirut and made their way overland to Jerusalem. From Damascus, Flaubert wrote Bouilhet about a "Dictionnaire des idées reçues" (Dictionary of Received Ideas), a compendium of popular beliefs and clichés that would be arranged in such a way that the reader would not know whether or not he was being mocked. He would work on this project all his life, intending to place it in the second volume of *Bouvard et Pécuchet* (1881; translated, 1896). In the same letter (4 September 1850) is found one of his best-known aphorisms: "L'ineptie consiste à vouloir conclure" (Stupidity consists of seeking to conclude).

From Syria the companions made their way through Turkey, Greece, and Italy, where Mme Flaubert came to meet her son. Together they visited Rome, Florence, and Venice, returning to Croisset in June 1851. Flaubert had ingested "plein le ventre de couleurs" (a bellyful of colors); he had seen the Pyramids, the Holy Sepulcher, and the Parthenon. He had also spent most of his inheritance on the trip. In July, Du Camp wrote to ask what Flaubert was writing—was it the story of "Mme Delamarre," which he thought very beautiful?

This is an allusion to Flaubert's source material for *Madame Bovary*. Eugène Delamare was an obscure medical officer, a former student of Dr. Flaubert, whose second wife, Delphine, had two affairs and died, leaving her husband with a daughter and enormous debts. Louise Pradier, the sculptor's wife, could also have served as a model. What is of more importance than Flaubert's source is the fact that he had taken up with Louise Colet once more, and that his frequent letters to her serve as a kind of log of the novel's composition. The writing of *Madame Bovary* was wholly to absorb Flaubert from its beginning on 19 September 1851 until he sent off the manuscript to Du Camp on 30 April 1856.

The story begins with the slow-witted Charles Bovary, a country health officer, who takes as his second wife Emma Bovary, the dissatisfied and pretty daughter of a well-to-do farmer. Unsatisfied in her marriage and yearning for a love and an existence that she can find only in the romantic books she devours, Emma is completely bored and frustrated. (In a witty piece entitled "The Kugelmass Episode" [1977] that takes off on the *Madame Bovary* story line, Woody Allen describes the couple as a "paramedic married to a jitterbug.") They move to Yonville-l'Abbaye, where their neighbor is the grotesque and pompous pharmacist Homais, whose "enlight-

ened" attitudes are invariably expressed in platitudes. The local priest cannot fathom Emma's dilemma, and her mother-in-law is hostile. Disappointed that she gives birth to a daughter rather than a son, she finds no joy in motherhood. She flirts gingerly with a lawyer's clerk, Léon Dupuis. She attends an agricultural fair in the company of a rakish country squire, Rodolphe Boulanger, and is seduced by him during a horseback ride in the woods.

Emma is further disillusioned and humiliated when Charles botches a clubfoot operation. Rodolphe tires of Emma's demanding nature and abruptly abandons her on the eve of a planned flight to Italy. Emma falls into a deep depression but eventually recovers. On a trip to the Rouen opera she reencounters Léon, who entices her into an affair that begins with a ribald carriage ride around town. Emma travels frequently to Rouen for clandestine rendezvous with Léon, spends and borrows profligately, and becomes mired in despair and debt. As the bailiffs arrive to seize the family goods, Emma takes arsenic and dies a painful death. Afterward, Charles discovers her love letters to Rodolphe. He blames his misfortune on no one, or rather on fate, and soon dies. The orphaned little Berthe will be condemned to the grim world of nineteenth-century child labor. Homais receives the Legion of Honor.

All the characters of *Madame Bovary* are strongly drawn, and the novel alternates between moments of savage satire and deeply moving, lyrical passages. In fact, the novel can be viewed as being structured around a series of dramatic episodes: Emma's wedding feast, where the guests spend sixteen gluttonous hours at the table; the ball at La Vaubyessard, the episode which, the narrator tells the reader, made a "hole" in her life; the agricultural fair, with its double discourses of seduction; Emma's encounters with the emblematic Blind Man; her meeting in the Rouen cathedral with Léon and ensuing lovemaking in the carriage; her last appeal to Rodolphe and her suicide. Linking all the episodes is Emma's incessant yearning for a nameless fulfillment and a capacity for wishing herself other than she is, a characteristic that an early critic, Jules Gaultier, dubbed *le bovarysme*.

Virtually all of the characters' names say something about them. The "bovine" metaphor of oxlike, cud-chewing existence is encoded in the Bovary name; Rouault, Emma's maiden name, contains the French word for wheel, and thus gestures to the patterns of repetition and enclosure in her constricted life; Léon, unlike his namesake Leo, is scarcely leonine—rather, he is timorous and indecisive. And, in a subtle comeuppance visited upon him at the novel's end, Léon will marry a Mlle Léocadie Lebœuf (Léocadie The Ox).

Flaubert's name has long been linked to realism, and *Madame Bovary* has long figured as a sacred text of literary "mimesis" (the representation of reality). The earliest recorded use of the term *realism* came in a Parisian periodical of 1826. Having defined it as a "literary doctrine . . . that would lead to the imitation not of artistic masterpieces but of the originals that nature offers us," the journalist added that realism "might well emerge . . . as the literature of the nineteenth century, the literature of truth." Realism was not to achieve wide currency until the 1850s, however, and then it would be used in conjunction with a certain style in painting, in particular the paintings of Gustave Courbet. *Realism* was rarely used without the epithet *sordid* or *vulgar.*

As F. W. J. Hemmings observes in *The Age of Realism* (1974), historians have linked the rise of realism to the abandonment, by influential thinkers and philosophers in the nineteenth century, of the solid belief in transcendental values that had hitherto framed the European worldview. Thus the Marxist critic György Lukács once called the novel "the epic of a world forsaken by God," and indeed realism depends on a willing suspension of belief, on the part of reader and writer, in an intervening deity, whose mediations in this world might shape human fates. In order to be convincing, the characters in a novel must be shown to be working out their own destinies independently of God's will: "To the marriage of realism and positivism (or determinism) there is no obstacle, but realism and fatalism make uneasy bedfellows."

Now Flaubert refused to think of himself as a realist. The author of *Saint Antoine* had undertaken his new subject as an antidote to his own lyrical flights, and had done so upon the strong urging of his friends. In one of his most frequently quoted letters to Colet (16 January 1852), he wrote, "Il y a en moi, littérairement parlant, deux bonshommes distincts: un qui est épris de *gueulades,* de lyrisme, de grands vols d'aigle, de toutes les sonorités de la phrase et des sommets de l'idée; un autre qui fouille et qui creuse le vrai tant qu'il peut, qui aime à accuser le petit fait aussi puissamment que le grand, qui voudrait

vous faire sentir presque *matériellement* les choses qu'il reproduit" (There are inside me, literarily speaking, two distinct fellows: one who is smitten by *shouts,* by lyricism, by great eagle flights, by all the sonorities of the sentence and the loftiness of ideas; another who probes and digs into the true as best he can, who loves to underscore the little fact as powerfully as the big one, who would wish to make you feel almost *physically* the things he is reproducing). He had failed to fuse the two sides of his nature in *Saint Antoine* and the first *Education sentimentale*; now it was time to succeed or "jump out of the window."

But the heavy realistic component of the new work made him protest that the whole Bovary business was inimical to his temperament. He complained in 1856 that people thought him drawn to reality, whereas "je l'exècre" (I loathe it). And later, in an 1876 letter to George Sand, he wrote, "J'exècre ce qu'on est convenu d'appeler le *réalisme,* bien qu'on m'en fasse un des pontifes" (I loathe what people call realism, although I'm supposedly one of its pontiffs). To Colet he grumbled constantly about the vulgarity of his subject matter, the platitude of his characters, and the difficulty of finding *le mot juste*—or precise word and phrasing.

He wrote Colet on 17 October 1853 that he was tortured by the book, that it gave him stomach pains and made him want to vomit: "Je crois qu'aujourd'hui je me serais pendu avec délices, si l'orgueil ne m'en empêchait. Il est certain que je suis tenté parfois de foutre tout là et la *Bovary* d'abord. Quelle sacrée maudite idée j'ai eue de prendre un sujet pareil! Ah! Je les aurai connues, les *affres* de l'Art!" (I think that today I would have hanged myself with delight if pride hadn't stopped me. What's certain is that I'm sometimes tempted to say to hell with it all, beginning with the *Bovary* woman. What a damn cursed idea of mine it was to pick such a subject! Ah! I'll have learned all about the *torments* of Art!). Why did he persist? It was out of sheer artistic devotion (24 April 1852): "J'aime mon travail d'un amour frénétique et perverti, comme un ascète le cilice qui lui gratte le ventre" (I love my work with a frantic and perverted love, as the ascetic the hair shirt that scratches his belly).

Yet the torments of art yielded a masterpiece that confounded the critics of 1857, puzzled as they were by the author's successful combination of artistic, nuanced phrasing with an "immoral," though banal, subject—adultery. And yet for Flaubert there were no intrinsically beauti-

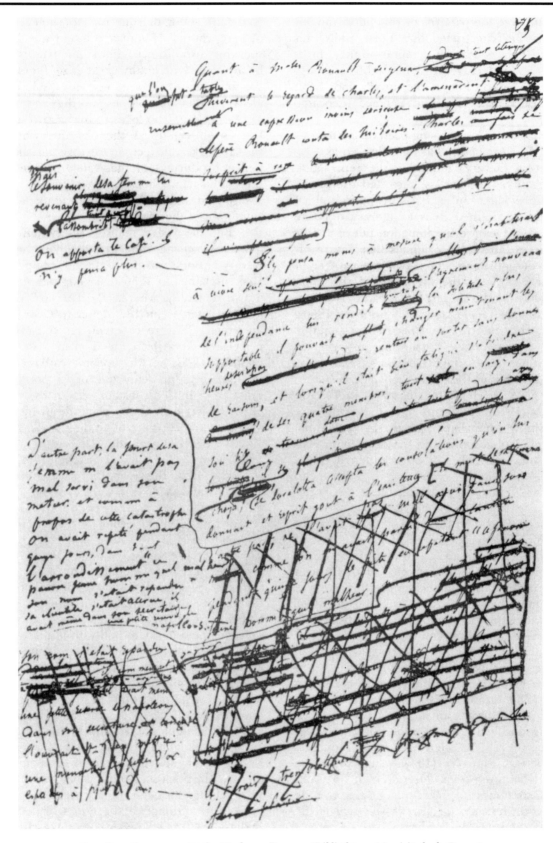

Page from the manuscript for Madame Bovary *(Bibliothèque Municipale de Rouen)*

ful or ugly subjects, for all was in the style, style being, as he put it, "in itself an absolute way of seeing things." Flaubert's cult of form, which brought him aesthetically close to the doctrine of *l'art pour l'art* (art for art's sake) and the school of poets known as *le Parnasse,* led him to conceive his celebrated ambition of writing "un livre sur rien" (a book about nothing) in which style alone would be the sustaining element (letter to Colet, 16 January 1852).

Alison Fairlie has written that realism, as practiced by Flaubert, can be understood as a manner of reacting against the traditional Romantic novel with its flights of fancy and its emphasis on the fantastic, the ideal, and the exceptional. It sought to create the illusion of observing impartially the events of an average life. Balzac and Stendhal had already exploited the possibilities offered by the triviality of daily life; but their characters were exceptional beings whose lives were filled with exciting events. They succeeded or failed in spectacular ways. Such was not to be the case with Emma Bovary.

Emma would have been better matched with a character such as Chateaubriand's René or a Lamartinian lover, or in a suicidal role as beautiful as that of Chateaubriand's Atala. But failure in love alone does not determine Emma's downfall; she has money problems, is pursued by creditors and bailiffs, and dies amid emetics and vomiting. The very possibility of the dramatic seems constantly to be denied her. When she thinks that her husband Charles may surprise her with her lover Rodolphe, she breathlessly asks him if he has his pistols. Rodolphe uncomprehendingly asks her why. "Mais . . . pour te défendre, reprit Emma.—Est-ce de ton mari? Ah! le pauvre garçon!" (But . . . to defend yourself, replied Emma.—You mean against your husband? Oh, the poor fellow!).

Her desire for luxury, for a life of excitement and social sophistication, is satisfied only by a single night spent at a ball in an elegant country château. In his plans Flaubert had thought of having her visit Paris, but the book restricts her to the provinces, where she can only buy maps of the capital and trace imaginary itineraries with her finger. Flaubert thus subjects his characters to what Baudelaire called a "dureté systématique" (systematic harshness).

Moreover, Flaubert wrote that the hardest thing in art is not to make people laugh or weep, but to make them dream (26 August 1853). An object long contemplated acquires an interest of its own (16 September 1845). It is unnecessary to inflate the objects of the material world with artificial dignity and grandeur; the artist's task is to extract from the humblest object its suggestive value. Thus in Charles's fantastic schoolboy cap one can see the symbol of his stupidity: "une de ces pauvres choses dont la laideur muette a des profondeurs d'expression comme le visage d'un imbécile" (one of those poor things whose silent ugliness has depths of expression like the face of an imbecile).

One of Flaubert's strongest aesthetic beliefs concerned narration. He was adamant that the novelist should maintain neutrality and that the author's personality should remain absent from the novel (this is one of his chief differences with his predecessors in the development of French realism, Balzac and Stendhal). Of course Flaubert put much of his own temperament into his works—the most famous assertion concerning the identity of his protagonist remains "Madame Bovary, c'est moi" (*I* am Madame Bovary)—but Flaubert does so in an impersonal manner. His most memorable formulation of this tenet comes in a letter to Colet (9 December 1852): "L'auteur, dans son œuvre, doit être comme Dieu dans l'univers, présent partout, et visible nulle part" (The author in his work must be like God in the universe: everywhere present and nowhere visible). "It is above all else," writes Hemmings, "this finely balanced mixture, where Emma is concerned, of empathy and critical objectivity that has earned the novel its celebrity as the first masterpiece of the realist esthetic."

The absence of the author does not mean that he has no opinions; on the contrary, as Flaubert wrote, he is, like the deity, omnipresent. But how is one to detect authorial presence or judgment? Sometimes this poses no problem, since the platitudes of Homais and the schemes of Lheureux are obvious or transparent. Patterns of recurrence give objects significance: a statuette of a priest reading his breviary that stands in Emma's yard deteriorates progressively in harsh weather and then falls off the moving van and is smashed; it symbolizes the breakup of her marriage to Charles. A representation of Cupid appears in each of the three parts of the novel, but in the last one it is "smirking."

In other scenes the author's meaning may be less accessible. Flaubert worried that a "poetic" conversation between Léon and Emma (when they first meet at the beginning of part 2) might be taken seriously, whereas he intended it

Louise Colet, whose letters from Flaubert record his progress on Madame Bovary *(drawing by an anonymous artist)*

to be grotesque. In such instances Flaubert sets up rather visible ironic counterpoints, making sure in this particular scene, for example, that the "poetic" is offset by a "practical" conversation simultaneously taking place between Charles and Homais. Homais's pompous claims to scientific expertise are deflated by his inability to convert temperature scales. His comments about the financial ease of the local farmers are belied by their manifest poverty. Léon's lyrical description of the natural beauty of Swiss waterfalls is undercut by his own remark that his experience is second-hand, derived from a cousin's account. This example of direct speech (dialogue) suggests a general rule for reading *Madame Bovary*: all dialogue should be read as satire. The proof comes in the grand agricultural fair scene—a truly bravura piece—where the elevated and the vulgar are ostensibly set at odds, only to be conflated in the awarding of a prize for the best manure.

Here another problem arises, one that Flaubert was also highly conscious of: how to reproduce the mediocrity of everyday speech and yet still capture its evocative tones, its lingering charm, even its underlying poetry. Easy enough, one might say, to depict the surface of human speech and to stigmatize its inadequacies; more

daunting by far to convey its subtextual and virtually immaterial allure. As Gothot-Mersch writes in her 1971 edition of *Madame Bovary*, "Les cœurs pleins vibrent sous les mots vides" (Full hearts are throbbing under the empty words).

An uncharacteristic authorial intervention in *Madame Bovary* reveals just how strongly Flaubert felt on this point. As Emma affirms her love in embarrassingly overwrought terms, Rodolphe discounts her protestations, hearing in them only the hackneyed endearments of his previous mistresses, "comme si la plénitude de l'âme ne débordait pas quelquefois par les métaphores les plus vides, puisque personne, jamais, ne peut donner l'exacte mesure de ses besoins, ni de ses conceptions, ni de ses douleurs, et que la parole humaine est comme un chaudron fêlé où nous battons des mélodies à faire danser les ours, quand on voudrait attendrir les étoiles" (as if the fullness of the soul does not sometimes overflow in the emptiest metaphors, since no one, ever, can give the exact measure of his needs, nor of his conceptions, nor of his sorrows, and since human speech is like a cracked drum on which we beat out melodies fit to make bears dance, when one would wish to move the stars).

The main problem, then, is the lack of "fit" between sentiment and expression. In an attempt to remedy this problematic relationship, Flaubert had recourse to the syntactic resources of the language itself, and perfected what was later to be called the "free indirect style" (FIS; the "free" indicates that once launched, it requires no verbs of thinking or saying). This is an intermediate style that is situated somewhere between direct and indirect style. It allows Flaubert, as Brombert writes, "to formulate clearly that which, in the character's mind, remains unformulated or only half-formulated." Thus the author glides imperceptibly between the confused, half-articulated concepts of the characters and his own artistic and polished expression of the same concepts. Its effect on readers is to place them simultaneously on the inside and on the outside of the character.

After the catastrophic clubfoot operation, the text focalizes on Emma's disgust with her husband's potential: "Comment donc avait-elle fait (elle qui était si intelligente!) pour se méprendre encore une fois? (Just how had she managed [she who was so intelligent] to be mistaken once again?). The reader must here reflect: who exactly states that Emma is intelligent? It is a third-person statement, but would the narrator make such an assertion? FIS offers the potential for irony and lyricism, and it is Flaubert's most admired stylistic achievement. Harry Levin praises this internalization of the narrative for achieving a paradoxical "eloquent banality," the sensation that speech is both caricature and poetry.

Alison Fairlie makes the important point about FIS that its characteristic French tense is the imperfect (or the conditional), a tense reserved in French for describing the real background conditions of events or scenes. Since the imperfect also serves to describe Emma's inner thoughts, the effect is one of shuttling without distinction between reality and illusion. And that interweaving of the real and the dream is what gives *Madame Bovary* its strongest appeal.

When the novel was finished, Du Camp and Laurent Pichat, then editors of the *Revue de Paris*, asked to publish it in serial form, intending to cut the risqué scenes (such as the carriage ride) to avoid the wrath of the imperial censor. But expurgation brought them the wrath of Flaubert, and the censor did not fail to prosecute them on charges of immorality. Flaubert suspected political persecution and was personally outraged (16 January 1857): "Je dois aller m'asseoir (pour crime d'avoir écrit en français) sur le banc des filous et des pédérastes" (I must take my seat [for the crime of having written in French] on the bench of pickpockets and pederasts). He feared that he would be found guilty by the court, but his lawyer (Sénard, to whom *Madame Bovary* is dedicated) presented a brilliant defense, and the defendants were acquitted. The novel, then assured of a succès de scandale, was published in two volumes in April 1857.

Before this, at the time he completed *Madame Bovary*, Flaubert returned to his *Saint Antoine*, eventually publishing some excerpts of the finished second version in Théophile Gautier's *L'Artiste* (December 1857). But now he feared more censorship and prosecution, and so he turned away from modern life to antiquity, to Carthage. As always, Flaubert undertook serious documentation for the new work, in libraries in Rouen and Paris. The first chapter of *Salammbô* (1862; translated, 1886) was started in October 1857. He needed to see the sites of his novel for himself, and so he undertook his second and last trip to North Africa, shipping out from Marseilles in April 1858 on a two-month voyage that took him to eastern Algeria and Tunisia. By June he was back in Croisset, studying his travel notes and hard at work. It was to take him until February 1862 to finish it.

During the *Salammbô* years, Flaubert was an established literary personality who frequented figures such as Sainte-Beuve, Baudelaire, Edmond and Jules Goncourt, George Sand, Ernest Renan, and many others; after the publication of *Salammbô* he was also well received in imperial society, particularly in the circle of Princess Mathilde, the emperor's cousin.

Almost nothing was known about Carthage, but this would leave room for Flaubert's historical imagination to work. His principal source would be Polybius's *General History*, and the plot would tell of the revolt of mercenary armies after the defeat of Carthage in the first Punic War (third century B.C.) and the bloody repression that ensued. The passion of a mercenary leader, Mâtho, for a Carthaginian princess, Salammbô, would provide the matrix of the novel's binary structure.

The novel opens with a banquet in the gardens of Hamilcar in Megara, a suburb of Carthage. The mercenaries, or "Barbarians," are suspicious of the Carthaginians, who are unable to pay them off and who in turn are wary of the soldiers, a motley group of Africans of all sorts, of Greeks and Gauls, and other races. They do not understand one another's languages, and this increases the confusion. Drunken mercenaries avenge themselves by killing the sacred fish, a sacrilege that brings Salammbô out of her apartments to berate the mob. The soldiers cannot understand her ancient Chadian dialect, but they watch her descent from the palace in fascination. Narr'Havas, the Numidian, and Mâtho, the Libyan, are particularly struck by her appearance and become rivals. Mâtho is counseled by a freed slave, the crafty Greek named Spendius.

Eventually, the soldiers are convinced to leave Carthage, but they meander about and set up camp not far away. Hostilities break out when the pay issue cannot be settled, and the Barbarians return to bivouac beneath the city walls. Salammbô emerges onto her terrace at night to worship the moon goddess Tanit, "Reine des choses humides" (Queen of all things humid). She is consumed by a vague yearning; she would like to leave her body, be only a breeze or a moonbeam. She wants to visit the sanctuary and see a veil, the zaïmph, sacred to Carthage and its fate. It is said that the touch of the veil kills the profane, but Mâtho and Spendius penetrate the town through the viaduct and steal it from the temple. The alarm is raised; guarded by the zaïmph, Mâtho braves the howling crowds and leaves the city. He is now the undisputed mercenary leader. The Carthaginian army with its elephants routs the Barbarians, but the general, Hanno, does not follow up his victory and is in turn put to flight by a counterattack of flaming swine.

At this point the suffete, Hamilcar Barca (father of Salammbô), returns to take charge of Carthage. A man of enormous wealth, Hamilcar worships the terrible god Moloch, "the devourer." He plots revenge against the Barbarians—"Périssent dix mille Barbares plutôt qu'un seul d'entre nous" (Let ten thousand Barbarians perish rather than one of us)—and his Punic armies defeat Spendius at the battle of Macar. But Carthage turns against him when he is surrounded by four Barbarian armies, and threatens to immolate his daughter. The high priest of Tanit, Schahabarim, urges Salammbô to recover the zaïmph from Mâtho. After performing an erotic and mystical dance with the sacred python, she sets out for the mercenaries' camp. There she gives herself to the Barbarian: "Moloch, tu me brûles!" (Moloch, you are burning me!). And yet, upon retrieving the veil, "elle restait mélancolique devant son rêve accompli" (she remained melancholy before the fulfillment of her

dream). Narr'Havas betrays the Barbarians to serve Carthage, and Salammbô is promised to him.

The Barbarians lay siege to Carthage; Spendius cuts the aqueduct, and the Carthaginians suffer from hunger and terrible thirst in the heat. In order to appease Moloch, the Carthaginians sacrifice the infant sons of the nobility. (Hamilcar manages to substitute a slave's child for his own son Hannibal.) The frenzied noise of the slaughter attracts the Barbarians, who look on in horror. Rain falls and thunder rumbles: "C'était la voix de Moloch; il avait vaincu Tanit; et, maintenant fécondée, elle ouvrait du haut du ciel son vaste sein" (It was the voice of Moloch, who had conquered Tanit; and now made fertile, she opened her vast womb from the heights of the sky).

With renewed courage, the Carthaginians manage to escape by sea and to trap the Barbarians in the Pass of the Axe. Carnage, cannibalism, starvation, and death are their fates, and lions eat the survivors. Mâtho is captured by Hamilcar and forced to run the gauntlet of the massed, frenzied Carthaginians. "Le principe femelle, ce jour-là, dominait, confondait tout: une lascivité mystique circulait dans l'air pesant" (This day the female principle dominated and confounded all: a mystical lascivity circulated in the heavy air). By the time Mâtho reaches Salammbô, he is scarcely recognizable as a human being, yet she feels attracted to him. Torn to pieces by the mob, he falls dead; a priest of Moloch rushes forward to cut out his heart and offers it to the sun.

The populace roars in exultation: "Carthage était comme convulsée dans le spasme d'une joie titanique et d'un espoir sans bornes" (Carthage was as if convulsed in the spasm of a titanic joy and limitless hope). Narr'Havas encircles Salammbô's waist and raises his cup to the genius of Carthage. Salammbô rises to drink also, but she falls backward dead, "blême, raidie, les lèvres ouvertes, et ses cheveux dénoués pendaient jusqu'à terre. Ainsi mourut la fille d'Hamilcar pour avoir touché au manteau de Tanit" (pale, stiff, her lips parted, and her unbound hair hanging down to the ground. So died the daughter of Hamilcar for having touched the mantle of Tanit).

Even with its appalling bloodthirstiness, *Salammbô* was an immediate success. Despite its setting in a remote and little-known historical period, it managed to address many contemporary concerns, as Anne Green has shown. Flaubert's

Lithograph by Odilon Redon for La Tentation de Saint Antoine. *The picture illustrates a passage describing a demon with a head of death and a crown of roses.*

publisher Michel Lévy had paid him eight hundred francs for the rights to *Madame Bovary*; for *Salammbô*, Lévy offered ten thousand. *Salammbô* costumes became popular and were worn to court balls. Flaubert's photograph was taken by Nadar, and he began to attend the Magny literary dinners (where he met Ivan Turgenev). He began work with Bouilhet on a fairy play, *Le Château des cœurs* (House of Hearts), which was to be refused by several theater directors and never performed. He was invited to the Tuileries and eventually (in 1864) to Compiègne, the preferred residence of Napoleon III. Empress Eugénie wrote that he was admired for his talent and erudition.

Flaubert's clinical interest in pathology comes to the fore in *Salammbô*, displayed in scenes of sadism and orgies of killing and bloodlust. The violence is unending. Lust, betrayal, mystical sensuality, and the unsteady antithesis of Civilized and Barbarian are themes of the work. (The indifferentiation of Civilized and Barbarian was moreover a favorite theme of literary

decadence.) Flaubert's old preoccupations with the Orient and its ferocious gods, and with the themes of inaccessibility, sacrilege, and mystical yearning, reappear here.

Emma and Salammbô are really sisters under the skin. Salammbô experiences only disillusionment when she at last possesses the zaïmph; it is the same with Emma's disenchantment in marriage: "Et Emma cherchait à savoir ce que l'on entendait au juste dans la vie par les mots de félicité, de passion et d'ivresse, qui lui avaient paru si beaux dans les livres" (And Emma tried to understand what precisely was meant in life by the words bliss, passion, and ecstasy, which had seemed so beautiful to her in books).

Flaubert's style in *Salammbô* is chiseled, lapidary, and Parnassian. It focuses on hard surfaces, jewelry, and sculpted, exotic perfections of a neurotic allure, on shimmer and plastic forms. Its gaze alternates between the petrified and the putrified. And a terrible sameness underwrites this world, a lassitude that the Ancients knew as taedium vitae. "Ah! vous comprenez l'embêtement de l'existence, vous!" (Ah! you understand the boredom of existence!), he wrote Baudelaire, the poet of spleen (ennui). Flaubert early wrote of his own "melancholy of the barbarian races."

In 1864 Flaubert's niece Caroline married Ernest Commanville. Her departure left only Flaubert and the aging Mme Flaubert in Croisset. She continued to support him financially. Another work had been decided on, and Flaubert settled into his study to begin ("ce cabinet du travail obstiné et sans trêve . . . témoin de tant et de si grands labeurs" [this cabinet of obstinate and relentless work . . . witness to so many great labors], as the Goncourts described it after a visit the year before). Soon he was putting in fourteen-hour days. This modern novel, the composition of which was to keep him "in harness" from 1864 to 1869, would be *L'Education sentimentale*—another masterpiece. Flaubert described it in this way (6 October 1864): "Je veux faire l'histoire morale des hommes de ma génération; 'sentimentale' serait plus vrai. C'est un livre d'amour, de passion; mais de passion telle qu'elle peut exister maintenant, c'est-à-dire, inactive" (I want to write the moral history of the men of my generation; "sentimental" would be truer. It's a book about love and passion, but about passion such as it can exist today, that is, inactive). Documentation and research led to long studies of the revolution of 1848 (it has been remarked that he had personally "attended" only its February days), feminist movements, means of transportation under the July Monarchy, neo-Catholic thought, stock-market operations, and diphtheria; he traveled to Fontainebleau, to a porcelain factory, to Melun and Montereau.

His research did not prevent him from leading an active social life. He traveled to London in 1865 and 1866 to visit, respectively, Juliet Herbert and his childhood friends Gertrude and Harriet Collier. In 1866 he was decorated with the Legion of Honor, and George Sand came for a visit to Croisset. In 1865 he had visited the Schlesingers in Baden-Baden, and in 1867 he may have seen Mme Schlesinger again in France. He attended a ball given in Czar Alexander II's honor at the Tuileries. Work continued apace, and on 16 May 1869 *L'Education sentimentale* was finished. He gave readings of his new work in Princess Mathilde's salon. To his great distress, both Bouilhet and Sainte-Beuve died before its publica-

tion in November. (Lévy paid him sixteen thousand francs for the work.)

As Flaubert had indicated, *L'Education sentimentale*, was to be the story of the failure of Flaubert's generation as seen through its protagonist, Frédéric Moreau. The story begins in 1840, as the eighteen-year-old Frédéric's boat is leaving Paris. Frédéric has been sent to visit his uncle in Le Havre and is on his way home to Nogent-sur-Seine. He has just finished school and will spend the summer in the provinces. The trip is uneventful, even languid, as the boat slowly makes its way upstream past the modest houses that dot the banks of the Seine. Frédéric is in a pensive and somewhat melancholy mood: "Il trouvait que le bonheur mérité par l'excellence de son âme tardait à venir" (He found that the happiness deserved by the excellence of his soul was long in coming).

His travel companions are of a common appearance, and the decks are strewn with scraps of food and trash, yet in the midst of this bourgeois mediocrity he is suddenly visited by an "apparition," a Beatrician vision of a comely, dark woman so striking that his fate is sealed in a single moment. "Quels étaient son nom, sa demeure, sa vie, son passé? Il souhaitait connaître les meubles de sa chambre, toutes les robes qu'elle avait portées, les gens qu'elle fréquentait; et le désir de la possession physique même disparaissait sous une envie plus profonde, dans une curiosité douloureuse qui n'avait pas de limites" (What was her name, her home, her life, her past? He longed to know the furniture in her room, all the dresses that she had worn, the people whom she frequented; and even the desire of physical possession disappeared in a deeper yearning, in a painful curiosity that had no limits).

This is Mme Arnoux, the archetypal maternal-erotic figure whose image had long ago imprinted itself on Flaubert's psyche in the encounter with Mme Schlesinger. (Her Christian name, like the character's, was Marie.) Mme Arnoux is a vision of loveliness in her straw hat with ribbons fluttering in the wind. Her oval face is framed by black hair, and her straight nose and chin are sharply outlined against the blue sky. Her fingers are so fine that light seems to traverse them. "Elle ressemblait aux femmes des livres romantiques" (She looked like the women in Romantic books). A black nanny brings her daughter to her, and this leads Frédéric to surmise that his exotic vision must be of Creole, or Andalusian, origin. In fact she is the wife of Jacques

Arnoux, the vulgar and philandering proprietor of a shop and journal oxymoronically entitled *L'Art industriel* (Industrial Art).

Frédéric returns to Paris for law school, which bores him. He shares a room with his impoverished Nogent friend, Deslauriers, and dabbles in literature with the idea of writing a novel. The two friends (who stick together throughout the novel despite many fallings-out) imagine that they will conquer Parisian society like heroes out of a Balzac novel. They make an assortment of acquaintances: Sénécal, the dogmatic socialist; Hussonnet, the bohemian journalist; Pellerin, the second-rate painter; and Dussardier, the good-hearted worker who embodies the generous and naive qualities of the 1848 revolutionaries.

Frédéric fails his law exams. He has become an intimate of the Arnoux household and timidly worships his idol without declaring himself. His hopes fail, and one night he thinks of throwing himself from a bridge into the Seine; but the parapet is broad, and out of "lassitude" he renounces the attempt. Frédéric is invited to dine with an influential banker, M. Dambreuse, who has political interests in Nogent, but he prefers to attend Mme Arnoux's birthday party at her country house in Saint Cloud. An incident reveals Arnoux's infidelity, and Frédéric returns to Paris with Mme Arnoux, alone in a carriage with her sleeping daughter.

Back in Nogent, Frédéric's mother reveals that family finances are grim. He can no longer live in Paris and must take a position at home as a law clerk. A little neighbor girl, Louise Roque, develops a crush on him. Finally he is saved from provincial existence by the death of his wealthy uncle; he can return to Paris after all. When his mother inquires what he will do there, he answers "Rien!" (Nothing!).

In part 2 Frédéric leads a leisurely existence. He buys an apartment, a carriage, and a horse and enjoys the life of a fashionable man-about-Paris. He frequents the Arnoux household once again; their financial position is perilous, and M. Arnoux has become a faience merchant. M. Arnoux takes him to a masked ball and introduces him to a courtesan, Rosanette Bron. He attends soirees at the house of M. and Mme Dambreuse. He is now paying court to Mme Arnoux and Rosanette but cannot seduce either.

Political unrest is in the air; Frédéric largely ignores it except to the extent that he is obliged to listen to Sénécal. He meets a young nobleman, M. de Cisy, whose great concern is "avoir du ca-

Caricature of Flaubert by Eugène Giraud
(Bibliothèque Nationale)

chet" (having tone), and promises Deslauriers money to feed his political ambitions by starting a newspaper. But on learning that M. Arnoux is in debt and may have to leave Paris, he gives money to keep his ideal love from departing. A misunderstanding leads to a comic duel with M. de Cisy. Frédéric's investments in coal mining with M. Dambreuse turn sour, and his reduced fortune forces him to consider marriage with Louise Roque.

Learning of his engagement, Mme Arnoux becomes jealous and at last recognizes that she loves Frédéric. An idyllic interlude ensues, during which she receives him at her house at Auteuil, but these tender meetings remain platonic. Demands for political reform now fill prerevolutionary Paris. Frédéric is determined to possess Mme Arnoux and rents an apartment for the purpose. Her son's croup keeps her from the rendezvous, and out of bitter frustration Frédéric seeks out Rosanette, who is astonished at his new forcefulness ("Je suis à la mode, je me réforme" [I'm in fashion; I've reformed]); he takes her to the apartment. During the night his weeping awakes Rosanette; he explains that his tears come from being too happy: "Il y avait trop longtemps que je te désirais!" (I wanted you for so long!).

Part 3 begins with the early days of the revolution of 1848. Frédéric and Hussonnet are more or less spectators (as Flaubert and Du Camp had been in reality) and follow the rampaging mobs into the Tuileries palace. "Les héros ne sentent pas bon!" (Heroes don't smell good!), remarks Hussonnet. But Frédéric finds the people "sublime," and, characterized by the narrator as an "homme de toutes les faiblesses" (a man of every weakness), he is drawn into political agitation. He presents himself as a candidate to a revolutionary organization, the "Club de l'Intelligence," but his appearance is preempted by a "patriote de Barcelone" who cuts him off with a speech delivered entirely in Spanish.

Disgusted with politics, Frédéric enjoys an unplatonic idyll with Rosanette in Fontainebleau. After their return to Paris, he makes up with Mme Arnoux but is interrupted at a crucial moment by the sudden appearance of a possessive Rosanette. Next Frédéric becomes the lover of Mme Dambreuse. M. Dambreuse dies. Since political reaction is in the air, marriage with Mme Dambreuse would mean a great fortune for Frédéric. But M. Dambreuse has cut his wife out of his will. About this time Arnoux's business affairs go completely awry, and despite Frédéric's attempts to save them, the Arnouxes are obliged to leave Paris. Out of loyalty Frédéric breaks with both Rosanette (their illegitimate child dies in infancy) and Mme Dambreuse.

It is 2 December 1851, the day of Louis-Napoleon Bonaparte's coup d'état. Frédéric thinks of Louise Roque and returns to Nogent, but he arrives just in time to see her and Dussardier emerge from their marriage in the village church. He returns to Paris. The police are breaking up political protests against the coup. Dussardier refuses to budge and cries "Vive la République!" He is run through by a policeman's sword, and Frédéric recognizes the killer: Sénécal, whose evolution from revolutionary to reactionary is now complete.

All of this action takes place before the next-to-last chapter of the novel. Now comes what Marcel Proust referred to admiringly as its "blanc" (blank space). As this example of temporal acceleration demonstrates, Flaubert had discovered the compressibility of time and could consequently or-

chestrate the rhythms of his novel to great aesthetic effect:

> Il voyagea.
> Il connut la mélancolie des paquebots, les froids réveils sous la tente, l'étourdissement des paysages et des ruines, l'amertume des sympathies interrompues.
> Il revint.
> Il fréquenta le monde, et il eut d'autres amours encore. Mais le souvenir continuel du premier les lui rendait insipides; et puis la véhémence du désir, la fleur même de la sensation était perdue. Ses ambitions d'esprit avaient également diminué. Des années passèrent; et il supportait le désœuvrement de son intelligence et l'inertie de son cœur.

> (He traveled.
> He experienced the melancholy of steamers, cold awakenings under the tent, the tedium of landscapes and ruins, the bitterness of interrupted friendships.
> He returned.
> He went into society, and he had still other loves. But the constant memory of the first one made them insipid; and besides, the vehemence of desire, the very flower of feeling was lost. His intellectual ambitions had also declined. Years passed; and he endured the idleness of his mind and the inertia of his heart).

In March 1867 Frédéric is suddenly visited by Mme Arnoux. They take a walk through the streets of Paris. Back in the apartment Mme Arnoux removes her hat; her hair has turned entirely white. "Ce fut comme un coup en pleine poitrine" (It was like a blow straight to his chest). Yet Frédéric falls to his knees to affirm his eternal love. Suspecting that she is about to yield at last, he feels revulsion and something like fear of incest. He does not want to "dégrader son idéal" (degrade his ideal); he turns away from her and begins rolling a cigarette. So Mme Arnoux places a maternal kiss on his forehead, cuts off a lock of her hair for him, and leaves. "Et ce fut tout" (And that was all).

In the last chapter, Frédéric and Deslauriers have reconciled again and are chatting by the fireside. They sum up their lives and their friends'. Pellerin, the "future Veronese," has become a photographer. Rosanette has been widowed and gone fat. The two friends, "celui qui avait rêvé l'amour, celui qui avait rêvé le pouvoir" (the one who had dreamt of love, the one who had dreamt of power), wonder how they could have failed. ("Les Fruits secs" [The Desiccated Fruits] was the novel's original title.) They go back over their youth to an incident in Nogent in the summer of 1837. An escapade that took them timidly to the bordello of "the Turkish woman" ended in flight and embarrassment for the pair of adolescents they then were. They reconstruct all the details of the adventure, and then Frédéric exclaims—and he is echoed by Deslauriers: "C'est là ce que nous avons eu de meilleur!" (That was the best thing in our lives!).

As stated, Flaubert carried out extensive historical research on the bourgeois regime of the July Monarchy. (He once famously signed a letter "Gustavus Flaubertus Bourgeoisophobus.") His fictional account is often taken as a historical record or document in itself, and indeed one of his fears was that the characters might be engulfed by the historical background. Yet *L'Education sentimentale* says nothing about Bonapartism or the dynamic liberal Catholic movements of the time, and relatively little about its numerous socialist doctrines. Sénécal is a sinister caricature of the doctrinaire socialist.

The book is certainly deeply autobiographical, but in no way could it be considered a roman à clef. It is the record of the education of his generation, one that Flaubert felt could never carry to completion its generous ambitions and hopes, either in the sentimental or the political realm. The word *quarantehuitard* (Forty-eighter), coined to designate a revolutionary of 1848, has a pejorative suffix suggesting ineffectiveness. The novel is structured to march in counterpoint with history so that, for example, Frédéric's multiple sentimental failures (with Mme Arnoux, Rosanette, Louise, and Mme Dambreuse) coincide with (and appear to culminate in) the failure of the Second Republic and its overthrow by Bonaparte.

Politics and political speechifying always put Flaubert into a satirical mode, and this novel is no exception. The Club de l'Intelligence episode shows speech in the arena of revolutionary egalitarianism degenerating into babble and logorrhea, and the hypocrisy of conservative political concerns in M. Dambreuse's salon is equally mocked. The prostitution of ideas, or the profanation of dreams, is what most strikes the reader of *L'Education sentimentale*, and the imagery of prostitution and that of circularity (as in *Madame Bovary*) run side by side throughout the book.

The coincidence of these concepts may be seen in "historical" incidents such as the sacking of the Tuileries, where whores adorn themselves

in Legion of Honor ribbons, and where escaped prisoners roll in the royal princesses' beds as a consolation for not being able to rape them. In the purely fictional realm, Frédéric takes Rosanette into a chamber lovingly prepared for Mme Arnoux. The salon of the wealthy Mme Dambreuse (which resembles Rosanette's) is depicted in terms of a bordello, and M. Dambreuse is described as having bowed and scraped before every government, for he had acclaimed Napoleon, the Cossacks, Louis XVIII, 1830, the workers, and every other regime, cherishing power with such love that "il aurait payé pour se vendre" (he would have paid to be able to sell himself). The bordello scene of the end is the long-deferred explanation of an allusion to a "low house" in the beginning of the novel, and this circular return is the opposite of forward movement or thrust. It brings the reader back to adolescence and underscores the lack of moral growth in the characters, the lack of sentimental progress, and thus gives an ironic twist to the title.

Indeed, neither lubricity nor ambition seems to lead anywhere. It has been noted that Frédéric's voyage in the opening scene is virtually the antithesis of the itinerary of a true adventure. The boat is not heading downstream for the open sea, but upstream, inland, in a reversal that points to a kind of psychological inertia or solipsism. Frédéric's only itinerary is in fact aimlessness, reflected in his immense random walks across Paris and in the evolution of his plans. A reader of romantic texts, like Emma (indeed, Emile Faguet called him the spiritual son of Charles and Emma Bovary), Frédéric early abandons the writing of a novel called "Sylvio, le fils du pêcheur" (Sylvio, the Fisherman's Son) because its plot is more reminiscent of Musset than the arriviste heroes of Balzac and Stendhal that Deslauriers cites as models of Parisian success. He ponders whether he should become a great poet or a great painter and decides on painting (it will take him closer to Mme Arnoux).

In an example of the potential that FIS offers for irony, one finds the following: "Il avait donc trouvé sa vocation! Le but de son existence était clair maintenant, et l'avenir infaillible" (Thus he had found his vocation! The purpose of his existence was now clear, and his future infallible). Finally, when Frédéric unexpectedly inherits his uncle's fortune (and he does so not because his own efforts have succeeded, but because the uncle has died intestate), his announced ambition is reduced to a single word:

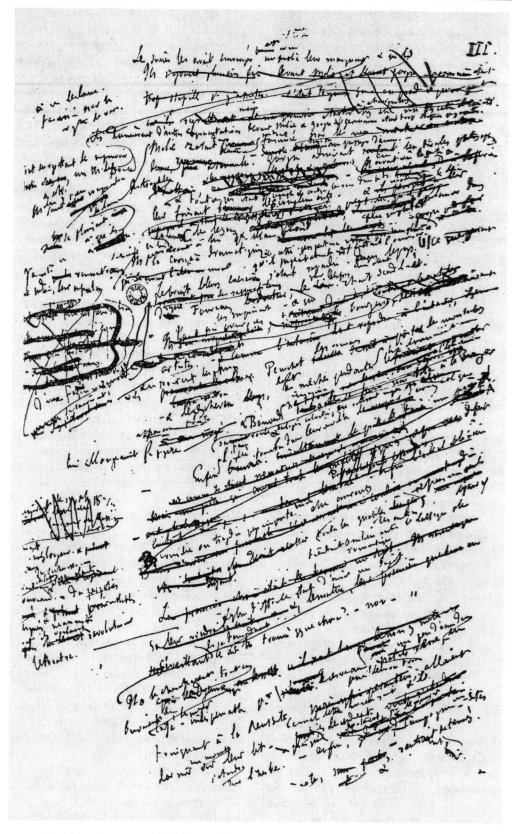

Page from the manuscript for Bouvard et Pécuchet *(Bibliothèque Municipale de Rouen)*

"Rien!" (Nothing!). Thus Frédéric is widely referred to as a *velléitaire* (one who has only weak intentions and cannot resolve to act).

If indeterminacy, fragmentation, and discontinuity are the hallmarks of the postmodern, then *L'Education sentimentale* offers much to sustain the views of scholars, such as Jonathan Culler, who maintain that Flaubert set out deliberately to block recuperation, that is, the reflex that assigns meaning to all fictional events. "Action," such as it exists in *L'Education sentimentale*, is summarized in the ironic portrait of a curious minor character, the actor Auguste Delmar, whose most imposing stance is a pose: hand on heart, left foot forward, eyes lifted skyward, he wears a laurel crown and attempts to project a look of fascination into his gaze. He stands as a model of the circular imagery of the novel, for his great stage success comes with a role that has him lecturing Louis XIV and predicting 1789. Thereafter, the same role is fabricated for him: an English brewer who rails against Charles I; a student from Salamanca who curses Philip II; and his best role, that of heartbroken father denouncing "la Pompadour."

His success is so complete that popular biographies are written of him. He is seen as a latter-day Saint Vincent de Paul mixed with Brutus and Count de Mirabeau. "On disait: 'Notre Delmar.' Il avait une mission, il devenait Christ" (People would say 'Our Delmar.' He was a man with a mission, he was turning into Christ). His electoral platform, expounded at the Club de l'Intelligence, is to pacify the mobs by showing them his profile. His greatest admirer, the procuress Mlle Vatnaz, claims that he represents the very genius of France, the people. She claims that he has a humanitarian soul and understands the sacred role of art. The last glimpse of Delmar portrays him declaiming a humanitarian poem about prostitution. Spelling variations in his name (Delamare, Dellamarre, Delmas, Belmar) seem to point to the most famous of French political proverbs: "Plus ça change, plus c'est la même chose." It is hard not to conclude that the staginess and essential hollowness of this fraudulent character stand for all the self-delusions besetting the generation of 1848.

Though *L'Education sentimentale* is rich in satire, and though its protagonist is a "failure," his love for Mme Arnoux is redemptive in the sense that it alone allows the ideal to persist in the face of disillusion. Frédéric's passion waxes and wanes, but even in the last scene, where motive

and emotion are most ambiguously portrayed, Mme Arnoux retains, white hair and all, her hold over his dreams and senses. The tenacity with which Flaubertian characters hold to their illusions is legendary. They seem to do so with considerable justification, for fulfillment brings weariness and disenchantment. In *Madame Bovary*, the narrator warned about this: "Il ne faut pas toucher aux idoles: la dorure en reste aux mains" (One must not lay hands on idols: the gilt rubs off on one's hands). Thus adultery brings to Emma only "toutes les platitudes du mariage" (all the platitudes of marriage), and Salammbô's finally touching the zaïmph brings only disappointment. The dream accomplished is its end. What an irony to consider that Frédéric Moreau alone would seem wise in his refusal to "degrade his ideal!"

In Flaubert's ironic vision, abstention is the closest one may come to satisfaction. Jean-Pierre Richard has noted that after the "apparition" of the opening scene, Mme Arnoux is mainly experienced as an absence, or at best, as an evanescent presence. "We hear her move behind a partition, we glimpse her profile behind a drapery: only her echo or her shadow can be possessed. Her house is full of intervening objects: screens, fans, lampshades." This very space of deferral constitutes Flaubert's opportunity to inscribe scenes of great tenderness, particularly the idyllic days that Frédéric and Mme Arnoux spend in their clandestine trysts in Auteuil, trysts of perfect intimacy and innocence. The sense of what might have been is the strongest impression this novel leaves its readers, and if, for the survival of the dream, *nothing* is always better than *something*, then its mode of deferral bestows upon *L'Education sentimentale* its enduring poetic qualities. *L'Education sentimentale* is the reliquary of romanticism. The storehouse of fine sentiments has been petrified, shriveled like so many *fruits secs,* or transformed into clichés. In this sense the moderns are no longer "believers" in the Romantic religion of perfect love; thus it is only through irony's oblique approach that Flaubert can pay nostalgic homage to the ideal.

The public reception awaiting his new novel was not brilliant, and Flaubert had to be satisfied with a succès d'estime. Only in recent years has *L'Education sentimentale* come into its own as the true masterpiece of the realist canon. Flaubert soon returned to work on *Saint Antoine* and spent Christmas of 1869 with George Sand in Nohant. The years from 1869 to 1872 were to be difficult ones for him, and for France; first, more deaths: Bouilhet in 1869, and in 1870 a close friend, Jules Duplan, then Jules de Goncourt as well. The Franco-Prussian War, a catastrophe for France, broke out in July. Flaubert was appointed a lieutenant in the National Guard, but the Prussians had reached Rouen by December, and Croisset was eventually occupied. Flaubert was profoundly depressed and became more misanthropic than ever.

After the signing of the armistice in January 1871 he refused to wear his Legion of Honor. After a visit to Princess Mathilde in exile in Brussels, Flaubert returned to Croisset to work on *Saint Antoine* and to busy himself with Bouilhet's unpublished works. Elisa Schlesinger, now a widow, had come to Trouville for a visit and was invited to Croisset, but their farewell scene had already been written in the penultimate chapter of *L'Education sentimentale*. (Flaubert's last extant letter to her is dated 8 October 1872.) Mme Flaubert's health was declining, and family finances were becoming more and more alarming. Mme Flaubert died in April 1872, and Flaubert was deeply grieved. George Sand was to write him a most moving letter on this occasion. In September he switched publishers, as Georges Charpentier bought the rights to his works from Lévy and was promised the definitive *Saint Antoine* and the new work now under way, *Bouvard et Pécuchet*. Théophile Gautier died in October.

The year 1873 was largely devoted to theatrical activities. Flaubert attempted to ready an unfinished play by Bouilhet and undertook a political comedy of his own, *Le Candidat* (1874; translated as *The Candidate*, 1904); neither was successful. While Charpentier brought out *La Tentation de Saint Antoine* in March 1874 (surprisingly, sales were good), the "bear" of Croisset was throwing himself into documentation for *Bouvard et Pécuchet*. One of Flaubert's sources for information on the routines of copy clerks was the son of his old playmate from youth, Laure Le Poittevin. This was Guy de Maupassant, then employed as a clerk in the Ministry of the Navy in Paris. Flaubert became quite fond of young Guy, who served a kind of literary apprenticeship under the master.

Inevitably, it was rumored that Maupassant the "disciple" was in reality Flaubert's son, and it is a fact that illegitimacy is a recurrent theme in Maupassant's works. He has left a record of a Sunday reception in Flaubert's apartment in the rue Murillo: the visitors were Turgenev, Hippolyte

Taine, Alphonse Daudet, Emile Zola, and Edmond de Goncourt; and Flaubert stupefied them with his "prodigious erudition." Henry James attended one of these Sundays in 1875 (by then Flaubert had moved to the same apartment house as the Commanvilles, in the rue du Faubourg Saint-Honoré). That was the year of his nephew's near bankruptcy, which Flaubert heroically helped to stave off by selling his single large asset, a farm at Deauville. It was feared that Croisset might have to be sold as well, but happily this was not necessary. After this debacle Flaubert would live the remainder of his life in straitened circumstances.

In March 1876 Louise Colet died. By then Flaubert had finished a short work that he entitled "La Légende de Saint Julien l'hospitalier" ("The Legend of Saint Julian the Hospitaler") and had begun work on a second tale, "Un Cœur simple" ("A Simple Heart"), intended for George Sand. But his great friend died in June before she could read the work. Flaubert also planned a third short work, "Hérodias"; the first two were published separately in periodicals in 1877 (Flaubert needed money), and in April of that year Charpentier brought them out together under the title *Trois contes* (translated as *Three Tales*, 1923).

The tales are placed in three different chronological settings and locations. "Un Cœur simple" is set in contemporary France, "Saint Julien" in a generalized Middle Ages, and "Hérodias" in the Near East in the time of John the Baptist. They all present the old Flaubertian yearning for escape from self as the characters thrust toward mystical transcendence.

The most accessible of the tales is "Un Cœur simple," probably the most anthologized of all Flaubert's writings. (It is also the most poignant of the *Trois contes*, although poignancy is not the essence of Flaubert.) It tells the story of a peasant girl, Félicité, who loyally serves the same mistress for more than fifty years. "Pendant un demi-siècle, les bourgeoises de Pont-l'Evêque envièrent à Mme Aubain sa servante Félicité" (For a half-century, the women of Pont-l'Evêque envied Mme Aubain her servant Félicité). This much-admired opening sentence affords quick insight into the richness of Flaubert's style. Its syntactical end point identifies the focus of the tale, the maidservant Félicité, and "Felicity" is a name remarkable enough to encourage the reader to see if *happiness* will be her lot. It also imparts information regarding geographical setting (Pont-l'Evêque sounds like a Norman place-name) and social class (*bourgeoises*) that will figure in the tale. The choice of the term *half-century* over the equally possible *fifty years.* shows Flaubert's sense of duration and temporality at its acutest, for "half-century" is psychologically much longer; it is *le mot juste.*

As a young orphan girl from the country, Félicité is taken in by a widow, Mme Aubain, who finds in her the perfect servant for one hundred francs a year. She is loyal and hardworking, and frustrated in a series of loves. Jilted by her fiancé, the farmhand Théodore, she lavishes her inarticulate affection on Paul and Virginie, the children of Mme Aubain. But Virginie dies young, and Paul goes off to boarding school. Her beloved nephew Victor, a sailor boy, is lost to yellow fever on a voyage to Havana. She cares for Polish refugees and devotes herself to alleviating the final suffering of an outcast, old Father Colmiche.

One day Mme Aubain is given a parrot, Loulou. He becomes Félicité's constant companion. In time Félicité turns deaf, and the only voice that reaches her is the parrot's. In her isolation, he has become almost a son, a lover. When he dies, she has him mounted. Struck by his resemblance to the dove in a stained glass window (symbol of the Holy Ghost), she begins to pray to him. Mme Aubain dies and leaves her a small income. Félicité is allowed to stay in her room, stuffed with remembrances of her loves, as the empty house slowly decays around her. Loulou is now moldy and worm-eaten. Her end approaches, and the priest allows Loulou to be placed on the altar of repose set up in the courtyard for the Corpus Christi procession. She bids him a tender farewell, and as she expires in wafts of incense from the ceremony below, "elle crut voir, dans les cieux entrouverts, un perroquet gigantesque, planant au-dessus de sa tête" (she believed she saw, in the opened heavens, a gigantic parrot, hovering over her head).

Many readers have felt that Flaubert's incarnation of the Holy Ghost in the body of a parrot constitutes a satire of religious thought. He was, after all, a relentless mocker of all parrotry, the mindless repetition of clichés, and conceived as one of his earliest projects a "Dictionnaire des idées reçues." Emma's consultation with the priest in *Madame Bovary* ends in an empty repetition of the catechism ("baptized, baptized, baptized"), and it has been said that many of the characters in his world are infected with psittacosis—parrot fever. And Sartre remarked in *L'Idiot de la famille* that "Flaubert ne croit pas qu'*on parle: on est parlé*" (Flaubert does not believe that *one speaks: one is spoken*). Language infects one with thought in reverse, thought being not the origin but rather the product of words. Loulou's very name is made of repetition, and one scene in particular, where Mme Aubain's visitors admire him while wondering why he is not called "Jacquot" (French for "Polly"), has been termed a "closed circuit of inanity" by Victor Brombert.

Irony seems to pervade the tale at every pass, and nowhere more obviously than in Flaubert's onomastic practices: Félicité finds felicity in extremis perhaps, but not on this earth; her fiancé, Théodore, is hardly a "gift of God" nor is Mme Aubain an *aubaine* (a godsend). And yet Flaubert himself, an unbeliever, maintained that he respected religion and that his tale was not at all ironical, but on the contrary, "very serious and very sad." "Je veux apitoyer, faire pleurer les âmes sensibles, en étant une moi-même" (I want to move people to pity, to make sensitive souls weep, being one of them myself). Moreover the tale was written for George Sand in specific response to her regret that Flaubert's fictional practice masked his true feelings in impassivity.

Thus the story is finely balanced between tenderness and irony. Félicité suffers in silent abnegation and gives every appearance of leading a saintly existence in her capacity for love and charity. She bestows her gifts on the children, on her ungrateful mistress, on the sick, and on strangers, and she performs authentic deeds of self-sacrifice, as when she heroically saves the entire Aubain family from an attack by a bull. She might well become the matter of a saint's life herself—"Saint Felicity Slaying the Bull." Pious and modest, she seems to recall a youthful project of Flaubert, to tell the story of a Flemish virgin who lives her whole existence in mystical devotion. If Félicité's belief is illusion, it does not fail to comfort her to the end of her life, including the ultimate visionary appearance of the gigantic parrot. She certainly dies in odor of sanctity. Félicité shares this with Frédéric Moreau, that neither suffers the loss that inevitably ensues upon the possession of an ideal—no matter how decrepit that ideal has become.

The second of the tales, "Saint Julien," opens with a depiction of the stability of Julien's world. His father is a great lord, and the paternal manor is a safe and prosperous place. Soon after Julien's birth, a mysterious hermit appears to the mother and tells her to rejoice, for her son will be a saint. The next day a Gypsy beggar stammers prophetic words to the father: "Ah, ah! ton fils! ... beaucoup de sang! ... beaucoup de gloire! ... toujours heureux! la famille d'un empereur" (Ah, ah! Your son! ... Much blood! ... Much glory! ... Always happy! The family of an emperor). Neither parent tells the other, but each respects the child as if he were marked by God. They take great care for him, and he receives a thorough education.

One day Julien kills a little white mouse in the church and furtively throws its body away. Next he strangles a wounded bird: its dying convulsions fill him with ecstasy. He takes up venery and becomes an expert hunter. One morning he indulges in an orgy of killing: deer, badgers, peacocks, birds, foxes, hedgehogs, and lynx—Julien mercilessly slays them all. He comes to an amphitheater filled with stags, where he wreaks carnage until at last he spies a buck, a doe, and their fawn. He sends arrows into them all, but the dying buck springs forward and, to the tone of a tolling bell, confronts Julien: "Maudit! maudit! maudit! Un jour, cœur féroce, tu assassineras ton père et ta mère!" (Accursed, accursed, accursed! One day, cruel heart, you will kill your mother and father!). Julien rejects the stag's prophecy, "Non! non! non!" And then he pauses: "Si je le voulais, pourtant?" (But what if I wanted to?). He abandons hunting, but in two separate accidents he narrowly misses killing his mother and father, and he flees the castle in dread of the prediction.

Julien becomes a great soldier, and eventually, to reward his services, the Emperor of Occitania offers him his daughter in marriage. Julien languishes; he would like to hunt again, but he may not, believing that the fate of his parents is bound to the killing of animals. But at his wife's urging, he does set off to hunt. During his absence his mother and father come to seek him out, and their daughter-in-law offers them her own bed. In a nightmarish scene, Julien is unable to kill any animals, who surround him and accompany him in sinister silence back to the palace. There Julien mistakes his father for a lover and his mother for his wife. In a burst of uncontrollable rage, he slays them both.

A repentant Julien wanders, a beggar, through many lands. He seeks ever greater acts of mortification, but his suffering cannot be

Monument to Flaubert in his home city of Rouen
(Musée des Beaux-Arts de Rouen)

eased. Finally he becomes a boatman beside a perilous river. In all weather Julien carries travelers across it, asking nothing for his dangerous service. He lives in abject poverty. One stormy night, from across the river, a voice cries out his name three times. It is a leper, whom Julien ferries back to his hut. The leper demands food and drink, and Julien gives him what he has. He is cold and demands that Julien lie naked by him for warmth. Julien does his will: he stretches himself out on top of him, mouth to mouth, breast to breast. The leper clasps him tight, the roof flies off, the heavens unfold, and Julien rises face to face with Jesus Christ, who bears him off to heaven. "Et voilà l'histoire de saint Julien l'Hospitalier, telle à peu près qu'on la trouve, sur un vitrail d'église, dans mon pays" (And that is the story of Saint Julien the Hospitaler, more or less as it can be found in a stained glass window of a church in my land).

Several familiar themes are to be found in the tale. The first is the linking of sexuality and religion or death, particularly in the killing of the white mouse in church and later the pigeon. Julien hastily mops up the drop of blood the mouse leaves behind and almost guiltily disposes of the little carcass, saying nothing to anyone. But he immediately starts to kill birds with his blowpipe, and he is happy as they rain down upon his shoulders. The death of the pigeon is recounted in overtly sexual terms: "Les convulsions de l'oiseau faisaient battre son cœur, l'emplissaient d'une volupté sauvage et tumultueuse. Au dernier roidissement, il se sentit défaillir" (The convulsions of the bird made his heart beat and filled it with a wild and tumultuous ecstasy. At its last stiffening, he felt himself fainting).

The apparent reciprocity between destruction and creation is a plausible variant reading of these same events, and the history of nineteenth-century literary decadence constantly views the "Barbarian" as a longed-for injection of vigor that will regenerate a stagnant society. Violence then becomes a remedy for the impasse of positivism and the exhaustion of an overcivilized society: decadent works are filled with episodes of gratuitous cruelty. This was one of the preoccupations of *Salammbô*, whose prose style, with its emphasis on heavy, overloaded descriptions, is often termed lapidary. This accentuation of the artificial at the expense of the natural, or the man-made at the expense of the human, would become the hallmark of the masterpiece of decadence, Joris-Karl Huysmans's *A rebours* (1884; translated as *Against the Grain*, 1922).

Julien's inward contradictions are made literal in the incompatible double prophecy of his infancy. It is the symbol of Julien's paradoxically double nature, his capacity for savagery and sainthood, for good and evil, for creation and destruction. In more specifically psychoanalytic terms, William J. Berg has shown that the Freudian concepts of displacement and reversal are at work in the tale. As Julien has himself admitted his patricidal leanings ("But what if I wanted to?"), the latent Oedipal conflict cannot be denied. It would unfold as follows: while it would be unthinkable for Julien to kill his father, the stag (synecdoche for all animals) provides a socially acceptable substitute. Moreover, the stag is described as a "patriarch." When Julien kills the animals, he escapes from his position of inferiority with regard to the Father (reversal).

During Caroline's wedding trip in 1845, Flaubert had written down a nightmare about animals (in his *Notes de voyage* [Travel Notes, 1910]): he was walking in a great forest with his mother when they noticed monkeys in the trees and in their path. They were all looking at him; soon he was surrounded by monkeys, and one of them took him by the hand. Flaubert shot the monkey, which screamed and bled. Then his mother asked him, "Pourquoi le blesses-tu, ton ami? qu'est-ce qu'il t'a fait? ne vois-tu pas qu'il t'aime? comme il te ressemble!" (Why do you wound your friend? What has he done to you? Don't you see that he loves you? How similar he is to you!). And Flaubert awoke feeling that he was of the same nature as the animals and fraternizing with them in a tender and pantheistic communion. Thirty years later the guilt of 1845 was shifted to Julien.

The narrative tone of this tale comes closest to what one might properly expect in a legend; it is that of a dreamworld where supernatural events are common and time has been suspended. Although the narrator says that he has taken his tale from a stained glass window, it is known from the research of Benjamin F. Bart and Robert F. Cook that Flaubert's source was a printed description. The setting of "Saint Julien" is an idealized Middle Ages, picturesque and mysterious despite all its killing. The reader feels distanced from this world because of the obscure psychology of the characters and the stylistic features of the narrative, such as the exotic or archaic vocabulary of venery and falconry. Its very tone of historical affirmation is distancing ("C'est lui, et pas un autre, qui assomma la guivre de Milan et le dragon d'Oberbirbach" [It was he, and no other, who slew the serpent of Milan and the dragon of Oberbirbach]). In Julien's legend, the naive and the erudite are interwoven, the real and the surreal overlap with ease, and Julien's final flight heavenward in the arms of his Saviour is narrated with a matter-of-fact sense of wonder.

Even though "Hérodias" closely follows documentary sources (and thus is the most "historical" of the *Trois contes*), it is marked by condensation, ellipsis, and obscurity. Significantly, it is the tale most admired by the historian Taine, who said it was the real Judea in A.D. 30. And although Edmond de Goncourt called it a "gaudy mosaic," he and his brother had earlier written this in their journal (24 October 1864): "Le roman, depuis Balzac, n'a plus rien de commun avec ce que nos pères entendaient par roman. Le roman actuel se fait avec des *documents*, racontés ou relevés d'après nature, comme l'histoire se fait avec des documents écrits. Les historiens sont des raconteurs du passé; les romanciers, des raconteurs du présent" (The novel, since Balzac, has had nothing more in common with what our fathers understood by novel. The novel today is made with *documents*, narrated or gathered from nature, just as history is made with written documents. Historians are tellers of the past; novelists, tellers of the present).

In a letter of 19 June 1876, Flaubert joked that he was becoming one of the pillars of the temple: "Après Saint Antoine, Saint Julien; et ensuite saint Jean-Baptiste; je ne sors pas des saints. Pour celui-là, je m'arrangerai de façon à ne pas 'édifier.' L'histoire d'Hérodias, telle que je la comprends, n'a aucun rapport avec la religion. Ce qui me séduit là-dedans, c'est la mine officielle d'Hérode (qui était un vrai préfet) et la figure farouche d'Hérodias, une sorte de Cléopâtre et de Maintenon. La question des races dominait tout" (After Saint Anthony, Saint Julien, and then Saint John the Baptist; I can't get out of the saints. For this one, I'll manage so as not to 'edify.' The story of Herodias, the way I understand it, has no connection with religion. What fascinates me in this is the official appearance of Herod [who was a real prefect] and the fierce appearance of Herodias, a sort of Cleopatra and Maintenon. The racial question dominated everything). Sources in art for "Hérodias" included the Saint John sculpture on the Rouen cathedral and Perugino's *Beheading of Saint John*, which he had seen in Perugia in 1851.

The characters of "Hérodias" are taken from Roman and biblical history: the scheming and ambitious Herodias (a Jezebel, the saint calls her), who has divorced one uncle to marry another; Antipas, her husband (a son of the great Herod), the Tetrarch of Galilee; Vitellius, the Roman Proconsul; his decadent son and favorite of the Emperor Tiberius, the gluttonous Aulus; the fulminating prophet John the Baptist (here called Iaokanann); Salome, the daughter of Herodias and her first husband; and many others. The Gospel story of Salome's dance and John's decapitation are the center of the tale, but the atmosphere of tension, of religious and political suspicion and intolerance, is reminiscent of *Salammbô*. Flaubert no doubt drew on his memory of

Kuchuk Hanem and her lustful Dance of the Bee for Salome, and the old theme of profanation arises in John's beheading. As the head is passed around the banquet table, torches are extinguished, tears roll down the Tetrarch's cheeks, and the guests hurriedly make their exit. The head is placed before Aulus, who is awakened: "Par l'ouverture de leurs cils, les prunelles mortes et les prunelles éteintes semblaient se dire quelque chose" (Through the opening of their lashes, the dead pupils and the dulled pupils seemed to speak to one another).

Herodias was also a subject treated by Stéphane Mallarmé in the 1860s, but after Flaubert's tale and Gustave Moreau's paintings, interest shifted more to Salome. Oscar Wilde wrote a one-act play (in French) that served as the libretto (in German translation) for Richard Strauss's opera *Salome* (1905), and Sergey Diaghilev mounted a ballet on the theme in 1913. Gratuitous cruelty, decadence, profanation, and the cycle of destruction and regeneration compose the familiar yet exotic preoccupations of "Hérodias."

The unity of *Trois contes* is a much-debated question; it is certainly a problematic unity, to be found (if it exists) in a presentation of varieties of religious experiences, a triptych of saints' lives. Or perhaps it should be located in the yearning to escape from self, in the quest for transcendence that haunts the protagonists of the Flaubertian universe.

Flaubert now returned to *Bouvard et Pécuchet*. The *Dictionnaire des idées reçues* had been mentioned while he was on his trip to the Orient, and the subject of the two copyists dates from 1862. *Bouvard et Pécuchet* would remain unfinished, but it was published in 1881, only one year after Flaubert's death. His early title for the novel was "Les Deux Cloportes" (The Two Woodlice). It offers a cautionary tale of intellectual frustration.

The two woodlice, the copy clerks Bouvard and Pécuchet, meet one sultry summer evening on the boulevard Bourdon in Paris. They immediately take a liking to one another, so that when Bouvard comes into an inheritance and Pécuchet retires, they decide to leave Paris to live in the countryside. At their place in Chavignolles, they begin to study and experiment with agriculture; soon they pass to arboriculture, then to ornamental gardening, chemistry, anatomy, medicine, astronomy, natural sciences, geology, archaeology, and history. Their ambition is encyclopedic. In each domain they are frustrated, for in each they discover contradictions and flaws.

The two friends are immersed in politics with the revolution of 1848, and in affairs of the heart. They take up gymnastics and study animal magnetism, spiritism, and philosophy. "Alors une faculté pitoyable se développa dans leur esprit, celle de voir la bêtise et de ne plus la tolérer" (Then a pitiable faculty developed in their minds, that of seeing stupidity and no longer tolerating it). They go on to religion and the adoption of a pair of miscreant children; but everything leads to failure. In the plans for the unfinished last chapter, they return to copying. They have a double desk made, purchase copybooks and writing instruments, and then "Ils s'y mettent" (They go to it). A second volume of *Bouvard et Pécuchet*, a *sottisier*, or compendium of stupidities, was to have consisted almost entirely of quotations. It would have exposed the contradictions and bêtises of their readings.

Harry Levin has called *Bouvard et Pécuchet* a "*Bildungsroman* in reverse." Bouvard's name recalls the bovine, and Pécuchet's name (from *pecus* [cattle]) yokes him to the same destiny. The research that the partners carry out, it has often been remarked, is effected with a Flaubertian pertinacity, and their enthusiastic inquiries could be taken as a caricature of the Hermit of Croisset's own multifarious investigations.

Nothing could be more like their creator than their interest in bêtises. The *Dictionnaire*, Sartre wrote, was a strange work of more than a thousand entries, but in the end, who was the butt of it all? "Personne. Ou plutôt si: un homme. Le plus curieux, c'est qu'il *est* visé et ne semble pas s'en rendre compte. C'est l'auteur lui-même" (No one. Or rather yes: one man. The most curious thing is that he *is* the butt and does not seem to realize it. It is the author himself). For Lionel Trilling, Bouvard and Pécuchet "are the *reductio ad absurdum* of our lives in culture . . . " (*The Opposing Self*, 1955). But are they finally comic or tragic in their willingness to persist? The pessimism of the book, and Flaubert's characteristic infusion of irony, make debate fruitless. They are simply exemplars of modernity.

Bouvard et Pécuchet is certainly a self-reflexive book, one whose reading retraces its own composition. For Brombert, it marks the impasse of fiction, that is, the limits of traditional realistic narrative. The work calls into question, and destroys, all pretense of narrative authority, for it makes it impossible to pinpoint with certainty the narrative instance, or the source of the narrating voice. The use of FIS here breaks down demarcations, and often the numerous summaries in the book cannot be confidently attributed to a character, a treatise, or a narrator. Utterances become free-floating and produce the *simulation* of an imitation.

By upsetting the foundations of classical mimesis, in which copy and model, imitator and imitated are clearly situated with respect to one another, *Bouvard et Pécuchet* displaces the very concept of origin and truth. Signs darken and become opaque; meaning is obscured, and one is left with the unending circulation of words. Roland Barthes—in a passage so often quoted that Anne Herschberg-Pierrot wonders if it has become a cliché itself—wrote in *S/Z* (1970) that one never knows if Flaubert is responsible for what he writes (if there is a subject *behind* his language); the essence of Flaubert's writing is to "empêcher de jamais répondre à cette question: *Qui parle?*" (prevent one from ever answering this question: *Who is speaking?*).

Flaubert's last years were a mixture of worries over money and health, and devotion to friends and work. The great events of 1879, for example, were a fractured leg (he was cared for by a new, devoted friend, his neighbor Edmond Laporte), receipt of a rather meager official pension of three thousand francs, and the reading of *War and Peace* (1865-1869), which Turgenev "the Muscovite" had sent him. In early 1880 he was on chapter 10 of *Bouvard et Pécuchet,* and serial publication of his fairy play, *Le Château des cœurs,* had commenced. He read the manuscript of Maupassant's short story inspired by the Franco-Prussian War, "Boule de suif" (Butter Ball, 1879). Although Maupassant had published little before age thirty, this story brought him instant fame, and Flaubert duly hailed it as a masterpiece of composition, of comedy, and of observation. He read Zola's *Nana* (1879) and found it "Babylonian." Earlier, of *L'Assommoir* (1877; translated as *Gervaise (L'Assommoir),* 1879), he had wryly observed that Zola was becoming "une *précieuse* à l'inverse" (a *précieuse* in reverse).

No admirer of naturalism, he wrote Maupassant that it was an empty word, an "ineptitude" exactly like "realism." He smiled upon learning that Du Camp had been elected to the French Academy. For Easter weekend, Flaubert had as houseguests in Croisset his publisher Charpentier, Daudet, Goncourt, Maupassant, and Zola. The last Saint Polycarp's dinner was held in

April. This was an annual dinner honoring Flaubert, who professed an ironic identification with this early bishop of Smyrna, famous for his lament, "My God, my God, what a century you have placed me in!" On 8 May, Flaubert suffered a stroke and died.

Elisa Schlesinger lived until 1888. Flaubert's niece Caroline had custody of his papers; she had remarried, and as Mme Franklin-Grout lived in Antibes until her death in 1931.

The Russian critic Mikhail Bakhtin wrote in a long essay on "Discourse in the Novel" that the nineteenth century created "an important novel-type in which the hero is a man who *only* talks, who is unable to act and is condemned to naked words." The passage could apply to Frédéric Moreau, to Emma Bovary, to Bouvard and Pécuchet. But it is not only the pessimism of failure or the inadequacy of words that is figured in Flaubert's writings. One is most alert to a particular admixture of emotion and irony. Thus during the *Bovary* years he had written to Colet (20 March 1852): "Toute la valeur de mon livre, s'il en a une, sera d'avoir su marcher droit sur un cheveu, suspendu entre le double abîme du lyrisme et du vulgaire (que je veux fondre dans une analyse narrative)" (All the worth of my book, if it has any, will be in having learned to walk straight along a hair, suspended between the double abyss of lyricism and vulgarity [which I wish to fuse in a narrative analysis]). That fusion is what constitutes the pleasure of his text, from *Madame Bovary* to *L'Education sentimentale* and "Un Cœur simple."

In addition to his advances in technique, Flaubert's legacy to the modern writer is one of tenacity, of devotion to task. He established the familiar image of the artist-as-priest. Proust thought him a "génie grammatical" (grammatical genius) and paid him homage by including a pastiche of his style in the "Lemoine Affair" section of his *Pastiches et mélanges* (1919). Franz Kafka admired him excessively. Sartre was totally obsessed, writing thousands of pages about Flaubert. (His only novel of distinction, *La Nausée* [1938; translated as *Nausea*, 1949], owes much to *Bouvard et Pécuchet*.) A generation of Latin American novelists found inspiration in him; Mario Vargas Llosa devoted an entire work to him (*The Perpetual Orgy*, 1975). He is the writer's writer in his meticulous planning and his refusal to settle for less than *le mot juste*. He left works that have continued to attract the attention of critics and literary theorists of stature. His practice enacts in advance the dilemmas of the modern writer: the crisis of representation, the inadequacy of language, the stoic awareness of humanity's entanglement in words.

Letters:

Correspondance (4 volumes, Paris: G. Charpentier, 1887-1893; 5 volumes, Paris: L. Conard, 1910; 9 volumes, 1933; 4 volumes, 1954); 3 volumes, edited by Jean Bruneau (Paris: Gallimard, Bibliothèque de la Pléiade, 1973-1991);

Flaubert in Egypt, translated and edited by Francis Steegmuller (Chicago: Academy Chicago Limited, 1979);

The Letters of Gustave Flaubert, 2 volumes, translated and edited by Steegmuller (Cambridge, Mass.: Harvard University Press, 1980-1982).

Bibliography:

D. J. Colwell, *Bibliographie des études sur G. Flaubert*, 4 volumes (Surrey, U.K.: Runnymede, 1988-1990).

Biographies:

Philip Spencer, *Flaubert, A Biography* (London: Faber & Faber, 1952);

Enid Starkie, *Flaubert. The Making of the Master* (London: Weidenfeld & Nicolson, 1967);

Benjamin F. Bart, *Flaubert* (Syracuse: Syracuse University Press, 1967);

Starkie, *Flaubert. The Master* (London: Weidenfeld & Nicolson, 1971);

Jean Bruneau and Jean A. Ducourneau, eds., *Album Flaubert* (Paris: Gallimard, 1972);

Herbert Lottman, *Flaubert. A Biography* (Boston: Little, Brown, 1989).

References:

Charles Bally, "Le Style indirect libre en français moderne," *Germanischromanische Monatsschrift*, 4 (1912): 549-556, 597-606;

Maurice Bardèche, *L'Œuvre de Flaubert* (Paris: Les Sept Couleurs, 1974);

Julian Barnes, *Flaubert's Parrot* (New York: McGraw-Hill, 1985);

Benjamin F. Bart and Robert F. Cook, *The Legendary Sources of Flaubert's "Saint Julien"* (Toronto & Buffalo: University of Toronto Press, 1977);

Bart, ed., *Langages de Flaubert* (Paris: Lettres Modernes, 1976);

Charles Baudelaire, "Madame Bovary," in *Œuvres complètes,* edited by Yves Le Dantec and Claude Pichois (Paris: Gallimard, 1968), pp. 647-657;

Albert Béguin, "En relisant *Madame Bovary,*" *Table Ronde* (27 March 1950): 160-164;

William J. Berg, Michel Grimaud, and Georges Moskos, *Saint/Oedipus Psychoanalytical Approaches to Flaubert's Art* (Ithaca, N.Y.: Cornell University Press, 1982);

Leo Bersani, *Balzac to Beckett. Center and Circumference in French Fiction* (New York: Oxford University Press, 1970);

Geneviève Bollème, *La Leçon de Flaubert* (Paris: Julliard, 1964);

Victor Brombert, "*L'Education sentimentale:* articulations et polyvalence," in *La Production du texte,* edited by Claudine Gothot-Mersch (Paris: Union Générale d'Editions, 1975), pp. 55-69;

Brombert, "Flaubert and the Temptation of the Subject," *Nineteenth-Century French Studies,* 12 (1984): 280-296;

Brombert, "Lieu de l'idylle et lieu du bouleversement dans *L'Education sentimentale,*" *Cahiers de l'Association Internationale des Etudes Françaises,* 23 (1971): 277-284;

Brombert, *The Novels of Flaubert. A Study of Themes and Techniques* (Princeton: Princeton University Press, 1966);

Jean Bruneau, "L'Avant-dernier Chapitre de *L'Education sentimentale,*" *Nineteenth-Century French Studies,* 12 (1984): 322-327;

Bruneau, *Les Débuts littéraires de Gustave Flaubert, 1831-1845* (Paris: A. Colin, 1962);

Stratton Buck, *Gustave Flaubert* (New York: Twayne, 1966);

Charles Carlut, *La Correspondance de Flaubert. Etude et répertoire critique* (Columbus: Ohio State University Press, 1968);

Carlut, ed., *Essais sur Flaubert en l'honneur du professeur Don Demorest* (Paris: A. G. Nizet, 1979);

Alberto Cento, *Commentaire de "Bouvard et Pécuchet"* (Naples: Liguori Editore, 1973);

Cento, *Il Realismo documentario nell' "Education Sentimentale"* (Naples: Liguori Editore, 1967);

Pierre Cogny, *"L'Education sentimentale" de Flaubert. Le monde en creux* (Paris: Larousse, 1975);

Dorrit Cohn, *Transparent Minds. Narrative Modes for Presenting Consciousness in Fiction* (Princeton: Princeton University Press, 1978);

Jonathan Culler, *Flaubert. The Uses of Uncertainty* (Ithaca, N.Y.: Cornell University Press, 1974);

Raymonde Debray-Genette, "Génétique et poétique: le cas Flaubert," in *Essais de critique génétique,* edited by Louis Hay (Paris: Flammarion, 1979), pp. 21-67;

Debray-Genette, ed., *Flaubert à l'œuvre* (Paris: Flammarion, 1980);

D. L. Demorest, *L'Expression figurée et symbolique dans l'œuvre de Gustave Flaubert* (Paris: Les Presses Modernes, 1931);

George L. Dillon and Frederick Kirchhoff, "On the Form and Function of Free Indirect Discourse," *Poetics and Theory of Literature,* 1 (1976): 431-440;

Maxime Du Camp, *Souvenirs littéraires,* in Flaubert's *Œuvres complètes,* 2 volumes, edited by Bernard Masson (Paris: Editions du Seuil, 1964);

Alfred G. Engstrom, "Flaubert's Correspondence and the Ironic and Symbolic Structure of *Madame Bovary,*" *Studies in Philology,* 46 (1949): 470-495;

Alison Fairlie, *Flaubert: Madame Bovary* (London: Arnold, 1962);

Shoshana Felman, "Illusion réaliste et répétition romanesque," in *La Folie et la chose littéraire* (Paris: Editions du Seuil, 1978), pp. 159-169;

Flaubert et le comble de l'art (Paris: Société d'Edition d'Enseignement Supérieur, 1981);

Flaubert: Proceedings of the Wisconsin Symposium of October 1980, special issue of *Nineteenth-Century French Studies,* 12 (Spring 1984);

Flaubert. Revue d'Histoire Littéraire de la France, 4/5 (July-October 1981)—colloquium organized by the Société d'Histoire Littéraire de la France for the Flaubert Centenary;

Gérard Genette, "Silences de Flaubert," in *Figures* (Paris: Editions du Seuil, 1966), pp. 223-243;

Michal Peled Ginsburg, *Flaubert Writing. A Study in Narrative Strategies* (Stanford: Stanford University Press, 1986);

Raymond Giraud, ed., *Flaubert. A Collection of Critical Essays* (Englewood Cliffs, N.J.: Prentice-Hall, 1964);

Claudine Gothot-Mersch, "De *Madame Bovary* à *Bouvard et Pécuchet.* La parole des personnages dans les romans de Flaubert," *Revue d'Histoire Littéraire de la France,* 81 (1981): 542-562;

Gothot-Mersch, *La Genèse de "Madame Bovary"* (Paris: José Corti, 1966);

Gothot-Mersch, "Sur le narrateur chez Flaubert," *Nineteenth-Century French Studies,* 12 (1984): 344-365;

Anne Green, *Flaubert and the Historical Novel* (Cambridge: Cambridge University Press, 1982);

Gustave Flaubert, proceedings of the "Journée Flaubert," University of Fribourg (Fribourg: Editions Universitaires, 1981);

Stirling Haig, *Flaubert and the Gift of Speech* (Cambridge: Cambridge University Press, 1986);

Haig, "History and Illusion in Flaubert's 'Un Cœur Simple,' " in *The Madame Bovary Blues* (Baton Rouge & London: Louisiana State University Press, 1987), pp. 116-143;

F. W. J. Hemmings, ed., *The Age of Realism* (Harmondsworth, U.K.: Penguin, 1974);

Anne Herschberg-Pierrot, "Le Cliché dans *Bouvard et Pécuchet,*" in *Nouvelles recherches sur "Bouvard et Pécuchet" de Flaubert* (Paris: Société d'Edition d'Enseignement Supérieur, 1981), pp. 31-37;

Herschberg-Pierrot, "Cliché, stéréotypie et stratégie discursive dans le discours de Lieuvain," *Littérature,* 36 (1979): 88-103;

Herschberg-Pierrot, "Problématiques du cliché—sur Flaubert," *Poétique,* 11 (1980): 334-345;

Henry James, *Essays in London and Elsewhere* (New York, 1893);

Hans Robert Jauss, "Literary History as a Challenge to Literary Theory," *New Literary History,* 2 (Autumn 1970): 7-37;

Hugh Kenner, *Flaubert, Joyce and Beckett. The Stoic Comedians* (Boston: Beacon Press, 1962);

Diana Knight, *Flaubert's Characters. The Language of Illusion* (Cambridge: Cambridge University Press, 1985);

Dominick LaCapra, *"Madame Bovary" on Trial* (Ithaca, N.Y. & London: Cornell University Press, 1982);

Harry Levin, *The Gates of Horn. A Study of Five French Realists* (New York: Oxford University Press, 1963);

Marguerite Lips, *Le Style indirect libre* (Paris: Payot, 1926);

Jean-Claude Mallet, ed., *Flaubert à l'œuvre* (Paris: Flammarion, 1980);

Brian McHale, "Free Indirect Discourse: A Survey of Recent Accounts," *Poetics and Theory of Literature,* 3 (1978): 249-287;

Jean-Pierre Moussaron, "Une Etrange Greffe," in *Flaubert et le comble de l'art* (Paris: Société d'Edition d'Enseignement Supérieur, 1981), pp. 89-109;

D. C. Muecke, *Irony and the Ironic* (London & New York: Methuen, 1982);

Robert J. Niess, "On Listening to Homais," *French Review,* 51 (1977): 22-28;

Roy Pascal, *The Dual Voice. Free Indirect Speech and Its Functioning in the Nineteenth-Century European Novel* (Manchester, U.K.: Manchester University Press / Totowa, N.J.: Rowman & Littlefield, 1977);

Dennis Porter, "Flaubert and the Difficulty of Reading," *Nineteenth-Century French Studies,* 12 (1984): 366-378;

Laurence M. Porter, ed., *Critical Essays on Gustave Flaubert* (Boston: G. K. Hall, 1986);

Christopher Prendergast, "Flaubert: Quotation, Stupidity and the Cretan Liar Paradox," *French Studies,* 35 (1981): 261-277;

Prendergast, *The Order of Mimesis* (Cambridge: Cambridge University Press, 1986);

La Production du sens chez Flaubert, Colloque de Cerisy (Paris: Union Générale d'Editions, 1975);

Marcel Proust, "A propos du 'style' de Flaubert," in *Contre Sainte-Beuve,* edited by Pierre Clarac (Paris: Gallimard, 1971), pp. 586-900;

Michel Raimond, "Le Réalisme subjectif dans *L'Education sentimentale,*" *Cahiers de l'Association Internationale des Etudes Françaises,* 23 (1971): 299-310;

Jean-Pierre Richard, "La Création de la forme chez Flaubert," in *Littérature et sensation* (Paris: Seuil, 1954), pp. 119-219;

Michael Riffaterre, "Flaubert's Presuppositions," *Diacritics,* 11 (1981): 2-11;

Jean Rousset, *"Madame Bovary* ou 'le livre sur rien,' " in *Forme et signification* (Paris: José Corti, 1962), pp. 109-133;

Jean-Paul Sartre, "La Conscience de classe chez Flaubert," *Temps Modernes,* 21 (May 1966): 1921-1951; (June 1966): 2113-2153;

Sartre, *L'Idiot de la famille: Gustave Flaubert de 1821 à 1857,* 3 volumes (Paris: Gallimard, 1971-1972); translated by Carol Cosman as *The Family Idiot: Gustave Flaubert, 1821-57,* 4 volumes (Chicago: University of Chicago Press, 1981-1991);

Albert Thibaudet, *Gustave Flaubert. Sa vie, ses romans, son style* (Paris: Plon, 1922; revised edition, Paris: Gallimard, 1935);

Margaret G. Tillett, *On Reading Flaubert* (London: Oxford University Press, 1961);

Stephen Ullmann, "Reported Speech and Internal Monologue in Flaubert," in *Style in the French Novel* (Cambridge: Cambridge University Press, 1957), pp. 94-120;

P. M. Wetherill, "Flaubert et les incertitudes du texte," in *Flaubert: La Dimension du texte,* edited by Wetherill (Manchester, U.K.: Manchester University Press, 1982), pp. 255-270;

D. A. Williams, "Flaubert—'le premier des non-figuratifs du roman moderne'?," *Orbis Litterarum,* 34 (1979): 66-86;

Williams, *The Hidden Life at its Source. A Study of Flaubert's "L'Education Sentimentale"* (Pickering, North Yorkshire: Hull University Press, 1978).

Papers:

Flaubert's papers are at the Bibliothèque Nationale (Paris), the Bibliothèque Historique de la Ville de Paris, the Bibliothèque Municipale de Rouen, and the Musée Flaubert (Canteleu-Croisset).

Théophile Gautier

(30 August 1811 - 23 October 1872)

Albert B. Smith
University of Florida

SELECTED BOOKS: *Poésies* (Paris: Rignoux, 1830); enlarged, with *Poésies diverses* and *España,* in *Poésies complètes* (Paris: Charpentier, 1845);

Albertus, ou l'âme et le péché, légende théologique (Paris: Rignoux, 1833); enlarged, with other collections, in *Poésies complètes* (Paris: Charpentier, 1845);

Les Jeunes-France, romans goguenards (Paris: E. Renduel, 1833); enlarged, to include *Œuvres humoristiques* (Paris: V. Lecou, 1851);

Mademoiselle de Maupin, double amour, 2 volumes (Paris: E. Renduel, 1835); translated as *Mademoiselle de Maupin* (New York: Carlton House, n.d.);

La Comédie de la mort (Paris: Desessart, 1838); enlarged, with other collections, in *Poésies complètes*;

Une Larme du diable (Paris: Desessart, 1839);

Tra los montes (Paris: V. Magen, 1843); republished as *Voyage en Espagne* (Paris: Charpentier, 1845);

Les Grotesques, 2 volumes (Paris: Firmin-Didot, 1844);

Nouvelles (Paris: Charpentier, 1845);

La Croix de Berny, roman steeple-chase, 2 volumes, by Gautier and Vicomte Charles de Launay (Delphine de Girardin), Jules Sandeau, and Joseph Méry (Paris: Pétion, 1846); translated by Florence Fendall and Florence Holcomb as *The Cross of Berny, or Irene's Lovers* (Philadelphia: Porter & Coates, 1873);

Les Roués innocents (Paris: Desessart, 1847); republished with *Jean et Jeannette* (Paris: L. Hachette, 1863);

Militona (Paris: Desessart, 1847); republished in *Un Trio de romans* (Paris: V. Lecou, 1852); translated by Mrs. Benjamin Lewis as *Juancho, the Bullfighter* (New York: Cassell, 1890);

Les Deux Etoiles, 2 volumes (Brussels: Tarride, 1848); republished as *Partie carrée,* 3 volumes (Paris: H. Souverain, 1851); republished as *La Belle Jenny* (Paris: Michel Lévy, 1865); translated by Lucy Arrington as *Four Destinies* (New York: Hurst, n.d.);

Jean et Jeannette, histoire rococo (Paris: Baudry, 1850); republished in *Un Trio de romans* (Paris: V. Lecou, 1852);

Italia (Paris: V. Lecou, 1852); enlarged as *Voyage en Italie: Italia* (Paris: Charpentier, 1875);

La Peau de tigre (Paris: H. Souverain, 1852);

Emaux et camées (Paris: Eugène Didier, 1852; enlarged edition, 1853); definitive edition

Théophile Gautier, circa 1856 (photograph by Nadar)

(Paris: Charpentier, 1872); translated by Agnes Lee as *Enamels and Cameos and Other Poems* (New York: Sproul, 1903);

Constantinople (Paris: Michel Lévy, 1853);

Théâtre de poche (Paris: Librairie Nouvelle, 1855); enlarged, with other plays and ballet scenarios, as *Théâtre: mystère, comédies et ballets* (Paris: Charpentier, 1872);

Le Roman de la momie (Paris: Hachette, 1858); translated by Mrs. Anne T. Wood as *The Romance of the Mummy* (New York: J. Bradburn, 1863);

Histoire de l'art dramatique en France depuis vingt-cinq ans, 6 volumes (Paris: Hetzel, 1858-1859);

Le Capitaine Fracasse, 2 volumes (Paris: Charpentier, 1863); translated by M. R. Ripley as *Captain Fracasse* (New York: Holt, 1880);

Spirite, nouvelle fantastique (Paris: Charpentier, 1866); translated as *Spirite: A Fantasy* (New York: A. L. Burt, n.d.);

Voyage en Russie, 2 volumes (Paris: Charpentier, 1867);

Histoire du romantisme (Paris: Charpentier, 1874);

Mademoiselle Dafné de Montbriand, eau-forte dans la manière de Piranèse (Paris: Charpentier, 1881).

Collections: *Works*, 12 volumes, translated and edited by F. C. de Sumichrast (Boston: C. T. Brainard, 1900);

Œuvres complètes, 11 volumes (Geneva: Slatkine Reprints, 1978).

PLAY PRODUCTIONS: *Giselle, ou les Wilis* (ballet), by Gautier, Jules-Henri Vernois de Saint-Georges, and Jean Coralli Peracini, music by Adolphe Adam, Paris, Théâtre de l'Académie Royale, 28 June 1841;

La Péri (ballet), by Gautier and Peracini, music by Joseph Burgmüller, Paris, Théâtre de l'Académie Royale, 17 July 1843;

Un Voyage en Espagne, by Gautier and Paul Siraudin, Paris, Théâtre des Variétés, 21 September 1843;

Le Tricorne enchanté, Paris, Théâtre des Variétés, 7 April 1845;

La Juive de Constantine, by Gautier and Noël Parfait, Paris, Théâtre de la Porte-Saint-Martin, 12 November 1846;

Pierrot posthume, by Gautier and Siraudin, Paris, Théâtre du Vaudeville, 4 October 1847;

Regardez, mais ne touchez pas, by Gautier and Bernard Lopez, Paris, "Second" Théâtre-Français (Odéon), 20 October 1847;

Pâquerette (ballet), by Gautier and Arthur Saint-Léon, music by M. Benoît, Paris, Opéra, 15 January 1851;

Gemma (ballet), music by Nicola Gabrielli, Paris, Théâtre Impériale de Musique, 31 May 1854;

Yanko le bandit (ballet), music by M. Deldevez, Paris, Théâtre de la Porte-Saint-Martin, 22 April 1858;

Sacountalâ (ballet), music by Ernest Reyer, Paris, Opéra, 14 July 1858.

SELECTED PERIODICAL PUBLICATIONS: *La Morte amoureuse*, Chronique de Paris (23 June 1836, 26 June 1836);

Le Petit Chien de la marquise, Figaro (19 December 1836, 23 December 1836, 24 December 1836);

La Chaîne d'or, ou l'Amant partagé, Chronique de Paris (28 May 1837, 11 June 1837);

Fortunio, Figaro (28 May 1837 - 24 July 1837);

Une Nuit de Cléopâtre, Presse (29 November 1838 - 6 December 1838);

Le Roi Candaule, Presse (1 October 1844 - 5 October 1844);

Arria Marcella, Revue de Paris (1 March 1852);

Avatar, Moniteur Universel (29 February 1856 - 3
    April 1856);
Jettatura, Moniteur Universel (25 June 1856 - 23
    July 1856).

Théophile Gautier was one of the best
known and most highly respected literary per-
sonalities in France in the nineteenth century.
Among writers of the time, he counted as friends
Victor Hugo, Alexandre Dumas *père*, Honoré de
Balzac, Gustave Flaubert, Edmond and Jules de
Goncourt, Charles Baudelaire, and, from his earliest school days in Paris, Gérard de Nerval. Gautier and the expatriate German poet Heinrich
Heine saw one another regularly. The painter
Eugène Delacroix appreciated Gautier's criticism,
as did the composers Hector Berlioz and
Giacomo Meyerbeer. Gautier and the critic
Charles-Augustin Sainte-Beuve regarded one another fondly as fellow veterans of the Romantic
struggles of the 1830s. Contemporary painters,
sculptors, and playwrights courted Gautier as the
newspaper reviewer in the best position to promote their works.

Gautier also enjoyed respect as a poet. Indeed, it was primarily his poetry that created a
niche for him in nineteenth-century literary history. His collection *Emaux et camées* (1852; translated as *Enamels and Cameos and Other Poems*,
1903) went through an exceptional six editions in
twenty years. Because of its visual inclination and
its emphasis on formal perfection, the collection
inspired the Parnassians of the 1860s and, at the
end of the century, the Modernismo poets of
Spanish America. Baudelaire's dedication of *Les
Fleurs du mal* (1857; translated as *Flowers of Evil*,
1909) reveals the veneration in which Gautier the
poet was held: "Au poëte impeccable, au parfait
magicien ès lettres françaises, à mon très-cher et
très-vénéré maître et ami Théophile Gautier,
avec les sentiments de la plus profonde humilité,
je dédie ces fleurs maladives" (To the impeccable
poet, to the perfect magician in letters, to my
dear and revered master and friend Théophile
Gautier, with the deepest humility I dedicate
these sickly flowers). When, at Gautier's death,
the editor Alphonse Lemerre invited contributions to a memorial volume honoring the author
of *Emaux et camées*, no fewer than eighty contemporaries sent poems, among them the acknowledged greats of the day—Hugo, Charles-Marie-
René Leconte de Lisle, Stéphane Mallarmé, and
the English poet Charles Swinburne.

Gautier's rejection of an ideological mission
in art and his call for a nonutilitarian outlook in
the artist made him recognized as a leader in the
"art for art's sake" movement. His preface to *Mademoiselle de Maupin, double amour* (1835; translated
as *Mademoiselle de Maupin*) stands as the principal
manifesto of *l'art pour l'art*, with its uncompromising claim that art in whatever form has no other
aim and no other morality than the creation of
beauty.

Gautier was born in Tarbes, in southwestern
France, on 30 August 1811. When he was three,
the family relocated to Paris, where his father,
Pierre, took a post as a government functionary.
At the age of eleven, the boy enrolled in the
Collège Louis-le-Grand; then, after an unhappy
experience as a boarding student there, he
moved as a day student to the Collège Charlemagne. It was here that he met Gérard Labrunie,
later known by his pen name, Gérard de Nerval,
who became his lifelong friend; and it was during this period that he began to study painting
and to write poetry. In 1829 Gérard introduced
Gautier to the already-famous Hugo. Dazzled by
Hugo's presence and position as leader of the
new Romantic school, Gautier enthusiastically supported Hugo's theatrical offensive with his flamboyant participation at the premiere of Hugo's
play *Hernani* (25 February 1830), a performance
that marked victory in the campaign to gain critical respect for Romantic drama.

By now Gautier had given up painting for poetry. His first collection of poems appeared in
July 1830, just at the moment of the July Revolution and the attendant overthrow of the Restoration monarchy. At least in part because of circumstances, the collection drew little attention.
Gautier appears to have been scarcely daunted;
he continued writing verse, including the collections *Albertus* (1833) and *La Comédie de la mort*
(The Comedy of Death, 1838).

Gautier was now part of the Parisian literary and artistic bohemia. With Nerval, Pétrus
Borel, and other would-be artists and writers, Gautier formed the Petit Cénacle, delighting in a bois-
terously defiant campaign to "shock the bourgeoisie." This group gradually merged into the
so-called Groupe du Doyenné. New members
joined in their free-living ways, their eager quest
for critical recognition—on their own terms—
and their continuing efforts to unsettle the middle class. Gautier was not above exploiting his bohemian associations. In *Les Jeunes-France, romans
goguenards* (The Young-France, Stories in a Jest-

ing Manner, 1833), he evoked their escapades and their assaults on middle-class values, all the while poking tender fun at their more absurd eccentricities.

Gautier was also gaining a reputation as a literary historian of sorts. His series of articles "Exhumations littéraires" (later entitled *Les Grotesques*, 1844) introduced many little-known French authors, principally from the baroque era. Gautier's interest went to these marginalized writers because they stood at the opposite pole from the great authors of French classicism and because they displayed a certain irregularity in their art, a quality that held particular appeal for the young Romantic—and one that he did not hesitate to inject into his own works.

By publicizing these rejected authors, Gautier was sure to annoy die-hard classicists among his contemporaries. His role as a provocateur did not stop here. His first full-length novel, *Mademoiselle de Maupin*, in addition to its defiant preface-manifesto, contained erotic elements certain to shock the prudish among the literary public.

But Gautier was beginning to see that he could not continue exclusively in this vein: he had at last to face up to reality and find steady employment. Having already displayed a solid knowledge of art and artistic technique in occasional critical articles and already enjoying recognition as a verbal talent, he found in 1836 a post as art critic for Emile de Girardin's new daily newspaper, the *Presse*. In 1837, with Nerval, he also began to share the duties of theater reviewer for the *Presse*. Gautier soon took over full responsibility for the theater column; and every week for nineteen years, except for periods of absence now and then from Paris, he turned in to Girardin a review of current theatrical offerings.

In the spring of every year, he produced a series of articles in which he presented and judged the paintings and sculptures being exhibited in the annual Salon show. Gautier held the two positions on the *Presse* until 1855, when he left his sometimes bumpy association with Girardin to take over the art and drama columns of the *Moniteur Universel*, the semiofficial organ of the Second Empire. Here he remained until 1869, when he joined the new government-sanctioned daily, the *Journal Officiel*. His tenure there was short. With the German victory in the Franco-Prussian War in 1870, the empire fell, and the *Journal Officiel* ceased publication. Two independent dailies, however, the *Gazette de Paris* and the *Bien Public* (Commonweal), were happy to employ Gau-

Self-portrait of Gautier in 1830 (Musée Carnavalet)

tier; so he was able to pursue his journalistic work until a few months before his death in 1872.

Gautier was never happy as a journalist. His responsibilities kept him from what he considered his true calling, poetry. Regular deadlines and frequently deadly dull subjects for review made him feel trapped in a life of inescapable monotony. Yet he knew he had to carry on his professional activities: increasing financial demands—two sisters to support, two former mistresses to maintain (he *did* have a sense of responsibility!), three children to rear—forced him to keep his shoulder to the journalistic wheel.

He was nevertheless able to break the routine from time to time. Travel offered him a happy means of escaping the monotony of journalism and the prosaic quality he found in modern French life. At the same time it permitted him to satisfy his impulse for excitement, and the travel accounts he sent back to Paris for publication helped him to meet the demands on his pocketbook. He learned the pleasures of travel in 1836 during a brief tour of Belgium with Nerval. In 1840 he took a five-month trip to Spain, whose exotic qualities had long attracted him. Then, for two months in 1845, he toured the French colony of Algeria. In 1850 he visited Italy, and in 1852 he satisfied a long-standing desire to journey to the Middle East. Traveling all the way to Constantinople, Gautier returned by way of Athens and Venice. If Spain had charmed him with its contemporary exoticism, the ancient monuments of Greece awed him. He wrote to a friend that Athens had left him in a state of transport, that next to the Parthenon everything else seemed crude and barbarian, that one felt oneself to be a savage before the radiant, serene marbles of the temple.

A journey to Russia from 1858 to 1859 was something of a business trip: as the leading Parisian art critic, Gautier, under the patronage of Czar Alexander II, was to document the art of Russia and draft an impressive illustrated volume, *Trésors de l'art de la Russie* (Russian Art Treasures, never completed). Another official trip in 1869 took Gautier to Egypt. Sent to cover the inauguration of the Suez Canal, he had expected to find the opportunity to visit a country that had always fascinated him. He was disappointed: official functions and an injury sustained during the ship crossing combined to hobble his movement and thus to frustrate his anticipations.

Journalism never got such a hold on Gautier that he had to give up creative writing. His travels provided material for his poetry and his fiction. His imagination supplied a vast array of subjects that he incorporated into works in a variety of forms, for Gautier was a polygraph. In an age marked by inventive diversity, when authors tried their hand in many different genres, Gautier stood out for his manifold endeavors. In addition to his poetry, travel literature, and criticism, he managed to produce a multitude of short stories, novelettes, and novels. He also proposed a theory for a unique dramatic form, a comedy of fantasy, and he wrote several plays in this vein. Finally, surpassing anything his contemporaries were achieving in the way of creative diversity, Gautier conceived several ballet scenarios. *Giselle* (1841), with music by Adolphe Adam, has been one of the most popular ballets of all time and a standard repertory piece throughout the world.

Gautier's last years were scarcely happy. Journalism was becoming ever more tiresome. His refusal to approve his daughter Judith's marriage in 1866 resulted in severely strained relations in his family. The Prussian siege of Paris in 1870 and the subsequent civil strife in 1871 brought physical trials, domestic displacements, fears for the safety of family members, and uncertainties in his professional life. His health was deteriorating. Here again, he sought escape, not in exoticism, but in a nostalgic return to his festive days as a young partisan of the Romantic cause. He was writing his recollections of this happy time when he died on 23 October 1872. The unfinished *Histoire du romantisme* (History of Romanticism, 1874) remains as one of Gautier's most precious legacies.

It is impossible to separate Gautier's fiction from his other works: the same themes recur, whether in a short story or ballet scenario, a novel or travel account. Indeed, the themes themselves are all related, turning on a fundamental conflict between ideal and reality. From the earliest narratives to the works written near the end of his career, Gautier's fiction is marked by the portrayal of protagonists in search of an ideal, the realization of which, they believe, will bring them supreme happiness. In the earlier works the desired good is an ideal of perfect beauty to be enjoyed in the here and now. Later the focus shifts to an ideal of beauty belonging to a distant past, which can be enjoyed only in the imagination. In the late novelette *Spirite* (1866; translated as *Spirite: A Fantasy*), the ideal assumes an immaterial character. Union with it is to be realized only through an exclusively spiritual approach.

The nature of beauty naturally changes with the shift from a tangible to a spiritual good. Beauty in the early works lies in perfection of form, in a perfect harmony of parts and lines. Moreover, it requires a rich setting accompanied by handsome accessories. The protagonist of *La Morte amoureuse* (1836; translated as *The Dead Leman*, 1903) is drawn to the courtesan Clarimonde not only for her dazzling physical beauty but also for everything around her—splendid clothing, opulent surroundings, and a lavish life-style. The quest for perfect beauty thus implies a particular ethical outlook. Gautier's early protagonists are materialists, requiring sensuous satisfaction, full and immediate.

In those works in which beauty resides in a remembrance of forms past, experienced through an intense play of the imagination, the form envisioned retains fundamentally the same character—it is perfect in line and equilibrium. The ethos of the idealist also remains essentially unchanged. Clarimonde had identified herself as beauty, youth, and life; Arria Marcella, of the novelette by the same name, written in 1852, associates her pagan spirit with much the same character when she declares, "Je crois à nos anciens dieux qui aimaient la vie, la jeunesse, la beauté, le plaisir" (I believe in our ancient gods who loved life, youth, beauty, and pleasure). But the setting of beauty is conceived in ethnic terms. It is an entire past civilization that attracts Gautier's hero.

Material beauty plays little or no role in the late ideal. The spirit that makes itself known to Gautier's hero in *Spirite* is barely perceptible, a being recognized not through the senses but through some visionary capacity resembling second sight. While the spiritual orientation may enhance the aesthetic sense, even formal beauty loses its allure. The idealist is interested only in severing his attachments to the material world, so that he can enjoy the felicities promised by the otherworldly existence.

In Gautier's works materialistic and imaginative approaches to happiness encounter many obstacles, all of which work to frustrate full and enduring satisfaction. These are components of a theme characterized by a strong antipathy toward modern reality, whatever form it may take. In any of the works involving an ideal of beauty, it is what Gautier represents as the severe morality of the modern age that blocks attainment of happiness. This morality, according to the narratives, is traceable to the establishment of Christianity as the dominant force in Western culture. Christianity, fostering an almost exclusive preoccupation with the soul, has brought about an atrophy of modern mankind's sensuous impulse. The result is not only a stern morality that condemns materialistic pleasures but also a firm hostility to beauty, grandiosity, and magnificence, which permits what Gautier represents as a pervasive tolerance for ugliness. Gautier's works return again and again to the idea that modern European civilization is degraded, without any sensitivity to—or interest in—beauty. Worse, the modern spirit consciously acts to smother the aesthetic drive.

Obstacles also include the human subjection to time and its ravages. Apparently Gautier could not reconcile himself to the fact that impermanence is an inescapable feature of existence. This may indeed explain his representation of attempts to recapture a golden age dominated by the veneration of beauty. Such efforts are of course doomed from the outset: the mind is never strong enough to maintain its hold on the past; and this ideal, too, falls victim to the prevailing morality.

Obstacles also exist within the individual seeker. The human tendency to satiety with material pleasures brings an unavoidable diminution of pleasure. Or some defect in the personality may prevent union with the ideal. Gautier represents in *Jettatura* (The Evil Eye, 1856) a protagonist whose visual sense is literally evil, creating disorder around him and wreaking the worst havoc of all in causing the death of the woman he loves. Disillusion with a sensuous approach to happiness is clear in *Jettatura*. In the context of past failures to achieve happiness through the senses, and considering the success through a spiritual orientation depicted in a work to come, the protagonist's decision to blind himself and thus remove his deadly means of pleasure appears as a rejection of materialism. At the same time Gautier's representation of the beloved as a being revealing an ever more ethereal nature already anticipates the immaterial pleasures of *Spirite*.

These same themes are evident throughout Gautier's writings. The idealism of certain characters in the ballets parallels that found in the fictional heroes. Antipathy to the modern world surfaces in all of the genres that Gautier practiced. It appears regularly in his criticism. His dissatisfaction with things around him explains the escapism implicit in the stories that evoke Spain or ancient Egypt, and explicit in his travel literature. His apparent obsession with impermanence— with the deterioration of men and things caused by the passage of time—is visible in his evocations of the enduring monuments of Egypt and in poems such as "L'Art" (1857, in *Artiste*), which assigns to poetry itself the mission to combat the ravages of time.

Indeed, Gautier's preoccupation with themes of impermanence has led some critics to see him exclusively as a frightened man for whom the only reality was death. Such a view might be justifiable if it were not for the equally strong element of humor in Gautier. But a difficulty arises here, too. How could Gautier allow himself to inject humorous episodes and ironic asides into works whose themes are clearly serious? Some would say that the humor is a psychological defense. Others might suggest that humor allowed Gautier to show that he was not taken in by the pathos of the subject he was treating. Still others would simply sidestep the issue, saying that Gautier was a man of paradox. Critics troubled by the coexistence of humor and seriousness in Gautier may well be tyrannized by a classical view of literature that insists on the separation of tones. It is worth remembering that Gautier was a friend of Hugo, who, in the preface to his play *Cromwell* (1827), enunciated precisely the desirability of mingling tones and genres in a single work. By mixing humorous and solemn elements, Gautier could well have been following the precepts of his master. Certainly he was not a slave to such traditions as would forbid the juxtaposition of opposing elements in the same work.

Whatever the reasons, the presence of humor in all of Gautier's works is undeniable. It dominates plays such as *Une Larme du diable* (A Tear Shed by the Devil, 1839) and *Le Tricorne enchanté* (The Magic Three-Cornered Hat, 1845). It is a significant element in the novels *Mademoiselle de Maupin* and *Le Capitaine Fracasse* (1863; translated as *Captain Fracasse*, 1880). Humorous observations are scattered throughout the travel literature. Even in unusually serious works such as *Jettatura*, *Avatar* (1856), and *Spirite*, Gautier was not loath to introduce ironic incongruities.

Gautier's irony has been related to that brand of humor erected into a philosophical outlook by the German August Wilhelm von Schlegel and known by the qualifier "Romantic." Indeed, much of the comic element in Gautier would appear to partake of Romantic irony. Gautier—or his narrator—frequently stands above and at a distance from the material being treated. He often deflates his characters or his subject or treats them in a burlesque manner. He is flippant to the point of irreverence. He taunts his reader. Narrators are frequently self-conscious of their roles as personages just as fictitious as the characters whose stories they are telling. The detached narrator emphasizes that his story is only a story and is not to be taken for reality. Narrators and characters digress to present material that may be of some interest but that serves not at all to move the story forward.

The use of irony, however, is only one mark of Gautier's innovative spirit. Like many of his contemporaries, he eagerly experimented, seeking out new subjects and trying out new literary forms and means of expression. When, in 1835, he proposed the creation and development of a new form of comedy, he did so not by means of a treatise or preface but through the words of a principal personage in his novel *Mademoiselle de Maupin*, itself typifying the new genre, albeit in narrative form. *Mademoiselle de Maupin* contains examples of further experimentation in its mingling of forms of discourse. The novel begins in the epistolary mode; then, once the reader has come to expect a plot-by-letters, Gautier suddenly switches to a verbal exchange presented in the form of a dramatic dialogue—reported in a letter! Later, a third-person narrator introduces himself, apologizes for his intrusion, and takes over the management of the story.

An unusual example of experimentation is evident in the novel *La Croix de Berny* (1846; translated as *The Cross of Berny*, 1873). The subject, a woman's difficulties caused by her unwitting inspiration of love in three men, all friends, is banal enough. What is significant is that this is a novel, epistolary in form, written by four different hands—Gautier, Delphine de Girardin, Jules Sandeau, and Joseph Méry—a *roman-steeplechase* (steeplechase novel) in which each author assumes the role of a character and attempts by his or her narration to put narrative hurdles in the path of the others.

Gautier not only experimented with the so-called *genre fantastique* but found in it a happy vehicle for the representation of the quest for an ideal that occupied such an important place in his work. The fantastic was a genre that the French of the 1830s eagerly borrowed from German literature, in particular the narratives of E. T. A. Hoffmann. As a rule, fantastic works depicted the intrusion of supernatural phenomena into a fictional universe conceived as a reproduction of the real world. Gautier, on the other hand, though not exclusively, tended to narrate the stories of individuals from the real world who inexplicably find themselves transported to another order. Fantastic beings served Gautier as symbols for the kind of ideal his protagonists imagined, and as concretizations of the obstacles that interfered to frustrate the idealist's quest for happiness. In *Arria Marcella*, for example, the hero suddenly finds himself in a Pompeii restored to the form it had just before its destruction in the first century. Here he meets the beautiful Arria Marcella, who died in the eruption of Vesuvius and whose form, cast in congealed ash and preserved in a Neapolitan museum, has already infatuated him. The reader is led to understand that she symbolizes all that was beautiful and vibrant in pagan civilization. On the other hand, her father, who intrudes to block the protagonist's union with the lovely Pompeian, is a convert to Christianity, and, as such, he symbolizes that ascetic morality that Gautier blamed for the grim modern hostility to aestheticism.

One of the most evident features in Gautier's writings is exoticism. It may be contemporary, as in his evocations of the countries that he visited; or it may involve an imaginative reconstruction of earlier times, whether the world of ancient Greece or a period closer to Gautier—the age of Louis XIII or the frivolous time of Louis XV. Whatever the time or place, Gautier seeks to situate his reader in a world made as palpable as exceptional verbal talent will permit. That description of course dominates has led some critics to view the plots of the exotic narratives as mere skeletons on which Gautier hung verbal paintings. Though such a judgment is probably too severe, it is a fact that description is an essential element in Gautier. He describes cities, with their buildings, their monuments, and their street scenes. He depicts interiors in minute detail. He evokes scenes in nature. Pictures of ceremonies, processions, and crowd scenes abound. Gautier focuses, too, on costume, listing and describing in detail the exotic objects of clothing that his characters wear. He is careful to use correctly the technical vocabulary particular to the time, the milieu, or the activity.

Gautier attempts, furthermore, to render the subject *culturally* vivid. Having visited Spain, he was able in *Militona* (1847; translated as *Juancho, the Bullfighter*, 1890) to re-create not only physical objects but also diverse elements of Madrid culture—the bullfights, *tertulias* (literary salons), outdoor markets, knife fights, and the life of the upper classes and the life of the *manolos*, or members of the working class. A feature that has received scant attention from Gautier scholars is his use of style as a means of exotic representation. In his exotic fiction, he causes his characters to speak in a manner consistent with the time and place of the story. The speech of the eighteenth-century nobles in *Jean et Jeannette* (1850) is suitably characterized by a certain artificiality and preciosity and by frequent allusions to such mythological figures as were common in the art and literature of the time. Likewise, the dialogue in *Le Capitaine Fracasse* is conceived to fit the social position of the characters within the frame of a mannered, rather artificial discourse associated with the baroque period. Even the style of the narrator belongs to the time in which the action is set: he too embodies the exoticism of the subject, with a preciosity of expression and a use of figures and allusions that recall the language of works from the preclassical seventeenth century.

Allusion is, in fact, a distinguishing mark of Gautier's literary discourse. Without appearing pedantic, he displays—as if compulsively—an excep-

tionally broad culture. His writings, whatever the genre, abound in references to works from a variety of literatures and periods, to events and personages from ancient history to modern, to mythology and folklore, and to painters, sculptors, and works of art from diverse ages and lands. He is reported to have underscored his emphasis on description by stating that he was a man for whom the visual world existed; he was undeniably an author for whom a vast culture existed, and he required his readers to possess the same culture if they wished to appreciate him fully.

Gautier began his career as a writer of fiction with the fantastic tale *La Cafetière* (The Coffee Urn), published in a literary review, the *Cabinet de Lecture* (The Reading Room), in 1831. The first-person narrator recounts a series of unusual events that occurred in an old Norman manor house he was visiting. Just after retiring for the night, he became aware that figures from the eighteenth-century portraits and tapestries in his room were coming to life and organizing a soiree, conversing, taking coffee from a beautiful porcelain coffee urn, and dancing to the music of a small ensemble that had stepped down from one of the tapestries. The narrator reports that he was at first naturally startled at what was happening but that he soon joined in the gaiety. He found himself particularly attracted to a beautiful girl in the group. They danced, then sat down to talk.

Infatuated with her beauty and charm, he was delighted at the ease with which they communicated with one another: it was as if their souls interpenetrated, without need for words. His enchantment was suddenly interrupted, however, when at dawn the dancing stopped, and his lovely companion fell unconscious at his feet, disappearing among the shards of the coffee urn, mysteriously broken. The narrator also collapsed, stunned by this abrupt turn. The next morning his friends found him unconscious on the floor of his room, surrounded by the fragments of the shattered urn. Later, when the narrator, a budding artist, tried to sketch the urn from memory, his host noted with surprise that the drawing resembled his sister, who had died two years before from a seizure following a night of dancing. The narrator now sadly realized that he had experienced a love not only impossible to recapture but impossible to discover again in the real world.

La Cafetière set the form and tone of the many fantastic narratives to come. From *La Morte amoureuse* to *Avatar* and *Jettatura*, Gautier repre-

Honoré de Balzac (left) and Gautier (right) with the actor Frédérick Lemaître in 1840 (watercolor attributed to Gérard Grandville; from Jacques Nathan, ed., Encyclopédie de la littérature française, *1952)*

sented protagonists discovering full and intense love in fantastic settings, but almost immediately losing the source of felicity through an unexpected interruption of their delight. In *La Cafetière* the narrator simply does not have the capacity to maintain his hold on an attractive time past. In other fantastic works, other forces, external as well as internal, prevent lasting union with the personage symbolizing a given ideal. Not until he composed *Spirite* did Gautier introduce a protagonist who finds satisfaction at once total and enduring.

Mademoiselle de Maupin also depicts characters seeking an ideal. Here, Gautier uses the epistolary form to have his main personages report on their respective quests, the Chevalier d'Albert for an ideal of perfect beauty, Madelaine de Maupin for unswerving love. The story ends unhappily. Though d'Albert discovers his ideal of beauty in Madelaine, he is unable to hold her for very long: she disappears, unwilling to watch him fall victim to satiety and to the inevitable disappointment that he will experience—and reflect back to her—as age undermines her beauty. Madelaine

herself never finds—and never expects to find—the kind of perfect love she requires.

In 1837 Gautier published the novelette *Fortunio*. Here the roles of idealist and ideal are reversed. Fortunio is depicted as the perfection of male beauty and is surrounded by all of the accessories that Gautier attached to beauty at this time—incredible wealth, a fabulously rich and beautiful dwelling in the exotic style of India, elegant clothing, the ability to satisfy material desires at the snap of a finger, and an enticing air of mystery. Gautier represents the idealist in the form of the beautiful courtesan Musidora, who, once she has met the rather aloof Fortunio, can conceive of no greater happiness than enjoying his enduring love. She is disappointed. Fortunio belongs to another world, indeed another order. He cannot abide the drabness and the prosaic spirit of modern Europe; and, recognizing that Musidora herself is somehow tainted by her origins if not her profession, he abandons her to return to his native India.

Fortunio is thus another story of a failed quest. The subject also served Gautier as a means for introducing the theme, common in his works, of antipathy for the present. In addition, he used his narrative to exploit that vein of exoticism so widespread in his oeuvre.

Gautier's "exotic" narratives that remove the reader in time include *Le Petit Chien de la marquise* (The Marquise's Little Dog, 1836), *Jean et Jeannette*, and *Le Capitaine Fracasse*, all of which take the reader back in French history; and *La Chaîne d'or, ou l'Amant partagé* (The Golden Chain, or The Shared Lover, 1837), *Une Nuit de Cléopâtre* (One of Cleopatra's Nights, 1838), *Le Roi Candaule* (King Candaule, 1844), and *Le Roman de la momie* (1858; translated as *The Romance of the Mummy*, 1863), which evoke milieus belonging to antiquity.

Le Roman de la momie is at once typical and unique, for it displays an exoticism both contemporary and remote in time. While its frame story situates the action in contemporary Egypt, its embedded main narrative removes the reader to the ancient Egypt of the time of Moses. Gautier, who had not yet visited Egypt in 1857, based much of his description on books that the scholar Ernest Feydeau had made available to him. The frame story reviews the archaeological explorations of two contemporary Europeans. When the narrator has them penetrate into an undiscovered burial monument, he describes at length the complex inner structure of the tomb, the different chambers that the explorers visit, the sarcophagus they discover, and the mummy it contains.

A text they find in the sarcophagus constitutes the main narrative, the story of Tahoser, the beautiful Egyptian girl mummified in the burial crypt. Tahoser loves a handsome stranger whom she sees from time to time in the streets of Thebes. At the same time, she inspires the passion of the mighty pharaoh. On the other hand, the stranger Poëri, the pharaoh's intendant, loves the Hebrew woman Ra'hel. The plot turns on the respective attempts of Tahoser to capture Poëri's affection and of the pharaoh to make himself loved by Tahoser. In this part of the narrative, Gautier endeavored not only to re-create verbally the ancient Egyptian capital and its life but also to convey the sense of grandiosity and solidity he associated with Egyptian civilization. The subject also allowed him to repeat the comparisons he seemed compelled to find between attractive civilizations from the past and his own dull and uninspired time.

Gautier's fictional works that transport the reader to an exotic present include *Militona, Les*

Deux Etoiles (1848; translated as *Four Destinies*), and *Mademoiselle Dafné de Montbriand, eau-forte dans la manière de Piranèse* (Mademoiselle Dafné de Montbriand, Etching in the Manner of Piranesi, 1881). *Militona* is typical both of this form of exotic fiction and of Gautier's general proclivity for mingling humor and gravity in the same work. The scene is set in Madrid. Don Andrés de Salcedo, a well-to-do young socialite, is engaged to Doña Feliciana Vasquez de los Rios, herself quite wealthy and modish; but he becomes infatuated with Militona, a pretty young girl he meets at a bullfight, and he begins an investigation to learn where she lives.

Not in the least put off by the discovery that she is a *manola* living in a working-class district, Andrés attempts to communicate with her; but in so doing he attracts the attention of the torero (bullfighter) Juancho, himself jealously in love with Militona. The rivalry at last comes to a head when Juancho and Andrés engage in a knife fight in which the furious bullfighter wounds the nobleman and leaves him for dead in the street in front of Militona's house. The remainder of the story recounts how she finds Andrés and cares for him, how they fall in love and marry, and how Juancho, despondent at his loss, allows himself to be gored to death in a corrida.

Throughout the narrative the reader encounters allusions to Spanish customs, food, national characteristics, architecture, and well-known monuments. By the structure that he gives to the story, Gautier is able to introduce his readers to different Spanish milieus. Through several episodes set in Feliciana's apartment, he evokes the life of the Madrid upper classes. To reach Militona in her milieu, Andrés assumes the disguise of a working-class *madrileño* (Madrilenian) so as to enter her neighborhood unnoticed— and so as to permit Gautier to describe the open-air market where Andrés purchases his *manolo* clothing and the poor quarter where Militona lives. Gautier situates the initial meeting between Andrés and Militona at a bullfight, giving himself the opportunity to evoke the pageantry and the action associated with a typical corrida. He represents the crowd on its way to the arena, the stir of the spectators in the stands, the ceremonious beginning of the bullfight, and the choreographed movements of the toreros. Throughout, Gautier makes full use of appropriate technical terms and even the argot of the bullring.

Although the representation of Andrés's and Militona's tender love and of Juancho's jealousy, despair, and suicide gives the novel a serious, even tragic, tone, Gautier does not refrain from injecting an occasional note of humor or irony into the narrative. His narrator frequently intrudes to call attention to his role as narrator and thus to signal that the story is only a story. He consistently makes fun of Feliciana's comically misplaced attempts to ape the latest styles and manners of England. When Andrés disappears in pursuit of Militona, Feliciana's father notifies the police. The authorities assign to the case two detectives who can only be characterized as Spanish versions of the Keystone Kops. They regularly misinterpret evidence. Their logic is flawed beyond reason. In their failures they are always at pains to cover their mistakes by some implausible explanation. They attempt to impose themselves not by intelligence but by pompous speech. Their reconstruction of Andrés's disappearance makes of the young socialite a dangerous political conspirator threatening the stability of the government. They are thoroughly annoyed to learn later that Andrés has only been on a mission of love. Finally, they are portrayed as cowards: their comic terror when approaching Juancho to arrest him serves as the ultimate deflation of these guardians of the Spanish peace.

As on other occasions, Gautier makes frequent use of literary and artistic allusion. In the description of the ugly duenna who accompanies Militona, he recalls the monstrous female figures in the engravings of Francisco de Goya. Before undertaking the description of a particular locale, the narrator ironically alludes to François Rabelais and Balzac, who, he says, would have exaggeratedly given their readers an "enumeration" of four pages; then he himself devotes sixteen pages to his representation of the bullfight at which Andrés first speaks to Militona! The evocation of certain costumes brings allusions to Fracasse and Matamore, braggart soldiers from the commedia dell'arte. To suggest the sinister quality of a street scene at night, Gautier alludes—perhaps mistakenly—to Rembrandt's painting *The Nightwatch* (1642), which often serves him when he wishes to convey a sense of foreboding.

If *Militona* is typical of Gautier's purely exotic narratives, *Le Capitaine Fracasse* presents a quasi-historical exoticism with a twist of romance. Like the vast majority of his fictional pieces, *Fracasse* appeared first as a feuilleton, a serialized form, in the *Revue Nationale et Etrangère* (late 1861 to mid June 1863). The work appeared later in 1863 in two volumes. Gautier had been

An 1839 caricature that mocks Gautier's coiffure

promising this novel since the time of *Mademoiselle de Maupin*, in 1835, and had even received advances on its publication. The editor François Buloz had gone so far as to take Gautier to court in an attempt at forcing compliance with the contract, and Gautier had been spared restitution of the advance and a fine only by the intervention of a wealthy admirer who settled the matter out of court. More disappointed expectations had prevented the appearance of the novel until 1861.

The exoticism in *Le Capitaine Fracasse* lies in Gautier's attentiveness to the re-creation of a segment of early-seventeenth-century French life. The narrator evokes in detail the frequently uncertain existence of itinerant actors. Tracing their wanderings from the provinces to Paris permits Gautier to explore the life of the upper and middle classes as well as the low, rough-and-ready ways of robbers and swords-for-hire. The narrator introduces the reader to the interiors of country inns, Parisian hotels, castles, and pothouses. In addition, he imagines the activities of the time—hunting parties, highway robberies, public hangings, and improvised theatrical productions. Gautier's concern to place his reader in the 1630s extends even to geographical detail. When, for example, he represents the actors' entry into Paris, he takes them along a route that conforms exactly to the seventeenth-century plan of the capital, naming and precisely situating locales and structures, most long gone or renamed in 1861.

Gautier gave his novel the structure of a romance. Verisimilitude, then, is not a quality to be expected in characterization or plot. The principal characters all belong to the nobility, and the protagonists are uniformly noble in spirit. The principal male personage, Sigognac, is a destitute provincial nobleman who must make an initiatory journey and overcome a series of obstacles, material and moral, in order to achieve the good fortune with which romance must end. The heroine, Isabelle, who appears as a common actress, turns out to be the illegitimate daughter of a prince. The love that develops between the two personages is pure to a fault.

The action follows Sigognac's travels with a theatrical company from the southwestern provinces to Paris, where the troupe gains recognition, where Sigognac proves his nobility of blood and spirit, and where some of the major uncertainties are clarified. Threats to the eventual union of the lovers recur at every stage of the journey, then are realized when the lustful duc de Vallombreuse kidnaps Isabelle. Sigognac and his fellow actors save her by attacking the castle where she is a prisoner and killing or neutralizing her kidnappers, including Vallombreuse, who is mortally wounded. A coincidental recognition scene, occasioned by the identification of a ring that Isabelle carries, brings reunion with her noble father—and the discovery that Vallombreuse was her brother!

A new threat—reminiscent of such plays as *The Cid* (1637), by the dramatist Pierre Corneille, who coincidentally was producing his plays in Paris at the time of this story—separates the lovers again: Sigognac, as the killer of his beloved's brother, realizes that he cannot now hope to marry Isabelle; so he sadly returns to his dilapidated manor house in Gascony to resume his life of poverty, now all the more cheerless because he can never expect the happiness that chance has wrenched from him. However, who should appear one day but Vallombreuse, miraculously recovered. Having undergone a complete—if implausible—change of character, he wishes to make amends for earlier offenses by helping Sigognac to reestablish his fortune and by bringing him together again with Isabelle.

It is easy to understand why French aunts and uncles have, since the nineteenth century, chosen *Le Capitaine Fracasse* as a gift for young readers. The adventure is exciting. The style is racy, and the language is rich. If the romance has a moral, it is that constancy in the pursuit of a worthy goal pays off and that nobility of spirit is to be preferred above all else.

Yet the work also has something to say to older readers, to those interested in finding a more sophisticated message and perhaps additional clues to the author's mentality. The fact that Gautier had had the story of *Fracasse* in mind since the 1830s is significant. His original interest in setting the action during the reign of Louis XIII coincides exactly with his study of the irregular authors from this period in preparation for *Les Grotesques*. That he centered the action of *Fracasse* on the life of a contemporary troupe of itinerant actors reflects his enthusiasm for the baroque theater, which assumed theoretical form in his call for a fantasy comedy in *Mademoiselle de Maupin*.

Indeed, Gautier used his novel as a vehicle for the further expression of his ideas on dramatic form and the art of the theater. In numerous digressions he has his characters discuss the art of acting and the relationship between the theater and life. Finally, the fact that he republished the original manifesto several times over the years and the fact that he never abandoned the story of *Fracasse* show that his enthusiasm for a comic drama based on models popular in the baroque era—including the comedies of William Shakespeare—never flagged. Only such dramatic types as the irregular comedies of the preclassical period and the equally irregular Italian comedy—Fracasse himself is a commedia character—could save the French theater from the weary realism and the prosaic middle-class values that Gautier saw taking over the French stage of his day.

Like *Mademoiselle de Maupin*, *Le Capitaine Fracasse* gives novelistic form to Gautier's ideal theater. It is a narrative depicting types rather than psychologically complex characters. The plot development depends as much on coincidence as on neat cause-effect progression. Unmotivated digressions regularly interrupt the action. Ironic tricks of all kinds, including frequent and substantial intrusions by the narrator, undercut both story and characters. Finally, Gautier reveals a distinct preoccupation with style, often at the expense of content.

Fracasse thus gave Gautier the opportunity

to promote a type of literary expression opposed to what he viewed as the uninspired forms of his day. It permitted him yet again to indulge his stylistic bent. And it satisfied his escapist compulsion. Its quasi-historical exoticism allowed him to remove himself from the present and at the same time to create perhaps another of those verbal obstacles to the inexorable movement of time that he regarded as the true legacy of art.

Builders of the canon have been unwilling to place Gautier among the major authors of nineteenth-century French literature. If one compares his poetry to that of the acknowledged giants of the time, the judges may be correct. Gautier does not approach Hugo for variety and richness; he does not in his poetry achieve Baudelaire's profound expression of despairing idealism; he does not have the adventurous poetic spirit of Mallarmé or Arthur Rimbaud.

It is rather Gautier's fiction that makes him worthy of inclusion among the great writers of the nineteenth century. He is unique in his engaging use of irony, in his unflagging defense of art, and in his concentration on beauty. In his personal manner, he is representative of romanticism by his experimental impulse and especially by his idealism, which he never lost in the midst of contemporary threats. Marcel Voisin, whose judgment of him is the most balanced of all recent views, considers Gautier to be not only a distinguished author in his time but an estimable figure worthy of a higher position in a broader context. Summing up Gautier by images of sun and night reminiscent of the critical and philosophical work of Gaston Bachelard, Voisin presents him as a man seeking to control a tension that he, his contemporaries, and many moderns embody, the tension between ontological optimism and anguish produced by the dark fear that human beings are nothing in a meaningless universe. Gautier, to his everlasting credit, proposed art as the way to equilibrium. Voisin's final assessment of Gautier confirms why the old Romantic deserves a place among the major authors of French literature: "Thanks to his literary achievements, Théophile Gautier, by revealing himself to us, all of himself, speaks to us about ourselves, our anxieties and our hopes, about human beings eternally divided between the sunlight and the night."

Letters:

Correspondance générale, 6 volumes to date, edit-

ed by Claudine Lacoste-Veysseyre (Geneva: Droz, 1985-   ).

Bibliography:

Charles-Victor-Maximilien-Albert, Vicomte de Spoelberch de Lovenjoul, *Histoire des œuvres de Théophile Gautier*, 2 volumes (Paris: Charpentier, 1887).

Biographies:

Adolphe Boschot, *Théophile Gautier* (Paris: Desclée de Brouwer, 1933);

Joanna Richardson, *Théophile Gautier, His Life and Times* (New York: Coward-McCann, 1959).

References:

Edwin Binney, *Les Ballets de Théophile Gautier* (Paris: Nizet, 1965);

Claude Book-Senninger, *Théophile Gautier, auteur dramatique* (Paris: Nizet, 1972);

René Bourgeois, "Théophile Gautier, ou les traces de Thalie," in his *L'Ironie romantique: Spectacle et jeu de Mme de Staël à G. de Nerval* (Grenoble: Presses Universitaires de Grenoble, 1974), pp. 151-172;

Bulletin de la Société Théophile Gautier (1979-   );

Pierre-Georges Castex, "Gautier et son angoisse," in his *Le Conte fantastique en France de Nodier à Maupassant* (Paris: José Corti, 1962), pp. 214-247;

Ross Chambers, *"Spirite" de Gautier: une lecture* (Paris: Minard, 1974);

Bernard Delvaille, *Théophile Gautier* (Paris: Seghers, 1968);

L'Esprit Créateur, issue on Gautier, 3 (Spring 1963);

Europe, issue on Gautier, 601 (May 1979);

Albert J. George, "Gautier," in his *Short Fiction in France, 1800-1850* (Syracuse: Syracuse University Press, 1964), pp. 166-188;

Richard B. Grant, *Théophile Gautier* (Boston: Twayne, 1975);

René Jasinski, *Les Années romantiques de Théophile Gautier* (Paris: Vuibert, 1929);

Georges Matoré, *Le Vocabulaire et la société sous Louis-Philippe* (Geneva: Slatkine Reprints, 1967);

Georges Poulet, "Théophile Gautier," in his *Etudes sur le temps humain* (Paris: Plon, 1950), pp. 278-307;

Revue d'Histoire Littéraire de la France, issue on Gautier, 72 (July-August 1972);

Jean Richer, *Etudes et recherches sur Théophile Gautier prosateur* (Paris: Nizet, 1981);

Joseph Savalle, *Travestis, métamorphoses, dédoublements: Essai sur l'œuvre romanesque de Théophile Gautier* (Paris: Minard, 1981);

Marie-Claude Schapira, *Le Regard de Narcisse: Romans et nouvelles de Théophile Gautier* (Lyon: Presses Universitaires de Lyon, 1984);

Albert B. Smith, *Ideal and Reality in the Fictional Narratives of Théophile Gautier* (Gainesville: University of Florida Press, 1969);

Smith, *Théophile Gautier and the Fantastic* (University, Miss.: Romance Monographs, 1977);

Robert Snell, *Théophile Gautier: A Romantic Critic of the Visual Arts* (Oxford: Clarendon, 1982);

Michael C. Spencer, *The Art Criticism of Théophile Gautier* (Geneva: Droz, 1969);

P. E. Tennant, *Théophile Gautier* (London: Athlone, 1975);

H. van der Tuin, *L'Evolution psychologique, esthétique et littéraire de Théophile Gautier: Etude de caractérologie littéraire* (Paris: Nizet, 1933);

Marcel Voisin, *Le Soleil et la nuit: L'Imaginaire dans l'œuvre de Théophile Gautier* (Brussels: Editions de l'Université de Bruxelles, 1981).

Papers:

The Bibliothèque Spoelberch de Lovenjoul (named for Gautier's bibliographer) contains a substantial collection of manuscripts, contemporary copies of Gautier's works (with autographs, marginal notes, etc.), letters, and documents relating to the author and his family. Housed for years in the Musée Condé at Chantilly, the collection was later moved to the Institut de France in Paris.

Victor Hugo

(26 February 1802 - 22 May 1885)

Timothy Raser
University of Georgia

SELECTED BOOKS: *Ode sur la naissance de Son Altesse Royale monseigneur le duc de Bordeaux* (Paris: Boucher, 1820);

Odes et poésies diverses (Paris: Pélicier, 1822);

Odes (Paris: Persan, 1823);

Han d'Islande, anonymous, 4 volumes (Paris: Persan, 1823); translated as *Hans of Iceland* (London: J. Robins & Co., 1825);

Nouvelles Odes (Paris: Ladvocat, 1824);

Odes et ballades (Paris: Ladvocat, 1826; enlarged edition, Paris: Hector Bossange, 1828);

Bug-Jargal (Paris: Urbain Canel, 1826); translated as *The Slave-King* (Philadelphia: Carey, Lea & Blanchard, 1833);

Cromwell (Paris: Ernest Flammarion, 1827);

Ode à la colonne de la place Vendôme (Paris, 1829);

Les Orientales (Paris: Charles Gosselin et Hector Bossange, 1829);

Le Dernier Jour d'un condamné, anonymous (Paris: Gosselin et Bossange, 1829); translated by Sir P. Hesketh Fleetwood as *The Last Days of a Condemned* (London: Smith, Elder & Co., 1840);

Hernani, ou l'Honneur castillan (Paris: Mame et Delaunay-Vallée, 1830); translated as *Hernani; or, The Honour of a Castilian* (London: W. Sams, 1830);

Notre-Dame de Paris, 2 volumes (Paris: Charles Gosselin, 1831; enlarged edition, Paris: Renduel, 1832); translated by A. L. Alger (Boston: Estes & Lauriat, 1832);

Marion de Lorme (Paris: Charpentier, 1831);

Les Feuilles d'automne (Paris: Renduel, 1831);

Le Roi s'amuse, drame (Paris: Eugène Renduel, 1832); translated as *The King's Fool* (London: J. Clements, 1841);

Lucrèce Borgia, drame (Paris: Eugène Renduel, 1833); translated by W. T. Haley as *Lucretia Borgia, a Dramatic Tale* (London: J. Clements, 1842);

Victor Hugo (photograph by Nadar)

Marie Tudor, drame en trois journées (Paris, 1833);
Claude Gueux (Paris: Everat, Imprimeur, 1834);
Littérature et philosophie mêlées, 2 volumes (Paris: Renduel, 1834);
Angelo, Tyran de Padoue (Paris: J. Hetzel, 1835); translated by Charles Reade as *Angelo* (London: H. Lacy, 1851);
Les Chants du crépuscule (Paris: Renduel, 1835); translated by George W. M. Reynolds as *Songs of Twilight* (Paris: French, English & American Library, 1836);
Les Voix intérieures (Paris: Renduel, 1837);
Ruy Blas (Paris: H. Delloye, 1838); translated as *Ruy Blas. A Romantic Drama* (London: T. H. Lacy, 1860);
Le Retour de l'empereur (Paris: Furne et Cie., [n.d.]);
Les Rayons et les ombres (Paris: Delloye, 1840);
Le Rhin, 2 volumes (Paris: Delloye, 1842); translated by D. M. Aird as *The Rhine* (London: D. Aird, 1843);
Les Burgraves, trilogie (Paris: E. Michaud, 1843);
Œuvres oratoires de Victor Hugo, 2 volumes (Brussels: Tarride, 1852);

Napoléon-le-petit (Brussels: Tarride, 1852);
Les Châtiments (Brussels: Henri Samuel et Cie., 1853);
République universelle, démocratique et sociale. Anniversaire de la révolution de 1848. 24 février 1855 (Jersey: Imprimerie universelle, 1855);
Les Contemplations, 2 volumes (Brussels: Pierre-Jules Hetzel, 1856);
La Légende des siècles, 1ʳᵉ série. Histoire. Les Petites Epopées, 2 volumes (Brussels: Hetzel, Méline Cans et Cie., 1859); translated by Geo. S. Burleigh as *The Legend of the Centuries* (New York, 1874);
John Brown (Paris: E. Dentu, 1861);
Les Misérables, 10 volumes (Brussels: Lacroix, Verboeckhoven et Cie., 1862); translated by Lascelles Wraxall (London: Hurst & Blackett, 1862);
William Shakespeare (Brussels: Lacroix, Verboeckhoven et Cie., 1864); translated by A. Haillot (Boston: Estes & Lauriat, 1864);
Les Chansons des rues et des bois (Brussels: Lacroix, Verboeckhoven et Cie., 1865);
Les Travailleurs de la mer, 3 volumes (Brussels: Lacroix, Verboeckhoven et Cie., 1866); translated as *The Toilers of the Sea*, 2 volumes (Boston: Dana Estes, 1866); enlarged French edition (Paris: J. Hetzel et A. Quantin, 1880-1889);
La Voix de Guernesey (Guernsey: T.-M. Richard, 1867);
L'Homme qui rit, 4 volumes (Brussels: Lacroix, Verboeckhoven et Cie., 1869); translated as *The Man Who Laughs* (Boston: Dana Estes, 1869);
L'Année terrible (Paris: Michel Lévy, 1872);
Actes et paroles I, Avant l'exil (Paris: Michel Lévy, 1872);
Quatrevingt-treize, 3 volumes (Paris: Michel Lévy frères, 1874); translated by Frank Lee Benedict and J. Hain Friswell as *Ninety-three* (London: Sampson Low, Marston, Low & Searle, 1874);
Actes et paroles II, Pendant l'exil (Paris: Michel Lévy, 1875);
Actes et paroles III, Depuis l'exil, 1870-1876 (Paris: Calmann-Lévy, 1876);
Histoire d'un crime, déposition d'un témoin (Paris: Calmann-Lévy, 1877); translated by T. H. Joyce and A. Locker as *The History of a Crime; The Testimony of an Eye-Witness* (New York: Hurst, 1877);
La Légende des siècles, Nouvelle série, 2 volumes (Paris: Calmann-Lévy, 1877);

L'Art d'être grand-père (Paris: Calmann-Lévy, 1877);

Le Pape (Paris: Calmann-Lévy, 1878);

La Pitié suprême (Paris: Calmann-Lévy, 1879);

Religions et religion (Paris: Calmann-Lévy, 1880);

L'Ane (Paris: Calmann-Lévy, 1881);

Les Quatre Vents de l'esprit, 2 volumes (Paris: J. Hetzel et A. Quantin, 1881);

Torquemada (Paris: C. Lévy, 1882);

La Légende des siècles, Tome cinquième et dernier (Paris: Calmann-Lévy, 1883);

L'Archipel de la Manche (Paris: Calmann-Lévy, 1883).

Collections: *Œuvres de Victor Hugo*, 20 volumes (Paris: E. Renduel, 1832-1842);

Œuvres de Victor Hugo, 16 volumes (Paris: Furne et Cie., 1841);

Œuvres complètes de Victor Hugo, 48 volumes (Paris: J. Hetzel et A. Quantin, 1880-1889);

Œuvres complètes de Victor Hugo, 45 volumes, edited by Paul Meurice, Gustave Simon, and Lécile Daubray (Paris: Ollendorf, Albin Michel, 1902-1951);

La Légende des siècles, La Fin de Satan, Dieu, edited by Jacques Trachet (Paris: Gallimard, Bibliothèque de la Pléiade, 1950);

Les Misérables, edited by Maurice Allen (Paris: Gallimard, Bibliothèque de la Pléiade, 1951);

Œuvres poétiques, 3 volumes (Paris: Gallimard, Bibliothèque de la Pléiade, 1964);

Œuvres complètes, édition chronologique, 18 volumes (Paris: Le Club Français du Livre, 1967-1970);

Notre-Dame de Paris and *Les Travailleurs de la mer*, edited by Jacques Seebacher and Yves Gohin (Paris: Gallimard, Bibliothèque de la Pléiade, 1975);

Œuvres complètes, 15 volumes to date (Paris: Laffont, Collection Bouquins, 1985-   ).

PLAY PRODUCTIONS: *Amy Robsart*, Paris, Théâtre de l'Odéon, 13 February 1828;

Hernani, Paris, Théâtre Français, 25 February 1830;

Marion de Lorme, Paris, Théâtre de la Porte-Saint-Martin, 11 August 1831;

Le Roi s'amuse, Paris, Théâtre Français, 22 November 1832;

Lucrèce Borgia, Paris, Théâtre de la Porte-Saint-Martin, 2 February 1833;

Marie Tudor, Paris, Théâtre de la Porte-Saint-Martin, 6 November 1833;

Angelo, Tyran de Padoue, Paris, Théâtre Français, 28 April 1835;

La Esmeralda, Paris, Théâtre de l'Académie royale de musique, 14 November 1836;

Ruy Blas, Paris, Théâtre de la Renaissance, 8 November 1838;

Les Burgraves, Paris, Théâtre Français, 7 March 1843.

OTHER: *Paris*, Introduction to *Paris-Guide*, by Hugo (Paris: Librairie Internationale, 1867).

No century of French literature has been better represented by a single author than the nineteenth, and no writer better personifies the French nineteenth century than Victor Hugo. His life span corresponds closely to the century's limits; for fully fifty years Hugo wrote abundantly, and when he died, the nation honored him with the ceremonies ordinarily reserved for heads of state. Hugo was a royalist, a Bonapartist, a republican; he usefully supported or actively opposed all the governments that took shape during his lifetime; he saw two monarchies, two republics, two empires, two revolutions, a coup d'état, and the Commune, with its bloody repression. Not simply was Hugo an observer of and participant in his times, he was also one of the most prolific writers in history, but, unlike many other prolific writers, his works are both varied and important; he was a poet, a novelist, and a playwright. It can even be argued that his poems, novels, and plays are among the best that the French nineteenth century offers (even if, in the latter category, Hugo's excellence depends largely on the mediocrity of his competitors' offerings). One of his poetry collections (*Les Contemplations*, 1856) ranks among the most beautiful ever written, and his novel *Les Misérables* (1862) is universally acknowledged as a masterpiece. The length of Hugo's works is daunting: eighteen fifteen-hundred-page volumes of works, fragments, letters, and drawings constitute the reference edition.

Some publication statistics might give an idea of the extent and duration of Hugo's achievement: during his lifetime Hugo's works were published three times more frequently than those of other Romantic writers (including Alfred de Musset, Alfred de Vigny, and Stendhal), and five times more often than those of mid- and late-century writers (including Gustave Flaubert, Emile Zola, Arthur Rimbaud, and Charles Baudelaire). During the same time his works were published twice as often as those of French classical authors: Jean de La Fontaine, Jean Racine, and

Hugo in 1829 (etching by Achille Devéria)

Nicolas Boileau. More recently, from 1960 to 1971, he was the second most-published dead author in France (200 editions), following only Honoré de Balzac (373 editions), and was published more often than Alexandre Dumas *père* (129), Molière (122), or Stendhal (115). *Les Misérables* was the most widely published novel from that decade (108 editions), if various abridged editions can be counted.   ·

Hugo has of course known periods of neglect: his poetry was virtually forgotten between 1915 and 1939; if his *Les Contemplations* outsold Baudelaire's *Les Fleurs du mal* (1857; translated as *Flowers of Evil*, 1909) during the nineteenth century, the latter was published far more frequently than the former between 1915 and 1939 (47 editions to 1). During his lifetime, and for many years thereafter, he was recognized as a poet: in 1950, for example, 49.5 percent of his works published were poetry, while only 32.5 percent were novels; in 1975, 5.3 percent were poetry, while 86.7 percent were novels. Even though the name Victor Hugo is no longer (as the poet Stéphane Mallarmé said it was) *personally* a synonym for literature, his works have endured, having weathered significant periods of neglect. He has now found new readers, and a new identity.

That he excelled in almost every field he touched makes the task of the critic harder, for it is difficult to know where to start, and which works to single out as most important. Hugo wrote novels from his earliest to his latest years, and his novels are, from the beginning, revealing of his deepest preoccupations. While his later novels demonstrate technical mastery and poetic qualities achieved only after years of work, his novels, taken as a group, reveal more about his development and evolution than the other genres to which he put his hand.

It would be inaccurate, however, to pretend that Hugo's reception, both contemporary and current, was one of unalloyed appreciation and admiration: he was a man with many enemies and detractors, and this qualification is true today. Indeed, when asked who was the greatest French poet of the nineteenth century, the novelist André Gide is said to have retorted, "Victor Hugo, hélas!" (Victor Hugo, alas!). While many scholars have made Hugo the subject of their lifework, many others have ignored him, to the point where critic Harold Bloom can claim that "Victor Hugo remains absurdly unfashionable and neglected by his nation's most advanced critics." The sheer size of Hugo's work, the duration of his dominance, and the extent of his influence could give both competitors and critics ample reason to seek greatness elsewhere.

It might be useful then to consider some of the other celebrated comments made about Hugo. Tellingly, many of these are quips, one-liners whose concision contrasts neatly with the amplification that Hugo gave to all his pronouncements. Many observers try to deflate the Hugolian balloon, but in so doing produce the very contrasts that Hugo used and thus exemplify the author's power, even among his detractors. Perhaps the most famous of these quips is the twentieth-century writer Jean Cocteau's "Victor Hugo était un fou qui se croyait Victor Hugo" (Victor Hugo was a madman who thought he was Victor Hugo).

Indeed, Hugo was self-obsessed, and this obsession could be qualified, especially in the later years, as mania. There are many grounds for such comments: in *William Shakespeare* (1864), for example, Hugo lists the geniuses of humanity and cross-references them to individual nations and epochs. The place for modern France is conspicuously vacant, as if inviting itself to be filled. In *Les Travailleurs de la mer* (1866; translated as *The Toilers of the Sea*, 1866), as in *Notre-Dame de*

Paris (1831; translated, 1832), he describes a reef as a giant, rocky *H*, "espèce d'immense H majuscule" (a kind of immense capital *H*). Hugo's drawings, interesting in their own right, often include stormy landscapes where a geological formation crumbles into plain or sea: this formation is sometimes none other than the name *Victor Hugo*. Excessive modesty was not one of Hugo's failings.

It could also be said that Hugo had no followers. Baudelaire went so far as to judge that what influence Hugo had was pernicious, sapping the originality of those who came too close: "C'est M. Victor Hugo qui a perdu M. Boulanger—après en avoir perdu tant d'autres . . . " (It's Mr. Victor Hugo who has ruined Mr. Boulanger, after having ruined so many others . . .). Certainly Hugo, despite his admirers, never created a new aesthetic, such as the one begun by Baudelaire and continued by Mallarmé and Paul Valéry. Hugo may have simply lived too long: by the time he died, in addition to his own children, those who would have taken up where he left off were already dead or, perhaps, even worse, had simply been left behind.

Hugo's popularity—the sales of his works to a wide audience, his appreciation by ordinary readers—is also a mixed blessing. Jean-Paul Sartre was openly envious of this achievement: "Hugo, sans doute, a eu la rare fortune de pénétrer partout: c'est un des seuls, peut-être le seul de nos écrivains qui soit vraiment populaire" (Hugo, no doubt, had the rare good fortune to be read everywhere: he's one of our only, perhaps our only writer who has been truly popular). André Breton tried to minimize Hugo: "Victor Hugo est surréaliste quand il n'est pas bête" (Victor Hugo is a surrealist when he isn't stupid). Hugo's ability and tendency to speak to the greatest number, albeit at the expense of using platitudes and stereotypes, elicited a dismissive response from the founder of the new surrealist school. Sartre's envy and Breton's misgivings can easily be laid to the account of his immense success.

It has often been claimed that Hugo's works are fantastic, that they fail to achieve the verisimilitude—psychological or descriptive—characteristic of the novel. Richard B. Grant, writing about the early books, points out the ambiguity of the word that Hugo used to qualify these works, and argues that *roman* should be translated as "romance," not "novel." While the novel tries to represent "real people" through the analysis, description, and evolution of character, the ro-

mance deals in archetypes and tends toward myth. Thus, while charges that Hugo's characterization is poor are accurate, they miss an important point: Hugo sought to represent a general, archetypal reality, more akin to myth than to modern novels.

Critics have attacked the very structures of Hugo's novels, specifically the author's use of and purpose in using antithesis. Here again Baudelaire is the most articulate critic: "M. Victor Hugo laisse voir dans tous ses tableaux, lyriques et dramatiques, un système d'alignement et de contrastes uniformes. L'excentricité elle-même prend chez lui des formes symétriques" (Mr. Victor Hugo allows one to see in all his pictures, lyrical and dramatic, a uniform system of alignment and contrast. Eccentricity itself becomes symmetrical in his works). Here, too, the critic is entirely right: Hugo does make extensive use of contrast, opposition, and antithesis. It should be pointed out, though, that these devices are as indicative of an artistic intention as they are of an individual style. This in turn detracts from the realism of his works, while giving them an idiosyncratic aspect (Baudelaire's objection), but it does allow him to represent great abstractions concretely. In *Mimesis: The Representation of Reality in Western Literature*, Erich Auerbach acknowledges the power of effect that Hugo achieved through these devices, even if they, at the same time, deny verisimilitude to his representation of reality: "in dealing both with historical and contemporary subjects, he elaborates the stylistic poles of the sublime and the grotesque, or other ethical and aesthetic antitheses, to the utmost, so that they clash; in this way very strong effects are produced, for Hugo's command of expression is powerful and suggestive; but the effects are improbable and, as a reflection of human life, untrue."

The reservations regarding Hugo—his egotism, his idiosyncrasies, his use of types, his popularity, his desire to achieve strong effects—could all be subsumed under one word: *melodrama*. Hugo's novels please or displease depending on one's attitude to this crude, effective, moralizing genre, and they are, if not melodramas, at least melodramatic, for Hugo makes extensive, even abusive, use of reversals, recognition scenes, and stark contrasts to stir the emotions of his readers. Furthermore, Hugo loves to reveal pure good and evil. If, following Peter Brooks, one accepts that melodrama is the "expressionism of the moral imagination," Hugo's works are plainly melodramatic: the simple oppositions so favored

Page from one of Hugo's school notebooks (Bibliothèque Nationale)

by the writer consistently give rise to moral interpretations. However, it must also be noted that these devices go beyond morality and give concrete expression to other intangibles: fate, history, time. Hugo uses the devices of melodrama to represent what cannot be represented, to figure the sublime.

Among the many photographs of Hugo, there is one, taken when he was fifty-four during his exile at Guernsey, that shows him in a pose of meditation, eyes heavy-lidded, almost closed. Its legend reads—perhaps in deliberate self-parody—"Victor Hugo écoutant Dieu" (Victor Hugo listening to God). Perhaps because of this picture, or maybe because of his practice of spiritualism from 1855 to 1856, Sartre once called Hugo "the favorite interviewer of God." The picture's legend and Sartre's witticism make one smile, but there is an important grain of truth in both. Hugo *did* listen to God, if by that last word one understands those invisible forces that escape human control and defy rational apprehension.

It is possible to synthesize Hugo's many and varied works with a reference to the author's larger-than-life persona. The biographer André Maurois has called this projection of Hugo's self "Olympio," and it is to be found in all his works, poetic and topical, dramatic and novelistic. Such an approach has much to recommend it but tends to make the author's works reflections of his personality, and even a persona as gigantic as Olympio cannot hope to account for Hugo's texts. Yet Hugo's overriding ambition is clear: to give concrete representation to the invisible forces that shape human lives—fate, history, society, cruelty, revolution. Perhaps more so than any other writer, Hugo put a face on these forces and made them recognizable.

Victor Hugo's father, Joseph-Léopold Sigisbert Hugo, was born the son of a master carpenter in Nancy in 1773. At fifteen he cut short his schooling, in which he had acquired a useful knowledge of Latin and mathematics, to enlist in the king's army, only to find shortly thereafter that he was serving a new master: the revolutionary government, or Convention. As a junior officer he was sent in 1793 to the Vendée region of Brittany to put down an antirevolutionary insurrection, and he was rapidly promoted to the rank of captain. There, in 1796, he met Sophie Trébuchet, the orphan daughter of a sea captain, raised with royalist sympathies by her aunt. Despite their political differences, the young people fell in love and married on Adjutant-Major Hugo's birthday, 15 November 1796.

They moved to Paris, where they lived for two years before the birth of their son Abel, followed in 1800 by the birth of a second son, Eugène. There they met Victor de Lahorie, who aided Hugo's political ambitions and who became Sophie's lover: General Lahorie was to be her third son's godfather. Joseph was called back to active duty and served in the Army of the Danube. With Napoleon's rise to power and the ensuing premium put on military service, the family's moves became more frequent, and Joseph's stays at home became rare; nevertheless, a third son, Victor-Marie Hugo, was born in Besançon on 26 February 1802, a child so sickly that the midwife declared he would not live.

Whether because both Joseph and Sophie had taken lovers, or because of their differences of personality, or because of Joseph's long absences from home, their marriage suffered, and the children were brought up by their mother in different garrison towns. In 1805 Mme Hugo and her sons joined Joseph in Italy, where he had just captured the famous guerrilla Fra Diavolo. In 1811 her husband was promoted to general in the army of King Joseph of Spain (Napoleon's brother), with salary to match. With the prospects of high social station and material comfort before them, the family took the long trip to Madrid.

While it was the king's wish to see the Hugos together, when Sophie arrived in Madrid, she found that her husband had no desire to leave his mistress, Catherine Thomas, and after three months of disputes the couple resolved on divorce, under the terms of which Mme Hugo would have custody of Eugène and Victor, while Count Hugo (the title was conferred in 1810 by King Joseph of Spain) kept Abel. In March of 1812, after several difficult months in Madrid, Mme Hugo returned to Paris with Eugène and Victor. Meanwhile, her friend Lahorie had participated in a conspiracy against Napoleon and was executed six months after their return. Mme Hugo rejoiced at Napoleon's fall, even if it did mean that her ex-husband's pay was cut by half, and her handsome allowance accordingly stopped. Mme Hugo's natural reaction to this event might account for Victor's early hatred of the emperor, his preoccupation with the death penalty, and the fascination with exile that appeared so early and so often in his work.

NOTRE-DAME
DE PARIS.

PAR VICTOR HUGO,

TROISIÈME ÉDITION.

PARIS,
CHARLES GOSSELIN, LIBRAIRE,
RUE SAINT-GERMAIN-DES-PRÉS, N° 9.
M DCCC XXXI.

Cover for the third edition (1831) of the romance that became known as The Hunchback of Notre Dame

As schoolboys, first in the Pension Cordier, then in law school, the Hugo brothers collectively did very well, all possessing great aptitude for study. Prior to their trip to Spain, Mme Hugo had given them Spanish grammars and dictionaries, and these sufficed for them to learn the language. Nevertheless, Victor soon decided that the law was not for him. In 1816, according to his wife's much later biography, he decided on a literary vocation, exclaiming, "Je veux être Chateaubriand ou rien!" (I want to be [François-René de] Chateaubriand or nothing!), referring to the great author who was then at the pinnacle of his success. In 1817 a poem submitted by Victor to the Académie Française received an honorable mention. Encouraged, the boys founded a journal together, the *Conservateur Littéraire*, which appeared regularly between December 1819 and

March 1821, most of whose work was done by Victor, who, under pseudonyms, wrote more than a hundred articles, twenty-two poems, and a short story, "Bug-Jargal," published in five short installments in May and June of 1820.

As Victor's literary talent had been developing, he had also fallen in love with his childhood friend Adèle Foucher; unfortunately, his brother Eugène had also become enamored of her. By April 1820 Victor and Adèle were very much in love, but when Adèle's parents learned of this, they forced the situation: either they must marry or break off. What resulted was a year's separation, letters, secret meetings, and much unhappiness. When Victor's mother died of pneumonia in June 1821, he proposed to Adèle and was now accepted by her parents. On 12 October 1822 the couple was married, but that night Eugène, who had been showing signs of unbalance, destroyed his furniture with a saber and was eventually interned in June 1823. The cost of his treatment in the asylum was shared by Victor and Abel until Eugène's death in March 1837. No doubt the madness that cut short Eugène's life, complicated by literary and amorous rivalries, had a deep effect on Victor, expressed in some beautiful poems. It is also quite likely that the rival "brothers" that people Hugo's novels—Bug-Jargal/d'Auverney, Han/Ordener, Quasimodo/Jehan—recall this early misfortune.

Hugo's first novel, *Han d'Islande* (1823; translated as *Hans of Iceland*, 1825), was written during his and Adèle's courtship and published shortly after their marriage. The first edition, anonymous, came out in February 1823 and was followed by a second in July of the same year. A third edition appeared in 1829. Following the example of Sir Walter Scott, Hugo set his novel in the past, in seventeenth-century Norway, and indulged the taste for convoluted plot, violent action, and horror that reigned in 1823. The outrageousness of the plot is far more amusing in the text than in outline.

Briefly put, *Han d'Islande* is the story of Ordener Guldenlew's unsuccessful effort to find documents that will reinstate his lover's father, Schumacker. Ordener, son of the vice-king, travels Norway to find the outlaw Han, thinking that the latter has the needed documents, not knowing that Han is present at every point along his itinerary. His efforts having failed, he claims responsibility for an uprising falsely fomented in Schumacker's name by Schumacker's enemy Ahlefeld, and he rescues lover and father, albeit at risk to his own life. At the last moment the lost documents surface, treachery is revealed, Ordener is spared, Schumacker is reinstated, and Ordener marries his beloved Ethel.

Even if one accepts the plot's implausibility—and there are surprises, recognitions, digressions, and reversals too numerous to mention—its characterizations are outlandish. Han, for example, destroys an entire regiment of soldiers because one of their number has precipitated his son's death; Han drinks blood from his son's skull and eats the flesh of Ahlefeld's son Frédéric. Obviously, the realistic portrayal of life in Norway was not Hugo's main concern.

More important are aspects of the work's construction: the plot is divided into two equal parts, the meeting of hero and monster taking place at the very center. Characters are presented as couples: Ordener and Han are good and bad foci of activity; Ethel is matched in her hopeful virtue by the despairing wickedness of Ahlefeld's wife; Ahlefeld, vindictive and cunning, is paired with Schumacker, who has lost his trust of his fellowmen. Clearly, such couples prepare the reader for a resolution where good and evil will finally be recognized for what they are, behind appearances that have misled characters and readers of the story. Therefore, *Han d'Islande* is a melodrama, and this might account for nineteenth-century appreciation and twentieth-century bemusement.

One theme that runs through the story is inherent both to melodrama and to Hugolian narrative: the number of reversals that take place. Ahlefeld comes to Han's cave to manipulate the outlaw, only to find his own son dead on the floor; Ahlefeld sends his lackey Musdoemon to his death only to find that that very lackey fathered the Frédéric he thought was his son. Musdoemon, in turn, anticipates his release from prison only to find that the executioner (his brother, by the way) has come for him. There are as many such moments as there are characters in the story; Hugo loves to create situations where a fundamental change can occur in a person's view of things, moments of conversion where what one thought was true turns out to be false, where falsehood becomes truth.

A striking image of this occurs well into *Han d'Islande* when Ordener, looking at the landscape of Lake Sparbu, sees the lake's surface as a window, not a mirror: "C'est comme si un abîme prodigieux, perçant le globe de part en part, laissait voir le ciel à travers la terre" (It's as

An 1833 caricature of Hugo by Pétrus Borel
(Musée Victor-Hugo)

though a huge abyss, piercing the globe from one side to the other, allowed one to see the sky through the earth). Such moments occur frequently in Hugo's works and are central to his understanding of himself (as in *Les Contemplations*) and of his characters (as in *Les Misérables*). Here Hugo is inviting his readers to see the events of *Han* differently, in a way that will enable them to take this fable more seriously.

Han is nothing if not gory; its central character's exploits are cruel, savage, and gratuitous. But if one does not insist on Han as the center of the story, his deeds are no longer mere hyperboles of evil. No matter how unpleasant they are, Han's actions hardly apply to Hugo's readers. Another gory current to the story pertains to institutionalized cruelty. The reader gets a close look at the executioner's trade; a high official (Ahlefeld) sacrifices multitudes of miners for the sake of a palace intrigue. Han, by contrast, kills only a regiment; indeed, Han does eat human flesh but so, it would seem, does the judicial system. The cruelty of both blind institutions and the too-lucid persons who hide within them is such that one must conclude that there are two monsters in Norway, and that of the two, Han—who, significantly, is small of stature—is the lesser one. This extraordinary adventure has a false bottom hiding something of far greater value, and it would be a mistake to dismiss it as an exercise in expressing adolescent fantasies.

Soon after the publication of *Han d'Islande*, in June 1823 Hugo published an article on Scott's *Quentin Durward* (1823), in which he made large advances in his conception of literary realism. Hugo admired Scott's historical accuracy and erudition (his own works were rather skimpily researched), but even more he admired Scott's "drama," which he defined as scenic composition, neither continuous narration nor epistolary fragmentation. This principle of composition, forcing the reader to imagine plot relations behind the scenes, is more lifelike and less tedious. Such a novel, he admits, would be more faithful to the laws of poetry than to those of history, but it would give French literature its own epic: "C'est le roman, à la fois drame et épopée, pittoresque mais poétique, réel mais idéal, vrai mais grand, qui enchâssera Walter Scott dans Homère" (It is the novel, simultaneously drama and epic, picturesque but poetic, real but ideal, true but great, that will encompass Walter Scott in Homer). Here, in a nutshell, Hugo states his definition of the novel: antithetical in construction, dramatic in conception, tending toward epic, and the whole subservient not to historical but to poetic truth.

Hugo's article on *Quentin Durward* appeared in the *Muse Française*, a royalist, Catholic journal that aspired to elaborate the poetic principles exemplified by Chateaubriand. Hugo's friend Emile Deschamps edited the journal; its contributors comprised a group that met on Sundays in the home of the librarian Charles Nodier, and it was here that many of Hugo's early poems were first read. Two collections of *Odes* date from this period; 1824 was also the year of his daughter Léopoldine's birth.

Despite the conservative character of the *Muse Française*, Hugo's political opinions had begun to change. Since his mother's death he had come to know his father better, and slowly he came to appreciate Count Hugo's achievements and, simultaneously, to feel misgivings about being a royally subsidized poet. Nonetheless, when in 1825 King Charles X was crowned, Hugo went to Rheims with Nodier to attend the

coronation and to compose an ode on the subject. In this climate of mixed feelings on the subject of monarchy, Hugo revised his short story "Bug-Jargal" and, augmenting it fivefold, made of it his second novel. It was published in February 1826.

Bug-Jargal (translated as *The Slave-King*, 1833) is a story of brotherhood and friendship between the enslaved son of an African king and the nephew of a colonial tyrant. Both love the same woman; both are generous and noble in thought and deed; both honor their word at the risk of their lives. Here, too, plot is convoluted and characterization is flat. D'Auverney learns that a powerful slave, Pierrot, is in love with his fiancée but is so impressed by Pierrot's nobility that he intercedes on the latter's behalf when the slave is condemned to death. In gratitude, Pierrot saves d'Auverney and Marie during the slave uprising that engulfs Haiti in August 1791. Taken prisoner by the insurgent slaves, d'Auverney is able to measure Pierrot's power, intelligence, and courage by comparison with the cynical manipulations of the slaves' other leaders, Biassou and the Obi. As the story unfolds, d'Auverney realizes that Pierrot is actually Bug-Jargal, son of an African king, and more worthy of admiration than any of his colonial masters.

As in *Han*, there are horrors, surprises, and reversals. The executions of captured colonists are particularly gruesome—daggers and saws are used; the docile Pierrot turns out to be the commanding Bug-Jargal; d'Auverney, who thought he was betrayed by Bug-Jargal, actually unconsciously betrays his friend. The novel appears to be an adventure story set in an exotic location, telling of male virtues: strength, courage, self-sacrifice.

However, there is another layer to it, one that has to do with its historical setting. By an irony of history, the slave revolt in Haiti took place during the French Revolution and was put down by men professing the values of that time: liberty, equality, fraternity. Certainly, *Bug-Jargal* asks difficult questions about the Revolution. At the surface the cruelty with which various Frenchmen propose to put down the insurrection is astounding. One, who has already killed some of his slaves in order to terrify the others, proposes to surround the city with the heads of executed slaves. To be sure, fraternity does not go far here, and this attitude toward blacks is a far cry from the brotherhood of d'Auverney and Bug-Jargal. It is no accident that the "citizen-general" who proposes this terrorism is a "citizen" (a supporter of the French Revolution), nor is it an accident that the action involves beheading: an allusion to the Reign of Terror is sure. The question thus arises: how can the proponents of social change (citizens) justify the killing that produces that change? To put down the insurrection they must deny the legitimacy of the very means that empower them.

Hugo's critique of the Revolution goes beyond the events of 1789-1793 to encompass the philosophy of the Enlightenment. Indeed, the French Revolution was made in the name of principles that had been elaborated and defended over the course of the preceding century: liberty, equality, fraternity. When, however, the colonists try to expound these principles to the insurgent slaves, they are met with blank incomprehension. Pleading for his life now, the "citizen-general" explains that his services as an "economist" would make him invaluable to his black captors, but where the white man would devise policies to allocate scarce resources, the black man sees no shortage: "Quand j'ai besoin de charbon, je brûle trois lieues de forêt" (When I need charcoal, I burn three leagues of forest). Nature is finite for one, inexhaustible for the other; more poignantly, the white man, who has no respect for human life, treats nature with respect, while the black's disregard for nature is coupled with an exact understanding of human suffering.

What becomes apparent is the extent to which Hugo's new vision is ironic. Not simply does he see each event from two sides as in *Han*, he shows how each position implies its contrary. Furthermore, this irony, seemingly applied to race relations in a far-off land, has more to do with France than it would seem. An epilogue to the novel tells how d'Auverney is condemned by the Convention for having told an antirevolutionary story, but the warrant for his arrest comes too late: he has just died fighting for the government that condemned him. Hugo's feelings about the Revolution are decidedly ambivalent, for *Bug-Jargal* is a story of praise for revolutionary principles of equality that expresses misgivings about revolutionary violence.

An image—present in both versions of the story—expresses this ambivalence perfectly. As he is led to his planned execution, d'Auverney sees a tree growing in a waterfall: "L'humidité qui imprégnait ses racines l'empêchait seule de mourir, tandis que la violence de la cataracte lui arrachait successivement ses branches nouvelles,

et le forçait de conserver éternellement les mêmes rameaux" (The water impregnating its roots alone prevented it from dying, while the waterfall's violence continuously tore off its new branches, forcing it forever to keep the same branches). The water nourishes the tree and prevents it from dying, but its violence also prevents it from growing and reaching any kind of maturity.

At the end of 1826, Hugo published a new collection of poetry, *Odes et ballades*, which further removed him from the royalism of his earlier *Odes*. The collection took up Romantic preoccupations: historical inspiration and technical perfection. This collection attracted considerable attention, notably that of the young Charles-Augustin Sainte-Beuve, critic for the *Globe*, whose admiration led him to an acquaintance with Victor and Adèle. Encouraged in his romanticism, Victor wrote a long (six-thousand-line) drama, *Cromwell*.

This work, three times the length of most classical plays, was too long to be performed and instead was published on 15 December 1827. The *Globe* devoted an entire issue to it and its long preface, in which the editors found both a statement of political principles and a theory of romanticism. In 1829 Hugo returned to poetry with *Les Orientales*, featuring poems of "oriental"—that is, exotic—inspiration. The preface likens poetry to a Spanish city, the variety of whose architectural influences, Western and Arabic, sacred and profane, corresponds to the eclecticism of poetry. This collection was particularly appreciated by Pierre Leroux, also of the *Globe*.

During the same years that Hugo was writing about faraway places (*Les Orientales*), distant times (*Odes et ballades*), and historical subject matter (*Cromwell*), he was becoming increasingly interested in something both very near and very timely: the death penalty. As a child in Spain, he had seen a man about to be garroted as well as the dismembered, crucified body of the guerrilla Mina; upon his return from Spain, his mother's lover had been executed; in France the waning years of the Bourbon monarchy saw increased efforts to revise the penal system. Nevertheless, the death penalty was still venerated, even if employed less than it had been a decade earlier, and Hugo spoke out against it in his short novel *Le Dernier Jour d'un condamné* (translated as *The Last Days of a Condemned*, 1840), published anonymously in February 1829. In its third and fourth editions, it was accompanied by a prefatory

An 1833 etching by Célestin Nanteuil showing Hugo surrounded by vignettes of his works (Musée Victor-Hugo)

"Comédie à propos d'une tragédie" (Comedy about a Tragedy), justifying its subject and its form.

To a certain extent, the title of the work tells it all: the novel describes the last days in the life of a man condemned to death. A first-person diary, it relates an anonymous writer's last week, his memories of his sentencing, and his stay in prison during appeal. On his last day he speaks with a distracted priest, his own daughter, and a convict who takes his coat. He makes a final appeal for mercy, but it is denied. The text's last words are "Quatre heures" (Four o'clock), the time of his scheduled execution.

What aroused attention to the work, aside from its macabre subject, was that Hugo refused to specify the man's crime, or to recount his biography. Instead, he focused entirely on what occurs after sentencing. The issue is not whether *this* man ought or ought not to be beheaded, either because of his crime or because of mitigating circumstances, but whether *any* man should be executed. As he states in his 1832 preface to the work, his point was to show that the penalty is inherently cruel, regardless of the crime it punishes, for the life lived after sentencing is a life of suffering. He accordingly refuses to get sidetracked on the different, but much more pathetic, issue of individual justice.

Consequently, the work is purely introspective. The man tells how the thought of death changes his perception of the world and others' perception of him. Some of these changes are subtle; others are not. His life, for example, is divided into two periods: before and after sentencing. His consciousness is also split. In a famous scene where he watches prisoners being chained, he is able to pity others, but he is unable to endure the attention he arouses when identified as the *condamné* (condemned man). The person he thinks about most is the king, obviously because this man can pardon him, but also because a mere thirty-eight years earlier, King Louis XVI had traveled the road he is to travel. At the prison hospital, doctors revive him from a fainting fit in order to ensure that his health is good enough for him to die. Just hours before the execution, he receives a visit from his daughter. Not recognizing him, she tells him her father is dead. Simply put, he has outlived himself; both dead and alive, each perception he has of this split is a source of pain.

In contrast with this message are what one could call the novel's missing appendages: chapter 47, entitled "Mon histoire" (My Story), is missing (and was never written, despite calls from Hugo's publisher Charles Gosselin for its inclusion), as are, of course, the story's conclusion and any indication of what crime the man might have committed to merit the death penalty. Antitheses are typical of Hugo's writing; elisions are not. Indeed, it would not be going too far to call antithesis the "life" or the "heart" of Hugo's thought: the figure is so prevalent that one could disqualify a text as Hugolian if it did not make use of antithesis or reversal. In the works of a writer whose use of complementary pairs is so extensive, the figure of elision—incompleteness—is thus all the more striking. It is as if something has died, and that is the point of its use in *Le Dernier Jour d'un condamné*.

Nodier qualified *Le Dernier Jour d'un condamné* as a "bad dream"; several critics found fault with the anonymous author's decision to leave out any narration of the man's life or crime. Jules Janin argued that an individual drama said nothing against the death penalty in general and pleaded with the author for more "pleasant" literature. The death penalty remained nevertheless a constant subject of Hugo's thought, running through *Les Misérables* and *Quatrevingt-treize* (1874; translated as *Ninety-three*, 1874).

The year 1829 was very busy for Hugo. In addition to publishing *Le Dernier Jour d'un condamné*, he wrote a play, *Marion de Lorme*, a historical drama about a duel in the time of Richelieu, only to learn that its performance was to be prohibited by the government because of its portrayal of a vacillating King Louis XIII; he also wrote the play *Hernani* (1830; translated, 1830) and oversaw much of its production. This interest in the theater had largely to do with the income it could provide. After Léopoldine's birth in 1824, the Hugos had had two sons: Charles, born in 1826, and François-Victor, born in 1828. In 1830 Mme Hugo was to have a second daughter, Adèle.

Hernani was a great success, but this success was achieved only after a "battle" during which Hugo's proponents, young members of the Romantic movement, systematically cheered the play and drowned out its opponents—literary conservatives—for the first weeks of its performance. In the success following those first performances, Hugo neglected to give the option of first refusal to Gosselin, publisher of *Le Dernier Jour d'un condamné*, and in order to rectify this breach of contract, promised Gosselin a new novel for January 1831, thus agreeing to write a major work in less than a year. The July Revolution (1830), during which the Bourbon monarchy was replaced by the house of Orléans, interrupted this work, and Gosselin granted Hugo a short respite. The manuscript was published on 16 March; it was entitled *Notre-Dame de Paris*.

The novel, set in Paris in 1842, recounts three men's love and one woman's hatred for a young Gypsy dancer, Esmeralda, who in turn loves a fourth man: the handsome soldier Phoebus. The men incarnate different classes of medieval society: Quasimodo, the cathedral's hunchbacked bell ringer, represents the lower classes; Claude Frollo, the cathedral's deacon and Quasimodo's guardian, represents the clergy; Pierre Gringoire, an unappreciated author, is marginalized, as unable to participate in society

as he is to consummate his marriage of convenience to Esmeralda. Complementing the three men is an old woman, Paquette Chantefleurie, whose baby was stolen years ago by Gypsies, and who has vowed an undying hatred for that group. Phoebus wins Esmeralda's heart and, at the moment of fulfilling his passion for her, is struck by Frollo, but Esmeralda is the one who is charged with murder (even though Phoebus survives) and sorcery. Tried and convicted, Esmeralda is rescued by Quasimodo, only to fall into the hands of Paquette, who recognizes her as her long-lost daughter Agnès, but too late. Esmeralda is arrested again and hanged; Quasimodo, understanding Frollo's role in this judicial murder, throws his master from the cathedral's tower, only to wander off to Esmeralda's pauper's grave, and to die with her body in his arms.

The plot is undoubtedly both sentimental and melodramatic. The diabolical priest, the handsome, free-living soldier, and the devoted but deformed hunchback all spring from the repertory of popular fiction, and it is easy, reading for the plot alone, to dismiss the novel. Indeed, English critic John Ruskin was so outraged by Hugo's portrait of his cherished medieval city that he labeled the book "disgusting." Nonetheless, it was an immediate success, going into several editions in two years; the "eighth" edition (published by Renduel) includes three chapters Hugo had withheld from Gosselin in hopes of raising the book's price.

Critics agree that it is not the plot, but the evocation of the Middle Ages that constitutes the center of the novel's interest, and the statement that the cathedral is its main character is of great validity. Two chapters in particular are singled out for praise: "Notre-Dame de Paris" and "Paris à vol d'oiseau" (A Bird's-eye View of Paris). In the first Hugo claims to evoke the cathedral, not as it is in 1832, but as it was in 1482, before the ravages of time and man. Then, it was incomparably more beautiful than now, and if it has suffered through the centuries, it is not due to any weathering, but to revolutions, restorations, and changes of fashion. Notre-Dame appears as a worn masterpiece from another era, a work bridging two periods (Romanesque and Gothic), and bringing that sense of transition to the present day. The other chapter describes Paris as it was 350 years prior to the book's publication and evokes the many quarters, churches, and monuments of the medieval city, its narrow confines and its outlying

*Caricature of Hugo by Benjamin Roubaud, 1841. The great man of letters has his right foot on the
Théâtre Français, while his left is on the Académie Française (Musée Victor-Hugo).*

towns. Hugo opposes this vision to the more recent developments of Parisian geography and deplores the Renaissance and its effects. Just as
time has damaged the cathedral, each century
has taken with it much of Paris's medieval
beauty.

What becomes more apparent as one reads
Notre-Dame de Paris is that its deep subject is decline: that of the cathedral and Paris, to be sure,
but also that of the monarchy (in an often-noted
scene, the king asks when his time will come), of architecture (Claude Frollo foretells the demise,
with the advent of the printed book, of the cathedral as a source of knowledge), and of individual resolve (Frollo slowly gives in to his diabolical
impulses). Hugo refers to this process as
'ΑΝΆΓΚΗ, or fate: this is the word Frollo scratches
on the wall when Esmeralda haunts his thoughts;
this is the principle the priest invokes when, fascinated, he watches a fly perish in a spider's web.
The fly's predicament symbolizes his own passion
for Esmeralda as well as Esmeralda's own inabil-

ity to extricate herself from the judicial system,
the cathedral's demise in the web of printed
words, and the monarchy's futile struggle in the
web of history. It is important here not to con-
fuse fate with progress: to be sure, the decline of
the monarchy or of superstition can be understood as the coming of a better order. The force
that Hugo describes as 'ΑΝΆΓΚΗ, however, is
blind, careless of whether it produces good or
evil. Fate brings the printed book but also the guillotine; Frollo's death but also Esmeralda's; the
end of monarchy but also revolution.

Even in this work "d'imagination, de caprice
et de fantaisie" (of imagination, caprice, and fantasy), there is a strong current of social commentary, and the themes of judicial cruelty, of institutional blindness, and of social upheaval are never
far from the surface. At the very moment that
Louis XI's Flemish visitor reassures him (ironically, in the fortress of the Bastille) that monarchy will last for some time to come, the criminal rabble of Paris is assaulting Notre-Dame—

nominally the king's responsibility to defend—and this violence must be put down with even more violence. When Esmeralda is tried for sorcery, she at first denies knowledge of the black art but, upon being tortured, confesses to having killed a man still alive and is condemned to death on the basis of this confession, citations from books of necromancy, and the testimony of her pet goat. The comedy of this trial only makes its tragic outcome more poignant. However one looks at the novel—from the point of view of its description, or its characterization, or its social commentary—Hugo tells a story of relentless fatalism, of a vanishing world's resignation to its own disappearance.

When *Notre-Dame de Paris* was published, Hugo's friend Vigny expressed his pleasure at the novel. The poet Alphonse de Lamartine called its author "le Shakespeare du roman" (the Shakespeare of the novel) but faulted it for its insufficient expression of religious belief. Charles de Montalembert criticized it for the quality that Hugo deliberately sought in his plays: "ce mélange continuel du grotesque au tragique" (this continual mixture of the grotesque and the tragic).

Three years after *Notre-Dame de Paris*, Hugo was to write one last story before falling silent as a novelist for almost three decades. This short story, *Claude Gueux*, published in July 1834, was based on what actually happened to the convict Claude Gueux from 1830 to 1832. Gueux was harassed by his jailer, whom, after careful deliberation, he killed. After attempting suicide he was tried and guillotined. Here again Hugo brings up the question of the death penalty in its most acute form. The story is revolting—both Gueux's action and the law's reaction—for by portraying Gueux's decision to murder his jailer as a trial and execution, Hugo forces an awful judgment. If one condemns Gueux, it must be because he has taken another man's life, and thus the death penalty is unjust; if, on the other hand, one accepts the death penalty, it must follow that one accepts Gueux's action, for his victim was tried and duly executed. However one looks at it, the story leaves its reader ill at ease with the death penalty.

From 1834 until 1862, Hugo was to concentrate on the theater, poetry, and politics. This period, extraordinarily productive, was also extraordinarily eventful, but was nevertheless interrupted by almost a decade during which Hugo, surprisingly, did not publish much of anything.

In an essay on Hugo's novels, it is possible to mention his poetry, theater, and political statements only in passing. These were the genres in which Hugo worked during this period, and it would be a mistake to think that their cursory treatment here implies a smaller importance. The poems of *Les Feuilles d'automne* (Autumn Leaves, 1831) poignantly express his distress at learning of Adèle's love for Sainte-Beuve; those of *Les Chants du crépuscule* (1835; translated as *Songs of Twilight*, 1836) and *Les Rayons et les ombres* (Sunlight and Shadows, 1840) tell of his love for Juliette Drouet, while his admiration for Napoleon comes forth strongly in *Les Voix intérieures* (Inner Voices, 1837). Each of these collections would have made a lesser poet proud, but they are overshadowed nonetheless by the later *Contemplations*.

During the decade of the 1830s, Hugo was also very successful in the theater, where he tended to concentrate on historical drama. The 1833 titles *Lucrèce Borgia* and *Marie Tudor* speak for themselves; *Marion de Lorme* finally was performed in 1831; *Le Roi s'amuse* (translated as *The King's Fool*, 1841), which represented King François I in a very unfavorable light, was prohibited after its first performance in 1832. *Angelo, Tyran de Padoue* (1835; translated as *Angelo*, 1851) involves jealousy and power in Renaissance Padua. *Ruy Blas* (1838; translated, 1860) is perhaps Hugo's best-known play. It recounts the incongruous love of a lackey for the queen of Spain, his rise to power, and his abrupt fall. While certain themes—fate, virginity, death, and class conflict—recur in the plays, Hugo's dramas differ from his novels (except *L'Homme qui rit* [1869; translated as *The Man Who Laughs*, 1869]) through their insistence on political power.

During the production of *Hernani*, Hugo's friend Sainte-Beuve became interested in Mme Hugo and in time became her lover, a love that was to leave Hugo open to other interests. During rehearsals of *Lucrèce Borgia*, Hugo met the actress Juliette Drouet, who played the minor role of the Princesse Negroni, and the two fell in love.

Their relationship was to last fifty years, consecrated by a "wedding" (actually an oath of continued support) in 1839, marked each year on 16 February (the anniversary of their first night together) by a written expression of love in a book reserved for that purpose, and punctuated, during their first decade, by yearly summer vacations together. Juliette was to become, for all intents and purposes, Hugo's second wife, serving

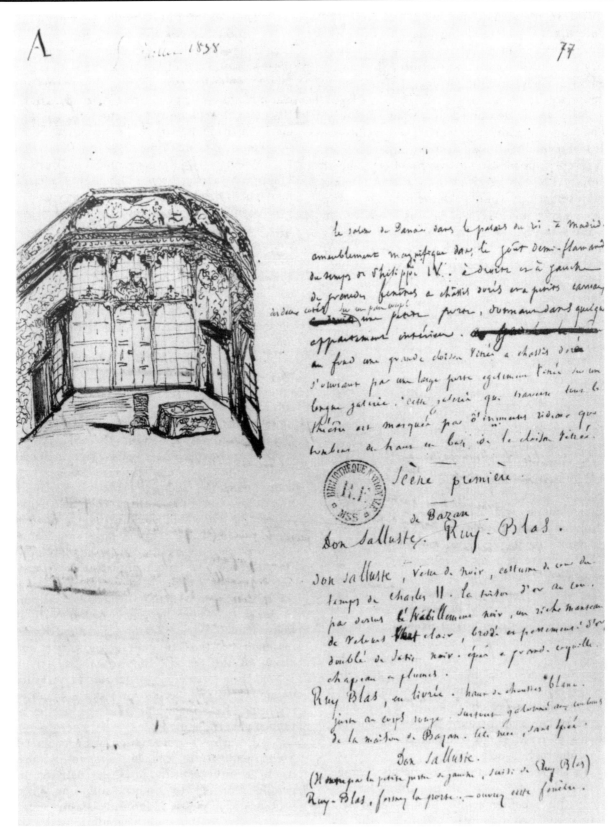

Page from the manuscript for Ruy Blas, *with Hugo's sketch of a set design for the first act (Bibliothèque Nationale)*

as his secretary, abandoning her career and public life for his, and following him into exile, yet she was received in his house only in 1867, after thirty years of devotion and sacrifice. She can be seen as a model for the virtuous fallen women Hugo places in his novels.

The 1840s accounted for what might be called Hugo's worldly success. His play receipts enabled him finally to live free from financial worries (even if, in his later years, he often claimed penury); he was received into the Académie Française, a crowning achievement for any French writer, in 1841; and he was made a peer of France in 1845. However, this worldly success came close to jeopardizing his success as an artist, and the same decade also brought a series of personal defeats and tragedies that shook him profoundly, preparing the way for the rejuvenation of his writing that was to occur during the Second Empire, the period of his exile from France (1851-1870).

His 1843 play, *Les Burgraves*, portraying archetypal characters of German mythology, was a commercial flop. By the tenth performance its receipts were only one-third of those of a competing play by Racine, at a time when theatergoers were not particularly fond of the seventeenth-century playwright. With that failure Hugo ceased writing for the stage (even if he later wrote plays to be read). His use of the melodramatic mode, with its excesses and contrasts, had always aroused criticism, but by 1843 it was simply not palatable to the theatergoing public.

That same year his daughter died in singularly pathetic circumstances. Married in February at the age of nineteen, she and her husband drowned in September while her father was vacationing with Juliette in Spain. Stepping from the stagecoach on the way home in the French town of Soubise, Hugo read in a newspaper that Léopoldine Vacquerie, née Hugo, had died five days previously in a boating accident. Absent when his daughter died, unaware of her death until days later, all because he was vacationing with his mistress, Hugo could hardly have been more vulnerable to self-reproach.

In 1845, shortly after receiving his peerage, he was discovered in compromising circumstances with a painter's wife, Léonie Biard, who was to spend two months in prison for adultery, while Hugo, as a peer, could not be prosecuted. In June 1846 Juliette's daughter Claire, age twenty, died of tuberculosis.

These events caused Hugo to suspend his literary production for five years, and it was only the anger he felt over Louis-Napoleon Bonaparte's coup d'état of December 1851 that caused him to publish again. During this period, however, Hugo was not entirely inactive. After the flagrante delicto he went into seclusion in Juliette's apartment, where he began work on a novel entitled at that time "Misères" (Miseries).

When in 1848 the government of King Louis-Philippe was overthrown, Hugo was elected a member of the Assemblée constituante (Constituent Assembly), charged with framing a constitution for the new republic. The Second Republic came to be, and Hugo was elected a deputy of the legislative assembly in May 1849. Louis-Napoleon Bonaparte was elected president in December 1849, but when Hugo realized the president's hidden ambitions, he became less than pleased with Bonaparte's political role. In 1850 and 1851 the writer moved to a position of outright opposition to Bonaparte. When on 2 December 1851 the president abrogated the constitution, Hugo knew he was in danger, and after several unsuccessful attempts to organize resistance to the coup d'état, he fled to Brussels on 11 December. Juliette joined him three days later.

There he immediately started work on his account of the coup d'état, *Histoire d'un crime* (1877; translated as *The History of a Crime*, 1877), and followed it soon after with a pamphlet entitled *Napoléon-le-petit* (1852). This publication made things difficult for the Belgian government, which sought good relations with its more powerful neighbor, so Hugo, anticipating expulsion, left Brussels in August 1852 for the island of Jersey in the English Channel, where he was joined by his wife. There he established himself at a house named Marine-Terrace, and fueled still by his anger over the coup (and the subsequent declaration of the Second Empire on 2 December 1852), Hugo wrote *Les Châtiments* (The Punishments, 1853), a collection of satirical poems denouncing the crimes and misdeeds of the new French government.

At Marine-Terrace, Hugo was a magnet for French expatriates, political exiles, and admirers. As the months went by, however, many of these people returned to France, following various promises of amnesty. Hugo thus became isolated in his exile. At this time he undertook the revision of a group of poems, adding many of new inspiration. *Les Contemplations*, the spiritual autobiography of a poet, was centered around the death

Caricature of Hugo by Honoré Daumier

of Léopoldine, with lighthearted, lyrical works in a section called *Autrefois* (before) and more pessimistic, philosophical works in the other part, *Aujourd'hui* (today). Between these sections lies a date: 4 September 1843, Léopoldine's death day. This collection, containing some of the most beautiful works Hugo wrote, is often considered his poetic masterpiece. It first appeared in April 1856. Perhaps because it was a work of pure poetry coming on the heels of the invective of *Napoléon-le-petit*, or perhaps simply because it was his first lyrical work since *Les Rayons et les ombres*, it was widely appreciated and sold well.

Nevertheless, Hugo had not ceased to be involved in politics. His entire nineteen-year exile was a political statement, and many times he refused to return to France until Napoleon III left power. He also insisted on his political beliefs locally. In 1853 he protested the bungled execution of a death sentence on the neighboring island of Guernsey; in 1855 he criticized a state visit by Napoleon III to England. Shortly thereafter he was asked to leave Jersey, and he and his

family left for Guernsey on 31 October 1855. There he purchased a dwelling called Hauteville-House, which he decorated ornately and returned to many times after his exile ended in 1870.

On the back cover of *Les Contemplations*, Hugo announced two great poems: *Dieu* (God) and *La Fin de Satan* (The End of Satan). These grand titles, however, discouraged Hugo's Belgian publisher Pierre-Jules Hetzel, who suggested that he instead concentrate on other projects, notably a series of "petites épopées" (small epics) that would tell the story of man. This collection came to be known as *La Légende des siècles* (1859; translated as *The Legend of the Centuries*, 1874), and each of its parts corresponds to a major division of history. This book features the touching and simple "Booz endormi" (Booz asleep), and the other poems are similarly visual, portraits of a moment in time. The work was to be complemented by two other series of poems with the same title (1877 and 1883).

At this point Hugo decided once again to look at the manuscripts of "Misères," composed between 1845 and 1848. The subjects of social injustice, punishment, and redemption had been close to the surface of *Le Dernier Jour d'un condamné* and *Claude Gueux*; they were also present in many of his poems and *Notre-Dame de Paris* and were visible, if not in the plots, at least in the allusions of many of his plays. This novel, finally called *Les Misérables*, would be the subject of Hugo's efforts until July 1861; he sold the exclusive rights to it for twelve years to the Belgian publisher Alfred Lacroix for three hundred thousand francs. In order to ensure that it was read in its entirety, Hugo refused to serialize it. The book, published in the spring of 1862, was an amazing financial success. Some reviewers criticized *Les Misérables* for its length, its digressions, its philosophy, and especially for its social message, difficult for the partisans of the government to accept from that government's most illustrious exiled citizen.

Les Misérables is of course a vast work, fifteen hundred pages in most editions. Its events span a sixteen-year period between 1815 and 1832, relating the story of an ex-convict's attempt to rejoin society; the story of a fallen woman's child's fate; the story of a young man's conversion to his estranged father's Napoleonic convictions; and, above all, the story of these good characters' nemeses: Javert, an overly zealous policeman; Thénardier, a veteran corrupted by his poverty; and Gillenormand, an aging aristocrat, unable to recognize his grandson's idealism for what it is.

Though long, the plot is ultimately simple: Jean Valjean, an ex-convict, is so astounded by the charity of Bishop Myriel that he is converted to goodness, but not, however, before committing one last crime, the theft of a coin from a small boy. Under an assumed name, he becomes a prominent citizen of another town, where his good works are so conspicuous that he becomes its mayor. There he intervenes on behalf of an unwed mother, Fantine, who has been obliged to leave her daughter, Cosette, in the care of the Thénardiers. It is too late, however, to save Fantine from her illness. But Valjean, obliged to reveal his identity to save another man's life, ransoms Cosette from the mercenary Thénardiers and goes into hiding in Paris. There they live peacefully for several years but are finally detected by the policeman Javert, who is determined to arrest Valjean for his last theft.

Cosette, now a woman, falls in love with Marius, a young man devoted to his father's memory and desirous therefore of helping Thénardier, who many years earlier, and entirely by accident, had saved his father's life while looting the bodies on the battlefield of Waterloo. During the insurrection of 1832, Valjean saves both Marius and Javert; the latter, incapable of reciprocating or understanding Valjean's generosity, commits suicide. Marius marries Cosette. Thénardier's last effort to extract money from Valjean fails when, attempting to blackmail Marius, he learns that Marius is fully aware of his father-in-law's past.

There is much more to the novel than this sketch can tell; many characters have gone unmentioned, and many turns of plot and descriptions have not been acknowledged. Of Hugo's novels *Les Misérables*, set for the most part in the recent past and in Paris, would have to be considered the most realistic. The detail with which the writer describes the Thénardiers' run-down inn in Montfermeil, the neighborhood of the *masure Gorbeau* (Gorbeau hovel) where Valjean lives, the barricades of 1832, and the chain gang that Valjean and Cosette see while walking in Paris all present a vision that is either recognizable or highly plausible. The work, started in 1845, was of a world that the author admittedly only knew through memory, but one that his readers could also remember. However, such realism is not straightforward: even the most detailed and pre-

cise of Hugolian descriptions tends toward a symbolic or mythic generality.

When the fallen Fantine leaves Paris with the infant Cosette in order to find work elsewhere, she comes across an inn where children play under a sort of wagon. The vehicle is described thus:

> Les ornières avaient donné aux roues, aux jantes, aux moyeux, à l'essieu et au timon, une couche de vase, hideux badigeonnage jaunâtre assez semblable à celui dont on orne volontiers les cathédrales. Le bois disparaissait sous la boue et le fer sous la rouille. Sous l'essieu pendait en draperie une grosse chaîne digne de Goliath forçat.

> (The ruts in the road had given the wheels, the rims, the hubs, the axle, and the shafts a coating of mud, a hideous yellow wash rather similar to the one intentionally used to adorn cathedrals. The wood disappeared under mud, as the iron did under rust. Under the axle was draped a heavy chain worthy of Goliath taken prisoner.)

The mud, the rust, and the chain are all details that make the image vivid. At the same time the allusions to cathedrals and to Goliath suggest that this wagon is much more than a mere setting for the children's play. Heavy, brooding, and sinister, it seems to loom over the children like poverty itself, a presence so massive that it could hobble Goliath or corrupt the church. There is a tendency in all of Hugo's works to make even the smallest details speak, and when they do, they speak of moral concerns.

What is plain, even in this sinister depiction of life in the underclasses, is that this is a novel of redemption: Valjean, Fantine, and Marius all seek to be worthy of trust put in them, and each one finds it exceedingly difficult. This is not just a matter of doing good. As mayor of Montreuil sur Mer, Jean Valjean rebuilds the town's economy, provides jobs, and ensures public virtue, but he still cannot rest easy. When a vagrant is charged with Valjean's crime, the latter must acknowledge his true name and return to prison. When, after saving Javert's life, he is once again apprehended by the policeman, Valjean does not resist. And not simply does he accept Marius as Cosette's beloved, he saves the young man's life by carrying him for hours through the Paris sewers. In order to be redeemed, one must first be humbled; only then one becomes good. To rise, one must first descend, socially, psychologically, and morally.

This novel about redemption is also, necessarily, about the forces that work against happiness; after all, its title is *Les Misérables*. These forces are formidable, as in the case of Jean Valjean. He resurrects the town of Montreuil sur Mer; he allows Fantine to die happy; he rescues Champmathieu; he brings up Cosette as his daughter; he saves the life of a sailor; he even rescues his persecutor. Each new proof of goodness serves only to show how relentless man is in refusing to acknowledge his brother's ability to improve. For instance, how can Fantine raise herself up after giving herself to a worthless cad? She uses all her earnings to pay the Thénardiers' vicious requirements; she sells her hair, her front teeth, and finally her body. For her, society is particularly cruel, and she must die with her goodness recognized only by Jean Valjean. These almost superhuman efforts prove that the oppressive forces of society are as much the subject of the novel as its nominal heroes.

In some cases these forces are particularly relentless, so much so that they must be called fate. Some characters are incapable of regeneration; their only contribution is misery. Such is the case of Thénardier. Although he and his wife are paid by Fantine, they mistreat Cosette and raise their requirements to exorbitant levels. When Jean Valjean meets their extravagant demands and claims Cosette, he only rekindles their hatred. They hate him for taking a child they despised at a price they themselves set. Each brush with goodness only makes them more determined in their malevolence. If, for Hugo, radical change is the prerogative of freedom, this incapacity for change could serve as his definition of fate, in *Les Misérables* and elsewhere.

In its original edition, *Les Misérables* consisted of five parts, divided into ten volumes; its publication took place in three installments (3 April, 15 May, and 3 June 1862). Like Hugo's plays, the publication and reception were organized by the author's friends and family to produce the greatest effect, and these efforts succeeded, even in the country that Hugo had left eleven years earlier. Mme Hugo wrote of groups of workers splitting the cost of the ten volumes in order to read it in turn. On 15 May, the publication date of parts 2 and 3, a crowd of booksellers stood before the printing house at six in the morning and was so large that police were needed to maintain order.

Frontispiece by Hugo for his poetry collection featuring les petites épopées *(little epics)*

Critics, however, were not as pleased. Many found fault with the novel's digressions, especially the flashback to Waterloo. Jules Barbey d'Aurevilly denounced it for its "socialism"; Baudelaire praised it for its symbolic and poetic qualities, but in a later letter claimed that he had not meant a word of his review. Hippolyte Taine dismissed Hugo as insincere, and his success as an event soon to pass. Sainte-Beuve, coming to his ex-friend's defense, admired Hugo's popular success and his monumental stature.

Although Hugo had been in exile for ten years when *Les Misérables* was published, the novel undoubtedly reflects a strong attachment to France and to the past. It presents a detailed picture of the Paris of Hugo's youth; it deals with events that Hugo knew of firsthand. Perhaps owing to the circumstances of its composition in addition to its message, *Les Misérables* expresses a longing for France: pre-Second Empire France to be sure, but France nonetheless. In October 1862 Hugo was already thinking of another novel, *Quatrevingt-treize*, but decided to hold off in order to leave "space" for *Les Misérables*. Personal considerations also prevented taking up a new novel. His wife Adèle's publication of her husband's biography (in June 1863) required his attention, and in October his daughter Adèle, enamored of a British lieutenant, Alfred Pinson, ran off to Canada, where she hoped to marry him. Soon afterward, the Hugos learned that Pinson, already married, had no intention of marrying Adèle, and slowly it became apparent that Adèle was mentally unbalanced. She followed Pinson to Barbados and did not return to France until 1872.

In April 1864 Hugo published—to accompany his son François-Victor's translation of Shakespeare's works—a preface entitled *William Shakespeare*, in which he sought to define poetic genius. The preface, which became a book, attracted attention for its Olympian view of great poets, among whom Hugo cited Homer, Job, Aeschylus, and Isaiah. Many critics saw in the indication of only one Frenchman—François Rabelais—an invitation for Hugo's name to be added to the list.

With the completion of this work Hugo was free to start another novel, and this one was not nostalgic, but an expression of his preoccupations on Guernsey. Originally entitled "L'Abîme" (The Abyss), the novel came to be known as *Les Travailleurs de la mer*. In July 1865 he signed a contract with his Belgian publisher Lacroix for the publication of the novel and a collection of poetry, *Les Chansons des rues et des bois* (Songs of the Streets and the Woods). This collection of erotic poetry was actually published before the novel, in October 1865; sensual rather than meditative in character, it complements the philosophical thrust of the earlier *Contemplations*.

When Hugo presented the novel's manuscript for publication, Lacroix suggested leaving out a lengthy preface describing the Channel Islands. This part, "L'Archipel de la Manche" (The Channel Archipelago), was considered by Hugo to be a "portal" to the novel but was reincorporated with it only in the 1883 edition of his collected works. Not only did Hugo conceive of this work—preface and narrative—as a totality, he also grouped it with *Notre-Dame de Paris* and *Les Misérables* to compose a trilogy on the subject of fate: "Un triple ananké pèse sur nous, l'ananké des dogmes, l'ananké des lois, l'ananké des choses. Dans *Notre-Dame de Paris*, l'auteur a dénoncé le premier; dans *Les Misérables*, il a signalé le second; dans ce livre, il indique le

troisième" (A triple destiny weighs down on us, the destiny of dogmas, the destiny of laws, and the destiny of things. In *Notre-Dame de Paris* the author denounced the first; in *Les Misérables* he noted the second; in this book he indicates the third). Each novel tells of a struggle against an overwhelming force: in *Notre-Dame de Paris* that force is superstition, incarnated in the judicial system; in *Les Misérables* it is law, personified by Javert; in *Les Travailleurs de la mer* it is mute nature, instantiated in the sea.

The story's imagery and mythological resonances form its center. A young man, Gilliatt, in love with the daughter (Déruchette) of a steamship owner (Mess Lethierry), goes off alone to the reef where the latter's ship—*La Durande*—has been stranded through the machinations of its evil mate, Clubin. There, for ten weeks, Gilliatt battles the elements to save the ship's steam engine, even risking death just before returning to land: an octopus tries to kill him as it has killed Clubin. He returns to land triumphant, handing over the engine to Mess Lethierry along with the owner's lost fortune, only to learn that in his long absence Déruchette has fallen in love with a young preacher. He aids the two to elope and then, staring at the sea, allows the tide to drown him.

In its simplicity, its opposition of a hero to primeval forces, its strangeness of setting, and its hero's virtue and self-sacrifice, this is certainly the most mythical of Hugo's novels. Perhaps for this reason Hugo grouped it with *Les Misérables* and *Notre-Dame de Paris*. In many of Hugo's earlier works, he describes the city as an ocean; here, the sea is like Paris: a reef resembles Notre-Dame, and the waves resemble the city's crowds. Many other parallels have been drawn, but the point is that this novel prolongs, in a more schematic outline, a play of great forces present in more realistic guise elsewhere.

The plot is recognizable: through feats of strength, perseverance, and intelligence, a young man reaches maturity. Gilliatt is a pure hero, but inasmuch as his efforts are supposed to win Déruchette's hand, the story is sexual. All of Gilliatt's work is a labor of love; whatever he does is a sublimation of desire. His retrieval of the *Durande* is tantamount to a conquest of Déruchette; Hugo notes that the names for boat and daughter are derived from one root. At the same time, however, Gilliatt's feats betray a great fear of sex: he prefers the boat to the girl and readily abandons Déruchette to his rival. This

*Hugo's house on the place Royale, Paris, now the
Musée Victor-Hugo*

fear comes out quite plainly in his combat with the octopus, in the description of which Hugo insists on the feminine pronoun *elle* (she/it): "Elle n'a pas d'os, elle n'a pas de sang, elle n'a pas de chair. Elle est flasque. Il n'y a rien dedans. C'est une peau. On peut retourner ses huit tentacules du dedans au dehors comme des doigts de gants. Elle a un seul orifice, au centre de son rayonnement" (It has no bones, it has no blood, it has no flesh. It's limp. There's nothing in it. It's a skin. You can turn its eight tentacles inside-out like the fingers of a glove. It has only one orifice, at the center of its rays). Gilliatt's feat is like that of a knight—Perceval—who must overcome obstacles, retrieve an object, and remain pure while doing so. The familiarity of this quest goes far in making a poetic epic—whose strangeness is matched only by its language and setting—seem realistic.

If anything, Hugo's exile had consolidated his reputation in a way he had not enjoyed prior to 1851. The sales of *Les Contemplations* and *Les Misérables* had been gratifying. Hugo, while keep-

ing the family purse strings pulled tight, was nonetheless commanding high prices for his works, and *Les Travailleurs de la mer* was no exception. Lacroix paid him 120,000 francs for it and *Les Chansons des rues et des bois*; in fact, Hugo was able to turn down two handsome offers for prepublication serial rights. When it was later published in serial form, its presence boosted the circulation of the newspaper the *Soleil* from 28,000 to 80,000. Like *Les Contemplations*, *Les Travailleurs de la mer* offered no objectionable social commentary, enabling many critics to admire it without reservation. The young Emile Zola praised it for its "vision." It even influenced consumer tastes: octopus appeared on restaurant menus, and as an ornament for ladies' fashion.

The following year, Paris was the site of an Exposition Universelle. Despite the fact that Hugo had not set foot in France for fifteen years, he wrote a preface for a guide to the city (*Paris Guide*) published for the occasion. Surprisingly, the empress Eugénie is said to have suggested that a play by Hugo be performed (for the first time since the coup d'état) in order to commemorate the Exposition. *Hernani* was accepted and performed on 20 June 1867 to enthusiastic crowds. As before Hugo's exile, Mme Hugo took particular interest in the production and attended its first performance. A reprise of *Ruy Blas*, by contrast, was prohibited but took place in Brussels in 1868.

In the summer of 1868, Mme Hugo, sixty-nine years old, suffered an apoplectic seizure and died two days later, on 27 August. Hugo accompanied the body of his wife to Quiévrain, on the French/Belgian frontier. She was buried in Villequier, next to her daughter Léopoldine.

During the years 1866, 1867, and 1868, Hugo had been working on a new novel, initially entitled "Par ordre du roi" (By Order of the King), later to be published as *L'Homme qui rit*. Like the three earlier novels, this was to form part of a trilogy, whose subject was not fate, but history; its elements were to be aristocracy, monarchy, and revolution, and *L'Homme qui rit* represented the first.

In order to depict the aristocracy, Hugo set his novel in early-eighteenth-century England, for it was there, he claimed, that the privileges and abuses of this class were most developed. The story is that of a young boy, Gwynplaine, abandoned on the coast of England in 1690. Disfigured by *comprachicos* (child buyers), he has been left to die. Instead, he stumbles upon a baby girl (Dea), rescues her, and in turn is rescued by an itinerant philosopher, Ursus. Years later the three have become a troupe of actors, putting on an allegorical mystery play in the working-class quarters of London. There, the Duchess Josiane sees their performance and becomes perversely enamored of Gwynplaine. An obscure and devious underling, Barkilphedro, learns that Gwynplaine is none other than the son of a banished lord, Clancharlie, since deceased, and is as such a peer of England. Apprised of this, Queen Anne orders her enemy Josiane to marry Gwynplaine. Gwynplaine flees Josiane in horror and on the night he is invested in the House of Lords rises to make an impassioned speech on behalf of the lower classes. His disfigurement, however, causes only laughter. Humiliated, Gwynplaine leaves Parliament for the docks, where he finds his beloved Dea dying. He steps into the water to die as her soul rises to heaven.

In many respects this is the most dramatic and the most Hugolian of novels. The action is set in the past, among the rulers of a foreign power, and involves a love born of power and contrast, the story of a grotesque hero and a woman whose beauty is matched only by her depravity. Themes found in *Hernani*, *Notre-Dame de Paris*, *Marie Tudor*, and *Ruy Blas* are all found here.

The subject of *L'Homme qui rit* is suffering: that of the people, under the oppression of the aristocracy; that of children, abused by an exploitative society; that of reformers whose solutions cannot be implemented; that of exiles. This is the import of Gwynplaine's speech before the assembled lords and the meaning of his disfigurement; beneath his permanent smile lies a mutilated soul. This suffering is figured in a horrendous image when Hardquanonne, the *comprachico* who carved the smile on Gwynplaine's face and disarticulated his joints, is in his turn tortured. The sheriff slowly places a great pile of stones on his chest until, almost crushed, he confesses his crime.

But if the novel is about suffering, it is also about the causes of that suffering, and these are by no means abstract. Gwynplaine's disfigurement was brought about by royal edict, at the "bon plaisir" (good pleasure) of King James II. Then too, when Queen Anne orders Josiane to marry Gwynplaine, it is at her "plaisir royal" (royal pleasure). What is striking here is that, well before Sigmund Freud, Hugo unites pleasure so tightly with pain, as if one person's plea-

sure depends on another's pain, or even more perversely (as in Josiane's case), the fact that one person (Anne) takes pleasure (in marrying Gwynplaine and Josiane) means that another (Josiane) can no longer take pleasure in doing what she wants to do.

What Hugo suggests then is that the relation of lords to people is erotic, that the lords use the people for their pleasure. So much is evident in the infatuation Josiane conceives for Gwynplaine, and in the assignation she gives him. Furthermore, even if this relation is erotic, it is by no means for the mutual benefit of the classes involved. It is pleasurable for the lords only when its inequality humiliates the people. This would be the meaning of Josiane's loss of interest in Gwynplaine when she learns that he is her equal: where there is equality, there is no desire and no pleasure.

As can well be imagined, *L'Homme qui rit* attracted criticism. Barbey d'Aurevilly wrote two hostile articles, the first criticizing the "asthmatic" style, the second asserting that *Victor* Hugo should be renamed *Victus* (vanquished). Even Hugo conceded that the novel was a failure, stating that he had "abused" the genre: "J'ai voulu en faire une épopée. J'ai voulu forcer le lecteur à penser à chaque ligne" (I tried to make an epic of it. I tried to force the reader to think about every line). Even contemporary critics are unsure about *L'Homme qui rit*: John Porter Houston has qualified it as "outlandish"; Richard B. Grant has asserted that it is "an extremely bad piece of writing." The novel appears to be a work of erudition—Hugo did considerable research before writing—but many of its purported "facts," such as the existence of the *comprachicos*, are pure invention. Yet its vices as well as its virtues are quintessentially Hugolian: the extraordinary plot, conceived with little regard for conventional verisimilitude; the sheer pleasure the author took in writing it; and the density of its imagery—these all could have been produced only by Hugo.

L'Homme qui rit was published in April and May of 1869. Many events were occurring in France during that year that would prevent Hugo's continuation of his projected trilogy: Napoleon III's empire was weakening; yet another amnesty was proposed to Hugo (and rejected); the French government haltingly evolved toward a parliamentary system. During this period the publishers of the *Evénement*, Hugo's pre-Empire newspaper, founded another opposition journal, the *Rappel*; Hugo approved but abstained from

Le Grand Chemin de la postérité *(1841), lithograph by Benjamin Roubaud, who depicted Hugo as the standard-bearer for a mélange of French writers (Musée Victor-Hugo)*

participating. When in July 1870 France declared war on Prussia, Hugo realized that the Empire's end was near and accordingly traveled to Brussels, where he was living when the French forces were defeated at Sedan and the Third Republic was proclaimed. On 5 September 1870 Hugo arrived in Paris to a tumultuous welcome.

The years 1870 and 1871 involved as much political activity on Hugo's part as those of the Second Republic. Initially, in September 1870 he called on the French to push back the Prussians and enlisted (at age sixty-eight) in the National Guard. After the armistice of January 1871, he was elected a deputy from Paris. In the Chamber of Deputies he argued against the terms of the proposed peace treaty and the expulsion of Giuseppe Garibaldi. Unsuccessful, he resigned. While Victor was in Bordeaux (where the government was meeting), his son Charles died. When Paris declared the Commune, the Third Republic repressed it savagely; at this point Hugo offered his house in Brussels as an asylum for escaped communards. He was promptly expelled from Belgium, and during the summer of 1871 he stayed in Luxembourg.

The following year, in February, his daughter Adèle returned from Barbados, where she had followed Lieutenant Pinson; she was interned at the asylum of Saint Mandé. His son François-Victor was to die of tuberculosis at the end of 1873. It was becoming apparent that, just as he had eclipsed his brothers, he was going to outlive his children; it was also becoming clear that he was overshadowing most of the other writers of his century.

There was little Hugo could do but continue. In March 1872 *Ruy Blas*, with Sarah Bernhardt in the role of Marie de Neubourg, was performed with great success in Paris; in April, Hugo published his poetic account of the events of 1870-1871, *L'Année terrible* (The Terrible Year). He returned to Hauteville-House in August with Juliette and François-Victor. He was to remain there until July 1873; during this year he wrote *Quatrevingt-treize*.

During the years of exile and before, as the case of Léonie Biard shows well, Hugo had liaisons with many women—visitors, admirers, and servants. During the year 1872-1873 Juliette Drouet herself engaged the young Blanche Lanvin as a laundress, and Hugo unexpectedly fell more deeply in love with her than with previous lovers; so much so that, in July 1873, Juliette demanded Blanche's dismissal, and so much so that, for his part, Hugo left Guernsey to rejoin Blanche in Paris a month later. Their correspondence was to end only with Blanche's (unhappy) marriage in 1879. Blanche typifies the fascination that vulnerable young women held for Hugo, which found frequent expression in his works: Esmeralda, Fantine, and Dea are all literary precursors of this experience.

For whatever reasons, the year spent in Guernsey was very productive. The manuscript of *Quatrevingt-treize* was finished by June 1873, and the novel was published in February of the following year. There can be no doubt that the fratricidal turmoil of the Commune contributed to Hugo's thought on that other episode of internecine combat, the Reign of Terror, designated in French by the number *93*, an abbreviation of

1793. This was the year of the radicalization of the French Revolution: from a short-lived constitutional monarchy, the government of France became a republic; the king was beheaded; nobles emigrated; and royalist regions of France, notably the Vendée in Brittany, revolted against the Parisian government. Region against region, Frenchman against Frenchman, government against government: the parallels with the events of 1870-1871 could hardly be clearer.

Despite its allegorical status, however, the novel is far better grounded in reality than any novel since *Les Misérables*; its plot eschews some of the more overt symbolism of *L'Homme qui rit* and *Les Travailleurs de la mer*. An uncle set against his nephew, a woman separated from her children, a priest serving the Revolution, a teacher spying on his student: in *Quatrevingt-treize*, Hugo uses metaphors of division to depict revolutionary struggle. An old aristocrat, the Marquis de Lantenac, lands, with British help, in Brittany, where he succeeds in arousing an insurrection. In Paris, Jean Marat, Maximilien Robespierre, and Georges Danton, members of the powerful Comité de salut public (Committee for Public Safety), delegate Cimourdain, an ex-priest, to put it down. Cimourdain, in turn, enlists Gauvain, Lantenac's own nephew, to do the job. After some initial success Gauvain traps his uncle in an old fortress, where the marquis and his remaining forces hold some children hostage. After a bloody battle, Lantenac escapes from the burning fortress but turns back to rescue the children, albeit at risk to his own life. He is captured; but Gauvain, wishing to show that the Revolution can match the mercy shown by the representative of the Old Regime, allows Lantenac to escape. Gauvain is executed, and Cimourdain commits suicide.

As in *Les Misérables*, conversion is a central feature of *Quatrevingt-treize*. Lantenac, the bloodthirsty commander of royalist forces, sacrifices his chance to escape and regroup in order to rescue children adopted by the revolutionary army. Gauvain, devoted to the Revolution even if he is of noble extraction, lets the marquis escape precisely because of the latter's noble, self-sacrificing gesture; the marquis in turn is dumbfounded by this nobility on the part of a revolutionary officer. These reversals and conversions have another side, however: they bring out the extraordinary rigidity of the characters' personalities, which remain inflexible until a conversion brings them to a radical change. There are no gradual

Sarah Bernhardt as Doña Sol in an 1877 revival of Hernani *(photograph by Nadar). Hugo was in his seventies when he began an affair with this great actress.*

evolutions here; revolution is all.

After a sailor on board the corvette *Claymore* succeeds in bringing a loose cannon under control, Lantenac honors him for his feat of courage but has him shot for allowing the cannon to roll free in the first place. Lantenac's adhesion to discipline is absolute, and his fanaticism incarnates an ideology. The same is true of Cimourdain, the priest-become-revolutionary: he loves his disciple Gauvain, but also loves the republic, and must therefore sacrifice his personal bond to his political belief when he learns of Gauvain's treason. Gauvain himself is inflexible. He believes in the Revolution because of its humanitarian ideals and must therefore free his uncle for the good deed he has done—proving the Revolution's capacity for mercy—rather than kill him for the atrocities he has committed in the past, and might very well commit in the future.

Hugo (center) with his family in Guernsey

A lengthy description of Paris in 1793, indicating fashions, prices, and customs, serves likewise to give form to the revolutionary ideology, for colors indicate political conformity, prices signify acceptance of a new economic order, and new heroes indicate new ideals. The plot, characters, and descriptions—though less than realistic in any modern sense—tend to present a vast, undefinable force that sweeps through the pages, and that must be called "revolution." It is never seen, but its effects and side-effects are. Similarly, on board the *Claymore*, it is not the ocean, but rather the loose cannon rolling about inside the ship, demolishing the vessel and maiming its crew, that commands attention. This blind force is the subject of *Quatrevingt-treize*.

The reception of *Quatrevingt-treize* was, as usual, mixed. On one hand it was denounced and misunderstood: Amédée Achard called it an "apologie de la Commune" (an apology for the Commune); Barbey d'Aurevilly asserted that it revealed Hugo's royalist sentiments. On the other hand it was a popular success: its sales and those of *L'Année terrible* reinforced each other; in April 1874 *Quatrevingt-treize* was serialized in the *Rappel*, whose circulation jumped from 50,000 to 89,500.

In 1872 Hugo also published the first volume of his *Actes et paroles*, his various contributions to the political life of his country—speeches, articles, and letters. The series was continued in 1875, with the publication of his many pronouncements from the years of exile, and the following year, his contributions from 1870 onward. These publications contributed to his own political activities, which were ongoing. In January 1876 he was elected to the Senate, where he argued for amnesty for the participants in the Commune; in 1878 he opposed President Marie Edmé Patrice de MacMahon and was instrumental in obtaining his resignation. His creative life continued too: in 1877 he published the new series of *La Légende des siècles* and *L'Art d'être grand-père* (The Art of Being a Grandfather), a collection of poems.

On the night of 27 June 1878, Hugo suffered a stroke, the effects of which at first appeared to be slight. He complained a day later of feeling "stunned" and expressed the desire to get back to work, but could not quite get over its effects. A trip to Guernsey that was to last four months still did not produce the hoped-for convalescence. Juliette, now seventy-two, began to take control of Hugo's private life, and especially (doing for him what he had done for her during the first years of their love) watched over all his meetings and correspondence. While Hugo was able to host banquets, to attend meetings of the Académie Française, and, occasionally, to write verse, his creative life was by most definitions over.

There nonetheless remained a vast amount that Hugo had never published, and this was slowly made available. Among these works was *L'Archipel de la Manche*, which Hugo had proposed to Lacroix in 1865, only to have his publisher discourage publication. When in 1883 a large edition of his collected works was published, this prologue was finally added to the novel that it had been intended to introduce. In 1881 a collection of old poems, *Les Quatre Vents de l'esprit* (The Four Winds of the Spirit), was published, while in 1883 the last series of *La Légende des siècles* appeared. A severe article by Zola captures the resentment of Hugo's continued presence on the literary scene that was gathering at the time: "Victor Hugo est devenu une religion en littérature, je veux dire une sorte de police pour le maintien du bon ordre.... Etre passé à l'état de religion nécessaire, quelle terrible fin pour le poète révolutionnaire de 1830" (Victor Hugo has become a literary religion, I mean a sort of police force for maintaining order.... To have become a necessary religion, what a terrible end for the revolutionary poet of 1830). Certainly, there is much to be found in these late publications; however, by 1880 many young writers preferred not to find it there.

In 1881 France feted the beginning of Hugo's eightieth year, putting up a triumphal arch on the Avenue d'Eylau, where he lived; hundreds of thousands of admirers filed under his windows on 26 February, his birthday. The end was nearing, however. Juliette died of cancer in May 1883, and Hugo survived his lover by only two years. On learning of his death on 22 May 1885, the Senate and Chamber adjourned; a day of mourning took place on 31 May, when Hugo's body lay in state beneath the Arc de Triomphe. A million mourners lined the route the hearse followed as it carried his remains from the Arc de Triomphe to the Pantheon.

Letters:

Victor Hugo intime: mémoires, correspondances, documents inédits (Paris: Marpon et Flammarion, 1885);

Lettres de Victor Hugo aux Bertin. 1827-1877 (Paris: Nourrit et Cie., 1890);

Correspondance (Paris: Calmann Lévy, 1896-1898);

Correspondance entre Victor Hugo et Paul Meurice, preface by Jules Claretie (Paris: Fasquelle, 1909);

Lettres à Juliette Drouet, 1833-1883, edited by Jean Gaudon (Paris: Pauvert, 1964);

Victor Hugo publie "Les Misérables" (Correspondance avec Alfred Lacroix, août 1861 - juillet 1862) (Paris: Klincksieck, 1970);

Correspondance entre Victor Hugo et Pierre-Jules Hetzel, 1 volume to date, edited by Sheila Gaudon (Paris: Klincksieck, 1979-);

Correspondance familiale et écrits intimes, 2 volumes to date, edited by Jean Gaudon (Paris: Laffont, 1988-).

Bibliographies:

John Parker Anderson, "Bibliography," in Sir Frank Thomas Marzials, *Life of Victor Hugo* (London: W. Scott, 1888), pp. i-xxix;

Abbé Pierre Dubois, *Bio-bibliographie de Victor Hugo de 1802 à 1825* (Paris: H. Champion, 1913);

Maximilian J. Rudwin, *Bibliographie de Victor Hugo* (Paris: Société d'Edition "Les Belles Lettres," 1926);

Elliott Mansfield Grant, *Victor Hugo: A Select and Critical Bibliography* (Chapel Hill: University of North Carolina Press, 1967);

Patricia A. Ward, *Carnet bibliographique Victor Hugo (œuvres et critique, 1978-80)* (Paris: Minard, 1985);

D. J. Adams and A. R. W. James, "Bibliographie sommaire des œuvres de Hugo traduites en anglais de son vivant," in *Victor Hugo et la Grande Bretagne: Actes du deuxième colloque Vinaver* (Liverpool: Francis Cairns, 1986).

Biographies:

Raymond Escholier, *La Vie glorieuse de Victor Hugo* (Paris: Plon, 1928);

Pierre Audiat, *Ainsi vécut Victor Hugo* (Paris: Hachette, 1947);

Jean Delalande, *Victor Hugo à Hauteville-House* (Paris: Albin Michel, 1947);

Escholier, *Victor Hugo, cet inconnu* (Paris: Plon, 1951);

Henri Guillemin, *Victor Hugo par lui-même* (Paris: Editions du Seuil, 1951);

André Maurois, *Olympio, ou la vie de Victor Hugo* (Paris: Hachette, 1954); translated by Gerard Hopkins as *Olympio: The Life of Victor Hugo* (New York: Carroll & Graf, 1956);

Photograph of Hugo in 1869 on the balcony of Hauteville-House, Guernsey

Pierre Angrand, *Victor Hugo raconté par les papiers d'Etat* (Paris: Gallimard, 1961);

Frances Vernor Guille, *Adèle Hugo: Journal d'exil*, 3 volumes (Paris: Minard, 1968-1985);

Charles Baudouin, *Psychanalyse de Victor Hugo* (Paris: Armand Colin, 1972);

Alain Decaux, *Victor Hugo* (Paris: Perrin, 1984);

Danièle Gasiglia, *Victor Hugo. Sa vie, son œuvre* (Paris: Editions Frédéric Birr, 1984);

Adèle Hugo, *Victor Hugo raconté par Adèle Hugo*, edited by E. Blewer (Paris: Plon, 1985).

References:

Pierre Albouy, *La Création mythologique chez Victor Hugo* (Paris: José Corti, 1963);

Erich Auerbach, *Mimesis: The Representation of Reality in Western Literature*, translated by Willard R. Trask (Princeton: Princeton University Press, 1946);

Jean-Bertrand Barrère, *La Fantaisie de Victor Hugo*, 3 volumes (Paris: José Corti, 1949-1960);

Charles Baudelaire, *Œuvres complètes*, 2 volumes (Paris: Gallimard, Bibliothèque de la Pléiade, 1975-1976);

Harold Bloom, "The Breaking of Form," in *Decon-struction and Criticism*, edited by Bloom (New York: Seabury Press, 1979), pp. 1-37;

André Breton, *Manifestes du surréalisme* (Paris: Gallimard, 1975);

Hugo Brochu, *Amour/Crime/Révolution. Essai sur "Les Misérables"* (Montreal: Presses de l'Université de Montréal, 1974);

Victor Brombert, *Victor Hugo and the Visionary Novel* (Cambridge, Mass.: Harvard University Press, 1984);

Brombert, "Victor Hugo's Condemned Man: Laughter of Revolution," *Romanic Review*, 70 (1979): 119-132;

Peter Brooks, *The Melodramatic Imagination: Balzac, Henry James, Melodrama, and the Mode of Excess* (New Haven: Yale University Press, 1976);

Jean Cocteau, *Œuvres complètes*, 11 volumes (Lausanne: Marquerat, 1946);

Jean Gaudon, *Le Temps de la contemplation* (Paris: Flammarion, 1969);

Claude Gély, *Les Misérables de Hugo* (Paris: Hachette, 1975);

Pierre Georgel, *La Gloire de Victor Hugo* (Paris: Editions de la réunion des musées nationaux, 1985);

Richard B. Grant, *The Perilous Quest: Image, Myth, and Prophecy in the Narratives of Victor Hugo* (Durham: Duke University Press, 1968);

Kathryn M. Grossman, *The Early Novels of Victor Hugo: Towards a Poetics of Harmony* (Geneva: Droz, 1986);

Stirling Haig, "From Cathedral to Book, From Stone to Press: Hugo's Portrait of the Artist in *Notre-Dame de Paris*," *Stanford French Review*, 3 (Winter 1979): 343-350;

W. Wolfgang Holdheim, "The History of Art in Victor Hugo's *Notre-Dame de Paris*," *Nineteenth-Century French Studies*, 5 (Fall-Winter 1976-1977): 58-70;

John Porter Houston, *Victor Hugo* (Boston: Twayne, 1988);

Jean Mallion, *Victor Hugo et l'art architectural* (Paris: Presses Universitaires de France, 1962);

Jean Maurel, *Victor Hugo philosophe* (Paris: Presses Universitaires de France, 1985);

Jeffrey Mehlman, *Revolution and Repetition: Hugo/Marx/Balzac* (Berkeley: University of California Press, 1977);

Suzanne Nash, *"Les Contemplations" of Victor Hugo: An Allegory of the Creative Process* (Princeton: Princeton University Press, 1976);

Nash, "Writing a Building: Hugo's *Notre-Dame de Paris*," *French Forum*, 8 (May 1983): 122-133;

Sandy Petrey, *History in the Text: "Quatrevingt-treize" and the French Revolution* (Amsterdam: John Benjamins, 1980);

Henri Peyre, *Hugo* (Paris: Presses Universitaires de France, 1972);

Jean-Paul Sartre, *Situations, II* (Paris: Gallimard, 1948);

Paul Savey-Casard, *Le Crime et la peine dans l'œuvre de Victor Hugo* (Paris: Presses Universitaires de France, 1956);

Jacques Seebacher, "Gringoire, ou le déplacement du roman historique vers l'histoire," *Revue d'Histoire Littéraire de la France*, 75 (March-June 1975): 308-320;

Seebacher, "Le Système du vide dans *Notre-Dame de Paris*," *Littérature*, 5 (February 1972): 95-106;

Anne Ubersfeld, *Le Roi et le bouffon: Etude sur le théâtre de Hugo de 1830 à 1839* (Paris: José Corti, 1974);

Paul Zumthor, *Victor Hugo, poète de Satan* (Paris: Laffont, 1946).

Papers:
Hugo's papers are located in the Bibliothèque Nationale (Paris), the Maison Victor Hugo (Paris), the Villequier Museum, the Library of the University of Manchester (England), the Vianden Museum, and the Spoelberch Lovenjoul Collection (Chantilly).

Prosper Mérimée
(28 September 1803 - 23 September 1870)

Scott D. Carpenter
Carleton College

BOOKS: *Théâtre de Clara Gazul, comédienne espagnole,* as Clara Gazul (Paris: A. Sautelet, 1825; enlarged edition, Paris: H. Fournier jeune, 1830); translated as *The Plays of Clara Gazul, a Spanish Comedian* (London: G. B. Whittaker, 1825);

La Guzla, ou choix de poésies illyriques recueillies dans la Dalmatie, la Bosnie, la Croatie et l'Herzégovine, anonymous (Paris: F.-G. Levrault, 1827);

La Jaquerie, scènes féodales, suivie de La Famille de Carvajal, drame (Paris: Brissot-Thivars, 1828);

1572. Chronique du temps de Charles IX (Paris: Alexandre Mesnier, 1829); republished as *Chronique du règne de Charles IX* (Paris: H. Fournier jeune, 1832); translated as *1572. A Chronicle of the Times of Charles the Ninth* (New York: G. & C. & H. Carvill, 1830);

Mosaïque (Paris: H. Fournier jeune, 1833); translated by Emily Waller and Mary Dey as *The Mosaic* in *The Novels, Tales and Letters of Prosper Mérimée* (New York: Frank Holby, 1905);

La Double Méprise (Paris: H. Fournier, 1833); translated by William Arnold as *The Double Mistake* in *The Novels, Tales and Letters of Prosper Mérimée*;

Notes d'un voyage dans le midi de la France (Paris: Fournier, 1835);

Notes d'un voyage dans l'ouest de la France (Paris: Fournier, 1836);

Notes d'un voyage en Auvergne (Paris: Fournier, 1838);

Notes d'un voyage en Corse (Paris: Fournier jeune, 1840);

Essai sur la guerre sociale (Paris: Firmin-Didot frères, 1841);

Colomba (Paris: Magen et Comon, 1841); translated anonymously (Boston: Phillips, Sampson, 1856)—original contains *Les Ames du purgatoire* and *La Vénus d'Ille,* translated by Olive Palmer and Waller as *Souls in Purgatory* and *The Venus of Ille* in *The Novels, Tales and Letters of Prosper Mérimée;*

Prosper Mérimée, circa 1866

Etudes sur l'histoire romaine, 2 volumes (Paris: Victor Magen, 1844);

Notice sur les peintures de l'église de Saint-Savin (Paris: Imprimerie royale, 1845);

Monuments historiques (Paris: Imprimerie royale, 1846);

Carmen (Paris: Michel Lévy frères, 1847); translated by Thomas Diven (Chicago: Donnelly, Grasset, Loyd, 1878)—original contains *Arsène Guillot* and *L'Abbé Aubain,* translated by Mary Loyd and Edmund Thompson as *Arsène Guillot* and *The Abbé Aubain* in *The Novels, Tales and Letters of Prosper Mérimée;* orig-

193

inal enlarged as *Nouvelles* (Paris: Michel Lévy frères, 1852);

Histoire de Don Pèdre Ier roi de Castile (Paris: Charpentier, 1848); translated as *The History of Peter the Cruel, King of Castile and Leon* (London: R. Bentley, 1849);

Episode de l'histoire de Russie. Les Faux Démétrius (Paris: Michel Lévy frères, 1853); translated by Andrew R. Scoble as *Demetrius the Impostor. An Episode in Russian History* (London: Richard Bentley, 1853);

Les Deux Héritages suivis de L'Inspecteur général et des Débuts d'un aventurier (Paris: Michel Lévy frères, 1853);

Mélanges historiques et littéraires (Paris: Michel Lévy frères, 1855);

Architecture gallo-romaine et architecture du moyen-âge: Instructions du Comité historique des arts et monuments, by Mérimée, Albert Lenoir, Auguste Leprévost, and Charles Lenormant (Paris: Imprimerie impériale, 1857);

Les Cosaques d'autrefois (Paris: Michel Lévy frères, 1865);

Dernières nouvelles (Paris: Michel Lévy frères, 1873); translated by Waller and Louise Paul in *The Novels, Tales and Letters of Prosper Mérimée*;

Portraits historiques et littéraires (Paris: Michel Lévy frères, 1874);

Etudes sur les arts au Moyen Age (Paris: Michel Lévy frères, 1875);

Mémoires historiques (Paris: Bernouard, 1927);

Histoire du règne de Pierre le Grand suivie de l'Histoire de la fausse Elisabeth II, edited by Henri Mongault and Maurice Parturier (Paris: Conard, 1947).

Collection: *Théâtre de Clara Gazul, Romans, Nouvelles* (Paris: Gallimard, Bibliothèque de la Pléiade, 1978).

PLAY PRODUCTIONS: *L'Amour africain*, Paris, Théâtre des Nouveautés, 11 July 1827;

Le Carrosse du Saint-Sacrement, Paris, Comédie Française, 13 March 1850.

OTHER: Théodore-Agrippa d'Aubigné, *Aventures du baron de Fæneste*, edited by Mérimée (Paris: P. Jannet, 1855);

Pierre de Bourdeille, seigneur de Brantôme, *Œuvres complètes*, edited, with an introduction, by Mérimée (Paris: P. Jannet, 1858-1895);

Ivan Turgenev, *Pères et enfants*, preface by Mérimée (Paris: E. Fasquelle, 1863);

Turgenev, *Nouvelles moscovites*, translated by Mérimée and Turgenev (Paris: J. Hetzel, 1869)—contains "Annouchka," "Le Juif," "Pétouchkoff," "Le Chien," "Le Brigadier," "Histoire du Lieutenant Yergounof," "Apparitions";

Turgenev, *Fumée*, preface by Mérimée (Paris: J. Hetzel, n.d.).

Few authors have divided the opinions of readers more than Prosper Mérimée. His stories and novellas are remarkable for their punch and playfulness, but some critics have accused Mérimée of lacking the breadth and substance necessary for the "more serious" genre of the full-length novel. Hailed by some as the master of short prose, he is dismissed by others as a dilettante. Perhaps most renowned for his innovations in narrative technique, he is also impressive for his extraordinary versatility, adding to his reputation as a writer of fiction the credentials of historian, linguist, archaeologist, and translator. He is best remembered, however, for his creative works, the most famous of which, *Carmen*, is best known today in the operatic form Georges Bizet gave it in 1875. Many of Mérimée's lesser-known works are not only fascinating in their own right, but are also important for the transitional role they play in literary history.

Mérimée seemed always on the fringe of the arts. Although strongly committed to the Romantic movement as a youth, he maintained a certain aloofness in his literary endeavors. This reserve, which he was to exhibit increasingly in his personal life, has been interpreted as a defense mechanism: the overly sensitive Mérimée would appear to have refused to invest himself fully in his literary creations in order to avoid identifying with their possible rejection. Accordingly, his first works, *Théâtre de Clara Gazul, comédienne espagnole* (1825; translated as *The Plays of Clara Gazul, a Spanish Comedian*, 1825) and *La Guzla* (The Guzla, 1827), were in part mere literary hoaxes in which the author hid behind unlikely pseudonyms. However, these spoofs drew considerable attention and approbation in Parisian literary circles, and Mérimée was soon launched on a fertile literary career. Still, even during his most prolific period, from 1829 to 1841, he was careful to maintain the illusion that writing was for him but a pastime. Like his father before him, Mérimée distanced himself from his art by taking on increasingly onerous administrative duties, and by 1847 his literary production had ground to a halt. Professional studies, translations, and historical pieces were to occupy him until 1866, when he returned to creative writing for the last years of his life.

Mérimée maintained a curiously ambivalent relationship with the literary community, and although he held a seat in the prestigious Académie Française from 1844 on, he gradually distanced himself throughout his life from many major literary personages. Initially allied, for example, with such incompatible figures as Stendhal and Victor Hugo, his relationship with both men went sour, and he never spoke of their work without expressing reservations. In 1870, upon reading Gustave Flaubert's *L'Education sentimentale* (1869; translated as *Sentimental Education*, 1898), he wrote to his friend Eugène Viollet-le-Duc: "N'y a-t-il personne qui pût lui donner un bon conseil et le tirer d'une vilaine ornière où il s'engage sans avoir l'air de s'en apercevoir?" (Is there no one to give him a bit of advice and pull him out of the rut he seems to have unwittingly gotten himself into?).

This aloofness can also be sensed in Mérimée's prose, especially in the detached narrators that became his trademark, often playing the role of outsiders reporting on events distant in time or space. His works are marked by a spare, sometimes almost journalistic style, accented with local color and a piercing view of human psychology, often made ironic by a reserved narrator. Always something of a maverick, Mérimée relished subverting traditional forms and preying on the expectations of the naive reader. This playfulness amounted to nothing less than the deliberate subversion of the aesthetics of his time, an aesthetics whose limits he was constantly testing.

Prosper Mérimée was born on 28 September 1803, at 7 Carré Sainte-Geneviève, near the Pantheon in Paris. He was the only child of Jean-François-Léonor Mérimée and Anne-Louise Mérimée, née Moreau. His parents, both of liberal political inclination, had strong ties to the artistic community. An artist of some renown, Léonor came in second in the competition for the prestigious Prix de Rome in 1787 and third in 1788. Though a competent painter, Léonor harbored no delusions of grandeur, and by 1795 he had begun to renounce his creative work in favor of a series of primarily administrative posts in cultural institutions, which were to occupy and support him for the rest of his life. Anne Mérimée had acquired some modest celebrity of her own as an author of children's stories (including an adaptation of *Beauty and the Beast*), and she was also

a skilled portraitist. Both parents were unbelievers, and Mérimée, accordingly, was neither baptized nor given any religious upbringing. Although his parents were not fawning, they provided a nurturing and affectionate setting, as evidenced by the fact that Mérimée lived with them until their deaths in 1836 (Léonor) and 1852.

In 1812, at the age of eight, Mérimée entered the Lycée Napoléon (later the Lycée Henri IV), where he proved to be a competent though uninspired student. His pursuits were varied and did not always correspond to the academic program. Throughout his adolescence he tried his hand, with mediocre results, at drawing and painting. Early on he showed a gift for languages, garnering a few school prizes for Latin and Greek, and learning English and Italian at home. He took his baccalaureate in August 1819 and at his father's insistence enrolled in the Faculté de Droit (Law School) at the University of Paris in November of the same year.

Also important during these early years was the young Prosper's sentimental education. Aside from a brief infatuation with a certain Mlle Dubost in 1810, his first serious romantic interest seems to have been Fanny Lagden, the elder of two English sisters who took art lessons from Mme Mérimée. Their romance was short-lived, but the two remained in contact, and much later Fanny was to devote her life to the growing needs of her aging suitor; the two are buried together in the cemetery at Cannes. Mérimée also cultivated a small circle of distinguished male companions during his early years, including Jean-Jacques Ampère (son of the scientist André-Marie), Charles Lenormant (later an eminent linguist and archaeologist), and Adrien de Jussieu (son of the famous botanist Antoine-Laurent).

While working toward his law degree, which he took in 1823, Mérimée found himself once again distracted from the academic program by other pursuits, this time more literary. With Ampère he undertook a translation (which has been lost) of the works of Ossian, and he began to frequent the social and literary salons of Paris. It was in this milieu that he met, among others, Stendhal, with whom he was to have a long friendship. Stendhal encouraged his young friend's literary aspirations, and in 1822, in the salon of Emmanuel Viollet-le-Duc (the father of the architect Eugène-Emmanuel), Mérimée gave a reading of his "Cromwell," a prose play embracing Stendhal's theories about Romantic theater.

If the play met with a cool reception, this was perhaps not because of its lack of literary merit: the nervous Mérimée is reputed to have read so quickly and monotonously that the listeners could scarcely follow the action. In any case, Mérimée decided not to publish the piece, and it has since been lost.

In 1824 Mérimée published a small spate of articles on Spanish theater. He praised above all the realism pervading the Spanish stage, especially insofar as it unfettered theater from the burdensome unities and *convenances* (conformities) of classical doctrine. Around the same time he had been trying his own hand at this new kind of theater, and in 1825 he gave his first reading of two playlets, *Les Espagnols en Danemarck* (Spaniards in Denmark) and *Une Femme est un diable* (A Woman is a Devil), at the salon of Etienne Delécluze. Mérimée's execrable delivery seemed to doom the pieces to obscurity, but Ampère intervened to give a second reading, which met with enthusiasm. Readings of other playlets followed, and in June of that year the collection appeared under the title *Théâtre de Clara Gazul*. Mérimée shrouded the volume in playful mystery, attributing the plays to a Spanish actress named Clara Gazul, whose works were supposedly introduced and rendered into French by the unlikely Joseph L'Estrange. Delécluze provided the frontispiece of the volume, a portrait of Clara, who bears a striking resemblance to the young Mérimée.

Théâtre de Clara Gazul consists of eight plays (six in the original edition) of varying length and subject matter. The prologue to the first play puts the author, Clara herself, onstage, where she ridicules the arbitrary conventions of French theater and the narrow-mindedness of a public that cannot appreciate a play unless it is divided into acts, relegates physical action to the wings, and restricts itself to the tales of people who died at least four hundred years ago. "Et s'ils n'étaient morts que depuis trois cent cinquante ans, est-ce que la comédie ne pourrait pas être bonne?" she asks the poet; "C'est difficile," comes the reply (And if they had been dead for only 350 years, couldn't the play be any good?—It's a problem).

Mérimée demonstrates throughout the volume that the real problem lies in the mindless application of the conventions that stifled French theater. At one point or another he succeeds in breaking all the rules, supplanting the alexandrine with realistic prose dialogue, and blending comedy and tragedy. He also does not hesitate to put violence on the stage: in one play (*L'Amour*

Mérimée in 1825, at the funeral of Gen. Maximilien-Sébastien Foy, where he served as a pallbearer (sketch by David d'Angers; Musée d'Angers)

africain [African Love]) a character kills both his best friend and his wife; in another (*Inès Mendo, ou le préjugé vaincu* [Inès Mendo; or, Prejudice Defeated]) a reluctant executioner cuts off his own right hand rather than behead his daughter's lover. Although these plays were not intended for the stage (only two were produced—with dismal results—in Mérimée's lifetime), they served to announce the arrival of Romantic theater, predating the better-known contributions of Hugo, Alfred de Musset, and Alexandre Dumas *père*. They also introduce themes that will continue to find favor with Mérimée, including the struggle against power and convention, the hypocrisy of religious orders, and various forms of betrayal. Women in *Théâtre de Clara Gazul* occupy two opposite roles, either innocent victims or scheming, lively seductresses. In this latter category one finds prototypes for Carmen, the quintessential femme fatale. One can also note certain of Mérimée's stylistic tics, such as the motif of oranges, which he often uses both as local color and as a symbol of feminine sensuality. This, too, will resurface much later in *Carmen*.

During the late 1820s Mérimée led an easy and bawdy life, often in the company of Stendhal, Musset, and the English lawyer Sutton Sharpe. He spent a good deal of time in brothels when not actively courting a mistress. One seduction led to a duel in 1828; for reasons that were unclear (Mérimée enjoyed being enigmatic), he refused to fire and was wounded in the left arm. In spite of these time-consuming occupations, including excursions to London, his literary production did not suffer, and the period from 1827 through 1829 saw the publication of a collection of ballads, two more plays, a novel, and his first short stories.

The first of these works, *La Guzla*, was another literary hoax, a fabricated "translation" of Illyrian verse published anonymously. So masterful was Mérimée's handling of folkloric material and the elements of local color that the ruse was not uncovered until the following year. Mérimée seems to have set little stock by this work: he later claimed to have written it in order to amass the funds necessary to travel to that part of Europe. However, Suzanne Bernard has pointed out that these "translations" are important as the first instance of prose poetry. Alan William Raitt has shown how Mérimée plays on the collection's prosaic qualities in the double entendre of his subtitle: *choix de poésies illyriques* (Choice of Illyrian/Unlyrical Poems). In 1828 Mérimée published *La Jaquerie, scènes féodales* (The Jaquerie, Feudal Scenes), a long play about the peasant rebellion in France in the late fourteenth century, symptomatic of his own initially liberal tendencies. *La Jaquerie* contained a shorter drama, *La Famille de Carvajal* (The Carvajal Family), an adaptation of the story of Beatrice Cenci.

In 1829 Mérimée produced his first major work in prose, the historical novel *1572. Chronique du temps de Charles IX* (translated as *1572. A Chronicle of the Times of Charles the Ninth*, 1830). Both an imitation and something of a parody of Sir Walter Scott's novels, the *Chronique* examines the events leading up to the Saint Bartholomew's Day Massacre (24 August 1572), during which French Catholics slaughtered their Protestant compatriots. Mérimée clearly views the massacre as one of the most senseless tragedies French history has to offer. He is careful to underscore the fact that it is a question of an internal, civil confrontation, and this links the play to the cycle of revolutions in which France was caught in Mérimée's own time.

The novel focuses on the fratricidal nature of such conflicts, following two brothers divided by religion: the young Protestant Bernard de Mergy and the apostate George. George is in fact an anachronism, a fundamentally Voltairean figure (much like Mérimée himself), who has embraced Catholicism solely for practical reasons. He helps his brother earn favor in both the Protestant and the Catholic factions, and participates in protecting him on the night of the massacre. Somewhat predictably, during the siege of the Protestant stronghold of La Rochelle, Bernard is responsible for his own brother's death, which can be seen as emblematic of the folly of this historic episode.

In the *Chronique*, Mérimée brought considerable erudition to bear on his fiction, a combination that would become a hallmark of his prose. In the preface he describes the work as an attempt to respond to certain historical questions, but the result is clearly not a treatise. The gruesomely detailed descriptions of the slaughter of the Protestants seem calculated to inspire horror in the reader, which Mérimée heightens by sallies of macabre humor at particularly inappropriate moments. That he is more interested in manipulating than educating his reader is best seen in the chapter "Dialogue entre le lecteur et l'auteur" (Dialogue Between the Reader and the Author), in which the author steadfastly refuses to satisfy the reader's curiosity about the important historical personages lurking in the margins of the *Chronique*. He further disarms the reader (and undercuts the drama of George's death) by a rapid conclusion that refuses to supply any kind of denouement: Bernard's fate and that of his mistress are left in the hands of the reader. These deliberately contrived passages and the rather two-dimensional characters demonstrate Mérimée's debt to the eighteenth-century novel, especially to such works as Denis Diderot's *Jacques le Fataliste et son maître* (1796; translated as *James the Fatalist and His Master*, 1797). The lighthearted passages seem to exhort the reader not to take the book too seriously; in the context of a subject whose gravity Mérimée seems to want to assert, this would appear an infelicitous technique. In other works Mérimée was to use narrative detachment more forcefully.

The *Chronique* could hardly have been better timed: a year after Mérimée brought forth this account of the repressive measures of

Charles IX, a reactionary Charles X started maneuvering to free the monarchy from its constitutional foundations. The result was the July Revolution, which replaced Charles X with the more liberal regime of Louis-Philippe. Although Mérimée had nothing to do with the uprising (he had been in Spain from June to December 1830), his liberal tendencies were by now well known, and he had well-placed friends, including Stendhal. After serving a brief and uneventful stint in the National Guard, he took on his first administrative post, heading up the office of the secretary-general of the navy. This was the beginning of Mérimée's long and very dedicated career as a bureaucrat, and over the next few years he rose rapidly through the ranks, adapting easily to a bewildering array of responsibilities. He was finally appointed inspector-general of historic monuments in May 1834, a post he was to discharge actively for more than twenty years.

Although extremely conscientious, Mérimée often found his professional duties excruciatingly dull, and he compensated for this by intensifying the activities of his ribald personal life. Not surprisingly, he found little time for his literary pursuits, and although he published *Mosaïque* (translated as *The Mosaic*, 1905) in June 1833, this did not constitute new work. The majority of the short stories, ballads, and articles that make up the heterogeneous collection had been written in 1829 or 1830, and had already appeared individually in the *Revue de Paris* or the *Revue Française* between 1829 and 1832.

It is not clear how Mérimée happened to try his hand at the short story, for the genre was fairly uncommon at this time; in any case, the young writer was to find his niche here. Mérimée's compression of stories to a few pages lent them a verve and energy quite unfamiliar to readers better acquainted with Honoré de Balzac's long descriptions and digressions. Mérimée despised useless details. A main effect of this spare style is that it moves one through the story faster than one can process it, and the emotional charge of the ending is heightened by the reader's unpreparedness.

The best example of this technique is perhaps the first story of the collection, "Mateo Falcone." A tale of fierce Corsican honor, "Mateo Falcone" tells the story of a young boy, Fortunato, who conceals an outlaw from the police, but who later sells out to the authorities. His father, Mateo, is outraged at this dishonorable conduct, and brushing aside his wife, he takes his

son out to the woods for punishment. When Mateo tells the youth to say his prayers, Fortunato begs his father to spare him. Mateo calmly waits till the prayers are finished, and as Fortunato gets up to go to his father's knees, Mateo shoulders his gun and fires. Mérimée's cool, disinterested narration clashes with the brutality of the scene itself, resulting in a narrative detonation that parallels that of Mateo's rifle.

The diversity of the works in *Mosaïque* bears witness to Mérimée's eclectic interests as well as to his prowess at a wide range of styles: "Vision de Charles XI" (The Vision of Charles XI), a reconstruction of a seventeenth-century premonition, marks Mérimée's entrance into the genre of the fantastic; "Fédérigo" partakes of the folktale, invoking a curious blend of Christian and Greco-Roman mythologies. Perhaps the only unifying element of all the stories is a recurrence of such themes as honor, jealousy, and treachery, usually overlaid with acutely ironic narration.

Less ironic are the four *Lettres d'Espagne* (Letters from Spain), only the first three of which are included in the original edition. Each of these letters, drafted for the *Revue de Paris* during Mérimée's 1830 trip to Spain, attempts to overturn the prejudices and received ideas about a given aspect of Spanish life. Following in the tradition of Charles-Louis de Secondat, Baron de Montesquieu's *Lettres persanes* (1721; translated as *The Persian Letters*, 1750), Mérimée enjoys occasionally upsetting prevailing French sentiments of superiority. Thus the letter on bullfighting, far from decrying the brutality of this "sport," ends up praising it as the highest form of tragedy—an artistic laurel the French liked to reserve for themselves; his report of a hanging culminates with a consideration of the superiority of the Spanish penal system. The last letters, on thieves and witches, are especially important for the background material they were later to provide for *Carmen*. All in all the works of *Mosaïque* figure as Mérimée's literary coming of age, serving to consolidate his reputation among contemporaries as a master.

In the middle of 1833 Mérimée met Jenny Dacquin, a young French girl who had been writing him under an English pseudonym. He was immediately taken with her, and their continued correspondence was to assume romantic undertones. Mérimée clearly had more than a platonic interest in his charming correspondent, but it is unsure whether Dacquin ever yielded. In any event, she was to remain Mérimée's friend and confidante until his death in 1870. In 1874 she published two volumes of his letters under the title *Lettres à une inconnue* (translated as *Letters to an Unknown*, 1905), and they provide the most reliable panorama of his activities over the course of thirty-seven years.

A man of multiple interests, Mérimée had been pursuing other romantic possibilities in 1833, including the novelist George Sand. The general consensus is that the relationship culminated in a disastrous one-night stand, Sand reporting that "l'expérience manqua complètement" (the experiment failed miserably). Either to salvage some benefit from the misadventure, or to counter possible doubts about his virility, Mérimée memorialized the event by using it as the basis for his first novella, *La Double Méprise* (1833; translated as *The Double Mistake*, 1905).

This heavily fictionalized account revolves around the young and unhappily wed Julie de Chaverny. She is just beginning to respond (rather unenthusiastically) to the overtures of a young suitor, when her friend Darcy returns from six years of foreign service. She is irresistibly drawn to the equally smitten Darcy, and by the end of the day this dragon of virtue has given herself to Darcy during a nocturnal carriage ride. Moments after the act, however, Julie realizes her mistake: she had seen this as the first step of their lives together, while Darcy views her coldly as a simple conquest. Profoundly troubled, overwhelmed with shame and disgust, she does not survive the shock of this disillusionment, dying in a matter of days.

La Double Méprise was in general poorly received by the public on the grounds of *invraisemblance* (improbability), and there seems to have been little appreciation of Mérimée's skillful, humorous subversion of Romantic conventions, of which he shows the cynical underside. The offhand, rapid conclusion detailing Julie's demise is less a poorly executed climax than a full-blown caricature of the traditional "wasting away" of disgraced or unhappy protagonists, such as Jean-Jacques Rousseau's frail heroine in *Julie, ou La Nouvelle Héloïse* (1761; translated as *Julia, or the New Eloisa*, 1773). Here, perhaps more than in any of his earlier works, Mérimée succeeds in giving his narrative voice a well-shaped character—and one that, by its stark contrast with the tale it recounts, provides a major source of narrative tension.

With his appointment to the inspector-generalship of historic monuments, Mérimée

CARMEN

Poster for the first production (1875) of Georges Bizet's opera version of Mérimée's 1847 novel

began a series of annual tours of various regions of France, doing his best to inventory the thousands of historic structures in need of repair or protection. Nothing if not thorough, he took exhaustive notes, ostensibly addressed to the minister of the interior, but which he also generally edited and published for the learned community. More than anyone else he was responsible for bringing to public attention the plight of a significant portion of the French patrimony, and his responsibilities were soon expanded to include supervision of restoration projects, often undertaken with the collaboration of Viollet-le-Duc.

In 1834, the first year of his position, he spent nearly five months cataloguing monuments in the south of France, the results of which appeared the following year as *Notes d'un voyage dans le midi de la France* (Notes on a Trip in the South of France). This time was necessarily lost for any kind of creative endeavor. Partly because of his increased responsibilities, partly for fear of not being able to maintain his already considerable reputation, and partly because he had never held writing to be a serious occupation, Mérimée's literary production began to slow down dramatically. Nevertheless, what was lost in quantity was often more than compensated for by quality, as some of Mérimée's finest works were to appear in the years to follow.

Les Ames du purgatoire (translated as *Souls in Purgatory*, 1905), a modest novella written before he began his new duties, appeared in the *Revue des Deux Mondes* (15 August 1834). Given the life of dissipation Mérimée had been leading since 1830, it seemed appropriate that in this work he should take on the legend of Don Juan, but the result is somewhat infelicitous. For instance, Mérimée focuses on the Don Juan de Maraña myth, which differs from the Don Juan de Tenorio version principally in its ending: de Maraña repents and dies practically a saint. Mérimée strives, perhaps too hard, to cast the legend in the light of psychological realism. Thus Don Juan's libertine life-style is depicted as a reaction to his rearing by the opposed and rigid forces of a devout mother and a soldiering father.

Fascinated and terrified as a child by a painting of the torments of purgatory, the young Don Juan soon loses himself in ventures guaranteed to make these torments a reality. After a life of excess he returns to the vacant family manor, where he is once again captivated by the forgotten painting. Soon after, he has a vision of his own death and of phantoms awaiting his arrival in purgatory, and this vision marks the beginning of a new life. Although technically beyond reproach, this tale has never earned warm praise. It is marred by the unavoidable monotony of Don Juan's accumulation of conquests, and the redemption motif (already surprising for someone of Mérimée's Voltairean upbringing) clashes oddly with the irony and cynicism cultivated throughout the body of the work. Its importance lies primarily in the artful integration of elements of psychology, narrative realism, and the supernatural: these were to come together more fruitfully in later tales.

The next years were given over increasingly to other pursuits. Mérimée's professional responsibilities expanded, and travel continued to consume his time. In addition to a two-month sojourn in England in 1835, he regularly spent many months on the road for his tours of historic monuments, the notes of which appeared in due course (*Notes d'un voyage dans l'ouest de la France* [Notes on a Trip in the West of France, 1836], *Notes d'un voyage en Auvergne* [Notes on a Trip in Auvergne, 1838], and *Notes d'un voyage en Corse* [Notes on a Trip in Corsica, 1840]). His social life was enhanced by the arrival in Paris of a Spanish friend, the Countess de Montijo, whom he had met in 1830 during his first trip to Madrid. Both he and Stendhal frequented this household, delighting in particular the countess's daughter Eugenia, the future bride of Napoleon III. Early in 1836 Mérimée succeeded in seducing Valentine Delessert, who was to remain his mistress for many years. Amid this pleasant and rather carefree period there occurred a single devastating event: the death of Mérimée's father, Léonor, in September 1836.

Contrary to appearances, Mérimée's inspector-generalship was not detrimental to his literary life. Although the quantity of his production had diminished sharply, during the period from 1837 to 1845 he completed what are generally held to be his finest works of fiction. Furthermore, his growing erudition in history and archaeology was to enhance the incisive and coolly authoritative narrative voice he had long cultivated. On 15 May 1837 he published in the *Revue des Deux Mondes* what he was to consider his masterpiece, *La Vénus d'Ille* (translated as *The Venus of Ille*, 1905), inspired in part by a statue he came across during his tour of Brittany.

It is a first-person account by a Parisian archaeologist (the narrator is a caricature of Mérimée) of his visit to the tiny village of Ille, at the foot of the Pyrenees. The unsuspecting narrator surprises his host, Monsieur de Peyrehorade, in the midst of a twofold commotion: the imminent wedding of his boorish son Alphonse, and the recent unearthing of a bronze statue of Venus. The statue figures increasingly throughout the story as a disruptive element in the tranquil existence of this Mediterranean village. After it topples upon one of the excavators, the Venus gives rise to rampant ill will, which is heightened by its jeering expression. Distaste soon turns to superstition as vandals claim the statue threw their stones back at them, and anxiety and fear spread among the credulous.

Of course, the presence of a goddess of love during wedding preparations suffices to entwine the two strands of the plot, and on the morning of the ceremony, Alphonse places his wedding band on the statue's finger in order to improve his grip during a tennis game. He inadvertently leaves the ring after the game and has to make do with a substitute during the ceremony. That night he is crushed to death in his wedding bed, and the account of his delirious bride suggests that the statue itself entered the room, as if to embrace its groom. This explanation is swept aside by the authorities, but the clues are insufficient for a precise reconstruction of the events. Finally, in an epilogue, the narrator reports that the crime has never been solved.

La Vénus d'Ille has been hailed as the finest example of "fantastic" literature, a genre that dabbles in the supernatural but ultimately hesitates between a rational and a supernatural explanation. Mérimée's handling of the situation is superb: Peyrehorade's odious, womanizing son is a particularly inviting victim, and there is no shortage of suspects. In particular, Alphonse's adversary on the tennis court, who has sworn vengeance for an ignominious defeat—and who is of the same stature and complexion as the bronze Venus—draws the attention of the authorities; but his alibi is unshakable. The narrator himself, who demonstrates a clear distaste for Alphonse, has been put forth by critics as a possible culprit. At the same time, evidence for a supernatural denouement accumulates, and "rational" logic is gradually challenged by the suggestive power of details on which Mérimée does not even comment.

For example, the bezel of the ring is shaped like two hands coming together, a miniature form of the metallic embrace the statue seems to return. Even the narrator, a stalwart champion of the rational, feels himself oddly touched by the "superstitious terror" spreading through Ille. The fundamental indecisiveness of the tale caters to Mérimée's penchant for subverting readers' expectations and leaving endings inconclusive. Ultimately a whole series of oppositions pitting pagan against Christian, past against present, rational against irrational, and love against death is left fundamentally unresolved, which makes *La Vénus d'Ille* strangely disturbing reading even today.

Although Mérimée did not immediately continue in the vein of the fantastic, he was soon to capitalize on some of the thematic elements of *La Vénus d'Ille*. In 1839 he included in his annual tour a trip to Corsica, less to evaluate the island's monuments than to glean material for a new piece. The happy result was *Colomba* (1841; translated, 1856), a story focusing on the Corsican tradition of the vendetta. Like *La Vénus d'Ille*, *Colomba* derives its tensions from a set of oppositional pairs, the most obvious of which is two feuding families. More interestingly, it confronts barbarity with civilization, and custom with change.

When the young Orso della Rebbia returns home after years on the mainland, he hopes to break out of the cycle of revenge in which his family has been engaged with the Barricinis; he thus plans not to challenge the suspicious official explanation of the murder of his father two years earlier. However, his sister, Colomba, an incarnation of Corsican ferocity, masterminds a retaliation upon the Barricinis, drawing her brother toward his traditional role of avenger. Her ruthlessness extends so far as to provoke an attack by the Barricinis upon her brother, and when Orso finds himself ambushed, he is forced to fire upon his attackers in self-defense. So, as the cycle of retaliation is finally broken, and Orso is legally exculpated, the oppositions seem to be resolved: the Barricini family is annihilated, and civilized law is restored.

Yet in typical Mériméan style, the resolution is not so neat, and disturbing undertones remain. The triumph over the Barricinis is not achieved by Orso's civilized politics of desistance, but rather by Colomba's savage vengefulness, which she expresses by way of her brother and in the disguise of a lawful response. The faint wailings of the decrepit Barricini patriarch at the end of the novella remind the reader that justice has not been done, and that the civilized law of the mainland has become little more than a new tool for the perpetuation of ancient custom. Now a recognized master of psychological portraiture, Mérimée capitalizes on his study of human emotion, which he depicts as resurging through new channels when other forms of expression are forbidden or repressed.

Colomba achieved critical acclaim from the highest official sources, Charles-Augustin Sainte-Beuve calling it Mérimée's most beautiful, most perfect work. The precise attention to detail, the unity of development, and especially the dilemma of personal inclination versus social obligation cast *Colomba* as a new classic, "au vrai sens du mot" (in the true sense of the word).

Not surprisingly, this apparent aesthetic conservatism met with a cold reception from Mérimée's former mentor. As early as *La Vénus d'Ille*, Stendhal thought that Mérimée was getting timid in his writing, and regretted that the verve of his early works had been sacrificed to dry precision. He also found that Mérimée himself was becoming somewhat insufferable, and after 1839 the re-

Self-portrait of Mérimée (from Robert Baschet, Du romantisme au Second Empire: Mérimée [1803-1870], *1958)*

lationship between the two men cooled considerably. Certainly many of Mérimée's contemporaries found the author stuffy, with a high idea of himself. That his airs primarily compensated for a deep-seated insecurity can be seen in his craving for the public signs of success.

Although he feigned mild indifference for official honors, he campaigned hard behind the scenes for his election to the Académie des Inscriptions et Belles-Lettres in 1843, going so far as to write a historical study, *Essai sur la guerre sociale* (Essay on Social War, 1841), expressly to round out his qualifications. So fretful was he over election to the Académie Française in 1844 that he arranged to have a rather provocative story about a prostitute, *Arsène Guillot* (translated, 1852), published in the *Revue des Deux Mondes* on 15 March, the day after the election. This way it could serve either as a sign of his indifference should he not be elected or, in the opposite case, as an assertion of his intent to maintain his ribald, independent spirit within the staid institution.

In 1844 Mérimée published an expanded version of his historical work *Etudes sur l'histoire romaine* (Studies of Roman History) and began to examine Gypsy customs and language. The fruits of this study were to come together with aspects of the *Lettres d'Espagne*, and with the author's re-

cent penchant for deadly heroines, to produce *Carmen* (1847; translated, 1878). Although it drew unenthusiastic reviews in its day, this novella is undoubtedly the Mérimée title best known to today's public, which is most familiar with it through the operatic or film versions.

Like *La Vénus d'Ille*, *Carmen* marries the themes of love and death: the central narrative focuses on the tragic fate of Don José, a young and hotheaded cavalry officer who is lured in spite of himself into a life of dishonor and banditry by a Gypsy temptress. In the tradition of the Abbé Prévost's *Manon Lescaut* (1731), Carmen follows a cycle of passion, indifference, and infidelity, all of which suffice to render José insanely possessive and jealous. The further he strays from the law, killing two of Carmen's lovers and plotting against the third, the more José rages against the spell the diabolical beauty has cast upon him. Finally he takes control, threatening to stab her if she does not remain faithful. Carmen, however, sees death as infinitely preferable to surrendering her freedom, and she offers her bosom to the blade; José strikes twice.

The drama of *Carmen* is heightened by Mérimée's ingenious narrative frame. As in *La Vénus d'Ille* the narrator is a bookish archaeologist, and he crosses paths with both Don José and Carmen during a research trip to Spain. When he passes through Cordoba several months later, he learns that José is currently in prison, awaiting execution. He pays him a visit in his cell. Now, after the dry, impassive monologue of the narrator, José's monumental story emerges, painfully recounted by the outlaw himself and rendered all the more poignant by the impending death sentence. Reminiscent of the staccato style of "Mateo Falcone," Carmen's death hits the reader hard and fast, occupying only a few lines. The story ends immediately thereafter with José turning himself in to the authorities.

Carmen first appeared in the *Revue des Deux Mondes* (1 October 1845). When it was published in book form, Mérimée appended an epilogue in which the unruffled narrator moves without comment to a discussion of certain Gypsy customs and expressions. This imperturbability has been seen variously as undercutting the whole impact of José's tragedy, or as elevating it by its contrast. In any case, the simple disjunctiveness of the conclusion compounds the unsettled sense of José's saga. The best of Mérimée's stories betray the conventional aesthetics of the well-told tale in this way, refusing to conclude in any fully satisfying fashion.

In 1846 Mérimée wrote a pair of short stories: "L'Abbé Aubain" (translated as *The Abbé Aubain*, 1905), which was published in the *Constitutionnel* (24 February), and "Il Viccolo di Madama Lucrezia" (translated as "The 'Viccolo' of Madam Lucrezia"), which did not appear until the publication of *Dernières nouvelles* (1873; translated in *The Novels, Tales and Letters of Prosper Mérimée*, 1905). But *Carmen* was to be his last major creative piece for more than twenty years. His departure from fiction coincided closely with the first signs of a break with Valentine Delessert, who had been his mistress and faithful reader for the past decade. More than this, though, Mérimée had always been ambivalent about the merits of literature, and he now gave himself over increasingly to historical and archaeological studies, and somewhat later to the translation of Russian authors.

During the revolutionary months of 1848 he again served with the National Guard, and his reactions to the popular uprising showed that over the years the young maverick had moved toward political conservatism. Although distraught by the ferocity of civil unrest, he was prepared to defend the system that had served him so generously. Accordingly, he supported the presidency and empire of Louis-Napoleon, and his position was enhanced in 1853 when Napoleon wed Mérimée's young friend Eugenia de Montijo, who then became Empress Eugénie. At Eugénie's insistence, Mérimée accepted a nomination to the Senate. Although he tried, unsuccessfully, to fight the most repressive press laws, and even attempted to have the censorship case against Charles Baudelaire dismissed, his implicit support of the regime earned him great disfavor among such opposition writers as Hugo.

By the late 1850s Mérimée's health and spirits were in decline. His mother had died in 1852, and he was now zealously cared for by his childhood friends, the Lagden sisters. Disenchanted with the parasitic existence of a courtier, he sought solace primarily in the new field of Russian studies, in which he had first dabbled in the late 1840s. During this period he was to play an important role in introducing Russian culture to the French. He wrote extensively on Russian authors and put out many translations, working especially closely with Ivan Turgenev. He also produced two volumes of Russian history, *Episode de l'histoire de Russie. Les Faux Démétrius* (1853; trans-

lated as *Demetrius the Impostor. An Episode in Russian History*, 1853) and *Les Cosaques d'autrefois* (Cossacks of Yesteryear, 1865). While these attested to Mérimée's continued interest in history, they may also have contained a commentary on the present, especially in the case of the first of these titles: a certain amount of cheek was required to write about imperial impostors during a regime that clearly rode on the coattails of the Napoleonic empire.

Starting in 1856 Mérimée began to winter in the South, usually in Cannes. By 1862 his respiratory problems had worsened, and he tried cures at various spas, feeling no relief except from a compressed air treatment he happened upon in 1868. As his list of dead friends lengthened, he considered his own demise imminent, and for years he suffered from bouts of morbidity.

In 1866, for reasons Mérimée himself did not understand, he returned to fiction, writing three stories in the last four years of his life. Originally intended as mere parlor entertainment for the guests of the imperial court, they are among the finest of Mérimée's works. "La Chambre bleue" ("The Blue Chamber"), written in 1866 and published in *Dernières nouvelles*, is a lighthearted tale of forbidden love between two young, inexperienced lovers. This romantic adventure, entailing an overnight excursion from Paris, appears to become entangled in another, more sordid story: the supposed murder, in the adjoining room of the hotel, of the Englishman the couple had encountered on the train.

The story culminates in a flurry of panic as the lovers attempt an escape in order to avoid the publicity the crime will surely draw. But at the crucial moment of their evasion, Mérimée defuses both tension and fear. The murder proves illusory: the "blood" they had spied seeping under the door between the rooms was but the mess from a spilled bottle of port. The trick of this piece is that it undermines the reader's expectation of a typically Mériméan disastrous ending. Paradoxically, the happy ending itself becomes disquieting for readers familiar with Mérimée's earlier works, for it seems to undermine the anticipated connection between love and death. Mérimée does, in fact, link the two, but he manages it by way of a complicated, marginal paralleling of his story with the tragic myth of Pyramus and Thisbe; once again he destabilizes the reader by decentering the thrust of his story.

For *Lokis* (published in *Dernières nouvelles*), his last dalliance with the fantastic, Mérimée was to borrow heavily from *La Vénus d'Ille*: one finds the same narrative frame, the same tension between the rational and the supernatural, and the same indecisive conclusion. Here, however, the struggle is not between male and female forces, but between the rational and bestial natures at battle within every individual. The setting, in accord with the author's recent interest in Eastern Europe, is remote Lithuania, where the learned Parisian narrator is the guest of the young Count Michel Szémioth. As in *La Vénus d'Ille*, there is a marriage in the offing, between the Count and the playful mademoiselle Iwinska. Szémioth also has his hands full taking care of his mother, who has been deranged since she was carried off by a bear some nine months before giving birth to her son, whom she has since associated with the beast who brutalized her.

Although Szémioth strikes the narrator as a soundly rational being, certain irregularities (a penchant for tree climbing, the fear he inspires in dogs and horses) suggest a curious instance of crossbreeding. Something along these lines seems to be confirmed by the ending: the morning after the nuptials, Iwinska is found partially devoured in the wedding bed, and the count has vanished. The narrator concludes with an explanation of the etymological bond between the name *Michel* and *lokis*, the Lithuanian word for *bear*. Although Mérimée does not maintain the same indecisiveness in this ending as in *La Vénus d'Ille*, the conclusion of *Lokis* can be even more disturbing. The story's explicit ruminations on human psychology serve to turn the reader away from what is already an outrageous supernatural explanation; but to discount the supernatural is to opt for a troubling psychological interpretation, thus acknowledging a fundamental duplicity of human nature, the delicate balance of which can be easily upset.

Mérimée's fascination with the underside of human nature, and with the interrelationship between what would later be called the conscious and the unconscious, reached its zenith in his last story, "Djoûmane" (published in *Dernières nouvelles*), in which a cavalry officer leaving for night patrol becomes entangled in a web of increasingly improbable events, all of which revolve around a young Algerian girl and a snake. At the climax the girl changes into one of the narrator's fellow officers, who, it turns out, is waking him up: he has fallen asleep during the excursion.

Mérimée in 1865 (photograph by Desideri)

Close reading of the story's introduction, preceding the company's departure, demonstrates that Mérimée had grasped the profound influence of the waking state upon the dream, as well as the subtle metaphoric and metonymic operations of what Sigmund Freud would later call the dreamwork. Indeed, the very title "Djoûmane" resonates with the Arabic *tourdjouman*, or "interpreter," thus highlighting the notion of symbolic transformation. In "Djoûmane," Mérimée had come full circle, leaving dry realism for a Romantic vision that had not seen its equal since Gérard de Nerval.

"Djoûmane" never made it to the imperial court, for Mérimée's health was failing rapidly. With the declaration of the Franco-Prussian War, he turned his diminished energies to matters of state, trying to unite the disparate factions of the government for a more effective resistance. He once said that he did not think he would be able to survive a French defeat, and on the evening of 23 September 1870, three weeks after France's capitulation, he expired in his bed at his summer residence in Cannes.

The last stories were collected posthumously in 1873, under the title *Dernières nouvelles*. Save for the collection of some pieces previously seen only in periodicals, this was to remain the extent of Mérimée's posthumous publications: in May 1871 his house had been torched during the uprising of the Paris Commune (probably because of his association with the imperial regime), and his papers were lost. Because of the turmoil of the current political situation, his death drew slight immediate attention, but when calm was restored, the critical world began to scurry to collect Mérimée's massive correspondence. Not until well after the turn of the century had enough documents become available to produce the coherent vision of Mérimée's extraordinarily variegated life and work that was to emerge in Pierre Trahard's monolithic, four-volume study.

Mérimée's oeuvre has drawn steady critical attention, even enjoying a resurgence of interest in the late twentieth century. Although best known as the founder of the modern short story, he also played important roles in the development of other genres, launching Romantic theater in *Théâtre de Clara Gazul*, inaugurating the prose poem in *La Guzla*, and refining the historical novel in *1572. Chronique du temps de Charles IX*.

Early criticism tended to praise works where Mérimée was not writing like himself, that is, where he was not playing games with his reader by the use of surprise endings or unreliable narrators. Games, however, have a newfound respectability in the late twentieth century, and this has led to Mérimée's reevaluation. These quirks in his writing, far from being cheap tricks or shortcomings, have been gradually recognized as indications of an extraordinary sensitivity to the rules governing the interaction between text and reader. Mérimée persistently challenged established aesthetic codes, regularly subverting readers' expectations. Usually working within the framework of literary realism, he routinely disrupted the transparent representation that realism generally sought to transmit. In so doing he challenged the reading aesthetic of passive reception, and can thus be seen as one of the precursors of the modern novel.

Letters:

Lettres à une inconnue (Paris: Michel Lévy frères, 1874); translated by Olive Palmer as *Letters to an Unknown* in *The Novels, Tales and Letters of Prosper Mérimée* (New York: Frank Holby, 1905);

Lettres à une autre inconnue (Paris: Michel Lévy frères, 1875);

Correspondance générale, edited by Maurice Parturier, volumes 1-6 (Paris: Le Divan, 1941-1947); volumes 7-17 (Toulouse: Privat, 1953-1964).

Biographies:

Pierre Trahard, *La Jeunesse de Prosper Mérimée (1803-1834)*, 2 volumes (Paris: E. Champion, 1925);

Trahard, *Prosper Mérimée de 1834 à 1853* (Paris: H. Champion, 1928);

Trahard, *La Vieillesse de Prosper Mérimée* (Paris: H. Champion, 1930);

Alan William Raitt, *Prosper Mérimée* (New York: Scribners / London: Eyre & Spottiswoode, 1970);

Maxwell Smith, *Prosper Mérimée* (New York: Twayne, 1972);

Jean Autin, *Prosper Mérimée, écrivain, archéologue, homme politique* (Paris: Perrin, 1983).

References:

Ora Avni, "Et la chose fut: *La Vénus d'Ille* de Mérimée," *Poétique*, 12 (April 1981): 156-170;

Avni, "Mystification de la lecture chez Mérimée: Lira bien qui rira le dernier," *Littérature*, 58 (May 1985): 29-41;

Jean Bellemin-Noël, *Vers l'inconscient du texte* (Paris: Presses Universitaires de France, 1979);

Frank Paul Bowman, *Prosper Mérimée; Heroism, Pessimism, and Irony* (Berkeley: University of California Press, 1962);

Patrick Brady, "Déguisement et déshabillage: La structuration symbolique de la *Chronique du règne de Charles IX*," *Francofonia*, 4 (Autumn 1984): 73-81;

Scott Carpenter, "Diversions in Reading: Esthetics and Mérimée's 'La Chambre bleue,'" *French Forum*, 14 (September 1989): 303-310;

Pierre-Georges Castex, *Le Conte fantastique en France de Nodier à Maupassant* (Paris: Corti, 1951);

Jacques Chabot, *L'Autre Moi* (Aix-en-Provence: Edisud, 1983);

P. Cogman, "The Narrators of Mérimée's *Carmen*," *Nottingham French Studies*, 27 (November 1988): 1-12;

Barbara Cooper, "Mérimée's *La Jaquerie*: Time, History, and the 'Pleating' of the Text," in *L'Hénaurme Siècle: A Miscellany of Essays on Nineteenth Century Literature,* edited by Will McLendon (Heidelberg: Carl Winter Universitätsverlag, 1984), pp. 27-34;

Kathryn Crecelius, "Narrative as Moral Action in Mérimée's *Colomba*," *Nineteenth-Century French Studies,* 14 (Spring-Summer 1986): 225-237;

Robert Dale, *The Poetics of Prosper Mérimée* (The Hague: Mouton, 1966);

Jean Decottignies, "Lokis. Fantastique et dissimulation," *Revue d'Histoire Littéraire de la France,* 71 (January-February 1971): 18-29;

Europe, issue on Mérimée, 557 (September 1975);

Gillian Horrocks, "A Semiotic Study of *Carmen*," *Nottingham French Studies,* 25 (October 1986): 60-72;

Laurence Porter, "The Subversion of the Narrator in Mérimée's *La Vénus d'Ille*," *Nineteenth-Century French Studies,* 10 (Spring-Summer 1982): 268-277;

Luc Rasson, "L'Impossible Disjonction: Dit et non-dit dans 'Lokis' de Prosper Mérimée," *Nineteenth-Century French Studies,* 12-13 (Summer-Fall 1984): 81-94;

Tobin Siebers, "Fantastic Lies: Lokis and the Victim of Coincidence," *Kentucky Romance Quarterly,* 28 (1981): 87-93;

Eileen Sivert, "Prosper Mérimée: Isolation and Fear of Self," *Language Quarterly,* 15 (1977): 53-65;

Pierre Trahard, *Prosper Mérimée et l'art de la nouvelle* (Paris: Nizet, 1952).

Henry Murger
(Louis-Henri Murger)
(27 March 1822 - 28 January 1861)

Harry Redman, Jr.
Tulane University

BOOKS: *La Vie de bohème* (Paris: Dondey-Dupré, 1849);

Scènes de la vie de jeunesse (Paris: Michel Lévy frères, 1851); translated anonymously as *Life in Bohemia* (N.p.: Mossant, Vallon, 1900); translated anonymously as *Love in the Latin Quarter* (New York: Avon, 1948);

Scènes de la bohème (Paris: Michel Lévy frères, 1851); republished as *Scènes de la vie de bohème* (1852); translated by George B. Ives as *Bohemian Life* (Philadelphia: G. Barrie & Son, 1899); translated by Ellen Marriage and John Selwyn as *The Latin Quarter* (London & Glasgow: Collins Clear-Type Press, 1899);

Le Pays latin (Paris: Michel Lévy frères, 1851);

Le Bonhomme Jadis (Paris: Michel Lévy frères, 1852);

Scènes de la campagne: Adeline Protat (Paris: Michel Lévy frères, 1853);

Propos de ville et propos de théâtre (Paris: Michel Lévy frères, 1853);

Le Roman de toutes les femmes (Paris: Michel Lévy frères, 1854);

Ballades et fantaisies (Paris: Michel Lévy frères, 1854);

Les Buveurs d'eau, Scènes de la vie d'artiste (Paris: Michel Lévy frères, 1855);

Le Dessous du panier (Paris: Michel Lévy frères, 1855);

Le Dernier Rendez-vous (Paris: Michel Lévy frères, 1856);

Les Vacances de Camille, Scènes de la vie réelle (Paris: Michel Lévy frères, 1857);

Madame Olympe (Paris: Michel Lévy frères, 1859);

Le Sabot rouge (Paris: Michel Lévy frères, 1860);

Henry Murger, 1854 (photograph by Nadar)

Le Serment d'Horace (Paris: Michel Lévy frères, 1861); translated by Brander Matthews as *Cuttyback's Thunder* in *Comedies for Amateur Acting* (New York: D. Appleton, 1880);

Les Nuits d'hiver (Paris: Michel Lévy frères, 1861); translated by Arthur C. Kennedy as *Winter Nights* (London: Gowans & Gray, 1923);

Les Roueries de l'ingénue, Scènes de la vie de théâtre (Paris: Naumbourg, 1861);

Le Roman du capucin (Paris: Librairie Nouvelle, 1868).

PLAY PRODUCTIONS: *La Vie de bohème*, with Théodore Barrière, Paris, Théâtre des Variétés, 22 November 1849;

Le Bonhomme Jadis, with Michel Carré, Paris, Comédie Française, 21 April 1852;

Le Serment d'Horace, with Lambert Thiboust, Paris, Théâtre du Palais Royal, 28 November 1860.

Henry Murger was born on 27 March 1822 at 17, rue St-Georges in Paris. When the house was demolished several years later, the parents and their little son moved to what is now 61, rue Taitbout. At the new address as at the previous one, Murger's father, a tailor, served as concierge. Several famous literary, artistic, and musical personalities lived in the building, so that, while the family was not wealthy, the boy grew up in a rather cultivated atmosphere. In other respects, however, his education left a great deal to be desired. His formal schooling was lackadaisical, and he was always conscious of the fact. He never learned to punctuate correctly. At fifteen he went to work as a solicitor's clerk. Secretly, because his father disapproved, he began writing poetry. He also began to meet various young artists and writers, all hungry but ambitious bohemians.

Drawn to one another because of their similar interests and material situations, they banded together and called themselves the Buveurs d'Eau (Water Drinkers), some of the members being unable to afford to drink anything but water. Later Murger would devote a book to them. Very much at home in such company, he was to remember these young men nostalgically, writing about them over and over again, bringing them to life with their mistresses, their sorrows, and their occasional triumphs. Though not Water Drinkers, Charles Baudelaire and Gustave Courbet were soon to take their place among Murger's impecunious associates. While he had no real political views then or later, one of the men he knew and cultivated at about this time was Eugène Pottier, who was to write the lyrics to the "Internationale" (1871).

Murger was not a successful law clerk. When the solicitor for whom he worked, Cadet de Chambine, not surprisingly, dismissed him, one of the tenants on the rue Taitbout, the author Etienne de Jouy, found him another job. Thus it was that, for a time, he became the secretary of Count Jacques Tolstoy, a Russian agent. There was little work and little remuneration, with the result that the young man continued to be almost as destitute as ever. To make matters worse, his father, who did not like his friends, decided to turn him out, leaving him to live by whatever expedients he could. Now and then he shared rooms with others more or less in his own predicament. Among these chance roommates were Adrien Lelioux and Jules Husson (Champfleury).

Meanwhile, Murger had fallen in love. He was seventeen; Marie Fonblanc, a grisette (the name given, in the first half of the nineteenth century, to young working girls), was seven years older than her adolescent lover. She was also married, her spouse being a fairly successful career thief. Murger's liaison with her lasted until 1841. After their separation the lovers returned to one another several times, but nothing serious came of their reconciliations. Murger never forgot Marie, but his heart had been broken. At least the relationship netted him two charming novelettes, *Les Amours d'Olivier* (The Loves of Olivier, published in *Scènes de la vie de jeunesse*, 1851), and *Le Dernier Rendez-vous* (The Final Rendezvous, 1856), plus the poem "Chanson de Musette" (1851).

But Murger's solitude did not last. Various women came and went in the young man's life. There was an interlude, which is supposed to have been platonic, with a Danish woman who appears to have been a person of means and culture. She was blonde, and her name was Christine, but not much is known about her. The relationship was short-lived, in any case. Soon Murger was consoling himself with others. One of the most important was another grisette, Lucile Louvet. Like Marie, she had been mar-

ried. As with Marie also, the relationship was episodic, the bohemian bliss punctuated with quarrels and reconciliations. In 1847 the lovers parted, but not for long. The following winter, mortally ill with tuberculosis, Lucile Louvet turned to Murger for help. Although strapped himself, Murger took her in and cared for her. Through connections, he was able to have her admitted to La Pitié Hospital, where she died a month later.

Later, thinking about her, he grew to love her even more as he recalled their happier days. He came to love her more in retrospect than he had when they actually lived together. She was to be the principal model for Mimi in *Scènes de la bohème* (1851; translated as *Bohemian Life*, 1899). Murger has been accused of callousness toward her during her final weeks, but, having had her admitted to the hospital, he could have done little more for her than he did. Visitors were allowed only once a week, and even then he was too poor to take her flowers. When she died, he could not afford a cemetery plot, and she went to a pauper's grave. Ill himself, he went into St-Louis Hospital a short time after she died.

Lucile's last illness coincided with the Revolution of 1848. In Paris, with Louis-Philippe deposed and in flight, anarchy reigned. It was to take the Provisional Government weeks to restore a semblance of order. Getting around in the capital during the upheaval was not always easy. Moreover, at this time Murger had the chance to make a little money, some of which could be used to help the sick woman in the event she survived. Count Tolstoy asked his secretary to keep an eye on what was happening and to report events. This Murger did, attending republican clubs, observing, and making reports to his patron, who in turn passed the material on to Saint Petersburg.

After Louvet's death Murger went on to other loves; women were a necessary part of his life. That he had mistresses, that he had a whole series of them, is startling in view of his unprepossessing looks and demeanor. His precarious, erratic existence had taken its toll on his appearance. One male contemporary described him, still quite young, as short, awkward, coarse, ugly, and almost bald, with a long, unkempt beard that looked as if it had faded. Add to this that he was dirty. With women, moreover, he was shy, yet they found him attractive. He was a skilled conversationalist, and perhaps this is what won their hearts.

Whatever the case, Louvet had many successors. All were grisettes; some were seamstresses, and some made artificial flowers for a living. Sooner or later, all made their way into their lover's novels. There was a Juliette, blond and tubercular, who was followed by various others. The most important was the one who lasted, Anaïs Latrasse. Like some of her predecessors, she had been married. She became Murger's mistress around 1852, remaining her lover's companion until his death nine years later.

At thirty, if he had not exactly settled down, Murger had become a man with whom it was at least possible to live. Thanks to the success of his novels, there was also a bit of money, though not much. In 1851 he had begun writing for the influential *Revue des Deux Mondes*, where many of the novels appeared as serials before publication in book form. He also worked for the *Moniteur de la Mode* at this time and was art and drama critic for the *Artiste*. Arsène Houssaye, editor of the *Artiste*, persuaded him to start spelling his first name with a *y* instead of an *i*, since *Henry* looked more exotic than *Henri* and would be more apt to catch a reader's eye. Houssaye was less successful in getting him to put a diaeresis over the *u* in *Murger*.

Before long Murger and Anaïs were ensconced in a rather placid domestic life, dividing their time between Paris and Marlotte, a pleasant village in Fontainebleau Forest where the couple lived first at an inn and later in a house the author rented. Murger was happy and productive. He liked the rural atmosphere, and it inspired him. Anaïs's husband having ruled out the idea of a divorce, Murger could not legalize his liaison. A devoted wife in all but name, Anaïs proved to be an able ambassador between him and his publishers. It was not to last long, however. Murger's health had never been robust, and the years of chronic dissipation, poverty, and malnutrition would catch up with him, undermining what stamina remained, later. In August 1841, only nineteen, Murger had done an initial stint in a hospital; scarcely more than a year later, he was back. There would be many such visits.

Early in January 1861, he took an apartment at 16, rue Neuve-des-Martyrs, now rue Manuel. Hardly settled in, he went to work correcting the proofs for his volume of verse *Les Nuits d'hiver* (1861; translated as *Winter Nights*, 1923). Soon he began to experience violent cramps in his left leg. Several doctors agreed that the trou-

An 1856 caricature of Murger by Etienne Carjat

ble was arteritis, which would soon be complicated by purpura, and ordered him back to the hospital. This time it was to the Maison Dubois, where he checked in on 26 January. Word quickly spread that the famous author was desperately ill. During the next two days, racked with pain and hallucinating, he received many callers, one of them an emissary from Count Alexandre Walewski, minister of fine arts. Not quite thirty-nine but prematurely aged, he died on 28 January.

The funeral, paid for by the government, took place three days later and was attended by several thousand mourners, including several members of the French Academy. Michel Lévy, the deceased's publisher, had already distributed advance copies of *Les Nuits d'hiver* to the important critics, thus insuring that each obituary would be at once a death notice and, in all likelihood, a highly favorable review. Murger was buried in Montmartre Cemetery. On the tombstone that was eventually erected stands a woman's figure, for which Mariette Roux, the Musette of *Scènes de la bohème*, is said to have posed. A bust was placed in the Luxembourg Gardens in 1895.

As for Anaïs Latrasse, the photographer Nadar raised enough money for her to open an antique shop on rue Taitbout, where her lover had spent his boyhood. She lived on until 1917, dying at the age of ninety.

Murger's elaborate funeral and the huge crowds attending it are indicative of the place this writer occupied in French literature at the time he died, although posterity has not ratified the enthusiasm he aroused in his contemporaries. Murger had come a long way, but he had not gone as far as he would have liked. His beginnings had been difficult. Because of his parents' scant resources, he had to go to work early. As a result, his education suffered, an obstacle he was never able to overcome. Moreover, because he knew no other social milieus at close hand, he had no choice but to write about the band of poor but determined young men, all committed to one of the arts, among whom he had been forced to live. And, of course, he wrote about the unassuming, sometimes devoted working-class girls who intermittently shared their lives until one of the parties cast the other aside and went on to other things.

While these people furnished him his material, Murger did not really like living among them and aspired to more elevated social circles. As soon as he had scored his first theatrical success, he moved to the Paris Right Bank. Here and there *Scènes de la bohème* and *Scènes de la vie de jeunesse* (translated as *Life in Bohemia*, 1900) contain harsh words aimed at the Water Drinkers. His early newspaper articles now and then derided socialism and its proponents, not to mention those whose lot socialism might have alleviated. Still, had Murger ever achieved genuine material success and established himself in an easier, prettier world, it would have ruined him as an author, leaving him nothing to write about. Bohemians he knew; the middle classes and the aristocracy he did not really understand.

As was the case with Théophile Gautier and so many other contemporaries, journalism proved to be Murger's basic means of support. Writing for newspapers and magazines helped make it possible for the author to break into creative writing. Early on he contributed poems and a whimsical tale, "Les Amours d'un grillon et d'une étincelle" (The Loves of a Cricket and a Spark, 1845), to the *Moniteur*. With this delightful story he discovered that he was a better prose writer than he was a poet. Most of his short stories, novelettes, and novels initially appeared in

periodicals. One of the first periodicals with which he was associated was the *Corsaire*, for which he wrote "Un Envoyé de la providence" (1845-1849). It was to be the second of the *Scènes de la bohème*.

With the *Comédie humaine*, Honoré de Balzac had popularized "scenes" in French literature. Alfred Assollant, Octave Feuillet, and other novelists continued to use the term and exploit the idea. Murger, along with the others, used the term and idea, but with a difference. Each of the "scenes" in his novels is generally self-contained and can easily stand alone as a short story or novella. Murger's first collection of this kind was *Scènes de la vie de jeunesse*. The most memorable of these "scenes" probably is the novelette *Le Bonhomme Jadis*, a sentimental look at the bohemian world the author was striving to put behind him. Both the book and the novelette were an instant success.

Houssaye, Murger's former editor at the *Artiste*, had become the director of the Comédie Française. Impressed with *Le Bonhomme Jadis*, he urged his young protégé and friend to turn it into a one-act comedy. Murger acted on the suggestion and, with Michel Carré, converted his novella into an entertaining curtain raiser that, on occasion, can still be seen at the Comédie Française. With an outstanding cast, it was first produced there on 21 April 1852. Gautier thought it superb. Another novella in *Scènes de la vie de jeunesse* is *Les Amours d'Olivier*, in which the author recounted his liaison with Marie Fonblanc. *Le Dernier Rendez-vous*, which narrates the final episode, was written in 1851. It appeared in the *Revue des Deux Mondes* in 1852 and was published as a book in 1856.

Claude et Marianne came out in installments in the *Revue des Deux Mondes* in 1851. Later Murger published it as a volume, changing its title to *Le Pays latin* (The Latin Quarter, 1851), though it is generally referred to as *Claude et Marianne*. *Scènes de la campagne: Adeline Protat* (Country Life Scenes: Adeline Protat) ran as a *Revue des Deux Mondes* serial in 1852, appearing in book form in 1853. It is the story of a painter named Lazare who, with his dog, lives in Fontainebleau Forest, where he falls in love with a local girl, the innkeeper's daughter. Thinly disguised, the characters are Murger, Anaïs, and one of their pets, all in their rural paradise at Marlotte. At about the same time Murger published *Propos de ville et propos de théâtre* (Town Talk and Theater Talk, 1853), a series of comic anecdotes and silhouettes treating the social, literary, and theatrical worlds. Most of the material had appeared earlier in the *Corsaire.*

Murger's next book was *Le Roman de toutes les femmes* (Every Woman's Novel, 1854). With this novella the author included several others: *Stella, Margareth, Le Mausolée* (The Mausoleum), and *Le Stabat Mater.* All had been written about a decade earlier and show the still obscure young author imagining a series of rich, aristocratic characters, denizens of a world he beheld only at a great distance. Though not typical of his work, the stories have an undeniable charm. Next came *Les Buveurs d'eau,* subtitled *Scènes de la vie d'artiste* (Scenes of the Artistic Life). As so often happened, it appeared piecemeal in the *Revue des Deux Mondes* (1853 and 1854), then in book form a little later (1855). It deals with the adventures of the young bohemians among whom the author moved while doing his literary apprenticeship.

After this, tireless and needing money as much as ever, Murger published *Le Dessous du panier* (The Bottom of the Basket, 1855), perhaps his least-known novel. *Le Dernier Rendez-vous,* the sequel to *Les Amours d'Olivier,* was another matter and an instant success. As usual, readers saw it first in the *Revue des Deux Mondes* (1852), although *Les Amours d'Olivier* had come out in the *Evénement. Les Vacances de Camille, Scènes de la vie réelle* (Camille's Holiday, Scenes from Real Life), Murger's most personal novel and one of his most successful, appeared in the *Revue des Deux Mondes* from 15 April 1857 to 1 June 1857, followed by volume publication later the same year.

Not surprisingly, Camille and Théodore, a painter, look very much like Anaïs Latrasse and Henry Murger. Several scenes in the country, particularly well executed, bear witness to the author's continuing attraction to rustic life. Murger's liaison with his mistress was by now well established, and it shows in Camille, the writer's most devoted heroine. When the author died, he had started work, with Paul Siraudin, on a dramatic adaptation of the novel.

Madame Olympe (1859), although readable and entertaining, added little to his stature as a man of letters. In 1860 he offered his public *Le Sabot rouge* (The Red Horseshoe), which had come out in installments in the *Moniteur.* It is a story about avarice, lechery, and murder, and the characters, realistically portrayed, are remarkably credible. Psychologically, the novel shows the author at his best. Once more the action takes place in Fontainebleau Forest, where villagers gather at an inn called Le Sabot rouge. This was the last novel Murger completed. After his death Houssaye published *Les Roueries de l'ingénue, Scènes de la vie de théâtre* (The Ingenue's Tricks, Scenes from Theater Life, 1861). Left unfinished, it was probably completed by Houssaye, who also wrote the introduction. In 1868 another novel appeared, *Le Roman du capucin* (The Capuchin's Novel). Set in Italy, it deals with thwarted love ending in suicide and is narrated by a kindly monk experienced in matters of the heart. Before book publication, the story ran as a serial in the *Figaro* from 27 September 1868 to 23 October 1868.

Murger had brought out *Ballades et fantaisies* in 1854. Some of his poems are in prose, making him, along with Aloysius Bertrand, Maurice de Guérin, and Baudelaire, one of the prose poem's early practitioners. His last contribution to the *Revue des Deux Mondes* (1 January 1860) was a prophetic poem, "La Ballade du désespéré" (The Ballad of the Despairing Man), in which Death knocks at the writer's door, and the visitor calls out:

Ouvre, j'apporte
Pour tous les maux la guérison.

(Open up. For all ills
I bring the cure).

Weary of life, the poet invites his guest in, telling him that he has been expected. Following Murger's death a year later, the poem appeared again, the last piece in *Les Nuits d'hiver,* for which Murger had been correcting the proofs when he died. This collection, which does not contain all of his poetry, is a selection of verse written at different times, some of the items going back to when he was eighteen and experiencing the pangs of first love. The poetry is fairly good but demonstrates that Murger had been right in deciding that prose was his real medium. Included in the volume is the delightful "Chanson de Musette."

Quickly set to music, the "Chanson de Musette" had appeared elsewhere. Readers had seen it in the book for which Murger is chiefly remembered, *Scènes de la bohème.* While at the *Corsaire,* Murger had written a piece called "Un Envoyé de la providence." This sketch, concentrating on Marcel, a starveling painter, and Schaunard, an equally penniless composer, appeared on 9 March 1845. Readers had to wait until 6 March

Mariette Roux (seated), the model for Musette in Scènes de la vie de bohème, *with her sister (photograph by Nadar)*

1846 for the second episode. The third came out on 9 July of the same year. The episodes were popular, and after that they became more frequent. The last one dates from 21 April 1849.

Meanwhile, new characters were added. Rodolphe, a poet, made his appearance, as did Francine, Mimi, Musette, and others. For the most part, the men, all poor at first, were students, artists, or writers. The women, all grisettes, some tender and appealing, some pert and impudent, were working girls or artists' models. The characters' love involvements were casual, their adventures episodic, their psychology superficial. There was sentiment and even pathos, but except for the death of Mimi, Rodolphe's tubercular little mistress, most of the action was comic, though not without an occasional spurt of realism. The world in which these people lived was not new, according to the author. In Paris it was at least as old as François Villon and Pierre Gringore, who had moved about in it too.

It was some time before it occurred to Murger to do anything more with the "scenes"

he had written. Then one of his readers, a minor dramatist named Théodore Barrière, sensing that they had dramatic potential, approached Murger with the idea of collaborating on a play based on his sketches. Together the two men hammered out *La Vie de bohème* (Bohemian Life), which was staged at the Théâtre des Variétés on 22 November 1849. Prince Louis-Napoleon Bonaparte was in the audience, as were Gautier, Théodore de Banville, Jules Janin, and a host of other literary personalities. The play was a hit, and Murger was a celebrity.

Deciding to assemble the *Corsaire* sketches in a volume, he wrote a preface for it and produced the novel, if it can be called that, on which his fame principally rests. Published by Michel Lévy in 1851, it ran through numerous editions. Initially, Murger called it *Scènes de la bohème* (Scenes of Bohemia) but quickly changed his mind. From 1852 onward, its title was *Scènes de la vie de bohème*. It kept its enthusiastic reading public to the end of the century. Though that public dwindled, there were many editions until the middle of the twentieth century. In February 1893 two Milan newspapers announced that Giacomo Puccini and Ruggiero Leoncavallo were each writing operas based on it. Puccini's *La Bohème* was the first to be staged (Turin, 1 February 1896). Leoncavallo's had its premiere in Venice on 6 May 1897. It was successful enough at first but lost ground as Puccini's version slowly won the hearts of operagoers. Puccini and his librettists chose to emphasize Mimi's pathetic death, which has made people unfamiliar with the novel assume that Murger's work is uniformly tragic, instead of being the generally carefree series of episodes that it really is.

La Vie de bohème was not Murger's sole theatrical venture. *Le Serment d'Horace*, a clever one-act vaudeville written in collaboration with Lambert Thiboust, opened at the Théâtre du Palais Royal on 28 November 1860, shortly before the author's death, and was enthusiastically received. When Murger died, he had written one act of a play he intended to call "Scènes de la vie d'artiste" (Scenes of the Artistic Life). In addition, there was a melodrama with a plot that combined *Adeline Protat* and *Le Sabot rouge*. It was to be called "Les Paysans" and had already been conditionally accepted at the Théâtre de la Gaîté. Other plays, neither performed nor published, include "Pipelet et Cabrion."

Not all of Murger's work has been collected or published. In addition to the plays listed above, several other works were left unfinished. The *Figaro* listed some of them at the time of the author's death. Nadar and his collaborators printed selections from the correspondence, but not all of it, in their *Histoire de Murger* (1861). Not all of the plays appeared in the so-called *Œuvres complètes*, a designation that Michel Lévy frères gave new editions of his works. *Les Nuits d'hiver* contains only a sampling of the poetry, some of which remains unpublished. Regrettably, Murger's art and drama criticism has never been collected either and lies buried in the pages of the *Artiste*.

By the time he died, Murger was virtually a public figure. Readers, including the waifs he immortalized, adored him, and most of his fellow writers held him in considerable esteem. To contemporary readers he seems dated, however. Those who people his fictional world are no longer of much interest. Nowadays—art having become a brisk business with no room in it for dreamers turning out art for art's sake—those struggling to survive in the art world, however

Victor Massé, Charles-Augustin Sainte-Beuve, Jules-Amédée Barbey d'Aurevilly, Murger, and Charles Baudelaire, in a detail from the painting Panorama *(1889), by Alfred Stevens and Henri Gervex (from Catherine Boschian-Campaner, Barbey d'Aurevilly, 1989)*

picturesque, have lost their appeal. Moreover, just as the situations in which they are presented lack variety, there is a certain sameness in the bohemians Murger portrayed. What they do not lack, though, is spontaneity. In the midst of woes they realize they must take in stride, the characters in Murger's work manage to be lighthearted, witty, and entertaining. Jules and Edmond de Goncourt might scoff, but this is all most contemporaries demanded. Murger even had his imitators, such as Henri Perron d'Arc.

In short, to the general reader and even to the cultivated one, Murger was a great man, universally acclaimed. Important writers such as Victor Hugo and Gautier admired him. A member of the Société des Gens de Lettres, Murger, had he lived, would almost certainly have been elected to the Académie Française. As early as 1856 he inspired a biography. Adding its admiration to that of the public, the government awarded him the Legion of Honor and gave him a sumptuous funeral. The *Figaro* devoted several articles to him at the time of his death, noting the luminaries who attended the funeral and those who contributed to the cost of erecting a monument over his grave. Later that same year an article was devoted to him in the important *Nouvelle Biographie générale*.

Letters:

Adrien Leliou, Félix Tournachon (Nadar), and Léon Noël, *Histoire de Murger* (Paris: Hetzel, 1861);

Gabriel Clouzet, "Lettres inédites d'Henry Murger," *Figaro*, 4 March 1911.

Bibliography:

Peter J. Edwards, "La Revue *L'Artiste* (1831-1904). Notice bibliographique," *Romantisme*, 67 (First Trimester 1990): 110-118.

Biographies:

Eugène de Mirecourt, *Henry Murger* (Paris: Havard, 1856);

Adrien Leliou, Félix Tournachon (Nadar), and Léon Noël, *Histoire de Murger* (Paris: Hetzel, 1861);

Georges Montorgueil, *Henry Murger, romancier de la bohème* (Paris: Bernard Grasset, 1928);

Robert Baldick, *The First Bohemian: The Life of Henry Murger* (London: Hamish Hamilton, 1961).

References:

Marius Boisson, *Les Compagnons de la vie de bohème* (Paris: Tallandier, 1929);

Alfred Delvau, *Henry Murger et la bohème* (Paris: Bachelin-Delflorenne, 1866);

Claude Foucart, "De la conversation romanesque à l'air d'opéra," in *Oper als Text*, edited by Albert Gier (Heidelberg: Carl Winter, 1986), pp. 277-287;

B. Mirekine-Guetzévitch, "Henry Murger agent secret de la Russie pendant la Révolution de 48," *Nouvelles Littéraires*, 12 November 1927;

Arthur Moss and Evalyn Marvel, *The Legend of the Latin Quarter* (New York: Beechhurst Press, 1947);

Marie-Louise Pailleron, *François Buloz et ses amis* (Paris: Calmann-Lévy, 1920);

Charles de Ricault d'Héricault, *Murger et son coin* (Paris: Trémaux, 1896);

André Warnod, *La Vraie Bohème de Henry Murger* (Paris: Dupont, 1947).

Charles Nodier
(29 April 1780 - 27 January 1844)

Grant Crichfield
University of Vermont

SELECTED BOOKS: *Discours prononcé à la Société des Amis de la Constitution de Besançon, le 22 décembre 1791* (Besançon: Simard, 1791);

Discours de M. Nodier fils, âgé de douze ans, prononcé à la Société des Amis de la Constitution, séante à Besançon lors de sa réception (Besançon: Simard, 1792);

Dissertation sur l'usage des antennes dans les insectes, et sur l'organe de l'ouïe dans les mêmes animaux, by Nodier and F. M. J. Luczot (Besançon: Briot, 1798);

Charles Nodier à ses concitoyens (Besançon, 1800);

Bibliographie entomologique, ou catalogue raisonné des ouvrages relatifs à l'entomologie et aux insectes, avec des notes critiques et l'exposition des méthodes (Paris: Moutardier, 1801);

Pensées de Shakespeare, extraites de ses ouvrages (Besançon: Métoyer, 1801);

Les Proscrits (Paris: Lepetit et Gérard, 1802); revised and enlarged as *Stella, ou les Proscrits, suivi de la Lettre d'un solitaire des Vosges, de la Filleule du Seigneur, de la Vision, et de Fanchette* (Paris: Gide, 1808); revised and enlarged as *Stella, ou les Proscrits* (Paris: Gide, 1820);

La Napoléone (Paris: Février, 1802);

Le Dernier Chapitre de mon roman (Paris: Cavanagh, 1803);

Le Peintre de Saltzbourg, journal des émotions d'un cœur souffrant (Paris: Maradan, 1803; revised and enlarged edition, Paris: Gide, 1820);

Essais d'un jeune barde (Paris: Cavanagh, 1804);

Prophétie contre Albion (Paris: Cavanagh, 1804);

Les Tristes, ou Mélanges tirés des tablettes d'un suicide (Paris: Démonville, 1806);

Dictionnaire raisonné des onomatopées françaises (Paris: Démonville, 1808; revised and enlarged edition, Paris: Delangle, 1828);

Archéologue ou système universel et raisonné des langues. Prolégomènes (Paris: Didot, 1810);

Questions de littérature légale. Du plagiat, de la supposition d'auteurs, des supercheries qui ont rapport aux livres. Ouvrage qui peut servir de suite au dictionnaire des anonymes et à toutes les bibliogra-

Charles Nodier (portrait attributed to Joseph Franque; Musée de Besançon)

phies (Paris: Barba, 1812; revised and enlarged edition, Paris: Crapelet, 1828);

Dictionnaire de la langue écrite, ACC (Paris: Crouillebois, 1813);

Histoires des sociétés secrètes de l'armée, et des conspirations militaires qui ont eu pour objet la destruction du gouvernement de Bonaparte, anonymous (Paris: Gide, 1815); translated as *History of the Secret Societies of the Army: and of the Military Conspiracies Which Had for Their Object the Destruction of the Government of Napoleon* (London: Longman, Hurst, Rees, Orme & Brown, 1815); translated as *History of the Secret Societies of the Army,* introduction by Charles M. Lombard (Delmar, N.Y.: Scholars Facsimiles & Reprints, 1978);

Le Vingt-et-un janvier (Paris: Le Normant, 1816);

215

Des Exilés (Paris: Gide, 1818);

Jean Sbogar, 2 volumes, anonymous (Paris: Gide, 1818; revised and enlarged, 1820); translated by Percival Gordon [Peter Irving] as *Giovanni Sbogarro. A Venetian Tale*, 2 volumes (New York: C. S. Van Winkle, 1820);

Thérèse Aubert (Paris: Ladvocat, 1819);

Adèle (Paris: Gide, 1820);

Le Vampire, mélodrame en trois actes, by Nodier, Carmouche, and Jouffroy (Paris: Barba, 1820);

Mélanges de littérature et de critique, 2 volumes (Paris: Raymond, 1820);

Voyages pittoresques et romantiques dans l'ancienne France, 12 volumes, by Nodier, J. Taylor, and Alphonse de Cailleux (Paris: Didot, Gide, 1820-1846);

Promenade de Dieppe aux montagnes d'Ecosse (Paris: Barba, 1821); translated as *Promenade from Dieppe to the Mountains of Scotland* (Edinburgh: W. Blackwood / London: T. Cadell, 1822);

Smarra, ou Les démons de la nuit, songes romantiques, traduit de l'esclavon du comte Maxime Odin (Paris: Ponthieu, 1821);

Trilby, ou le Lutin d'Argail. Nouvelle écossaise (Paris: Ladvocat, 1822); translated as *Trilby, The Fairy of Argyle*, with introduction by Nathan Haskell Dole (Boston: Estes & Lauriat, 1895);

Infernalia, anonymous (Paris: Sanson, Nadau, 1822);

Essai critique sur le gaz hydrogène et les divers modes d'éclairage artificiel, by Nodier and Amédée Pichot (Paris: Gosselin, Ladvocat, Ponthieu, 1823);

Dictionnaire universel de la langue française, 2 volumes, by Nodier and V. Verger (Paris: Belin-Mander, 1823);

Bibliothèque sacrée grecque-latine (Paris: Thoisnier-Desplaces, 1826);

Catalogue d'une partie de livres rares, singuliers et précieux dépendant de la bibliothèque de M. Charles Nodier (Paris: Merlin, 1827);

Poésies diverses (Paris: Delangle, 1827);

Examen critique des dictionnaires de la langue française, ou Recherches grammaticales et littéraires sur l'orthographe, l'acception, la définition et l'étymologie des mots (Paris: Delangle, 1829 [1828]);

Mélanges tirés d'une petite bibliothèque, ou Variétés littéraires et philosophiques (Paris: Crapelet, 1829);

Histoire du roi de Bohême et de ses sept châteaux, suivie de Les Aveugles de Chamouny et de L'Histoire du chien de Brisquet (Paris: Delangle,

1830); republished as *Les Sept Châteaux du roi de Bohême. Les Quatre Talismans* (Paris: Lecou, 1852);

Souvenirs, épisodes et portraits pour servir à l'histoire de la Révolution et de l'Empire, 2 volumes (Paris: Levavasseur, 1831);

Œuvres complètes, 6 volumes (Paris: Renduel, 1832)—volume 1 comprises *Jean Sbogar*; volume 2 comprises *Le Peintre de Saltzbourg*; *Le Suicide et les pèlerins*; *Les Méditations du cloître*; *Adèle*; *Thérèse Aubert*; volume 3 comprises *Smarra*; *Note sur le rhombus*; *Le Bey Spalatin*; *La Femme d'Asan*; *La Luciole*; *Trilby*; *La Filleule du Seigneur*; *Une Heure, ou La Vision*; *Le Tombeau des grèves du lac*; *Sanchette, ou Le Laurier-rose*; *Histoire d'Hélène Gillet*; volume 4 comprises *La Fée aux miettes*; *Le Dernier Chapitre de mon roman*; volume 5 comprises *Rêveries* (*Miscellanées*; *Des types en littérature*; *Du fantastique en littérature*; *De l'amour et de son influence*; *De quelques phénomènes du sommeil*; *M. de La Mettrie, ou les superstitions*; *De la perfectibilité de l'homme et de l'influence de l'imprimerie sur la civilisation*; *De l'utilité morale de l'instruction pour le peuple*; *De la fin prochaine du genre humain*; *De la palingénésie humaine et de la résurrection*); volume 6 comprises *Mademoiselle de Marsan*; *Le Nouveau Faust et la nouvelle Marguerite*; *Le Songe d'or*;

Souvenirs de jeunesse, extraits des Mémoires de Maxime Odin (Paris: Levavasseur, 1832);

Œuvres complètes, volumes 7 and 8 (Paris: Renduel, 1833)—volume 7 comprises *Le Dernier Banquet des Girondins*; *Recherches sur l'éloquence révolutionnaire*; volume 8 comprises *Souvenirs et portraits: Souvenirs* (*Euloge Schneider*; *De la réaction thermidorienne, et des compagnies de Jéhu*; *De la maçonnerie et du carbonarisme*; *Les Prisons de Paris sous le Consulat*); *Portraits* (*Les Colonels Founier et Foy*; *Le Général Malet*; *Le Colonel Oudet*);

Examen critique par M. Ch. Nodier, des lettres à Julie sur l'entomologie par M. E. Mulsant (Paris: Méquignon-Marvis, 1833);

Littérature du Moyen-Age. Notice sur le Romancero français (Paris: de Brun, 1833);

Œuvres complètes de Charles Nodier, volumes 10 and 12 (Paris: Renduel, 1834)—volume 10 comprises *Souvenirs de jeunesse* (*Séraphine*; *Thérèse*; *Clémentine*; *Amélie*; *Lucrèce et Jeannette*); volume 12 comprises *Notions élémentaires de linguistique, ou Histoire abrégée de la parole et de l'écriture, pour servir d'introduction à l'alphabet, à la grammaire et au dictionnaire*;

Discours prononcés dans la séance publique tenue à l'Académie française pour la réception de M. Charles Nodier, le 26 décembre 1833 (Paris: Didot, 1834);

Recueil de notices bibliographiques, philologiques et littéraires par Charles Nodier (Paris: Techener, 1834-1835);

Institut royal de France. Discours prononcé, au nom de l'Académie française, par M. Ch. Nodier; le 23 août 1835, jour de l'inauguration de la statue de Cuvier, à Montbéliard (Paris: Didot, 1835);

La Seine et ses bords (Paris: Everat, 1836);

Vocabulaire de la langue française, extrait de la dernière édition du Dictionnaire de L'Académie, publié en 1835, by Nodier and M. Ackermann (Paris: Didot, 1836);

Une Corbeille de rognures, ou Feuillets arrachés d'un livre sans titre (Paris: Tournai, 1836);

Inès de Las Sierras (Paris: Dumont, 1837);

Veillées de famille. Contes instructifs et proverbes moraux en français, en italien, en anglais et en allemand. Ouvrage nouveau à l'usage de la jeunesse de tous les pays, by Nodier and Michaud, 2 volumes (Paris: Allardin, 1837);

Œuvres complètes, volume 11 (Paris: Renduel, 1837)—comprises *Contes en prose* (*Polichinelle*; *Le Bibliomane*, translated by Mabel Osgood Wright as *The Bibliomaniac* [New York: J. O. Wright, 1894]; *Voyage de Kaout' t' chouck*; *Sibylle Mérian*; *Lidivine*; *Baptiste Montauban*; *Jean-François les Bas-bleus*; *Piranèse*; *Les Fiancés*; *La Combe de l'homme mort*; *Paul ou la ressemblance*; *Trésor des Fèves et Fleur des Pois*, translated as *Bean Flower and Pea Blossom* [London: Chapman & Hall, 1846; New York: D. Appleton, 1852]; *Le Génie bonhomme*, translated as *Genius Goodfellow*, with *The Wood Cutter's Dog* [London: Chapman, 1846; New York: D. Appleton, 1852]; *L'Homme et la fourmi*); and *Contes en vers* (*Le Trésor ou les trois hommes*; *Le Courrier de Potemkin*; *Les Furies et les Grâces*; *Babouk ou l'homme heureux*; *Retirez-vous de mon soleil*; *Dioclétien*; *Le Fou de Pirée*; *Le Poète et le mendiant*; *L'Inscription*; *Un Mot de César*; *L'Ambre*; *Le Bengali*; *L'Elu et le damné*; *Epilogue*);

Les Quatre Talismans, conte raisonnable, suivi de La Légende de sœur Béatrix (Paris: Dumont, 1838);

La Neuvaine de la Chandeleur et Lydie (Paris: Didot, 1839);

Œuvres complètes, volume 9 (Paris: Magen et Comon, 1841)—comprises *Souvenirs* (*Charlotte Corday*; *Saint-Just et Pichegru*; *Suites d'un mandat d'arrêt*); *Portraits* (*Pichegru*; *Réal*; *Fouché*);

Journal de l'expédition des Portes de Fer (Paris: Imprimerie royale, 1844);

Description raisonnée d'une jolie collection de livres (Nouveaux mélanges tirés d'une petite bibliothèque) (Paris: Techener, 1844);

Franciscus Columna (Paris: Techener, Paulin, 1844); translated by Theodore Wesley Koch as *Francesco Colonna: A Fanciful Tale of the Writing of the Hypnerotomachia* (Chicago: R. R. Donnelly, 1929);

Souvenirs de la Révolution et de l'Empire, 2 volumes (Paris: Charpentier, 1850).

Editions and Collections: *Contes fantastiques* (Paris: Charpentier, 1850);

Romans (Paris: Charpentier, 1850);

Souvenirs de jeunesse (Paris: Charpentier, 1850);

Contes de la veillée (Paris: Charpentier, 1853);

Nouvelles, suivies des Fantaisies du dériseur sensé (Paris: Charpentier, 1853);

Moi-même. Roman qui n'en est pas un, tiré de mon portefeuille gris-de-lin. Pour servir de suite et de complément à toutes les platitudes littéraires du dix-huitième siècle, edited, with an introduction, by Jean Larat (Paris: Champion, 1921);

Contes, edited, with an introduction, by Pierre-Georges Castex (Paris: Garnier, 1961);

Œuvres complètes, 12 volumes (Geneva: Slatkine, 1968);

Une Œuvre méconnue de Charles Nodier: Faust imité de Goethe, edited, with an introduction, by Ginette Picat-Guinoiseau (Paris: Didier, 1977);

La Fièvre et autres contes, edited by Jacques-Remi Dahan, postface by Jean-Luc Steinmetz (Langres & Lille: L'Homme au Sable/Thierry Bouchard, 1986);

Cours de belles-lettres, tenu à Dole de juillet 1808 à avril 1809, edited, with an introduction, by Annie Barraux (Geneva: Droz, 1988).

OTHER: Jean-Baptiste François Xavier Cousin de Grainville, *Le Dernier Homme, ouvrage posthume*, 2 volumes, edited, with an introduction, by Nodier (Paris: Ferraaîné et Deterville, 1811);

Jean de la Fontaine, *Fables de La Fontaine, avec un nouveau commentaire littéraire et grammatical*, 2 volumes, commentary by Nodier (Paris: Eymery, 1818);

Cyprien Bérard, *Lord Ruthwen, ou les Vampires*, 2 volumes, introduction by Nodier (Paris: Ladvocat, 1820).

TRANSLATIONS: Lady Mary Hamilton, *La Famille du duc de Popoli. Mémoires de M. de Can-*

telmo son frère, 2 volumes, translated by Nodier (Paris: P. Didot l'aîné, 1810);

Hamilton, *Le Village de Munster*, translated by Nodier (Paris: A. A. Renouard, 1811);

Hamilton, *Auguste et Jules de Popoli, suite des Mémoires de M. de Cantelmo*, 2 volumes, translated
by Nodier (Paris: A. A. Renouard, 1812);

Charles Robert Maturin, *Bertram, ou Le Château de
Saint-Aldobrand*, translated by Nodier and J.
Taylor (Paris: Gide, Ladvocat, 1821);

John Tobin, *Lune de miel*, translated by Nodier in
Chefs d'œuvre des théâtres étrangers, volume 1
(Paris: Rapilly, 1827);

Oliver Goldsmith, *Le Vicaire de Wakefield*, translated by Nodier (Paris: Bourgueleret, 1838).

Contradiction is a term that characterizes
not only Charles Nodier's personality but also his
oeuvre, philosophy, politics, and, ultimately, his
place in the French canon. On the one hand, he
was a man born of the Enlightenment; his lifelong work on botany, entomology, linguistics,
and dictionaries exemplifies his appreciation, pursuit, and advancement of learning based on the
tradition of eighteenth-century philosophical and
scientific inquiry. One of his foremost concerns
was the organization of knowledge in order to
make it more accessible. His bibliophilia was
founded on this interest; his lexicons also illustrate it, as do his insect collections and his profession as a librarian.

But, on the other hand, this was a person
who often railed at the notion that positivistic science could explain the mysterious, spiritual dimension of human experience or provide satisfactory
answers to the deepest human fears and questions about the unknown. In his fantastic texts
and in some essays, he proposes that only spiritual transformation through the imagination and
its dreams, and ultimately its art, can reveal hidden truths and lead to inner fulfillment. Some aspects of Nodier's reputation reflect these apparent dichotomies. While his endeavors on the
dictionary of the Académie française and on linguistic topics, such as onomatopoeia or a theory
of natural language, were cornerstones of his prestige during his lifetime, they are now often considered to have only historic interest. And while
some elements of his literary production, such as
La Fée aux miettes (The Crumb Fairy, 1832), went
unnoticed by his contemporaries and others,
such as *Histoire du roi de Bohême et de ses sept
châteaux* (The Story of the King of Bohemia and
His Seven Châteaus, 1830), were virtually forgot-

ten for a century or more after their first publication, they have been rediscovered by modern literary theoreticians and are now the focal point of a
renewed critical interest in his entire production.

Much of Nodier's authority with his contemporaries rested on his proposals for a new literature that would reject the hallowed tenets of neoclassicism and open itself to fresh content and
form in order to be able to reflect the mentalities
and realities of postrevolutionary France. Although he never produced a work considered to
be a great literary masterpiece, he is nevertheless
recognized as a writer and thinker whose texts
were not only sometimes popular, but also, more
importantly, influential and forerunners of much
that was to come in the nineteenth and twentieth
centuries. As early as 1800, Nodier played a role
in the introduction of romanticism into France,
and he became the leader of the new movement
by the 1820s. He championed ideas and writers
from abroad, especially Germany and England,
and even Illyria; he was among the earliest
French proponents of William Shakespeare, Sir
Walter Scott, and, later, Slavic literature. Like
Germaine de Staël, he promoted a literature
based on current concerns and problems. This
meant, for example, the inclusion of subjects
from foreign and also national traditions beyond
classicism, the recognition of the glories of the
texts and monuments of the Middle Ages and
the Renaissance, the inclusion of Christian values
and themes, and the development of regional
and historical specificity. A leader of the new
movement by his ability to present novel ideas convincingly, he gathered around him, and often
helped, other artists and thinkers at the brilliant
salon he held at the Bibliothèque de l'Arsenal,
which became, for a while, the center of the
French Romantic school.

At the core of Nodier's philosophy, aesthetics, and fiction is the notion of the imagination.
Throughout his work, he stresses the fundamental importance of dreams and the fantastic to psychic well-being. In his fiction he tries to imitate
the qualities and effects of these elements, both
agreeable and nightmarish, through innovations
in content and form. He created texts that rede-
fine space and time, that are structured on digres-
sion, free association, lack of sequence, irony,
and verbal invention. Well ahead of the Symbolists, Sigmund Freud, and the Surrealists, Nodier
attempted to explore the inner, unconscious life
of the individual. These texts were also an expression of his philosophical and religious ideas, built

Nodier pictured at his favorite pastime (lithograph by Tony Johannot). In 1844 an anonymous critic for the Siècle *dubbed him "the Don Juan of bibliomania."*

on palingenetic concepts of illumination and passage to superior levels of inner awareness, integration, and ecstasy. Nodier, then, reinvigorated the *conte fantastique* (fantastic short story) by giving it a philosophical and psychological orientation. Through both form and content, Nodier set the stage for writers such as Gérard de Nerval, Guy de Maupassant, Théophile Gautier, Arthur Rimbaud, Lautréamont (Isidore Ducasse), and André Breton.

But Nodier's political views often seemed opposed to his aesthetic program, and this contrast affected his role in a Romantic movement that considered itself to be closely allied to politics. In this regard, and like many people of his own time and others in similar circumstances, Nodier underwent a thorough change—nearly an about-face—between his youth and his middle years. He shifted from adolescent Jacobin to active anti-Jacobin, then to anti-Bonapartist jailed for his writings, and by his early thirties he became a functionary of the empire and an editor of one of its official organs, the *Télégraphe Officiel*. With the fall of Napoleon, he claimed to have been a royalist all along, sought and received letters of nobil-

ity, and managed to secure favorable positions throughout the Restoration. In 1830, again in trouble with the authorities for his political texts, he was saved by the revolution of that summer and remained in favor through the July Monarchy until his death.

Some accused him of lacking genuine politics beyond self-interest; others claimed he was naive or, worse, a hypocrite, a person willing to change historical fact for personal gain. However, after his period as a young revolutionary, he clearly became very much the ultraroyalist. His conservatism was based on the feeling that a constitutional monarchy was a great advance over the absolute rule of the old regime and that only it, allied with the Church, could guarantee order, human dignity, prosperity, liberty, and an improvement in the arts. But, at the same time, in his aesthetics he advocated a very liberal opening toward innovative conventions and themes to create a literature that would mirror new social realities. Many viewed such stances as conflicting; his literary contemporaries often saw romanticism as a kind of liberalism in the arts that could be reflected only by liberal politics. Differences such as these were partly to blame for Nodier's estrangement from Victor Hugo and, by 1830, for Nodier's loss to him as chief of the Romantics. While Nodier was, and remains, a multifaceted, often enigmatic figure, he was and continues to be a "legend" because of his originality and his influence on the course of French thought and literature.

Jean Charles Emmanuel Nodier was born in Besançon on 29 April 1780 to Suzanne Paris and Antoine Melchior Nodier. As children, Charles and his only sibling, Elise, born in 1784, lived with their mother in Poligny while their father practiced law in Besançon during the week and joined them on weekends and holidays. On 12 September 1791, two weeks after giving up his post as mayor of Besançon to become president of the Département du Doubs, Antoine legally married Suzanne, formerly his housekeeper, thereby legitimizing Charles and Elise. The family's heretofore clandestine existence ended with the parents' marriage. After the death of Antoine's mother, the Nodiers occupied her house at 11 rue Neuve (now rue Charles Nodier) in Besançon.

The young Charles resented being left with his mother, whom he resembled physically but disliked strongly, and missed his father, whom he adored. Suzanne was reputed (some say unjustly) to be cold, brusque, stingy, illiterate, and fanatical. Charles probably inherited from her not only his physical features, but also a predisposition to Addison's disease, which would explain the abnormal skin pigmentation that they shared. The weakness, rapid fatigue, irritability, nervousness, gastrointestinal upsets, and hypoglycemia that plagued Charles throughout his life may have been associated with this disease as well.

Charles's education progressed rapidly, and his political and literary activities began early. Antoine, formerly a professor, was the brilliant young Charles's only tutor until he was ten years old. Reading Michel de Montaigne by the age of eight and philosophy by nine, Charles easily wrote themes in both French and Latin by the time his father sent him to the Pension Mathieu. Soon thereafter the child prodigy's abilities were recognized both in and out of school. Chosen as the pension's representative at the Fête de la Fédération, Charles delivered a political address that gained him some local glory, a feeling he never forgot. The next year (1791) he gave a speech in praise of liberty to the Jacobins' Club, Les Amis de la Constitution, in Besançon; it was printed afterward and thus became his first published work. Impressed with him, the Jacobins invited Charles to join their ranks in 1792; the printing of his reception speech was his second publication by the age of twelve.

Revolutionary events did, of course, touch Charles's life in many ways over the course of his youth; they profoundly influenced his political and philosophical thinking and determined some of his important literary themes. In 1789 his mother was one of the most enthusiastic members of the women's revolutionary club, Les Amies de la Constitution; Antoine was also a fervent supporter of the Revolution and a member of the Jacobin Club. As a judge, to pursue forcefully enemies of the Revolution, he moved his court and guillotine out of Besançon to try insurgents around the region, and condemned many to death. Charles, at age thirteen, observed some of his father's trials and several executions. These events made a deep impression on him at the time; they certainly planted seeds both of an increasing horror at the violence of the Revolution and of the themes of execution and death that would pervade his later literary production.

After that dramatic summer of 1793, the *accusateur public* (public prosecutor) from Strasbourg, Euloge Schneider, a demagogic, defrocked priest and friend of Antoine, stayed at the Nodier home and thus came to know Charles

well. At that time and later that year, when Charles went to see him in Strasbourg, Schneider shared with him his erudition, especially about Greek texts, including the works of Anacreon. But Schneider's own downfall (at the hands of Louis Saint-Just) was in progress and led finally to his execution. During this trip Charles also visited the Rhine headquarters of his father's friend Gen. Jean-Charles Pichegru and lived briefly under the camp conditions of the army. These and other events were included by Nodier in many of his texts, such as *Souvenirs et portraits de la Révolution française* (Souvenirs and Portraits of the French Revolution, 1833); they also form the basis of a play by Alexandre Dumas *père* about this period in Alsace, *Les Blancs et les bleus* (1867-1868; translated as *The Whites and the Blues*, 1895), a drama dedicated to Nodier and in which he is a character.

Nodier made his last Jacobin speech, possibly authored by his father, in Besançon on 10 Thermidor 1794. In a style similar to that of Maximilien Robespierre, Charles eulogized the young heroes Joseph Barra, the Vendean who had defied royalists, and Agricola Viala, of Marseilles, who had died fighting counterrevolutionaries. But because Charles's speech in late July for the fete declared by Robespierre coincided with the latter's condemnation, the local reaction was hostile to both Nodiers. As a consequence of the change in the political atmosphere of Besançon, Antoine sent Charles to stay with a family friend, the engineer Justin Girod de Chantrans, in exile in the countryside at Novillars, near Besançon. Girod gave him fatherly companionship and enlightened, systematic training in literature, history, mathematics, botany, and entomology. With him, Nodier hunted butterflies and other insects, examined them inside a makeshift laboratory, and studied about them in his library. Nodier also read Johann Wolfgang von Goethe and Laurence Sterne, Jean-Jacques Rousseau and Shakespeare; these writers' influence would remain central to Nodier's literary works and theories. He remembered this late summer of 1794 as a carefree, idyllic time and gained two interests that became lifelong passions: entomology and books.

A revolutionary experiment in secondary education attracted Nodier early in 1796. He enrolled at the Ecole Centrale in Besançon, where courses were taught by Joseph Droz, Glo de Bresses, and Victor Proud'hon, and where he concentrated on his new interest in science. Here he helped found a secret society called Les

Philadelphes. This was a young men's literary club with rituals and mystic signs taken from the Freemasonry his father knew. Other members included Charles's good friend and fellow scientist Luczot de la Thébaudais, an engineer eleven years older than he, with whom he published an essay on insects in 1798; Charles Weiss, who was to be Nodier's close friend all his life; Pierre and Joseph Deis; Charles Pertusier; and later, a twenty-five-year-old army captain, Jacques Joseph Oudet, whom Nodier idolized.

This club, turning its attention as well to pranks, carousing, and political—especially anti-Jacobin—acts, overturned Besançon's guillotine (which city fathers had decreed permanent). A more dangerous act occurred a year later, on 12 August 1799, when Nodier, Weiss, and a few other Philadelphean friends staged, on the Promenade de Granvelle, a skit they had authored in which they satirized and denounced the Jacobins—this only two days after Nodier's father had addressed the newly revived Jacobin Club of Besançon. While the others were arrested and Weiss was sent to prison for six weeks, Nodier took refuge with acquaintances away from Besançon. Through his father's intervention and his own retraction, Charles avoided similar treatment. However, he lost the post of assistant librarian that his father had helped him acquire at the Ecole Centrale in October 1798.

The late 1790s were troubled years not just for Nodier's politics, but also his physical and emotional health. He drank heavily and took and abused opium, which probably contributed to bouts of malaise, acute melancholia, and thoughts of death. He swung frequently from one extreme to another: sometimes timid (especially with women), weak-willed, and depressed; at others excitable, fickle, hypersensitive, brazen, and impudent; or again vivacious, charming, full of imagination, and a good storyteller who spoke distinctly and expressed himself clearly and convincingly. He continued his creative efforts: an unfinished autobiography, *Moi-même. Roman qui n'en est pas un, tiré de mon portefeuille gris-de-lin. Pour servir de suite et de complément à toutes les platitudes littéraires du dix-huitième siècle* (Myself: A Novel Which Is Not Really One, Taken from My Flax Gray Portfolio. To Serve as a Sequel and Complement to All the Literary Platitudes of the Eighteenth Century, 1921).

In this text, written in 1800, he imitated his favorite authors, such as Crébillon *fils* (Claude-Prosper Jolyot de Crebillon), Rousseau, Denis Diderot, and Jean-Baptiste Louvet de Couvray, and included prose and verse in a *galante* style, translations of Sallust and Virgil, and bibliographical essays. In 1800 he founded a newspaper, the *Bulletin Politique et Littéraire du Doubs*; his attacks in it against Jacobins led to a lawsuit that he won. But his pamphlet *Charles Nodier à ses concitoyens* (Charles Nodier to His Fellow Citizens, 1800) denigrated old Jacobins in the Besançon city government; the mayor's response derided Charles's literary pretensions and reviewed both Antoine's zealous activities during the Reign of Terror and his illicit relationship with Suzanne Paris and, thus, Charles's birth out of wedlock. This affair inflamed passions on both sides to an intolerable level. Charles, who published no riposte, left—or was sent by his father—in December 1800 for his first visit to Paris.

Nodier stayed in a modest room at the Hôtel de Hambourg, 70 rue de Grenelle-Saint-Honoré, and his stay in Paris was filled with literary and social activities that he loved. Allowed to visit Napoleon's apartments and libraries, he published, with the encouragement of the naturalist Jean-Baptiste de Lamarck, his *Bibliographie entomologique* (Entomological Bibliography, 1801). He met and fell in love with Lucile Messageot, who was the stepdaughter of one of his father's colleagues and married to the painter Jean Pierre Franque. Charles was soon to make her the heroine of *Le Peintre de Saltzbourg* (The Painter of Salzburg, 1803), reminiscent of Goethe's *Die Leiden des jungen Werthers* (1774; translated as The Sorrows of Werther, 1779), and Franque later painted an idealized portrait of Nodier.

Having exhausted his funds after three months, Nodier went back to Besançon, his former post at the library, and renewed creative activity. He published a collection of apothegms, *Pensées de Shakespeare, extraites de ses ouvrages* (Thoughts of Shakespeare Taken from His Works, 1801), and thereby made his mark as one of the first of his time truly to appreciate the Bard; this book foreshadowed the popularity Shakespeare would gain in France later in the century. Nodier admired the grandeur of Shakespeare's vision, as well as his moral instruction and his use of the dream, the fantastic, and the marvelous. These qualities would also be at the center of Nodier's literary concerns. Other activities that year included the writing of plays, at least one of which he coauthored with Francis, pseudonym of Baron Marie-François d'Allarde.

Nodier seized an opportunity to return to Paris, where he stayed at the Hôtel de Béarn, rue Coq-Héron. He soon joined the Franques in attending meetings of the *méditateurs*, or meditators (referred to by artists as *les primitifs*), a group of the painter Jacques-Louis David's students. They wanted to reform society through a life modeled on the ancient philosophers and through a renewal of the arts. These mystics followed their leader, Maurice Quaï, who had an important influence on Charles by generating in him enthusiasm for Pythagoras and by tracing out to him the supposed evolution of Christian love from Pythagoras to Plato, and even to Hinduism. While these notions would appear later in works such as *La Fée aux miettes*, Nodier's interest in mysticism certainly went back to his childhood and his father's Freemasonry, and to his encounter at home with the illuminist Jacques Cazotte, and thus with Rosicrucian concepts. This time in Paris the young Nodier met many illuminist leaders, such as Nicolas de Bonneville, translator of German Romantic works and proponent of German illuminism and a special form of Pythagoreanism that proposed worship of nature rather than gods.

This second Parisian sojourn was brought to an end by an act of political defiance and publication of a novelette. He clandestinely circulated the satirical *La Napoléone* (1802), which he had written in Besançon, but Napoleon's police took no notice of his defiant ode at this time. Nodier also published *Les Proscrits* (The Outcasts, 1802), a short novel that includes some of the attack against tyranny that appears in *La Napoléone*, but which is also much more than a political piece. This text is really Nodier's first work of imaginative literature, and it reflects his love for Goethe's romanticism and tearful pessimism, and, specifically, his *The Sorrows of Young Werther*, which Nodier considered the first modern novel. Nodier's heroine, Stella, a kind of female Werther, has been unfaithful to her husband in exile and, as a result, commits suicide. Like François-René de Chateaubriand's Atala, Stella was another character type that became familiar in the literature of that time. While Nodier's novel knew a certain, if brief, success, he remained disappointed in it because he thought it bad and trivial. This sort of self-denigration was a characteristic that remained with him all his life.

In the spring of 1802, Charles returned to Besançon, where he worked on *Le Peintre de Saltzbourg*. A good, productive period there

Frontispiece by Tony Johannot for Smarra, ou Les démons de la nuit

earned him his parents' permission to return to Paris in the fall of 1803, where he found a room at the Hôtel de Berlin, 25 rue des Frondeurs. This stay began positively with the publication of *Le Peintre de Saltzbourg* followed by *Méditations du cloître* (Meditations of the Cloister). *Le Peintre de Saltzbourg* is an epistolary novel concerning the frustrated love of Charles Munster and Eulalie. He leaves to visit his native village for a few weeks, but is reported to have died. Eulalie then honors a commitment inspired by her dying mother to marry the melancholic Spronck. The novel ends melodramatically when Charles's return coincides with Spronck's death. Eulalie refuses Charles and retires to a convent, and he, in turn, is found dead in the flooding Danube.

Typical of Nodier's early fiction, this sentimental novel reflects the strong influence of *Werther* and Rousseau but tends to the cliché. Its plot leads to the kind of denouement seen in many other Romantic texts, and its dominant themes of life's travails, the solace to be found in nature, the beauties of church bells, and the refuge offered by monasteries and convents are also typical of such texts. But this novel does announce a key theme that recurs in Nodier's later works: the impossibility of union for young lovers in this world. *Le Peintre de Saltzbourg* defines as well a clear parallel to Nodier's personal situation vis-à-vis Lucile Franque. The very brief *Méditations du cloître* is an apology for the religious life and a lament that it has become a refuge from worldly disillusionment. Both texts also reflect themes presented by Chateaubriand, in Nodier's opinion a literary genius, in *Génie du christianisme* (1802; translated as *The Genius of Christianity*, 1802), and *Atala* (1801; translated, 1802).

Nodier's life took a dramatic turn after the publication of *Le Peintre de Saltzbourg*. Tragically, both his mentor, Quaï, and Lucile Franque died. For Nodier, these deaths meant that the structures of his social and intellectual lives suddenly crumbled. As he had done during his previous stay in Paris, he returned to the prostitutes in the gardens of the Palais Royal and, as a result, contracted gonorrhea for the second time. Then *La Napoléone* appeared in a London émigré paper, the *Ambigu*, in October 1803. Copies quickly appeared in Paris, and Napoleon's police attempted to ascertain, but did not discover, the identity of the author. Perhaps fearing the publisher would be arrested for it, perhaps wanting some political glory, Nodier wrote to the police to admit his authorship of the anti-Bonaparte piece. He was arrested on 23 December, treated for his medical problems, and ultimately incarcerated for thirty-six days. After efforts by his friends and his father, and the composition of a pro-Napoleonic piece, *Prophétie contre Albion* (Prophecy against Albion, 1804), Nodier was released by the first consul (who was probably unaware that this was the author of *La Napoléone*). He was freed on 26 January 1804 and ordered back to Besançon to live under paternal and police surveillance.

Before his arrest Nodier had also published *Le Dernier Chapitre de mon roman* (The Last Chapter of My Novel, 1803), an eighteenth-century-style libertine story in the tradition of Crébillon *fils*. Just before leaving Paris, he managed to write about a dozen articles for the *Décade Philosophique* and to publish *Essais d'un jeune barde* (Essays of a Young Bard, 1804). *Essais* contains varied passages, such as rapturous Ossianesque prose and poetry, more *pensées* of Shakespeare, and tributes to Quaï and Franque.

After a year of good behavior within the confines of Besançon, Nodier began to lobby for permission to leave for Paris. His request was not only denied, but, for political reasons, he fell again under police surveillance. He had taken to frequenting the Café Marullier, which was known as the haunt of both Jacobins and royalists and their sympathizers. There he met some of the men with whom he became involved in what he later termed the "Conspiration de l'Alliance" (Conspiracy of the Alliance) to capture and assassinate Napoleon. Several of the conspirators were arrested, but Nodier fled and hid in the mountains of the Jura. His father, again politically embarrassed by his son, promised officials to bring Charles back, but failed to do so.

Although he was considered by police and local officials to be an excitable, impudent man, an anarchist, a bad novelist, an opium user, a possible epileptic—but not a political leader—Charles's name was, after several months, removed from the police wanted list. (A police report of this period describes Nodier as six feet tall, with brown eyes; short, curly, chestnut hair; prominent nose; protruding chin; large mouth; and oval face; he carried his head a little to one side and walked in an indolent manner.) Having gained permission to leave Besançon but still under surveillance, he spent several months visiting relatives and friends in neighboring villages. In Dole he met his future wife, Désirée-Liberté, daughter of his father's good friend Judge Charve; Charve's stepdaughter was Nodier's former love, Lucile Franque.

In 1806 Nodier published *Les Tristes, ou Mélanges tirés des tablettes d'un suicide* (The Sad Ones, or Miscellanies Taken from the Tablets of a Suicide). This volume is a collection of short texts; some are reminiscent of Goethe, Ossian, and Friedrich von Schiller; there are also essays, romances, and tributes to Franque and the *méditateurs*. However, one of the pieces, *Une Heure, ou la vision* (One O'Clock, or The Vision), stands apart for its originality and its importance in Nodier's literary evolution and that of French literature. The mad, epileptic hero of *Une Heure* is thoroughly disillusioned with the world and possesses extraordinary powers to communicate directly with the unknown—in this case, with his beloved dead wife, who calls him from a star of pure light.

This eerie, tightly woven, sentimental tale introduces the first in the line of Nodier's exemplary, innocent characters who are epileptics, lunatics, children, or poets, and who have supersensitive faculties that enable them to see higher truths. *Une Heure* is the earliest text in which

Nodier explores the themes of the occult and extrasensory powers, which became landmarks of his fiction: the potentials of sleep and dream and the menace and freedom they represent; the liberation offered by the imagination versus ordinary existence; and the innocence and omnipotence of love. His supernatural fiction was his greatest source of literary brilliance; it earned him a place as a precursor of French romanticism and of fantastic and dream literature, and it also marked him as one of the most original writers of his time.

The year 1808 brought turning points for Charles. After falling into political disgrace and losing his judgeship (as did Charles's future father-in-law, Monsieur Charve), Antoine died in October. Meanwhile, during that summer, Charles was bringing his life onto a more steady track. In July he finally obtained release from police surveillance, although he still was not allowed in Paris. In late August he married Désirée, an event that seems to have had a stabilizing effect on him. It brought an end to his involvement with dubious friends, political cafés, and conspiracies. Aware of his new responsibility as a husband, and of the far-reaching power of Napoleon and his police, he associated in Dole only with people such as his father's magistrate acquaintances, or his new friend, the writer Benjamin Constant, who could help him socially and literarily.

In early July of that same summer, Charles obtained permission to give a public course in Dole on ancient and modern literature, philosophy, grammar, and natural history. He discussed and displayed his keen appreciation for Shakespeare, Dante, Torquato Tasso, Miguel de Cervantes, and medieval French comedy, among other topics. His course proved a great success and brought him enormous satisfaction; but, after repeating it in early 1809, he never taught again, for various circumstantial and financial reasons. Finally published in 1988 as *Cours de belles-lettres* (Course on Great Literature), this course was an early expression of Nodier's thoughts on the importance of such elements as foreign literatures, medieval and Renaissance cultures, and definition of genre. It established him as one of the first champions of romanticism in France and remains an important document for the development both of that new movement and of his own thought.

Also in 1808, Nodier published a work that reflects another aspect of his multifaceted interests: *Dictionnaire raisonné des onomatopées françaises*

(Analytical Dictionary of French Onomatopoeia). This erudite book is an example of the important contributions Nodier made to linguistics over the course of his life. In fact, it was officially adopted as a title to be included in the libraries of the recently created state lycées.

The end of his course in Dole, the denial of a request to give it in Dijon, his marriage, and the death of his father all meant that Nodier was in debt and, more than ever, needed to find a way to earn his living. He entertained such varied possibilities as immigration to Louisiana, a position in Egypt, and a postal job in Lons-le-Saunier. But a truly interesting opportunity presented itself in the summer of 1809, and Charles accepted. In Amiens the expatriate, erudite Englishman Sir Herbert Croft needed a scholarly assistant and secretary to help him in his preparation of a new edition of the *Fables* of Jean de La Fontaine (1668-1694); by coincidence, Charles was working on a commentary of the same text. By early September, he and Désirée moved into the apartment Sir Herbert provided, along with board, servants, horse and carriage, and a generous salary.

Once installed in the rue Gloriette, Nodier set to work and soon realized how overwhelming the demands of his post were to be. Working up to eighteen hours a day, he translated into French the long, mediocre novels of Lady Mary Hamilton, Sir Herbert's wife. Nodier also performed for him such tasks as the tedious correction of the traditional punctuation in Horace's texts, the translation of Samuel Johnson's *Lives of the Poets* (1779-1781), the preparation of the new edition of the *Fables*, the planning of a new printing press, and the constant taking of dictation (even during meals). In addition to ceaseless, tiresome work, there was increasing discord in the Croft household; more seriously, the English couple was having major financial problems. As a result Sir Herbert was never able to pay Charles after the first quarter. Finally, the Crofts' demands on Nodier's time and energy prevented him from completing his own projects. In 1810 Nodier was able to extricate himself from this impossible situation, and he and Désirée went to live in the Charve family home in Quintigny. The experience with Croft did, however, teach Charles a sense of respect for detail, accuracy, and authenticity for the texts on which he worked. Elected to the Academy of Amiens, Charles left with affection for the city's citizens as well as for Sir Herbert, with whom he maintained a warm correspondence, and about whom he later wrote the story *Amélie* (1834).

The next two years were secure and peaceful ones for Charles among friends and relatives in the quiet town of Quintigny, in the Jura. Marie Antoinette Elisabeth was born to him and Désirée on 26 April 1811, their only child to survive to adulthood. Nodier, who was to be an outdoorsman for many years, walked extensively in the region, collecting plants and insects, and reading along the way. His writing and research continued with articles on epic poetry in the *Journal du Jura*, work on his edition of La Fontaine's *Fables*, an edition of Jean-Baptiste de Grainville's *Le Dernier Homme* (The Last Man) in 1811, and philological essays. This period was perhaps marred only by his sense that, at the age of thirty, he had not acquired the recognition that he ought to have, and by occasional bouts of ill health. Preoccupied throughout his life with headaches, insomnia, general weakness, and melancholia, he often was convinced that death was near. Nevertheless, in 1812 he was able to bring out his *Questions de littérature légale* (Legal Questions on Literature), whose success was so long-lived that he published a second, expanded edition sixteen years later. This is a collection of essays on such literary problems as imitation, plagiarism, allusion, and forgeries, and on a method of textual dating and attribution based on historical information and internal evidence. His work was seen as groundbreaking in a little-known field, and its appeal was augmented by the sense of discovery he gave to the authentication and establishment of texts. Later that year his abilities and achievements were recognized in his home city when he was elected to the Academy of Besançon.

In the fall of 1812 Nodier obtained through his future brother-in-law a post that was not only precisely the sort he had been looking for, but which also led to adventure and an important new perspective on himself and his culture. He became the municipal librarian and editor of the *Télégraphe Officiel* in the Illyrian city of Laybach (Ljubljana). Now an official appointee of Napoleon's empire, he was a long way from his earlier status in Paris and Besançon with the imperial police. Traveling via Switzerland and northern Italy, Charles, Désirée, and Marie arrived in Ljubljana in early January 1813, and Charles set to work immediately.

Formerly a paper of record for government acts and decrees, the *Télégraphe Officiel* was transformed by Nodier—with the knowledge of his superior Joseph Fouché, formerly of Napoleon's police (and who had imprisoned Nodier in Paris)—into a journal for Slovenian national and cultural awareness. He encouraged publication of works concerning all aspects of Illyria: history, geography, botany, entomology, folklore, literature, art, and language. Owing to his editorial policies, he frequented local educated society, especially the Baron Sigismund de Zoïs's salon, where, for the first time, he heard discussions of all subjects from non-French points of view. With respect to his literary opinions Charles became more convinced than ever of the central influence of German romanticism on contemporary European and French literature. He also learned about Serbo-Croatian literature, elements of which appear in his later work.

In both salon and official life, Nodier's good qualities shone through: diplomacy, charm, quick wit, vivaciousness, and imagination. But official life—and its required dress—also ate through his income, in spite of a salary seven times the one Croft was to have paid him, plus that sum again for expenses, and in spite of yet another appointment as inspector of the national lottery. At the collapse of Napoleon's grip on the region in August 1813, Nodier and his family were forced to leave. After a brief stay in Trieste to publish the last issues of the *Télégraphe*, they traveled back to France and arrived in Quintigny poor, tired, and injured (Désirée had broken her leg).

Fortunately, Nodier obtained a post with the *Journal de l'Empire* in Paris; he left Quintigny in November 1813, and Désirée and Marie soon followed, to live at 17 rue des Trois Frères. A literary critic for the paper, he wrote as well on general literary and political questions. He was an audacious and well-respected commentator, his perspicacious judgment and intense interest in both new and foreign works preparing him well for the role he would play in the Romantic debate. Between 1814 and 1820, through his forum at the *Journal*, he wrote in favor of the new romanticism, frequently quite alone in his opinions and often in direct opposition to those of his editors. Nodier also ghostwrote reviews for the gravely ill Julien-Louis Geoffroy and, upon his death in 1814, replaced him as drama critic. After the Restoration the paper became the *Journal des Débats*; his articles provided him a good income for a growing family. The Nodiers' son, Térence, was born in 1814; a sickly child, he died in 1816.

During the Hundred Days of 1815, Nodier published a historical novel, *Histoires des sociétés secrètes de l'armée* (translated as *History of the Secret Societies of the Army*, 1815). This work, which appeared anonymously, is based on various conspiracies against Bonaparte. Written both as an expression of his anti-Bonapartist sentiment and as a tribute to his old comrade, Oudet, who died in Napoleon's service at the battle of Wagram in 1809, Nodier's novel creates a society of Philadelphes with several thousand members who permeate the army and pose a serious threat to the emperor. In this *Histoire* some facts about known intrigues are leavened by fiction: Nodier, for example, has Oudet assassinated by Napoleon's agents at Wagram, with the result that grief-stricken soldiers commit suicide on his grave. While this was entirely false, many readers believed it and, much to Nodier's amusement, still discussed it years later.

Having anonymously written a strong piece in the *Journal des Débats* against Napoleon's return to power, Nodier was in danger when the emperor did in fact return. Summoned by the police—again Fouché—he refused to recant and instead stood by his true royalist opinions. After another anti-Bonapartist article by him in the *Nain Jaune* (Yellow Dwarf, or Pope Joan) in May 1815, he and his family accepted the refuge offered by a fellow bibliophile and supporter of the Restoration, the duc de Caylus, at the Château de Buis outside Paris in Ville d'Avray. In recognition of his loyalty to the *ultras* in 1814, Charles had received from the king the Ordre du Lys; after the installation of Louis XVIII, Nodier obtained letters of nobility and a secure place on the *Journal des Débats*.

While Nodier's political conservatism was manifest in many of his actions and writings, another facet of his thought revealed itself in his novel *Jean Sbogar* (translated as *Giovanni Sbogarro. A Venetian Tale*, 1820), published anonymously in 1818. This text gained immediate popularity; in 1820 it went into a second, luxury edition. The protagonist, Sbogar, is a conspirator and bandit who lives mysteriously in his Illyrian castle. This anarchist hero fights social injustice and struggles against restrictive legal and social definitions. Sbogar proves the nobility of his character by a refusal to marry his love, Antonia, because to do so would ruin her reputation, and, thus, his own. Because of his decision, Antonia decides to enter a convent to await death and a reunion with him in the afterlife. The novel comes to a close when Jean escapes police by throwing himself into the sea. This text is based on a theme that runs through many of Nodier's works: a love that is impossible in this world and that can be fulfilled only in another existence. Also in *Jean Sbogar*, Nodier evokes the exoticism of lands he has visited and can thus relate with truth and precision. In this case, Illyria provides the colorful backdrop for the novel's action; in other texts, it would be Scotland, and in yet others the regional specificity of Normandy or his native Franche-Comté. And, as in some of his early literary pieces, Nodier's interest in foreign literatures permeates *Jean Sbogar*: the influence of Goethe's *Werther* is again evident, and so is that of Schiller's *Brigands* (1782).

Nodier claimed that the political implications of *Jean Sbogar* were responsible for the failure of a project making him professor of political economy at the new Lycée Richelieu in Odessa. While there, he would also have directed a press and acted as editor of a journal. He even moved from Paris to Quintigny to await final arrangements that never came through. Also in 1818, Charles finally published the commentaries on La Fontaine that he had begun ten years earlier. This two-volume work was well received and became an important scholarly reference on La Fontaine. The Nodiers returned to Paris in October 1818, this time to 1 rue de Choiseul; while he was eventually reimbursed for his expenses caused by the Odessa project, he would be plagued until 1835 by a bad debt he had foolishly cosigned before the Odessa project. Money matters were always a problem for him; he lent easily, often naively, and he borrowed and repaid in the same way, which led more than once to bitterness.

In 1819 Nodier's novel *Thérèse Aubert* came out and soon went into a second edition. This work marked a departure from his earlier novels dealing with the tragically frustrated love of a pure heroine and a sensitive hero—inspired by Goethe's *Werther* and Rousseau's *Julie, ou La Nouvelle Héloïse* (1761; translated as *Julia, or The New Eloisa*, 1773)—toward his more mature later novels. Though still a work about unhappy love, *Thérèse Aubert* is remarkable for a new ability to portray characters more precisely, more individually, and to analyze the subtleties of love's development and manifestations. Setting the novel's action during uprisings in the Vendée and western France, Nodier incorporated in his scenic descriptions many of the observations of Normandy he had made during his trip in 1818. The hero, Adolphe, having lost both his parents to the Ter-

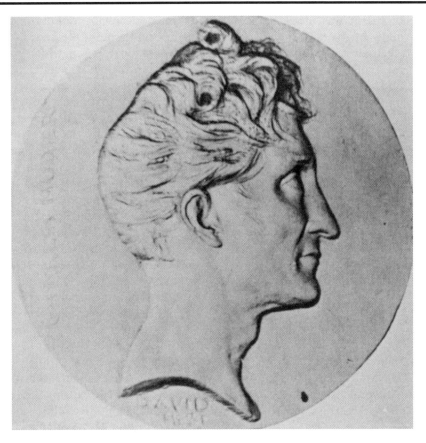

Medallion of Nodier in 1831 by David d'Angers

ror, joins the royalists; he thus becomes a kind of outlaw à la Jean Sbogar. Like many of the revolutionaries Nodier portrays in a favorable light in his works, Adolphe's two teachers support the Revolution, but fall victim to it, as does the revolutionary father of Thérèse Aubert, who had sheltered and fed Adolphe.

The theme of unrequited love reappears in Nodier's short epistolary novel *Adèle* (1820). In their letters, Gaston de Germancé and his friend Edouard de Millanges exchange notions of perfect love, which one can experience only on an ideal plane, in a life beyond the earthly one. The novel's introduction formulates the tension Nodier sees between the ideal and the material, societal conditions; this is a dichotomy that historical and social changes heightened in the revolutionary and postrevolutionary periods. The ideality human beings can sense creates feelings that are impossible either to define precisely or to satisfy. Furthermore, this phenomenon manifests itself in literature as a *vague* (vagueness) of morality and sentiment. Nodier's description harks back to ideas presented by Chateaubriand, Staël, and other writers; the *méditateurs* he knew in

Paris as a youth; and such philosophers as Pierre Ballanche and Louis de Bonald. Nodier's formulation of the problem of the ideal became well known and influential during the rest of the century.

As a young man, Nodier had tried writing for the theater, both alone and in collaboration with others; he had also begun to explore fantastic themes in *Une Heure*. In 1820 he combined these interests with the knowledge of vampire stories that he gained in Illyria. He adapted a tale by Cyprien Bérard, *Lord Ruthwen, ou Les Vampires*, for a play entitled *Le Vampire*. This was one of the first French plays about Dracula, and it was very successful. The following year Nodier continued his work in a similar vein by collaboration with Baron Isidore Justin Séverin Taylor on an adaptation of a tragedy by the major English gothic writer Charles Robert Maturin: *Bertram, ou Le Château de Saint-Aldobrand*. Through these plays and his critical writings, Nodier played an important role in the introduction to France of foreign writers, such as Maturin, and of foreign and fantastic subject matter, such as vampire legends. But Nodier's interest in the *frénétique* that texts such as *Le Vampire* represent was brief; he soon moved on to other modes of the fantastic.

Nodier also developed his central place in the new Romantic movement through channels other than literary and critical writing. Increasingly he led gatherings of writers at his home, attended by, among others, Alphonse de Lamartine; the melodramatist René-Charles de Pixérécourt; Hugo, with whom he developed a stormy friendship; and Dumas *père*, a lifelong friend whom he met by chance at a performance of *Le Vampire*. As pilot of the new literary school and throughout his life, Nodier personally helped many writers and thinkers—aspiring, struggling, or forgotten—by his articles, reviews, and personal influence. Hugo, Alfred de Vigny, Alfred de Musset, and Bonneville were among the beneficiaries of such aid.

The year 1821 brought opportunity and tragedy for Charles. The Nodiers' second son, Amédée, was born that year but lived only a few months. In the summer Charles was able to travel via London to Scotland, a trip that furnished material for several later publications. With his friends Taylor, Alphonse de Cailleux, and the painter Jean-Baptiste Isabey, he went to the land of two of his most beloved authors, Ossian (James Macpherson), and Scott. They failed to meet Scott, but afterward Nodier wrote and published *Promenade de Dieppe aux montagnes d'Ecosse* (1821; translated as *Promenade from Dieppe to the Mountains of Scotland*, 1822). This volume, illustrated by Isabey and others, is a journal and guide composed of descriptions, entomological information, and impressions. Imitated in France and poorly judged in the *Edinburgh Review*, this book reveals a Nodier who at once misses home and family just as soon as he leaves them but who also has the ability to seize and express poetically the exotic aspects of a place.

Smarra, ou Les démons de la nuit (Smarra, or Demons of the Night, 1821) is, more than any other, the text that established Nodier's literary reputation. It was presented as an Illyrian work translated by Maxime Odin. Nodier explains in his preface that the term *Smarra* in Slavic regions means *nightmare* as well as *vampire* and that he considers this text, a pastiche of Apuleius, Dante, Shakespeare, and John Milton, to belong to the serious fantastic rather than the inferior *frénétique* of the popular vampire stories written by himself and others. *Smarra* is the account of Lorenzo, who, in the arms of his beloved Lisidis, falls asleep and experiences night terrors. In his

dream he loses his identity and becomes Lucius, transported from a pleasant Lombardy to a sinister Thessaly. Images, which are sometimes sensual (and which reappear in texts such as *La Fée aux miettes*), succeed one another: young girls, spectral figures, demons, and his dead friend Polémon. Polémon tells his story of being delivered to Smarra by the sorceress Méroé and her magic ring. The nightmare worsens when Lucius, accused of Polémon's murder, is beheaded and then watches his own head roll; he also sees Smarra and Méroé tear out Polémon's heart. Lorenzo finally awakens to the comforting presence of Lisidis and the realization that he was simply having bad dreams. Nodier tries to imitate a nightmare through content, inconsistencies, and digressive structure (misunderstood and criticized by his contemporary readers). He tries to create the impression of composing the narrative in an unconscious, nearly trancelike way. His innovations in technique and his efforts to explore the unconscious in *Smarra* put Nodier well ahead of his time. This text remains one of the keystones of French dream literature, a precursor of Nerval (who admired Nodier), the Symbolists, and the automatic writing of the Surrealists a century later.

Nodier continued in early 1822 in the fantastic vein, combined with the exoticism of Scotland, in *Trilby, ou le Lutin d'Argail* (translated as *Trilby, The Fairy of Argyle*, 1895). This time, however, the tone is lighter. Trilby is a sprite who takes refuge in the house of Dougal, a Scottish fisherman. Having fallen in love with Jeannie, the Scot's wife, Trilby keeps their poor cottage clean, and the husband prospers. While the innocent Jeannie is dreaming, Trilby speaks to her, declaring his feelings and encouraging her to abandon herself to him. The worried couple decides to have him exorcised by an old monk, Ronald, who threatens to imprison him in a tree for a thousand years should he ever return. Consequently, the husband's fish catches cease; the wife becomes morose. Her dreams, now sensual, transform the playful, sweet will-o'-the-wisp into a strong, handsome man who frankly desires to possess her. Because she has suppressed her once-free dreams of Trilby, her new ones create guilt, anxiety, and frustration. Thus, both *Smarra* and *Trilby* represent two sides of the same coin in that they enact repressed psychic elements: Smarra is the terrifying, oppressive embodiment of hidden fears; Trilby seems at first the innocent, cajoling representation of controlled desires, but is ultimately more destructive than Smarra. Also, while Nodier returns in this Scottish tale to a theme he often treated in his Wertherian novels—that is, impossible love—he abandons in both *Smarra* and *Trilby* the sentimentality that permeates texts such as *Les Proscrits*. *Trilby* was so successful that a woman's Trilby hat became a fad, and three theatrical adaptations of his story were put on nearly simultaneously in Paris in the spring of 1823. In critical opinion, *Trilby* remains one of the very best of Nodier's fictional works.

Nodier wrote other texts in 1822, including *Infernalia*, a collection of tales of terror, witchcraft, magic, and demonology. These stories are in the tradition of Cazotte but are generally judged inferior to *Trilby*. But this year also marked the beginning of a hiatus in his literary production. His life remained active, his position among the Romantics became increasingly central, and his critical and linguistic publications continued. The public had to wait until 1830 for his next work of literature, *Histoire du roi de Bohême et de ses sept châteaux*.

Nodier's activities in 1823 included collaboration with Hugo and others on a new Romantic periodical, the *Muse Française*; continued writing for the conservative journal the *Quotidienne*; the triumph of his play *Le Vampire*; and a collaboration with Amédée Pichot on *Essai critique sur le gaz hydrogène et les divers modes d'éclairage artificiel* (Critical Essay on Hydrogen Gas and the Various Methods of Artificial Lighting).

But 1824 brought a major change in Nodier's life: appointment by Charles-Philippe, Comte d'Artois, as librarian at the Arsenal in Paris, where he was to live for the rest of his life. Soon after moving, the Nodiers' personal responsibilities grew because Charles's sister, Elise, and her seven-year-old daughter came to live with them. Charles could easily pursue his passion for books at the Arsenal and also during his evening strolls to the *bouquinistes* (booksellers) on the nearby quais of the Seine. In his apartments at the Bibliothèque de l'Arsenal, his salon became the first of the important Romantic *cénacles* (literary circles) and was thus the very center of the young movement in Paris between 1824 and 1827. Over these and later years, Charles and Désirée's brilliant gatherings, described vividly by Dumas *père*, brought together writers such as Hugo, Vigny, Honoré de Balzac, Gautier, Musset, Marceline Desbordes-Valmore, Delphine and Sophie Gay, Laure Junot (Duchesse d'Abrantès), and Louise Colet; the philosophers Charles Fourier and Ballanche; the painters Achille and

Eugène Devéria, the Johannot brothers (Charles, Alfred, and Tony), David d'Angers, and Eugène Delacroix; the critic Gustave Planche; and Charles's old friend and protector Jean de Bry. Visitors such as Victor and Adèle Hugo found the Nodiers' home to be lively, welcoming, and warm; Charles and Désirée's hospitality, congeniality, wit, and intelligence made it the rare place where people could come together from both sides of the classical-Romantic and conservative-liberal debates. Charles put his *invités* at ease with his charm and his superb abilities as a conversationalist. While his contemporaries often got the impression of laziness or diffidence from his stooped posture, ambling walk, and drawling speech, they were delighted and fascinated by the tales he told, by his skill as a raconteur.

Nodier had met Hugo in 1823 at a public meeting of the Société Royale de Bonnes Lettres. Their friendship flourished over the next few years: Hugo frequented Nodier's salon; they traveled together to the coronation of Charles X in Rheims in 1825 (for which Charles was historiographer and Victor poet laureate); and that same year they took another trip together, with their families (who also got on well with each other), to visit Lamartine at his home near Lyons and then on to Switzerland (Geneva and Lausanne). Nodier championed Hugo's early works, initiated him on Shakespeare, and was ultimately an important influence on the young genius. Hugo, the disciple, in recognition of this master, dedicated works to Nodier (as did Lamartine and Dumas).

But serious problems developed in the friendly relationship between two of the leaders of the Romantic school. Hugo's efforts to move the focal point of the Romantics from Nodier's salon to his own was successful, and hurt Charles keenly. Prior to this, though, Nodier, possibly owing to several months of debilitating illness, remained virtually silent on the publication of Hugo's all-important *Préface de Cromwell* (1827). That same year Hugo established his own *cénacle* at the rue Notre-Dame-des-Champs and took many of the young Romantics with him from the Arsenal. The following year Hugo removed Nodier's name from the dedication to *Odes et ballades* (1828), then from other individual poems. In 1829 Nodier published a bitter article on Hugo's *Les Orientales* in the *Quotidienne*. By 1830 Nodier saw Hugo as a bit of an egomaniac, who had pushed aside his aging, former mentor, protector, and friend to set himself up as leader of the young Romantics. But when Hugo's *Hernani* opened in 1830, Nodier attended the premiere (the password there of the Young Turks was "Nodo hierro," known to be a play on Nodier's name, among other things). Charles stated in letters that he did not much like the play, but he stayed quiet, in the main, about it. In following years Nodier, for reasons of intrigue, opposed one of Hugo's bids for entry to the Académie française. But he and Hugo never openly broke; they even became friendly again, and in the end Hugo was a pallbearer at Nodier's funeral.

In 1828 Nodier completed and submitted *Histoire du roi de Bohême et de ses sept châteaux*. This novel is a fusion of diverse elements: a satire of contemporary society, including an autocratic king and the Académie française, under the guise of the Institut de Tombouctou; a pastiche of Nodier's most revered writers, including Cervantes, Cyrano de Bergerac, Jonathan Swift, Montaigne, Jacques Amyot, Clément Marot, and most notably François Rabelais and Sterne; mock-serious narration with an erotic undertone; playful linguistic invention; and parody of the Wertherian sentimental epistolary novel he himself previously loved and wrote. If *Histoire du roi de Bohême* echoes the irony, the verbal richness, the extravagances, and the digressive, episodic, rambling structures of Rabelais and Sterne, Nodier's text—through its linguistic experimentation and use of space and time—makes him a forerunner of poets such as Stéphane Mallarmé, Rimbaud, and Guillaume Apollinaire. He gives free reign to his abilities in language, inventing new words that are often derived from the onomatopoeia he thought to be the base of human language. He arranges them on the page so as to suggest spatially an object or interrelationships between terms; for example, he includes in his prose a poem about a coach and horses, written entirely in onomatopoeic syllables.

Nodier loosely structures the novel around the timid, innocent Théodore, King of Bohemia, and his efforts to visit his seven castles somewhere near Spain. Traveling with Don Pic de Fanferluchio and Breloque, he must first decide how to reach their destination: their imagination, aided by wine and betel leaves, will serve them better than ordinary means of transportation. Their voyage functions as a framework for the many characters, adventures, extravagances, and discoveries that follow. In 1831 Balzac wrote a "Lettre sur Paris" for the *Voleur* in which he ranks Nodier's novel with his own *Physiologie du mariage* (1826; translated as *Physiology of Marriage*, 1899)

and Stendhal's *Le Rouge et le noir* (1830; translated as *The Red and the Black*, 1913) as "poignantes moqueries" (poignant mockeries) that are representative of the times. For Balzac, these works catch the essence of a dying society and reflect the inner thoughts of an old nation awaiting a reinvigorated social organization. Recent critics tend to emphasize the complexity and the modernity of *Histoire du roi de Bohême*.

The year 1830 brought financial problems and personal readjustments for Nodier. On 9 February his beloved Marie married Jules Mennessier. In order to provide her dowry, Charles was obliged to sell the personal library he had so lovingly collected. For political reasons arising from the publication of *Souvenirs et portraits de la Révolution française* (April-July, *Revue de Paris*) concerning the roles of himself and others in the events of the 1790s, his literary pension was reduced, then eliminated; he was dismissed as librarian in July. But the revolution of that same month brought about a change of regime, and his post was saved; Nodier armed himself and stayed to defend the Arsenal during the revolution. A cousin, Lt. Gen. Claude-Pierre Pajol, was appointed governor of Paris, and this in turn guaranteed Nodier's position. At the conclusion of the uprising, while leaving the Arsenal, he, who abhorred violence, interceded in a quarrel between an apple merchant and her brutish son. As a result Nodier's leg was broken, and he was bedridden for two and a half months. At that time responsible for the support of nine people, he turned all the more earnestly to writing.

In November 1830 his important essay *Du fantastique en littérature* appeared in the *Revue de Paris*. Here he defined the ideas on the fantastic he had been evolving since *Une Heure* and *Smarra*, and which he would continue to elaborate over the 1830s in the rich production of some of his best literary works, such as *La Fée aux miettes*. In *Du fantastique en littérature*, Nodier traces manifestations of the fantastic in literature from antiquity to his own day. He enunciates the principle that a penchant for the marvelous is an innate quality of humankind and, further, that it is an essential instrument of life, quite possibly the only compensation for the miseries caused by society. For Nodier (in fact, a superstitious person), superstition is the science of elevated things. He says that purely rational man is at the lowest level of a philosophical classification of human beings; the second level, a zone midway between materiality and ideality, is occupied by the

Nodier's daughter, Marie (portrait by Achille Deveria; from Hubert Juin, Charles Nodier, *1970)*

poet, who lives in the former but can see the latter; and the Ideal, or God, is at the apex of the cosmos and is the goal of the imagination. The divinely inspired genius can perceive the spiritual world; the fantastic is the passage from the material to the ideal spheres, and this event effects a complete renewal in the subject.

While Nodier explored conventional fantastic themes, such as vampires, in his earlier frenetic texts (*Le Vampire*), he was searching for a new fantastic, which, different from overly optimistic fantasy, would be a serious *fantastique*, one based on the profound collective dreams of a people, one that would facilitate a "progression imaginaire." This would be like that introduced by E. T. A. Hoffmann, one that has the variety and truth of dreams, finds its source in the psyche, and is an integral part of the narrative. For Nodier, there are three types of fantastic: the "histoire fantastique fausse" (false fantastic story), which depends on the double credulity of the teller and the public, as in a traditional fairy tale;

the "histoire fantastique vague" (vague fantastic story), which leaves one in a state of dreamlike doubt; and the "histoire fantastique vraie" (true fantastic story), which would be physically impossible and yet entirely believable, one which "ébranle profondément le cœur sans coûter de sacrifices à la raison" (profoundly shakes the heart without costing any sacrifices from reason).

Nodier continued his work on the theory of the fantastic in 1831 with the publication of *M. de La Mettrie ou les superstitions* (October, *Revue de Paris*). Here he develops his notion that superstition is a fundamental characteristic of human beings and that it fulfills the yearning to know the ideal. Nodier's significant essay *De quelques phénomènes du sommeil* (On Some Phenomena of Sleep) had appeared in the *Revue de Paris* in February. In it he proposes the concept that sleep and the semiconsciousness one experiences just before it are privileged states. One loses contact with the material world and is thus in a special zone where the imagination can operate freely, and where one easily experiences the fantastic. For Nodier, the fantastic is a salutary, integrating event for the psyche because it enables knowledge of an exalted plane of existence. This essay is an important early definition for fantastic and also dream literature. In 1831 Nodier's writings of note also included his *Mémoires de Maxime Odin* (July, *Revue de Paris*), later retitled *Souvenirs de jeunesse* (Memories of Youth, 1832), a collection of portraits of young girls of whom the narrator is sometimes the lover. *De l'amour et de son influence, comme sentiment, sur la société actuelle* (On Love and on Its Influence, as a Feeling, on Present-day Society, 1832) is seen by some as a kind of defense of his incestuous feelings for his daughter, Marie; in this text he tries to show that in the Golden Age of the Garden of Eden, Eve was simultaneously the sister and the daughter of Adam.

The spring of 1832 brought a cholera epidemic to Paris, and the Nodiers escaped for the duration to the Mennessiers' home in Metz. Charles continued the efforts he had begun in 1824, repeated in 1830 and twice in 1832, toward admission to the Académie française. He based his case for investiture principally on his work on linguistics and lexicography, such as the *Examen critique des dictionnaires de la langue française* (Critical Examination of French Dictionaries, 1828). When the sixth edition of the *Dictionnaire de l'Académie Française* appeared in 1831, Nodier wrote a series of articles in the *Temps*, and in his *Miscellanées, variétés de phi-*

losophie, d'histoire et de littérature (Miscellanies, Varieties of Philosophy, History, and Literature, 1832), he attacked the *Dictionnaire* as being hopelessly out-of-date and incorrectly organized. On the merits of such work, Nodier was elected to the Academy in October 1833 to fill the seat the dramatist Jean-Louis Laya had occupied.

Nodier's literary production virtually exploded in 1832 and 1833; working very late into the night, as was his habit, he produced more than a dozen short stories and novelettes, supplemented by several important essays and articles. Many of these texts were published from 1832 until 1837 in the volumes of his *Œuvres complètes*. Reprinted by Slatkine in 1968, this remains the most comprehensive and accessible single edition of Nodier's work. *Mademoiselle de Marsan* (1832), published in volume six, is a novel that again portrays Maxime Odin, who—much like Nodier himself at various times—is a naturalist, now in the Adriatic region, resisting domination by foreign powers such as Napoleon and the Austrians. The action is set around 1808 and features the Carbonari, an Italian underground organization that believed that clandestine, subversive activities were the only possible means to achieve its goals of social and political reform. This element reflects Nodier's support of secret societies—from the Philadelphes, the méditateurs, and the Freemasons to groups of political conspirators—as a means for change. Maxime, already pursued by Napoleon's police, becomes involved with the independence movement of Mario Cinci, Doge of Venice, and thus with the Carbonari, and with Diane de Marsan, the lover of Cinci. In the end the movement is defeated, the leaders imprisoned or killed. But the Carbonari live on to continue their struggle against tyranny in Europe. The subtlety and passion of the characters of *Mademoiselle de Marsan* generally do not measure up to those of such personae as Jean Sbogar, and the technique and style do not present the level of interest of a text such as *Histoire du roi de Bohême*; its appeal today is principally historic.

La Fée aux miettes appeared in volume four of *Œuvres complètes*. Virtually unnoticed at that time, it is now considered Nodier's masterpiece and, as such, has received serious critical attention in the past quarter-century. This is a fantastic tale introduced by a narrator who tells a friend about a trip to Scotland, where he discovers the special truth madmen can possess. In an insane asylum, the narrator meets Michel, who then relates his life story. As a somewhat melan-cholic child in Granville (Normandy), he meets an extraordinarily old, ugly, but sprightly woman called the Crumb Fairy. After a growing friendship with Michel, the Fairy tells him that she wants to become his wife and share her fortune with him, but only on the condition that he find a way for her to return to her home in Scotland. Michel agrees. At this point the Fairy gives him a diamond-studded gold locket containing a portrait of the beautiful Belkiss, whose likeness is really—and unbeknownst to Michel—that of the young Crumb Fairy. While Michel falls in love with the perfect woman this image represents, over several years he nevertheless proves his commitment to the Crumb Fairy by many adventures designed by her to test him (gifts of gold coins and her near drowning, among others).

After a series of bizarre events in Greenock, the Fairy takes him to her fabulous cottage, where they live blissfully for six months. Then she reveals to him that she will die within the year unless he fulfills his final mission: to find the one mandrake that will sing him a pretty song of his childhood and that will not only unite them forever but also enable her to become again the young and beloved Belkiss of the portrait. Michel's *récit* ends a year later, at the last moment before sunset—also the moment of his narration—and he is still searching. Later the frame narrator says that Michel is said to have been saved by the Princess Mandrake, married the Queen of Sheba, and become Emperor of the Seven Planets.

La Fée aux miettes is a richly suggestive text that has lent itself to a wide variety of provocative interpretations, ranging from biographical to narrational, philosophical to structural: a roman à clef with Michel as Nodier; a *récit* of Nodier's veiled, incestuous yearnings for his daughter; an allegory based on alchemical, or again Freemasonic, rites and symbols; a representation of a process of psychic integration; a work whose fundamental circular structures support an evolution toward spiritual fulfillment; a text based on numerical structures that form overarching metaphors for an ultimate goal of unity; and a story in which dreams are meaningful and fundamental. These are a few examples of recent approaches to the work, approaches that suggest its charm and universality. It is now seen as a landmark in the development of the traditions of fantastic and dream literature as well as the fairy tale in the nineteenth century.

Nodier published several essays in 1832. *Des types en littérature* (On Types in Literature, in *Œuvres complètes*, volume five) is a discussion of great literary character types and a reprise of a few of his basic notions on French romanticism. In addition to indicating his idea of the best *types*—including characters by Pierre Corneille, Molière, Rabelais, and Voltaire—he declares that neoclassicism has restricted the creation of *types* by French writers. He says that foreign authors, such as Goethe, in *Werther*, and especially British writers, such as Shakespeare, Henry Fielding, Samuel Richardson, and Scott, have a more open mentality than the French and have thus produced the greatest number and variety of types.

Two other essays published in 1832 remain crucial to a comprehension of Nodier's thought. In *De l'utilité morale de l'instruction pour le peuple* (*Œuvres complètes*, volume five), he writes on his ideas about the decline of humankind, caused in part by the corrupting influence of progress. He says that education, defined as reading, writing, and counting, has been of no true benefit. Only oral instruction, memories, and traditions of nature can impart true knowledge. *De la palingénésie humaine et de la résurrection* (August, *Revue de Paris*), provoked an answer by Balzac in his *Lettre à Charles Nodier*. In this essay Nodier formulated concepts that had interested him since childhood, which had numerous sources, and which he developed in many of his tales, from his early *Une Heure* to *La Fée aux miettes* and *Jean-François les Bas-bleus* (Jean-François the Bluestocking).

He knew Freemasonic ideas, and the Rosicrucian and alchemical ones associated with them, from his father and grandfather. As a child, he met Cazotte, Antoine's friend and frequent guest. Through their discussions Charles gained familiarity with the ideas of other illuminists, such as Louis-Claude de Saint-Martin and Martinez Pasqualis. While living in Paris as a young man Nodier investigated Pythagoreanism with the méditateurs; he knew such illuminists as Emanuel Swedenborg and Johann Lavater; the ideas on palingenesis of Ballanche and Charles Bonnet had an important and early influence on him.

In *De la palingénésie*, Nodier, like many other Romantics, says that humanity is unhappy because it can conceive of death and resurrection but cannot achieve the latter. This is because human beings are merely *êtres rationnels* (thinking beings), who can think about, but who are unable to sense, resurrection. On the biblical sixth day, still to come, God will create a new species, the *être compréhensif* (comprehensive being). This is a species like an angel, but different from human beings; man will be transformed into it, acquire new sensory organs, and evolve into the ultimate, permanent *état résurrectionnel* (state of resurrection). This last state will be one of happiness, love, and integration in an eternal present moment. Such palingenetic notions inform most of Nodier's later oeuvre.

From the early 1830s until his death, Nodier produced many fictional texts, perhaps best understood when grouped by thematic "cycles." Nodier wrote at least four types of tales during this period. The first is a cycle of seers or "Innocents." These stories present a character who, by virtue of being pure and simple, is able to understand the fantastic. Nodier said that the madman or the child, living in a state of innocence, can recount the fantastic. This *fantastique* is about illusions that are true, a primordial paradise that offers refuge and consolation to the weary in an age of skepticism. Because its hero is a lunatic, *La Fée aux miettes* is generally placed in the cycle of the Innocents. Other stories in this group are *Histoire d'Hélène Gillet*, *Le Songe d'or* (The Dream of Gold), *Jean-François les Bas-bleus*, and *Baptiste Montauban ou l'idiot* (Baptiste Montauban, or The Idiot).

In *Histoire d'Hélène Gillet*, Nodier incorporates a historical setting (1624) with a true event (Monique Saquel's possibly unjust accusation of infanticide in 1820; Nodier and other writers interceded for her), adding elements of the fantastic and reflections of the abhorrence of capital punishment that he acquired during the Terror. The virtuous, beautiful, and rich Hélène Gillet is drugged and raped. After giving birth to a child, she falls into a coma, during which her infant is stolen. She awakens and later learns her child has been found dead. Accused of murder, Hélène is condemned to death. But Grandjean, the executioner, takes pity on her and cannot accomplish his task. The enraged mob then kills him; his wife finishes his job, but the throng turns and murders her too. An aversion to the death sentence is a theme that recurs in Nodier's texts: in *La Fée aux miettes*, the falsely accused Michel is saved at the last moment by the Crumb Fairy from the executioner and the bloodthirsty crowd; in *Smarra*, the dream-narrator recounts his own awful guillotining; in *Souvenirs et portraits de la Révolution*, Nodier describes Euloge Schneider's execution.

In *Le Songe d'or*, characters respond according to their disposition to a treasure of gold. A fakir, a lawyer, a brigand, a woodcutter (named Xaïloun), and the wise old poet Lockman all die after their encounter with the gold, but God saves Xaïloun "à cause de son innocence et de sa simplicité" (because of his innocence and simplicity). Lockman is resurrected by an angel because he is a poet and sage. *Jean-François les Bas-bleus* is the story of a tailor's son whose education has come to naught. Finding him to be incapable of making sense of the material world or rational thought, people think him mad. But, when confronted with questions of the imagination and the spiritual world, he demonstrates a profound understanding; at the end of the tale, he is able to predict the future. The title character of *Baptiste Montauban* is another solitary, gentle figure. Rebuffed in love, he retreats from the world and develops a special communication with animals. After his death, his soul lives on in a state of pure being.

In certain ways opposed to his stories of innocents are the tales that feature the *dériseur sensé* (sensible mocker). Again, such categories are in no way exclusive; elements typical of this cycle also appear in many of his other texts. In this group of stories, Nodier mordantly criticizes and satirizes the notions of progress, perfectibility, and society, as he also does in his essays *De la perfectibilité de l'homme* (On the Perfectibility of Man, 1832), *De la fin prochaine du genre humain* (On the Near End of the Human Species, 1832), and *De l'utilité morale de l'instruction*, and, in a milder tone, in his novel *Histoire du roi de Bohême*. The most important of the *dériseur sensé* stories are *Léviathan-le-long* (*Revue de Paris*, November 1833), *Zérothoctro-Schah* (probably written in 1833, but not published until 1961), and *Voyage pittoresque et industriel dans le Paraguay-Roux et la Palingénésie australe* (*Revue de Paris*, February 1836). Nodier called the first two "histoires progressives" (progressive stories), that is, tales that follow a continuous story line, which, in fact, also includes the third text.

As in the eighteenth-century *conte philosophique* (philosophical tale), his characters undergo many mishaps and adventures that illustrate his philosophical points. Berniquet and others embark on the ship *Le Progressif* and head for the idyllic island of Patagonia to find the perfect man and the perfect society. The various characters and adventures, some fantastic, provoke discussions of subjects ranging from palingenesis to

Caricature of Nodier as a bibliophile, by Benjamin Roubaud

progress, education, medicine, and the Académie française. Finally, the idea of perfectibility is shown to be faulty; it is resurrection for which humankind yearns, and Zoroaster provides the key to its achievement. *Voyage pittoresque* is an attack on various social institutions, such as banks, the post office, railways, the king, the representative system of government, and the judicial system.

A third cycle of stories can be called the "mystical" works. This group certainly includes the short stories *Lydie ou la résurrection* (Lydie, or the Resurrection, *Revue de Paris*, April 1839) and *Franciscus Columna* (1844; translated as *Francesco Colonna*, 1929); some critics also include *Paul ou la ressemblance* (Paul, or the Resemblance, 1836) and *La Légende de sœur Béatrix* (The Legend of Sister Beatrix, *Revue de Paris*, October 1837). Nodier wrote all the texts of this cycle in the last eight years of his life. The emphasis on his idea of love and life in the hereafter distinguishes the mystical tales. Having shed his physical self through death, man will find eternal happiness in a resurrected state. For Nodier, love finds both its source and its fulfillment in an ideal realm. While it may have sensual dimensions, it remains a pure, innocent emotion and can be fulfilled only in the life after death.

Lydie ou la résurrection is a tale that expresses perhaps better than any other Nodier's ideas on palingenesis and the nature and power of love. Lydie has lost her husband in a fire, and she is considered by the villagers to be mad because she is convinced that he returns to her at night. He comes in the form of an angel that appears from a bright light. He tells her that he is in an intermediate state, between earth and resurrection; this is the palingenetic *état compréhensif*. Lydie finds great consolation in her vision; it enables her to continue living because she is convinced that death is not to be feared, and that reunion with her husband and eternal fulfillment await her. *Franciscus Columna* further develops Nodier's idea of the purity of love. The artist Franciscus, soon to become a monk, loves the cultured, beautiful, and rich Polia. They avow their love for each other but do not marry because they want to preserve the innocence of their love. At the end, in an ecstatic state dominated by thoughts of her, Franciscus passes to perpetual bliss.

Paul ou la ressemblance is a tale of filial love. The title character is approached by an old man who is convinced Paul is his son because Paul closely resembles the man's child, now dead, but whom the Virgin has announced to be still alive. Paul declines the man's offer of adoption, money, and love in order to stay with his own family. The tale contains passages about the nature of love and resurrection, and attacks on positivism and rationalism. In *La Légende de sœur Béatrix*, Sister Béatrix saves a man who is really her childhood love. Persuaded to leave with him, she ends up an abandoned, miserable beggar. She returns to her former convent, where the Virgin has taken her place. The Virgin tells her to don her former habit; she is thus transformed to her previous innocence.

The tales in the fourth group do not clearly fall into one of the other "cycles." The fantastic appears in many, such as *Inès de Las Sierras* (1837), a story of a ghost (Inès) representing the ideal, fatal, and eternal love of Lieutenant Sergy. *L'Amour et le grimoire* (Love and the Magic Book, *Revue de Paris*, October 1832) is a tale of diabolism whose fantastic tone is light, recalling the eighteenth-century libertine tale perhaps more than the serious fantastic story. Several texts are fairy tales, such as *Trésor des Fèves et Fleur des Pois* (1837; translated as *Bean Flower and Pea Blossom*, 1846). These resemble children's tales, while others are for adults, such as *La Fée aux miettes* and *Trilby*.

In his tales Nodier wanted to collect and preserve the legends, myths, and fables that spring from anonymous people. He had started with Slovenian folklore and literature in the *Télégraphe Officiel*, and he continued with increasing fervor as his life advanced. He was one of the first of his time to say that dialects could produce great literature, and he fought against legal proposals to suppress regional patois in France.

From 1833 to 1835 Nodier devoted most of his energy to the Académie française. As an *académicien* and *rapporteur* (reporter) of its dictionary, he wrote a series of articles reversing his former attacks on it. But his reduced literary activity of 1834 and 1835 was also caused by illnesses that kept him in bed for a month in the summer of 1834, three months in the spring in 1835, and again that winter. Diagnosed in December 1835 as having chronic nephritis (a diagnosis that was not entirely correct, but a condition that would be the cause of his death), he was ordered to reduce his activities dramatically. This meant giving up his daily sorties in search of rare books, his frequent evenings at the theater, and the hours spent at his favorite cafés and restaurants. He did manage to publish *Notions élémentaires de linguistique* (Elementary Notions of Linguistics) in 1834. That same year he founded, with the bookseller J. J. Techener, the important *Bulletin du Bibliophile*, a magazine for book lovers. As always, he maintained a voluminous correspondence with such friends as Charles Weiss and such literary figures as Lamartine. He also found the strength for a trip with Désirée to Belgium in late spring 1835; it turned out to be a kind of triumphal tour that he found surprising but gratifying.

Nodier's health deteriorated rapidly from the mid 1830s until his death. By late 1836 he had a cataract and needed strong glasses to see; he had gone deaf in one ear and had only partial hearing in the other; he trembled violently when writing; and he walked laboriously. Nevertheless, he maintained a prolific literary output through the 1830s, continued work at the Académie française, and maintained his correspondence. On 6 December 1843 he collapsed while returning from voting at the Hôtel de Ville, a civic duty he refused to neglect, and never again left his bed; he died on the evening of 27 January 1844. Until the last moment, Nodier was surrounded by friends and visitors to the Arsenal. He remained lucid, witty, considerate, warm, charming, and peaceful, with the wife, daughter, grand-children, and books that he loved at his side.

Letters:

Alexandre Estignard, *Correspondance inédite de Charles Nodier, 1796-1844* (Paris: Librairie du Moniteur Universel, 1876);

Boyer de Sainte-Suzanne, *Notes d'un curieux* (Monaco: Imprimerie du Journal de Monaco, 1878), pp. 339-417;

Léonce Pingaud, *Lettres de Charles Weiss à Charles Nodier* (Paris: Champion, 1889);

Gustave Simon, "Charles Nodier: lettres inédites à Victor Hugo," *Revue Mondiale*, 177 (1927): 329-339; 178 (1927): 11-17;

Jacques-Remi Dahan, *Correspondance croisée* (Bassac: Plein Chant, "Collection de l'atelier furtif," 1987).

Bibliographies:

Jean Larat, *Bibliographie critique des œuvres de Charles Nodier, suivie de documents inédits*, in his *La Tradition et l'exotisme dans l'œuvre de Charles Nodier (1780-1844). Etude sur les origines du romantisme français* (Paris: Champion, 1923);

Edmund J. Bender, *Bibliographie des œuvres, des lettres et des manuscrits de Charles Nodier; suivie d'une bibliographie choisie des études sur Charles Nodier, 1840-1966* (Lafayette, Ind.: Purdue University Studies, 1969);

Sarah Fore Bell, *Charles Nodier, His Life and Works: A Critical Bibliography, 1923-1967* (Chapel Hill: University of North Carolina Press, 1971);

Laurence M. Porter, "The Present State of Nodier Studies," in *The French Short Story*, edited by Phillip Crant (Columbia: University of South Carolina Press, 1975), pp. 199-205;

Raymond Setbon, "Le Dossier Nodier," *Romantisme*, 15 (1977): 92-107;

Jean Richer and Jean Senellier, "Charles Nodier: remarques et compléments bibliographiques," *Studi francese*, 24 (1980): 93-102;

Marie-Claude Amblard, "Compléments aux bibliographies des œuvres de Nodier," in *Charles Nodier. Colloque du deuxième centenaire. Besançon, mai 1980* (Paris: Les Belles Lettres, 1981), pp. 265-274;

Didier Barrière, "Bibliographie," in *Nodier l'homme du livre. Le rôle de la bibliophilie dans la littérature* (Bassac: Plein Chant, "L'Atelier du XIXᵉ siècle," 1989), pp. 199-309.

Biographies:

Marie Mennessier-Nodier, *Charles Nodier, épisodes et souvenirs de sa vie* (Paris: Didier, 1867);

Léonce Pingaud, *La Jeunesse de Charles Nodier: les Philadelphes* (Besançon: Dodivers, 1914);

Alfred Richard Oliver, *Charles Nodier: Pilot of Romanticism* (Syracuse: Syracuse University Press, 1964);

Hubert Juin, *Charles Nodier* (Paris: Seghers, 1970).

References:

Albert Béguin, *L'Ame romantique et le rêve. Essai sur le romantisme allemand et la poésie française* (Paris: José Corti, 1963), pp. 336-345;

René Bourgeois, "Charles Nodier ou les charmes de Clio," in *L'Ironie romantique: spectacle et jeu de Mme de Staël à Gérard de Nerval* (Grenoble: Presses Universitaires de Grenoble, 1974), pp. 173-218;

Pierre-Georges Castex, "Nodier et ses rêves," in *Le Conte fantastique en France de Nodier à Maupassant* (Paris: José Corti, 1951), pp. 121-167, 420-423;

Charles Nodier. Colloque du deuxième centenaire. Besançon mai 1980 (Paris: Les Belles Lettres, 1981);

"Charles Nodier l'annonceur," *Cahiers du Sud*, 37 (1950): 353-386;

Grant Crichfield, "Full Circle(s) in Nodier's *La Fée aux miettes*," *French Forum*, 9 (May 1984): 200-211;

Crichfield, "Nodier's Numbers: Multiplicity, Acceleration, Unity in *La Fée aux miettes*," *Nineteenth-Century French Studies*, 17 (Fall-Winter 1988-1989): 161-169;

Europe, issue on Nodier, 58 (June-July 1980);

Lucienne Frappier-Mazur, "Les Fous de Nodier et la catégorie de l'excentricité," *French Forum*, 4 (January 1979): 32-54;

Gérard Genette, "Onomatopoétique," in *Mimologiques. Voyage en Cratylie* (Paris: Seuil, 1976), pp. 149-181;

Miriam S. Hamenachem, *Charles Nodier: Essai sur l'imagination mythique* (Paris: Nizet, 1972);

Bettina L. Knapp, "Charles Nodier—The Crumb Fairy: A Heiros Gamos or a Sacred Marriage of Sun and Moon," in *Dream and Image* (Troy, N.Y.: Whitston, 1977);

Jean Larat, *La Tradition et l'exotisme dans l'œuvre de Charles Nodier (1780-1844). Etude sur les origines du romantisme français* (Paris: Champion, 1923);

André Lebois, *Un Bréviaire de compagnonnage: "La Fée aux miettes"* (Paris: Archive des Belles Lettres, 1961);

Hans Peter Lund, *La Critique du siècle chez Nodier* (Copenhagen: Akademisk Forlag, 1978);

Rudolph Maixner, *Charles Nodier et l'Illyrie* (Paris: Didier, 1960);

Robert J. Maples, "Individuation in Nodier's *La Fée aux miettes*," *Studies in Romanticism*, 8 (Autumn 1968): 43-64;

Max Milner, *Le Diable dans la littérature française de Cazotte à Baudelaire. 1772-1861*, 2 volumes (Paris: José Corti, 1960);

Hilda Nelson, *Charles Nodier* (New York: Twayne, 1972);

Laurence M. Porter, *The Literary Dream in French Romanticism: A Psychological Interpretation* (Detroit: Wayne State University Press, 1979);

Porter, "The Stylistic Debate of Charles Nodier's *L'Histoire du roi de Bohême*," *Nineteenth-Century French Studies*, 1 (Fall 1972): 21-32;

Jean Richer, *Autour de l' "Histoire du roi de Bohême"* (Paris: Archives des Lettres Modernes, 1962);

Charles-Augustin Sainte-Beuve, "Charles Nodier," in *Portraits littéraires (1844)*, in *Œuvres*, volume 2 (Paris: Gallimard, Bibliothèque de la Pléiade, 1960), pp. 297-333;

Daniel Sangsue, *Le Récit excentrique (Gautier, de Maistre, Nerval, Nodier)* (Paris: José Corti, 1987);

Marcel Schneider, *La Littérature fantastique en France* (Paris: Fayard, 1964);

Auguste Viatte, *Les Sources occultes du romantisme: illuminisme-théosophie, 1770-1820*, 2 volumes (Paris: Champion, 1928);

Jules Vodoz, *"La Fée aux miettes." Essai sur le rôle de l'inconscient dans l'œuvre de Charles Nodier* (Paris: Champion, 1925).

Papers:
The most important collection of Nodier's papers is at the Bibliothèque municipale de Besançon; the Bibliothèque Nationale and the Bibliothèque de l'Arsenal, both in Paris, hold additional manuscripts.

George Sand
(Amantine-Aurore-Lucile Dupin)

(1 July 1804 - 8 June 1876)

David A. Powell

Hofstra University

SELECTED BOOKS: *Rose et Blanche*, by Sand and Jules Sandeau, 5 volumes (Paris: Renault, 1831);

Indiana, 2 volumes (Paris: Roret et Dupuy, 1832); translated by George B. Ives (Philadelphia: Barrie & Son, 1900);

Valentine, 2 volumes (Paris: Dupuy, 1832); translated by Ives (Philadelphia: Barrie & Son, 1900);

Lélia, 2 volumes (Paris: Dupuy, 1833); revised edition, 1 volume (Paris: Bonnaire, 1839); translated by Maria Espinosa (Bloomington: Indiana University Press, 1978);

Jacques (Paris: Bonnaire, 1834);

Leone Leoni (Paris: Bonnaire, 1835); translated by Ives (Philadelphia: Barrie & Son, 1900);

André (Paris: Bonnaire, 1835);

Simon (Paris: Bonnaire, 1836);

Lettres d'un voyageur (Brussels: Scribe, Tecmen & Compagnie, 1837); translated by Eliza A. Ashurst as *Letters of a Traveller,* edited by Matilda M. Hays (London: E. Churton, 1847); translated by Sacha Rabinovitch and Patricia Thomson (Harmondsworth, U.K.: Penguin, 1987);

Mauprat (Paris: Bonnaire, 1837); translated by Stanley Young (London: Heinemann, n.d.); translated by Hays (London: E. Churton, 1847);

Spiridion (Paris: Bonnaire, 1839; revised edition, Paris: Perrotin, 1842);

Les Sept Cordes de la lyre (Paris: Bonnaire, 1840); translated by George A. Kennedy in *A Woman's Version of the Faust Legend: The Seven Strings of the Lyre* (Chapel Hill: University of North Carolina Press, 1989);

Gabriel (Paris: Bonnaire, 1840);

Le Compagnon du Tour de France, 2 volumes (Paris: Perrotin, 1841); translated by Hays as *The Companion of the Tour of France* (London: Churton, 1847);

Horace (Paris: L. de Porter, 1842);

Consuelo (Paris: L. de Porter, 1843); translated by Francis G. Shaw, 2 volumes (Boston: W. D. Ticknor, 1846); translated by Fayette Robinson (Greenwich, Conn.: Fawcett, 1961);

Teverino (Paris: Calmann-Lévy, n.d.; Brussels: Société Belge de Librairie, 1845);

La Comtesse de Rudolstadt (Paris: L. de Porter, 1844); translated by Francis G. Shaw (Boston: Ticknor, 1847);

Jeanne (Brussels: Hauman, 1844);

Le Meunier d'Angibault (Paris: Desessart, 1845); translated by Mary E. Dewey as *The Miller of Angibault* (Boston: Roberts, 1863);

Isidora (Paris: Souverain, 1846);

Le Péché de Monsieur Antoine (Brussels: Lebèque et Sacré fils, 1846);

La Mare au diable (Paris: E. Proux, n.d. [1846]); translated by Antonia Cowan as *Devil's Pool* (London: Blackie, 1966); translated by Frank Porter as *The Haunted Pool* (Berkeley, Cal.: Shameless Hussy Press, 1976);

Lucrezia Floriani (Paris: E. Proux, 1846);

François le champi (Brussels: Meline, Cans & Compagnie, 1848); translated by Eirene Collis as *The Country Waif* (Lincoln: University of Nebraska Press, 1977);

La Petite Fadette, 2 volumes (Paris: Michel Lévy, 1849); translated as *Little Fadette. A Domestic Story* (London: G. Slater, 1849); translated by Hays as *Fadette. A Domestic Story* (New York: Putnam, 1851); translated by Eva Figes as *Little Fadette* (London: Blackie, 1967);

Le Château des Désertes (Paris: Michel Lévy, 1851);

Les Maîtres sonneurs (Paris: Cadot, 1853); translated by Katherine Wormeley as *The Bagpipers* (Boston: Little, Brown, 1890);

Histoire de ma vie, 4 volumes (Paris: Lecou, 1854-1855); partial translation by Maria E. McKaye as *My Convent Life* (Chicago: Academy Chicago, 1977); partial translation by Dan Hofstadter as *My Life* (New York:

George Sand, circa 1864 (photograph by Nadar)

Harper & Row, 1979); translated and edited by Thelma Jurgrau as *Story of My Life* (Binghamton, N.Y.: SUNY Press, 1991);

La Daniella (Paris: Librairie nouvelle, 1857);

Elle et lui (Paris: Hachette, 1859); translated by Ives as *She and He* (Philadelphia: Barrie & Son, 1900);

Le Marquis de Villemer (Paris: Naumbourg & Paetz, 1860-1861);

Valvèdre (Paris: Michel Lévy, 1861);

Tamaris (Paris: Michel Lévy, 1862);

Mademoiselle la Quintinie (Paris: Michel Lévy, 1863);

Le Dernier Amour (Paris: Michel Lévy, 1867);

Mademoiselle Merquem (Paris: Michel Lévy, 1868);

Césarine Dietrich (Paris: Michel Lévy, 1871);

Nanon (Paris: Michel Lévy, 1872);

Contes d'une grand-mère, volume 1 (Paris: Michel Lévy, 1873); volume 2 (Paris: C. Lévy, 1876); translated by Margaret Bloom (Philadelphia & London: Lippincott, 1930);

Ma Soeur Jeanne (Paris: Michel Lévy frères, 1874); translated by R. S. Crocker as *My Sister Jeannie* (Boston: Roberts, 1874).

Editions and Collections: *Œuvres complètes de George Sand*, 24 volumes (Paris: Bonnaire,

1836-1840); 1 volume (Paris: Magen et Comon, 1841); 2 volumes (Paris: Souverain, 1842);

Œuvres complètes de George Sand, 16 volumes, revised by Sand (Paris: Perrotin, 1842-1844; Paris: Garnier, 1847);

Œuvres complètes de George Sand illustrées par Tony Johannot et Maurice Sand, 9 volumes (Paris: Hetzel, 1851-1856);

Œuvres de George Sand, 109 volumes (Paris: Hetzel-Lecou, 1852-1855; Paris: Michel Lévy, 1856-1857);

Questions d'art et de littérature (Paris: C. Lévy, 1878);

Questions politiques et sociales (Paris: C. Lévy, 1879);

Masterpieces of George Sand, 20 volumes, translated by George B. Ives (Philadelphia: Barrie & Son, 1900-1902);

Voyage en Auvergne, in *Œuvres autobiographiques*, 2 volumes, edited by Georges Lubin (Paris: Gallimard, 1970-1971);

Œuvres complètes, 33 volumes, edited by Lubin (Paris: Aujourd'hui / Les Introuvables, 1976-1979);

George Sand: In Her Own Words, translated and edited by Joseph Barry (Garden City, N.Y.: Doubleday, 1979).

PLAY PRODUCTIONS: *Cosima*, Paris, Théâtre-Français, 29 April 1840;

François le champi, Paris, Odéon, 23 November 1849;

Claudie, Paris, Théâtre de la Porte-Saint-Martin, 11 January 1851;

Le Mariage de Victorine, Paris, Gymnase, 26 November 1851;

Mauprat, Paris, Odéon, 28 November 1853;

Le Marquis de Villemer, Paris, Odéon, 29 February 1864;

La Petite Fadette, Paris, Opéra-Comique, 15 September 1864.

For seventy-five years after her death, George Sand was preemptorily dismissed as a writer of adolescent fiction, not worthy of serious study, "une écriveuse" (a woman scribbler). The only titles that had made an impact were *La Mare au diable* (1846; translated as *Devil's Pool*, 1966) and *La Petite Fadette* (1849; translated as *Little Fadette*, 1967), deemed appropriate for teenage girls. Readers of Marcel Proust knew *François le champi* (1848; translated as *The Country Waif*, 1977) for its prominent place in the opening pages of his *Du côté de chez Swann* (1913; translated as *Swann's Way*, 1922), though this did little initially to invite a serious critical investigation of Sand's oeuvre. Sand predicted she would fall from popularity if she failed to keep her name before the public. And even though she produced more than eighty novels, two dozen plays, three volumes of short stories, and many political tracts, even though she continued writing and publishing until her death, she was quickly forgotten.

Sand occupied a most important, transitional position in the French novelistic tradition. She stands alongside Honoré de Balzac for her mixture of romantic and realistic ideals and approaches, though she is more sincere and more didactic than the Tourengeau author. She also takes her place alongside Gustave Flaubert, a generation earlier, though much more sincere and more moralizing than the Norman novelist. In addition, she enjoyed close relationships with many well-known artists in Paris, such as Franz Liszt, Alfred de Musset, Eugène Delacroix, Frédéric Chopin, Heinrich Heine, and Ivan Turgenev, to name but a few. There is no doubt that she reflected the artistic and cultural activities of the capital as well as the ideological concerns of her day.

During her lifetime, George Sand was, with Eugène Sue and Balzac, one of the most widely read French authors. Wherever her novels were serialized, in the *Revue des Deux Mondes*, in the *Presse*, or in several other journals, she enjoyed a faithful following. Her popularity among her contemporaries can be explained by two distinct reasons: feminist and socialist ideology and personal reputation. Sand's novels and plays frequently extol the contributions of women to society and defend women's right to happiness. She also attacks the status quo of nineteenth-century French society, from marriage to the archaic hierarchy of the class system. At the same time, Sand's private life did not go long unnoticed in Parisian circles, and from the moment her gender was discovered (she often sported male student's garb), her personal life became a curiosity for many.

During her lifetime, Sand was widely read and acclaimed. She repeatedly pleased her readership, and many of her works had several reprintings. After her death, however, other contemporary authors took her place in the hearts of the public, and she was soon forgotten by readers and critics alike. Not until the late 1950s was there a resurgence of interest in the Berrichon writer, and even then critical analyses focused largely on the autobiographical nature of her writing. Attacks on marriage in her novels and especially her own sexual freedom led to rather brutal assessments of her work. André Maurois's biography, *Lélia, ou la vie de George Sand* (Lélia, or The Life of George Sand, 1952) offers an unsophisticated and misogynistic interpretation of that novel as an explanation of Sand's entire life. Shortly after Maurois's biography came one by Pierre Salomon, *George Sand* (1953), which focuses largely on Sand's love and sex life. He makes the traditional attempts to link life and works and often sees her novels as a fictional transposition of episodes in her life. He has little interest in Sand as a creative mind or a literary innovator.

Since the late 1960s, not uncoincidentally at the same time as the rise of the modern feminist movement, critics have paid more attention to George Sand and her writings. The next decade witnessed the establishment of literary societies devoted to the study of Sand's works (The Friends of George Sand at Hofstra University and Les Amis de George Sand in Paris) as well as several important new editions of her novels and essays, though many still remain to appear in modern, critical editions. Some noteworthy biographies appeared around the centenary of Sand's death, including those by Curtis Cate, Francine Mallet, and Joseph Barry. Sand's novels are now receiving serious consideration by prominent literary critics, and her tenuous position in the French literary canon is being redefined.

George Sand began life as Amantine-Aurore-Lucile Dupin, on 1 July 1804, born in Paris to a couple from opposite social backgrounds. Her mother, Sylvie Delaborde, was the daughter of a Parisian bird seller; her father, Maurice Dupin, was an illegitimate descendant of Frederic-Auguste de Saxe, King of Poland. They had wed less than a month before their daughter's birth. Aurore's father began a brilliant career in Napoleon's armies, but his life ended abruptly in a riding accident near his home at Nohant (Berry) when Aurore was only four years old. Aurore's mother, at odds on all counts with her mother-in-law, Marie-Aurore Dupin, eventually gave in to the financial arrangement Mme Dupin the elder proposed; Sylvie left Aurore in Nohant and returned to Paris.

Aurore thus grew up with her strict grandmother, who, despite her Voltairean ideals, sent her granddaughter to convent school in Paris. There Aurore abandoned her childhood religious invention, Corambé, the androgynous deity

*Sand in 1830 (portrait by Eugène Delacroix;
Musée Carnavalet)*

to whom she had built a natural altar in the woods behind Nohant. At the Convent of the English Augustinians she had a revelation and contemplated taking vows but was quickly and earnestly discouraged by her confessor and a nun who had befriended her.

Quite concerned at her granddaughter's newfound penchant for religious devotion, Mme Dupin brought Aurore back to Nohant. She hoped to teach Aurore to take her place as mistress of Nohant, but she fell ill and died less than a year later. Aurore, who was seventeen, was forced to live in an unsatisfactory arrangement with her mother in Paris. During an escapist visit with friends outside of Paris, Aurore met the man who would take her away from this unpleasant life: Casimir Dudevant. They were married in August 1822, and Aurore gave birth to a son, Maurice, on 30 June 1823.

Aurore soon regretted her marriage. Casimir, who was not a good companion and did not share her intellectual curiosities, spent most of his time hunting and drinking with Hippolyte Chatiron, Aurore's half brother. On a trip to the Pyrenees and then to the Dudevant estate outside

of Bordeaux, Aurore met Aurélien de Sèze, a dashing young man with inspiring poetic and intellectual attributes. He is often assumed to be Aurore's first great love. When the Dudevants returned to Nohant, Aurore was reunited with her childhood friend Stéphane Ajasson de Grandsagne, who is reputed to be the father of her second child, Solange, born 13 March 1828.

Two years later another Berrichon returned from his studies in Paris and caught Aurore's fancy: Jules Sandeau. Jules's lively intellect and youthful charms corresponded precisely to Aurore's needs of the moment. Jules returned to Paris; at the same time, Aurore found a letter in which Casimir explained his low opinion of his wife. She confronted him and promptly left for Paris (January 1831) with a modest pension from her husband.

Life in Paris with Jules was exciting, and Aurore enthusiastically took advantage of the cultural offerings of the capital. She discovered she could garner inexpensive tickets to the theater if she dressed as a male student; this habit soon established a reputation for the burgeoning writer and became her insignia. She was not above exploiting the obvious marketing advantages of such curiosity. Although she first began crossdressing for practical reasons, she continued the suggestive habit even after her identity was wellknown. She enjoyed shocking people, gaining a reputation as provocative because she smoked in public, most often cigars or a pipe. She once appeared at one of the regular dinner parties at Magny's (a famous Parisian restaurant of the era) dressed in a scarlet Persian outfit, sporting a sword at her side and smoking a cigar. Musset, whom she had met shortly before at Charles-Augustin Sainte-Beuve's, was quite intimidated by her outfit and demeanor. Such dress and behavior gave rise to rumors concerning Sand's morals, rumors fueled by her bold separation from her husband to live in Paris with her lover.

Aurore began to write at this time. Jules had already embarked on a writing career and encouraged Aurore to join him in a few collaborative efforts, including the full-length novel *Rose et Blanche* (1831). During her return visit to Nohant and her children in the summer of 1831, Aurore wrote her first solo novel, *Indiana* (1832), which soon set her apart from her lover. Aurore and Jules had published together under the joint pseudonym "J. Sand." Now Aurore's editor wanted her to continue with a similar name, so she adopted "G. Sand," "G." for "George," which reminded Sand of her earthbound roots in Berry. "George Sand" soon became the name associated with the new author.

In *Indiana*, Sand deplores the fate of women in marriage. The nineteen-year-old eponymous character, growing weary with her dull life as the wife of a retired army officer, is smitten with the charming Raymon de Ramière, who is having an affair with Indiana's Creole maid, Noun. The latter, pregnant with Raymon's child, discovers his attempts to seduce Indiana and drowns herself. Indiana also attempts suicide, though she never succumbs to Raymon's wiles. Followed by her English cousin, Sir Ralph, Indiana returns to her native Isle of Bourbon, planning to jump off a cliff; out of an ill-explained dedication, Ralph plans to join her. In an appended conclusion now considered an integral part of the text, Indiana and Ralph recognize and declare their love for each other just before their uncompleted suicidal jump. Thereafter they lead a Rousseauistic existence on the island, far from the harmful influence of French society.

Indiana was hailed as a successful novel in the Balzacian mode, in terms of structure and plot. The female characters, however, have much more depth and sensitivity than the men. Indiana's tiresome hesitations implicitly reflect her circumstances; Noun's brash reaction signals a decisiveness of which Indiana is incapable. Raymon is cleverly designed to elicit the reader's scorn. He resembles the socialite Rastignac of Balzac's fictional world, though with less of a sense of historical development. The novel's ending seems abrupt and implausible. Although the return to Bourbon establishes a sense of closure, the final pages give the reader a pseudopastoral depiction of the merits of country life in opposition to the ills of society. Sir Ralph remains sketchy to the end. He lurks in Indiana's surroundings as a shadow, without being fleshed out; when he suddenly decides to accompany her to Bourbon, he becomes a principal character, with almost no preparation. His dedication to Indiana, though touching, verges on incest and largely repeats the older man / younger woman match of her marriage.

Valentine (1832) constitutes Sand's first attempt at depicting life in the provinces. Bénédict, a simple but intelligent peasant, falls in love with the aristocratic but uncomplicated Valentine. Their love is simple, chaste, and mostly implicit. Although Valentine marries someone of her rank, the marriage remains unconsummated, and

she continues to see Bénédict, chastely, during her husband's long absences. The situation is made awkward by Valentine's half sister, Louise, who is the unwed mother of a young boy, Valentin. She, too, has feelings for Bénédict, but she sacrifices them for Valentine's sake, even though she knows her half sister's love can never be expressed. The confusion of emotions and social constructs—aristocracy versus peasantry; love versus honor; faithfulness versus personal desires; education and culture versus Philistine pretentions; appearances versus reality—makes this novel a perspicacious examination of society in general and of provincial society in particular. Nothing specifically points to Berry in *Valentine*, but the emphasis on country folk to the exclusion of Parisian society already marks Sand's determination to devote her talents to the study of her people.

Rather jealous of Sand's two novels and a short story, "Melchior," published in the *Revue de Paris* (July 1832), Sandeau sank into despair, marked by a lack of productivity. They soon parted, and Sand's autonomous career began. But in her determination to gain independence through writing, further bolstered by her recent successes, she suffered from great anxiety because of her personal situation. According to the Napoleonic Code, she risked losing her homestead, Nohant, and the custody of her children to her husband if she left him definitively. She began to doubt herself and felt she had nowhere to turn, not even the church. From the depths of this despair she produced *Lélia*, undoubtedly one of her most innovative and challenging novels.

Lélia, published in late July 1833, is a confused repository of Sand's ill feelings, an attempt to define unhappiness with men, disappointment with herself, and disenchantment with society, religion, and indeed life in general. From a plan for a short story concerning a repentant ex-gambler, the novel developed into a disquisition on a woman's inability to satisfy her desires. Lélia's unwillingness to separate Sténio, the poet she loves and who loves her, from other men leads her down a road of denial, uncertainty, self-doubt, and self-destruction. Lélia's long-lost sister, Pulchérie, embodies the hedonism Lélia refuses to recognize. Pulchérie finally seduces Sténio for Lélia's sake. Lélia, now in a convent, explains to Sténio the futility of hoping for any response from her; Sténio drowns himself in despair. Magnus, who has fallen in love with Lélia, fails to answer Sténio's calls for help; he holds himself responsible for the young poet's death. He charges Lélia with political scheming, which also implicates the Cardinal; the latter poisons himself, and Lélia is sentenced by the Inquisition and dies.

Sand was quite fond of what she considered her one metaphysical novel, though she was plagued by the enormity of doubt it communicated. She was also troubled by the unfavorable and sometimes hostile reception it received. Over the next six years, she struggled to revise *Lélia* to make it a more acceptable, less pessimistic work. Not only did she wish the novel to please the public, but she also feared harmful repercussions on her impending trial for legal separation from Casimir. In 1839 a revised edition of *Lélia* appeared. In the optimistic new ending, the title character becomes an abbess. Sand's recent introduction to the religious writer Félicité-Robert de Lamennais, Pierre Leroux, Franz Liszt, and the Berrichon lawyer Michel de Bourges certainly influenced her revision of *Lélia*.

Musset was one of Sand's fans, and he greatly admired *Lélia*. Shortly after its publication he met her at a dinner party arranged by Sainte-Beuve. Sand and Musset began a liaison in the summer of 1833. During a walk in the forest at Fontainebleau, Musset suffered a seizure and had hallucinations that seemed to presage his early death. In December the romantic couple left for Italy, a lifelong dream for both. Once in Genoa, however, Sand fell ill, and Musset searched the streets for distraction. When they moved on to Florence, Sand had recovered and set to work, but Musset's habits were already well established. Sand handed him her research on powerful Renaissance families in Florence, which she had used to draft "Une Conspiration en 1537," and urged him to accomplish some worthwhile work. He soaked up local color in Florence and used that familiarity to remold Sand's draft, producing one of the most famous plays of the Romantic era, *Lorenzaccio* (1834).

By the time the couple reached Venice, relations were already strained. Musset fell ill and was apparently near death. Sand called in a young doctor, Pietro Pagello, who was fascinated by the mysterious French female writer. Their affair reportedly began while Musset lay on his sickbed, only meters away. When Musset felt well enough, he and Sand agreed that it would be better if he returned to Paris. She stayed in Venice and began a full-blown relationship with Pagello.

During the few short months of this liaison, Sand began writing what would become her first

autobiographical work, *Lettres d'un voyageur* (1837; translated as *Letters of a Traveller*, 1847). Originally consisting of only three letters written to Musset about her thoughts and discoveries in the Veneto, this work grew to include a series of twelve letters written between 1834 and 1836 to various friends and colleagues, expressing a gamut of emotions, from nostalgia to melancholy, from fear to anger, and comprising thoughts on suicide, religion, and music. Sand used the device of a masculine narrator, yet there is no doubt that the central "I" and the author are one and the same.

The "Venetian" letters offer a valuable insight into Sand's interest in "effets de réel" (realistic devices), as she freely describes the details of Venetian fetes, the musical talents of gondoliers, and the costumes of women of all social strata. This attention to detail would serve her well in her quasi-realist depictions of life and people in Berry in her famous rustic novels. The remainder of the letters treat the nature of travel. She extols the need to bring a fresh outlook to one's perception of the world. She writes Giacomo Meyerbeer an adulatory and well-informed letter on his opera *Les Huguenots* (1836), displaying her knowledge of contemporary music. She also refers to Liszt's link between music and the written word, an important association for Sand's own creative world.

After an untidy and embarrassing ending to the Pagello relationship, Sand, now splitting her time between Paris and Nohant, began legal proceedings against her husband. As divorce was not an option, the most she could hope for was a legal separation that would return to her all her property and the custody of her children. The series of trials was unpleasant; fortunately for Sand, public opinion swayed the judges in their final decision, and she won her case.

Throughout this period (1835-1836), Sand received legal counsel from Bourges. Their relationship, which soon became a liaison, provided a new source of inspiration for Sand, since Michel persuaded her to develop a political discourse in her writing to reflect the world around her. Though the political subtext of Sand's works is evident from the start, there is a marked change at this time as its expression became more explicit.

Mauprat (1837) transforms into fiction many of Sand's burgeoning political and feminist concerns of this tumultuous period. Edmée Mauprat talks her way out of a rape by her cousins with the help of the youngest cousin, Bernard Mauprat. She proves to be the superior and dominant character of the novel. While she is not Sand's first strong woman, she is perhaps the first willfully dominant woman of Sand's universe. Bernard falls in love with her, but Edmée will not accept his declaration of love until he proves himself worthy of her. She designs for him a rigorous rehabilitation program of general education and social training. She even sends him away to America for several years and charges him with continuing his education while abroad. When he returns, there are legal problems between the upper and lower branches of the family. The trial scenes display a realism inspired by Sand's own ordeal in court the year before. The novel does end with Edmée and Bernard's union, but there is no doubt that Edmée successfully and rightfully maintains her dominant role. This text can be seen as Sand's declaration of feminism, more explicitly militant than in any previous work.

About this time Sand managed to wrangle from her friend Liszt an introduction to Chopin. The young, very Catholic Polish musician was at first intimidated by the strong, unconventional Frenchwoman, but he soon gave in to her seductions and to his own desires. They agreed to try out their relationship away from the piercing eyes of Parisian gossipmongers and spent the winter of 1838-1839 in Majorca. There Chopin composed, among other works, his series of preludes, and Sand finished *Spiridion* (1839), a novel on which she had been working for several months.

Spiridion, which she started while revising *Lélia*, depicts the conflict between Sand's fervent spiritualism and her uncertain religious affiliations. The novel traces one man's search for the true religion; Leroux's influence shines through. There was later some speculation that he had written parts of the book; these charges were disproven in Jean Pommier's *George Sand et le rêve monastique: "Spiridion"* (George Sand and The Monastic Dream: "Spiridion," 1966). The Romantic notion of progress serves as an underpinning to the hero's quest for religious truth. Born and raised Jewish, he converts first to Protestantism, then to Catholicism, changing his name with each new incarnation. Disillusioned with the lack of piety among his fellow monks, Spiridion decides he must go beyond Catholicism, but fear of the Inquisition forces him to write down his vision and secretly to pass the manuscript on to a devoted disciple. Three generations later, the manuscript is unearthed by a young monk, Angel. Labeled *Hic*

Self-portrait of Sand, 1831 (from Joseph Barry, Infamous Woman: The Life of George Sand, *1977)*

est veritas!, it displays the influence of *The Imitation of Jesus Christ* by Thomas à Kempis (fifteenth-century) and the Gospel of St. John. A revised version of *Spiridion* appeared almost four years later.

Sand now embarked on projects springing from another interest: socialism. After Bourges urged her to greater political militancy, she gradually incorporated in her writing more explicit commentary on social ills and her dream for an egalitarian community. The first work in this socialist strain, *Simon* (1836), presents only skeletal issues with little development. In *Le Compagnon du Tour de France* (1840), Sand demonstrates her ability to insert socialist theory into a narrative. Influenced by Agricol Perdiguier's book, *Le Livre du compagnonnage* (The Book of Guilds and Trade Associations, 1839), Sand's *Compagnon* laments the failings of the guild system while admitting the damage often wreaked by overly zealous idealists.

Pierre Hugenin, a master carpenter, represents the innocent socialist who has no pretense to reform. His posture as a tolerant yet careful idealist serves as a literary device to allow sometimes long expositions on socialist theory. A romantic interest parallels the socialist struggle: Pierre falls in love with and is loved by Yseult de Villepreux. Despite her aristocratic name, she and her grandfather are devoted to a democratic ideal. However, the reader discovers that the comte de Villepreux actually harbors Orléanist sympathies. When he discovers his granddaughter's attachment to a carpenter, he reminds Yseult of her promise never to marry a commoner, a promise she does not break. This ending lacks any naive foreshadowing of social ills; there remains, however, an undercurrent of hope.

Horace (1842) continues this social commentary, though along less ambitious lines. Paul Arsène, a working-class provincial, rubs elbows unpretentiously with bourgeois students in Paris. Sand attempts to prove through this character that different classes can coexist peacefully. Horace represents another type, the bourgeois who amasses debts in his attempts to become part of aristocratic society; he fails miserably and goes to Italy to start life afresh. Sand's condemnation of the social climber is not total; at the novel's close, Horace has a clear understanding of his hypocrisy and deceit. She also allows him the hope of a new beginning. The socialist discourse in *Horace* displays a thorough awareness of contemporary Saint-Simonian activities (based on the ideas of Claude-Henri de Rouvroy, Comte de Saint-Simon) in Paris. While Sand communicates a certain intellectual curiosity alongside a clear, almost religious dedication to the new socialism, one also detects a warning against trends in political movements.

Le Meunier d'Angibault (The Miller of Angibault, 1845) and *Le Péché de Monsieur Antoine* (The Sin of Monsieur Antoine, 1846), both minor works in Sand's corpus, present various forms of the socialist dream. The first discusses the issue of whether money obtained immorally can be used for moral purposes. Henri Lémor struggles against his father's devotion to accumulating wealth as well as his own love for an aristocratic woman, Marcelle de Blanchemont. Henri makes amends for his father's swindlings, bankrupting himself in the process. Only when he finds out that Marcelle was left penniless by her deceased husband can he hope for happiness. In the second novel, Monsieur Antoine hides his noble name and raises his daughter, Gilberte, with democratic ideals. She falls in love with Emile Cardonnet, who shares and indeed fosters her socialist dreams. Several theoretical discus-

sions, not always seamlessly woven into the narrative, clarify the dominant socialist theme.

In all the so-called socialist novels, several social classes bear some of the responsibility for conflict, pointing to a need for social leveling and democratization. Sand often considered that country folk demonstrated a greater comprehension of democracy, a conviction which led her to embark on a series of novels devoted to life in the central provinces of France (mostly Berry and Creuse) and to the needs and desires of their people. Three novels traditionally make up the "rustic" series: *La Mare au diable*, *François le champi*, and *La Petite Fadette*. They showed Parisian readers an aspect of French life unfamiliar to them, though her presentation is far from realistic in a Flaubertian sense. Sand's idealization of peasant life remains one of the benchmarks of provincial literature, inspiring such novelists as Thomas Hardy, Charlotte Brontë, George Eliot, and Leo Tolstoy. At the same time, Sand's peasant paradise has given rise to some criticism: commentators often find fault with her "effets de réel," which are sometimes anachronistic or ageographical, or charge her with using a middle-class, patronizing tone. Her rustic novels deserve, however, a serious reading.

In Sand's first attempt at the provincial / peasant novel, *Jeanne* (1844), the title character is coveted by three men: an English nobleman, Sir Arthur; a French nobleman, Guillaume; and a French bourgeois, Léon. The vulgar Léon insults Jeanne in his bungled attempts at seduction. Sir Arthur declares his love openly and honestly; Guillaume, Sir Arthur's best friend, represses his love, ostensibly out of respect for Arthur and Jeanne. None of the love interests is developed, though Jeanne is quite moved by Sir Arthur's respect and love for her. Like Chateaubriand's Atala, Jeanne promised her dying mother not to marry, and she dies keeping the promise. Jeanne represents Sand's ideal: a simple, uneducated woman who displays a natural intelligence and a solid moral constitution. Her character would be further developed with Nanon almost thirty years later. The finely woven mixture of Christianity with superstition and regional legends gives this novel its distinctive flavor and provides a valuable insight into peasant beliefs.

La Mare au diable, a novel often given to girls for wholesome reading, depicts the complex confusion that besets a widower strongly encouraged by his family to seek a new wife and mother to his children. While the search concentrates purely on finding someone who will carry out the function of a good wife and mother, Germain finds himself sharing his woes, repeating especially how much he misses his wife, with a young neighbor, Marie. Meanwhile, Marie is beginning her adult life and is discovering the dangers the world holds for women. In a long discussion by a lakeside, the famous "devil's pool," both reveal their disillusions and disappointments to each other, and in so doing realize how well they complement each other. An appendix to the novel, *Les Noces de campagne* (The Country Wedding), gives a detailed account of their wedding and is often cited as one of Sand's most sincere attempts to document Berrichon life in fiction.

François le champi tells the story of a foundling, François, who is taken in by Madeleine Blanchot. When her mean-spirited husband sends him away, François obtains employment on a farm at some distance. Later, when M. Blanchot dies, François returns to assist Madeleine in her time of grief. He finds her bedridden, unable to perform any household functions. While nursing her and putting her affairs in order, he gradually realizes his love and devotion for her, which she returns. They marry despite the hint of incest, which led to scandal when the novel was first published. As a foundling, François is an outsider and suffers from the stigma, though he does not understand it. In a way his separation from Madeleine and subsequent return bring him a more forthright, less suspicious allure: he comes back as a young adult, for whom the absence of history is somewhat less troublesome than for a child. The separation from Madeleine in time and space also distances him from her and diminishes the incestuous shadow.

La Petite Fadette tackles directly the issue of superstition and "witch doctoring" in Berry. Fadette, a poor young girl who lives in a hovel in the woods, crosses the path of bourgeois twins, Landry and Sylvinet, an encounter which forces the issue of social class. Fadette helps Landry find his brother, who is lost in the woods; Landry is then beholden to her and struggles with the moral conflict of indebtedness to someone who inspires fear and disgust in him. Ashamed that he tried to shirk his responsibility of gratitude, Landry regrets his judgment. He gets to know Fadette and learns to like and respect her; he even falls in love with her. Despite disapproval from friends and family, and especially the strong jealousy of Sylvinet, they marry.

Paganism is pitted against Christianity in *Fadette*. Taking up again the theme introduced in *Jeanne*, Sand weaves into the narrative on sorcery a subtle argument about the outsider. Fadette refuses to conform to traditional expectations, which are somewhat foreign to her anyway because of her background. Unable to tolerate difference, the village children mock her clothes and her backward ways. These prejudices inform Landry's initial reaction to Fadette's mysterious powers. Albeit didactic and moralistic, *La Petite Fadette* is perhaps one of Sand's finest works on the issue of tolerance and acceptance.

Les Maîtres sonneurs (1853; translated as *The Bagpipers*, 1890), though not traditionally considered one of the "romans champêtres" (rustic novels), takes place in Berry and neighboring Bourbonnais. It explores the complex nature of personal and social problems, successfully dispelling the patronizing Parisian view of "simple provincial life." Joseph, who becomes a master bagpiper in the course of the novel, expresses his love, and his frustration at this unrequited love, through his ingenious musical improvisations. Sand examines communication through music, with special emphasis on folk music and improvisation. Once again she uses the theme of the outsider; Joseph's inability to express himself earns him the reputation of being a backward child. Once he proves his capacity for expression through music, he becomes defensive and almost defiant in his musical prowess. However, even among other musicians, Joseph remains an outsider, largely because of his arrogance, but also because of his gift of improvisation, which sets him apart from more ordinary musicians.

Sand's masterpiece, *Consuelo* (1843), and its sequel, *La Comtesse de Rudolstadt* (1844; translated, 1847), combine elements of the musical novel, the Gothic novel, the Bildungsroman, and the historical novel. *Consuelo* follows the title heroine, inspired by Sand's close friend Pauline Viardot, through her preparations for a singing career during the mid eighteenth century, her stint as a private music tutor, her debut and disillusionment with the theater, and her initiation into a secret society. Consuelo is an orphan whose beautiful voice earns her a place in a convent music school with the famous maestro Porpora. Her purity, in musical style as well as in morality, places her above those around her, which causes Consuelo several problems. Repelled by the people in the theater, to whom her friend and betrothed, Anzoleto, has become attached, she leaves Venice to take a job as private music tutor to a Bohemian aristocratic family, the Rudolstadts. The young baron, Albert, an erudite but strange son of the family, believes he is the reincarnation of several famous Bohemian revolutionaries. In Consuelo, he finds the messianic answer to his long-awaited dream. They understand each other through musical expression and appreciation. Music and politics are linked through purity in the ideological theme of this novel.

Albert falls in love with Consuelo, and she recognizes that she is fond of him; but his aunt makes it clear he is not to marry a commoner, so Consuelo keeps her desires to herself, indeed hidden from even herself. Sensing an awkward situation, she leaves the Rudolstadt home to travel on foot to Vienna, where Porpora has relocated. En route she meets a young musician who seeks instruction from the two people of the musical world he admires most: la Porporina (Consuelo) and Porpora. The young man is Joseph Haydn. Together they travel to Vienna and find Porpora, who takes her to Berlin on an opera contract, but she is urgently called back to the Rudolstadt castle, where Albert is dying. His aunt, convinced he is dying of a broken heart, consents to the marriage with Consuelo; Consuelo agrees, also hoping to save Albert's life. All efforts are in vain: Albert dies, and Consuelo promises the aunt never to use her noble title. This scene brings to a poignant head the bitterness of class struggles inherent in the relationship.

Consuelo pleases the Berlin operagoing public, but her refusal to accommodate Frederick the Great puts her in prison. She profits from her incarceration by composing and maintaining the purity of her voice. Concurrently, Albert's comrades, "les Invisibles," examine Consuelo's moral and political fiber to see whether she could become a member of their secret society, a Freemason type of organization aiming to topple unjust despots. This sequence of events is often interpreted as a prefiguration of the French Revolution. Albert has not really died, and he mysteriously frees Consuelo from prison without her knowing who he is. She is inducted into "les Invisibles" after she proves to Albert's mother, Wanda—the only other female member of the secret society—that she does love Albert.

Consuelo loses her voice, a loss that to her seems to be the answer to her troubles; she devotes herself to Albert and their children as they roam throughout Eastern Europe, preaching the love of humanity through music. Albert plays the violin while Consuelo composes some music, but mostly she interprets Albert's music for the public.

Consuelo is a microcosm of Sand's universe. The prerevolutionary setting allows, paradoxically, for a rich political and social commentary on contemporary France, for while Sand's attack on the class system does focus on an aristocratic family, her plea for an egalitarian society suggests the socialism of the 1830s and 1840s. The atmosphere of eighteenth-century underground movements, clearly exemplified by the Masoniclike group of "les Invisibles," contributes as much to the Gothic flavor of the novel as to its function as historical fiction. The idealist strain is also reminiscent of many socialist tracts of the period, and it reflects the tone Sand often used to convey socialist dreams.

The aesthetic aspect of the novel provides an equally rich backdrop to commentary on the role of the artist in society, the attitude of the artist toward art, and the artist's response to the public. La Corilla, Consuelo's rival on the stage as well as in the heart of her betrothed, embodies the perfect opera star: a magnificent instrument, a well-trained technique, and a healthy reserve of sentimentality tempered by the gift of (false) sincerity. But she too often gives the public just what it wants: embellishments. Anzoleto also courts the public, an approach he learns from la Corilla. His character is similar to that of Célio in *Le Château des Désertes* (The Désertes Château, 1853), who also sings for the public, but without the sincerity of emotion the music requires. Consuelo prefers to reserve embellishments for the exigencies of music, thus forcing the public to appreciate the artist's standards.

On the feminist score, *Consuelo* presents a strong, mature heroine, one who forges her way in a difficult profession without resorting to feminine wiles. Consuelo is contrasted to la Corilla on every level: artistic integrity, feminist policies, and general morals. Furthermore, Consuelo proves herself intelligent—to the contrary of the stereotypical artist concerned only with her music—and digests a large bibliography of Masonic writings. The enigmatic loss of voice near the end of the novel continues to give rise to various critical interpretations, but Consuelo remains the dominant figure at the end of the novel, even though Albert receives the important musical focus.

One of Sand's earliest literary endeavors, *Voyage en Auvergne* (1829), includes a plan to compose her memoirs; she even sketched an outline. Eighteen years later she began drafting the story of her life, but its composition was interrupted by the Revolution of 1848 and the coup d'état in 1851. Finally, in late 1854 *Histoire de ma vie* (translated as *Story of My Life*, 1991) appeared serially and almost simultaneously in volume form. At first public reaction to *Histoire de ma vie* showed disappointment; readers had expected details about people and events. Numerous critics also denigrated the lengthy opening section, which deals mostly with Sand's father. Nonetheless, Sand's autobiography offers a wealth of information as well as insight into her universe, at least from the perspective of Sand at age fifty.

After the long section on her ancestors, approximately five hundred pages in the Pléiade edition, where she explains that "everything is history," Sand turns to her own life. The reader learns about her intellectual growth during her years at the convent of the English Augustinians in Paris, of her grandmother's death, and of her precipitous marriage to escape the dominion of her mother. She tells very little about Jules Sandeau or Musset. And the major phase of her writing career occupies relatively few pages, with few details.

Sand does devote a few short chapters to individuals: Marie Dorval, Delacroix, Sainte-Beuve, Luigi Calamatta, and Charles Didier. Michel de Bourges also is the topic of quite a large section. In the last two chapters of the memoirs, Chopin occupies center stage. Sand describes the trip to Majorca and dwells on Chopin's ill health. Finally, the break with Chopin corresponds with the end of the autobiography.

Also in an autobiographical vein, though Sand always denied it, her novel *Elle et lui* (1859; translated as *She and He*, 1900) depicts her tempestuous affair with Musset. Here Sand explores the friendship between two artists. Thérèse and Laurant's ill-defined relationship is interrupted by Dick Palmer, who clearly recalls Pagello in the "affaire de Venise" (Venetian affair). The artists' attitudes toward their work reflect what is known about Sand's industriousness and Musset's need for inspiration. Musset tells his version of the stormy affair with Sand in *La Confession d'un enfant du siècle* (*1836; translated as Confession of a Child of the Century,* 1892), usually held to be a fair, contrite recounting. *Elle et lui*, however, was immediately attacked as unjustly harsh on the Musset character.

Sand in 1833 (drawing by Alfred de Musset; Institut de France, Foundation Lovenjoul)

Perhaps because Musset had died just two years before publication of *Elle et lui*, the public was more apt to protect his reputation; and the public was always ready to find fault with a woman with Sand's reputation for ruthlessly using men to her advantage. Musset's brother, Paul, added to the hue and cry by publicly condemning Sand's novel; he then countered with a novelistic version of his own, *Lui et elle*, which appeared barely six weeks later. *Elle et lui* does not rank among Sand's best work. The artistic context, which offers an ideal vehicle for aesthetic commentary, goes underdeveloped; after the initial exposition, it is hardly important that the two protagonists are even artists. Yet the autobiographical aspect of the novel provides valuable insight into Sand's memoirs and her attitudes toward them.

Le Marquis de Villemer (1860-1861), which garnered great public and critical accolades, examines attitudes of a different sort: class struggles within the nobility. Because of unfortunate circumstances, Caroline de Saint-Géneix finds herself in dire financial straits. Unashamed, she assumes the job of private secretary to Madame la marquise de Villemer. Urbain de Villemer, son of the marquise, is an intellectual, occupied with writing a history of the atrocities of the French aristocracy. He falls in love with Caroline and tells his mother so. The mother, proud and jealous of Caroline's rank, bans her from the house.

Urbain finds her a modest job in Creuse, where she encounters a couple who have adopted a small child. She loves the child and cares for him. It is eventually revealed that the child is Urbain's from an affair with a married woman, who has died. Caroline and Urbain ultimately marry with everyone's approval. Sand uses traditional oppositions in French society for her social commentary: Paris versus the provinces; high nobility versus lower nobility; arrogance versus modesty; and hierarchy versus egalitarianism. Barely eight years into the Second Empire, the French liberal public gladly adopted this work as a declaration of social rights and aspirations.

The novel's success gave Sand the idea to adapt it for the stage. In 1864 *Le Marquis de Villemer* opened at the Odéon. Once again the work was a great success. Two important differences separate the play from the novel. First, Urbain's illegitimate son becomes the child of a secret marriage. Second, Urbain is not writing a defamatory book on the French nobility, though his political colors do peek through the family armor. While the play is thus less striking from the political perspective, Sand was obliged to adapt the egalitarian theme to the standards of the theatergoing public, which was largely Parisian upper middle class.

Sand had been dabbling in the theater since *Cosima* (1840), a financial and critical disaster. While the text provides some excellent material on Sand's notion of women being caught in the prison of marriage, the play lacks clear direction and a dramatic sense. But she did not stop writing for the theater; Sand adapted several of her novels for the stage, the most successful, after *Le Marquis de Villemer*, being the reworkings of her rustic novels. *François le champi*, produced at the Odéon in 1849 by Victor Bocage, established for Sand a reputation as the rustic realist of the Paris stage. The decor, props, and music developed for the production of *François* created a fresh interest in the theater. Sand also rewrote *Mauprat* for the stage (1853); *La Petite Fadette* was set to music and produced in 1864. These adaptations not surprisingly betray the original novels, usually for reasons of staging and dramatic interest.

Sand wrote two significant closet plays that hold particular interest for their themes and ideology. *Les Sept Cordes de la lyre* (1839; translated as *The Seven Strings of the Lyre*, 1989) deals with Sand's thoughts on the mystico-religious capacity of music. The heroine, Hélène, is the only woman in the text and the only mortal character to understand music. She is able, through the beauty of music, to convert Albertus, the cynical philosophy teacher, to a belief in love and possibly in a supreme being.

Gabriel (1840) depicts a main character whose gender or gender identification is always in question. Brought up in Renaissance Italy for reasons of inheritance to believe she is a boy, Gabrielle discovers the deception at age seventeen. She sets off to find her cousin, Astolphe, the rightful, or at least the lawful, heir, and she falls in love with him. Astolphe is confused by his own attraction to his cousin, who is still dressed as a man, until he discovers her true gender in a Carnival scene brilliantly drawn with a double cross-dressing quid pro quo. Gabrielle eventually finds she cannot negotiate two genders. The one that she was brought up to be empowers her in all aspects of her life; she cannot fully integrate the other, which she sincerely wants to be and tries to assume, because of the hypocrisy of her circumstances. Neither of these plays has ever been produced.

Of the plays Sand originally wrote for the stage, perhaps *Claudie* (1851) is the best known. Here Sand tackles the plight of the unwed mother, surrounded by well-meaning bigots and self-serving hypocrites. Sand uses once again a rustic setting. *Claudie* presents concerns of interest to all women, especially the problem of "reputation." Claudie, though a strong woman, also suffers from ill-placed guilt. There is a happy ending, but it is attained with difficulty. The play was a great success.

Strong women were Sand's strong suit. Nearly all her novels of the later period (1860-1876) offer levelheaded, determined women. *Mademoiselle Merquem* (1868) presents a well-established woman, the patron and idol of the small Norman village where she lives. She is attracted to a younger man, Armand, who must learn the difference between pure and impure love before she will agree to a union. In several ways this novel recalls the training process in *Mauprat*, though here there is more emphasis on the woman's pride and her position in the village. In *Césarine Dietrich* (1871), Sand introduces a less confident heroine, one who seeks to seduce through intellectual curiosity. The novel turns around the notion of the Protestant tradition for intellectual pursuits and Césarine's struggle to assert herself within and despite this heritage.

Nanon (1872) is undoubtedly Sand's most interesting portrayal of a strong woman from this period. After the 1871 Commune, with which Sand was less than sympathetic, she chose a Revolution-era setting for this novel. Nanon finds herself amid several conflicts in the confusion of the post-Revolution fervor: clergy versus Jacobins; aristocrats versus peasants; principled people versus profiteers. Nanon, a young peasant woman who learns to read, saves the aristocratic novice Emilien, who can hardly read. Nanon also purchases property, thanks to the new post-Revolution laws, manages a large tract of land, and proves herself capable in financial negotiations. Nanon not only bears the responsibility of all the major decisions in the novel, she also enjoys the greatest growth. She profits from all the potential advantages of the postrevolutionary period in ways most peasants did not. The novel is a mixture of historical fiction and feminist idealism that works on the structural and narrative levels; somewhat unreliable in matters of historical accuracy, it nevertheless succeeds in creating a positive view of country women, of women in general, and a hope for a future egalitarian France.

In the last four years of her life, Sand devoted much of her time and energy to her granddaughters. She wrote for them a series of stories, collected in two volumes, *Contes d'une grand-mère* (A Grandmother's Stories, 1873 and 1876). The stories place mostly little girls in situations where they learn acceptance of themselves and of others. Introspection balanced with concern for others, courage, and a high degree of imagination make these some of Sand's most interesting characters. Her emphasis on the wonders of language is most striking. From the jargonistic vocabulary of some stories to the invented, nonhuman language used to communicate with statues or birds in other stories, language learning carries strong significance in Sand's universe. Another recurring theme in the stories is change. The young characters undergo many metamorphoses, even death; yet Sand portrays change as something good, something to accept and to anticipate. These stories remain relatively unknown, yet they recapitulate many of Sand's themes and the philosophy of life encountered throughout her oeuvre.

Sand treated many of the dominant concerns of her day, including socialism and religion. She read Leroux and Lamennais; she was familiar with Charles Fourier, Saint-Simon, and Barthélemy Enfantin. Like most novelists who attempted to superimpose socialist theory on a narrative structure, or sometimes vice versa, Sand did not eschew didacticism, though she was not overly idealistic. The edifying strain of Sand's writings appears throughout her career and has been the source of some recent criticism. For the context in which she wrote, however, one can hardly say Sand exaggerates, and she certainly never condescends.

Socialist concerns in the 1830s and 1840s were never very far from religious issues. Sand, who never subscribed to Fourier's materialist ideology, was in constant search of the true religion. She never practiced Catholicism in any regular manner, with the exception of her years in the convent of the English Augustinians; indeed, she constantly criticized the Church and explored other possibilities of religious expression. While her anticlericalism is less virulent than that of some other Romantic authors, Sand held little respect for the clergy, an attitude that comes out in a few works, particularly in *La Daniella* (1857).

When Sand's son, Maurice, and his wife, Lina Calmatta, had their marriage rededicated by a Protestant minister, Sand began to explore seriously the advantages of Protestantism over Catholicism. Unfortunately she encountered only a variety of Calvinist dogmas, each as strict if not stricter than the stringencies of Catholicism. Unable to find any acceptable alternative, Sand remained a Catholic to her death, but in name only. This presented a problem when she died, for her daughter, Solange, insisted Sand be buried with full last rites according to church custom. Lina, to whom Sand had always felt much closer than to her own daughter, maintained that a Catholic burial was the last thing Sand would have wanted. Maurice was not much help in resolving the matter, and George Sand received final rites in the Catholic tradition.

Another issue that attracted Sand to the egalitarian aspects of socialism was the place of feminism. Her feminism has been questioned by commentators from Flora Tristan to late-twentieth-century critics, but the circumstances in which Sand was struggling must be considered. Her most defiant and most constant feminist position was against the prisonlike oppression of marriage. Criticized on this score from the publication of her first novel, *Indiana*, to her last days, Sand often specified that she believed in an egalitarian union between a man and a woman, but she stipulated that marriage as it existed under the Napoleonic Code promoted the oppression of women. Many of her novels grapple with this issue (*Indiana*, *Valentine*, *André*, *Jacques*, *Consuelo*, *Mademoiselle la Quintinia*, *Le Dernier Amour*, and *Mademoiselle Merquem*, to highlight the most obvious ones), and a few plays treat the same topic, including *Cosima*, *Claudie*, and *Le Marriage de Victoria*. The female characters always hesitate (or regret they did not hesitate) to engage themselves in a social contract that removes all political, social, and psychological sense of individuality.

Of further concern for critics of Sand's feminism was her refusal to run for office. A group of women from the *Voix des Femmes*, a militant newspaper, nominated Sand as a delegate in the first elections after the 1848 revolt. Sand declined in an open letter to the editor of the *Réforme*. (Her nomination had been announced publicly without direct contact with Sand.) She explained elsewhere at the same time that she was against universal suffrage; with women's education in the deplorable state of the 1850s, how could one hope for women to make intelligent choices in elections? Their votes would therefore simply reflect the voice of their husbands. Until women received a better education, she believed that they should not vote; and until women could vote, she could not run for public office.

One area where Sand undisputedly made her mark is the provincial novel. Unlike Balzac, she was able to introduce the Parisian readership to even the most unfamiliar details of a life hitherto virtually unknown to them, different in mores, in traditions, and even in language. Her attempts to weave Berrichon dialect into a French narrative, though not always satisfactory, underscored the multiculturalism of mid-nineteenth-century France. Sand's conscious efforts to keep the culture of "la Vallée noire" alive and authentic bear testimony to her dedication to egalitarianism without any sense of undue exploitation. The "romans champêtres" have much to say about Berry and the Berrichons, but even more about Parisians and their attitudes toward provincials.

Sand is at once representative of and unique in the French literary canon. Her individuality, though perhaps not evident in all her prolific production, shines through in many works. Her indisputable influence on other writers

Sand at age thirty (portrait by Eugène Delacroix; from André Maurois, Lélia: The Life of George Sand, *1953)*

(Willa Cather, George Eliot, Elena Gan, and Turgenev) further attests to her stylistic and thematic prowess. Her death was a blow to many, even to Victor Hugo, who never wasted much breath or ink on her during her life. He wrote a stirring eulogistic message: "Je pleure une morte et je salue une immortelle.... George Sand était une idée; elle est hors de la chair, la voilà libre; elle est morte, la voilà vivante" (I mourn a dead woman and I hail an immortal woman.... George Sand was an idea; she is outside of the realm of the flesh, now she is free; she is dead, now she is alive).

Sand remains one of the most important novelists of the nineteenth century. She is well on the way to being assured her proper place in the novelistic tradition. She will certainly be remembered for having forged a way in a profession dominated by men. She will always be remembered as a woman writer who brought to the attention of the reading public the social status of women and country folk.

Letters:

Correspondance, 25 volumes, edited by Georges Lubin (Paris: Garnier, 1964-1991);

Gustave Flaubert and George Sand, *Correspondance*, edited by Alphonse Jacobs (Paris: Flammarion, 1981).

Bibliographies:

Vicomte Charles Spoelberch de Lovenjoul, *George Sand: Etude bibliographique sur ses œuvres* (Paris: Leclerc, 1914);

Annarosa Poli, *George Sand vue par les Italiens: Essai de bibliographie critique* (Paris: Didier, 1965);

Robert A. Keane and Natalie Datlof, "George Sand and the Victorians: Bibliography," *George Sand Newsletter*, 1 (1978): 5-6;

Gaylord Brynolfson, "Works on George Sand, 1964-1980: A Bibliography," in *George Sand Papers: Conference Proceedings, 1978*, edited by Datlof (New York: AMS, 1982), pp. 189-233;

David A. Powell, "Selected Bibliography," in *The World of George Sand*, edited by Datlof, Jeanne Fuchs, and Powell (New York: Greenwood Press, 1991), pp. 271-278.

Biographies:

Wladimir Karénine, *George Sand: Sa vie et ses œuvres*, 4 volumes (Paris: Ollendorff et Plon, 1899-1926);

André Maurois, *Lélia, ou la vie de George Sand* (Paris: Hachette, 1952); translated by Gerard Hopkins as *Lélia: The Life of George Sand* (New York: Harper, 1953);

Pierre Salomon, *George Sand* (Paris: Hatier-Boivin, 1953);

Curtis Cate, *George Sand* (Boston: Houghton Mifflin, 1975);

Francine Mallet, *George Sand* (Paris: Grasset, 1976);

Joseph Barry, *Infamous Woman: The Life of George Sand* (Garden City, N.Y.: Doubleday, 1977);

Renee Winegarten, *The Double Life of George Sand, Woman and Writer: A Critical Biography* (New York: Basic Books, 1978);

Donna Dickenson, *George Sand: A Brave Man— The Most Womanly Woman* (Oxford: Berg, 1988).

References:

Simone Balayé, "Consuelo: Déesse de la pauvreté," *Revue d'Histoire Littéraire de la France*, 74 (1974): 614-625;

Paul Groves Blount, *Sand and the Victorian World* (Athens: University of Georgia Press, 1979);

Thierry Bodin, "Balzac et Sand: Histoire d'une amitié," *Présence de George Sand*, 13 (February 1982): 4-21;

Bodin, "Le Dossier de *Elle et Lui*," *Présence de George Sand*, 29 (May 1987): 6-62;

Frank Paul Bowman, "George Sand, le Christ et le royaume," *Cahiers de l'Association Internationale des Etudes Françaises*, 28 (May 1976): 243-262, 374-376;

Yvette Bozon-Scalzitti, "Vérité de la fiction et fiction de la vérité dans *Histoire de ma vie*: Le projet autobiographique de George Sand," *Nineteenth-Century French Studies*, 12 (Summer/Fall 1984): 95-118;

Denise Brahimi, "Ecriture / Féminité / Féminisme: Réflexions sur trois romans de George Sand," *Revue des Sciences Humaines*, 168 (October/December 1977): 577-588;

Germaine Brée, "George Sand: The Fiction of Autobiography," *Nineteenth-Century French Studies*, 4 (Summer 1976): 438-449;

Lucien Buis, *Les Théories sociales de George Sand* (Paris: Pedone, 1910);

Jean Cassou, "George Sand et le secret du XIXᵉ siècle," *Mercure de France* (December 1961): 601-618;

Léon Cellier, *Parcours initiatiques* (Neuchâtel: La Baconnière, 1977);

Cellier, ed., *Hommage à George Sand* (Paris: PUF, 1969);

Cellier, ed., *La Porporina: Entretiens sur "Consuelo"* (Grenoble: Presses Universitaires de Grenoble, 1976);

Kathryn Crecelius, *Family Romances: George Sand's Early Novels* (Bloomington: Indiana University Press, 1987);

Crecelius, "Writing a Self: From Aurore Dudevant to George Sand," *Tulsa Studies in Women's Literature*, 4 (Spring 1985): 47-59;

Michael Danahy, "George Sand, Women and the World of Work," *George Sand Newsletter*, 3 (1980): 36-41;

Natalie Datlof, ed., *The George Sand Papers* (New York: AMS Press, 1980, 1982);

Béatrice Didier, "Le Corps féminin dans *Lélia*," *Revue d'Histoire Littéraire de la France*, 76 (1976): 634-643;

Didier, "Femme / Identité / Ecriture: A propos de l'*Histoire de ma vie* de George Sand," *Revue des Sciences Humaines*, 168 (October/December 1977): 561-576;

Didier, "L'Image de Voltaire et de Rousseau chez George Sand," *Revue d'Histoire Littéraire de la France*, 79 (1979): 251-264;

Didier, "Sexe, société et création: *Consuelo* et *La Comtesse de Rudolstadt*," *Romantisme*, 13-14 (1977): 155-166;

Lucienne Frappier-Mazur, "Code romantique et résurgences du féminin dans *La Comtesse de Rudolstadt*," in *Récit amoureux*, edited by Didier Coste and Michael Zénaffa (Paris: Editions du Champ Vallon, 1984);

Frappier-Mazur, "Desire, Writing and Identity in the Romantic Mystical Novel: Notes for a Definition of the Feminine," *Style*, 18 (Summer 1984): 328-354;

Frappier-Mazur, "Nostalgie, dédoublement et écriture dans *Histoire de ma vie*," *Nineteenth-Century French Studies*, 17 (Spring/Summer 1989): 265-275;

Jean Gaulmier, ed., *Hommage à George Sand* (Strasbourg: Presses Universitaires de Strasbourg, 1954);

Janis Glasgow, *Une Esthétique de comparaison: Balzac et George Sand. La Femme abandonnée et Métella* (Paris: Nizet, 1978);

Jeanne Goldin, ed., *George Sand: Voyage et écriture* (Montreal: Presses de l'Université de Montréal, 1988);

Tatiana Greene, "George Sand, hérétique," in *George Sand: Collected Essays*, edited by Glasgow (Troy, N.Y.: Whitston, 1985), pp. 139-158;

Reinhold R. Grimm, "Les Romans champêtres de George Sand: l'échec du renouvellement d'un genre littéraire," *Romantisme*, 16 (1977): 64-70;

Léon Guichard, *La Musique et les lettres au temps du romantisme* (Paris: Presses Universitaires de France, 1955);

Marie-Jacques Hoog, "Du rêve à l'écriture chez George Sand," *George Sand Newsletter*, 5 (Fall/Winter 1982): 47-50;

Henry James, *French Poets and Novelists* (London: Macmillan, 1878);

James, *Notes on Novelists* (New York: Scribners, 1914);

Jean-Pierre Lacassagne, *Histoire d'une amitié: Leroux et Sand, d'après une correspondance inédite 1836-1866* (Paris: Klincksieck, 1973);

François Laforge, "Structure et fonction du mythe d'Orphée dans *Consuelo* de George Sand," *Revue d'Histoire Littéraire de la France*, 84 (1984): 53-66;

Madeleine L'Hopital, *La Notion d'artiste chez George Sand* (Paris: Boivin, 1946);

Georges Lubin, "La Liaison Musset-Sand," *Revue d'Histoire Littéraire de la France*, 73 (1973): 99-112;

Francine Mallet, "George Sand et la musique," *Présence de George Sand*, 10 (February 1981): 32-38;

Gay Manifold, *George Sand's Theatre Career* (Ann Arbor, Mich.: UMI, 1985);

Thérèse Marix-Spire, *Les Romantiques et la musique: Le cas George Sand (1804-1838)* (Paris: Nouvelles Editions Latines, 1955);

Gita May, "Des *Confessions* à *Histoire de ma vie*: Deux auteurs à la recherche de leur moi," *Présence de George Sand*, 8 (May 1980): 40-47;

Arlette Michel, "Structures romanesques et problèmes du mariage d'*Indiana* à *La Comtesse de Rudolstadt*," *Romantisme*, 16 (1977): 34-45;

Nancy K. Miller, "Writing (from) the Feminine: George Sand and the Novel of Female Pastoral," in *The Representation of Women in Fiction*, edited by Carolyn Heilbrun and M. Higonnet (Baltimore: Johns Hopkins University Press, 1981);

Marc Marcel Moret, *Le Sentiment religieux chez George Sand* (Paris: Marcel Vigné, 1936);

Nicole Mozet, "Signé 'le voyageur': George Sand et l'invention de l'artiste," *Romantisme*, 55 (1987): 23-32;

Mozet, "Le Voyageur sandien en quête d'un lieu d'écriture," *Etudes Françaises*, 24 (1988): 41-55;

Isabelle Naginski, "George Sand: Gynographie et androgynie," *Bulletin de la Société des Professeurs Français d'Amérique* (1983-1984): 21-36;

Naginski, *George Sand: Writing for Her Life* (New Brunswick, N.J.: Rutgers University Press, 1991);

Naginski, "*Lélia*: Novel of the Invisible," *George Sand Studies*, 7 (1984-1985): 46-53;

Annarosa Poli, *L'Italie dans la vie et dans l'œuvre de George Sand* (Paris: Colin, 1960);

Jean Pommier, *George Sand et le rêve monastique: "Spiridion"* (Paris: Nizet, 1966);

David A. Powell, "Discord, Dissension, and Dissonance: The Initiation in Sand's *Les Maîtres sonneurs*," *George Sand Newsletter*, 6 (1987): 54-62;

Powell, *George Sand* (Boston: Twayne, 1990);

Powell, "Improvisation(s) dans *Consuelo*," *Revue des Sciences Humaines*, no. 226 (April-June 1992): 117-134;

Marie-Jeanne Rabine, "George Sand: La formation et l'éducation d'une femme écrivain," *Women and Literature*, 4 (1976): 2-17;

Marie-Paule Rambeau, *Chopin dans la vie et l'œuvre de George Sand* (Paris: Les Belles Lettres, 1985);

Pierre Reboul, *Errements littéraires et historiques* (Paris: Presses Universitaires de Lille, 1979);

Nancy Rogers, "Slavery as Metaphor in the Writings of George Sand," *French Review*, 53 (1979): 29-35;

Gérard Schaeffer, *Espace et temps chez George Sand* (Neuchâtel: La Baconnière, 1981);

Naomi Schor, "Female Fetishism: The Case of George Sand," in *The Female Body in Western Culture: Contemporary Perspectives*, edited by Susan Rubin Suleiman (Cambridge, Mass.: Harvard University Press, 1985);

Schor, "Idealism in the Novel: Recanonizing Sand," *Yale French Studies*, 75 (1988): 56-73;

Schor, "Reading Double: Sand's Difference," in *The Politics of Gender*, edited by Nancy K. Miller (New York: Columbia University Press, 1986), pp. 248-269;

Armand Singer, ed., *West Virginia George Sand Conference Papers* (Morgantown: West Virginia University Press, 1981);

Eileen Boyd Sivert, "*Lélia* and Feminism," *Yale French Studies*, 62 (1981): 45-66;

Albert Sonnenfeld, "George Sand: Music and Sexualities," *Nineteenth-Century French Studies*, 16 (Spring/Summer 1988): 310-321;

Eve Sourian, "Les Opinions religieuses de George Sand: Pourquoi Consuelo a-t-elle perdu sa voix?" in *George Sand: Collected Essays*, edited by Glasgow (Troy, N.Y.: Whitston, 1985), pp. 127-138;

Anna Szabó, "La Figure du savant dans les romans de George Sand," *Studia Romanica*, 12 (1986): 105-112;

Szabó, "La Révolution à la lumière d'une autre: *Nanon* de George Sand," in *Révolution française et romantismes européens*, edited by Simone Bernard-Griffiths (Naples: Nella Sede dell'Instituto, 1989);

Patricia Thomson, *Sand and the Victorians: Her Influence and Reputation in Nineteenth Century England* (New York: Columbia University Press, 1977);

Françoise van Rossum-Guyon, ed., *George Sand: Recherches nouvelles* (Amsterdam: CRIN, 1983);

Pierre Vermeylan, *Les Idées politiques et sociales de George Sand* (Brussels: Editions de l'Université de Bruxelles, 1984);

Simone Vierne, "George Sand et le mythe initiatique," in *George Sand: Collected Essays*, edited by Glasgow (Troy, N.Y.: Whitston, 1986), pp. 288-305;

Vierne, ed., *George Sand* (Paris: CDU-SEDES, 1983);

Debra Linowitz Wentz, *Les Profils du Théâtre de Nohant de George Sand* (Paris: Nizet, 1978);

Dorothy Zimmerman, "George Sand and the Feminists of the 1830's and 1840's in France," *George Sand Newsletter*, 4 (1981): 20-24.

Papers:
The Collection Spoelberch de Lovenjoul, Chantilly, includes manuscripts of many of Sand's novels and plays, articles and fragments of her diaries, as well as letters and contracts. This is the most extensive collection of Sand's works. The Bibliothèque Nationale houses several manuscripts of novels and correspondence as well as private date books. The Bibliothèque historique de la Ville de Paris possesses manuscripts of several novels, private journals, and correspondence, as well as some school notebooks from Sand's youth. There is also a list of Berrichon vocabulary that Sand gathered. Other manuscripts can be found at the Château de Nohant and in the Bibliothèque George Sand in La Châtre (Berry).

Etienne de Senancour
(16 November 1770 - 10 January 1846)

Martha Noel Evans
Mary Baldwin College

BOOKS: *Les Premiers Ages. Incertitudes humaines* (N.p., 1792);

Sur les générations actuelles: Absurdités humaines (Paris, 1793);

Aldomen, ou le bonheur dans l'obscurité (Paris: Leprieur, 1795);

Rêveries sur la nature primitive de l'homme, sur ses sensations, sur les moyens de bonheur qu'elles lui indiquent, sur le mode social qui conserverait le plus de ses formes primordiales (Paris: La Tynna, 1799; revised and enlarged edition, Paris: Bertrand, 1809; revised edition, Paris: Ledoux, 1833);

Oberman (Paris: Cérioux, 1804); revised and enlarged as *Obermann* (Paris: Charpentier, 1840); translated by A. E. Waite as *Obermann* (New York: Brentano, 1893);

De l'amour considéré dans les lois réelles et dans les formes sociales de l'union des sexes (Paris: Cérioux et Bertrand, 1806; revised and enlarged edition, 2 volumes, Paris: Abel Ledoux, 1834);

Valombré, comédie en 5 actes et en prose (Paris: Cérioux, Barba, Capelle et Renaud, 1807);

De Napoléon (Paris: Beaupré, 1815);

Observations critiques sur l'ouvrage intitulé "Génie du christianisme" suivies de quelques réflexions sur les écrits de M. de B. [onald], relatifs à la loi du divorce (Paris: Delaunay, 1816);

Libres méditations d'un solitaire inconnu sur le détachement du monde et sur d'autres objets de la morale religieuse (Paris: Mongie et Cérioux, 1819); republished as *Libres méditations d'un solitaire inconnu sur le détachement du monde et sur divers objets de la morale religieuse* (Paris: Boisjolin, 1830);

Résumé de l'histoire de la Chine (Paris: Lecointe et Durey, 1824);

Résumé de l'histoire des traditions morales et religieuses chez les divers peuples (Paris: Lecointe et Durey, 1825);

Résumé de l'histoire romaine, 2 volumes (Paris: Lecointe et Durey, 1827);

Isabelle (Paris: Abel Ledoux, 1833);

Etienne de Senancour, 1843 (painting by Henri Blanc-Fontaine; from André Monglond, Le Journal intime d'Oberman, *1947)*

Petit vocabulaire de simple vérité (Paris: Place Saint-André-des-Arts, 1833).

Although Etienne de Senancour published many philosophical, historical, and critical works during his lifetime, he has gained a place in literary history principally as the author of *Oberman* (1804), a novel prized and promoted, along with François-René de Chateaubriand's *René* (1805) and Benjamin Constant's *Adolphe* (1816), by the younger generation of French Romantics as an expression of the unhappiness, frustration, and disillusionment termed *le mal du siècle* (the sickness of the century). The legend of Senancour's suffering and hesitant hero thus contributed to shaping a literary current dominant in French letters through the middle of the nineteenth century. Influenced strongly by Jean-Jacques Rousseau's *Julie, ou La Nouvelle Héloïse* (1761; translated as *Julie, or the New Eloisa*, 1773) and Jacques Bernardin de Saint-Pierre's *Etudes de la nature* (Nature Studies, 1784-1788), *Oberman* is distinguished from the contemporary works of Chateaubriand and Constant both by its epistolary form and by the major role played by nature in the hero's sensibility. As a member of the generation of émigré writers, which could be described simultaneously as postrevolutionary and pre-Romantic, Senancour constitutes an important transitional figure linking the philosophy and aesthetics of the eighteenth century with those of the Romantic period.

The same destiny of frustration and metaphysical suffering Senancour described in his fictional hero characterized the life of the author as well. The only child of elderly parents, Senancour spent a lonely and unhappy childhood in Paris. Timid and inept in social interactions, he took refuge in reading and in solitary walks in the country. When his father, who had himself considered a career in the church, insisted that his son enter Saint-Sulpice Seminary, the nineteen-year-old Senancour fled Paris a month after the fall of the Bastille. Unable for financial reasons to realize his dreams of travel to exotic lands, the young man went instead to Switzerland and, after adventuring on foot through the Alps, settled in Fribourg. There Senancour met a young Swiss woman and, pressured by her parents, quickly married. Two children, disillusionment, and regrets soon followed.

Having returned to Paris to reconcile with his parents and to look after his affairs, Senancour fell in love with the married sister of a close friend. Misinterpreting letters his wife had received from Senancour, Marie Walckenaer's elderly husband challenged her putative lover to a duel. Although an understanding was reached before the duel took place, Senancour was obliged to end his visits to the household. The one and only love of his life was thus not only impossible, but came to an end in humiliation and embarrassment. For the rest of his life, the dreams of ecstatic encounter associated with Mme Walckenaer and the bitterness of love denied would haunt Senancour's writing.

Although he risked arrest and was in danger of being put on the list of émigrés, Senancour nevertheless went back and forth between France and Switzerland several times. When at their death his parents left him a "fortune" of worthless assignats, Senancour found himself virtually without resources and was forced to take a position as the tutor of Sophie Houdetot's grandchildren in Paris. For the first time in his life, he began to enjoy refined society as he encountered it in the Houdetot salon and made friends among the philosophers and intellectuals who frequented it. This short period of happiness and security was soon interrupted, however, by an urgent summons from his wife's family in Fribourg. Senancour returned to discover that, although he had been absent from Switzerland for more than a year, his wife had just given birth to a son. The disillusioned and bitter Senancour returned to Paris a changed man: not only was his health damaged by the aftereffects of a foolhardy adventure in the Alps (transposed in a fictional account in the 1840 edition of *Oberman*), his marriage was clearly over, and he was without money and position. At the age of thirty-three, Senancour gave up his dreams of happiness and settled down in Paris to the obscure and solitary life that would occupy the rest of his days.

His first major book, *Rêveries sur la nature primitive de l'homme* (Musings on the Primitive Nature of Man, 1799), had, however, attracted a promising reception. Imbued both with the spirit of Rousseau and the sensualist philosophy of the late-eighteenth-century philosophers known as Idéologues, Senancour sets forth the project of his book in the opening sentence: "J'ai vu la nature mal interprétée, j'ai vu l'homme livré à de funestes déviations: j'ai cru entendre la nature, j'ai désiré ramener l'homme" (I have seen nature ill interpreted, I have seen man given to fatal deviations: I believed I heard nature, I wished to bring man back).

But while Senancour believes the meretricious attractions of society have led man astray from his true destiny, he does not wish to return to a savage state. Rather, he hopes to discover what institutions might be appropriate for what he calls, in a highly significant phrase, "l'homme social de la nature" (the social man of nature). Going against the grain of contemporaries such as Germaine de Staël, who was staunchly promoting the doctrine of perfectibility, Senancour expresses the hope of effecting a retrograde movement that would strip human society of unnecessary luxuries and commotion. Against the unhealthy "fermentation of the city," Senancour poses the ideal of the small, rural, "patriarchal" society he had observed in Switzerland.

Although Senancour investigates fundamental moral, philosophical, and social questions in the *Rêveries*, the very form of his writing reveals his resistance to traditional philosophy and, especially, to a Cartesian notion of reason or soul separate from the body. His meditative style, reminiscent both of Rousseau and Michel de Montaigne, is purposefully adopted to demonstrate both the superiority of "dreaming" over logical discourse and the fruitfulness of sensitivity to bodily perceptions and sensations.

Indeed, if man has gone astray, has fallen prey to "fatal deviations," the remedy Senancour proposes is a reconnection with the vital forces of nature. This reconnection will enable man to rediscover his original or "primitive" nature and thus to take his rightful place in the universal harmony of the cosmos. Senancour's program therefore includes an appeal for a double discipline: on the one hand, a withdrawal from the "factitious" products of an economy based on the production of surplus goods, and, on the other, a yielding to the flow of sensations and emotions generated by the beauties of nature. According to Senancour, the apparent mobility of feelings to which the sensitive man is subject will, through an effect of harmonic resonance with the rhythms of the universe, create a new sense of permanence and peace.

In the *Rêveries*, Senancour strives, then, not only to convince his readers by reasoned argument, but also, and more importantly, to entice them by re-creating the very effects of permanence and peace that are his ideal. The author's prose itself thus becomes a part of his argument: the majestic ternary rhythms, the incantatory repetitions and accumulations, and the descriptions of nature strangely stripped of all contingent detail simultaneously represent and reproduce the primordial language of primitive man. Senancour exhorts his readers to listen to and to experience "le mugissement des torrents fougueux, dans la sécurité des vallées; la paix des monts en leur silence inexprimable, et le fracas des glaciers qui se fendent, des rocs qui s'écroulent, et de la vaste ruine des hivers" (the roaring of impetuous torrents in the security of valleys; the peace of the mountains in their inexpressible silence, and the din of glaciers splitting, of rocks crumbling, and the vast ruin of winters).

Senancour's haunting eloquence, founded on rhythm, paradox, and the suggestive allegorization of natural objects, plays an equally central role in the novel that would eventually be seen as his major work. At the time of its publication in 1804, however, *Oberman* went almost unnoticed. Barely mentioned in the press, and then negatively, *Oberman* attracted few readers until some twenty years after its publication, when it was rediscovered by Charles-Augustin Sainte-Beuve, George Sand, Honoré de Balzac, Stendhal, Franz Liszt, Gérard de Nerval, and others, and became the object of a sort of cult.

The lack of contemporary notice is understandable, however. Senancour's reticence about personal revelation, his reluctance to yield to popular forms, and his very fidelity to the project of discovering "primitive" man all combined to strip this "novel" almost entirely of plot, incidents, and characters. *Oberman* is a novel in a kind of zero state, or, as the author himself would have it, it is not a novel at all. In the introduction, in which Senancour speaks as the fictional "editor" of the letters, he states: "Ces lettres ne sont pas un *roman*. Il n'y a point de mouvement dramatique, d'événemens préparés et conduits, point de dénouement; rien de ce qu'on appelle l'intérêt d'un ouvrage" (These letters are not a *novel*. There are no dramatic movement, no events prepared and developed, no denouement; nothing of what is called the interest of a work).

What many critics have regarded as the weaknesses of *Oberman* thus appear to be part of a conscious project on the part of the author, a project that reveals simultaneously Senancour's steadfastness to his own ideals and the paralyzing effects of his refusal to yield to common desires. According to the author himself, *Oberman* was not intended to draw a popular audience, but rather to appeal to a public of "adepts," to a "few scattered people in Europe" capable of responding to the thoughts, feelings, and passions of a discouraged and isolated man in search of the truth.

Written in part during Senancour's stay at the Houdetots' and finished after the disastrous discovery of his wife's adultery, *Oberman* is comprised of a series of letters written over a period of ten years to an unnamed recipient. There are some obvious parallels between the life of the fictional hero and the novel's author: they both run away from home at the age of nineteen; they both go to Switzerland; they are both troubled, reticent men with souls in turmoil. The apparent autobiographical qualities of *Oberman* led not only to the Romantics' equation of author and hero, but also, later, to the mining of the novel for information about Senancour's life (especially in André Monglond's *Journal intime d'Oberman*

Frontispiece from the second edition (1808) of Senancour's De l'amour, *an examination of love and sexuality*

[1947]). Senancour himself persisted in resisting this equation, however, and was particularly unsettled by visits from admirers in the 1830s who expected to find Oberman living on the rue de la Cérisaie.

Although Senancour claimed to be writing in the name of a fictitious hero, Oberman's letters closely resemble Senancour's *Rêveries* both in form and style. What differentiates the two works, and what makes *Oberman* a novel, in spite of the author's demurrals, is its structure as both a quest narrative and a *Künstlerroman* (artist's novel): the hero leaves home and family in search of the meaning of life, and decides in the end to become a writer. *Oberman* is also a novel of personality and, as such, eloquently inscribes the anxieties of a generation whose youth was marked by the collapse of social order, by isola-

tion from family and friends, and, perhaps most importantly, by the sudden blocking of future expectations. Like Chateaubriand's René and Constant's Adolphe, Senancour's Oberman feels that he has been robbed of his future, and he responds in similar ways: he feels that his will has been paralyzed, that he is old before his time, and, in even more painful images, that he is witnessing his own death. Although the Revolution is nowhere mentioned in *Oberman*, the effects of that cataclysmic event have been internalized and fictionalized as a personal, emotional, and metaphysical crisis.

The feeling of being cut off from the world of the living is not, however, only a torment for Oberman. In a paradoxical way, it is also a choice. Insofar as city life and the social organization of the polis represent for Oberman precisely what has gone amiss in human life, the solitary Alpine heights represent the promise of discovering a reality independent of man, and Oberman goes in search of that cosmic unity. In a striking episode recounting his ascent of the Dent du Midi, Oberman symbolically strips his mind and body of the accoutrements of civilization in order to communc with the purified cosmos represented by the austere Alpine landscape. His quest appears to be fulfilled; in an ecstatic experience of union, he becomes one with the silent universe revealed on the mountaintop and has the impression "de subsister dans le changement même" (of subsisting in the very midst of change).

But the impression of living in an eternal present cannot last, and Oberman must descend into the valley, taking up again "la longue chaîne des sollicitudes et des ennuis" (the long chain of solicitudes and cares). The inanimate universe with which he has ecstatically fused is in the end a promised but foreign land, an uninhabitable refuge.

The rest of the novel recounts Oberman's efforts to come to terms with the ineluctability of his ideal, and to discover a way of living in a world where time and language hold sway. This "world of the plains," as he calls it, thus becomes a puzzle to be solved or, more precisely, a dream to be interpreted. Like dreams, the world is made up for Oberman of disparate experiences and objects that hold promise of meaning, but whose relationships and logic remain elusive. This sense of a promised but withheld truth turns Oberman's encounters with both the exterior landscape of nature and the interior landscape of ideas and sensations into the extraordinarily haunting and suggestive images that have continued to attract readers to this austere, uneven, but eventually unforgettable novel.

Oberman's quest takes him back to the city, then to Fontainebleau, and finally back to Switzerland, where he builds a house he calls Imenström. He lives there with Fonsalbe, the disillusioned and world-weary brother of Mme Dellemar, the woman whom one eventually learns Oberman has secretly loved all his young life. Although he is still haunted by a sense of his own uselessness and by the hopelessness of ever understanding the nature of things, Oberman nevertheless establishes at Imenström a kind of dream house—much like Julie de Wolmar in Rousseau's novel *Julie, ou La Nouvelle Héloïse*—in which he plays the role of the beneficent head of a well-regulated but modest household. Having succeeded in "circumscribing" his desires, Oberman turns his attention to the simple pleasures of life that are within his grasp.

The dark, distressed tone of the novel changes at this point, and Oberman even indulges in unaccustomed frivolity and humor, spinning universal theories that he then unravels in a self-mocking gesture. He and Fonsalbe also "play" with sleep and explore the universe of dreams. As part of this playfulness, Oberman recounts a dream he has had that, in spite of the jocular tone, unlocks for the reader many of the secrets of the hero's elusive motivations. In the dream, a mountain chain, touched by the white-hot ring of Saturn, turns into a wild, frightening, undulating sea. This "great disaster" is observed by the dreamer from a height that distances him from the "lugubrious" events he is witnessing. In the following letter, without preamble, Oberman affirms to his correspondent that he will never marry.

The dream and its juxtaposition with the issue of marriage suggest that the mountains, in particular, and nature, in general, have been all along for Oberman a sexually charged and potentially dangerous female presence whose awakened passion comprises a terrifying spectacle. Retrospectively, the reader can understand what has not been clear to the narrator himself—that his insistence on being a superior observer, precisely an *Obermann*, is not only a philosophic stance, but also a defense against engagement in the world of adult eroticism. Oberman has made himself powerless because *all* action for him betokens this engagement. While the narrator has announced from the beginning his quest to discover the na-

ture of man, that purpose has been blocked not only by the inadequacy of human reason, but also by Oberman's fears of becoming a man in another sense.

This interpretation both of the dream and of the novel is corroborated by subsequent events and decisions. During a visit of Mme Dellemar to Imenström, Oberman realizes the nature of his love for her, but decides to renounce that love: "Elle et le désert, ce serait le triomphe du cœur. Non, l'oubli du monde, et sans elle, voilà ma loi" (She and the wilderness, that would be the triumph of the heart. No, to forget the world, and without her, that is my law). Later in the same letter, he asks himself, "Que faire donc? Je crois définitivement qu'il ne m'est donné que d'écrire" (What should I then do? I believe finally that the only thing I can do is write). And in the last part of the last letter of the novel, as Oberman goes on to discuss the kind of writing he will do, the reader slowly realizes that the first part of the project he describes is *Oberman* itself.

The structure of this barely novelesque novel is thus not only elusive, it is self-enfolding and recursive, and it sends the reader back to the beginning in a cycle of meaning that recalls the turning wheel of Saturn's ring. The author's reluctance to write a conventional novel now takes on a double meaning within the book, both as a defense against engagement in a love story and as a reflection of the novel's place in a larger writing project. Though rejecting a place in the world as a real father, Oberman intends to play a role as a symbolic patriarch through his writing on moral law.

Even though, unlike *René* and *Adolphe*, *Oberman* recounts a successful quest and the discovery of a vocation, it has taken its place in literary history with Chateaubriand's and Constant's novels principally as the expression of a tortured soul suffering from *le mal du siècle* (world-weariness). Whether the later Romantics' celebration of this aspect of Senancour's work set the tone for later critical work, whether the withholding nature of the novel's structure has given readers the sense of an author working against himself, or whether the very eloquence of the hero's anguish has overwhelmed other aspects of the book, Oberman has become a representative figure of the disillusioned, paralyzed, victim-hero of early-nineteenth-century French literature.

Senancour's own work followed the pattern announced in *Oberman*. Two years after the publication of the novel, Senancour published a collec-

Medallion of Senancour by David d'Angers (Musée d'Angers)

tion of essays on what he called "moral science." As the title *De l'amour* (On Love) indicates, Senancour asserts that love and the relations between the sexes form the central focus of man's ethical life. Here again the author characteristically combines philosophical meditations with intense passages of veiled personal revelations. Senancour's negative comments about marriage, his impassioned defense of divorce and free unions, and his frank discussions about erotic physical relations brought this book a certain *succès de scandale* while winning the marked admiration of the socialist thinker Charles Fourier.

Very little is known about Senancour's life during the twenty-five years following the publication of *De l'amour*. The waning of his creativity during this period was probably the result of financial problems as well as failing health. In order to support himself and his daughter, who was living with him in Paris, he was forced to concentrate his energies on journalism and commissioned works of history. At one point he even had to copy manuscripts and write business prospectuses

to make ends meet. Bad luck continued to pursue Senancour when in 1827 the second edition of a set of meditative essays, *Libres méditations d'un solitaire inconnu* (Free Meditations of an Unknown Solitary, 1819), was confiscated and the author was prosecuted for his audacious comments on Christianity and religious liberty. Although, paradoxically, *Libres méditations* represented Senancour's most positive approach to religious faith, his treatment of Jesus as a symbolic figure shocked the authorities, and Senancour was fined and condemned to nine months in prison. While he was acquitted on appeal, Senancour nevertheless demonstrated during the trials the steadfastness of his principles and his readiness to make personal sacrifices to defend them.

The belated "discovery" of *Oberman* by Sainte-Beuve and Sand led to new fame for Senancour late in life, to the republication of his early novel, and to the publication of another, his last, *Isabelle* (1833). It is not known when Senancour wrote *Isabelle*. References have been found indicating that Mme de Staël, whom Senancour admired, may have read an early version of the manuscript before her death in 1817. In any case, both the novel's epistolary form and the character of the eponymous heroine make it a companion piece to *Oberman*.

Isabelle has, in fact, been called "Oberman's sister." Like him, she expresses in her letters to a close friend her reluctance to marry, her difficulty in finding a place for herself in the world, her frustrations and unhappiness, and, finally, her decision to write a book. Not nearly as eloquent or moving as *Oberman*, *Isabelle* can also be differentiated from that novel by the dramatic episodes that take place—including a massacre of the heroine's friends and the man she might have loved—and by its tragic ending: while Isabelle climbs into the mountains and dies in a mysterious kind of semisuicide, the manuscript she has just completed and left with friends burns up in a fire.

Senancour became an invalid in his last years: he was deaf, almost totally paralyzed, and unable even to feed himself. He died in an *asile* (shelter) for old people at Saint-Cloud on 10 January 1846. Although Senancour was reluctant to see himself as a precursor of romanticism, that is precisely the place he has been assigned in literary history. A legend has formed around Oberman, who became to his cult followers a figure symbolizing the metaphysical suffering, the sensitivity to nature, and the impotence of the truncated destiny of the Romantic hero. The emphasis laid by critics and literary historians on the personality of Senancour's best-known hero has tended to obscure not only the philosophical content of his writing, which was the element the author himself most valued, but also the formal components of his literary production. It is perhaps sadly fitting that this reticent but uncompromising author, who never felt quite at home in the world, should continue to be both prized and, in his own terms, misread.

Bibliographies:

Joachim Merlant, *Bibliographie des œuvres de Senancour avec des documents inédits* (Paris: Hachette, 1905);

Béatrice Didier Le Gall, *L'Imaginaire chez Senancour*, volume 2 (Paris: Corti, 1966);

Jean Senelier, *Hommage à Senancour* (Paris: Nizet, 1970).

Biographies:

André Monglond, *Le Journal intime d'Oberman* (Paris & Grenoble: Arthaud, 1947);

Béatrice Didier Le Gall, *L'Imaginaire chez Senancour*, volume 1 (Paris: Corti, 1966).

References:

R. Bouyer, *Un Contemporain de Beethoven: Oberman, précurseur et musicien* (Paris: Fischbacher, 1907);

Van Wyck Brooks, *The Malady of the Ideal: Obermann, Guérin, Amiel* (Philadelphia: University of Pennsylvania Press, 1947);

Martha Noel Evans, "The Dream Sequences in Senancour's *Oberman*," *Symposium*, 32 (Spring 1978): 1-14;

Evans, "Le Thème de l'eau chez Senancour," *Revue des Sciences Humaines*, 107 (July-September 1962): 357-365;

A. Finot, *Essais de clinique romantique* (Paris: Houdé, 1947);

Ronald Grimsley, "Reflection and Irony in *Obermann*," *French Studies*, 25 (October 1971): 411-426;

Maurice Larroutis, "Monde primitif et monde idéal dans l'œuvre de Senancour," *Revue d'Histoire Littéraire de la France*, 62 (January-March 1962): 41-58;

Béatrice Didier Le Gall, *Senancour romancier: Aldomen, Oberman, Isabelle* (Paris: CDU Sedes, 1985);

Jules Levallois, *Une Evolution philosophique au commencement du 19e siècle (Senancour)* (Paris: Picard, 1888);

Levallois, *Un Précurseur: Senancour* (Paris: Champion, 1897);

Zvi Levy, *Senancour, dernier disciple de Rousseau* (Paris: Nizet, 1980);

Joachim Merlant, *Le Roman personnel de Rousseau à Fromentin* (Paris: Hachette, 1905);

Merlant, *Senancour, poète, penseur religieux et publiciste: Sa vie, son œuvre, son influence* (Paris: Fischbacher, 1907);

Gustave Michaut, *Senancour, ses amis et ses ennemis* (Paris: Sansot, 1910);

Marcel Raymond, "Senancour, deux expériences exemplaires," *Cahiers du Sud*, 385 (1966): 239-250;

Raymond, *Senancour: Sensations et révélations* (Paris: Corti, 1965);

Jean Senelier, *Hommage à Senancour* (Paris: Nizet, 1970);

Jean and Jérôme Tharaud, "Senancour," *Revue de Paris*, 54 (1947): 3-10;

Danielle Viéville-Carbonel, "Senancour et Camus, ou l'affinité de l'inquiétude," *Revue des Sciences Humaines*, 136 (1969): 606-615.

Papers:
No manuscript copies of Senancour's principal works are known. The manuscript of an unpublished version of *Libres méditations* can be found at the Abo Library in Turku, Finland. Lesser manuscripts and autograph letters are scattered in private collections and in the Sainte-Geneviève Library (Paris), the Historical Library of the City of Paris, the libraries of Besançon and Fontainebleau, and the Fribourg University Library, Switzerland.

Germaine de Staël
(Anne-Louise Germaine de Staël-Holstein)
(22 April 1766 - 14 July 1817)

Madelyn Gutwirth
West Chester University

SELECTED BOOKS: *Sophie, ou les sentiments secrets* (Paris, 1876);

Lettres sur les ouvrages et le caractère de J.-J. Rousseau (Paris, 1788); translated anonymously as *Letters on the Works and Character of Jean-Jacques Rousseau* (London: Robinson, 1789);

Jane Grey, tragédie en cinq actes et en vers (Paris: Desenne, 1790);

Réflexions sur la paix addressées à M. Pitt at aux Français (Paris, 1794);

Réflexions sur la paix intérieure (Paris, 1795);

Recueil de morceaux détachés (Lausanne: Durand, Ravanel et comp^e / Paris: Fuchs, 1795)— contains *Epître au malheur; Essai sur les fictions; Trois nouvelles: Mirza, ou Lettre d'un voyageur, Adelaïde et Théodore, Histoire de Pauline*;

De l'influence des passions sur le bonheur des individus et des nations (Lausanne: J. Mourer, 1796); translated anonymously as *A Treatise on the Influence of the Passions upon the Happiness of Individuals and of Nations* (London, 1798);

De la littérature considérée dans ses rapports avec les institutions sociales (Paris: Maradan, 1800); translated anonymously as *A Treatise on Ancient and Modern Literature* (London: G. Cawthorn, 1803);

Delphine (Geneva: J. J. Paschoud, 1802); translated anonymously as *Delphine* (London, 1803);

Corinne, ou l'Italie (Paris: Nicolle, 1807); translated by D. Lawler as *Corinne, or Italy* (London: Corri, 1807); translated by Avriel Gold-

Germaine de Staël (portrait by Baron Gerald; Musée de Versailles)

berger as *Corinne, or Italy* (New Brunswick, N.J.: Rutgers University Press, 1987);

De l'Allemagne, 3 volumes (Paris: Nicolle, 1810-1813; London: J. Murray, 1813); translated anonymously as *Germany* (London: J. Murray, 1813);

Réflexions sur le suicide (Stockholm: C. Delén, 1813);

Considérations sur les principaux événemens de la Révolution française, 3 volumes (Paris: Delaunay, 1818);

Dix années d'exil (Paris: Treuttel et Würtz, 1821); translated anonymously as *Ten Years' Exile; or, Memoirs of That Interesting Period of the Life of the Baroness de Staël-Holstein, Written by Herself* (London, 1821);

Des circonstances actuelles qui peuvent terminer la Révolution et des principes qui doivent fonder la république en France (Paris: Fischbacher, 1906).

Editions and Collections: *Œuvres complètes*, 17 volumes, edited by Auguste de Staël (Paris: Treuttel et Würtz, 1820-1821); volume 1 contains *Notice sur le caractère et les écrits de Madame de Staël*; *Lettres sur le caractère et les écrits de J.-J. Rousseau*; volume 2 contains *Réflexions sur le procès de la reine*; *Réflexions sur la paix, adressées à M. Pitt et aux Français*; *Réflexions sur la paix intérieure*; *Essai sur les fictions*; *Trois nouvelles*; *Zulma*; volume 3 contains *De l'influence des passions sur le bonheur des individus et des nations*; *Réflexions sur le suicide*; volume 4 contains *De la littérature considérée dans ses rapports avec les institutions sociales*; volumes 5-7 contain *Delphine*; volumes 8-9 contain *Corinne*; volumes 10-11 contain *De l'Allemagne*; volumes 12-14 contain *Considérations sur les principaux événemens de la Révolution française*; volume 15 contains *Dix ans d'exil*; volume 16 contains *Essais dramatiques*; volume 17 contains *Mélanges*;

Madame de Staël on Politics, Literature, and National Character, translated and edited by Morroe Berger (Garden City, N.Y.: Doubleday, 1964);

Les Carnets de voyage de Madame de Staël, edited by Simone Balayé (Geneva: Droz, 1971);

Madame de Staël: Choix de textes, thématique et actualité, edited by Georges Solovieff (Paris: Klincksieck, 1974);

Madame de Staël: An Extraordinary Woman. Selected Writings of Germaine de Staël, edited by Vivian Folkenlik (New York: Columbia University Press, 1987).

Germaine de Staël was born into a time of stormy change, and she suffered the buffetings,

in her life and in her writings, of its contradictory impulses. Her figure and her work acquire enhanced coherence if one considers her career as that of a person of exceptional gifts striving for what now would be viewed as a modern conception of womanhood—but a person hobbled and stranded at the crossroads: that intersection between the upper-class model of woman bequeathed to her by the Century of Light, and the popular drive toward the ideal of the equality of man that was to produce the French Revolution. But Staël has scarcely been envisaged in this light. The literary manuals have preserved the mention of her from her own day to this as one of the two women (the other being George Sand) worthy of canonic inclusion as figures essential to an understanding of romanticism in France.

Until the last quarter century, Staël was depicted almost invariably as the author of *De la littérature* (1800; translated as *A Treatise on Ancient and Modern Literature*, 1803) and *De l'Allemagne* (1810-1813; translated as *Germany*, 1813), works of enormous intellectual impact upon received ideas in their time, but bypassed by subsequent movements. Or else she has been that "Mistress to an Age" of J. Christopher Herold's 1958 biography, a gifted but hysterical harridan with nymphomaniacal tendencies, too active, ambitious, and pretentious for her own good. She was seen always as "The Great Female Exception," a posture she indeed assumed, and her example has been repeatedly summoned up in the ages since her death to provide a monitory caveat against an excess of female aspiration. One has only to cite, among many other commentators, Alphonse de Lamartine, in his *Souvenirs et portraits* (1871): "La charmante timidité de son sexe et de son âge, cette pudeur de l'âme, aussi rougissante que celle du corps, n'était jamais née en elle.... On regrettait un moment en elle cette innocence du génie qui s'ignore et doute de lui-même; on finissait par l'oublier au charme de son improvisation virile. Ce n'était plus une femme, c'était un poëte et orateur" (The charming timidity appropriate to her sex and her age, that modesty of the soul, as blushing as that of the body, never came to light in her.... People felt the want in her of that innocence of the genius who does not know his own powers, and doubts himself; they forgot this in hearing the charm of her virile improvisations. For she was no longer a woman, but a poet and orator).

Staël's continuing challenge to contemporary readers lies in the complexities of her case.

She was to be perhaps the last of the great salon women, virtually raised in the midst of a brilliant and rationalist conversational milieu. Yet just outside that milieu, and penetrating it more and more blatantly, a diffuse Rousseauist ethos had gained ground in popular opinion, bringing with it a tidal wave of emotionalism best exemplified, perhaps, by Jean-Jacques Rousseau's *Julie, ou La Nouvelle Héloïse* (1761; translated as *Julia, or The New Eloisa*, 1773), and on the eve of the Revolution, by another novel celebrating the beauty of the loss of the beloved, his disciple Jacques Henri Bernardin de Saint-Pierre's *Paul et Virginie* (1787; translated as *Paul and Virginia*, 1795). The Romantic revolt (sometimes termed pre-Romantic, in France) then taking place would sweep along the young (Staël was twenty-three as the Revolution began) in its tide of emotional rejection of the past. The "very bliss" of the new beginning William Wordsworth then felt to be under way fueled Staël's generation with an energy and a sense of possibility undreamed of before. For politics this would mean, to those who like Staël espoused an "enlightened" version of the Revolution, a cult of freedom, but one tempered by a sense of polity, of the commonweal, transcending the interest of the self. Yet that same impulse toward infinite possibility might, on the personal level, impel many toward an unbridled individualism, justified by the newly authorized realization of selfhood and the freshly legitimated joys of the pursuit of happiness.

Deeply embedded in the new bourgeois code that Rousseau articulated most effectively was a strictly dimorphic conception of gender. Women, as Rousseau averred in *Emile* (1762; translated, 1911), were to subordinate themselves strictly to husbands, even to tolerate injustice gladly at their hands. Furthermore, Rousseau advocated a strict separation of the sexes, in education and in life, ending only with the waning of the light of day. Of course this conception did not meet with universal approval. Most of all it conflicted with what one might term rococo social mores, such as those of the court and the salon, where women had enjoyed a distinct prominence in society during the eighteenth century. This presence of women in social life, however, certainly never amounted to the preeminence that has sometimes been imputed to them, as if they had indeed enjoyed a genuine "reign of women," a myth that Edmond and Jules de Goncourt, among others, would later popularize.

Germaine de Staël, on the brink of the era of modern republicanism, would combine the salon woman's social mastery with a powerful civic commitment and a Romantic fervor for the fulfillment of her talents and passions. But that fervor she worshiped with such intensity, calling it enthusiasm, which was to generate the energies prodding her to express what she would term her genius, was very nearly checkmated by the rival drive within her to succumb to the Rousseauist cult of the female vulnerability to love, a cult embraced by her age. All the remarkable work—political, fictional, critical—that she was to achieve, then, was wrought from within a tug-of-war between simultaneous drives toward freedom and dependency.

The Paris in which she was born and which she would forever regard as her natural element would, for the most part, never look upon her, or her parents before her, as anything but upstarts, parvenus from a foreign province, not even Catholics. Jacques Necker, her father, was the none-too-promising second son of a comfortable Protestant Genevese family. Sent out to Paris to the Genevese banker Thélusson as an apprentice, the young man succeeded beyond his family's expectations in the world of finance, becoming sole director of Thélusson's bank in 1765, at the age of thirty-three. Anne-Louise Germaine Necker would be born into a wealth that would never fail her needs, and that provided her with a portion of that amazing social aplomb that she was to exhibit to the public for so much of her life. Her mother, Suzanne Curchod de Nasse, four years Jacques Necker's junior, had been born to a pastor and his wife, Jeanne Gautier, in the Vaud district of Switzerland. Suzanne's father had so encouraged her lively intelligence, teaching her Latin and theology, as well as literature, that she would become somewhat celebrated in her own circle as a cultivated *précieuse*, a beautiful *bas-bleu* (bluestocking). The demise of her never-rich pastor father left Suzanne and her mother in straitened circumstances. Marriage was the only means of redress in their fortunes, and for a time the distinguished young Edward Gibbon was Suzanne's suitor; but his father found his son's marriage to an impoverished foreigner, no matter how comely and brilliant, an unseemly prospect. Suzanne was forced to assume a post as companion/governess in the family of Mme de Vermenoux, Genevese settled in Paris. To their house came Jacques Necker, originally attracted to Mme de Vermenoux, but in the end content to end up as the groom of a bride of more modest station.

Despite their unpromising beginnings, the Neckers had the highest ambitions accessible to Parisians: she to maintain an illustrious salon and entertain the most brilliant literati along with the highest society of the capital; he to become minister of finance, the most important post in the government of Louis XVI, if also that most vulnerable in a time of dwindling royal resources. Suzanne Necker's salon attracted a public including Denis Diderot, Jean-François Marmontel, Melchior von Grimm and the abbé Guillaume Raynal. Some Parisians, such as Voltaire, thought the couple less than enchanting—she, starchy; he, dull—but their salon effectively advanced his political aspirations and made the pair central players in the life of the city.

A striking feature of their salon was the inclusion of their little daughter Germaine, who was allowed to sit on a stool by her mother's side and interact with the visitors. Some commentators have said that Anne-Louise Germaine, who was born to the Neckers two years after their marriage, never had a childhood, and was thrust into the grown-up world almost from infancy. Her mother, rejecting Rousseau's ideas on the education of girls, professed she was raising her daughter "like Emile." In truth, she gave her an education much like her own, with solid translations of classical texts, history lessons, and religious instruction. A much-remarked upon feature of Louise's (as she was called until her marriage) childhood was a breakdown she suffered on the brink of adolescence. When Dr. Tronchin, the most celebrated physician of the age, was consulted, he ordered the child out of the city and its stimulations, to the country near Saint-Ouen, where she was to wear loose garments and not be made to study so assiduously. Her obsessive quality toward attachment was visible in the febrile joy she displayed when her cousin Catherine Rilliet-Huber came to join her at Saint-Ouen, to provide her with a playmate of her own age. Louise swore that they would never separate, showing Catherine a spontaneity of response altogether astonishing to this cousin, and offering to put on plays with her for entertainment. Rilliet-Huber also furnishes a picture of the young Germaine in the salon, where, although she remained silent as a dutiful child should do, her brilliant eyes (always conceded as her finest feature) darted about as she followed the exchange of ideas, re-

vealing how aptly she followed them, whether they were political or philosophic. At twelve she already thought of herself as a writer, and composed a playlet on the problems of life in Paris, a dramatization of her own situation as an exile from her place of birth, the first in a life that would become a series of exiles.

Following this crisis of early adolescence, Louise turned toward her father rather than her demanding mother to sustain her intense emotional nature. She found him receptive and loving, so much so that he would remain for her the one reliable polestar of her affective life. Her gratitude to him was to be replayed incessantly in the garlands of praise for his person and his policies that would festoon her works, to the malicious glee of the enemies of both, for whom they were a fertile source of mockery. This quasi-amorous attachment between Necker and his daughter stranded Suzanne Necker outside the warmth of the dyad they formed, and led to a permanent estrangement between mother and daughter.

Writing, since early on in a life mostly devoid of the companionship of other children, had represented a seductive inner voyage for Louise, as her youthful journal attests. Writing would always provide a place of unreason and protest, not quite fully censored, that she demanded as refuge from an uncomprehending world. The play, "Sophie, ou les sentiments secrets," written in 1786, illustrates her considerable skill at versification and her tendency to reify in fiction dilemmas too acute for her to confront directly. It explores, via an amorous triangle among a young woman and a couple who protect her, the anguish of her love, unrealizable, for her father and his for her.

A brilliant match in terms of her money and her family's prestige, Louise was less so as a Protestant and a woman of already demanding and decided personality. After much family dissent (Mme Necker had wished her to marry William Pitt, the Younger), a husband was found who combined the Protestant faith with an establishment in Paris (Louise was in no way prepared to move from there) and (modest) aristocratic rank and prestige, as well as connections to the court. Eric Magnus, Baron de Staël-Holstein, ambassador from the Swedish crown to France, seventeen years older than his bride, was handsome, courtly, cultivated, and vacuous. A womanizer and gambler, he was at first quite taken with his young wife. Once inside this marriage, Germaine, though less than enchanted with her

Jacques Necker, Mme de Staël's father (portrait by Joseph Sifrède Duplessis; from J. Christopher Herold, Mistress to an Age: A Life of Madame de Staël, *1958)*

spouse, from whom enchantment could not be expected—much as it might have remained ardently desired—threw herself into adult life. She opened her own salon on the rue du Bac, which rapidly became a center of intellectual and political exchange in the years after her 1785 marriage, and she wrote an informative chronicle of Parisian events for the king of Sweden, Gustave III. She also wrote another verse play in 1786, this time on the last days of Lady Jane Grey. This composition still conveys the highest conception of literary aspiration in the classical tradition, that of the writing of verse drama in the manner of Pierre Corneille, Jean Racine, and Voltaire. She explores the problematics of confronting the death of the beloved and of suicide, permanent features of the Staëlian oeuvre, with a sense of transcendent ethical commitment, like that of the Jane who had refused to recant her beliefs.

During this same period, Staël wrote her first critical work, *Lettres sur les ouvrages et le caractère de J.-J. Rousseau* (1788; translated as *Letters on the Works and Character of Jean-Jacques Rousseau*, 1789). These letters are a specific tribute, though not one without qualifications, to Rousseau's deep impact upon her outlook. Enthu-

siastically surveying his style, his *Discours sur les arts et sciences* (1750; translated as *The Effects of the Arts and Sciences With Regard to Manners*, 1773), his *Discours sur l'inégalité* (1755; translated as *On the Origin and Foundation of Inequality Among Mankind*, 1773), and his *Lettre à d'Alembert sur les spectacles* (1758; translated as *An Epistle to Mr. D'Alembert*, 1773) in the first of her letters, she goes on to engage in separate examinations of *La Nouvelle Héloïse*, of *Emile*, of Rousseau's political works, and of his interests in botany and music, ending with an interpretation of his character. Deeply imprinted by the Rousseauist vogue, her work is at once a fawning paean, a pleading attempt to achieve identification with the literate public's hero, and a subversive attempt, as a woman of letters, to assume his own mantle, a measure of which he could never have approved.

While strongly affirming her espousal of Rousseau's maternalism, which had achieved a massive consensus, she yet balks at his denigration of women, while never confronting it directly: "Je vois la nécessité de leur inspirer des vertus que les hommes n'ont pas, bien plus que celle de les encourager dans leur infériorité . . . " (I see a need to inspire in them virtues that men do not possess, much more than the need to encourage their inferiority . . .). She would prefer, she claims, to see women submitting to their destiny out of free choice rather than out of incapacity. And, in a move expressive of the problematics of her own life, she embraces Rousseau's distinctly articulated rejection of women such as herself: "S'il a voulu diminuer leur influence sur les délibérations des hommes, comme il a consacré l'empire qu'elles ont sur leur bonheur!" (If he wished to lessen [women's] influence upon men's deliberations, how he consecrated their power over men's happiness!). An informed and passionate exercise, these letters reflect Staël's tendency to grow, intellectually and emotionally, in full view of her audience.

Meanwhile, her worldly life remained such that a hidden life of literary effort would seem scarcely possible. After the birth of the first of her five children, Gustavine, her role as mother could be easily absorbed into an active social life of privilege, as was then the case for women of her class. A sickly child, this daughter would die in early childhood, leaving Staël free to pursue her passionate preoccupations with love, with politics, and, indissociable from this concern, with her father's career. Her marriage having already turned conventional, she sought solace elsewhere; her father's career having reached its apogee, she concentrated all her own aspirations on his success. And her contribution to it was no small one: her presence was a galvanizing force in any assemblage, her wit in speaking and her energy providing a focal point for any discussion, and her ease and agreeableness in social interaction soothingly reducing any sense of constraint that others might feel in confronting such palpable verbal and intellectual superiorities.

When Necker, in his last attempt to preserve the nation from ruin after the Estates General had met in May 1789, refused in June to turn against its decrees, a great popular demonstration arose to prevent him from withdrawing from power. Germaine had been in Versailles, aiding her mother in the social and administrative tasks attached to her father's ministry, had attended the opening of the Estates General, and was witness to the delirium of approval of her father. As she would write more than twenty-five years later in *Considérations sur les principaux événemens de la Révolution française* (Considerations on the Principal Events of the French Revolution, 1818), "Toutes ces voix, qui répétaient le nom de mon père, me semblaient celles d'une foule d'amis qui partageaient ma respectueuse tendresse" (All those voices repeating my father's name seemed like a crowd of friends who shared my respectful love for him). The tumult of such events, the glory of them coming so close to her, subsequently had an effect upon her much like that of a climb of Mount Everest, after which the rest of life seemed pallid and dull.

That there was an underside to this flirtation with political glory became manifest all too soon, as Necker was sent into exile by Louis XVI on 11 July. Suzanne and Jacques Necker mounted their carriage as if to go on their daily ride and did not stop until they reached Brussels, where their daughter joined them two days later. The reaction to this exile was to produce the fall of the Bastille. Necker would then return to power amid throngs of flower-bearing crowds, a return as heady or headier even than his previous apotheosis. Though this return was to be of short duration, these moments of heightened existence were to last forever in Necker's daughter's emotional economy, shaping her life.

Obsessed with the idea of partnership with a great man to whom she might semimaritally wed her talents and ambitions, who would be their instrument, Germaine became enamored of the handsome, aristocratically prestigious Count

Louis de Narbonne, with whom she had a son, Auguste de Staël, born in 1790. In pursuit of a ministerial post for Narbonne, she continued her political activity, opening her salon to persons of all political tendencies though herself preferring a somewhat Girondist posture, and supporting the establishment of a constitutional monarchy. With Narbonne's appointment as minister of war in 1791, Mme de Staël seemed to have triumphed; but events outsmarted her: he was dismissed in March 1792. Paris had become a perilous place for people of her class, whatever opinions they professed, but Staël remained in the city, aiding friends to cross the border by virtue of her money and her international contacts. Finally, seven-months pregnant with her second son, Albert, she fled—amid difficulties dramatically described in her *Considérations*—back to her deeply disappproving mother in Switzerland. There she stopped off only long enough to give birth to her baby in November, before departing in January to be with her lover Narbonne, in exile in England.

In a sort of tortured English idyll, she was to be entertained at Juniper Hall in Surrey, along with Narbonne, Charles-Maurice de Talleyrand, and Alexandre d'Arblay. She met the novelist Fanny Burney, whose celebrated musicologist father indignantly refused to allow his chaste daughter to share Staël's company, but a congenial acquaintance bloomed nonetheless.

From January to May 1793, a time of growing turmoil in France, Staël attempted to find her personal and political bearings by writing a new treatise, *De l'influence des passions sur le bonheur des individus et des nations* (1796; translated as *A Treatise on the Influence of the Passions upon the Happiness of Individuals and of Nations*, 1798), which she would continue working on during the next two years, years of deep disappointment, both sentimental and political.

The retreat in England ended as Staël returned to her parents' estate at Coppet (Switzerland), separating from Narbonne with deep regret, demanding imperatively that he write her regularly. In the region of Geneva, she made the acquaintance of Adolf, Count Ribbing, one of the regicides of Gustave III of Sweden, whom the baron de Staël had formerly served. A dashing aristocrat, neither characteristic being a matter of indifference to her, Ribbing fell ardently in love with Germaine. As Narbonne's defection became more patent, despite the desperation of her pleas to him, Germaine and Ribbing became lovers for a time, and she then displaced upon him all those ambitions for a political life *à deux* that she had formerly dreamed of achieving with Narbonne. During the summer of 1793, as the Terror came to invade the Revolution's agenda, she wrote a passionate and eloquent demand that the life of Marie Antoinette be spared, her *Réflexions sur le procès de la reine* (Reflections on the Trial of the Queen), which appeared in Paris in September. Of course this kindly and disinterested gesture had no effect, Staël and her political tendency had lost all credibility in Jacobin Paris, and the queen went to her death in mid October 1793, along with hundreds of others.

In May 1794 Suzanne Necker died, leaving her daughter, to whom she had refused to speak on her deathbed, with her bereft spouse. Her own horror of physical dissolution had been so great that she had arranged for her body and her husband's to be preserved in fluid in their funerary vault. The fall of Maximilien Robespierre in the summer of 1794 inspired Staël to compose a political pamphlet, *Réflexions sur la paix* (Reflections on Peace, 1795), an appeal to England to conclude a peace treaty with France before the spirit of conquest had run away with her homeland. With this political tract she hoped to return to post-Terror Paris.

After a final break with Narbonne, and during the lingering separation from Ribbing, on 19 September 1794 Staël made the acquaintance of Benjamin Constant in a fateful encounter at the home of mutual friends, the Cazanove d'Arlens, in Montchoisi, near Lausanne. To Germaine, he appeared not very prepossessing in looks, but "singularly witty." Constant, already a jaded character in his late twenties (a year younger than Germaine), had lived and studied in Scotland and Germany, been married and divorced, and had had several serious love affairs from which his father, a general, had felt the need to extricate him, a task Benjamin seemed unable to perform on his own behalf. Having returned to his native region, he had renewed his friendship with Isabelle de Charrière, a Dutch noblewoman married to a petty aristocrat, and a literary celebrity as the author of the exquisite novel *Caliste* (1785-1788).

Lucid and disabused, Charrière had a sensibility that matched Constant's well, and although he was of an age to have been her son, he had spent endless hours in her company in a sort of entente of the spirit. Charrière had little use for Staël, even before the Staël-Constant liaison

began, for the younger woman had paid the elder a visit and had the misfortune of displeasing her by her dress and her manners. Charrière and Constant had also complicitously mocked the style of Staël's plea for the queen's life. Now the older woman experienced the pain of seeing her young acolyte fall headlong and headstrongly in love with Germaine. Constant would write to Charrière in Germaine's defense: "J'ai rarement vu une réunion pareille de qualités étonnantes et attrayantes, autant de brillant et de justesse, une bienveillance aussi expansive, et aussi active, autant de générosité, une politesse aussi douce et aussi soutenue dans le monde, tant de charme, de simplicité, d'abandon dans la société intime" (I've rarely seen such a combination of astonishing qualities in anyone, so much brilliance and justness of mind, a concern for others as expansive and active, so much generosity, such a sweetness of social grace that is so sustained when she is with others, so much charm, simplicity, and self-abandon in intimacy). He decided to abandon Colombier, the Charrière estate, to seek out Germaine at Coppet.

But Germaine was not prepared to take him seriously. One March night in Mézery, where she had taken a house for the season, a sudden cry awakened all the inhabitants. The servants who rushed to discover its origin found Constant twisting in agony upon his bed. Lights went on, calls for help went out. At the sight of Germaine's cousin, Rilliet-Huber, Benjamin proclaimed that he was dying for his hostess's sake, and pleaded for her to come to him. Vomiting and foaming at the mouth, he was a dreadful sight, and Germaine was compelled to relent: "Vivez, vivez, cher Monsieur Constant, je vous en conjure" (Live, live, dear Mr. Constant, I beg you). After this scene she confessed to her cousin that she felt an invincible physical antipathy for this man that nothing could change. And yet, for lack of another companion, this peculiar, slight, redheaded chap, with his excellent mind and his learning surpassing her own (he had, after all, studied at universities in Erlangen and Edinburgh, which she could never have done) perforce began to seem to her to be that great man whose companion she might yet live to become.

Consequently, and despite that invincible repugnance, Constant ultimately had his way. Germaine and Benjamin traveled to Paris in May 1795, where she reopened her salon and prepared to renew her political life. But by August, in response to the publication of her *Réflexions sur la paix intérieure* (Reflections on Domestic Peace), the butcher Legendre pronounced a violent diatribe against her in the national convention, charging her with being a Circe, protecting émigré aristocrats, and corrupting the deputies she invited to dinner. By October she was forced into exile, and all of the year 1796 was spent in Switzerland. Allowed to return to France in 1797, she gave birth to a daughter, Albertine, in Paris in June.

Staël had completed her *De l'influence des passions* in the winter of 1795 in Coppet and Lausanne, while Constant labored over his *De la force du gouvernement actuel de la France* (1796; translated as *Observations on the Strength of the Present Government of France*, 1797). His link with Germaine had forged in him a furnace of ambition where no fires had ever kindled before. As to the treatment of her subject in *De l'influence des passions*, that literary fruit of the Revolution and of personal dismay, Staël divided them into public and private categories. The first treats such socially related impulses as the love of fame, ambition, vanity, vengeance, and partisan spirit. A shocking categorization here is her insistence upon situating love in this first part of her treatise, inasmuch as she chose to view it as but one more obsessively violent passionate affliction. The second section may be characterized as a sort of self-imposed apprenticeship, via writing, in wisdom: it deals with those feelings halfway between uncontrolled passion and the resources one might discover within oneself. Here one reads of friendship, of filial and conjugal love, and of religion.

Lastly one finds a treatment of the compensations offered by the presumably non- or anti-passionate love of study, charity, and philosophy. A rambling and at times painfully personal excursion—"Il me coûte de dire qu'aimer passionnément n'était pas le vrai bonheur" (It hurts me to say that loving passionately was not true happiness), she confesses—it contains, as do all her works, fine lapidary formulations, acute psychological observations, and ringing assertions. She ends her work on the passions affirming that "ce bonheur qu'on croit toujours trouver dans les objets extérieurs n'est qu'un fantôme créé par l'imagination, qu'elle poursuit après l'avoir fait naître, et qu'elle veut atteindre au-dehors, tandis qu'elle n'a existence qu'en elle" (that happiness we forever think we will find in external objects is but a phantom created by the imagination, which it pursues after having given

it birth; it seeks to reach it outside itself, whereas it has no existence but within).

This deepened exploration of the workings of the mind found another fruitful outlet in *Essai sur les fictions* (Essay on Fiction, 1795). Here she defends the still little-esteemed but much-read genre of the novel as a valuable one, and proposes that novelists turn away from their monomaniacal preoccupation with love. Ambition, pride, avarice, and vanity could and should, she thought, also become appropriate novelistic matter, and so she looks forward one day to reading about "the Lovelace of ambition," a challenge that Honoré de Balzac may well have taken up as he created his Eugène de Rastignac. Interestingly enough, Staël, who was otherwise so deeply drawn to meliorist politics, here proclaims ardently a doctrine of fiction for fiction's sake, even though she does not fail to note its ability to enlarge ideas. The only justification for a fiction, she holds, lies in the pleasure it gives; hence, if one has a moral or philosophic project in writing one, that project has to clothe itself in the seductive arts that charm the imagination. This exercise in criticism tested Staël's conception of the art of fiction, a process already engaged in her early tales. This teasing out of a critical grasp upon fiction would later come to maturity in her large novels. The back-to-back conceptions of *De l'influence des passions* and *Essai sur les fictions* made them parallel meditations on the limits of love and the power of passionate obsessiveness to warp life on the one hand, and, on the other, the compensations that the treatment of these same destructive forces by the controlled imagination might offer.

The last and most politically daring of Staël's texts before the century that was to be greeted with her *De la littérature* was to remain unpublished until the twentieth century. This was *Des circonstances actuelles qui peuvent terminer la Révolution et des principes qui doivent fonder la république en France* (On the Present Circumstances that Might Lead to an End of the Revolution, and on the Principles upon which the Republic Must Be Founded, 1906). Returning to France in 1797, Staël became politically active, as before, founding with Constant and others a constitutional group called the Club de Salm. During this period of the Directory, she met Napoleon Bonaparte on several occasions. Far from disapproving of him, she at first sought to collaborate with him. He, however, was unfailingly ungracious to her, making her deeply apprehensive in his presence. He, for instance, replied in nakedly misogynous terms to an admittedly foolish question she asked in company as to what sort of woman would exemplify for him the first among her sex by replying, "The one who had produced the most children!" With her canny perceptiveness about matters of state, she saw clearly that the future lay with the deliberate and ruthless Bonaparte. But with the coup d'état of Floréal (May 1798), a second despoiling of an election in two years, both Staël and Constant feared for the survival of representative government in France. The republic to which she aspires in *Circonstances* is one with firm institutions, insured by free elections. These, she sees, would be seriously undermined by the continuation of nationalistic adventurism, and she here assumes a resolutely antimilitarist posture. Believing, in her congenital optimism, that the battles against slavery, religious fanaticism, feudalism, and hereditary privilege had been won, she advocated a peaceful revolution, fostered by public education. This work, never truly completed, is both a sketchy foray into political theory and a political pamphlet, clearly intended to sway opinion at the moment.

Constant made countless corrections in Staël's text, which is something of a collaborative effort. Most of them, as editor Lucia Omacini has asserted, tended to moderate her more vigorous political stances, and to depersonalize her first-person remarks. But even with such emendations as he proposed, the work was outpaced by events, and could be published only in the twentieth century.

Meanwhile, Constant had taken up with the celebrated actress Julie Talma, while Germaine worked, from late 1798 and through 1799, on her *De la littérature*. As a male, Constant was now able to find a self-legitimizing role in government service, and, even as Napoleon ascended to sole power, became a member of the Tribunate. Yet his forthright speech there aroused the ire of Napoleon, with the result that the press, slavishly following the Consul's lead, unleashed some of those brutal attacks of which Germaine was frequently the object, this time upon both Constant and herself. The style of vituperation assumed by the newspaper *Journal des Hommes Libres* was typical: "Ce n'est pas votre faute si vous êtes laide, mais c'est votre faute si vous êtes intrigante.... Vous savez le chemin de la Suisse.... Emmenez votre Benjamin!" (It is not your fault if you are ugly, but it is your fault if you are an intriguer.... You know the route to Switzer-

land.... Take it with your Benjamin!).

If she was prepared to do so in the short run, it was to allow *De la littérature* to speak for her, as the first edition appeared in April 1800. To greet the new century, Staël had conceived a vast canvas within which she strove to place her construct of human evolution in Western culture as reconstituted through its literatures. In her preliminary discourse, she reflects that "la plupart des hommes, épouvantés des vicissitudes effroyables dont les événements politiques nous ont offert l'exemple, ont perdu maintenant tout intérêt au perfectionnement d'eux-mêmes, et sont trop frappés par la puissance du hasard pour croire à l'ascendant des facultés intellectuelles" (Most people, appalled by the atrocious vicissitudes to which political events have exposed us, have now lost all interest in their own perfectibility, and are too impressed by the power of chance to believe in the power of their intellectual faculties).

She consequently offers these meditations as an antidote to the wretched dispiritedness of her time, of which she gives a striking image in proposing her cultural cure: "Nous sortirions par degrés de la plus affreuse période de l'esprit public, l'égoïsme de l'état de nature combiné avec l'active multiplicité des intérêts de la société, la corruption sans politesse, la grossièreté sans franchise, la civilisation sans lumières, l'ignorance sans enthousiasme; enfin cette sorte de *désabusé*, maladie de quelques hommes supérieurs ... tout occupés d'eux-mêmes ils se sentent indifférents aux malheurs des autres." (We might emerge by degrees from the most frightful period for the public spirit—which combined an egoism of the state of nature with people's multiplicity of special interests, a corruption without civility, a vulgarity devoid of candor, a civilization without understanding, an ignorance without enthusiasm, in sum that species of *disaffection*, the malady of some superior men ... entirely preoccupied with themselves, and indifferent to the misfortunes of others).

Comparing the aristocratic France of 1798 with ancient Rome in its decline, she foresaw that the victory of the people would be only momentary, and that some centuries would be needed, during which their educational progress would have to be sustained by the now-vanquished segment of French society, before a true victory of the people could be proclaimed. In her argument, to the effect that the human spirit is perfectible, not intrinsically and permanently blemished,

Staël (right) depicted as the heroine of her novel Corinne *(painting by François Gérard; Musée de Lyon)*

she makes some material modifications (to be sure, not hers alone) to then-prevalent ideas of cultural history. European civilization (which for her is synonymous with all civilization) had not gone into eclipse between the fall of Rome and the Renaissance. She credits Christianity with having fostered the idea of conscience and its refinement through the art of the medieval era, which she views as favorable to the development of reason.

A loyal daughter of the Enlightenment, she would remain faithful to its precepts, even as she sought to conciliate it with faith. It was Christianity too, she thought, that had managed the fusion of North and South, the great schism that organizes her tableau. Indeed it is Christianity that makes her award her laurels of superiority to the literatures of the North, especially to English literature, and even more specifically, to William Shakespeare and to Ossian (she is entirely taken in by James Macpherson's forgery). This rehabilitation of the medieval and of the misty heroism of northern heroes was taken up by the French Romantic movement's poetic and architectural tastes, as Victor Hugo's *Notre-Dame de Paris* (1831) and Eugène-Emmanuel Viollet-le-Duc's "reconstructions" of France's medieval glories attest.

Like *Circonstances*, which was to lead to the permanent establishment of the republic in France, *De la littérature* has a deeply meliorist politico-cultural project. It was dedicated, beyond the present political perspectives, to a more enlightened public, for whom the idea that freedom of the mind and of the imagination was as essential to the republic as shoes and soap would not seem an absurdity. It is also a call for a return to the plentitude of language, after the loss of the signifier to republican platitudes and mantras, even though, unbeknownst to herself, the critic had herself internalized some of them. For Staël, the role that literature was called upon to perform must be nothing less than a sacred magistracy of mind and imagination. The Romantics of the next generation would perpetuate this view.

Yet the work could be belittled for its apparent special pleading for the superior mission of the writer that the author took herself to be, for the rights of "genius," and for the ritual obeisance she could not resist making to her sacred connection with her father, with its tribute to his transcendent gifts. Despite such problems, *De la littérature* was a huge success with the public, a second edition appearing in the same year as the first, and remaining timely enough to inspire sixteen printings during the course of the new century. Critical reception was, however, far more problematic than public acceptance, as might have been foreseen from Staël's already stalwart posture of opposition to Napoleon's government. François-René de Chateaubriand, with whom Staël's name would later come to be coupled as the chief literati of the first decades of the nineteenth century, and whose *Atala* (1801) had already made his a voice to be reckoned with, wrote a critique of her work after the publication of the second edition, in which Staël had attempted to respond to the criticisms raised against it.

Accusing her of seeing perfectibility everywhere, just as he himself saw Jesus Christ everywhere, Chateaubriand stated his dislike of Staël's mix of philosophy with religion. Although he accurately named some of the work's less readable qualities, he most especially found distasteful its pretensions to reasoning, for which he chides her in patronizing terms that smack of a misogynous distaste for the woman of intelligence. If he had the honor of knowing her, Chateaubriand remarks in his January 1801 *Mercure de France* critique, he would tell her: "Vous êtes sans doute une femme supérieure. Votre tête est forte et votre imagination pleine de charme.... Votre style a souvent de l'éclat, de l'élégance.... Mais malgré tous ces avantages, votre ouvrage est bien loin de ce qu'il aurait pu devenir. Le style en est monotone, sans mouvement, et trop mêlé d'expressions métaphysiques. Le sophisme des idées repousse, l'érudition ne satisfait pas, et le cœur est trop sacrifié à la pensée ... " (You are without a doubt a superior woman. You are strong of mind and your imagination is frequently full of charm.... Your style often has brilliance, elegance.... But in spite of all these qualities, your work is far from what it might have become. Its style is monotonous, static, and overfull of metaphysical expressions. The sophism of its ideas repels, its erudition fails to satisfy, and feeling is too sacrificed to thought ...). It was one of Staël's most endearing qualities that she never held a grudge, either against a critic or a lover. Her response was to offer Chateaubriand her friendship, a friendship that was to endure.

Still unwelcome in Paris, she continued to visit it for stays of varying length, on one of these visits finally effecting a legal separation from her spouse, whom she wished to divorce, divorce having been one of the extraordinary legislative reforms achieved in the early Revolution. Meanwhile, Staël had begun work on her first full-scale novel, *Delphine*, which she would describe in a letter as her "novel of women." Literature and novel writing may be thought of as at first providing an alternative to political life in Staël's career, a career reined in by her beloved father's reminders to her to "calm your ambition." He was no lover of women of letters, and had put the quietus on his wife's literary penchant, and mocked his daughter's habit of carrying about a portable desk, so that she might always be accessible to her family and never withdraw from its presence to write. He called her "M. de Sainte-Escritoire," bestowing on her writing activities a masculine title. Yet writing, though suspect, was still a less compromising and dangerous activity than political intrigue. And what had perhaps begun as a second-best enterprise would become more and more a primary passion, though even as the woman of letters she ultimately became, she would still retain a sense of the paradox of that posture for a woman. Her strategy for juggling that paradox lay in her assumption of the pose of Great Exception to the Feminine Rule, but *Delphine* is perhaps the only one of her fictional works to minimize that *folie des grandeurs* to which she clung elsewhere with such desperation.

Delphine poses the issue of women's right to individual opinions and passions, in the context of the very suppression of women's nascent rights that the Revolution would enact. Set in the early years of the last decade of the eighteenth century, from 1790 to 1792, it recounts the experiences of upper-class women confronting their lack of freedom through the tale of Delphine, the rich and free young widow of novelistic convention. An epistolary novel, it looks, as Charles-Augustin Sainte-Beuve was to observe, backward, in terms of style and substance, in contrast with the *Corinne* to come, a fully Romantic work.

Delphine embodies the struggle between an individual woman and social codes. Staël defended her choice of the early Revolution as her setting by observing that it presented the greatest possible barrier of opinion, so that neither Delphine, who flouts it, nor Léonce, who respects it, should seem totally in error. Delphine's character has been formed by her husband in name only, her protector M. d'Albémar, a man of the Enlightenment, who fought in the American Revolution. Since his death she has gone to live in Paris, where she achieves success and notoriety for her combination of charm, wit, personality, and generosity. A partisan of liberty, Delphine, as the consensus for female behavior would have insisted she do, makes no political pronouncements. These are instead stated within the novel by her friend M. de Lebensei. A Protestant educated in England and a member of the Constituent Assembly, he incarnates the man of action unfazed by trivial, capricious, and petty salon opinion.

A certain Mme de Vernon—a personage not unlike those female plotters of the eighteenth-century novel that find their culmination in Pierre Choderlos de Laclos's *Les Liaisons dangereuses* (*Dangerous Acquaintances*, 1782)—enchants Delphine with the grace of her manners and her perspicacity. Delphine agrees to provide Mme de Vernon's daughter Mathilde with a dowry, so that she may marry Léonce de Mondoville, a Spanish aristocrat Delphine has never seen. Once she has met the intense, attractive Léonce, they fall in love; but when Mme de Vernon conceals from Léonce some information that would prove Delphine innocent of having been unfaithful to him, Mathilde and Léonce marry. The remainder of the novel recounts Delphine's attempt to become a nun, Léonce's unsuccessful effort to prevent this, and, with Mathilde's death in childbirth, the inability of the couple to wed because of Léonce's Catholic scruples concerning Delphine's abandonment of her vows. Having volunteered for duty to defend the king, Léonce, as a royalist, is about to be shot before a firing squad when Delphine commits suicide, both protagonists thus expiring at the novel's close.

This skeletal summary in no way conveys the multiplicities of the novel, full of secondary plots and beautifully wrought portraits in the salon manner, with some of the bite of the character portraits by Jean de La Bruyère. The portraits of Mme de Vernon, Mlle d'Albémar, and Mme de Ternan are conveyed in the first person. The first character is a defense from the inside of the calculating woman, so dear a bugaboo to the Enlightenment novel; the second is the confession of an ungainly spinster whom society shuns; the third, that of Léonce's aunt, is an apologia by a disabused former society beauty who has become mother superior of the convent where Delphine takes refuge. All of these women, belonging to types that novelistic convention had depicted, if at all, as caricatures, are here endowed with disturbing life. The question of the legitimacy of divorce is given extended play, as the novel approves it verbally but negates it in its action.

But above all else, the question of freedom and its limits infiltrates the novel. A subtlety of observation makes Lebensei remark that "d'un âge à l'autre, il y a souvent dans le même caractère plus de différence, qu'entre deux êtres qui se seraient totalement étrangers" (from one age to another there is frequently more difference to be discerned in a single person than between two beings totally different from each other). This relativism dictates that freedom here is a species of *disponibilité*, of availability to change. In this work such freedom is a prime need of women, for whom the enunciation of principle is usually nothing but internalized enslavement. The novel curses these women's fate, and, with the death of the couple—dictated ultimately by Léonce's inability to espouse freedom and break out of the conformities of tradition—the work strives to make readers hate the damage wrought by rigid social constraints. One thinks of William Blake's proverb, "Damn braces; bless relaxes."

Everything that Staël had done to make her novel appear apolitical—setting it before the Terror, making it a love story devoid of all direct references to statecraft—could not protect her from Bonaparte's ire, eagerly seconded by the critical offensive. For the consul, who had just concluded the concordat with the pope, the work's anti-Catholicism could only have proven displeasing. And for all her evasion of the political, had Staël not dedicated her work to "la France silencieuse mais éclairée" (a France enlightened, though silent)? His comment on *Delphine* was to the effect that he no more liked women who made themselves into men than he cared for effeminate men. The *Mercure de France* held that *Delphine* spoke of love like a bacchante, of God like a Quaker, of death like a grenadier, and of morality like a sophist. The works were scarcely ever to be regarded as separate from the scandalous woman who had penned them. This notoriety helped propel this highly engaging novel from one to another of its twenty-one reprintings.

After having skirted for years what was for her the disaster of banishment, in 1803, as Staël was making for Paris in the hope that her novel had smoothed the way for her reentry, she stopped off on her route at Maffliers. There, while seated at table with a bunch of grapes in her hand, she received notification of her consignment to exile. On 25 October she turned away from France, and with Constant and her children, turned toward Germany. Her husband had died under her care, despite their estrangement.

Paris was closed to her. Her relations with Constant remained consistently stormy and ambiguous, both of them repeatedly seeking other lovers. This voyage to Germany would therefore be undertaken with the trepidation associated with a decisive break with the past, intensified by a sense of foreboding about leaving her aged father in Coppet. All of these factors were to lend this episode huge dimensions in Staël's life. In fact, Germany would effect an enormous reconstruction of her fragile pride, for wherever she went she was feted by princes and members of literate high society, many of whom had read and been impressed by her texts.

Although she had undertaken some study of German during a previous summer, her knowledge of that country and its culture was slim, as the sketchy chapter devoted to German literature in *De la littérature* attests. But her meeting with Wilhelm von Humboldt had altered her Parisian tendency to dismiss things German. The expatriate Frenchman and disciple of Immanuel Kant, Charles de Villiers, who came to meet her on her journey, proved an invaluable informant, as did Constant, who had studied in Germany, knew the language well, and had consented to stay with her until they reached Weimar. Staël recounts in *Dix années d'exil* (1821; translated as *Ten Years' Exile*, 1821) and in *Les Carnets de voyage* (Travel Notebooks, 1971), which she kept en route, her encounters in that city.

Greeted with great warmth by Charles Augustus, Duke of Saxe-Weimar-Eisenach, and the dowager duchess, Anna Amalia, who maintained an intellectual salon, she was to meet the deeply suspicious lions of the place: Christoph Wieland, Friedrich von Schiller, and finally, the grumpily wary Johann Wolfgang von Goethe. Although each of them trembled at the prospect of knowing her, and continued to hold some reservations concerning her intolerance of slowness and her peremptory questioning, all of them acknowledged her brilliance of speech, her pleasing simplicity of manner, and her surprising readiness to listen. Henrietta Knebel's assessment of 5 January 1804 illustrates the general warmth of her reception: "Son voisinage est une espèce de cure où l'on se rend comme à Carlsbad pour se sentir ensuite plus dispos et plus vivant. L'homme le plus vide d'idées ne pourrait dire qu'elle lui est à charge, tant elle s'entend bien à animer l'argile la plus grossière" (To be with her is a kind of cure like that for which we go to Carlsbad so as to return from it freshened and more alive. Even a man who was emptiest of all ideas could not find her oppressive, so well does she understand how to animate the most intractable clay). Staël received as much as she gave on this journey, which was crowned by a triumphant stay in Berlin. Hours of conversation, visits to plays and poetry readings, the company and near-permanent acquisition of the distinguished August Wilhelm von Schlegel as the Staël family's personal and intellectual factotum: these would come to fruition in *De l'Allemagne*, the work that was to culminate and crown Staël's career as a critic.

But that culmination was forced into abeyance. In Berlin, told only that her father was gravely ill, Staël interrupted her activity to rush in terror back to Coppet. In fact, he had already died, but Constant, who brought her the news, feared the effects on her nervous sensibility of the report of this death, which for her represented the most dreaded of all losses. On her return to Coppet, now her own dwelling, which had already taken on the aspect of a "Literary Estates General of Europe," she would continue the assembling of that coterie of intellectuals that would become known as the Groupe de Coppet. But she would also piously set about editing her father's manuscripts and compose and publish a eulogium of his life. These activities did not succeed in calming her restlessness of spirit, however, and at the end of 1804, in need of diversion from her single-minded grieving, she departed for Italy with Schlegel.

From December 1804 to May 1805 Staël traveled through Italy, another land for which she had initially felt little enthusiasm. In fact, her actual encounter with Italian society, less eager in its reception of her than that of Germany had been, depressed rather than pleased her. Among the admirers she did encounter was the poet Vincenzo Monti, whom she met at Milan. Though dutifully subjecting herself to the beauties of classical Italy and the glories of Italian Renaissance art, she would find herself infrequently moved by them. And yet her own crowning with the poet's laurel wreath, by the Arcadian Academy in Rome, cannot have displeased her: it certainly influenced her growing conception of the great novel she was preparing to undertake. A passing romance with the youthful Portuguese diplomat Pedro de Sousa Holstein, which could not, however, culminate in the long-lasting liaison she never ceased to crave, added its melancholy piquancy to her Italian foray.

Conférence de Mme de Staël, *gouache attributed to Philibert Louis Debucourt (Bibliothèque Nationale)*

Upon her return to Coppet, she began to write *Corinne, ou l'Italie* (1807; translated as *Corinne, or Italy*, 1807). Even before she composed *De l'Allemagne*, she embedded this novel in a *kulturgeschichtliche* grounding: in description of its arts, its customs, and its social mores, she would attempt to acquaint the French public with Italy's character. Of course, Italy, in the wake of the excavations of Pompeii and Herculaneum in the previous century, was popularly viewed as a place of history and mystery. Staël, ever alert to current vogues, would use this setting for her most remarkable work of fiction, and that fervor for the nation, its art, its people, and its past that had eluded her when she was on its soil now returned in force, as she fashioned the nation of her imagination in the image of the woman as hero, her supreme fantasy.

Its third-person narrative, breaking decisively away from the epistolary fiction of *Delphine*, relates a story whose action is greatly stripped down as compared with that of the previous novel. Oswald, Lord Nelvil, a young Englishman, is traveling in Italy with a French friend he has made along the way, to assuage his grief for the loss of his father. In Rome, visiting the Capitoline, he happens upon a fete in which the young woman poet Corinne is being crowned with the laurel wreath of Tasso. As he comes upon her on the staircase after the ceremony, her crown falls, and he returns it to her. As she looks at him, she perceives he is English and graciously answers his gesture in a flawless English accent, saying "Thank you." Corinne is deeply touched by this melancholy young man and includes him in her court of admirers, accompanying him to all the sights of the city, discoursing to him on the customs of the country, and on its history. A poet, she is an improviser (a kind of art very close to Staël's own conversational genius), and once before her public, she has only to be provided with a topic in order to spin a magical series of poetic variations upon it, as she strums her lyre. Her adoring public sees her as their national laureate, giving voice to the country's mystical essence.

But responsive as he is to Corinne's beauty and talents, Oswald's memories weigh upon him, and he finds himself unable to make a decisive commitment to remain with her. They travel together to Naples, a reminder, with its sulfurous volcano Vesuvius, of torment and sorrow. There Corinne does one of her improvisations, and there the lovers confess, each in turn, the secrets of their pasts. Oswald was caught in a web of deception in revolutionary Paris, having fallen in with a woman to whom he felt bound but who was merely toying with him, when his father, to whom he was devoted but whose wishes he had defied, died, leaving him with unresolved grief and much guilt. Corinne's story links her fatally with Oswald's own family. She is the half-Italian daughter of Lord Nelvil's best friend; Oswald's father had actually known her in her youth, and deemed her an inappropriate object for his son, much preferring that he wed her less flamboyant, modest and retiring half sister, Lucile. Deeply unhappy in the home of her father's repressive second wife, Corinne had fled her stifling English life for one of freedom and the expression of her gifts she has found in Italy.

Their confessions separate rather than bring Corinne and Oswald closer together. He goes back to England, where Corinne follows him; yet feeling herself no longer the glorious woman at the apogee of glory, but merely an abandoned lover, she cannot show herself to him there. She returns to Italy, falls ill, and moves toward death. Oswald, who has wed Lucile, has a daughter. He remains melancholy, for the spouses cannot communicate through their screen of sadness. They return to Italy, where Oswald hopes to see Corinne once more, but she rejects him, agreeing only to receive Lucile and the child, Juliette. As Corinne lies on her deathbed, she once more refuses to see Oswald. The narrator will neither blame nor absolve him.

In the writer's earlier tales *Mirza* and *Zulma* there had already been preliminary sketches for the kind of extraordinary figure one finds in Corinne. Mirza is not a mere woman, but a poet. And yet her lover, whom she has sheltered and taught all she knows, deserts her for a more traditional woman. *Corinne* proclaims a great destiny for its protagonist, but she is deprived of its fullness by her need for love. Her ability to sustain her vocation is undermined by the lover's withholding of it from her. Staël expresses the entrapment of the woman born into a society that had allowed its salon women to play their part in the great intellectual and political scenes of eighteenth-century life, but who now found themselves confronted by the idealization of a far narrower code of female conduct. This social evolution left some of these women mired in a social disapproval that thwarted their energies. In this novel Italy has a parallel profile: a nation once great, now despised, despite the grandeur of its achievements. And Oswald's England, that land that Staël herself so idealized as a place of freedom, is here instead an oppressive place for the woman of genius, a site of domestic hierarchy and order, furnishing a deadening contrast with the open-ended possibility of the easier, politically less evolved, but sunnier and more liberating Italy.

Corinne was a first as a novel of the failure of modern womanhood. Much admired by women readers, it went into many printings, appearing at a rate of one per year at mid century. Termed by Lamartine the "poets' novel," its coupling of mood with action and character constituted, despite its lengthy dissertations on the beauties of Italy, an extraordinary artistic fusion. After its publication Staël would be called Corinne everywhere, and did not reject that name, which reified her creation.

These latter years of the century's first decade witnessed a series of personal upheavals at Coppet, as Constant, secretly engaged to Charlotte von Hardenberg, would attempt to escape from Staël's hold upon him. At Coppet eminent visitors succeeded each other regularly, as amateur theatricals were performed by the inhabitants, and Constant, to the secret glee of the audience, would play Racine's Hippolyte to Staël's Phèdre. In these years Juliette Récamier, the most celebrated beauty of the time, engaged in a passionate friendship with the deeply susceptible Staël, and lived for long spells at Coppet, becoming one of its attractions. Constant worked on his sole great novel, *Adolphe*, and would read a portion of it in a company including Staël, who reacted with a burst of aggrieved outrage to its portrait of Ellénore.

The Coppet of those days was a place where food meant less than ideas. Wherever conversation had settled in, the servants would set up dinner or supper. Guests were left to their own devices, and no set schedule limited them. But whenever a serious controversy arose, their hostess would summon any of her guests she felt needed to resolve or clarify it. And conversation would hum on into the small hours of the night.

In December 1807, Staël left Coppet for Vienna, where she spent a brilliant season and had a love affair with the Viennese count Maurice O'Donnell. On her return she went again to Dresden and Weimar, and once back in Coppet, in July 1808, began work on *De l'Allemagne*.

If only for its chapter "On Classical Poetry and Romantic Poetry," this work would have enormous impact, for in it she posits in her synthetic way many conceptions that were to come together in Romantic art: the need of poetry to relate to a land, its history, and its ethos; the need of poetry to express states of inwardness; and the need of poetry to take wing on fantasy. Her discussion of the nature of taste, in which she inquires about its nature and vicissitudes, is a sort of early avatar of the method of Susan Sontag: "Le bon goût en littérature est comme l'ordre sous le despotisme, il importe de savoir à quel prix on l'achète" (Good taste in literature is like order under despotism; it is important to evaluate the price at which it is purchased). This work, more systematically of course than *Corinne*, reflects a global critical method encompassing a whole cultural nexus: historical, geographic, mythical, social, and political; and this is what makes it the pioneer text of interdisciplinary criticism. In terms of method alone, *De l'Allemagne* was a breakthrough more thorough and extraordinary than *De la littérature*. The fact that the author often attempts what she cannot altogether deliver is beside the point: it is the breathtaking conception, nearly realized, of describing a civilization that makes this work so impressive still.

Developing those insights on the literature of the North that had been voiced in *De la littérature*, specifically her dichotomy between literatures of the North and South, those of England and Germany as against those of Italy and France, she decides that the schism is less one between romanticism and classicism than between inspiration and imitation, and of course the former has primacy in her view. After giving voice to these theoretical considerations, Staël proceeds to discuss German poetry in the light of her grid. She thus praises Schiller and Goethe rather than Wieland, too gallicized for her taste, or Friedrich Klopstock. In her discussion of German drama, she does not fail to note the differences between the behavior of audiences in France and in Germany. She calls for a new theater, freed from the constraints of the three classical French unities, that would entail only unity of action. It was to be her own translations, imperfect as they were,

that would later give the closed-in French nation an idea of German letters, notably of Goethe's *Egmont* (1788) and Schiller's *Die Jungfrau von Orleans* (1801).

Far less confident in discussing philosophy, Staël nonetheless bravely attempted some account of developments in Germany for her French audience. Expressing respect for Gottfried Leibniz, she devotes most of her attention to Kant, whose idealism strongly appealed to her: since the categorical imperative bore some resemblance to her own liberal and Protestant credo of responsibility, she felt inclined to espouse it. Kant's tendency to globalize science, ethics, and the arts in a totalizing system also appealed to her own sense of synthesis. Yet she faults Kant for his excessive irony, obscurity, dryness, and severity.

A fourth section of *De l'Allemagne* is devoted to religion and enthusiasm, which for her are related categories. Here she advocates an "enlightened religion," purified of superstitious adjuncts. Despite her basic rationalism, she speaks of mysticism, which she had been exploring in a spirit of sympathy with visitors to Coppet such as Mathias Werner and Juliane von Krüdener. She would find in mysticism spiritual expansion and freedom for the individual spirit. And she chose to conclude *De l'Allemagne* on a prophetic note, sounding a pre-Whitmanian paean to enthusiasm: "Si l'enthousiasme enivre l'âme de bonheur, par un prestige singulier il soutient encore dans l'infortune; il laisse après lui je ne sais quelle trace lumineuse et profonde, qui ne permet pas même à l'absence de nous effacer du cœur de nos amis. Il nous sert aussi d'asile à nous-mêmes contre les peines les plus amères, et c'est le seul sentiment qui puisse calmer sans refroidir" (If enthusiasm inebriates the soul with happiness, through a singularity of its prestige it still sustains us in misfortune; it leaves an ineffably deep and luminous trace, which even absence cannot efface from the hearts of our friends. It serves as an asylum within us against the bitterest of troubles, and it is the only sentiment that can become calm without turning cold).

De l'Allemagne had been sent in parcels, as completed, to the emperor's censor for approval before it could be published. The first two volumes had been cleared, and the publisher Nicolle was sent the manuscript of the third on 15 August 1810. Staël, who was in residence at Chaumont pending approval of her request to come to Paris as her book appeared, was out on an excursion to a neighboring château when her son Auguste came to inform her that she would be given forty-eight hours to leave the country. Her book had been seized by the authorities. Anne Savary, Duc de Rovigo, the minister of police, wrote her with the reproof, "Your last work is not French." True, Staël had refused to add a few words to it complimentary to Bonaparte, so as to render it less unpalatable. Her text, despite its advocacy of rootedness in literature, in actuality enacts a quite contrary text, that of transcendence of nation. A European rather than a nationalistic French text, it was correctly interpreted by Bonaparte and his supporters as a demonstration of the nonsuperiority of the French, who had much to learn from German culture. Beyond that, the emperor was simply not prepared to tolerate the spirit of criticism. Had he not said, "Cette femme apprend à penser à ceux qui ne s'en aviseraient point ou qui l'avaient oublié" (This woman teaches people to think who would never have thought of it, or had forgotten how)? The entire printing of De l'Allemagne was reduced to pulp, and those in Paris who already had proofs of it were sought out to prevent its dissemination.

Returning willy-nilly to Coppet, Staël was to endure further trials. Her many flirtations had resulted in no lasting connection with a man, her link with Prosper Brugière, Baron de Barante, being something of an exception. For younger men her prestige remained a magnet, and she was not insensible to their appeal. But John Rocca, the young Swiss hussar who fell so desperately in love with her that they eventually married in a secret ceremony, was drawn less by her brilliance than by her kindness and gentleness. Now under unceasing surveillance by the police, none of her activities could pass without their notice during the year 1811, and so they duly noted her pregnancy and the birth of a son, Alphonse Rocca, in April 1812, facts that were so carefully managed by the principals that neither Geneva nor Staël's own children were aware of them. All of her letters were read. The new prefect of Geneva, Capelle, proposed that she write some complimentary words to the emperor on the birth of his heir, François-Charles-Joseph, King of Rome. Once more, she refused. Now fearing actual arrest, not merely continuing sequestration in her Swiss prison of a home, she planned her escape. After providing for her baby, like her father and mother before her, she and Albertine, wearing only their afternoon dresses, got into their car-

riage as if for a short drive, carrying fans. It was 23 May. Albert and John galloped alongside them. The plan worked; their departure was so skillfully executed that their absence went unnoticed until 2 June. The flight across Europe would take the family to Vienna, Moscow, Saint Petersburg, Stockholm, and, finally, to England.

In Sweden, Staël published Réflexions sur le suicide (Reflections on Suicide, 1813), dedicating it to the new Swedish king, Charles Jean Bernadotte, who became her candidate to replace Bonaparte as the end of his reign became imminent. In London, where she was apotheosized, she had the dubious pleasure of having three hundred visitors in four days sign up to meet her at her hotel. In Germany, De l'Allemagne was quickly translated, and although contemporary criticism varied and was sometimes pointed, none would be as harsh as a later critique by Heinrich Heine, who regarded the work as nothing less than a plague. Staël's objective had been, after all, an interpretation of Germany written for the French, and it was destined to have its deepest influence upon the philosophic cenacle of which Victor Cousin and François Guizot were prominent members. As before, Napoleonic opposition did nothing to impede the sale of the work and its republication: De l'Allemagne went into fifty-two printings.

Safely ensconced in England at the time of the invasion of France, and despite her long and painful opposition to Bonaparte, Staël felt real distress in the division of her loyalties, professing that she wished the general both victorious and dead. After his 31 March abdication, she was finally free to return home. But surprisingly, the Paris that had so long been her heart's desire no longer pleased her as it had. She saw the potential disaster in the return of the monarchy along with that of the exiled aristocracy, with its retrograde conceptions of government. Rocca's health was poor, and her own was beginning to fail. Yet the most draining betrayal was that of Juliette Récamier, the dear friend who had lived with her so long at Coppet. Récamier had first encouraged the passion of Staël's son Auguste, and then she did not see fit to reject a sudden burst of passionate love for her on the part of Constant. Staël's chief interest now lay in the antislavery campaign, for which she translated into French a manifesto by William Wilberforce.

Back in a Coppet that seemed no longer so confining, she undertook her last work, Considérations sur les principaux événemens de la

Staël, 1797 (drawing by Jean-Baptiste Isabey; Musée du Louvre)

Révolution française, published posthumously by her son Auguste. In that late season of her life, Staël became acquainted with George Gordon, Lord Byron. Summering on Lake Geneva, he was bemused by her, rather than repelled. But with summer's end, she and Rocca returned to Paris. There, while nursing her failing husband, she fell into a paralysis that worsened through the spring of 1817. Racked with pain, using the opium that had long been her comfort, she demanded a double dose of it from her faithful English attendant, Fanny Randall, and died in her sleep on Bastille Day. For all the historic events she had seen, all the changes of venue she had endured, all the relations with lovers and the friendships she had sustained, and all the published texts and masses of letters she had written, Staël was but fifty-one years old at her death. Her family buried her in the family tomb with her mother and father at Coppet.

Considérations pleased few except her friends. A work that suffers from the retrospec-

tive whitewash of memory, it yet contains colorful anecdotes and fresh perceptions of events. The account of the opening of the Estates-General reveals the youthful ardor of an eyewitness, and the story of her hairsbreadth escape from Paris in 1792 conveys the antagonism as well as the bravura felt by its principals. Staël's account of the history of her times dwells on errors and seeks to explain how events went as they did, in a sort of move of retrospective correction.

Posterity's view of Staël has been undeniably scarred by the frequent repetition, beginning in her own time and even in her own circle, of the imputation that hers was an androgynous nature. The *Actes des Apôtres*, a late-eighteenth-century satirical journal, referred to her as a hermaphrodite and a prostitute. Carlo Andrea, Count Pozzo di Borgo, would claim that she belonged neither to the sex one loved, nor to the sex that one esteemed. Prince Charles-Joseph de Ligne wrote a lengthy portrait of her as containing within herself a warring *Lui* and *Elle* (He and She): "*Lui* respecte l'amitié, *elle* rêve l'amour.... *Lui* a des principes fixes et invariables, *elle* forme des projets et ne s'arrête à rien.... *Lui* est patient et tranquille, *elle* inquiète et troublée" (*He* respects friendship, *she* dreams of love.... *He* has fixed principles, *she* forms plans and stops at nothing.... *He* is patient and calm, *she* is unquiet and troubled). The prince was, on the whole, more charmed by this combination than he was distressed by it, but the underlying accusation is one of having passed beyond nature's gender boundaries. And when posterity reads in Constant's diary his outbursts against her as a "man-woman," it may well wonder that someone so close to Staël could feel such profound self-justification in characterizing her in this way.

Of course Constant's texts are studded with many words of praise for her as well; but the interest of posterity has frequently been fixed on Staël's case as that of an anomaly among women. What few have taken into account is the climate of rigid sexual dimorphism of her period, and the deeply reactionary nature of the proto-Rousseauist revolution with regard to women. When Bonaparte said, with respect to her, that he expected subordination and respect for authority because it came from God, or that women were born to knit, he was speaking the masculine consensus of his time. Its animus was directed precisely at women such as Staël, who might have had political or other pretensions to individual thought, or have seen themselves as actors, not understanding their role as one entirely subordinated to family.

Staël was by no means unaware of this fierce intolerance, and once mused that people in a city she was about to visit, perplexed as to what she might be like, probably thought of her as some sort of devil. But for the most part, her chief strategy lay in turning away from the hatred directed at her person, though she would complain endlessly of the pain it gave her. She could not confront its mystery for her, and chose rather to behave as if she were in truth no monster but rather an exception: a perfectly natural person, but a genius, to whom all should be forgiven, even in a woman. In consideration of the barrage of harassment she had to endure, it was a miracle that she was able to preserve so much of her energy for the great work of the transition from court to republic. Oddly enough, one of the most unambiguous tributes to Staël would come from the utopian socialist Claude-Henri de Rouvroy, Comte de Saint-Simon, who wrote her an enthusiastic note: "Ce Bonaparte qui vous exile, ce Bonaparte qui dit que les femmes ne sont bonnes qu'à raccommoder des chausses, a-t-il produit des idées aussi utiles que les vôtres pour les progrès de l'esprit humain? Non. Je me sens révolté . . ." (This Bonaparte who exiles you, this Bonaparte who says that women are good only to mend trousers, has he produced ideas as useful as yours for the progress of the human spirit? No. How he revolts me . . .).

In the new European order, and the new dispensation for women of the end of the twentieth century, Staël may now stand forth as a troubled but ardent pioneer, who persisted in forging her literary vocation in spite of a pervasive climate of reproof. Close to the centers of power, she nevertheless remained marginal as a woman aspiring to influence upon her own and future times. She was thus well situated ontologically to the mapping and transcendence of borders of gender, genre, and geography. That pained rejection of barriers that characterizes both the style and the substance of every one of her texts, fictional, historical, critical, or political, is the quality that renders Germaine de Staël one of the earliest modernists of them all.

Letters:

Béatrice W. Jasinski, *Correspondance générale de Madame de Staël*, volumes 1-4 (Paris: Pauvert, 1960-1978); volume 5, *Première partie* (Paris: Hachette, 1982); volume 5, *Deuxième partie* (Paris: Hachette, 1985).

Bibliographies:

Paul-Emile Schazmann, *Bibliographie des œuvres de Mme de Staël et description d'après les exemplaires originaux des éditions françaises publiées de son vivant et des inédits posthumes* (Paris & Neuchâtel: Attinger, 1938);

F.-C. Longchamp, *L'Œuvre imprimé de Madame Germaine de Staël* (Geneva: Cailler, 1949);

Cahiers Staëliens, new series (Paris: Touzot, 1962-   ).

Biographies:

David Glass Larg, *Madame de Staël: La vie dans l'œuvre (1766-1800). Essai de biographie morale et intellectuelle* (Paris: Champion, 1924-1928);

André Lang, *Une Vie d'orages, Germaine de Staël* (Paris: Calmann-Lévy, 1958);

J. Christopher Herold, *Mistress to an Age: A Life of Madame de Staël* (Indianapolis: Bobbs-Merrill, 1958);

Pierre Cordey, *Mme de Staël, ou le Deuil éclatant du bonheur* (Lausanne: Rencontre, 1967);

Helen B. Posgate, *Madame de Staël* (Boston: Twayne, 1969);

Béatrice d'Andlau, *La Jeunesse de Madame de Staël* (Geneva: Droz, 1971);

Ghislain de Diesbach, *Madame de Staël* (Paris: Perrin, 1984);

Karyna Szmurlo, "Germaine de Staël," in *French Women Writers,* edited by Eva Martin Sartori and Dorothy Wayne Zimmerman (New York: Greenwood Press, 1990).

References:

Simone Balayé, *Madame de Staël: lumières et liberté* (Paris: Klincksieck, 1979);

Balayé, "Madame de Staël, Napoléon et la mission de l'écrivain," *Europe* (1969): 124-137;

Balayé, "Le Système critique de Mme de Staël: Théorie et sensibilité," *Revue de l'Université d'Ottawa* (1971): 542-555;

Helen Borowitz, "The Unconfessed Précieuse: Mme de Staël's Debt to Mlle de Scudéry. Terpsichore and Corinne," in her *The Impact of Art on French Literature, from Scudéry to Proust* (Newark: University of Delaware Press, 1985);

Robert Escarpit, *L'Angleterre dans l'œuvre de Madame de Staël* (Paris: Didier, 1954);

Geneviève Gennari, *Le Premier Voyage de Madame de Staël en Italie et la genèse de "Corinne"* (Paris: Boivin, 1947);

Avriel Goldberger, Madelyn Gutwirth, and Karyna Szmurlo, *Germaine de Staël: Crossing the Borders* (New Brunswick, N.J.: Rutgers University Press, 1991);

Gutwirth, *Madame de Staël, Novelist: The Emergence of the Artist as Woman* (Urbana: University of Illinois Press, 1978);

Gutwirth, "Madame de Staël, Rousseau, and the Woman Question," *PMLA*, 86 (January 1971): 100-109;

Gruffed E. Gwynne, *Madame de Staël et la révolution française: Politique, philosophie, littérature* (Paris: Nizet, 1969);

Etienne Hofmann, ed., *Benjamin Constant, Madame de Staël et le Groupe de Coppet* (Oxford: Voltaire Foundation / Lausanne: Institut Benjamin Constant, 1982);

Hofmann and Anne-Lise Delacrétaz, eds., *Le Groupe de Coppet et la révolution française* (Lausanne: Institut Benjamin Constant / Paris: Touzot, 1988);

Charlotte Hogsett, *The Literary Existence of Germaine de Staël* (Carbondale: Southern Illinois University Press, 1987);

Maija Lehtonen, "Le Fleuve du temps et le fleuve de l'enfer: Thèmes et images dans *Corinne* de Madame de Staël," *Neuphilologische Mitteilungen*, 68 (1967): 225-242, 391-408; 69 (1968): 101-128;

Lawrence Lipking, "Lord Byron's Secret: The School of Abandonment and Aristotle's Sister: A Poetics of Abandonment," in his *Abandoned Women and Poetic Tradition* (Chicago: University of Chicago Press, 1988);

Robert de Luppé, *Les Idées littéraires de Madame de Staël et l'héritage des lumières (1795-1800)* (Paris: Vrin, 1969);

Madame de Staël et l'Europe, actes du Colloque de Coppet (1966), preface by Jean Fabre and Balayé (Paris: Klincksieck, 1970);

Haydn Mason, "The Way Forward: Madame de Staël, *De la littérature*," in his *French Writers and Their Society, 1715-1800* (London: Macmillan, 1982);

Nancy Miller, "Performances of the Gaze: Staël's *Corinne or Italy*," in her *Subject to Change: Reading Feminist Writing* (New York: Columbia University Press, 1988);

Ellen Moers, "Performing Heroism: The Myth of *Corinne*," in her *Literary Women: The Great Writers* (New York: Doubleday, 1977);

André Monchoux, "Madame de Staël interprète de Kant," *Revue d'Histoire Littéraire de la France*, 66, no. 1 (1966): 71-84;

Roland Mortier, "Philosophie et religion dans la pensée de Madame de Staël," *Rivista di Letterature Moderne e Comparate*, 20, nos. 3-4 (1967): 165-176;

Carla Peterson, "*Corinne* and *Louis Lambert*: Romantic Myth Making," in her *The Determined Reader: Gender and Culture in the Novel from Napoleon to Victoria* (New Brunswick, N.J.: Rutgers University Press, 1986);

Georges Poulet, "La Pensée critique de Mme de Staël," in his *La Conscience critique* (Paris: Corti, 1971);

Jean Roussel, "La Critique de Madame de Staël," in his *Jean-Jacques Rousseau en France après la révolution, 1795-1830* (Paris: A. Colin, 1972);

Eve Sourian, *Madame de Staël et Henri Heine: Les deux Allemagnes* (Paris: Didier, 1974);

Jean Starobinski, "Mme de Staël et la définition de la littérature," *Nouvelle Revue Française*, 28, no. 168 (1966): 1054-1059;

Susan Tenenbaum, "The Coppet Circle: Literary Criticism as Political Discourse," *History of Political Thought*, 1 (Autumn 1980): 453-473;

Janet Todd, "Madame de Staël's *Delphine*," in her *Women's Friendship in Literature* (New York: Columbia University Press, 1980);

Marie-Claire Vallois, *Fictions féminines. Madame de Staël et les voix de la Sibylle* (Stanford: Anma Libri, 1987);

Auguste Viatte, "Madame de Staël et son entourage," in his *Les Sources occultes du romantisme: illuminisme-théosophie (1770-1820)*, volume 2 (Paris: Champion, 1965).

Papers:

The Bibliothèque Nationale, Paris, and the Château de Coppet, Coppet, Switzerland, hold original manuscripts of Staël's works.

Stendhal
(Marie-Henri Beyle)
(23 January 1783 - 23 March 1842)

James T. Day
University of South Carolina

BOOKS: *Lettres écrites de Vienne en Autriche, sur le célèbre compositeur Jh. Haydn, suivies d'une vie de Mozart, et de considérations sur Métastase et l'état présent de la musique en France et en Italie*, as Louis-Alexandre-César Bombet (Paris: Didot, 1814); republished as *Vies de Haydn, de Mozart et de Métastase* (Paris: Didot, 1817); translated by R. Brewin as *The Life of Haydn, in a Series of Letters written at Vienna, followed by the Life of Mozart, with Observations on Metastasio, and on the present State of Music in France and Italy* (London: John Murray, 1817); republished as *The Lives of Haydn and Mozart with Observations on Metastasio and on the present State of Music in France and Italy* (London: John Murray, 1818);
Histoire de la peinture en Italie, 2 volumes, as M. B. A. A. (Paris: P. Didot aîné, 1817);
Rome, Naples et Florence en 1817, par M. de Stendhal, officier de cavalerie (Paris: Egron, 1817; revised, 1827); translated anonymously as *Rome, Naples and Florence in 1817. Sketches of the present State of Society, Manners, Arts, Literature, etc. in these celebrated cities* (London: Colburn, 1818);
De l'amour, 2 volumes (Paris: Mongie, 1822); translated by Philip Sidney Woolf and Cecil N. Sidney Woolf as *On Love* (London: Duckworth, 1914);
Racine et Shakspeare (Paris: Bossange, Delaunay, Mongie, 1823; revised and enlarged edition, Paris: Dupont et Roret, 1825);
Vie de Rossini (Paris: Boulland, 1823); translated as *Memoirs of Rossini, by the author of the Lives of Haydn and Mozart* (London: Hookman, 1824); translated by Richard N. Coe as *Life of Rossini* (London: Calder, 1956);
D'un nouveau complot contre les industriels (Paris: Sautelet, 1825);
Armance, ou quelques scènes d'un salon de Paris en 1827, 3 volumes (Paris: Canel, 1827);

Stendhal, 1840 (portrait by Olaf Södermark; Musée de Versailles)

Promenades dans Rome, 2 volumes (Paris: Delaunay, 1829); translated by Haakon Chevalier as *A Roman Journal* (New York: Orion, 1957);
Le Rouge et le noir, chronique du XIXᵉ siècle, 2 volumes (Paris: Levavasseur, 1830); translated by E. P. Robins as *Red and Black, A Chronicle of the Nineteenth Century* (London: Smithers / New York: George H. Richmond & Son, 1898); translated by Charles Tergie as *Red and Black, A Story of Provincial France* (New York: Brentano, 1898); translated by Horace

B. Samuel as *The Red and the Black* (Toronto: McClelland, Goodchild & Steward, 1913);

Mémoires d'un touriste, 2 volumes (Paris: Dupont, 1838); translated by Allan Seager as *Memoirs of a Tourist* (Evanston, Ill.: Northwestern University Press, 1962);

La Chartreuse de Parme, 2 volumes (Paris: Dupont, 1839); translated by Robins as *La Chartreuse de Parme* (New York: George H. Richmond & Son, 1895); translated by C. K. Scott Moncrieff as *The Charterhouse of Parma* (New York: Boni & Liveright, 1925);

L'Abbesse de Castro (Paris: Dumont, 1839)—contains "Vittoria Accoramboni" and "Les Cenci"; enlarged as *Chroniques italiennes*, edited by Romain Colomb (Paris: Michel Lévy, 1855);

Romans et nouvelles (Paris: Michel Lévy, 1854);

Nouvelles inédites (Paris: Michel Lévy, 1855)—contains the first chapters of *Lucien Leuwen* under the title *Le Chasseur vert*; revised as *Lucien Leuwen*, edited by Jean de Mitty (Paris: Dentu, 1894); revised as *Lucien Leuwen*, edited by Henry Debraye (Paris: Champion, 1926-1927);

Journal de Stendhal, edited by Casimir Stryienski and François de Nion (Paris: Charpentier, 1888); revised as *Journal d'Italie*, edited by Paul Arbelet (Paris: Calmann-Lévy, 1911); enlarged as *Journal de Stendhal*, edited by Debraye and Louis Royer (Paris: Champion, 1923-1934);

Lamiel, edited by Stryienski (Paris: Quantin, Librairie Moderne, 1889);

Vie de Henry Brulard, edited by Stryienski (Paris: Charpentier, 1890); revised and enlarged, edited by Debraye (Paris: Champion, 1913);

Souvenirs d'égotisme, edited by Stryienski (Paris: Charpentier, 1892); translated by T. W. Earp as *Memoirs of an Egotist* (London: Turnstile, 1949); translated by Hannah and Matthew Josephson as *Memoirs of Egotism* (New York: Lear, 1949).

Collections: *Œuvres complètes de Stendhal*, 19 volumes (Paris: Michel Lévy, 1853-1855);

Œuvres complètes, 79 volumes, edited by Henri Martineau (Paris: Editions du Divan, 1927-1937);

Romans et nouvelles, 2 volumes, edited by Martineau (Paris: Gallimard, Bibliothèque de la Pléiade, 1952);

Œuvres complètes, 50 volumes, edited by Ernest Abravanel and Victor Del Litto (Geneva: Cercle du Bibliophile, 1967-1974);

Œuvres intimes, 2 volumes, edited by Del Litto (Paris: Gallimard, Bibliothèque de la Pléiade, 1981-1982).

Among the four greatest novelists of nineteenth-century France, Stendhal is noteworthy for the intensity of conscience and feeling in his characters, and for beginning his publication of fictional works later in life than did Honoré de Balzac, Gustave Flaubert, and Emile Zola. These two facts may have a common cause. Stendhal was unusually preoccupied with self-image, and as a result he was by turns timid or brazen, sensitive or cynical, evasive or forthright, never sure of how he was being perceived by others. These aspects of his personality appear in the portraits of his heroes and in his narrative technique, but they may also account for his waiting until age forty-four to publish his first novel. Having filled hundreds of pages in his diaries, and with nonfiction works already in print, he finally had the confidence to risk public scrutiny of a totally creative work. His sense of the craft of fiction developed quickly after the appearance of his novel *Armance* (1827), and his later novels have an important place in the development of literary realism. Stendhal's techniques of handling point of view and psychological portraiture are distinctive and have been much admired by critics and novelists.

During his lifetime Stendhal's works enjoyed much less popular success than those of contemporaries such as Eugène Sue, who is not considered very significant today, but they were well known to the cultured elite. Consequently he had a certain reputation in Paris salons, yet he did not derive a substantial income from his writing. Stendhal reflected that it was less desirable to have a wide following among his contemporaries than to appeal to readers in 1880 or 1935, and curiously, his choice of dates proved somewhat prophetic. Zola, in an essay first published in 1880, discussed Stendhal as one of his precursors (along with Balzac and Flaubert), and in 1882 an article by the novelist Paul Bourget, along with the influence of Hippolyte Taine's continuing enthusiasm, consolidated Stendhal's reputation in the French literary canon. By 1935 a growing critical industry of "Stendhaliens" had published a wealth of texts on and by their author. In his own time, however, Stendhal had to rely on work as a journalist, specialist in military supply, and French consul abroad to supplement income from publications and his father's estate.

But this may be a factor in the greatness of his best novels, which are admired for their combination of lofty sentiments and realistic portrayal of the socioeconomic milieu. Firsthand experience with military campaigns, commerce, and public administration no doubt provided him with a store of the small but significant details that contribute to the realism of his fiction. This experience and Stendhal's frequent presence at salon gatherings brought him into contact with diverse social and professional strata, with the result that, in writing his novels, he was not dependent on documentation or literary convention for the representation of social dynamics. Finally, his perpetual shortage of funds must have had a causal connection to his vision of personal happiness, which, in his writing at least, depended much less on material advantages than on the capacity to find pleasure in beauty, in strong emotion, in the expression of one's individual nature, and in contact with energetic personalities. This doctrine of the pursuit of happiness, or "la chasse au bonheur," became known by his term *beylisme*. Balzac, who, like Stendhal, had more financial ambition than finances, excelled at portraying the irresistible lure of lucre and its ravages; Stendhal's fiction stresses instead the inadequacy of wealth for authentic happiness and often dramatizes alternatives to financial satisfaction.

Money and personal happiness, then, are major themes in Stendhal's fiction. Since he wrote in the Romantic period, moreover, his works inevitably reflect many thematic preoccupations of his time: the superior soul, the aesthetics of solitude, the power of the will and the imagination, the myth of Napoleon, the dynamics of love, the individual's sense of personal honor, the uncertainties of fate, and so on. Yet Stendhal's understanding of human nature was considerably influenced by the so-called idéologues of the late eighteenth century, such as Antoine Destutt de Tracy and Pierre Cabanis, whose theories of psychology and ideation stressed physiology and language, continuing the nonmetaphysical orientation of Etienne de Condillac and Enlightenment thought. This influence gives rise in the novels to themes that are more Stendhalian than Romantic: reading, writing, and communication in general; spies, masks, pseudonyms, and hypocrisy; and the spontaneous, unexpected behavior of singular individuals.

Stendhal's technique and style are also quite characteristic. Unlike many Romantic contemporaries who strove to imitate the effusive lyricism of François-René de Chateaubriand, Stendhal claimed to prefer the directness of the *Code civil* (Civil Law). In a literary age of lush descriptions (Alfred de Musset once defined romanticism as "l'abus des adjectifs" [the abuse of adjectives]), Stendhal preferred action, dialogue, and analysis; consequently, his occasional portraits and descriptions are quite spare. To reveal the psyche of his characters he made extensive use of the interior monologue, a device uncommon in his time. These aspects of his technique have won twentieth-century admiration for his works, yet they often had a negative effect on reception of his novels among his contemporaries. Today, Stendhal's best-known titles are *Le Rouge et le noir* (1830; translated as *The Red and the Black*, 1913) and *La Chartreuse de Parme* (1839; translated as *The Charterhouse of Parma*, 1925). These novels, each with its own devoted following, stand in a small group of nineteenth-century French masterpieces. Also much admired today are Stendhal's two posthumous autobiographical works, *Vie de Henry Brulard* (Life of Henry Brulard, 1890), and *Souvenirs d'égotisme* (1892; translated as *Memoirs of an Egotist*, 1949). His anecdotal treatise *De l'amour* (1822; translated as *On Love*, 1914) is well known, as is his personal interpretation of romanticism, *Racine et Shakspeare* (1823).

Marie-Henri Beyle was born on 23 January 1783 in Grenoble to Joseph-Chérubin Beyle, a lawyer, and his wife, Caroline-Adélaïde-Henriette, née Gagnon. He was the first child in the family to survive, an earlier Marie-Henri having died a few days after birth the year before. Later siblings included Pauline, to whom Henri was very close, and Zénaïde, for whom he professed dislike. Letters written to Pauline after Henri left Grenoble at age sixteen are an important part of his collected correspondence. His mother died in 1790, when Henri was seven. Thanks to reminiscences in Stendhal's autobiographical works, much is known about his childhood memories. In a famous passage from *Vie de Henry Brulard*, he claims that, before his mother's death, he loved her ardently and desired to cover her body with kisses. Since the boy never had a good relationship with his father, whom Stendhal recalls as authoritarian, hypocritically conventional, and bourgeois, these details have been adduced as evidence of a powerful Oedipus complex, and in recent years there have been numerous Freudian analyses of his work.

Chérubin Beyle's dark, damp, and chilly house in Grenoble on the rue des Vieux-Jésuites (now 14, rue Jean-Jacques Rousseau) had been in the family since 1696. Stendhal recalls odious lessons in Latin with his live-in tutor, the abbé Raillane (who seems to have inspired a lifelong anticlericalism), and his longing for greater freedom in the repressive domestic atmosphere maintained by his maiden aunt Séraphie, who took over the child-rearing responsibilities of her deceased sister. Yet his childhood also had a bright side. Family legend held that his maternal grandfather, a respected physician who embraced the culture of the Enlightenment, had roots in Italy. His home in Grenoble, in which Henri Beyle spent a good portion of his childhood, was located at the intersection of the place Grenette and the Grande-Rue; it was brighter and more open than the paternal home and had a view of the mountains. These circumstances are no doubt the beginning of Stendhal's personal myth of Italy as a luminous place where the spirit is less oppressed by the hypocritical constraints of society. When young Henri was allowed outside, as on family outings in the country, he was capable of feeling immense happiness.

During the years of the French Revolution, Henri, captivated by the rhetoric of liberation from tyranny, followed the events enthusiastically, quite unlike his father, whose royalist sentiments earned him several months of incarceration. The newly created public school in Grenoble, l'Ecole Centrale, allowed Henri to interact extensively with peers (with one of whom he undertook a duel using pistols), and to excel at mathematics, which he looked upon as his ticket out of Grenoble. Indeed, in November 1799 he arrived in Paris, where he was supposed to sit for the entrance exam given by the Ecole Polytechnique. He did not take the exam, however, and instead benefited from the patronage of a powerful cousin, Pierre Daru, who obtained for him a position as clerk in a government office. Stendhal longed to write plays and become the Molière of his time; for the present he was being paid to write official letters for Daru's signature. A few months later Daru sent him, commissioned as a second lieutenant, across the Saint Bernard pass into northern Italy, where the Italian campaign was in progress. Having read voraciously during his childhood, Stendhal identified with the heroes of romances by Ludovico Ariosto and Torquato Tasso as he endured the perils and rigors of a soldier's lot on the way to Milan. He was enchanted, and the vivid memories of this experience would find their place in the composition of *La Chartreuse de Parme* nearly forty years later.

After some rewarding adventures in Milan and Lombardy, garrison life in the Italian Piedmont completely undid Henri's enchantment, and he came to miss the bourgeois refinements of the life he had deplored in Grenoble. In early 1802 he returned home on sick leave, then headed for Paris in April. He resigned from the army and spent his time reading, writing in the journal he had begun in 1801, attending the theater, and trying, with no success, to write verse plays. He followed an actress to Marseilles in 1805, hoping in vain to make a fortune in banking or business there, then returned to Paris, where he managed to regain favor with the Darus. Following the imperial armies with his cousin Martial Daru in 1806, he reached Berlin and Brunswick, passing through the town of Stendal, which he would later recall when coining his pseudonym. As a war commissioner he was charged with procurement, and later with the administration of occupied German territory. His functions took him to Vienna in 1809, then back to Paris in 1810, where he was named "auditeur au Conseil d'Etat" (auditor to the Council of State) and "inspecteur du Mobilier et des Bâtiments de la Couronne" (inspector of Crown buildings and furnishings). These were significant positions in the imperial bureaucracy and allowed him a fairly lavish life-style.

Yet Stendhal became restless, and he departed abruptly for Milan in 1811. There he had a brief but passionate love affair with Angela Pietragrua, whom he had admired at a distance during his earlier stay. Her beauty and exciting, unpredictable nature made a lasting impression on him. Renewed contact with the art of Italy inspired him to begin writing a history of painting after his return to Paris in November of 1811, but this work was interrupted by the disastrous Russian campaign of 1812, in which he participated as a supply commissioner and often-horrified observer. His fortunes were on the decline along with those of Napoleon, and after additional missions in Germany and brief stays in Milan and Grenoble, he was in Paris at the time of the restoration of the Bourbons to the throne in 1814. Released from his imperial functions with retirement at half-pay, he returned to

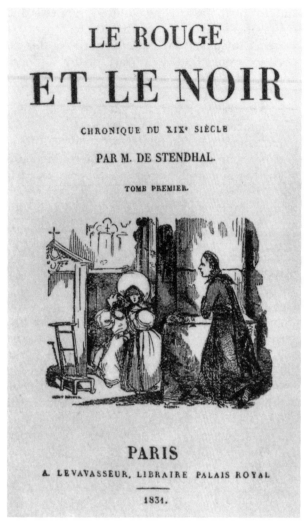

LE ROUGE ET LE NOIR

CHRONIQUE DU XIXe SIÈCLE

PAR M. DE STENDHAL.

TOME PREMIER.

PARIS

A. LEVAVASSEUR, LIBRAIRE PALAIS ROYAL

1831.

Title page for the novel—based on an actual murder case—that established Stendhal's literary reputation

Milan, where he lived for the next seven years.

In 1814 Stendhal's first book appeared, bearing the unwieldy title *Lettres écrites de Vienne en Autriche, sur le célèbre compositeur Jh. Haydn, suivies d'une vie de Mozart, et de considérations sur Métastase et l'état présent de la musique en France et en Italie* (translated as *The Life of Haydn, in a Series of Letters written at Vienna, followed by the Life of Mozart, with Observations on Metastasio, and on the present State of Music in France and Italy,* 1817), and fancifully attributed to a pseudonymous Louis-Alexandre-César Bombet. Sales were less than brisk, and three hundred unsold copies were republished in 1817 with a new binding and a much shorter title, by which the work is known today: *Vies de Haydn, de Mozart et de Métastase* (Lives of Haydn, Mozart, and Metastasio). The pseudonym was all the more appropriate in that

Stendhal's book had borrowed to the point of plagiarism from other sources, principally from Giuseppe Carpani's *Le Haydine* (1812). Carpani discovered the theft and complained in the French press, but the matter was never taken seriously. Comparison of Stendhal's text with Carpani's reveals much translation and adaptation, but also considerable originality in style, scope, and critical judgment. Having subsidized the printing, Stendhal lost money on the venture but found his calling.

This calling was to take something he had read as the pre-text for his own book, in which he would give the borrowed subject a personalized treatment. *Histoire de la peinture en Italie* (History of Painting in Italy, 1817) gave him additional practice in adapting and borrowing from written sources, but also in formulating aesthetic judgments. The two-volume work was attributed to M. B. A. A., for M. Beyle Ancien Auditeur (Mr. Beyle Former Auditor), and the second volume bore an epigraph borrowed from Oliver Goldsmith's *Vicar of Wakefield* (1766), if not from William Shakespeare's *Henry V* (1599): "To the happy few." Stendhal would use the epigraph regularly to identify the sensitive souls he hoped to have as readers. His third book, *Rome, Naples et Florence en 1817* (1817; translated as *Rome, Naples and Florence in 1817,* 1818), was attributed to "M. de Stendhal." Although for this work, which resembles a tourist guide, he continued to borrow freely from printed sources, such as the *Edinburgh Review* and works by Germaine de Staël, *Rome, Naples et Florence* relies especially on his own travel diaries and observations of the Italian temperament and mores. In addition, the book gave expression to the author's distinctive epicureanism. It earned a small profit as well, and was revised for a second edition in 1827.

During these years in Milan, Stendhal wrote, cultivated the arts, and traveled extensively in Italy, France, and England. He also suffered the throes of unrequited passion at the hands of Matilde Dembowski (whom Stendhal called Métilde), the wife of a Polish officer who had served in the French army before settling in Italy. Although legally separated from her abusive husband, she preferred Stendhal's close friendship to his offers of love. Her tender detachment and her sublime intransigence both exasperated and enraptured her would-be lover. Métilde became the embodiment for Stendhal of a certain feminine ideal, and he drew on aspects of her lofty character in portraying some of his heroines. The Métilde experience was also the basis of his treatise on the psychology of love, *De l'amour*, published about a year after the difficult political situation in Milan prompted his relocation to Paris.

The most famous passage in *De l'amour* is in the second chapter, devoted to the way in which love develops. Stendhal proposes an odd comparison between a tree branch left in a salt mine and the image of the beloved in the mind of the admirer: just as glimmering salt crystals will form on the branch, the person admired will acquire dazzling virtues in the mind of the lover. As Stendhal puts it, "Ce que j'appelle cristallisation, c'est l'opération de l'esprit, qui tire de tout ce qui se présente la découverte que l'objet aimé a de nouvelles perfections" (*Crystallization* is my term for the mind's capacity to discover new perfections in everything it notices about the object of its love). This is the fifth of seven stages of love, running from admiration, a sense of pleasure, hope, then love, through a first crystallization, then doubt, and finally a second crystallization. The book has other such schematic analyses, including the four types of love defined in the first chapter: love based on passion, conventions of taste, physical desire, and vanity. Often anecdotal in structure and epigrammatic in style, *De l'amour* was the most "literary" of his early works; its blend of analysis and narrative elements can be seen in his novels. *De l'amour*, unsigned but attributed to the author of *l'Histoire de la peinture en Italie* and *Vies de Haydn, Mozart et Métastase*, did not sell well, but it was reviewed in a few journals and had some influential readers, including Balzac, who borrowed from it for his *Physiologie du mariage* (1826; translated as *Physiology of Marriage*, 1899).

From 1821 to 1830 Stendhal lived in Paris, frequenting the salons of Marie-Joseph, Marquis de Lafayette, Destutt de Tracy, Cabanis, Etienne Delécluze, and others. He interacted with the major figures of the Restoration, particularly those with a liberal orientation, and acquired the reputation of being a witty (and sometimes irritating) conversationalist, jolly cynic, and engaging raconteur. His friendship with Prosper Mérimée, who published a portrait of Stendhal titled *H. B.* (1850), dates from these years. He met other Romantic writers in the salons and contributed to their movement a pamphlet, *Racine et Shakspeare*, first published in 1823, then revised and enlarged in 1825.

In this work devoted to theater he formulated a relativistic definition of romanticism that could apply to other genres as well: "Le *Romanticisme* [*sic*] est l'art de présenter aux peuples les œuvres littéraires qui, dans l'état actuel de leurs habitudes et de leurs croyances, sont susceptibles de leur donner le plus de plaisir possible. Le *Classicisme*, au contraire, leur présente la littérature qui donnait le plus grand plaisir possible à leurs arrière-grands-pères" (*Romanticism* is the art of providing societies with literary works that, with respect to the current state of their habits and beliefs, are capable of giving them the most pleasure possible. *Classicism*, on the other hand, provides them with literature that gave the greatest possible pleasure to their great-grandfathers).

Because of his attachment to the liberal ideals of the Enlightenment, Stendhal stood apart from the early French Romantics, who had a nostalgia for the traditional values of legitimate monarchy and church, which had been stigmatized during the turbulent revolutionary and Napoleonic years. The 1823 version of his pamphlet does not seem to have attracted wide attention. But French romanticism was already in the process of becoming more liberal, as it contended against the French Establishment's condemnation of the movement. The 1825 version of *Racine et Shakspeare* enjoyed a good measure of success and influence, including a favorable review in the liberal *Globe*, which had been founded only the year before. Stendhal's Romantic modernism, however, was not in the mainstream of the movement, which for the next few years was to continue producing theatrical works written in alexandrine verse and lacking in subtle psychological portraiture, such as Victor Hugo's *Hernani* (1830).

Around 1822 Stendhal began contributing articles on philosophy, society, and the arts to various journals in Britain and France, including the *Paris Monthly Review*, where they appeared in English translation. Two chapters of *Racine et Shakspeare* were based on such articles, and a piece on Gioacchino Antonio Rossini gave rise to a book-length project, *Vie de Rossini* (1823; translated as *Memoirs of Rossini*, 1824). A passionate music lover who had spent many happy evenings at La Scala in Milan, Stendhal praised Italian music over French for its manner of speaking to the heart. *Vie de Rossini* seems free of the borrowing that is characteristic of his earlier books, and the success of his article on the composer in the *Paris Monthly Review* was acknowledged, ironically, by plagiarized versions that appeared in British and Italian publications. In the early weeks of 1824 Stendhal was responding yet again to the call of Italy with his third extended stay in Rome.

Not long after his return to Paris, he was responding to another call: that of passion. By now his ardor for the disdainful Métilde Dembowski had waned enough for him to take an interest in Clémentine de Curial, whom he had met ten years earlier. The wife of a general who had been given the title of count by Napoleon in 1814, she is said to have avenged herself of her husband's infidelities and harsh treatment by having a series of affairs. Her stormy liaison with Stendhal lasted from 1824 to 1826 and was a source of exhilaration for the writer, who had little in common with "Menti." She was politically conservative, the mother of two daughters, and hostess to large social gatherings. She was also an ardent mistress, exchanged coded signals to prepare assignations, and once hid Stendhal in her country château for three days. Like Angela Pietragrua and Métilde before her, she provided him with personality traits and personal circumstances that were to be useful for developing female characters in his novels.

In the midst of this tumultuous relationship, Stendhal joined an ideological fray and published *D'un nouveau complot contre les industriels* (On a New Plot against Industrialists, 1825). Romantics who were heading leftward had been giving serious attention to theories of industrial socialism. Ever one to exalt the individual, Stendhal objected to the depersonalizing utilitarianism of these theories (the title of his pamphlet is ironic, since the "plot" is not *against* but *by* the industrialists). In this work he thus ran the risk of alienating liberal Romantics, just as he had antagonized some in the conservative faction with his praise of the English playwright in *Racine et Shakspeare*. Like Menti in these years, Stendhal was true only to himself.

In part to distract himself from dejection after her abrupt termination of their affair, he threw himself into the completion of his first novel, *Armance*. Following a pattern already established, and which he was to continue, Stendhal took the premise of his novel from another author's book. Henri de Latouche had published an anonymous novel, *Olivier*, in 1826; this in turn was based on an unpublished story of the same title by Claire de Durfort, Duchesse de Duras.

Her story, which became a subject of gossip in the salons of the day, treated the despondency of an impotent man who cannot reconcile his physical inadequacy with the love he feels for a woman. Latouche's book, as intended, was attributed by many to Mme de Duras. Stendhal reviewed the novel for the *New Monthly Magazine* and was planning to take *Olivier* as the title of his own version, but under the influence of Mérimée he changed his title, and the publisher added a subtitle, *ou quelques scènes d'un salon de Paris en 1827* (or, Scenes from a Paris Salon in 1827).

Considering his heartache following the breakup with Menti, dejection brought on by love was a theme with which he could readily identify. Moreover, he had experienced a few temporary bouts of impotence himself. Thus Octave de Malivert, the unfortunate hero of *Armance*, was derived immediately from the "Olivier" stories but was a partial reflection of his author as well (F. W. J. Hemmings suggests the term "self-caricature"). Octave has liberal tendencies and military aspirations, deplores cupidity, is unpredictable, loves his mother "avec une sorte de passion" (with a kind of passion), and is a graduate of the Ecole Polytechnique (which Stendhal was supposed to attend, but did not, after leaving Grenoble for Paris). Like future Stendhalian heroes, and doubtless like the author himself, Octave is capable of savoring the meditative solitude of a confined space: "Il regrettait vivement sa petite cellule de l'école polytechnique" (He deeply missed his little cell at the college of science and engineering). As befits a Romantic hero, however, he has certain Byronic attributes that Stendhal lacked: wealth, noble manners, physical attractiveness, and a brooding soul. Oddly, Octave's crucial impotence is never explicitly identified. The plot centers on his attempts to find a place for himself in his society, and accordingly, like Stendhal's other major fictional works, *Armance* incorporates structures of the Bildungsroman, or novel of formation.

A common feature in this genre is the effect of a love interest on the hero's development, and the bulk of *Armance* is in fact devoted to Octave's growing love for his distant cousin Armance de Zohiloff, whose condition as an orphan with little fortune has led her from Russia to the home of relatives in Paris. Octave has just benefited from a law granting indemnities to the families of noble émigrés whose wealth had been confiscated by the state before the restoration of Bourbon royalty in 1814. His father, who returned to France in 1814, has seen his modest resources increased by two million francs, and Octave is unpleasantly surprised to notice that the change of fortune instantly earns him greater consideration in the aristocratic salons. Armance has precisely the sort of integrity Octave admires, and she fears that the disparity in fortune will alienate Octave from her.

These social and economic obstacles are sufficient motivation for the vicissitudes of their courtship without the element of impotence, which does, however, help explain Octave's moody preoccupation with his self-image. In addition to such recurring Stendhalian themes as family relations, the crass pursuit of the almighty franc, intense self-scrutiny, and the isolation of lofty souls, *Armance* presents many facets of the problem of communication. The narrator comments several times on Octave's degree of success in expressing himself in the salons; there are numerous exchanges of letters and messages; and communication may involve deception or withholding of information. Without an explanatory editor's preface, a reader might well conclude that Octave's Romantic suicide in the final pages is not prompted by his "fatal secret," but by despair brought on by a letter forged to resemble Armance's handwriting, in which she is made to confess to a friend that she is marrying Octave only for his wealth and social position.

Before succumbing to poison on a ship bound for Greece, where he is supposed to participate in the liberation effort, Octave writes to Armance, reveals his secret (which, however, is not divulged to the reader), and encloses the forged letter. The act of writing, of self-revelation, is exalting: "Jamais Octave n'avait été sous le charme de l'amour le plus tendre comme dans ce moment suprême" (Never had Octave been so under the spell of heartfelt love as in this supreme moment). Because of a similar effect of writing on his own psyche, Stendhal presented variations of this theme in many of his works. Perhaps Octave's Pyrrhic triumph in finally communicating his secret had restorative power for the author's ego in the wake of the breakdown of communication with Menti.

The reading public and Stendhal's friends had a largely negative reaction to *Armance*, and the eight hundred to one thousand copies of the first printing found so few buyers that in 1828 the remainders were rebound and announced as a second edition. Stendhal's financial circumstances at this time were no better than the for-

tunes of his first novel. Henry Colburn, the British publisher who commissioned Stendhal's articles for journals such as *Paris Monthly Review, New Monthly Magazine, London Magazine*, and *Athenaeum*, had never been prompt in paying, and commercial relations with his French contributor began to break down altogether in 1827. Since 1822 these articles, which appeared anonymously in English, had accounted for up to two-thirds of Stendhal's annual income (contributions traceable to Stendhal were retranslated into French and published by Henri Martineau from 1935 to 1936 as five volumes of the Divan edition of the complete works).

Moreover, Stendhal's theater column for the *Journal de Paris* ceased in 1827, and in 1828 the government cut his military pension from 900 to 450 francs. His bachelor mode of living depended on elegant clothes, evenings at the theater and in prominent salons, meals in fashionable restaurants, and annual trips abroad; with these financial setbacks, how could he continue? He had suicidal thoughts and made out several wills, but his financial plight was resolved by the intervention of influential friends who obtained for him, in the wake of the Revolution of 1830, an appointment as consul in Italy. Stendhal had hoped to become a high official in the French provincial administration, but to avoid financial insecurity he left Paris for Italy in November 1830.

This response to necessity was not tantamount to defeat on the social and intellectual battleground of Paris. Stendhal departed as a man to contend with on the literary scene. And he had good reason to be pleased with his sheer productivity, for between *Armance* in 1827 and his departure in 1830, he produced two significant works, one a masterpiece, in addition to some stories and his last journalistic essays for Colburn, who apparently never paid for them. One of the two major works was the novel for which he is best known, *Le Rouge et le noir*; the other was *Promenades dans Rome* (1829; translated as *A Roman Journal*, 1957).

After publication of the second edition of *Rome, Naples et Florence* in 1827, Stendhal had leftover material from that project, which he decided to supplement with personal notes, library research, and imagination to create yet another book on Italy. *Promenades dans Rome*, although composed in Paris, provided a sense of immediacy by adopting the format of a travel journal. Full of anecdotes, descriptions of artworks, historical details, and cultural commentary, the book

Stendhal dancing while on a December 1833 trip down the Rhône (sketch by Alfred de Musset; from Robert Alter, A Lion for Love: A Critical Biography of Stendhal, 1979)

met with critical acclaim and modest commercial success. People talked about it, tourists consulted it, and, most importantly for Stendhal's reputation, reviews in journals recalled many of his previous titles. Perhaps the work's greatest value for Stendhal, however, was the opportunity it provided to refine his art of concise narration in the composition of the many tales, anecdotes, and stories that were included.

Just as *Promenades dans Rome*, like most of his previous works, relied in part on borrowed material, *Le Rouge et le noir* sprang from the account of a crime that Stendhal had read in the *Gazette des Tribunaux* (Journal of Criminal Cases). A blacksmith's son named Antoine Berthet had enjoyed the patronage of a local priest and went on to enroll in a Grenoble seminary. After leaving for reasons of health, he became a tutor to the children of a M. Michoud de la Tour. Berthet appeared to have an involvement with Mme Michoud and was dismissed from his functions. He returned to a seminary, was expelled, became a tutor for an-

other family, and was dismissed for having an affair with his employer's daughter. Berthet turned his frustration against Mme Michoud, sent her some threatening letters, and later shot her with a pistol during Mass, in the church of the priest who originally had helped him. For this crime he was sentenced to death. Stendhal's Julien Sorel differs from Berthet in important ways, but their stories have similar outlines.

Julien, the son of a sawyer, has learned Latin from the abbé Chélan, a sincere Jansenist who encourages him to put his intelligence to good use in the search for a station in life. Enamored of the Napoleonic legend and an avid reader of *Le Mémorial de Sainte-Hélène* (1823), in which Emmanuel de Las Cases detailed Napoleon's life and thoughts in exile, Julien longs for the opportunity to prove his merit in military endeavors. The times have changed for France, however, and the priesthood seems to be the best outlet for a poor but talented young man in 1830. (The choice between army and church has traditionally served to explain the *Red* and *Black* in the title of the novel, but other interpretations abound, and much has been written on the subject.) Julien will cnroll at the seminary in Besançon, but first he remains in Verrières, a town in the mountainous Jura region of eastern France, and moves into the home of M. de Rênal, whose children he tutors. Julien's scorn for his aristocratic employers determines him to seduce Mme de Rênal, but he falls in love with her in the process. He thinks of her often in the seminary, where his cell offers an exalting panoramic view of the mountainous countryside.

The seminary director, also a Jansenist, obtains for Julien a position as personal secretary to the marquis de la Mole in Paris. Like Berthet, Julien becomes involved with his employer's daughter, but his fortunes with the fiery Mathilde lead him to an army commission, marriage plans, and a promised dowry. These plans are disrupted by a letter received from Mme de Rênal, who, under the influence of her confessing priest, has denounced Julien as a seducer. He is overcome with fury and rushes to Verrières, where he shoots Mme de Rênal in church. Once in prison Julien reflects on his short life and realizes he has been looking for happiness in the wrong places. Mme de Rênal recovers, visits him, and their love is renewed. At his trial Julien's testimony includes a speech in which he stresses the differences between his status as an ambitious peasant, and that of the jurors, who are "des bourgeois indignés" (indignant middle-class citizens). His speech suggests suicidal intentions, and indeed, he will be guillotined.

If this brief synopsis of the novel's action shows the degree of Stendhal's fidelity to Berthet's story, it completely overlooks the thematic and psychological richness of the work. Julien's character reveals an odd combination of timidity and lofty pride, forthrightness and hypocrisy, endearing spontaneity and calculating self-interest. The polarity of these character traits recalls the antithetical colors of the title and points to a fundamental thread of dualism in the fabric of the novel. This dualism is quite evident in the main female characters, for Mme de Rênal is principled but tenderhearted, selfless, and unaffected, while Mathilde de la Mole is more disingenuous, self-conscious, and flamboyant. Mme de Rênal loves Julien for the innocence and vulnerability that he often tries to conceal; Mathilde loves him for his shrewdness, ambition, and heady unpredictability. Religion, like love, is viewed from a dual perspective: the Jansenist abbé Chélan and abbé Pirard are presented in the favorable light of sincerity, while l'abbé de Frilair and unnamed Jesuits are confined to the shadows of hypocrisy and secular ambition.

Ultimately, the novelistic enterprise itself displays contradictory tendencies, since imitation may be opposed to invention. This opposition emerges in part from representations of reading and writing in the novel. Julien's voracious reading leads him to interpret experience on the basis not of what he sees and feels spontaneously, but of models he has encountered in books. His thoughts and actions are often guided by the Napoleonic model, internalized especially from reading *Le Mémorial de Sainte-Hélène*, but Julien is also influenced by works of Jean-Jacques Rousseau and others. Stendhal's reader first meets Julien, in fact, perched high in the roof timbers of his father's sawmill, reading *Le Mémorial*. Reading, for Julien, provides access to the ideal world of the imagination and relief from the drudgery of working with his coarse father and brothers, who are illiterate.

It is in the real world that Julien must make his fortune, however, and his cynical side is quite clear-sighted about the shortcomings of society and the foibles of human nature. Stendhal's narrator, accordingly, furnishes a detailed and compelling tableau of the political, economic, and social dimensions of Julien's world. The importance of realism in the novel is further emphasized by

Stendhal's subtitle at the beginning of book one, *Chronique de 1830* (Chronicle of 1830), despite the absence in the work of any mention of the crucial revolution of 1830 and the end of the Bourbon regime. Yet Julien often turns to the ideal worlds that can exist only in the mind. This dichotomy is made explicit in a passage that describes his mental state during a time in prison when Mme de Rênal was unable to visit and console him: "Rien ne lui plaisait plus, ni dans la vie réelle, ni dans l'imagination" (He no longer took pleasure in anything, whether of real life or of the imagination). The real and the ideal have converged in his relationship with Mme de Rênal.

Stendhal's narrator touts the realist aesthetic in some direct statements, the most famous of which defines the novel as a mere reflector of reality: "Eh, monsieur, un roman est un miroir qui se promène sur une grande route" (Why, sir, a novel is a mirror that is carried along a highway). In other interventions as well, the narrator pretends to apologize for elements of the story that might in some way be objectionable, but that must be reported because they are part of the story's declared historical reality. Such protestations of "reality" in fact may call attention to the artifice that underlies the invented narration, yet without compromising fictional illusion. This convention in storytelling has thematic value in *Le Rouge et le noir*, for in highlighting the tension between fiction and reality that his narrator and readers must confront, Stendhal enlarges upon the dualism that informs Julien's choices between imitation and invention, cunning and spontaneity, and the real world and that of the imagination.

This dualism is visible in another of the narrator's favorite devices, ironic commentary. As Victor Brombert demonstrates at length in *Stendhal et la voie oblique* (Stendhal and the Oblique Path, 1954), the narrator often provides explicit or implicit judgment of the hero's thoughts or conduct, but with an ironic thrust. An apparently negative assessment of a moment of weakness for Julien may, for example, be an oblique form of praise for his sensitivity. Along these lines, as Shoshana Felman shows in *La "Folie" dans l'œuvre romanesque de Stendhal* ("Folly" in Stendhal's Fictional Works, 1971), the word *folie* (folly or madness) may be used to characterize the actions of major figures such as Julien or Mathilde, but the word must be interpreted to mean a generally praiseworthy independence of spirit that distinguishes the superior soul from individuals who cling to convention. The ironic judgments formulated by Stendhal's narrators in his novels are complex and must be construed with caution, but in *Le Rouge et le noir* this irony furthers the current of dualism, since irony is constituted by distancing from the object, and often expresses the opposite of what has been stated.

Erich Auerbach rightly praised Stendhal as an innovator for his realistic portrayal of sociopolitical conditions, yet the power of Stendhal's major novels no doubt derives from his skillful appropriation of known conventions and archetypal patterns. Julien's superiority in *Le Rouge et le noir* is suggested in a few scenes where he occupies a physically elevated position; the first of these is in the sawmill, where the reader meets him reading among the roof timbers. Julien and other Stendhalian heroes experience friction with their fathers and find themselves physically attracted to a mother figure. These Oedipal patterns, not surprisingly, have given rise to a considerable amount of biographical and Freudian criticism. More generally, Stendhal's protagonists follow the tradition of fictional closure, which entails the death or departure of the hero. Julien's ritual execution by the guillotine is but one of several ordeals he endures in the process of establishing his status as hero in a context of archetypal precedents. He dies, appropriately, with full assurance of the redeeming power of Mme de Rênal's love.

Le Rouge et le noir attracted a good deal of attention in the press and among readers inclined to discuss important books. The first printing of fifteen hundred copies (a better-than-average figure for the time) seems to have sold well, and Stendhal's literary reputation was finally established as he prepared to leave Paris in order to enjoy the security of a position as French consul in Italy. His political reputation in Italy was to cause him problems, however. Northern Italy was under Austrian control, and various nationalistic and liberationist Italian groups known to Stendhal were closely monitored. Suspecting Stendhal (and not without reason) of harboring hostile sentiments toward Klemens von Metternich and the Austrian administration, police authorities had already expelled him from Milan during a trip to Italy in January 1828.

In the last months of 1830 Stendhal endured further administrative difficulties in northern Italy en route to Trieste, where he was to assume consular duties. His official reception in Trieste was chilly, and at the end of a few weeks he was informed that Austria would not allow him to act as consul in that town. Thanks to the intervention of some influential friends, Stendhal was sent instead to Civitavecchia, where a consular position was approved in April 1831. Over the next several years he would be the object of suspicion and sporadic surveillance; he would complain of the monotony of his duties and of life in a provincial town; he would spend much time traveling in Italy and visiting Rome, only forty miles from Civitavecchia; and he would take his mind off his solitude by writing.

He wrote a good deal in Civitavecchia and during his escapes to Rome, but most of it was to be published after his death. Among the most important of his writings during this period are the posthumous autobiographical works *Souvenirs d'égotisme* and *Vie de Henry Brulard*, which convey the introspective delight taken by a solitary quinquagenarian in reliving significant moments of his past as he commits them to writing. The relations between remembrance, invention, and writing were of great interest to Stendhal, who stated in the opening pages of *Souvenirs d'égotisme* that he would be mindful not to subject his happy memories to excessive written analysis. Near the end of *Henry Brulard* he muses, in a similar vein, "Comment peindre le bonheur fou?" (How can one describe intense happiness?), and the unfinished work ends with a prophetic last line, "On gâte des sentiments si tendres à les raconter en détail" (Such tender feelings are ruined if they are recounted in detail). His fiction also contains occasional reflections on the inexpressibility of strong emotion. As a writer, Stendhal was committed to finding words to express experience and feeling, so his statements about the limitations of language and the writer's psyche must be taken with a rhetorical grain of salt. Stendhal does indulge in moments of analysis and critical self-scrutiny as he probes his memory during the autobiographical act, but his style in these works is indeed more anecdotal than analytical.

Paradoxically, his first autobiographical narrative starts not with childhood memories but with his stay in Paris after leaving Milan in 1821. This period of his life is the basis of *Souvenirs d'égotisme*, composed in 1832. The word *égotisme* had negative connotations for Stendhal, who expressed concern in the early pages of the work for the reader's reaction to "les éternels *Je* que l'auteur va écrire" (the eternal *I*'s that the author is going to write); similar reflections appear in *Vie de Henry Brulard*. *Souvenirs d'égotisme* is full of digressions, portraits of people he knew, disparag-

Stendhal in consular uniform, circa 1836 (portrait by Silvestro Valeri; from Joanna Richardson, Stendhal, *1974)*

ing comments on the political scene during the Restoration, insights into his temperament, ruminations over lost opportunities, recollections of his brooding after breaking up with Métilde Dembowski, observations on the act of writing, and reflections on his own mortality. Of particular interest in the last area is an epitaph he composed that proclaims his love in this life for Domenico Cimarosa, Wolfgang Amadeus Mozart, and Shakespeare, and pays tribute in Italian to his favorite city: "Errico [*Arrigo* in other variants] Beyle, Milanese; visse, scrisse, amò" (Henri Beyle, of Milan; he lived, he wrote, he loved). A similar epitaph was attached to his tomb in the Montmartre cemetery at his death in 1842.

Having written about himself in his extensive journals from 1801 to 1823, then in *Souvenirs d'égotisme* in 1832, Stendhal was ready to undertake the difficult task of recalling and narrating his childhood. After an abortive attempt in 1833 (he stopped after a few pages), he threw himself into the project in November 1835 and produced several hundred pages by March of the following year. Curiously, *Vie de Henry Brulard* opens with the statement (considered by critics to be false) that he is writing in 1832, still under the

spell of a glorious view of ancient and modern Rome, which, that very morning, inspired in him the thought that he was only three months away from his fiftieth birthday. A few paragraphs later, he claims to have resumed writing after a hiatus of three years. Various reminiscences and reflections occupy the next several pages, and the narrative of his childhood begins only with chapter 3. The choice of an autobiographical pseudonym similar to his own name and the concocted opening where he decides to take stock of his life after contemplating a view of the Eternal City point to an ambivalent attitude toward the project of tracing his identity back to his childhood.

Stendhal mentions a few joyous moments but dwells especially on his sense of loss after his mother's death and on his longing for greater freedom. He refers to his father and his Aunt Séraphie as "mes tyrans" (my tyrants) because of their reluctance to let him play outside with other children. In addition, he reveals an influence on his lifelong anticlericalism and agnosticism. Because young Henri overheard a priest attempting to console his bereaved father with the words "ceci vient de Dieu" (this is God's doing), the seven year old developed a grudge against God. Later he was to endure the "tyrannie Raillane" (Raillane tyranny) at the hands of the priest who was hired to be the boy's tutor. The intensity of Stendhal's negative impressions of his father and Raillane is suggested in such phrases as "Depuis vingt ans au moins je détourne les yeux avec horreur du souvenir de cette terrible époque" (For at least twenty years I have turned my eyes with horror from the memory of that terrible period), and "Ils ont empoisonné mon enfance" (They poisoned my childhood).

Henry Brulard and *Souvenirs d'égotisme* are both characterized by digressions, interruptions, contradictions, and announced omissions. Critics have tried to account for this fragmented composition in psychological, linguistic, and aesthetic terms. To such considerations must be added the fact that Stendhal never put the texts into finished form for publication. Their very spontaneity, however, often produces a ring of authenticity and results in some delightful passages. Readers who know the autobiographical works will inevitably discover in his novels various reflections of the author's own difficulties with parental and religious authority, his loves, aspirations, disappointments, and contempt for greed, vanity, and hypocrisy.

Another feature that is common to both genres under Stendhal's pen is attention accorded to reading and writing. In *Vie de Henry Brulard* he details his childhood readings and stresses the importance of books for molding his character. His view that reading can produce a more intense kind of experience than real-life events and encounters is epitomized in an often-quoted formulation: "Un roman est comme un archet, la caisse du violon qui rend les sons c'est l'âme du lecteur" (A novel is like a bow, and the violin that produces the sounds is the reader's soul). Yet in *Souvenirs d'égotisme* he goes one better with the statement that "pour qui a goûté de la profonde occupation d'écrire, lire n'est plus qu'un plaisir secondaire" (for whoever has enjoyed the profound occupation of writing, reading is only a secondary pleasure).

If Stendhal dwells in these works on the psychological benefits of autobiographical writing (self-discovery, the attendant acuity of "mental vision," the exaltation of reliving a cherished moment), he also admits to what might appear as limitations: namely, an inability to verbalize strong feeling, and a reluctance to engage in extended description. The first of these can in fact be seen as the inexpressibility topos, a rhetorical ploy by which a writer conveys the significance of that which he or she says cannot be put into words. In both his novels and his autobiographical writings, Stendhal has recourse to various formulas for expressing ineffable emotion. As for description, his style of writing in general privileged action, analysis, and dialogue over decor, which sets him somewhat apart from contemporaries such as Balzac. A confession in *Souvenirs d'égotisme* is telling: ". . . j'abhorre la description matérielle. L'ennui de la faire m'empêche de faire des romans" (. . . I abhor material description. My vexation with doing it keeps me from writing novels). Yet while writing the autobiographical works, his memory was flooded with scenes from his past in which material aspects and spatial arrangements were essential. Rather than spoil the visual memory with an attempt at verbalizing, Stendhal's solution, especially in *Henry Brulard*, was to produce a sketch of the scene. These sketches have been reproduced in the published versions of the works.

Between *Souvenirs d'égotisme* and *Vie de Henry Brulard*, Stendhal produced a major novel, his longest, although it was never put into final form for publication. Critics have differed as to whether this novel, *Lucien Leuwen* (1894), even

reached its ending. As one might expect, in light of the introspective writing that surrounded its production, this work has a strong autobiographical dimension. The pre-text of *Lucien Leuwen* goes back to an official leave of absence of three months that Stendhal took in Paris in the fall of 1833. He renewed contact with, among many other people, Mme Jules Gaulthier, who had tried her hand at a novel and wanted Stendhal's opinion of her work. He read the manuscript of "Le Lieutenant" after his return to Civitavecchia and sent a frank assessment of the novel's weaknesses to Mme Gaulthier, who never published the work. But in the process of thinking through possible revisions, Stendhal hit on the idea of rewriting her novel as his own. He borrowed the name Leuwen and material for the first few chapters, but the situations, characters, and style are unmistakably Stendhalian.

Lucien Leuwen is the story of a young officer who is stationed in the provinces. He endures boredom, awkward moments, and the joys and sorrows of love; he later becomes a secretary to the minister of the interior, suffers various disappointments and humiliations, and leaves Paris to work in a French embassy abroad. Variations on familiar Stendhalian themes are obvious in the novel. Lucien, like Octave de Malivert, was a student at the Ecole Polytechnique, but was expelled after being wrongfully accused of antigovernment activity. Political satire is so salient in the work, and Stendhal shows so much scorn for the regime of Louis-Philippe, that publication would have been difficult to arrange even if the manuscript had been completed. Family relations, as usual, are given much importance, but *Lucien Leuwen* presents a reversal of the typical antagonism between hero and father. Monsieur Leuwen, a wealthy banker, is a kindly and generous soul who deserves his son's respect. Lucien's apprenticeship in the provinces is reminiscent of Julien Sorel's, except that Lucien is of a higher socioeconomic rank. He nonetheless must encounter, in the unattractive garrison town of Nancy, repeated manifestations of provincial pettiness.

The ordeal of love is perhaps more cruel for Lucien than for any other Stendhalian protagonist. In Nancy he falls in love with a beautiful young widow, Mme de Chasteller, whose portrait owes much to Stendhal's beloved Métilde Dembowski. When he first catches sight of her, he falls from his horse in front of her window. Much later, he leaves Nancy abruptly for Paris after falling victim to a plot concocted by the wicked doctor Du Poirier, in which Lucien is made to see and hear enough to believe that Mme de Chasteller has just given birth to an illegitimate child that could not be his own! This ruse is similar in effect to the forged letter that causes Octave to misjudge the sincerity of Armance's love. Between these events that frame Lucien's courtship of Mme de Chasteller, he must face his own timidity and inexperience, not to mention the intimidating female companion whom Mme de Chasteller hires before allowing him to call on her. Lucien appears to be the least heroic of Stendhal's unheroic heroes.

This is especially true in the second part of the novel, in which Lucien is powerless to resist the political corruption in which he acquiesces. He feels stifled by the good intentions of his father, whose own waggish political ambitions occupy several chapters, and bewildered by the behavior of Mme Grandet, who is willing to trade sex for a political favor. Lucien is unable to withdraw from his world of dreary political and venal interests to some remote, elevated vantage point where he can contemplate beauty and his own sense of superiority; as Robert Alter puts it, "There is no tower in this landscape." Timidity in love, lost illusions in military life, tedious administrative functions, a sensitive heart forced into cynicism—these unheroic autobiographical elements in *Lucien Leuwen* were much on Stendhal's mind as he tried to cope with his situation in Civitavecchia. His health was declining, he had lost his teeth, he had recently resorted to reading glasses, he often felt isolated, and he hated his job.

One occasional bright spot was Giulia Rinieri, a much younger woman with whom, to his great surprise, he had begun a love relationship in Paris in 1830. Giulia was already twenty-nine and inexperienced in physical love, but her attraction to the corpulent writer, just three years shy of fifty, was so exhilarating that he considered marriage. An Italian diplomat in Paris, Daniello Berlinghieri, a friend of Giulia's Sienese family, was acting as her guardian. As Stendhal was leaving Paris in order to assume his consular functions in Italy, he left with Berlinghieri a letter requesting the hand of his wealthy and elegant ward in marriage. Berlinghieri withheld approval, and Giulia married a cousin in 1833, but her attachment to Stendhal persisted.

She and Berlinghieri returned to Siena in 1832 and received Stendhal for an extended visit; Stendhal visited her in Florence a month after her marriage, and the two had intimate reunions in Paris from 1836 to 1838, then in Florence after 1839. If Giulia was an occasional bright spot for Stendhal during the 1830s, he also had to endure the gloom of a tenacious shadow in the person of Lysimaque Tavernier, his chancellor at the consulate in Civitavecchia. As a lower-level employee Tavernier had cleverly shown great willingness to take over Stendhal's functions during the consul's frequent absences, but after his appointment as chancellor in 1834, he showed a side that was manipulative, insubordinate, and perfidious. Poor relations with Tavernier were one of the many reasons behind the extended leave Stendhal took from his post during the years 1836-1839.

These years were extraordinarily productive and culminated in a masterpiece, *La Chartreuse de Parme*. Stendhal had brought to Paris some Italian manuscripts containing narratives from the sixteenth and seventeenth centuries. Some of these he rewrote in French and published in periodicals. "Vittoria Accoramboni" appeared in the *Revue des Deux Mondes* in March 1837. It and other stories, along with "Vanina Vanini," which had appeared in the *Journal de Paris* in 1829, plus a few others were published posthumously as the *Chroniques italiennes* (Italian Chronicles, 1855). The longest and most noteworthy of the collection is the novella *L'Abbesse de Castro* (The Abbess of Castro, 1839). The tales are full of unbridled passion, bold gallantry, lust for revenge, and scenes of imprisonment. One of Stendhal's Italian manuscripts, "Origine delle grandezze della famiglia Farnese" (Origin of the Greatness of the Farnese Family), was the pre-text for *La Chartreuse*.

Another literary project during his leave from Civitavecchia was a biography of Napoleon, which remained unfinished. Stendhal's stated intention to write a book on Napoleon dates from a journal entry in 1802, and he wrote a good deal in 1817 and 1818 during his stay in Milan. Because of anti-Bonaparte sentiment during the Restoration, publication of such a work would have been difficult, but by the late 1830s the emperor's reputation was undergoing a rehabilitation (his remains were brought to the Hôtel des Invalides in 1840), and Stendhal began anew. However, he seems not to have had the heart for the research required for the project, and he devoted himself instead to the *Chroniques italiennes* and to *Mémoires d'un touriste* (1838; translated as *Memoirs of a Tourist*, 1962). Travel books were selling well at this time, and since Stendhal was receiving only half-pay during his leave of absence, his decision to capitalize on his experience is not surprising. He had always been an enthusiastic traveler, moreover, and preparation of *Mémoires* would give him the pleasure of visiting the French provinces, particularly the Loire valley, Normandy, and Brittany. The book was composed from personal notes, borrowings from source books, and his vast store of political opinions, aesthetic judgments, and social observations. Characteristically, the "narrator" is disguised as a traveling iron merchant, but this sort of mask was what gave Stendhal the freedom to be himself. The book is admired for an uninhibited style that fits the content in that it suggests the importance of freedom from constraint for the pursuit of happiness. *Mémoires d'un touriste* attracted considerable attention in the press and virtually sold out within two years. Stendhal, who would have enjoyed enlarging on this success, also journeyed extensively in the southern provinces, but instead of getting another volume or two out of those travel notes, he set about composing *La Chartreuse de Parme*.

When he had stopped working on *Vie de Henry Brulard* in 1836, he was in Italy, as was his youthful protagonist, for whom the year was 1800. Like *Lucien Leuwen*, the autobiography was never finished, but it had reached a natural stopping point. Young Stendhal was a second lieutenant in the French army and, having crossed the Little Saint Bernard pass, descended into northern Italy and discovered Milan: "Cette ville devint pour moi le plus beau lieu de la terre. . . . J'y ai passé quelques mois de 1800, ce fut le plus beau temps de ma vie" (That town became for me the loveliest spot on earth. . . . I spent a few months there in 1800, and it was the best time of my life). In Paris in 1838, Stendhal could resume his nostalgic recollection of the Italian campaign, and that is precisely the starting point of *La Chartreuse*.

There were in fact two Italian campaigns, both led by Napoleon. During the first, from 1796 to 1797, General Bonaparte fought on behalf of the Directory; during the second, in 1800, just after the coup d'état that had made him first consul, he reimposed French control after the battle of Marengo. The first chapter of *La Chartreuse* mentions both campaigns and presents the French as liberators who are received joyously by many in northern Italy. Stendhal creates a typical soldier, Lieutenant Robert, who is billeted at the

Stendhal, 1841 (drawing by Henri Lehmann; Musée Stendhal, Grenoble)

palace of the marquise del Dongo, whose husband has fled. Robert is so well received that he becomes the father of Fabrice del Dongo (called Fabrizio in a standard English translation), the hero of the novel! In Lieutenant Robert, Stendhal creates not only an exemplary case for his opening chapter, but also a wish-fulfilling alter ego, since young Henri Beyle in the second Italian campaign was a rather shy second lieutenant (he met Angela Pietragrua in Milan in 1800 but became intimate with her only in 1811). The childless author of 1838, about to beget his last completed novel, makes additional use of Robert to introduce favorite themes of bastardy and miscast paternal authority.

The first chapter also introduces Stendhal's most vigorous and noble-minded female character, Gina, sister of the marquis del Dongo, who marries her to the aristocratic Count Pietranera. The liberal count, much older than Gina, follows the French army in its retreat between the two Italian campaigns. Gina, whose capacity to love is only increased by hardship, accompanies him. The stage is set for an intricate plot that will showcase Stendhal's most characteristic themes, sentiments, and images. Disguises, false names, coded messages, presages and prophecies, political intrigue, spies, military ambition and disillusionment, happiness in prison, towering vantage points—these combine with a style more lyrical than that of *Le Rouge et le noir* to produce a novel that Stendhal obviously delighted in composing. So great was his enthusiasm, in fact, that he composed the five-hundred-page work, most of which he improvised while dictating to a scribe, in only fifty-two days.

Critical studies have shown how the power of Fabrice's story derives in part from well-articulated scenes and images that invoke the authority and grandeur of myth. To this dimension must be added the narrator's tender irony and his modes of Stendhalian self-consciousness. The plot itself, based on the sixteenth-century Alessandro Farnese chronicle and transposed to the Napoleonic and post-Napoleonic era, has twists that are by turns romantic, humorous, and spellbinding. Fabrice's story is essentially one of coming of age, but the prominence of Gina and her lover, Count Mosca, makes the work something more than a novel of formation.

Like Julien, Fabrice admires Napoleon, but Fabrice is in a position to join the emperor's army for the catastrophic battle of Waterloo. Stendhal privileged Fabrice's bewildered point of view in depicting the battle, rather than adopting the panoramic perspective of an omnipresent narrator, and this technique was to influence Leo Tolstoy and others. Gina, who harbors amorous sentiments for her younger nephew (one thinks of Mme de Rênal and Julien), intervenes to facilitate an ecclesiastical career for Fabrice. Because of political intrigue in Parma and his own escapades, Fabrice is imprisoned in the Farnese Tower, but his reaction is surprising: "Est-il possible que ce soit là la prison . . . on est ici à mille lieues au-dessus des petitesses et des méchancetés qui nous occupent là-bas" (Can this really be prison . . . here one is a thousand leagues above the pettiness and meanness that are inescapable down below).

After falling in love with Clélia Conti, the warden's daughter, and after exchanging various kinds of messages with Gina, Fabrice escapes with their help. He is eventually pardoned by the new prince of Parma and resumes his career in the church, not to mention his involvement with Clélia, who accepts his visits only in the dark, out of respect for a vow she made to the Virgin

Mary never to see Fabrice again. Fabrice and Clélia have a son, but paternity is always problematic in Stendhal, and the boy dies a few months after Fabrice has him abducted so that he can spend more time with him. Clélia dies of remorse, and Fabrice withdraws to an isolated monastery that echoes the title of the novel, then dies a year later. Gina, twice widowed (her second husband, the old and wealthy duke of Sanseverina, had accepted a marriage of convenience) and now the wife of Mosca, dies soon after Fabrice. Mosca, aging but wise, influential, and "immensément riche" (immensely wealthy), is alone. It would seem that happiness has eluded him.

The somewhat operatic plot twists of *La Chartreuse* are held together by a narrative medium that confers significance on the various elements. Luminous scenes alternate with dark ones, and characters such as Gina and Mosca worry about aging, while others such as Fabrice and Clélia enjoy the bloom of youth. Satirical scenes give way to drama, base sentiments confront lofty ones (at times in the same character), and disillusionment may follow noble aspirations. Stendhal's dualism in *La Chartreuse* combines romance and realism in his oddly coherent view of human nature and the difficult quest for happiness. His novel was paid the ultimate compliment in the form of Balzac's laudatory article of seventy-two pages, "Etudes sur M. Beyle," which appeared in the *Revue Parisienne* (25 September 1840).

Having begot the intensely personal *La Chartreuse*, he had to face the prospect of an imminent return to his post in Civitavecchia. There were a few months for work on some of the Italian stories, but in June 1839 he left Paris for Italy, no doubt dreading the administrative headaches and the insolence of his chancellor, Tavernier. It appears, however, that he made the best of his final years in Civitavecchia (1839-1841), hunting, cultivating friendships, spending much time in Rome, and reminiscing and enjoying the fruits of his literary reputation. He even indulged in one last romance with a new flame in 1840. A stroke in March 1841 gave him an intimation of mortality, and he began planning for a health leave to Paris. His writing projects included revisions to finished works as well as new undertakings, none of which was published before his death. Balzac had proposed some changes to *La Chartreuse* that would have produced a novel à la Balzac, and Stendhal toyed with some of these. His most important work was perhaps done on the unfinished *Lamiel* (1889), which was to be a novel of formation with a female protagonist. For various reasons such novels are rare in nineteenth-century France, and Stendhal was unable to resolve his problems of composition, despite his admiration for energetic, independent-minded women, which has attracted the interest of twentieth-century feminist critics.

Lamiel and other projects accompanied him to Paris in the fall of 1841, where his unhealthy appearance alarmed his friends. In March 1842 he gave further attention to *Lamiel*, and especially to one of the *Chroniques italiennes*, "Suora Scolastica," with which he was occupied on 22 March. That evening he suffered a stroke and collapsed on the sidewalk near the hotel where he was staying. His best story had reached its ending by the early-morning hours of the next day. Romain Colomb, his cousin, settled the estate and began overseeing the publication of his manuscripts. Stendhal's reputation continued to grow, and by the last decades of the century the "happy few" were numerous enough to guarantee him a permanent place in the French literary canon.

Letters:
Correspondance inédite, 2 volumes, with an introduction by Prosper Mérimée (Paris: Michel Lévy, 1855);
Lettres intimes, edited by Lesbros-Bigillion (Paris: Calmann-Lévy, 1892);
Souvenirs d'égotisme, with letters to Stendhal's sister Pauline, edited by Casimir Stryienski (Paris: Charpentier, 1892);
Correspondance, 3 volumes, edited by Adolphe Paupe and P.-A. Chéramy (Paris: C. Bosse, 1908);
Lettres à Pauline, edited by L. Royer and R. de la Tour du Villard (Paris: La Connaissance, 1921);
Correspondance, 10 volumes in *Œuvres complètes*, edited by Henri Martineau (Paris: Editions du Divan, 1933-1934);
Correspondance, 3 volumes, edited by Martineau and Victor Del Litto (Paris: Gallimard, Bibliothèque de la Pléiade, 1962-1968).

Bibliographies:
Adolphe Paupe, *Histoire des œuvres de Stendhal* (Paris: Dujarric, 1903);
Henri Cordier, *Bibliographie stendhalienne* (Paris: Champion, 1914);
Pierre Jourda, *Etat présent des études stendhaliennes* (Paris: Les Belles-Lettres, 1930);
Louis Royer, *Bibliographie stendhalienne: 1928-1935* (Paris: Editions du Stendhal-Club, 1930-1936);
Victor Del Litto, *Bibliographie stendhalienne: 1938-1952* (Grenoble: Arthaud, 1945-1955);
Del Litto, *Bibliographie stendhalienne: 1953-1956* (Lausanne: Editions du Grand Chêne, 1958);
Del Litto, "Bibliographie stendhalienne," in *Stendhal-Club* (October issues, 1958-);
Del Litto, *Bibliographie stendhalienne: 1957-1960* (Lausanne: Editions du Grand Chêne, 1967);
David V. Erdman, ed., *The Romantic Movement: A Selective and Critical Bibliography* (West Cornwall, Conn.: Locust Hill Press, 1988-).

Biographies:
Matthew Josephson, *Stendhal, or the Pursuit of Happiness* (Garden City, N.Y.: Doubleday, 1946);
Henri Martineau, *Le Cœur de Stendhal, histoire de sa vie et de ses sentiments* (Paris: Albin Michel, 1952-1953);
Victor Del Litto, *La Vie de Stendhal* (Paris: Albin Michel, 1965);
Michael Wood, *Stendhal* (Ithaca, N.Y.: Cornell University Press, 1971);
Gita May, *Stendhal and the Age of Napoleon* (New York: Columbia University Press, 1977);
Robert Alter, *A Lion for Love: A Critical Biography of Stendhal* (New York: Basic Books, 1979);
Michel Crouzet, *Stendhal, ou Monsieur Moi-même* (Paris: Flammarion, 1990).

References:
Robert M. Adams, *Stendhal: Notes on a Novelist* (New York: Noonday Press, 1959);
Erich Auerbach, "In the Hôtel de la Mole," in his *Mimesis: The Representation of Reality in Western Literature*, translated by Willard R. Trask (Princeton: Princeton University Press, 1953);
Maurice Bardèche, *Stendhal romancier* (Paris: La Table Ronde, 1947);
Georges Blin, *Stendhal et les problèmes de la personnalité* (Paris: Corti, 1958);
Blin, *Stendhal et les problèmes du roman* (Paris: Corti, 1954);
Victor Brombert, *The Romantic Prison: The French Tradition* (Princeton: Princeton University Press, 1978);
Brombert, *Stendhal et la voie oblique* (New Haven: Yale University Press, 1954);

Brombert, *Stendhal: Fiction and the Themes of Freedom* (New York: Random House, 1968);

Peter Brooks, "The Novel and the Guillotine, or Fathers and Sons in *Le Rouge et le noir,*" in his *Reading for the Plot. Design and Intention in Narrative* (New York: Knopf, 1984);

Gilbert Chaitin, *The Unhappy Few: A Psychological Study of the Novels of Stendhal* (Bloomington: Indiana University Press, 1972);

Michel Crouzet, *Stendhal et le langage* (Paris: Gallimard, 1981);

James T. Day, *Stendhal's Paper Mirror: Patterns of Self-Consciousness in His Novels* (New York & Bern: Peter Lang, 1987);

Victor Del Litto, *La Vie intellectuelle de Stendhal. Genèse et évolution de ses idées (1801-1821)* (Paris: Presses Universitaires de France, 1959);

Del Litto, ed., *La Création romanesque chez Stendhal,* Actes du XVIᵉ congrès international stendhalien (Geneva: Droz, 1985);

Del Litto, ed., *Stendhal-Balzac: réalisme et cinéma,* Actes du XIᵉ congrès international stendhalien (Grenoble: Presses Universitaires de Grenoble, 1978);

Béatrice Didier, *Stendhal autobiographe* (Paris: Presses Universitaires de France, 1983);

Gilbert Durand, *Le Décor mythique de "La Chartreuse de Parme"* (Paris: Corti, 1961);

Europe, issue on Stendhal, 61 (August-September 1983);

Shoshana Felman, *La "Folie" dans l'œuvre romanesque de Stendhal* (Paris: Corti, 1971);

Gérard Genette, "Stendhal," in his *Figures II* (Paris: Editions du Seuil, 1969); translated by Alan Sheridan as *Figures of Literary Discourse* (New York: Columbia University Press, 1982);

René Girard, *Deceit, Desire and the Novel: Self and Other in Literary Structure,* translated by Yvonne Freccero (Baltimore: Johns Hopkins University Press, 1965);

Raymond Giraud, *The Unheroic Hero in the Novels of Stendhal, Balzac and Flaubert* (New Brunswick, N.J.: Rutgers University Press, 1957);

Marcel Gutwirth, *Stendhal* (New York: Twayne, 1971);

Stirling Haig, *Stendhal: The Red and the Black* (Cambridge: Cambridge University Press, 1989);

F. W. J. Hemmings, *Stendhal: A Study of His Novels* (Oxford: Oxford University Press, 1964);

Ann Jefferson, *Reading Realism in Stendhal* (Cambridge: Cambridge University Press, 1988);

Georg Lukács, *Studies in European Realism,* translated by Edith Bone (New York: Grosset & Dunlap, 1964);

Francine Marill-Albérès, *Le Naturel chez Stendhal* (Paris: Nizet, 1956);

Henri Martineau, *L'Œuvre de Stendhal. Histoire de ses livres et de sa pensée* (Paris: Le Divan, 1945);

D. A. Miller, *Narrative and Its Discontents: Problems of Closure in the Traditional Novel* (Princeton: Princeton University Press, 1981);

Carol A. Mossman, *The Narrative Matrix: Stendhal's "Le Rouge et le noir"* (Lexington, Ky.: French Forum Publishers, 1984);

Christopher Prendergast, *The Order of Mimesis: Balzac, Stendhal, Nerval, Flaubert* (Cambridge: Cambridge University Press, 1986);

Jean Prévost, *La Création chez Stendhal. Essai sur le métier d'écrire et la psychologie de l'écrivain* (Paris: Gallimard, 1974);

Martine Reid, *Stendhal en images. Stendhal, l'autobiographie et "La Vie de Henry Brulard"* (Geneva: Droz, 1991);

Revue d'Histoire Littéraire de la France, issue on Stendhal, 84 (March-April 1984);

Jean-Pierre Richard, "Connaissance et tendresse chez Stendhal," in his *Littérature et sensation* (Paris: Editions du Seuil, 1970); translated by Paul A. Archambault as "Knowledge and Tenderness in Stendhal," in *Stendhal: A Collection of Critical Essays,* edited by Brombert (Englewood Cliffs, N.J.: Prentice-Hall, 1962);

Jean Starobinski, "Stendhal pseudonyme," *Temps Modernes,* 7 (October 1951): 577-617; republished in his *L'Œil vivant* (Paris: Gallimard, 1961); translated by B. A. B. Archer as "Truth in Masquerade," in *Stendhal: A Collection of Critical Essays,* edited by Brombert (Englewood Cliffs, N.J.: Prentice-Hall, 1962);

Stendhal-Club, quarterly (1958-);

Emile Talbot, *Stendhal and Romantic Esthetics* (Lexington, Ky.: French Forum Publishers, 1985).

Papers:

Stendhal's papers are at the Bibliothèque Municipale de Grenoble and the Bibliothèque Nationale, Paris.

Eugène Sue
(Marie-Joseph Sue)

(26 January 1804 - 3 August 1857)

Ian Pickup
University of Birmingham, England

SELECTED BOOKS: *Plik et Plok* (Paris: Renduel, 1831)—contains *Kernok le pirate* and *El Gitano*;

Atar-Gull (Paris: Vimont & Renduel, 1831); translated as *The Negro's Revenge; or, Brulart, the Black Pirate* (London: J. Clements, 1841);

La Salamandre, 2 volumes (Paris: Renduel, 1832); translated by Henry William Herbert as *The Salamander, a Naval Romance* (London: Bruce & Wyld, 1845);

La Coucaratcha, 4 volumes (Paris: Canel & Guyot, 1832-1834)—contains *Le Bonnet de Maître Ulrick*; *Voyage et aventures sur mer de Narcisse Gelin, parisien*; *Caballo negro y poerro blanco*; *Le Présage* (originally titled *Le Combat de Navarin*); *Craô*; *Mon ami Wolf*; *Relation véritable des voyages de Claude Belissan, clerc de procureur*; *Un Corsaire*; *Daja*; *Une Femme heureuse*; *Le Parisien en mer*; *Les Montagnes de la Ronda*; *Physiologie d'un appartement*; *M. Crinet*; and *Scènes dialoguées*;

La Vigie de Koat-Ven, 4 volumes (Paris: Vimont, 1833); translated as *The Temptation; or, The Watch Tower of Koat-Věn* (London: John Worthan, 1845);

Histoire de la marine française, 5 volumes (Paris: Bonnaire, 1835-1837);

Latréaumont, 2 volumes (Paris: Gosselin, 1838); translated as *Latréaumont; or, The Conspiracy* (Cincinnati: U. P. James, 1840[?]); revised and corrected by Thomas Williams as *Latréaumont; or, The Court Conspirator* (New York: B. Winchester, 1845); also published as *De Rohan; or, The Court Conspirator. An Historical Romance* (London: H. Colburn, 1845);

Arthur, journal d'un inconnu, 3 volumes (Paris: Gosselin, 1838-1839); translated by P. F. Christin as *Arthur* (New York: Harper, 1844);

Deleytar, 2 volumes (Paris: Gosselin, 1839)—contains *Arabian Godolphin*; translated as *The Godolphin Arabian; or, the History of a Thorough-*

Eugène Sue, 1836 (painting by François-Gabriel-Guillaume Lépaulle; Musée Carnavalet)

bred (New York: Winchester, 1845); *Le Juge*; *Le Législateur*; and *Kardiki*;

Le Marquis de Létorière (Paris: Gosselin, 1840); translated by Thomas Pooley as *The Marquis de Létorière; or, The Art of Pleasing* (New York: Burgess & Stringer, 1844);

Jean Cavalier, ou Les Fanatiques des Cévennes, 2 volumes (Paris: Gosselin, 1840); translated as *The Protestant Leader* (London: T. C. Newby, 1849);

Deux histoires, 2 volumes (Paris: Gosselin, 1840)—contains *Hercule Hardi*; *Le Colonel de Surville, histoire du temps de l'Empire*; translated by Elizabeth O'Hara as *The Duchesse de Bracciano* (London: Smith, Elder / Liverpool: Deighton & Laughton, 1850); *L'Idiot*; *Les Récifs de Saint-Mandry*; *L'Embuscade*; *Billet d'amour*; *Le Cadeau*; *L'Aveugle de Tullins*; and *Gandrini le Noir*;

Le Commandeur de Malte, 2 volumes (Paris: Gosselin, 1841); translated by Adelbert Doisy as *The Commander of Malta* (Belfast: Sims & McIntyre / New York: Harper, 1846);

Mathilde, 3 volumes (Paris: Gosselin, 1841); translated by Herbert as *Matilde; or, The Memoirs of a Young Woman* (New York: Winchester, 1843); translated as *Matilda; or, The Misfortunes of Virtue* (London: C. Daly, 1845);

Thérèse Dunoyer, 2 volumes (Paris: Gosselin, 1842); translated as *Therese Dunoyer* (New York: Winchester, 1843);

Paula Monti, ou l'Hôtel Lambert (Paris: Gosselin, 1842); translated as *Paula Monti; or, The Hôtel Lambert* (London: Chapman & Hall, 1845);

Les Mystères de Paris, 10 volumes (Paris: Gosselin, 1842-1843); translated by Charles Rochford as *The Mysteries of Paris* (London: Daly, 1844[?]);

Le Juif errant, 10 volumes (Paris: Paulin, 1844-1845); translated as *The Wandering Jew* (London: Chapman & Hall, 1844-1845); translated by D. M. Aird as *The Wandering Jew: A Tale of the Jesuits* (London: Bruce & Wylde, 1845);

Le Morne-au-diable, ou L'aventurier (Paris: Gosselin, 1845); translated as *The Female Bluebeard; or, The Adventurer* (London: Strange, 1845);

Martin l'enfant trouvé, 12 volumes (Paris: Pétion, 1846-1847); translated as *Martin, the Foundling; or, The Adventures of a Valet-de-chambre* (London: Appleyard, 1847);

Les Sept Péchés capitaux (Paris, 1848-1851)—contains *L'Orgueil. La Duchesse*, 6 volumes (Paris: Pétion, 1848); *L'Envie. Frédérik Bastien*, 4 volumes (Paris: Pétion, 1848); *La Co-*

lère. Tison d'enfer, 2 volumes (Paris: Pétion, 1849); *La Luxure. Madeleine*, 1 volume (Paris: Cadot, 1849); *La Paresse. Le Cousin Michel*, 1 volume (Paris: Cadot, 1849); *L'Avarice*, 1 volume (Paris: Michel Lévy, 1851); and *La Gourmandise*, 1 volume (Paris: Michel Lévy, 1851);

Le Républicain des campagnes (Paris, 1848);

Les Mystères du peuple ou Histoire d'une famille de prolétaires à travers les âges, 8 volumes (Paris: Maurice le Châtre, 1849-1857); translated by Mary L. Booth as *Mysteries of the People; or, The Story of a Plebeian Family for 2,000 Years* (New York: Clark, 1867); translated by Daniel and Solon Deleon [de Leon] as *The Mysteries of the People* (New York: New York Labor News Co., 1904-1916);

Les Enfants de l'amour, 4 volumes (Paris: Cadot, 1850);

La Bonne Aventure, 6 volumes (Paris: Michel Lévy frères, 1851);

Miss Mary, ou l'institutrice, 4 volumes (Paris: Cadot, 1851);

L'Amiral Levacher, 2 volumes (Paris: Permain, 1852);

Fernand Duplessis, ou Les mémoires d'un mari, 8 volumes (Paris: Cadot, 1852-1853);

Gilbert et Gilberte, 7 volumes (Paris: Cadot, 1853);

La Marquise Cornélia d'Alfi. Le Lac d'Annecy et ses environs (Annecy: Saillet / Paris: Cadot, 1853);

La Famille Jouffroy, 7 volumes (Paris: Cadot, 1854);

Le Diable médecin, 7 volumes (Paris: Chappe, 1855-1857);

Les Fils de famille, 9 volumes (Paris: Cadot, 1856-1857);

Les Secrets de l'oreiller, 7 volumes (Paris: Cadot, 1858-1860).

SELECTED PLAY PRODUCTIONS: *Latréaumont*, by Sue and Prosper Dinaux, Paris, Théâtre-Français, 26 September 1840;

Mathilde, by Sue and Félix Pyat, Paris, Théâtre de la Porte-Saint-Martin, 24 September 1842;

Les Mystères de Paris, by Sue and Dinaux, Paris, Théâtre de la Porte-Saint-Martin, 13 February 1844;

Martin et Bamboche, Paris, Théâtre de la Gaîté, 27 October 1847;

Le Morne au diable, Paris, Théâtre de l'Ambigu-Comique, 5 August 1848;

Le Juif errant, Paris, Théâtre de l'Ambigu-Comique, 23 June 1849.

OTHER: M. le baron de Mortemart-Boisse, *Histoire, voyages et scènes intimes*, preface by Sue (Paris, 1834);

Suau de Varennes, *Les Matelots parisiens*, preface by Sue (Paris, 1837);

Savinien la Pointe, *Une Voix d'en bas*, preface by Sue, in *Almanach du mois* (August 1844);

Wenceslas Ayguals de Izeo, *Marie l'Espagnole ou La victime d'un moine*, preface by Sue (Paris, 1846);

Alphonse Karr, *Raoul Desloges ou Un homme fort en thème*, preface by Sue (Paris, 1851);

Lettres sur la question religieuse en 1856, preface by Sue (Brussels: Méline et Cans, 1857).

SELECTED PERIODICAL PUBLICATIONS—
UNCOLLECTED: "Profession de foi de Sue, candidat à l'assemblée constituante," *Réforme*, 14 March 1848;

"Le Suffrage universel et la vile multitude au IIIe siècle," *Liberté de Penser*, 20 September 1850; also published in *Almanach du peuple pour 1851*;

"Réalités sociales. Etudes sur le prolétariat des campagnes. Jean-Louis le journalier," *Liberté de Penser*, 11 November 1850, January-February 1851; also published in the *Semaine*, 18 July, 23 July, 22 August 1851.

Eugène Sue was without doubt the most successful writer of serial novels in France during the first half of the nineteenth century. He had a huge following among the country's expanding reading public, particularly from the time of the publication, in the *Journal des Débats*, of *Les Mystères de Paris* (1842-1843; translated as *The Mysteries of Paris*, 1844). It is for this work that he is best remembered. A convert to socialism shortly before he embarked on the composition of this epic novel (it might be more accurate to refer to him as a *républicain-socialiste*), Sue littered his narrative with overtly didactic references to the plight of the poor, the criminal classes, prostitutes, and unhappily married women. Sue's firm insistence on issues that were topical at the time in part helps to explain why the man whom Jean-Louis Bory refers to as "le roi du roman populaire" (the king of the popular novel)—a novelist more successful than Alexandre Dumas *père* and even Honoré de Balzac in his heyday—fell into almost total oblivion in France by the early twentieth century. His reputation is once again ascending, and critical opinion is undergoing a major revision as the full significance of the popular novel and the

mass media of the nineteenth century is increasingly recognized. Much research remains to be done on Sue, but a clearer appreciation of his overall significance is already emerging.

Marie-Joseph Sue—Eugène Sue to the public at large—was born in Paris on 26 January 1804. The son of a famous surgeon, Jean-Joseph Sue II (1760-1830), and the grandson of another famous surgeon who bore the same name (medical practitioners in the family can be traced back to the reign of Louis XIV), Eugène Sue was the first child of his father's second marriage, to Sophie Tison de Rilly (the birth certificate refers to her more judiciously, given the historical moment, as Marie-Sophie Derilly). Eugène's godmother was the future Empress Joséphine, while his godfather was Joséphine's son, the future Prince Eugène de Beauharnais. Eugène's father rejoiced in the title "médecin en chef de la garde des consuls" (chief doctor to the consuls' guard).

The young Eugène certainly did not have a deprived childhood: the family, which moved from a luxurious apartment near the place Vendôme to a splendid house on the corner of the rue de Suresnes, was clearly not lacking in material wealth. Eugène did not, however, have a happy childhood. A rebellious, even maladjusted child, the future novelist constantly aroused the anger of his father, whose hopes and aspirations he was unable to fulfill. In a manner not totally dissimilar to that of Stendhal in *Vie de Henry Brulard* (Life of Henry Brulard, 1890), Sue was to examine his formative years in his autobiographical novel *Arthur, journal d'un inconnu* (1838-1839; translated as *Arthur*, 1844), in which the eponymous hero describes his difficult relationship with his father. Like Stendhal, Sue was to be deprived of his mother, who died when he was still quite young.

Sue's early education could in no sense be described as successful. A pupil at the Collège Bourbon, he worked erratically and was often in trouble with his teachers. Under constant pressure from his father to espouse the family tradition and become a medical practitioner, the adolescent Sue seems to have preferred drawing and the world of his own imagination. His family background (his father married three times, the last marriage taking place less than a year after the death of Eugène's mother) probably encouraged him to follow current fashion, inspired in part by George Gordon, Lord Byron, and to adopt a skeptical, even cynical, attitude toward life. Such an attitude was to leave its imprint on his juvenilia and is also apparent in *Arthur*.

Despite paternal pressure, Sue abruptly left school in 1821 with no formal qualifications (though he had won a prize for drawing the previous year). The young Eugène, who was much given to practical jokes, embarked on what was to remain a fairly low-level medical career. Working first as a supernumerary in the hospital where his father was such a distinguished practitioner, and later in the provinces when forced to abandon the family home by an exasperated father, he eventually found his way onto several ships of the French navy. According to Bory, he initially had the rank of "chirurgien auxiliaire de troisième classe" (auxiliary surgeon, third class). His voyages were many and varied, including duty on the warship *Breslau* during which he was present at the battle of Navarin (1827). He remained in the service until April 1830 (by which time his father had died), whereupon he returned to Paris after an absence of some seven years.

The next phase of Sue's life has been commented on at length by Dumas *père* and others. This period marks the beginning of his literary career, but it also gave rise to accusations that he was a womanizer, dandy, man-about-town, and spendthrift member of the Jockey Club. While there can be little doubt that he dissipated his inheritance by 1837 and that in so doing he showed a great propensity for elegant living, many of his alleged exploits—recounted in print soon after his death and reiterated uncritically in the twentieth century by such critics as Georges Jarbinet and Bory—have probably been embellished and exaggerated. What is undoubtedly true, however, is that when he turned his attention to prose fiction, Sue drew on his knowledge of the sea and some of the exotic places he had visited during his naval career.

Often credited as being the writer who, following in the footsteps of James Fenimore Cooper, introduced the maritime novel into France, Sue began his career with potboilers. Works such as *Kernok le pirate* (Kernok the Pirate, 1831), *El Gitano* (1831), *Atar-Gull* (1831; translated as *The Negro's Revenge; or, Brulart, the Black Pirate*, 1841), and *La Salamandre* (1832; translated as *The Salamander, a Naval Romance*, 1845) are composed of seafaring tales set in France, Spain, Portugal, Africa, the Azores, the Mediterranean, the West Indies, and India. Strong on violent action, endless vicissitudes, and base acts of piracy and debauch-

ery—but somewhat lacking in stylistic sophistication, psychological penetration, and narrative subtlety—these tales of the sea are best considered as the unoriginal, cynical creations of a young writer strongly influenced by current fashion and in search of a style or manner of his own.

The best known of these tales are *Atar-Gull* and *La Salamandre*. *Atar-Gull* is a story of slavery and revenge. The title character is sold into slavery in Africa before being taken by the pirate-cum-slave trader Brulart to Jamaica, where he works for a certain Tom Wil. Wil falsely accuses Atar-Gull's father of a crime and has him hanged; the remainder of the novel is concerned primarily with revenge. Atar-Gull, posing as a dedicated and trustworthy slave, provokes the horrific murder of his master's daughter by a giant snake, then causes his master to fall into penury through a series of vindictive acts. He reveals the extent of his treachery to the now mute Tom Wil after they have moved to France. Brulart adds an extra dimension to the work: addicted to opium and given to exotic, erotic dreams that he often mistakes for reality, this awesome pirate is finally hanged for a catalogue of heinous crimes. *La Salamandre* (the title refers to a corvette of the French navy) is also a tale of piracy, greed, cynicism, and eroticism, with the added ingredients of shipwrecks and an account of Oriental bliss. Both works are characterized by somewhat tedious and repetitive authorial interventions, by a systematic attempt to reproduce the language of seafarers, and by a singular absence of characters who successfully embody Christian morality.

By this stage in his career, Sue had proven to be a moderately successful man of letters and had even come to the attention of British critics, who recognized him as the chief French exponent of the naval romance. Between 1834 and 1837 he gave much time to his relatively unsuccessful *Histoire de la marine française* (History of the French Navy), a work published in five volumes beginning in November 1835. Despite such a setback, he could claim to be a fairly established, if not first-rate, literary figure. He counted among his acquaintances some of the most distinguished writers of the period: Balzac, Cooper, Charles Nodier, Alphonse de Lamartine, and Alfred de Musset.

At this point in his literary development Sue gave evidence of what was to become an increasingly pronounced feature of his work: the ability to adapt to changing literary fashion (and,

Nineteenth-century pipe bowl in Sue's likeness, attesting to his popularity (Musée Carnavalet)

of conformity to the unity of action, *Latréaumont* incorporates love stories, warfare, and a good deal of historical background before concentrating on a conspiracy, centered in Normandy, which fails badly. This leads to the death of Latréaumont and the arrest of the now ruined and woman-hating de Rohann, who is soon executed. This would not be the last time that Sue, a writer best remembered for his accounts of squalor and deprivation in contemporary France, endeavored to emulate Balzac and other members of his generation by turning to a more remote period of French history.

In marked contrast to *Latréaumont* is Sue's next and, in terms of narrative sophistication, arguably most accomplished novel, the autobiographical, psychological study *Arthur*. With the exception of the last three chapters, the novel appeared in installments in the *Presse* between December 1837 and June 1839. The *roman-feuilleton* (serial novel) was, by this date, beginning to have an effect on the way many French novelists constructed their works, but *Arthur* is not a genuine serial novel for two reasons: it does not appear to have been published in its entirety in installments, and it does not contain a scrics of pcripcteias that allow the writer to end each installment on a note of suspense. This is a technique of which Sue was to give ample evidence later in his career, in particular from the time of publication of *Les Mystères de Paris*.

Arthur is noteworthy for its psychological and autobiographical elements. Reflecting the tensions of the difficult relationship that the novelist had with his own father, the novel contains a clear thematic link with *Les Mystères de Paris*: Rodolphe's abortive attempt at patricide and his subsequent expiation of this much-regretted act are yet another fictional reworking of the traumas of Sue's youth. Sue's inability to form a lasting relationship with a member of the opposite sex is mirrored in the psychology of Arthur, who finds lasting belief in anything or anybody impossible to sustain. The work deserves greatest praise for its technical qualities because it provides a fascinating variation on the confessional style of writing that had so recently been given a new impetus in the work of the Romantics in general and of Musset in particular (*Confession d'un enfant du siècle* [1836; translated as *The Confession of a Child of the Century*, 1892]).

Arthur is composed of a series of first-person narratives, the most important being those of the eponymous hero. Presented as frag-

indeed, to incorporate in his writing his own changing views and outlook) and to modify his narrative style accordingly. This protean nature became apparent when, leaving behind his maritime adventures, Sue turned to French history with the publication of *Latréaumont* (1838; translated as *Latréaumont; or, The Conspiracy*, 1840[?]).

This novel, set during the reign of Louis XIV, delves into courtly intrigue, paints a most unflattering picture of the monarch, and describes scenes of aristocratic hunting. These attributes help to situate the work in a distinctive temporal and spatial setting. The central intrigue has its origins in the tense alliance forged between Latréaumont, a brutal, vice-ridden adventurer (who, like his creator, has squandered his inheritance), and M. de Rohann, a member of an aristocratic family with Protestant sympathies and a former master of the royal hounds, who now finds himself at odds with his king. Typical of Sue's work, with its shifting centers of interest and lack

ments of a journal, but also as retrospective analyses of key phases in his life, Arthur's own accounts draw heavily on the benefits of hindsight. Brought up in a remote country château, the hero is a rich heir who loses his mother during his adolescence. Assured by his misanthropic, dying father that the possession of money and a systematic mistrust of all human feelings constitute the key to life, Arthur finds himself involved in a succession of doomed relationships. Hélène, Mme la marquise de Pénâfiel, Lord Falmouth, and Mme la princesse de Fersen all contribute to the growing cynicism and misanthropy he feels. An adulterous and seemingly idyllic relationship with a young orphan called Marie, who is married to a brigand named Belmont, is brought to a premature end when Arthur, Marie, and their child are shot dead by the incensed husband. The narrative, which contains elements associated with the picaresque novel of the previous century, has a circular structure. The relevant gunshots are heard in the opening chapter, and the murders themselves are revealed in chapter 3. A succession of narrative voices, dominated by that of the hero, takes the reader through a series of separate relationships before returning to the point of departure: Arthur's death.

Arthur is, in the context of Sue's work as a whole, a fairly sophisticated narrative construct. Following the example of Abbé Prévost's *Manon Lescaut* (1731) and Benjamin Constant's *Adolphe* (1816), Sue's psychological study is introduced by a narrative voice extraneous to the main action. This anonymous first-person narrative is supplanted for a short time by that of a priest who had known Arthur in the closing years of his life. The opening of the work is therefore comparable to an exploration of Russian dolls, or of boxes of ever-decreasing size placed one inside the other. As one narrative voice follows another, the reader is taken in stages ever closer to the central narration, that of Arthur himself. The familiar device of the discovery of a manuscript in Arthur's hand does, however, have an unusual slant. The original narrator—who finds the manuscript in a secret compartment of an item of furniture—reveals that it is written in two stages and from two distinctive temporal perspectives. Arthur recounts his own life from the age of twenty: seven years of it are written retrospectively, while five years are related in a form close to that of a diary, which ends on the day before he is shot. The narrative viewpoint is further varied through the intercalation of letters, in differ-

ent handwriting, which are referred to in the text as "les pièces justificatives de ce singulier manuscrit" (the supporting evidence of this remarkable manuscript). The last narrative voice encountered is the same as the first: the discoverer of Arthur's manuscript recounts the fatal shootings at the end.

Such narrative complexity is unusual in the work of Sue, who was then at a prolific stage in his career. One work follows another in quick succession: *Deleytar* (1839; includes *Arabian Godolphin*; translated as *The Godolphin Arabian; or, the History of a Thoroughbred*, 1845), *Le Marquis de Létorière* (1840; translated as *The Marquis de Létorière; or, The Art of Pleasing*, 1844), *Jean Cavalier, ou Les Fanatiques des Cévennes* (1840; translated as *The Protestant Leader*, 1849), *Deux histoires* (Two Stories, 1840; includes *Hercule Hardi* and *Le Colonel de Surville, histoire du temps de l'Empire*; the latter translated as *The Duchesse de Bracciano*, 1850), and *Le Commandeur de Malte* (1841; translated as *The Commander of Malta*, 1846).

The year 1841 saw a significant upswing in the career of this increasingly popular novelist with the publication of *Mathilde* (translated as *Matilde; or, The Memoirs of a Young Woman*, 1843). What Sue had originally intended to be an extended short story became a serial novel, first published in the *Presse* between December 1840 and September 1841, and subsequently in book form between April and October 1841.

Like many of his contemporaries, Sue was by now paid by the column, or even by the line, for works inserted in daily newspapers of the sort that were already exerting a pronounced effect on the manner of composition of contemporary prose fiction. Rival newspapers stood or fell largely as a result of their ability to publish in daily installments works of fiction that were capable of attracting and retaining a large and increasingly lower-middle-class or working-class readership. In all likelihood, as in the case of his later serial novels, Sue had not finished—nor indeed worked out the development and ending of— *Mathilde* when publication was begun in the *Presse*.

The ramifications of this new mode of publication included increased emphasis on action and high drama; democratization and popularization of themes, characters, settings, and language; inclusion of a fairy-tale element; and structuring of each episode to end in a climax or moment of suspense. These are the hallmarks of what rapidly became almost a new literary genre. *Mathilde* does not have all of these ingredients in profusion, but it is a transitional, even pivotal, work in the career of Sue. Not only was it first published in serial form, but it also contains clear indications as to the direction Sue's writing was to take, even before his political conversion.

Mathilde is a young, rich, and beautiful noblewoman who is orphaned by the age of four and brought up by her aunt, the cruel and detestable Mlle de Maran. Uncorrupted by this perverse influence, Mathilde seems well suited to the rich Abel de Rochegune, who is deeply in love with her, but she is instead introduced by her aunt to the apparently suitable, but in reality debased, Gontran de Lancry. Naively believing that she loves Gontran, Mathilde marries him at the age of eighteen, only to discover her error soon afterward, when he leaves her for a life of debauchery in Paris.

Mathilde comes to realize that she loves M. de Rochegune. Bound by the ties of marriage, she resolves to seek a legal separation. But on discovering that Emma, the daughter of her best friend, is desperately in love with M. de Rochegune and is quite literally pining away, Mathilde sacrifices her feelings and arranges their marriage. She subsequently has to endure much suffering and hardship. She returns to her now impoverished husband, and he tries to sell her as a slave to his enemy M. de Lugarto, the embodiment of evil. After many vicissitudes Gontran is killed in a duel, and M. de Rochegune is widowed. This convenient turn of events allows the author to contrive a happy ending—a crucial ingredient of the fairy tale—for, after a suitable period of time has elapsed, M. de Rochegune finally marries Mathilde. A work that demonstrates the unacceptability of the laws governing marriage therefore ends with an assurance of idyllic wedlock.

Mathilde is not without interest both from a technical and a thematic point of view. As in the case of Arthur, the central narrative is placed inside a frame. The introductory narrative is composed of some sixty pages, the epilogue, of some fifty or so; the central section, which totals some fourteen hundred pages, comprises the memoirs of the heroine. No effort is made to identify the original narrator or to explain how he came to be in possession of the memoirs. Mathilde's memoirs are addressed to M. de Rochegune. The reader therefore assumes the role of this man who is to discover, through his own reading of

Mathilde's account of her life, the true feelings of the woman he loves.

The novel contains the moments of suspense and the sudden changes of fortune that are typical of the roman-feuilleton. It can also be viewed as a much-expanded version of the Cinderella story, as the critic Brynja Svane has pointed out. Also typical of the serial novel are Sue's use of the enigma or mystery, his frequent recourse to contrasts of setting, and his introduction of low-life characters alongside aristocratic ones.

Thematically, the novel prefigures some of the central strands of Les Mystères de Paris. In its treatment of love and an unhappy marriage, and in particular in its handling of the role of women, Mathilde anticipates the more overtly didactic utterances that the author was to make in his most celebrated novel. Sue took an increasing interest, particularly after his political conversion, in the lot of poor, sick, and unhappily married women, and there seems little doubt that Mathilde won for him a faithful audience of female readers.

The success of Mathilde added to Sue's growing reputation in France. This did not go unnoticed among British critics, one of whom had major misgivings about the work but described it nonetheless as "the most popular book of the season, the most universally read, and not undeservedly so." What was about to happen, however, would turn a successful career into one of complete triumph.

Sue had made the acquaintance of the revolutionary, social reformer, and playwright Félix Pyat (1810-1899) through the publisher Charles Ladvocat, and the two men were to collaborate on the stage version of Mathilde, which premiered on 24 September 1842. On 25 May 1841, when Sue went to the Porte-Saint-Martin for the premiere of Pyat's play Les Deux Serruriers (The Two Locksmiths), he found the opportunity to renew an old acquaintance. Pyat was evidently keen on familiarizing the novelist with what were at this juncture, for Sue, the unsuspected, admirable qualities of the urban poor. He therefore invited the author of Arthur to the house of an erudite workman named Fugères the following day. Spellbound by the literary insights and more particularly by the sociopolitical analysis of this workman, Sue listened with growing admiration to the lucid and cogent articulation of socialist ideas given by Fugères over dinner. As a result of this enlightening experience, according to his biographer Bory, Sue declared, "Je suis socialiste!" (I am a socialist!). Sue now needed little encouragement from Pyat to turn, in his works of fiction, from the aristocracy and the bourgeoisie to the lower echelons of society, in particular the working and criminal classes. The seeds of his most celebrated novel, *Les Mystères de Paris*, were sown by this dramatic experience in the home of a workman and by Sue's own growing rejection of the traditional values of the aristocracy and the mercenary attitudes of the socially dominant bourgeoisie. The dandy, man-about-town, and horse-racing enthusiast was now to turn his attention to the lowest strata of the Parisian underworld.

L'Aventurier ou la Barbe-Bleue (translated as *The Female Bluebeard; or, The Adventurer*, 1845; retitled *Le Morne-au-diable, ou L'aventurier* when published in book form in 1845), *Thérèse Dunoyer* (translated as *Therese Dunoyer*, 1843), and *Paula Monti, ou l'Hôtel Lambert* (translated as *Paula Monti; or, The Hôtel Lambert*, 1845) were all published in the press between November 1841 and July 1842. *Les Mystères de Paris* first appeared in the *Journal des Débats* between June 1842 and October 1843; it was published in book form by Charles Gosselin between September 1842 and December 1843.

The sales figures for *Les Mystères de Paris*—though incomplete and approximate—are most revealing. Between the publication date of the original Gosselin edition and the year 1880, some twenty-six French language editions appeared. If the average print run was 5,000 copies, then about 60,000 copies were sold within two years of the original publication. Sales figures for the *Journal des Débats* rose dramatically during publication of the serialized version of *Les Mystères*, and these probably reached between 20,000 and 25,000 subscribers before publication of the serial ended. Although it is impossible to calculate precisely the size of the reading public, three factors ensured that each copy of the novel reached a large audience: the widespread habit of two, three, or even five people sharing the purchase price of a book (still relatively expensive at the time); the growing accessibility of the serialized version of the novel in the flourishing *cabinets de lecture* (reading rooms); and public readings of the work in cafés, workshops, and other social venues. Pierre Orecchioni has estimated that *Les Mystères* was read or heard by 400,000 to 800,000 of the author's compatriots. This is an impressive figure because the country's total population at the time was about thirty-five million.

Les Mystères de Paris is a long, polycentric work that is didactic in tone and even proselytizing in its intentions. Set initially in la Cité—an insalubrious quarter of Paris whose narrow, winding streets house many of the capital's undesirables and criminal classes—the novel moves to a farm (Bouqueval), to a variety of provincial locations, and even to the principality of Gérolstein. Paris, however, remains the focal point of the work, but rather than the *faubourg* (suburb) Saint-Germain and the haunts of the aristocracy, it is the *tapis-franc* (low-life tavern), the rue du Temple, and the homes and seedy abodes of the underprivileged, of honest artisans, of prostitutes, and, above all, of the criminal classes that form the epicenter of what is essentially a socially explosive, proletarian novel.

Some of the main themes are foreshadowed in Sue's earlier works. The central character, Rodolphe, as he is known in his disguise as a workman who paints fans, passes under the name of comte de Duren in the aristocratic circles of Paris, but in reality is none other than the fabulously rich German prince Rodolphe of Gérolstein. A slim, athletic figure endowed with Herculean strength, Rodolphe emerges as the incarnation of Providence, a high-principled avenging angel who dispenses his own brand of justice to the detriment of all that is evil. He gives succor to the oppressed and the socially disadvantaged in an attempt to expiate the "crime" of drawing his sword on his father.

Mathilde and *Arthur* offer the most obvious prefigurations of the main themes. Rodolphe, like Arthur, is at odds with his father and has fallen in love with the unhappily married Clémence d'Harville. Sue thereby creates another opportunity to expatiate on the plight of unhappily married women and on the least acceptable aspects of the laws governing marriage in contemporary French society. Rodolphe ultimately finds marital happiness but only after the death of his wife, the treacherous Sarah, and the suicide of the epileptic young husband of Clémence. This happiness is, however, marred by the death of Rodolphe's long-lost daughter, who has been brought up in squalor and is finally unable to accept the life of luxury offered her. Her death reminds her father of his "crime" and leads him to question the ultimate worth of his expiatory zeal.

This thematic, if somewhat skeletal, summary of *Les Mystères de Paris* establishes clear links with Sue's earlier novels but does little to indicate the nature and scope of the truly socialist and pro-

Caricature of Sue in 1850, when he was a socialist candidate for the legislature

letarian aspects of the work. The most memorable characters—in addition to Rodolphe and his long-lost daughter, the redeemed prostitute known both as La Goualeuse and Fleur-de-Marie—are those who belong to the criminal and working classes of low-life Paris. Le Chourineur, a sympathetic but pathological criminal whose prowess with a knife is the origin of his sobriquet; La Chouette, a one-eyed, hook-nosed, wily, sadistic predator; Le Maître d'école, a hideous but knowledgeable character who is endowed with more intelligence than his underworld confederates; Tortillard, a heartless individual whose name has passed into popular speech, meaning a deformed cripple; Rigolette, le Squelette, and le Gros-Boîteux: these are the base characters who enthralled such a large reading public and whose language Sue examined at some length and to no little effect.

Sue described his aims in portraying the hidden realities of life in the slums and prisons of Paris: "Notre unique espoir est d'appeler l'attention des penseurs et des gens de bien sur de grandes misères sociales" (Our sole hope is that we will draw the attention of thinkers and of honest folk to some of the great afflictions of society). Sue was without doubt advocating sociopolitical reforms and propagating utopian and socialist ideas. Seeing in philanthropy and charity the key to a better future for the urban poor and criminal classes, the novelist criticizes a society that drives women to prostitution, men to crime, first-time offenders to recidivism as a result of a stay in prison, and unhappily married wives to distraction because of antiquated civil laws that preclude divorce.

Believing strongly in the notion of the noble poor, Sue follows in the steps of the utopian socialists of the period (the Saint-Simonians and Fourierists, for example) and portrays a model farm where workers are encouraged to improve their assiduity and increase their moral probity in an atmosphere of healthy competition. This reformist element, together with the providential interventions of the avenging angel Rodolphe, seems to have captivated readers from different strata of contemporary French society. Sue became something of a national celebrity and was seen as the new champion of the oppressed and underprivileged.

His next novel, *Le Juif errant* (1844-1845; translated as *The Wandering Jew*, 1844-1845), was also extremely successful. Published in serial form in the *Constitutionnel*, it increased the sales figures of the ailing paper from thirty-six hundred in June 1844 to about twenty-five thousand by July 1845. *Le Juif errant* is another long, polycentric work, but in addition to its socialist themes, it has a strong anticlerical dimension. It presents a forceful, systematic indictment of the Jesuits, who are accused of adopting thoroughly unscrupulous means of self-enrichment and of justifying, in their writings, theft, adultery, rape, and murder.

The legend of the Wandering Jew, Ahasvérus, is at the heart of the complex narrative, which is characterized by a seemingly endless stream of coincidences and chance meetings. The descendants of this cobbler—condemned by Christ to wander throughout eternity for having refused him water on his journey to Golgatha—all have a medal inviting them to a meeting in Paris where they are to receive their inheritance. This meeting had been arranged 150 years earlier by their ancestor Marius de Rennepont. A Protestant, Marius had been persecuted by the Jesuits but had nonetheless managed to invest fifty thousand écus in gold before being condemned to the galleys. It is the huge fortune resulting from this investment that is to be passed on to the rightful heirs.

The novel concentrates in turn on each of Marius's surviving descendants: the minors Rose and Blanche Simon, the manufacturer François Hardy, Prince Djalma, the artisan Jacques Rennepont, Adrienne de Cardoville (daughter of the comte de Rennepont), and the Christlike priest Gabriel Rennepont. The Rennepont family, persecuted by the Jesuits in a succession of horrific events worthy of the *roman noir* (Gothic novel), is finally exterminated. The family fortune is, however, prevented from falling into the hands of the Jesuits, and the Wandering Jew is ultimately redeemed through the death of his progeny.

The tone of *Le Juif errant* remains fundamentally reformist. Sue's paternalistic diagnosis of contemporary society identifies inadequate salaries as the root cause of the corruption and moral impoverishment of the poor and underprivileged. Maintaining a Saint-Simonian or Fourierist posture, but denying that what he describes is utopian, Sue examines the model factory of François Hardy with its associated living quarters for the workers. The novelist insists on the need for healthy working and living conditions for those who form the lowest strata of society and also calls for drastic improvements in the social and legal status of women. All of these reforms should be bolstered by improved education and carried out in a spirit of community and fraternity.

By the time of the publication of *Le Juif errant*, Sue's career had reached its peak. Other works followed (*Martin l'enfant trouvé* [1846-1847; translated as *Martin, the Foundling; or, The Adventures of a Valet-de-chambre*, 1847] and *Les Sept Péchés capitaux* [The Seven Deadly Sins, 1848-1851]), but the novelist's career underwent a dramatic transformation as a result of the political events of 1848. For Sue, the February Revolution seemed to herald the dawn of a new age, and he became an increasingly popular public figure, so much so that in the elections of 1850 he was pressured into standing as a socialist candidate. He was elected by a handsome majority as the deputy for the Department of La Seine.

Sue's new career, however, did little if anything to enhance his reputation: he showed no stomach for public debate and was much criticized for correcting the proofs of his works when the chamber was in session. He even did nothing to stop the passage of the *loi Riancey* (Riancey law), which sounded the death knell of the serial novel. After the coup d'état of 2 December 1851, and as a result of his political views, he was imprisoned for a short time. Although taken off the list of proscribed citizens through the intervention of the future Napoleon III, Sue preferred to seek exile in Savoy (not a French territory at the time), and he set up home in Annecy in January 1852. He died there on 3 August 1857 and was buried in the local cemetery.

During the final, political phase of Sue's career his writings reveal an insurrectionist stance, particularly in *Les Mystères du peuple ou Histoire d'une famille de prolétaires à travers les âges* (1849-1857; translated as *Mysteries of the People; or, The Story of a Plebeian Family for 2,000 Years*, 1867). In reality a series of novels, *Les Mystères du peuple* traces the origins and lineage of the Lebrenn family from 57 B.C. forward to the central plot, which begins in Paris in 1848. The paternalism of the earlier socialist works is finally eradicated; sympathetic aristocrats no longer have a positive role to play in Sue's fiction. While the novelist still refused to take up a position alongside out-and-out extremists, he now believed that only revolt or insurrection could bring about the reforms that he had advocated since *Les Mystères de Paris*. The former dandy and man-about-town—who in his youth had written with a predominantly aristocratic audience in mind—had finally moved beyond feelings of mere sympathy and pity for the victims of urbanization and industrialization to a position where, on paper if not in deed, he felt impelled to prescribe a more radical cure for the ills he perceived in French society.

Bibliographies:

René Guise, "Bibliographie chronologique d'Eugène Sue," *Europe*, 643-644 (November-December 1982): 167-180;

Brynja Svane, *Bibliographie des œuvres d'Eugène Sue. Le Monde d'Eugène Sue I* (Copenhagen: Akademisk Forlag, 1986).

Biographies:

Alexandre Dumas, *Mes Mémoires* (Paris: A. Cadot, 1852-1854);

Eugène de Mirecourt, *Les Contemporains: Eugène Sue*, in *Portraits contemporains* (Paris: Fayard, 1857);

Dumas, *Les Morts vont vite* (Paris: Michel Lévy, 1861);

Ernest Legouvé, *Soixante ans de souvenirs* (Paris: Hetzel, 1886);

Paul Ginisty, *Eugène Sue* (Paris: Berger-Levrault, 1929);

Pierre Valléry-Radot, *Chirurgiens d'autrefois. La Famille d'Eugène Sue* (Paris: R.-G. Ricou & Ocia, 1944);

Jean-Louis Bory, *Eugène Sue, le roi du roman populaire* (Paris: Hachette, 1962); republished as *Eugène Sue, dandy mais socialiste* (Paris: Hachette, 1973); republished as *Eugène Sue* (Paris: Hachette, 1979).

References:

Marc Angenot, "Roman et idéologie: *Les Mystères de Paris*," in his *Le Roman populaire* (Montreal: Presses de l'Université du Québec, 1975);

Nora Atkinson, *Eugène Sue et le roman-feuilleton* (Nemours: Lesot, 1929);

Jean-Louis Bachellier, "Le Sujet de la représentation—*Les Mystères de Paris* d'Eugène Sue" (Paris: Thèse de troisième cycle, 1977);

Roger Bellet, "Le Saltimbanque et l'instituteur dans *Les Misères des enfants trouvés*," *Europe*, 643-644 (November-December 1982): 78-91;

Roger Bozzetto, "Eugène Sue et le fantastique," *Europe*, 643-644 (November-December 1982): 101-110;

Emilien Carassus, "Le Mirliflore, le romancier et le socialiste," *Europe*, 643-644 (November-December 1982): 17-30;

Pierre Chaunu, *Eugène Sue et la Seconde République* (Paris: Collection du centenaire de la Révolution de 1848, 1948);

Jean-Paul Colin, "La Marquise n'est pas sortie ou L'Ecriture de la paresse chez Eugène Sue," *Europe*, 643-644 (November-December 1982): 92-101;

Dominique Desanti, "Sorcières et saintes, Sade et Sue," in Sue's *Les Mystères du peuple*, volume 2, edited by Régine Deforges (Paris: Régine Deforges, 1978), pp. i-x;

Liliane Durand-Dessert, "Avant-propos," in Sue's *Les Mystères du peuple*, volume 1, edited by Deforges (Paris: Régine Deforges, 1977), pp. v-xviii;

Umberto Eco, "Rhetoric and Ideology in Sue's *Les Mystères de Paris*," in his *The Role of the Reader* (Bloomington: Indiana University Press, 1979);

René Guise, "Les Débuts littéraires d'Eugène Sue," *Europe*, 643-644 (November-December 1982): 6-16;

Guise, "*Les Mystères de Paris*. Histoire d'un texte: légende et vérité," *Le Bulletin du Bibliophile* (1982): 358-374;

Guise, "Le Phénomène du roman-feuilleton 1828-1848. La crise de croissance du roman," Thèse d'état (Nancy, 1975—microfiches);

Georges Jarbinet, *"Les Mystères de Paris" d'Eugène Sue* (Paris: Société française d'éditions littéraires et techniques, Malfère, 1932);

Edgar Knecht, "Le Juif errant, éléments d'un mythe populaire," *Romantisme*, 9 (1975): 84-96;

Knecht, *Le Mythe du Juif errant* (Grenoble: Presses Universitaires de Grenoble, 1977);

Louise Fiber Luce, "The Masked Avenger: Historical Analogue in Eugène Sue's *Les Mystères de Paris*," *French Forum*, 1 (September 1976): 227-237;

Patrick Maurus, "Eugène Sue ou l'écriture référentielle," *Europe*, 643-644 (November-December 1982): 67-77;

Pierre Michel, "Sex-Pol Sue. Femmes et révolution dans *Les Mystères du peuple*," *Europe*, 643-644 (November-December 1982): 127-137;

John Moody, *Les Idées sociales d'Eugène Sue* (Paris: Presses Universitaires de France, 1938);

Michel Nathan, "Délinquence et réformisme dans *Les Mystères de Paris*," in *Paris au XIXᵉ siècle. Aspects d'un mythe littéraire*, edited by Roger Bellet (Lyons: Presses Universitaires de Lyon, 1984);

Nathan, "Socialisme cosmique et métaphysique du feuilleton," *Europe*, 643-644 (November-December 1982): 120-125;

Yves Olivier-Martin, "Structures de la fiction policière," *Europe*, 643-644 (November-December 1982): 47-55;

Pierre Orecchioni, "Eugène Sue, mesure d'un succès," *Europe*, 643-644 (November-December 1982): 157-166;

Ian Pickup, "Elements of Balzacian Portraiture in the Novels of Eugène Sue before *Les Mystères de Paris*," *Nottingham French Studies*, 26 (October 1987): 34-45;

Pickup, "The Language of Crime in Sue's *Les Mystères de Paris*," *Degré Second*, 1 (July 1977): 139-163;

Roger Ripoll, "Du roman-feuilleton au théâtre," *Europe*, 643-644 (November-December 1982): 148-156;

Ripoll, "Eugène Sue," *Europe*, 643-644 (November-December 1982): 3-5;

Charles-Augustin Sainte-Beuve, *Chroniques parisiennes* (Paris: C. Lévy, 1876);

Sainte-Beuve, "Eugène Sue," *Revue des Deux Mondes*, 15 September 1840, pp. 660-675;

Sainte-Beuve, *Portraits contemporains*, 3 volumes (Paris: Didier, 1846);

Brynja Svane, "Divertir et politiser. Le jeu du double discours dans *Le Juif errant*," *Europe*, 643-644 (November-December 1982): 56-66;

Svane, *Les Lecteurs d'Eugène Sue. Le Monde d'Eugène Sue II* (Copenhagen: Akademisk Forlag, 1986);

Svane, *Si les riches savaient! Le Monde d'Eugène Sue III* (Copenhagen: Akademisk Forlag, 1988);

Svane, "Structures narratives et tendances idéologiques: Une étude d'Eugène Sue: *Mathilde*," in *Actes du VIIIᵉ Congrès des Romanistes Scandinaves* (Odense, Denmark: Odense University Press, 1983), pp. 341-349;

Nils Evert Taube, *Etude sur l'emploi de l'argot des malfaiteurs chez les auteurs romantiques* (Uppsala, Sweden: Appelbergs Boktryckeri A.-B., 1917);

Anne-Marie Thiesse, "Ecrivain/public(s): les mystères de la communication littéraire," *Europe*, 643-644 (November-December 1982): 36-46;

Thiesse, "L'Education sociale d'un romancier—le cas d'Eugène Sue," *Actes de la Recherche en Sciences Sociales*, 32-33 (April-June 1980): 51-63;

L. Thoorens, "Mystères et Paris d'Eugène Sue," *Revue Générale Belge*, 93 (August 1957): 94-104;

Jean-Claude Vareille, "Il était une fois ou l'héritage impossible," *Europe*, 643-644 (November-December 1982): 111-119;

John S. Wood, "Les Maux de l'époque: Sue," in his *Sondages, 1830-48: Romanciers français secondaires* (Toronto: University of Toronto Press, 1965);

Wood, "Situation des *Mystères de Paris*," *Europe*, 643-644 (November-December 1982): 31-36.

Papers:

Most of Sue's manuscripts are in private collections. His letters to Honoré de Balzac are at the Bibliothèque Spoelberch de Lovenjoul, Chantilly.

Alfred de Vigny

(27 March 1797 - 17 September 1863)

Robert T. Denommé
University of Virginia

BOOKS: *Poèmes*, anonymous (Paris: Pelicier, 1822); enlarged as *Poèmes antiques et modernes* (Paris: Urbain Canel, 1826);

Eloa, ou la sœur des anges, mystère (Paris: Boulland, 1824);

Cinq-Mars, ou une conspiration sous Louis XIII, 2 volumes (Paris: Urbain Canel, 1826); translated by William Hazlitt as *Cinq-Mars: A Conspiracy under Louis XIII* (London: D. Bogue, 1847);

Othello, ou le More de Venise (Paris: Levavasseur, 1830);

La Maréchale d'Ancre (Paris: Gosselin, Barba, 1831);

Stello: Les consultations du Docteur-Noir (Paris: Gosselin, 1832); translated by Irving Massey as *Stello: A Session with Doctor Noir* (Montreal: McGill University Press, 1963);

Discours prononcés dans la séance publique tenue par l'Académie française pour la réception de M. le comte Alfred de Vigny, le 26 janvier 1846 (Paris: Didot, 1846);

Chatterton (Paris: Souverain, 1835); translated by Hazlitt as *Chatterton* (London: D. Bogue, 1847);

Servitude et grandeur militaires (Paris: Bonnaire et Magen, 1835); translated by F. W. Huard as *Military Servitude and Grandeur* (New York: Doran, 1919);

Les Destinées (Paris: Michel Lévy frères, 1864);

Journal d'un poète, edited by Louis Ratisbonne (Paris: Michel Lévy, 1867);

Daphné, edited by Fernand Gregh (Paris: Delagrave, 1913);

Mémoires inédits, fragments et projets, edited by Jean Sangnier (Paris: Gallimard, 1958).

Collections: *Œuvres complètes*, 8 volumes, edited by Fernand Baldensperger (Paris: Conard, 1914-1935);

Œuvres complètes, 2 volumes, edited by Baldensperger (Paris: Gallimard, Bibliothèque de la Pléiade, 1948);

Œuvres complètes, edited by Paul Viallaneix (Paris: Editions du Seuil, 1965);

Alfred de Vigny, circa 1854 (photograph by Nadar)

Œuvres complètes, edited by François Germain and André Jarry (Paris: Gallimard, Bibliothèque de la Pléiade, 1986).

PLAY PRODUCTIONS: *Le More de Venise*, Paris, Comédie Française, 24 October 1829;

La Maréchale d'Ancre, Paris, Odéon, 25 June 1831;

Chatterton, Paris, Comédie Française, 12 February 1835.

Alfred de Vigny strikes many readers as the least effusive and most reserved of the French Romantic writers. Unlike such counterparts as Alphonse de Lamartine and Victor Hugo, who boldly asserted their confidence as they set out to define the ideals of postrevolutionary France in their writings, Vigny resorted to the utilization of symbols to disguise his ambivalent feelings and changing attitudes concerning the predicament of the individual. His apparent reticence proceeded from a hesitation to commit himself wholeheartedly to the resolution of specific problems that beset French society during the Bourbon Restoration (1815-1830), the regime of Louis-Philippe (1830-1848), and the first decade of the Second Empire (1852-1861).

Vigny's evolution from the pessimistic posture of his earlier years to the cautious and qualified optimism expressed in the posthumously published *Les Destinées* (The Fates, 1864) resulted from his unflagging reflection on the human situation. His attitude stemmed from his own interpretation of history and his observations of reality. He affirmed in an 1835 entry in *Journal d'un poète* (Diary of a Poet, 1867): "Il est certain que la Création est une œuvre manquée ou à demi accomplie, et marchant vers sa perfection à grand'peine" (It is certain that the work of Creation has been badly botched; it remains half-done: it evolves so slowly and painfully toward perfection).

Vigny's oscillations emanated from the combination of unfortunate events in his personal life and of external circumstances that compelled him to adjust his identity as an aristocrat in a bourgeois society. His dilemma was that of a man torn between values linked to an extinguished past and values being shaped by conditions of his own day. By and large, he attempted to clarify his ideas and attitudes concerning existence through the intermediary of legendary, biblical, and historical personalities in his novels, plays, and poems. If such figures as Moses, Jesus, and Cinq-Mars serve as concretizations of specific points of view in his work, they are also used as convenient camouflages for the expression of his own emotions.

As a conscious technician, Vigny sought out the philosophical dimension of his own experience before transposing it in his writing. The personal ingredient in such implications, however, is the key to his identity as a Romantic writer. As manifestations of his ideas, the symbols often resorted to in his fiction and poetry would not always be identified clearly with the viewpoints that are developed. Vigny's deliberate distortions and anachronisms expose his need to adjust the symbols he employs in order to have them conform more readily to his own conceptions. Thus, the symbolic elements in his legendary, biblical, and historical figures sometimes constitute little more than flimsy disguises for his own attitudes. The study of Vigny's accomplishment, then, becomes the examination of the manner in which he conferred the imprint of his own personality on works that he complicated with symbolic meanings.

Alfred-Victor de Vigny was born on 27 March 1797 in Loches (southern Touraine) of aristocratic parents. His father, sixty years old at the time of his son's birth, was a retired captain and a wounded veteran of the Seven Years' War. Vigny's mother, twenty years younger than her husband, took complete charge of her only surviving child's early education in the apartment they occupied in the requisitioned palace of the Elysée-Bourbon in Paris from 1799 to 1804. His father stirred his imagination with tales of his military exploits. At the age of ten, Vigny enrolled as a day student in Monsieur Hix's boarding school, where he confronted classmates who taunted him for the particle *de* placed before his name. His parents impressed upon him the need for developing and preserving a feudal and moral sense of honor. The boy enjoyed listening to the elegant conversations of his parents and their friends, in which the glorious past was recollected and contrasted with the ignominy of their present situation.

Between 1811 and 1813, Vigny attended the lycée Bonaparte (today Condorcet), where he encountered the hostility of classmates but where he also distinguished himself at his studies. Since he excelled at mathematics, he decided to seek admission to the Ecole Polytechnique. Spurred on by the tales of his father's military exploits as well as by the excitement of the Napoleonic conquests, he opted for the career of a military officer in the imperial army. But when Napoleon's army was defeated by the European coalition and when the Bourbons returned to power, it was no longer necessary for him to attend the Ecole Polytechnique to realize his ambition. His mother obtained a commission for him in the king's royal guard in July 1814. But the seventeen-year-old second lieutenant experienced quick disillusionment with his army career. Vigny's first assignment in March 1815 was to escort Louis XVIII to Ghent, when Napoleon returned from Elba to France for the Hundred Days. After the return of the Bourbons in 1815, Vigny was transferred to the sixth regiment of the Royal Guard. From March 1816 through June 1823, he experienced the boredom and monotony associated with barrack living in a peacetime army. While stationed at such posts as Vincennes, Amiens, Versailles, Courbevoie, Rouen, Orléans, and Strasbourg, he read widely in literature, the Scriptures, and mathematics to fill the many hours of leisure at his disposal.

In 1820 Vigny renewed his friendship with Emile Deschamps, then an employee in the Ministry of Finance. He had played with Deschamps as a child when the two lived in the Elysée-Bourbon. Deschamps introduced Vigny to Victor Hugo, who had just founded the legitimist journal *Conservateur Littéraire*. Hugo immediately invited Vigny to become a contributor. Behind the virtual anonymity of his initials, Vigny published a highly favorable essay on Amédée Pichot's translation of the complete works of George Gordon, Lord Byron in the December 1820 issue of the journal. His essay focused in approving terms on Byron's articulate disdain of the present and his dire predictions for the future. Byron's frame of mind coincided closely with Vigny's in 1820. The same issue of the *Conservateur* also contained Vigny's poem "Le Bal" (The Ball), a variation on the carpe-diem theme and an imitation of the abbé Jacques Delille's strophic lyricism.

Hugo paid handsome tribute to Vigny's abilities as a poet. This constituted just the kind of encouragement he needed to switch to a career in writing. Moreover, Hugo's own resolve to rejuvenate the French lyric and to restore it to its primitive vigor corresponded to Vigny's own need to reconcile oppositions between the past and the present. Vigny began to attend meetings at the literary salon of Virginie Ancelot at the Hôtel de La Rochefoucauld in Paris, and later, when he was stationed in Rouen, those of Pierre Baour Lormian, where in 1821 he read two of his poems, "La Fille de Jephté" (Jephta's Daughter) and "La Somnambule" (The Sleepwalker).

Jacques and Virginie Ancelot took an immediate liking to Vigny and struck up a lasting friendship with him. Indeed, Vigny bequeathed his estate to their daughter, Louise-Edmée, who was born at the time he frequented their drawing room in Paris. It was also there that he met the poet Delphine Gay, who fell in love with the dashing military officer. Delphine's mother, Sophie Gay, devoted much energy to bringing the two young poets closer together. It is not known conclusively whether Vigny returned Delphine's affection. At any rate, Mme de Vigny forbade her son to marry for love alone and quickly discouraged his relationship with the young woman who was no better off, financially, than he.

In March 1822 Vigny published anonymously his first collection of verse, *Poèmes*, which attracted little attention. It consists of three cantos of "Héléna" followed by three groups of poems: "Poèmes antiques" (poems of antiquity), "Poèmes judaïques" (Judaic poems), and "Poèmes modernes" (modern poems). Vigny reworked several of these pieces and added six others to fit under slightly modified divisions for the definitive edition of 1826, published as *Poèmes antiques et modernes* (Ancient and Modern Poems).

News of French intervention in the Spanish war to ensure Ferdinand VII's return to the throne bolstered Vigny's spirits toward the end of 1822. Vigny, along with his regiment at Strasbourg, left for southwestern France in May 1823. While waiting, presumably, to cross the Pyrenees into Spain, he began work on a major project, "Eloa." He frequented the literary salon of Mme Paul Nairac, where he met Edmond Géraud, editor of a regional journal and unofficial head of the Bordeaux literati. Rumor of Vigny's alleged affair with Delphine Gay reached the southwestern city through the intermediary of Marceline Desbordes-Valmore, a poet of elegies and romances, who corresponded with Delphine's mother. The audience to whom the young officer read sections of his poem "Eloa" was impressed by his wit and demeanor. In December 1823 Vigny and his regiment were ordered to the province of Béarn instead of Spain, dashing all his hopes for a more glorious military career.

During his sojourn in the Béarn region, he completed the outline for his first historical novel, *Cinq-Mars* (1826). During this period, Vigny began to take frequent leaves without pay from the military. The leisure he enjoyed enabled him to complete his first major poem for publication. *Eloa, ou la sœur des anges* (Eloa, or Sister of the Angels, 1824) is an epic verse comprised of three cantos that relate how a young virgin, transformed into an angel by a tear shed by Christ over the death of Lazarus, attempts to redeem the fallen Lucifer. The 778-line poem concentrates on the themes of the beauty and nobility of human pity. Substantively inspired by John Milton's *Paradise Lost* (1667), *Eloa* also owes much to sections of François-René de Chateaubriand's *Génie du christianisme* (1802; translated as *The Genius of Christianity*, 1802). Vigny's characterization of Lucifer as comforter to mankind rather than as seducer recalls Byron's Lucifer in *Cain* (1821).

Critical reaction to *Eloa* was, on the whole, approving and even enthusiastic. Hugo's dithyrambic review in the *Muse Française* led the way: Vigny's career as a poet seemed to be on the rise.

In June 1824 Vigny rejoined his regiment at Bayonne and was subsequently given an assignment to Pau, where he met a young English woman, Lydia Bunbury, with whom he fell in love. After some maneuvering, he obtained Sir Hugh Bunbury's grudging consent to marry his daughter. But the marriage would eventually prove disappointing, for Lydia adapted poorly to married life; she grew obese after two miscarriages, became noticeably awkward, spoke very little French, and understood nothing of her husband's poetry. This caused Vigny to distance himself somewhat from Hugo and Deschamps as well as other friends he had frequented. Eventually, many took the poet's outer reserve for pretension and aloofness. In April 1825 Vigny requested extended military leave, thus, for all practical purposes, bringing his career as a soldier to an end.

After settling in Paris, Vigny gathered the poems he associated with his military experience into the volume *Poèmes antiques et modernes*. The collection included the verse published in 1822, with the exception of "Héléna," and the addition of six new poems. He assigned his pieces to three rubrics: "Livre mystique" (the mystical book), "Livre antique" (the book of antiquity), and "Livre moderne" (the modern book). His main purpose was to present philosophical ideas in short poems that assumed either an epic or dramatic dimension. He described the conception behind *Poèmes antiques et modernes* in an entry in his *Journal*: "Concevoir et méditer une pensée philosophique; trouver dans les actions humaines celle qui en est la plus évidente *preuve*" (Conceive an idea, meditate on a philosophical thought, then find in the history of human behavior that which will stand as the most evident *proof*).

Vigny's originality in *Poèmes antiques et modernes* stems from the way he employs fables and anecdotes to convey philosophically individual confrontations with destiny. Each poem underscores some important aspect of the human situation through the symbolic use of a fable or an anecdote. In "Moïse" (Moses) and "Le Déluge," to mention but the best-known pieces, the anecdotal ingredients are virtually overwhelmed by the intensity with which moral and metaphysical issues are introduced into the fabric of the poems. "Moïse," which is placed in the mystical book,

emerges clearly as the masterpiece of the collection. The poem succeeds handsomely in equating the biblical figure's predicament with that of the poet himself.

Vigny alters considerably the Moses of Exodus and the Book of Numbers to have him conform to his own negative conception of divine election. The Moses of his poem, unloved and misunderstood by men, offers psychological resistance to the will of God and bemoans the despair he experiences as a prophet. To be sure, the sentiment of despair evoked in "Moïse" is not to be found in the scriptural account but rather bespeaks the sentiment known as the *mal du siècle*, the complaint of dissatisfaction voiced by superior individuals in postrevolutionary society. The prophet's only solace is likened to the poet's: the work bequeathed by each will be acknowledged and appreciated only by posterity. The collection of poems elicited mixed popular and critical reaction. Whatever else, *Poèmes antiques et modernes* attested to the significant accomplishment of a poet whose verse was intricately linked to the mood and tenor of the new civilization being fashioned in the aftermath of the French Revolution.

From 1826 to 1830, Vigny resided in Paris, where he frequented the literary *cénacle* of Charles Nodier, whom he had met in 1823. In 1826 discussion centered on the historical novel and drama as genres susceptible of winning popular support in the Romanticists' campaign to reform and rejuvenate French literature. Vigny articulated his own ambitions concerning the historical novel in his *Journal*: "J'avais le désir de faire une suite de romans historiques qui seraient comme l'épopée de la noblesse, et dont *Cinq-Mars* était le commencement" (I wanted to write a series of historical novels that would be like the epic of the noble class, and of which *Cinq-Mars* marks the beginning). He finished only *Cinq-Mars, ou une conspiration sous Louis XIII* (1826; translated as *Cinq-Mars: A Conspiracy under Louis XIII*, 1847).

Vigny sought to avoid writing a historical novel in the manner of Sir Walter Scott, whose literary reputation was becoming fairly well known in France. He discussed his conception of the new genre in an essay written in 1827, which he subsequently had inserted as a preface to new printings and editions of *Cinq-Mars*. "Réflexions sur la vérité dans l'art" (Reflections on Truth in Art) claimed that *Cinq-Mars* depicted historical personalities in a manner diametrically opposed to that of Scott. Rather than relegate historical

Self-portrait of the young Vigny (Bibliothèque de la Comédie-Française)

spiracy against Richelieu to the retrospective optic of the novelist's own disenchantment during the final years of the Bourbon Restoration. The novel blurts out the view that the cardinal's actions as prime minister sowed the seeds for the Revolution of 1789. "Réflexions sur la vérité dans l'art" comes to grips with the problematics of the historical novel, whose subject concerns both art and history. The essay argues that the novelist should be free to simplify or modify the characters of personalities and adjust or reorder segments of historical truth to achieve a more strikingly symbolic interpretation of events.

In Vigny's estimation, history pursues both a moral and a philosophical goal. Great historical personalities ultimately serve as actors for mankind, since their actions are viewed as embodying ideas and attitudes on a symbolic level. It is the novelist's responsibility to appraise and reconstitute the facts of history in order to confer upon them specific forms for specific actions. Moreover, the writer of fiction contributes an aesthetic dimension by fashioning a certain unity or homogeneity in his narrative account. He corrects the fragmentation of historical time through the presentation of a moral and aesthetic synthesis. Thus, historical personalities become eclipsed by the ideas their behavior represents or illustrates: "L'art ne doit jamais être considéré que dans ses rapports avec sa *beauté idéale* . . . la vérité dont il doit se nourrir est la vérité sur la *nature humaine*, et non l'authenticité du fait" (Art must be considered only in its relationship with *ideal beauty* . . . the truth that underpins it is the truth of the observation of *human nature*, and not that of the authenticity of facts). Since history distorts factual truth through its fragmented approach, the novelist should be free to invent what approximates the ideal in order to achieve greater truth than simple factual truth itself.

Comprised of twenty-six chapters, *Cinq-Mars* recounts the conspiracy of 1639 against Cardinal Richelieu, who sought to concentrate the power of the French throne to the detriment of the noble class. Henri d'Effiat, marquis of Cinq-Mars, a young man in love with a princess, Marie de Gonzague, quests after greater political power and a higher social station so that he may marry her. When the cardinal wages war against Philip IV of Spain, Cinq-Mars sides with the nobles who oppose Richelieu's designs. The opening pages of the novel bring the reader to June 1639, when the young marquis is preparing to join the royal forces at Perpignan. Vigny imagines at the out-

characters to minor roles, Vigny assigned them pivotal functions in the action he wished to represent. *Cinq-Mars* portrays the weakening of seventeenth-century France's aristocracy as foreshadowing calamitous consequences in the event of its collapse. Vigny's thesis is that France urgently needed the aristocracy as a guiding force, and that Cardinal Richelieu's policies systematically undermined the French feudal system. In order to elucidate his ideas, he assigned personalities such as Louis XIII, Richelieu, Father Joseph le Clerc du Tremblay, and Henri d'Effiat de Cinq-Mars major roles to play in his historical fiction. But just as he had previously altered the image of Moses to have him meet the requirements of his viewpoint in the poem, Vigny resorts to some historical distortions and anachronisms in order to assert more forcefully his contentions in *Cinq-Mars*.

The justificatory preface unveils the novel's moral and didactic function. Vigny's personal biases actually shift the portrait of Cinq-Mars's conset a dialogue between the Maréchal de Bassompierre, out of favor with the cardinal, and de Launay, an avid supporter of the latter's policies. Bassompierre's eloquent defense of the role of the aristocracy (a blatant fabrication on Vigny's part, since the Maréchal had been imprisoned at the Bastille between 1631 and 1643) introduces the novel's thesis that the masses, unbridled by the aristocracy, would be capable of destroying French royalty.

On the road from Touraine to Perpignan, Cinq-Mars witnesses the trial and execution of Urbain Grandier at Loudun, burned at the stake on a trumped-up charge of witchcraft (his only crime was his voluble opposition to Richelieu's policies). Vigny situates the episode anachronistically in 1639 in order to establish the sharp antithesis between the marquis's innocent motives, at this juncture, and the judge Laubardement's unscrupulous designs as one of the cardinal's most active agents. Cinq-Mars also encounters his former tutor, the kindly abbé Quillet, whose advice brings into clear focus the moral sanction of the crusade undertaken by the young marquis:

> En portant votre épée, souvenez-vous qu'elle est à Dieu. Mais aussi, lorsque vous serez au milieu des hommes, tâchez de ne pas vous laisser tromper par l'hypocrite; il vous entourera, vous prendra, mon fils, par le côté vulnérable de votre cœur naïf.

> (When you wear your sword, remember that it belongs to God. But also, when you get into the company of other men, try not to let yourself be taken in by hypocrites; you will be surrounded by them, my son, and they will take hold of you by the most vulnerable side of your naive soul).

Quillet's counsel underscores a subtheme developed by Vigny in his novel: that men ultimately allow overriding passions to corrode their initial commitments to noble and sacred causes. This problem is reexamined at greater length when Cinq-Mars's loyal friend, de Thou, questions the motives of his actions.

Cinq-Mars arrives at Perpignan to find the city besieged by the enemy. He engages promptly in some skirmishes, and his bravery in battle comes to the attention of Louis XIII. At this point the novel's action shifts abruptly to Paris about two years later. The reader learns that the young marquis has become the king and queen's favorite squire at the Louvre palace. His hatred for Richelieu unabated, Cinq-Mars enlists the aid of Spaniards to form a coalition against the cardinal. But the latter, who exercises such control over the king and his courtiers, is informed of the conspiracy by his diabolical spy, Father Joseph, or the Eminence Grise. Frightened, the queen withdraws her support of Cinq-Mars's plot to overthrow Richelieu, and persuades Marie de Gonzague to refrain from marrying beneath her rank. Devastated by this turn of events, the young marquis allows himself to be taken prisoner. He is soon guillotined in Lyons along with his faithful friend, de Thou.

When one first encounters Cardinal Richelieu, he is in his rooms at the archbishop's palace in Narbonne, where blue, yellow, and red stained-glass windows give out a mysterious glow. Vigny highlights melodramatic features to condition his reader's reaction. The cardinal appears virtually moribund: one sees him coughing and spitting up blood at frequent intervals. He possesses a ghostlike demeanor, and despite large, soft eyes, his physical appearance inspires only dread and terror. In fact, Richelieu's portrait is deformed to the point of caricature. The same holds true for Father Joseph (actually an anachronistic personage, since he died in 1638), who has the countenance of a spider. Thus, the novelist's portraits of the prime minister and the notorious spy lend the narrative a sense of evil foreboding from the beginning. For the sake of the thesis he explores, Vigny's one-dimensional description of Richelieu casts him merely as a man consumed with overpowering ambition.

Contrary to all historical verisimilitude, Vigny invents a long dramatic monologue in which Richelieu voices the distress he has experienced as France's prime minister. He addresses God thusly: "Je renverse l'entourage du trône. Si, sans le savoir, je sapais ses fondements et hâtais sa chute! Oui, mon pouvoir d'emprunt m'a séduit" (I knock down the crown's entourage. If, without knowing it, I were undermining its foundation and hastening its fall! Yes, I have been seduced by my assumed power). But the cardinal's prayerlike confession quickly changes into an arrogant justification for his conduct, and the articulation of his initial anguish gives way to an affirmation of haughty self-confidence. The long monologue reveals to which lengths Vigny had recourse to deter his readers from posing their own hypotheses concerning the behavior of the aristocracy, behavior that may have contributed to the eventual downfall of the monarchy.

The novelist complicates the heroic character of his protagonist by having him debate with his friend de Thou his ambition vis-à-vis his political goal and his sentimental aspirations. Henri d'Effiat reveals the secret love he nurtures for Marie de Gonzague and hastens to explain: "Je le suis, ambitieux, mais parce que j'aime" (If I am ambitious, it is because I am in love). De Thou, scandalized by his friend's avowal, reproaches him for wanting to overturn the state for the sake of his own happiness. But Cinq-Mars's reply only increases de Thou's consternation: "Le bonheur de l'Etat s'accorde avec le mien" (The welfare of the State coincides with my own welfare). When the marquis later learns that the princess has abjured her love for him, he realizes that it was primarily his passion that motivated his desire to overthrow and supplant Richelieu. He finally admits his self-deception to de Thou, the embodiment of total sacrifice and abnegation in the novel. In a real sense, Vigny shapes the characters of the two historical figures to have them represent the two conflicting attitudes residing in his own personality. The young marquis is the soldier and the man of action while de Thou is the contemplative companion given to thought and meditation.

As a conspirator, Cinq-Mars maintains but a precarious balance between his political ambition and his sentimental aspiration. The novel abounds in tales of simulated military retreats, false uprisings, and wild rumors concerning the illnesses of the cardinal and Louis XIII and of their impending abdications. Vigny means to persuade his readers of Richelieu's dastardly designs concerning the aristocracy with so many accounts. Yet, it is the projection of his pervasive doubt concerning the efficacy of all social action that overwhelms the narrative's thesis in the end. All told, *Cinq-Mars* is less the story of the marquis's plot to overthrow the cardinal than it is the study of the contrastive personalities of Henri d'Effiat and de Thou.

The chapter entitled "La Partie de chasse" (The Shooting Expedition) presumes to single out the instability of the aristocracy under Richelieu and Louis XIII. The king's prolonged illness has made the people anxious. The narrator comments on the disarray at court: were Louis XIII to die, his imperious minister would easily assume full reign, since the parliament appears powerless to stop him. Vigny's evocation of the situation of seventeenth-century monarchical France begs a comparison with the position of the Bourbon Restoration in the 1820s. In the novelist's

Vigny in uniform as a royal guardsman (portrait attributed to the author's mother; Musée Carnavalet)

view, France lacked the kind of organized resistance required to offset the political consequences of Napoleon, just as the aristocracy of the time of Louis XIII lacked the resolve to combat the political machinations that threatened its own survival.

It is significant that in the last chapter the reader should meet up with Pierre Corneille and Milton, already encountered in an earlier chapter that purported to give a kaleidoscopic portrait of the society of Louis XIII. Their appearance coincides precisely with the moment of the executions of Cinq-Mars and de Thou in Lyons. A carnival atmosphere has invaded the streets of Paris; only the disturbing chants of a group of men crossing the quais give cause for concern. Corneille and Milton are visibly troubled by the shouts of one man: "Le Parlement est mort ... les seigneurs sont morts: dansons, nous sommes les maîtres ..." (Parliament is dead ... the feudal lords are dead: let us dance for we are now the masters ...). The crowd scene of 1642 foreshadows those that characterized subsequently the French Revolution: the rumblings of the mobs presage the drama that will occur some 150 years later.

Vigny ends his novel with the imaginary confrontation between Corneille and Milton, who provide the novel's moral conclusion as far as history is concerned. Milton's alleged involvement with the English Puritan Revolution of the 1640s presumably endows him with a clairvoyance that enables him to decipher the message of the murmuring men. Milton denounces Richelieu's political inadequacy for having allowed his power to become so intimately associated with a weak and wavering monarch. He predicts the ascendancy of another political figure who will prove to be more logical than the cardinal and achieve greater authority: "Je vais trouver un homme qui n'a pas encore paru, et que je vois dominé par cette misérable ambition; mais je crois qu'il ira plus loin. Il se nomme Cromwell" (I am going to find a man who has not yet appeared, and whom I see dominated by this miserable ambition; but I believe he will go farther. His name is Cromwell). The designation of Oliver Cromwell closes the novel, and Milton's words imply that once the monarchy has been sufficiently weakened and the aristocracy decimated, countries resort to uncompleted revolutions that revert to totalitarian regimes. The name of Napoleon is discernible under the filigree of Cromwell's name.

Cinq-Mars proved to be an immediate popular success in 1826. A second printing came out in June of the same year, and by 1827 Vigny counted thirteen printings in various formats, and this despite glaring shortcomings in the novel. Charles-Augustin Sainte-Beuve criticized the work severely in the *Globe*: he chided Vigny for his outrageous falsification of historical personalities and events and for the irritating anachronisms that undermined the narrative at crucial intervals. He alluded to chapter 20, "La Lecture" (The Reading), as a case in point. Vigny situates the episode in the salon of the celebrated courtesan Marion Delorme in 1642. Members of the audience listen distractedly to Milton as he reads from *Paradise Lost* (actually begun in 1665). In the background, a somewhat larger group listens in rapt attention to a libertine poet discuss Madeleine de Scudéry's "Carte de Tendre" (Map of Love) from *Clélie*, which she published between 1654 and 1661. Such anachronisms and sudden shifts in plot development were bound to disconcert the more discerning reader. Even the portrait of the main protagonist is, at times, skimmed over in rather cavalier fashion.

After the success of *Cinq-Mars*, Vigny took a more active part in the literary life of Paris. Besides, in the capital he was in a better position to gauge the restive political climate of the regime of Charles X. By September 1826 his wife Lydia had become chronically ill, and he devoted himself increasingly to caring for her. In 1827 signs appeared that a political revolution was likely to occur shortly. Vigny requested a military discharge for reasons of health; it was granted on 14 May. If the Romantic revolution during these years focused on the revitalization of the French theater, it was Hugo who first responded, with his drama *Cromwell* (1827) and its accompanying manifesto. The preface to *Cromwell* articulated Hugo's conception of the unity of opposites, the sublime and the grotesque, which he presented as the theoretical cornerstone for the new drama. Hugo's example encouraged Vigny to write for the theater.

Vigny was now eager to help make the work of William Shakespeare better known to French audiences. His cousin Bruguière de Sorsum had already translated some of the bard's plays into French, and there also had been previous translations. He set to work on a French-verse translation of *Romeo and Juliet* (1594) with Deschamps. But because Augustin Soulié's adaptation was scheduled for performances at the Odéon in June 1828, the project was indefinitely postponed. Undaunted, Vigny tackled a translation/adaptation of *Othello*, which he entitled *Le More de Venise*. It was accepted for performance at the Comédie Française, where it went into rehearsal in July 1829. Meanwhile, Hugo's *Hernani* had been accepted by the reading committee in October. After considerable discussion on which play should be produced first, Hugo withdrew his play in favor of Vigny's adaptation. The incident, as well as Hugo's growing liberalism, cooled the friendship between the two men. *Le More de Venise* opened on 24 October 1829, and ran for thirteen performances. It represented a significant critical success.

During the July Revolution (27-29 July) of 1830, Vigny became torn between his loyalty to the Bourbons and his deep-seated conviction that their cause was a bad one. The July Monarchy of Louis-Philippe put a virtual end to the myth of the legitimacy of the monarchy. He saw the July Revolution as a conflict between industrialists and financiers on one part, and the aristocrats and the king's army on the other. He experienced ambivalent feelings about the fall of the

Bourbons, and expressed shock over the scanndalous weakness of the royalty, while he voiced his admiration for the commitment and tenacity of the people. As a retired military officer, he volunteered to serve in the National Guard, which Louis-Philippe had set up to ensure order in the streets of the capital. At this juncture Vigny no longer believed in a return to a legitimist monarchy nor in the advent of a genuine republic. He considered the government of Louis-Philippe to be censorial and thus antidemocratic. The poem "Paris," which he completed in 1830 and published in 1831, underscores his concern for the need of widespread social reforms.

The last years of the Bourbon Restoration had proved unsettling for Vigny. He began to question his own values and beliefs. He became skeptical about the efficacy of all institutions, and he grew noticeably disturbed by organized religion, whose entrenched dogmas seemed hopelessly congealed, oblivious to progress and the march of time. Influenced by Benjamin Constant's *De la religion* (On Religion, 1824-1831) and Victor Cousin's *Cours de philosophie: Introduction à l'histoire de la philosophie* (Course of Philosophy: Introduction to the History of Philosophy, 1828), Vigny meditated on the distinction between religious feeling or sentiment on one hand, and religious forms or dogmas on the other. He was struck by the cleavage that occurred between religious form and feeling in times of great moral and social upheaval. At such crucial moments, religious forms and dogmas tended to be displaced by newer forms more flexibly attuned to meet the needs of new circumstances. Vigny singled out this phenomenon in an 1829 entry in his *Journal*: "Les formes religieuses ne peuvent absorber ni une tête puissante ni un cœur passionné. Le philosophe veut passer au delà, l'amant sentir davantage, aimer plus violemment, avec moins d'égoïsme" (Religious forms can absorb neither a powerful mind nor a passionate heart. The philosopher wants to go beyond cults and dogmas, and the lover wants to feel more intensely and to love more violently with less egoism). The writer's own liberation from confining forms enables him to pursue goals that plane over the contingencies of time and space. Vigny's notation goes a long way toward explaining the motivation behind his subsequent quest after "l'esprit pur" (pure spirit), a quest that informed all of his writing from that point on.

Begun in 1828 and published in the April 1831 issue of the *Revue des Deux Mondes*, the four

chapters that comprise the uncompleted novel *L'Alméh: Scènes du désert* (The Almeh: Desert Scenes) analyze the tenuousness of religious forms from the perspective created by Napoleon's 1797 expedition into Egypt. *L'Alméh* is set in the vicinity of Thebes. The opening scene describes a cold night in the desert. All appears motionless; in view are two colossi with mutilated heads, seated on thrones of black marble. Suddenly, a white mass approaches the statues. A man alights from a white elephant and enters a nearby tent. The Brahman is welcomed inside by the two occupants: an old man, and a young girl. The Brahman makes a long speech in Hindi, in which only the word *Brahma* is understood by the two Arabs. Vigny's point is that if the two occupants recognize the name of God, they fail to understand the context in which it is uttered. Wishing to communicate more fully with the Brahman, the sheik sends for the "Frank," who is conversant in many languages. He will serve as interpreter for the perplexed Arabs.

The three chapters that follow focus on the personalities of the mysterious "Frank," a disillusioned émigré from the French Revolution, and an elderly Jesuit missionary who has assumed the name of "Servus Dei." The narrative reveals that the Brahman, the Moslems, the Jesuit, and the dismayed interpreter have been brought together in the desert because of Napoleon's European conquests and his impending arrival in Egypt. The Jesuit inhabits a section of the palace of Medinet-Abu, originally the abode of the ancient pharaohs. When the reader first meets "Servus Dei," he is trying to alter the faded image of the Egyptian god Osiris, changing it with ochre paint into a representation more suitable for his new Christian converts. He readily admits to "Frank," the skeptical interpreter, that he must at times resort to the Koran to explain the New Testament to them. *L'Alméh* introduces the notion of religious syncretization that Vigny discusses at length in his *Journal* and exploits as a major theme in *Daphné* (1913), his other uncompleted novel.

Vigny complicates his concept of syncretization with an ironic dimension. The pathetic efforts of "Servus Dei" to transform the image of Osiris into a Christian icon prove futile, since the new image serves only as a thin disguise of the pagan image. By and large, *L'Alméh* is a dialectical confrontation between the skeptical interpreter and the Jesuit missionary concerning the permanence of religious feelings and the fragility of dogmas in the face of change. Their dialogue underscores the fundamental instability of cults and forms considered immutable and eternal by organized religions. In the end, all human institutions succumb to the caprices of time and space. Vigny's narrative carefully aligns religious forms with the evolving civilizations of different races, thereby divesting all dogmatic forms of any exclusive claim to divinity. The skeptical interpreter's refusal to treat the Jesuit with any kind of mocking condescension confers a tragic dimension upon *L'Alméh*. In its uncompleted state, the fragments of *L'Alméh* emerge as the novelist's troubling statement on the contamination of religious doctrines.

Vigny's thesis is that orthodox religions spring from the needs and circumstances of self-contained societies that exist in relative isolation from others. In *L'Alméh* the isolation of the upper Egyptian desert protects the type of orthodoxy being evolved by "Servus Dei" for his converts. But the momentary arrival of Napoleon and his forces threatens the survival of the Jesuit missionary's kind of Catholicism by their imminent destruction of the environment that ensured its growth and prosperity. The Napoleonic presence, the reader is informed, will bring to an end the isolation in which "Servus Dei" had succeeded in developing and preserving an exclusive religious orthodoxy in the desert. The efforts of the Jesuit missionary are destined to meet the same end as those of his Egyptian predecessors.

The four chapters comprising *L'Alméh* display all the trappings of a potential thesis novel: long, belabored descriptions of settings and situations, certain distortions of facts and events, and exaggerated contrasts that underscore points that are made. The opening chapter, especially, betrays Vigny's obvious admiration for Scott and James Fenimore Cooper. *L'Alméh* went virtually unnoticed by the critics of the time. These fragments strike the modern reader more as a treatise than as a genuine exercise in fiction.

In 1830 Lydia was diagnosed as suffering from lymphatism, which made her a total invalid. Later that year Vigny met the actress Marie Dorval, whom he had seen on the stage of the Théâtre de la Porte-Saint-Martin. Full of admiration for her talent as a thespian, he became quickly enamored of her, and arranged for a reading of his new drama, *La Maréchale d'Ancre* (The Wife of Marshal d'Ancre), on 5 and 7 October in her apartment. He wanted her to play the leading role in his drama, but other commitments prevented her from performing when it was scheduled to open at the Odéon on 22 June 1831.

This mutual disappointment did not deter them from entering into a passionate and lengthy liaison that lasted until 1838. Because of complications, the actual premiere of *La Maréchale d'Ancre* took place on 25 June 1831.

The spectacular success of Hugo's *Hernani* (1830) had encouraged Vigny to write an original drama that he considered to be in the manner of Shakespeare. Despite occasional commingling of tragic and comic features, this first excursion into historical drama proved to be less than satisfying theater. *La Maréchale d'Ancre* centers on the minority of Louis XIII, which Vigny described as bound by two assassinations: that of Henri IV at the beginning of the young king's regency and that of Concino Concini in its final year. Vigny takes considerable pains to alter historical facts in order to argue for the abolition of the death penalty in political matters. The dramatist's imagination had been sparked by the series of trials of some of Charles X's former ministers during the early months of 1830. As in *Cinq-Mars*, Vigny's philosophical idealism rearranges history so that it may better illustrate his social and moral thesis. The complicated plot weighs down the central action and fails to invest the principal characters with any appreciable dramatic intensity. The play received only tepid critical response and failed to impress its audience.

Beginning in 1832 Marie Dorval assumed a greater importance in Vigny's personal life. The author of *Cinq-Mars* found himself in an unexpected quandary. The minister of the interior suspected him of being a legitimist Carlist while the Palais Royal believed him to be a republican sympathizer. If the Revolution of 1830 did not markedly change his political philosophy, he turned his attention to the social problems besetting the regime of Louis-Philippe during the first half of the 1830s. Notations in his *Journal* reveal an increasing preoccupation with the plight of the individual in the fluctuating social and political environment of the times. The 1832 narrative *Stello: Les consultations du Docteur-Noir* (translated as *Stello: A Session with Doctor Noir*, 1963) is the fictional expression of at least part of his concern.

Stello intermingles fact with fiction in order to illustrate the poet's wretched predicament in the societies in which he attempts to exercise his function as an artist. Vigny argues that if the poet's misfortune stems in part from his idealism and anxiety, it emanates principally from the masses' refusal to acknowledge his mission in society. Stello, a young man given to fits of depression, feels that he has been singled out to be a poet. He consults Doctor Noir, whom he takes to immediately and whose advice he seeks out. Stello confesses his desire to become a poet committed entirely to the service of society. Doctor Noir, who fears that he is headed for a life of disillusionment, takes him on as a patient. He recounts to Stello the stories of the lamentable experiences of three poets in order to deter him from his project. Each account purports to show the tragic victimization of artists by societies that either scorned them, ignored them, or held them in contempt. These three narratives constitute the work's basic organization.

The pathetic demises of Nicholas Gilbert (1751-1780), Thomas Chatterton (1752-1770), and André Chénier (1762-1794) expose the poet's abuse by different governments: Gilbert by the monarchy of Louis XV; Chatterton by the English state, a constitutional government; Chénier by the Revolutionary government, supposedly democratic. When Stello registers his shock and dismay over the poet's situation, Doctor Noir provides him with the following prescription, should he persist in his plan: "Séparer la vie poétique de la vie politique" (Keep the poetical life separate from the political life). Of the three types of government mentioned, the first feared the poet, the second disdained him as a useless human being, while the third hated him and considered him an aristocrat. Doctor Noir's advice to Stello is that the poet should remain wary of political factions and all their puffed-up claims, and remain aloof from all sectarianism. The poet's only true mission is the production of his own work.

Vigny attributes different aspects of his own personality to Stello and Doctor Noir. Stello is the anxious and melancholic poet, while Doctor Noir is the reasonable and critical observer. They engage in a dialogue between sentiment and reason, the two reactions one may assume in the face of evil and adversity. In a real sense, most of the narrative serves as a kind of commentary on Stello's conception of his role as an artist:

Je crois fermement en une vocation ineffable qui m'est donnée, et j'y crois à cause de la pitié sans bornes que m'inspirent les hommes, mes compagnons en misère, et aussi à cause du désir que je me sens de leur tendre la main et de les élever sans cesse par des paroles de commisération et d'amour.

(I firmly believe in the ineffable vocation I have received, and I believe in it because of the limitless pity that the sight of men, my companions in wretchedness, inspires in me, and also because of the desire that I have to extend my hand to them in order to elevate them with words of love and commiseration).

Stello's poetic creed bears a striking resemblance to Vigny's own poetics after 1830, especially when he affirms belief in the value of the interior life and the work of the mind.

Doctor Noir begins with his narration of Gilbert's death, an account that is significantly at variance with historical facts. Stello is told that the young poet died of starvation on a litter of straw, symbolically grasping his quill pen in one hand and a stale piece of bread in the other. (Gilbert actually benefited from a royal pension, and died from wounds he suffered in a riding accident.) When Doctor Noir realizes that his story has merely served as an indictment of the indifference of the monarchy of Louis XV, he proceeds to relate the tragic story of the poet Chatterton's suicide. Doctor Noir explains how he had been drawn to Kitty Bell's modest bakery near the English Parliament, where he would frequently converse with her about a destitute young writer who had bequeathed her his manuscripts. The unknown poet took poison after learning that his plea for help had been rebuffed by the lord mayor of London, who condescended, nonetheless, to take him in his employ as a valet. The account of Chatterton's tragic death moves Stello to unleash an impassioned diatribe against the evils of society: "L'homme a rarement tort, et l'ordre social toujours" (Man is rarely to blame, and the social order is always to blame). After becalming Stello, Doctor Noir proceeds to relate how André Chénier met his death during the so-called democratic period of the Reign of Terror.

The twenty-two chapters that comprise the narrative dealing with Chénier's execution constitute the most successful part of *Stello*, both as a work of fiction and as a treatise on the relationship between the poet and society. Vigny's vivid descriptions of prison scenes at Saint-Lazare are especially memorable. The richly complex portraits of Chénier, Maximilien Robespierre, Louis de Saint-Just, Mme Marie Bérenger de Saint-Aignan, and Mlle Aimée de Coigny, to cite but the most noteworthy, contribute more effectively to the novel's thesis than the one-dimensional sketches of the protagonists in the two earlier narratives. Doctor Noir's report of his visits to the

Frontispiece for the first edition of Vigny's drama based on his novel Stello

prison and to the house of Robespierre endows the chapters with a striking visual immediacy.

Central to this third narrative is the story of Doctor Noir's interview with Robespierre and Saint-Just, in which the fate of Chénier is decided. Stello's mentor interrupts his description with an aside to point out that, in his view, terrorists are crazed and sick individuals, characterizing thus his handshake with Robespierre: "Je ne la pris pas comme d'un ami, mais comme d'un malade . . . je lui tâtai le pouls" (I shook his hand not as a friend's, but as a patient's . . . I took his pulse). Doctor Noir records Robespierre's views concerning the function of the poet in society:

> . . . Je les regarde comme les plus dangereux ennemis de la patrie. . . . Qui s'oppose à mes vues? Les écrivains, les faiseurs de vers qui font du dédain rimé. . . . La Convention doit traiter tous ceux qui ne sont pas utiles à la République comme des contre-révolutionnaires.

> (. . . I consider them the most dangerous enemies of the state. . . . Who opposes my views? Writers or these fabricators of verse who fashion rhymes out of disdain. . . . The Convention must treat all who are not useful to the Republic as counterrevolutionaries).

Robespierre reads aloud what Chénier allegedly wrote about the Reign of Terror from a scrap of paper supposedly retrieved by a prison guard. At that point the poet's brother and Doctor Noir realize that Chénier's fate has been sealed and that he will be guillotined.

At one point Doctor Noir stuns Stello with the admission that his stories about the three poets have been only half true. Through his fictional intermediary, the novelist once again justifies his distortions of historical facts for the sake of ideal truth. By way of conclusion, Doctor Noir informs Stello that poets throughout the ages suffered no harsher fates than those of antiquity. The chapter entitled "Le Ciel d'Homère" (Homer's Heaven) relates an imaginary confrontation between Plato and Homer, who had been banished from the former's republic. Homer explains to the philosopher what he conceived to be his function as a poet in society: "Vous me demandez quelles institutions, quelles lois, quelles doctrines j'ai données aux villes? Aucune aux nations, mais une éternelle au monde. —Je ne suis d'aucune ville, mais de l'univers" (You ask me which institutions, laws or doctrines I bequeathed to the cities? Nothing to any specific nation, but lasting doctrines for the world. —I belong to no city, but rather to the universe).

Doctor Noir elucidates the thesis that informs the novel: political power most often voices its suspicion of artists, for the objective of art is eternal truth, while power incarnates "le mensonge social" (social deception). He then juxtaposes the dated or relative significance of all types of governments, whether they be despotic or democratic, with the splendor of literary and artistic accomplishments. When he believes he has cured Stello of his fantasies, he makes out a prescription for the poet's well-being. Doctor Noir advises Stello to maintain his distance from specific political issues, and to dedicate himself completely to the production of works that have intrinsic artistic values. For art must never depend on arbitrary contingencies of time for its inspiration. The advice dispensed by Doctor Noir parallels closely Vigny's own attitudes on the matter during the July Monarchy, when he maintained that the poet's mission was to advance the cause of civilization through the force of his ideas as a thinker. Yet, Doctor Noir, as well as Vigny, cautions Stello: "La Neutralité du penseur solitaire est une *neutralité armée* qui s'éveille au besoin" (The Neutrality of the solitary thinker is an *armed neutrality* that should be aroused when needed).

Critical and popular response to *Stello* proved disappointing, and Vigny recorded his dismay about the work's reception in his preface to the dramatization of *Chatterton* in 1835. The narrative's rambling form disconcerted most readers, and critics such as Sainte-Beuve reproached the writer for his unacceptable transmutation of historical facts, while others assailed the biased portrayal of the Reign of Terror. A revival of interest in *Stello* occurred in the years following the Revolution of 1848, when the social theses of the narrative were reappraised. But *Stello* would have to wait until the twentieth century for an objective study of the work on its own terms.

Vigny grew increasingly annoyed by Marie Dorval's reported liaisons with other men, and their erstwhile passionate rendezvous in her apartment soon turned to scenes of mutual recrimination. Matters grew more complicated for the author of *Stello* when his mother suffered several attacks of apoplexy in 1833, leaving her partially paralyzed. She moved into her son's residence, where he assumed complete responsibility for caring both for his ailing wife and his disabled mother. Meanwhile, Dorval reproached Vigny for having done little to advance her career as an actress. Vigny set to work on a dramatization of the second narrative in *Stello* in 1834. The drama, *Chatterton*, was accepted by the reading committee of the Comédie Française, and Vigny managed to have the role of Kitty Bell assigned to Marie Dorval.

Chatterton premiered on 12 February 1835. The three-act drama takes up the thesis expounded in *Stello* by relating the story of the young English poet and Kitty Bell. Vigny creates a dramatic tension through the juxtaposition of historical violence and the innocent aspirations of his protagonist. The parallelism between the play's action, set in the London of 1770, and the conditions confronting a newly industrialized French society, invested *Chatterton* with a topical pertinence in 1835. As a portrait of the poet without any role to assume in an overwhelmingly utilitarian society, the drama reveals at the same time the predicament of the bewildered individual in an environment bereft of all moral and spiritual direction.

Marie Dorval enthralled critics and audiences with her stunning performance of a modest and gracious heroine. Indeed, the drama's greatest attribute is the manner in which Vigny crafted the role of the industrialist's wife. Her suggested complexity of character overshoots that of Chatterton, whose personality as the victimized artist remains insufficiently explored. *Chatterton* emerges, above all, as a thesis drama that subordinates character portraiture to the requirements of the message that is expounded.

Shortly after the triumph of *Chatterton*, Vigny published a collection of anecdotes on the nature of armies, *Servitude et grandeur militaires* (1835; translated as *Military Servitude and Grandeur*, 1919). If *Cinq-Mars* portrays the suffering of the nobleman in society, and *Stello* exposes the poet's victimization, *Servitude et grandeur militaires* describes the martyrdom of yet another modern pariah, the soldier. As an officer from 1814 to 1827, Vigny had ample opportunities to observe the selfless devotion of countless soldiers to their country. The narratives underscore a unique grandeur and magnanimity that shine through their silent obedience and unqualified respect of duty. The book is divided into two sections. The first, "Souvenirs de servitude militaire" (Recollections of Military Servitude), contains two anecdotes, "Laurette, ou Le cachet rouge" (Laurette, or the Red Seal) and "La Veillée de Vincennes" (The Night at Vincennes). The second section, "Souvenirs de grandeur militaire" (Recollections of Military Grandeur), contains a three-part narrative, "La Vie et la mort du capitaine Renaud, ou La canne de jonc" (The Life and Death of Captain Renaud, or The Malacca Cane). None of the three stories included in *Servitude et grandeur militaires* is factually true, but, as in *Cinq-Mars*, symbolic truth is greater than simple factual truth.

The essays that introduce the various anecdotes discuss the predicament of the modern soldier and reflect on the nature of wars. Vigny condemns the military establishment's centralization by Louis XIV's minister François Le Tellier, Marquis de Louvois, which separated the army from the mainstream of the nation, thus making it "une nation dans la nation" (a nation within the nation). The enlisted man became a pawn and a scapegoat, serving at the convenience of the people, who consider him a kind of official executioner. His steadfast loyalty to the nation has made of him a martyr of passive obedience: "Leur couronne est une couronne d'épines et, parmi les pointes, je ne pense pas qu'il en soit de plus douloureuse que celle de l'obéissance passive" (Their crown is a crown of thorns, and among its thorn bushes, I can think of none more painful than that of passive obedience). In Vigny's view, the soldier's dignity and grandeur emanate from his bondage and servitude. The narrative "Laurette, ou Le cachet rouge" elucidates what he means by passive obedience.

In *Servitude et grandeur militaires*, the narrator is the novelist himself, whose anecdotes spring directly from his own recollections. "Laurette, ou Le cachet rouge" is the story of a disconsolate old captain whose remorse for a crime committed twenty years earlier remains unabated. Commander of the brig *Marat* during the Directory of 1797, he relates his experience to the narrator, whom he had previously met on the road to Flanders in 1815. He tells how he had been ordered to take on two young deportees, a poet and his wife, and given a letter with a red seal to be opened once the ship had passed the equator. The envelope contained the order to execute the young man, an order that the commander obeyed despite his personal conviction that the young man was innocent of any crime. When Laurette, the poet's wife, then lapsed into a state of madness, the commander had himself transferred into the infantry so that he might care for the distraught young widow. Laurette followed him in a mule-drawn cart through his military campaigns. The narrator interjects the following comment at the end of the tale: "Cette rencontre me révéla une nature d'homme qui m'était inconnue . . . je la plaçai dès lors très haut dans mon estime" (That encounter revealed to me something about man that I had not known . . . from then on, I held it in my highest esteem). Vigny pays tribute to the selfless devotion to duty and to the complete abnegation of the soldier who sacrifices himself for the welfare of others.

The second anecdote, published in the section concerning military servitude, is prefaced by an essay on responsibility. Vigny discusses the problem that confronted the old captain in "Laurette, ou Le cachet rouge": obeying criminal orders. The situation is studied from several viewpoints, with the novelist arguing that the severity of military laws in times of war should give way to a certain flexibility in times of peace. He also discusses the "insouciante soumission" (heedless sub-

mission) of soldiers whose primary duty is to obey and carry out orders. The average soldier experiences a certain satisfaction in such servitude; since he need not preoccupy himself with deciphering complicated orders, he is able to maintain an admirable composure under most circumstances. "La Veillée de Vincennes" deals with a soldier's scruples and is meant to illustrate Vigny's thesis.

The narrator recalls a conversation he had with an aging warrant officer while he was garrisoned at Vincennes during the Restoration. The noncommissioned soldier reproached himself for not having completed his examination of all the shells in the powder magazine for the next day's inspection. The narrator is invited to attend an improvised family concert at his home that evening. The next morning, he is awakened by the noise of the terrible explosion of the powder magazine, accidentally set off by the warrant officer, who had been checking the shells in readiness for the morning inspection. The sketches of the old quartermaster and his superior officer, Timoléon, single out the resignation, candor, and goodness of career soldiers who live in self-effacement. The story of the noncommissioned officer, in fact, appears to contradict Vigny's prefatory essay on responsibility. The soldier in the story is held accountable for the powder magazine, and the officer Timoléon undertakes unusually heroic initiatives in the aftermath of the disastrous explosion. Thus, the apparent tranquillity and peace of mind enjoyed by the soldiers does not proceed from any categorical absence of responsibility. The novelist ends "La Veillée de Vincennes" with a ringing condemnation of the political nation's abject indifference to the heroic dimension in the soldier's servitude.

The best-known narrative, "La Vie et la mort du capitaine Renaud, ou La canne de jonc," appears in the section on recollections of military grandeur. This story best illustrates all of the themes of *Servitude et grandeur militaires*. The narrator relates an episode that occurred on the night of 27 July 1830, at the height of the Revolution. Walking along a deserted Parisian boulevard, he came upon a battalion of the National Guard, and recognized Captain Renaud, a former comrade-in-arms, by his malacca cane. The officer invites the narrator to sit with him on a nearby bench, and begins to recount the highlights of his army career. He bemoans the fact that he has never won any recognition for what he feels has been his long and distinguished ser-

Vigny, 1830 (portrait by Tony Johannot; from Madeleine Ambrière, ed.,
Correspondance d'Alfred de Vigny, *volume 2, 1991)*

vice in the military. He recalls his early days as a young soldier, when he served Napoleon as a page and had sworn blind obedience to the emperor. Just as he appeared headed for a brilliant career, he was taken prisoner at sea by Admiral Collingwood on the British warship *Victory*. Upon his liberation, he took part in the 1814 campaign to recapture the city of Rheims. During the night assault, he killed a Russian guard who turned out to be a fourteen-year-old boy whose only weapon had been a malacca cane. Renaud tells how he retrieved the cane from the dead youth and how he carried it from that time on as his sole weapon and as a symbol of his resolve never to kill again. He ends his story by informing the narrator that he is now the commander of a battalion in charge of maintaining order in the streets of the capital. He then leaves the narrator, who reflects on Renaud's situation as a soldier. He has found consolation by assuming the humblest of duties. The next month the narrator learns that he had been struck down in the line of duty by a youngster who bore an uncanny resemblance to

the young Russian victim. The wounded captain took the boy under his protection and provided for his future, demanding only that the youth pledge never to join the military. Captain Renaud died shortly after with his conscience considerably assuaged.

Each of the episodes recounted by Captain Renaud corresponds to a different stage in the officer's odyssey from his early attempts to achieve glory through military action to a sustained period of reflection and meditation. His ultimate inner purification leads him to selfless devotion to his country. Renaud's story records Vigny's own attempts to temper an earlier predisposition to equate the achievement of glory with military action. Each episode constitutes a kind of moral lesson that elevates the officer and brings him closer to a contemplative state of mind. The first anecdote tells of Napoleon's celebrated interview with Pope Pius VII at Fontainebleau from the shocked perspective of the young page hidden in an alcove. It alerts the reader to the notion of *séidisme*, or blind, fanatical, and superstitious attachment of one man to another during the Napoleonic campaigns.

Prior to the related episode, young Renaud, who had been overwhelmed by the prestige of his idol, had paid little attention to his father's words on the matter. The elder Renaud's farewell letter to his son analyzed the condition that accounted for such absolute surrender to the emperor: "Tel que je te connais, tu serais un Séide, et il faut se garantir du *Séidisme* quand on est français. . . . La source de ce défaut est un grand besoin d'action et une grande paresse de réflexion" (Knowing you as I do, you would be a Séide, and one has to be protected from *Séidisme* when one is French. . . . The source of this failing is a great need for action along with an accompanying reluctance to reflect on one's actions). In the case of Napoleon, the confusion was that between the man (seen chiefly as a symbol) and principle. Since Napoleon counted on his soldiers' unquestioning subjection to him, he deliberately fashioned a public image that disguised his own subjection to the vagaries of time and space.

In the anecdote, the hidden page perceives the emperor's dissimulation in his interview with the pope, and he can scarcely contain the expression of his shock and disbelief. He observes Napoleon's tantrum during a discussion of his forthcoming coronation as emperor and the possible relocation of the papacy at the Tuileries Palace. The young Renaud exclaims to his narrator: "Je sentis une tristesse toute nouvelle en découvrant combien la plus haute grandeur politique pouvait devenir petite dans ses froides ruses de vanité, ses pièges misérables et ses noirceurs de roué" (I experienced an altogether new sadness in discovering how much the highest political grandeur could become so small in its coldly calculated ruses of vanity, its miserable traps and its darkest cunning). The pope's piercing exclamations—"Commediante!" and "Tragediante!"—expose the preposterous hoax behind Napoleon's posturing. The emperor may have proved to be a clever manipulator of the will of his *séides*, but his strategies reveal, ultimately, that his vision is no clearer than that of his adherents.

In the second anecdote, Captain Renaud recalls his imprisonment on the British warship and the kind treatment he received. Commander Collingwood allowed him free run of the ship in exchange for his word that he would not try to escape. Renaud relates how he attempted to detect traces of egoism and personal ambition in the naval officer's behavior. He soon learns that Collingwood serves his country out of pure devotion. If his selflessness gives meaning to his own life, it has not spared him the disappointments of the ordinary individual. He has remained indefinitely at sea as a kind of prisoner on his own vessel. For lack of a suitable replacement, he remains at the helm of the battleship as a sentinel for his country. Collingwood gives the young soldier the following advice just before he liberates him: "Je n'ai qu'une chose à vous recommander, c'est de vous dévouer à un Principe plutôt qu'à un Homme" (I have only one thing to recommend to you, and that is that you devote yourself to a Principle rather than to a Man). Once liberated, Renaud resolves to maintain an ideological distance from Napoleon, whom he now recognizes to be consumed solely by his own ambition.

Before acceding to the interior life to which he henceforth aspires, Captain Renaud knows that he will have to renounce wars in which unconscious spilling of human blood occurs. He relates his experience in the attack of the Russian outpost near Rheims. He recalls the horrible slaughter of the sleeping soldiers and the gasping noise of the fourteen-year-old youngster he had killed: "Papa!" When the distraught Renaud points out the dead child to his colonel, the following discussion takes place:

—Regardez cela, dis-je; quelle différence y a-t-il entre moi et un assassin?
—Eh! sacrédié, mon cher, que voulez-vous? c'est le métier.
—C'est juste, répondis-je, et je me levai pour aller reprendre mon commandement. L'enfant retomba dans les plis de son manteau dont je l'enveloppai, et sa petite main ornée de grosses bagues laissa échapper une canne de jonc, qui tomba sur ma main comme s'il me l'eût donnée.

(—Look at that, I said; what is the difference between me and a murderer?
—Damn it, old chap, what can one do about it? It's part of the job.
—You're right, I answered, and I got up to resume my command. The child fell back into the fold of his coat in which I wrapped him, and his little hand, displaying large rings, let fall a malacca cane, which fell on my hand as if he had given it to me).

The tragic episode haunts Renaud and overwhelms him with a disgust for all killing. He relates how from that moment on he began his slow but persistent ascent to a more desirable spiritual state of being. Thus, his story becomes that of a dedicated professional soldier who eventually assumes an essentially pacifist posture in the aftermath of the July Revolution.

"La Vie et la mort du capitaine Renaud" is capped by a chapter entitled simply, "Conclusion," in which Vigny delineates the moral lesson contained in the three stories that comprise *Servitude et grandeur militaires*. What sustains the military man in his servitude is his own abnegation and obedience to duty. So too, Vigny underlines, what supports the modern individual, confronted by foundering moral codes and collapsed institutions, is the cult of honor that lies deeply embedded in the human conscience. Vigny envisions honor as a kind of virile religion, divested of any symbol, dogma, or ritual: "L'Honneur, c'est la conscience, mais la conscience exaltée. C'est le respect de soi-même et de la beauté de sa vie porté jusqu'à la plus pure élévation et jusqu'à la passion la plus ardente" (Honor is conscience, but in exalted form. It is self-respect and respect of the beauty of one's life brought to its highest elevation and to its most ardent passion). In *Servitude et grandeur militaires*, honor emerges as the cornerstone of the new kind of religion capable of conferring moral stability in a rapidly changing world. In sum, the three stories recount Vigny's own evolution as he pleads the soldier's cause increasingly from the point of view of a conscientious objector. The last story, especially, may be interpreted as an impassioned argument in favor of pacifism.

When *Servitude et grandeur militaires* was published in 1835, it ran counter to the main current of the times: the political regime had evolved toward greater social repression, the professional soldier enjoyed a measure of prestige, and the National Guard had become the preferred instrument of Louis-Philippe's July Monarchy. The narrative was accorded a generally cool critical reception. Sainte-Beuve's review in the *Revue des Deux Mondes* underscored some relatively small historical inaccuracies, and decried the deliberate defacement of Napoleon's portrait in the third story. Critics closer to the present who have witnessed several catastrophic wars bestow a tragic dimension on the teachings of the narratives. By the sobriety of its style, the eloquent containment of its analyses of the soldier's condition, and its lively, well-paced dialogue, this work, which the novelist once described as a funeral oration for the army of the Restoration, stands out as a distinguished prose masterpiece among his achievements.

In 1836 Vigny began work on a manuscript that he hoped, when finished, would be published as the first of a three-part narrative on Julian the Apostate, Philipp Melanchthon, and Jean-Jacques Rousseau, men of different eras who dealt with the question of religious fervor and sentiment. Initially conceived as a continuation of Doctor Noir's consultation in *Stello*, the fragments of *Daphné* were left unpublished in Vigny's lifetime. They were finally edited by Fernand Gregh in 1913. *Daphné* utilizes the same characters as *Stello* in the prologue and epilogue that frame the main narrative, a series of letters dating from the fourth century that have recently been discovered by a rich young man, Trivulce. Doctor Noir and Stello have been summoned to Trivulce's bedside. He has become feverishly troubled by what he read in the letters. The prologue is set in February 1831. As Doctor Noir and Stello make their way to the Latin Quarter, they witness the sacking of the archbishop's residence by the people of Paris. When they arrive at Trivulce's rooms, they find a manuscript—four letters written by a Jewish merchant, Joseph Jechaiah, to a friend in Alexandria, Benjamin Elul. The epistles are an account of the events he had witnessed in the suburb of Daphné, near Antioch.

Daphné is the story of Julian the Apostate, a figure who had fascinated Vigny ever since he was a young man. He declares in his *Journal*: "Si la métempsycose existe, j'ai été cet homme" (If there is such a thing as metempsychosis, I was that man). *Daphné* recalls the destiny of Julian, the nephew of Constantine, who had been raised in the Christian faith, which he subsequently renounced in favor of Greek paganism. Once emperor, he attempts to restore the rites and symbols of paganism in an area that had been recently converted to Christianity. Vigny borrows liberally from Edward Gibbon's *History of the Decline and Fall of the Roman Empire* (1776-1788) and Plato's *Dialogues*, as well as from the works of St. John Chrysostom, to fashion a personal version of Julian the Apostate that meets the requirements of the thesis he develops. He depicts Julian, for example, as a fervent and even mystical Christian in his early years, a fact that finds no corroboration in Gibbon's account.

The letters comprising Trivulce's manuscript describe Jechaiah's arrival in Daphné, where he proceeds to the house of his friend Libanius, a pagan philosopher who resides near the city's temple. Libanius speaks to two disciples, Jean Chrysostom and Basil, in the merchant's presence, sketching for them a portrait of Julian as an exalted mystic, tormented by analogies between paganism and Christianity. Both Chrysostom and Basil cannot understand why Julian should have rejected Christianity. Libanius's explanation astonishes the two disciples: "Dès qu'il n'a plus vu clairement dans Jésus de Nazareth la Divinité pure et le Verbe qu'il adorait, il n'a plus rien voulu de ce culte. Il a mal fait" (When he no longer saw clearly Jesus of Nazareth as the pure Divinity and the Word that he adored, he wanted nothing more to do with this cult. He acted wrongly). Just as Libanius expresses concern over the young emperor's determination to restore pagan cults, the door bursts open, and Julian enters the room with his faithful friend, Paul of Larissa. He proceeds to explain why he reconverted to paganism, describes his new faith in the Platonic Logos, and asks Libanius's counsel concerning his resolve to restore paganism to his realm. Julian believes that men will better themselves once they become disassociated from dogmas. Libanius condemns his enterprise as wrongheaded, since paganism has died, and only the Christians nurture a strong faith, however contaminated it may be with its contradictory dogmas. The masses should be allowed their new Christian symbols because of their need for some kind of metaphysical underpinning to safeguard and sustain their moral code.

It is important to realize that Julian, as poet, emperor, and military leader, experiences the solitary predicament of the pariah, misunderstood and unappreciated by his society. The account he gives of his political accomplishments is a succession of episodes in which his constituents misjudge his motives and misunderstand the significance of his authority. Vigny's Julian burns his poems in order to preserve the purity of his thoughts. Libanius reproaches him for having burned his poetry, which is the true source of his enthusiasm and exaltation, and he castigates him for not sincerely believing in the pagan deity whose cult he has attempted to restore. Libanius speaks for Vigny when he cautions Julian to conceive of his duty as that of preserving the human family, of protecting it against the kind of dissension and disunity that would spell its death. His actions have not contributed to the maintenance of the treasure of Daphné:

Si tout le monde fait ainsi, notre trésor va périr,
Julien, et tu sais ce que c'est que le Trésor de

MIROIR DROLATIQUE

Du comte de Vigny quand la tres noble muse

Caricature of Vigny by Lorentz

Daphné: c'est l'axe du monde, c'est la sève de la terre, mon ami, c'est l'élixir de la vie des hommes, distillé lentement par tous les peuples passés pour les peuples à venir: c'est la morale.

(If everyone acts in such a fashion, our treasure will perish, Julian, and you know what the Treasure of Daphné is: it is the world's axis, the sap of the earth, my friend, it is man's elixir of life, slowly distilled by past nations for future nations: it is the moral sense).

Crushed and disillusioned, Julian can only respond: "Je croyais mon œuvre meilleur" (I thought my work was better).

Libanius's reprimand disheartens Julian. He retreats from Daphné and leaves for Persia, where he soon will meet his death at the hands of the Christian barbarians he had once hoped to convert to paganism. The three remaining letters relate the uprising by the people of Antioch, the arrival of the barbarians, and Julian's tragic, quasi-suicidal death in battle. Libanius's long tirade in the first letter or chapter constitutes the essential part of the novel Vigny left unfinished.

Daphné resembles *L'Alméh* insofar as it also studies the moment when a dying religion encounters a nascent one, and the resulting confusion and contamination that occur from mixtures and borrowings. Libanius informs the residents of Daphné: "Ils ont noyé toutes leurs croyances dans toutes les corruptions. Les évêques d'Egypte adorent à la fois Jésus et Sérapis: que dire de plus!" (They have drowned all their beliefs in all corrupt practices. The bishops of Egypt adore Jesus and Serapis at the same time: what more can one say!). Julian's new mystical identification with Platonism, defined as the quest for a pure divinity without the assistance of symbols, registers as a protest against everything that confuses ideas and their representation. It is not far-fetched to see a parallelism in the attitude of Julian, the historical figure, and Vigny, the writer. When Julian becomes conscious of the waning of paganism, he resigns himself to virtual obliteration by the incipient barbarians. For Vigny in the 1830s, Christianity had arrived at the point where paganism was in A.D. 363. If, in order to rescue the permanent treasure of a basic moral sense, Julian abdicated politically before the new barbarians, Vigny, as a writer, labored to evolve a moral and social code that kept a safe distance from the fluctuating contingencies of everyday reality.

The epilogue of *Daphné* contrasts the situation in Asia Minor during the fourth century with that of Paris in February 1831. When Doctor Noir and Stello finish reading Trivulce's manuscript, they look at each other in a prolonged silence. Outside, a raucous crowd in the street is busy knocking down crosses. A carnival cortege parades toward the boulevards; singing and laughter permeate the atmosphere. Their hearts wrung with emotion, Stello and Doctor Noir leave the student's rooms to observe the mobs firsthand. Closer to the Seine, they watch children throwing books, pillaged from the archbishop's residence, into the river. The plunder recalls that of the temple of Daphné by the invading barbarians. They purchase a folio volume from a child, and begin to read Bar Hebraeus Abulfarage's lament on the burning of the library of Alexandria by the barbarians: "Tous deux lurent avidement ces belles paroles écrites dans le XIIIe siècle sur

l'événement des Barbares du VIIe" (The two avidly read these beautiful words written in the thirteenth century on the incidents of the barbarians in the seventh century). Stello and the Doctor return dejectedly to Trivulce's bedside.

Daphné begs the question: which religion, in the nineteenth century, will replace that which has been diminishing, to sustain humanity's moral integrity? Critical reaction to the publication of *Daphné* in 1913 ran the gamut from denunciations of the uncompleted novel as an anti-Christian work to laudatory commentaries praising Vigny's erudition and the firmness and purity of his descriptive prose. For some critics, *Daphné* emerges as a minor masterpiece of the nineteenth century.

If nothing else, *Stello, Servitude et grandeur militaires*, and *Daphné* point out that as a writer, Vigny felt ill at ease with the regime of Louis-Philippe. The year 1837 depressed him considerably: the bereavement he experienced at the death of his mother was aggravated by Lydia's physical deterioration. Now half blind, she could scarcely speak, and kept herself confined to her bed. Vigny attempted to resume his liaison with Marie Dorval in early 1838, but their rendezvous became quickly undermined by fits of jealousy on the part of the two lovers. By the end of March, Vigny took an interest in two young Americans from Charleston, South Carolina, who had arrived in Paris to study painting and music. He made love to Julia Dupré while his relationship with Dorval continued to worsen. By August he had broken off with the actress, and went into semiretirement in his country home, Maine-Giraud, in the department of Charente.

The author of *Daphné* grew increasingly estranged from two erstwhile friends, Hugo and Lamartine. He became annoyed and disconcerted by their facile pantheism. His literary production declined noticeably; by November 1838 he had completed only parts of the poem "La Mort du loup" (The Death of the Wolf). In 1841 he took up the cause of copyrights and literary ownership on behalf of French writers, pleading for more enlightened legislation. By year's end he received an invitation to present his candidacy for election to membership in the Académie Française. Rejected five times, presumably for lack of new publications, he finally won election on his sixth attempt in 1854 after having published in issues of the *Revue des Deux Mondes* such poems as "La Flûte," "La Sauvage" (The Savage

Woman), and "Le Mont des Oliviers" (The Mount of Olives).

In February 1848 Vigny was optimistic about the possible advent of a republican constitution, and he rallied to the causes of the revolution. He felt the time had come for him to act, and he announced his candidacy for election as delegate for the Maine-Giraud district. He refused, however, to wage an active campaign, and was overwhelmingly defeated at the polls. After the bloody reprisals of June 1848, he returned with Lydia to their property at Maine-Giraud. For five years he produced no new literary works. He devoted his energy instead to the exploitation of his land for the lucrative production of wine and brandy.

As an antiparliamentarian, Vigny declared himself to be a Bonapartist after the coup d'état of 2 December 1851. He judged Napoleon III to be the lesser evil threatening France at that time. During his years at Maine-Giraud and his intermittent stays in Paris, he engaged in frequent correspondence with the vicomtesse Alexandrine du Plessis, Mme Louis Ancelot-Lachaud, and Mlle Camilla Maunoir. In a letter to Alexandrine du Plessis, he likened his writing to Sisyphus' rock, which repeatedly rolled back despite his persistent efforts. When he returned definitively to Paris in 1854, he entered into a brief liaison with the poet Louise Colet. In 1858 he took up with Augusta Froustey Bouvard, forty years younger than himself. Despite their age difference, they fell deeply in love. The relationship lasted up to the time of his death.

Vigny had been ailing for some time from a stomach cancer, which confined him to his apartment. When Lydia died of a seizure on 22 December 1862, he was too incapacitated to attend her funeral. At the time of his own death on 17 September 1863, Augusta was eight-months pregnant. She gave birth to a son a little more than a month after her lover's death.

Vigny published one of his most celebrated poems, "La Bouteille à la mer" (The Bottle in the Sea), prior to 1848, but left unpublished "La Colère de Samson" (Samson's Anger), "Wanda," and "Les Destinées" (The Fates). He finished "Les Oracles" in 1862 and "L'Esprit pur" in 1863, straining during his final illness to complete what he dubbed his "philosophical poems." Final entries in his *Journal* reveal that during his last days, he was preoccupied with metaphysical questions. The eleven poems that comprise *Les Destinées* were published posthumously in 1864 by

his literary legatee, Louis Ratisbonne. Completed between 1838 and 1863, the poems focus on the individual's struggle with the forces of destiny, revealing themselves under such guises as fate, providence, and predestination. *Les Destinées* relates the poet's attempts to achieve a measure of freedom from the bondage of a dominating fate in order to accede to the heights of pure spirit. The collection is held together by the poet's expression of existential anguish and anxiety, dreams of a more ideal state of being, and emotional transports. Whatever mitigated optimism emerges from *Les Destinées* is attributable to the poet's final expression of a constructive stoicism or resignation to his plight as a human being. The primary message of the collection is that the modern individual must learn to adjust to his situation.

In the first poem, "Les Destinées," Vigny juxtaposes the messengers of ancient fatality with the guardianship of divine grace in Christianity. The liberation won by the coming of Christ is an illusory one. Only the designations have changed: grace supplants the Fates, but Christianity has only lengthened the leash of humanity without truly liberating it. *Les Destinées* highlights the poet's reactions to the human situation: he finds no solace in nature ("La Maison du berger" [The Shepherd's Hut]), nor in the love of woman ("La Colère de Samson"), nor in God ("Le Mont des Oliviers"). In the end, he adopts a stoic attitude that accepts suffering without complaining ("La Mort du loup"). If there is a ray of hope for the future, it rests on the ultimate triumph of ideas ("La Bouteille à la mer"). The longest and most ambitious poem, "La Maison du berger," celebrates solitude, reverie, love, and poetry. The second part of this 336-line work is cast in the form of a dialogue concerning the kind of verse that should result from reverie and meditation. Vigny recalls Doctor Noir's prescription to Stello. True poetry addresses the heaven's sun, love, and life, while false poetry records the activities of men of action at the impure crossroads of the city. True poetry is likened to a pure diamond in which ideas are conserved and allowed to show through. "L'Esprit pur" appropriately concludes the volume, which may by viewed as Vigny's final legacy.

In a real sense, all of Vigny's work from *Eloa* to *Stello*, *Servitude et grandeur militaires*, and *Daphné* leads up to the ringing affirmation of "L'Esprit pur." It asserts the writer's ultimate philosophical independence, which proclaims confidence that, in the end, the ultimate triumph will be that of mind over matter, the victory of spiritual values over material ones. The new religion he hails and celebrates in "L'Esprit pur" is that of the human spirit.

Letters:

Correspondance (1816-1863), edited by Emma Sakellaridès (Paris: Calmann-Lévy, 1905);

Correspondance (1822-1863), 2 volumes, edited by Léon Séché (Paris: Renaissance du Livre, 1913);

Lettres inédites d'Alfred de Vigny au marquis de La Grange, edited by Albert de Luppé (Paris: Conard, 1914);

Correspondance entre Sainte-Beuve et Alfred de Vigny: lettres inédites, edited by Louis Gillet (Paris: Kra, 1929);

Correspondance: 1816-1835, edited by Fernand Baldensperger (Paris: Conard, 1933);

Lettres d'un dernier amour: Correspondance inédite avec "Augusta" [Froustey Bouvard], edited by V.-L. Saulnier (Geneva: Droz / Lille: Giard, 1952);

Les plus belles lettres d'Alfred de Vigny, edited by Francis Ambrière (Paris: Calmann-Lévy, 1963);

Correspondance d'Alfred de Vigny (1816 - juillet 1830), volume 1, edited by Madeleine Ambrière (Paris: Presses Universitaires de France, 1989);

Correspondance d'Alfred de Vigny (août 1830 - septembre 1835), volume 2, edited by Madeleine Ambrière (Paris: Presses Universitaires de France, 1991).

Bibliography:

François Germain, *L'Imagination d'Alfred de Vigny* (Paris: Corti, 1961).

Biographies:

Ernest Séché, *Alfred de Vigny*, 2 volumes (Paris: Mercure de France, 1913);

Ernest Dupuy, *Alfred de Vigny: La vie et l'œuvre*, 2 volumes (Paris: Hachette, 1915);

Pierre Flottes, *Alfred de Vigny* (Paris: Perrin, 1925);

Robert de Traz, *Alfred de Vigny* (Paris: Hachette, 1928);

Fernand Baldensperger, *Alfred de Vigny: Contribution à sa biographie intellectuelle* (Paris: Belles Lettres, 1933);

Arnold Whitridge, *Alfred de Vigny* (London & New York: Oxford University Press, 1933);

Ernest Lauvrière, *Alfred de Vigny*, 2 volumes (Paris: Grasset, 1945);

Maurice Toesca, *Vigny, ou La passion de l'honneur* (Paris: Hachette, 1972);

Nicole Casanova, *Alfred de Vigny sous le masque de fer* (Paris: Calmann-Lévy, 1990).

References:

Jacques Barzun, *Berlioz and the Romantic Century*, 2 volumes (New York: Columbia University Press, 1969);

Fernande Bassan, "Un Drame historique de Vigny: *La Maréchale d'Ancre*," *Studia Neophilologica*, 51 (Winter-Spring 1978): 115-124;

Paul Bénichou, *Les Mages romantiques* (Paris: Gallimard, 1988);

Bénichou, *Le Sacre de l'écrivain: 1750-1830* (Paris: Corti, 1973);

Bénichou, *Le Temps des prophètes: Doctrines de l'âge romantique* (Paris: Gallimard, 1977);

Georges Bonnefoy, *La Pensée religieuse et morale d'Alfred de Vigny* (Paris: Hachette, 1944);

Frank Paul Bowman, "The Poetic Practices of Vigny's 'Poèmes philosophiques,'" *Modern Language Review*, 60 (July 1965): 359-368;

Bulletin de l'Association des Amis d'Alfred de Vigny, 18 numbers (Paris: Centre National des Lettres, 1975-1990);

René Canat, *Le Sentiment de la solitude morale chez les Romantiques et les Parnassiens* (Geneva: Slatkine, 1967);

Albert Cassagne, *La Théorie de l'art pour l'art en France chez les derniers Romantiques et les premiers Réalistes* (Paris: Dorbon, 1905);

P.-G. Castex, *Alfred de Vigny* (Paris: Hatier-Boivin, 1957);

Colloque Alfred de Vigny, *Vigny, les Pyrénées et l'Angleterre* (Pau: La Société des Sciences, Lettres et Arts, 1978);

Robert T. Denommé, "Alfred de Vigny, 1797-1863," in *European Writers: The Romantic Century*, volume 5, edited by Jacques Barzun (New York: Scribners, 1985), pp. 447-487;

Denommé, *Nineteenth-Century French Romantic Poets* (Carbondale & London: Southern Illinois University Press, 1969);

James Doolittle, *Alfred de Vigny* (New York: Twayne, 1967);

Marc Eigeldinger, *Alfred de Vigny* (Paris: Pierre Seghers, 1969);

Europe, issue on Vigny, 589 (1978);

D. O. Evans, "Alfred de Vigny and Positivism," *Romanic Review*, 35 (November 1944): 288-298;

Evans, *Social Romanticism in France* (Oxford: Clarendon, 1951);

Anne S. de Fabry, *Vigny: Le rayon intérieur ou la permanence de Stello* (Paris: La Pensée Universelle, 1978);

Pierre Flottes, *La Pensée politique et sociale d'Alfred de Vigny* (Paris: Les Belles Lettres, 1927);

Flottes, *Vigny et sa fortune littéraire* (Bordeaux: Ducrois, 1970);

François Germain, *L'Imagination d'Alfred de Vigny* (Paris: Corti, 1961);

Henri Guillemin, *Monsieur de Vigny: Homme d'ordre et poète* (Paris: Gallimard, 1955);

Charles Hill, "Vigny and Pascal," *PMLA*, 73 (December 1958): 533-579;

Bertrand de La Salle, *Alfred de Vigny* (Paris: Fayard, 1963);

Henri Lemaître, *Du romantisme au symbolisme: 1790-1914* (Paris: Pierre Bordas, 1982);

Henry Majewski, "The Second Consultation of the Docteur Noir: Alfred de Vigny's *Daphné* and the Power of Symbols," *Studies in Romanticism*, 20 (Winter 1981): 461-474;

Max Milner, *Le Diable dans la littérature française de Cazotte à Baudelaire* (Paris: Corti, 1960);

Milner, *La Littérature française: Le romantisme I: 1820-1843* (Paris: Arthaud, 1973);

Pierre Moreau, *Le Romantisme* (Paris: del Luca, 1957);

Claude Pichois, *La Littérature française: Le romantisme II: 1843-1869* (Paris: Arthaud, 1979);

Lawrence M. Porter, *The Renaissance of the Lyric in French Romanticism* (Lexington, Ky.: French Forum, 1978);

Georges Poulet, *Les Métamorphoses du cercle* (Paris: Plon, 1961);

Jean-Pierre Richard, *Etudes sur le romantisme* (Paris: Editions du Seuil, 1970);

Jacques-Philippe Saint-Gérand, *L'Intelligence et l'émotion: Fragments d'une esthétique vignyenne (théâtre et roman)* (Paris: Société pour l'Information Grammaticale, 1988);

Paul Viallaneix, *Vigny par lui-même* (Paris: Editions du Seuil, 1966).

Papers:

Vigny's papers and manuscripts are on deposit in the Fonds Ratisbonne at the Bibliothèque Nationale in Paris. Notebook D-631 can be found at the Bibliothèque Spoelberch de Lovenjoul at Chantilly.

Books for Further Reading

The following list includes books in English and French that deal with literary history in France in the nineteenth century, the genre of the novel during that period or as a whole, or more than one French fiction writer between 1800 and 1860, whether analytically in discrete chapters or synthetically. Many of these studies reflect or constitute the most up-to-date scholarship in the area. The reader wishing to pursue further studies can consult, in addition to the annual *MLA International Bibliography*, the following major bibliographies: Otto Klapp, *Bibliographie der französischen Literaturwissenschaft* (Frankfurt: Klosterman, 1960-), not annotated but very thorough and particularly good for European criticism; the bibliography in *Revue d'Histoire Littéraire de la France*, edited by René Rancœur (formerly a rubric of each issue, now printed as issue number 3 of each volume); David V. Erdman, *The Romantic Movement* (New York: Garland, 1980-1987; West Cornwall, Conn.: Locust Hill Press, 1988-); and *Critical Bibliography of French Literature: The Nineteenth Century*, 2 volumes (Syracuse: Syracuse University Press, 1993), a major annotated bibliography that completes the series begun by David C. Cabeen in 1947.

Abrams, M. H. *The Mirror and the Lamp: Romantic Theory and the Critical Tradition*. New York: Oxford University Press, 1953.

Allen, James Smith. *Popular French Romanticism: Authors, Readers and Books in the 19th Century*. Syracuse: Syracuse University Press, 1981.

Bernard, Claudie. *Le Chouan romanesque: Balzac, Barbey d'Aurevilly, Hugo*. Paris: Presses Universitaires de France, 1989.

Bersani, Leo. *Balzac to Beckett: Center and Circumference in French Fiction*. New York: Oxford University Press, 1970.

Bishop, Lloyd. *The Romantic Hero and His Heirs in French Literature*. New York: Peter Lang, 1984.

Bishop. *Romantic Irony in French Literature from Diderot to Beckett*. Nashville: Vanderbilt University Press, 1989.

Bowman, Frank Paul. *Le Christ des barricades, 1789-1848*. Paris: Le Cerf, 1987.

Bowman. *French Romanticism: Intertextual and Interdisciplinary Readings*. Baltimore & London: Johns Hopkins University Press, 1990.

Brombert, Victor. *The Hidden Reader: Stendhal, Balzac, Hugo, Baudelaire, Flaubert*. Cambridge, Mass. & London: Harvard University Press, 1988.

Brombert. *The Romantic Prison: The French Tradition*. Princeton: Princeton University Press, 1978.

Brooks, Peter. *Melodramatic Imagination: Balzac, Henry James, Melodrama, and the Mode of Excess*. New Haven: Yale University Press, 1976.

Brooks. *Reading for the Plot*. New York: Viking, 1984.

Cascardi, Anthony J. *The Bounds of Reason: Cervantes, Dostoevsky, Flaubert*. New York: Columbia University Press, 1986.

Castex, Pierre-Georges. *Horizons romantiques*. Paris: José Corti, 1983.

Chambers, Ross. *Mélancolie et opposition: Les débuts du modernisme en France*. Paris: José Corti, 1987.

Clark, Priscilla Parkhurst. *Literary France: The Making of a Culture*. Berkeley: University of California Press, 1987.

Cohn, Dorrit. *Transparent Minds: Narrative Modes for Presenting Consciousness in Fiction*. Princeton: Princeton University Press, 1978.

Danahy, Michael. *The Feminization of the Novel*. Gainesville: University of Florida Press, 1991.

Furst, Lilian R. *Counterparts: The Dynamics of Franco-German Literary Relationships, 1770-1895*. Detroit: Wayne State University Press, 1977.

Furst. *Fictions of Romantic Irony*. Cambridge, Mass.: Harvard University Press, 1984.

Graña, César. *Bohemian Versus Bourgeois: French Society and the French Man of Letters in the Nineteenth Century*. New York & London: Basic Books, 1964.

Hartman, Elwood. *French Romantics on Progress: Human and Aesthetic*. Madrid: José Porrúa Turanzas, 1983.

Houston, John Porter. *The Traditions of French Prose Style: A Rhetorical Study*. Baton Rouge & London: Louisiana State University Press, 1981.

Jones, Louisa E. *Sad Clowns and Pale Pierrots: Literature and the Popular Comic Arts in 19th-Century France*. Lexington, Ky.: French Forum, 1984.

Juden, Brian. *Traditions orphiques et tendances mystiques dans le romantisme français (1800-1855)*. Paris: Klincksieck, 1971.

Kelly, Dorothy. *Fictional Genders: Role and Representation in Nineteenth-Century French Narrative*. Lincoln: University of Nebraska Press, 1989.

Levine, George. *The Realistic Imagination*. Chicago: University of Chicago Press, 1981.

Majewski, Henry F. *Paradigm and Parody: Images of Creativity in French Romanticism—Vigny, Hugo, Balzac, Gautier, Musset*. Charlottesville: University Press of Virginia, 1989.

Martin, Andrew. *The Knowledge of Ignorance: From Genesis to Jules Verne*. Cambridge: Cambridge University Press, 1985.

McLendon, Will L., ed. *L'Hénaurme Siècle*. Heidelberg: Carl Winter Universitätsverlag, 1984.

Milner, Max. *Le Romantisme. I: 1820-1843*. Paris: Arthaud, 1973.

Mitchell, Robert L., ed. *Pre-Text/Text/Context: Essays on Nineteenth-Century French Literature*. Columbus: Ohio State University Press, 1980.

Muray, Philippe. *Le 19ᵉ siècle à travers les âges*. Paris: Denoël, 1984.

Pasco, Allan H. *Novel Configurations: A Study of French Fiction*. Birmingham, Ala.: Summa, 1987.

Paulson, William R. *Enlightenment, Romanticism, and the Blind in France*. Princeton: Princeton University Press, 1987.

Petrey, Sandy. *Realism and Revolution: Balzac, Stendhal, Zola and the Performances of History*. Ithaca, N.Y.: Cornell University Press, 1989.

Peyre, Henri. *What Is Romanticism?* Translated by Roda Roberts. University: University of Alabama Press, 1977.

Pichois, Claude. *Le Romantisme. II: 1843-1869*. Paris: Arthaud, 1979.

Planté, Christine. *La Petite Sœur de Balzac: Essai sur la femme auteur*. Paris: Éditions du Seuil, 1991.

Porter, Laurence M. *The Literary Dream in French Romanticism: A Psychoanalytic Interpretation*. Detroit: Wayne State University Press, 1979.

Poulet, Georges. *The Interior Distance*. Translated by Elliott Coleman. Baltimore: Johns Hopkins University Press, 1959.

Prendergast, Christopher. *The Order of Mimesis: Balzac, Stendhal, Nerval, Flaubert*. New York: Cambridge University Press, 1988.

Rieben, Pierre-André. *Délires romantiques: Musset, Nodier, Gautier, Hugo*. Paris: José Corti, 1989.

Romantisme et politique, 1815-1851. Paris: Armand Colin, 1967.

Sangsue, Daniel. *Le Récit excentrique: Gautier—De Maistre—Nerval—Nodier*. Paris: José Corti, 1987.

Schneider, Marcel. *Histoire de la littérature fantastique en France*. Paris: Fayard, 1985.

Schor, Naomi. *Breaking the Chain: Women, Theory, and French Realist Fiction*. New York: Columbia University Press, 1985.

Segal, Naomi. *Narcissus and Echo: Women in the French Récit*. Manchester, U.K.: Manchester University Press, 1988.

Steele, H. Meili. *Realism and the Drama of Difference: Strategies of Representation in Balzac, Flaubert, and James*. University Park & London: Pennsylvania State University Press, 1988.

Stern, J. P. *On Realism*. London & Boston: Routledge & Kegan Paul, 1973.

Terdiman, Richard. *Discourse/Counter-Discourse: The Theory and Practice of Symbolic Resistance in Nineteenth-Century France*. Ithaca, N.Y. & London: Cornell University Press, 1985.

Todorov, Tzvetan. *The Fantastic: A Structural Approach to a Literary Genre*. Translated by Richard Howard. Cleveland: Case Western Reserve, 1973.

Turnell, Martin. *The Novel in France*. New York: Vintage, 1958.

Van Tieghem, Philippe. *Petite histoire des grandes doctrines littéraires en France*. Paris: Presses Universitaires de France, 1960.

Viallaneix, Paul, ed. *Le Préromantisme: Hypothèque ou hypothèse?* Paris: Klincksieck, 1975.

Weinstein, Leo. *The Subversive Tradition in French Literature. I: 1721-1870*. Boston: Twayne, 1989.

Contributors

Norman Araujo ....*Boston College*
Scott D. Carpenter...*Carleton College*
Barbara T. Cooper...*University of New Hampshire*
Grant Crichfield ....*University of Vermont*
James T. Day ....*University of South Carolina*
Robert T. Denommé ....*University of Virginia*
Martha Noel Evans ....*Mary Baldwin College*
Madelyn Gutwirth...*West Chester University*
Stirling Haig...*University of North Carolina at Chapel Hill*
Will L. McLendon ....*University of Houston*
K. G. McWatters..*University of Liverpool*
Allan H. Pasco...*University of Kansas*
Ian Pickup..*University of Birmingham, England*
David A. Powell...*Hofstra University*
Timothy Raser...*University of Georgia*
Harry Redman, Jr. ....*Tulane University*
Albert B. Smith ....*University of Florida*
John R. Williams..*University of New Orleans*
Dennis Wood..*University of Birmingham, England*

Cumulative Index

Dictionary of Literary Biography, Volumes 1-119
Dictionary of Literary Biography Yearbook, 1980-1991
Dictionary of Literary Biography Documentary Series, Volumes 1-9

Cumulative Index

DLB before number: *Dictionary of Literary Biography*, Volumes 1-119
Y before number: *Dictionary of Literary Biography Yearbook*, 1980-1991
DS before number: *Dictionary of Literary Biography Documentary Series*, Volumes 1-9

A

Abbey Press DLB-49

The Abbey Theatre and Irish
    Drama, 1900-1945 ....DLB-10

Abbot, Willis J. 1863-1934 ....DLB-29

Abbott, Jacob 1803-1879 ....DLB-1

Abbott, Lyman 1835-1922 ....DLB-79

Abbott, Robert S. 1868-1940.........................DLB-29, 91

Abelard, Peter circa 1079-1142 ....DLB-115

Abelard-Schuman DLB-46

Abell, Arunah S. 1806-1888...............................DLB-43

Abercrombie, Lascelles 1881-1938.....................DLB-19

Aberdeen University Press Limited DLB-106

Abrahams, Peter 1919- DLB-117

Abrams, M. H. 1912- DLB-67

Abse, Dannie 1923- DLB-27

Academy Chicago Publishers...............................DLB-46

Ace Books...DLB-46

Achebe, Chinua 1930- DLB-117

Acorn, Milton 1923-1986 ....DLB-53

Acosta, Oscar Zeta 1935?- DLB-82

Actors Theatre of Louisville................................DLB-7

Adair, James 1709?-1783? DLB-30

Adam, Graeme Mercer 1839-1912......................DLB-99

Adame, Leonard 1947- DLB-82

Adamic, Louis 1898-1951 ....DLB-9

Adams, Alice 1926- Y-86

Adams, Brooks 1848-1927 ....DLB-47

Adams, Charles Francis, Jr. 1835-1915 ....DLB-47

Adams, Douglas 1952- Y-83

Adams, Franklin P. 1881-1960...........................DLB-29

Adams, Henry 1838-1918 ....DLB-12, 47

Adams, Herbert Baxter 1850-1901......................DLB-47

Adams, J. S. and C. [publishing house].........DLB-49

Adams, James Truslow 1878-1949 ....DLB-17

Adams, John 1735-1826 ....DLB-31

Adams, John Quincy 1767-1848 ....DLB-37

Adams, Léonie 1899-1988 ....DLB-48

Adams, Levi 1802-1832 ....DLB-99

Adams, Samuel 1722-1803.............................DLB-31, 43

Adams, William Taylor 1822-1897.....................DLB-42

Adamson, Sir John 1867-1950 ....DLB-98

Adcock, Betty 1938- DLB-105

Adcock, Betty, Certain Gifts..............................DLB-105

Adcock, Fleur 1934- DLB-40

Addison, Joseph 1672-1719...............................DLB-101

Ade, George 1866-1944.................................DLB-11, 25

Adeler, Max (see Clark, Charles Heber)

Advance Publishing Company............................DLB-49

AE 1867-1935..DLB-19

Aesthetic Poetry (1873), by Walter Pater DLB-35

Afro-American Literary Critics:
    An Introduction..DLB-33

Agassiz, Jean Louis Rodolphe 1807-1873 ....DLB-1

Agee, James 1909-1955 ....DLB-2, 26

The Agee Legacy: A Conference at
    the University of Tennessee
    at Knoxville Y-89

Aichinger, Ilse 1921- DLB-85

Aidoo, Ama Ata 1942- DLB-117

Aiken, Conrad 1889-1973 ....DLB-9, 45, 102

Ainsworth, William Harrison 1805-1882.........DLB-21

Aitken, Robert [publishing house] DLB-49

Akenside, Mark 1721-1770................................DLB-109

Akins, Zoë 1886-1958 ....DLB-26

Alain-Fournier 1886-1914....................................DLB-65

Alba, Nanina 1915-1968 ....DLB-41

Albee, Edward 1928- DLB-7

Albert the Great circa 1200-1280.....................DLB-115

Alberti, Rafael 1902- DLB-108

Alcott, Amos Bronson 1799-1888 ....DLB-1

Alcott, Louisa May 1832-1888 ....DLB-1, 42, 79

Alcott, William Andrus 1798-1859 ....DLB-1

Alden, Henry Mills 1836-1919 ....DLB-79

Alden, Isabella 1841-1930.............................DLB-42

Alden, John B. [publishing house]................DLB-49

Alden, Beardsley and Company...................DLB-49

Aldington, Richard 1892-1962.........DLB-20, 36, 100

Aldis, Dorothy 1896-1966.............................DLB-22

Aldiss, Brian W. 1925- DLB-14

Aldrich, Thomas Bailey 1836-1907
....DLB-42, 71, 74, 79

Alegría, Ciro 1909-1967 ....DLB-113

Aleixandre, Vicente 1898-1984 ....DLB-108

Aleramo, Sibilla 1876-1960 ....DLB-114

Alexander, Charles 1868-1923 ....DLB-91

Alexander, Charles Wesley
[publishing house]....................................DLB-49

Alexander, James 1691-1756 ....DLB-24

Alexander, Lloyd 1924- DLB-52

Alger, Horatio, Jr. 1832-1899 ....DLB-42

Algonquin Books of Chapel Hill DLB-46

Algren, Nelson 1909-1981 ....DLB-9; Y-81, 82

Allan, Andrew 1907-1974 ....DLB-88

Allan, Ted 1916- DLB-68

Allbeury, Ted 1917- DLB-87

Alldritt, Keith 1935- DLB-14

Allen, Ethan 1738-1789.................................DLB-31

Allen, Gay Wilson 1903- DLB-103

Allen, George 1808-1876...............................DLB-59

Allen, George [publishing house] DLB-106

Allen, George, and Unwin Limited.............DLB-112

Allen, Grant 1848-1899.........................DLB-70, 92

Allen, Henry W. 1912- Y-85

Allen, Hervey 1889-1949 ....DLB-9, 45

Allen, James 1739-1808................................DLB-31

Allen, James Lane 1849-1925........................DLB-71

Allen, Jay Presson 1922- DLB-26

Allen, John, and Company............................DLB-49

Allen, Samuel W. 1917- DLB-41

Allen, Woody 1935- DLB-44

Alline, Henry 1748-1784...............................DLB-99

Allingham, Margery 1904-1966 ....DLB-77

Allingham, William 1824-1889 ....DLB-35

Allison, W. L. [publishing house]................DLB-49

Allott, Kenneth 1912-1973............................DLB-20

Allston, Washington 1779-1843 ....DLB-1

Alonzo, Dámaso 1898-1990...........................DLB-108

Alsop, George 1636-post 1673 ....DLB-24

Alsop, Richard 1761-1815 ....DLB-37

Altemus, Henry, and Company DLB-49

Altenberg, Peter 1885-1919...........................DLB-81

Altolaguirre, Manuel 1905-1959 ....DLB-108

Aluko, T. M. 1918- DLB-117

Alurista 1947- DLB-82

Alvarez, A. 1929- DLB-14, 40

Amadi, Elechi 1934- DLB-117

Amado, Jorge 1912- DLB-113

Ambler, Eric 1909- DLB-77

*America: or, a Poem on the Settlement of the
British Colonies* (1780?), by Timothy
Dwight DLB-37

American Conservatory Theatre.....................DLB-7

American Fiction and the 1930s DLB-9

American Humor: A Historical Survey
East and Northeast
South and Southwest
Midwest
West DLB-11

American News Company DLB-49

The American Poets' Corner: The First
Three Years (1983-1986) Y-86

American Publishing Company.....................DLB-49

American Stationers' Company DLB-49

American Sunday-School Union DLB-49

American Temperance Union DLB-49

American Tract Society.................................DLB-49

The American Writers Congress
(9-12 October 1981).....................................Y-81

The American Writers Congress: A Report
on Continuing Business Y-81

Ames, Fisher 1758-1808 ....DLB-37

Ames, Mary Clemmer 1831-1884 ....DLB-23

Amini, Johari M. 1935- DLB-41

Amis, Kingsley 1922- DLB-15, 27, 100

Amis, Martin 1949- DLB-14

Ammons, A. R. 1926- DLB-5

Amory, Thomas 1691?-1788 ....DLB-39

Anaya, Rudolfo A. 1937- DLB-82

Andersch, Alfred 1914-1980.........................DLB-69

Anderson, Margaret 1886-1973 ....DLB-4, 91

Anderson, Maxwell 1888-1959.....................................DLB-7

Anderson, Patrick 1915-1979.....................................DLB-68

Anderson, Paul Y. 1893-1938 ....DLB-29

Anderson, Poul 1926- DLB-8

Anderson, Robert 1917- DLB-7

Anderson, Sherwood 1876-1941 ....DLB-4, 9, 86; DS-1

Andreas-Salomé, Lou 1861-1937 ....DLB-66

Andres, Stefan 1906-1970 ....DLB-69

Andrews, Charles M. 1863-1943 ....DLB-17

Andrews, Miles Peter ?-1814 ....DLB-89

Andrieux, Louis (see Aragon, Louis)

Andrian, Leopold von 1875-1951 ....DLB-81

Andrus, Silas, and Son DLB-49

Angell, James Burrill 1829-1916................................DLB-64

Angelou, Maya 1928- DLB-38

Angers, Félicité (see Conan, Laure)

The "Angry Young Men" DLB-15

Angus and Robertson (UK) Limited............................DLB-112

Anhalt, Edward 1914- DLB-26

Anners, Henry F. [publishing house] DLB-49

Anselm of Canterbury 1033-1109...............................DLB-115

Anthony, Piers 1934- DLB-8

Anthony Burgess's *99 Novels:* An Opinion Poll..................Y-84

Antin, Mary 1881-1949..Y-84

Antschel, Paul (see Celan, Paul)

Apodaca, Rudy S. 1939- DLB-82

Appleton, D., and Company DLB-49

Appleton-Century-Crofts...DLB-46

Applewhite, James 1935- DLB-105

Apple-wood Books...DLB-46

Aquin, Hubert 1929-1977 ....DLB-53

Aquinas, Thomas 1224 or 1225-1274..........................DLB-115

Aragon, Louis 1897-1982 ....DLB-72

Arbor House Publishing Company.................................DLB-46

Arbuthnot, John 1667-1735 ....DLB-101

Arcadia House...DLB-46

Arce, Julio G. (see Ulica, Jorge)

Archer, William 1856-1924 ....DLB-10

Arden, John 1930- DLB-13

Arden of Faversham DLB-62

Ardis Publishers Y-89

The Arena Publishing Company....................................DLB-49

Arena Stage..DLB-7

Arensberg, Ann 1937- Y-82

Arguedas, José María 1911-1969 ....DLB-113

Arias, Ron 1941- DLB-82

Arland, Marcel 1899-1986..DLB-72

Arlen, Michael 1895-1956..DLB-36, 77

Armah, Ayi Kwei 1939- DLB-117

Armed Services Editions...DLB-46

Arndt, Ernst Moritz 1769-1860....................................DLB-90

Arnim, Achim von 1781-1831.......................................DLB-90

Arnim, Bettina von 1785-1859......................................DLB-90

Arno Press DLB-46

Arnold, Edwin 1832-1904 ....DLB-35

Arnold, Matthew 1822-1888 ....DLB-32, 57

Arnold, Thomas 1795-1842 ....DLB-55

Arnold, Edward [publishing house]..............................DLB-112

Arnow, Harriette Simpson 1908-1986..........................DLB-6

Arp, Bill (see Smith, Charles Henry)

Arreola, Juan José 1918- DLB-113

Arrowsmith, J. W. [publishing house] DLB-106

Arthur, Timothy Shay 1809-1885.........................DLB-3, 42, 79

Artmann, H. C. 1921- DLB-85

Arvin, Newton 1900-1963 ....DLB-103

As I See It, by Carolyn Cassady.....................................DLB-16

Asch, Nathan 1902-1964 ....DLB-4, 28

Ash, John 1948- DLB-40

Ashbery, John 1927- DLB-5; Y-81

Ashendene Press DLB-112

Asher, Sandy 1942- Y-83

Ashton, Winifred (see Dane, Clemence)

Asimov, Isaac 1920-1992 ....DLB-8

Asselin, Olivar 1874-1937..DLB-92

Asturias, Miguel Angel 1899-1974...............................DLB-113

Atheneum Publishers..DLB-46

Atherton, Gertrude 1857-1948 ....DLB-9, 78

Athlone Press DLB-112

Atkins, Josiah circa 1755-1781 ....DLB-31

Atkins, Russell 1926- DLB-41

The Atlantic Monthly Press...DLB-46

Attaway, William 1911-1986...DLB-76

Atwood, Margaret 1939- DLB-53

Aubert, Alvin 1930- DLB-41

Aubert de Gaspé, Phillipe-Ignace-François
      1814-1841..DLB-99

Aubert de Gaspé, Phillipe-Joseph
  1786-1871..DLB-99

Aubin, Napoléon 1812-1890.........................DLB-99

Aubin, Penelope 1685-circa 1731.................DLB-39

Aubrey-Fletcher, Henry Lancelot (see Wade, Henry)

Auchincloss, Louis 1917- DLB-2; Y-80

Auden, W. H. 1907-1973........................DLB-10, 20

Audio Art in America: A Personal Memoir....................Y-85

Auernheimer, Raoul 1876-1948.................DLB-81

Augustine 354-430....................................DLB-115

Austen, Jane 1775-1817.............................DLB-116

Austin, Alfred 1835-1913............................DLB-35

Austin, Mary 1868-1934.........................DLB-9, 78

Austin, William 1778-1841..........................DLB-74

The Author's Apology for His Book
  (1684), by John Bunyan.........................DLB-39

An Author's Response, by Ronald Sukenick Y-82

Authors and Newspapers Association...............DLB-46

Authors' Publishing Company........................DLB-49

Avalon Books...DLB-46

Avendaño, Fausto 1941- DLB-82

Averroës 1126-1198..................................DLB-115

Avicenna 980-1037....................................DLB-115

Avison, Margaret 1918- DLB-53

Avon Books...DLB-46

Awoonor, Kofi 1935- DLB-117

Ayckbourn, Alan 1939- DLB-13

Aymé, Marcel 1902-1967.............................DLB-72

Aytoun, William Edmondstoune 1813-1865 ....DLB-32

B

Babbitt, Irving 1865-1933............................DLB-63

Babbitt, Natalie 1932- DLB-52

Babcock, John [publishing house]..................DLB-49

Bache, Benjamin Franklin 1769-1798 ....DLB-43

Bachmann, Ingeborg 1926-1973....................DLB-85

Bacon, Delia 1811-1859...............................DLB-1

Bacon, Roger circa 1214/1220-1292............DLB-115

Bacon, Thomas circa 1700-1768 ....DLB-31

Badger, Richard G., and Company.................DLB-49

Bage, Robert 1728-1801.............................DLB-39

Bagehot, Walter 1826-1877.........................DLB-55

Bagley, Desmond 1923-1983........................DLB-87

Bagnold, Enid 1889-1981............................DLB-13

Bahr, Hermann 1863-1934...................DLB-81, 118

Bailey, Alfred Goldsworthy 1905- DLB-68

Bailey, Francis [publishing house]................DLB-49

Bailey, H. C. 1878-1961 ....DLB-77

Bailey, Jacob 1731-1808.............................DLB-99

Bailey, Paul 1937- DLB-14

Bailey, Philip James 1816-1902....................DLB-32

Baillargeon, Pierre 1916-1967......................DLB-88

Baillie, Hugh 1890-1966..............................DLB-29

Baillie, Joanna 1762-1851............................DLB-93

Bailyn, Bernard 1922- DLB-17

Bainbridge, Beryl 1933- DLB-14

Baird, Irene 1901-1981...............................DLB-68

The Baker and Taylor Company DLB-49

Baker, Carlos 1909-1987.............................DLB-103

Baker, Herschel C. 1914-1990 ....DLB-111

Baker, Houston A., Jr. 1943- DLB-67

Baker, Walter H., Company
  ("Baker's Plays")..................................DLB-49

Bald, Wambly 1902- DLB-4

Balderston, John 1889-1954........................DLB-26

Baldwin, James 1924-1987.....................DLB-2, 7, 33; Y-87

Baldwin, Joseph Glover 1815-1864...............DLB-3, 11

Ballantine Books..DLB-46

Ballard, J. G. 1930- DLB-14

Ballou, Maturin Murray 1820-1895...............DLB-79

Ballou, Robert O. [publishing house] DLB-46

Balzac, Honoré de 1799-1855 ....DLB-119

Bambara, Toni Cade 1939- DLB-38

Bancroft, A. L., and Company.......................DLB-49

Bancroft, George 1800-1891...............DLB-1, 30, 59

Bancroft, Hubert Howe 1832-1918................DLB-47

Bangs, John Kendrick 1862-1922 ....DLB-11, 79

Banim, John 1798-1842...............................DLB-116

Banks, John circa 1653-1706.......................DLB-80

Bantam Books...DLB-46

Banville, John 1945- DLB-14

Baraka, Amiri 1934- DLB-5, 7, 16, 38; DS-8

Barbauld, Anna Laetitia 1743-1825............DLB-107, 109

Barbeau, Marius 1883-1969 ....DLB-92

Barber, John Warner 1798-1885...................DLB-30

Barbey d'Aurevilly, Jules-Amédée 1808-1889............DLB-119

Barbour, Ralph Henry 1870-1944 ....DLB-22

Barbusse, Henri 1873-1935.........................DLB-65

Barclay, E. E., and Company DLB-49

Bardeen, C. W. [publishing house]..............DLB-49

Baring, Maurice 1874-1945 ....DLB-34

Barker, A. L. 1918- DLB-14

Barker, George 1913-1991 ....DLB-20

Barker, Harley Granville 1877-1946...........DLB-10

Barker, Howard 1946- DLB-13

Barker, James Nelson 1784-1858...............DLB-37

Barker, Jane 1652-1727? DLB-39

Barker, Arthur, Limited DLB-112

Barks, Coleman 1937- DLB-5

Barlach, Ernst 1870-1938....................DLB-56, 118

Barlow, Joel 1754-1812........................DLB-37

Barnard, John 1681-1770......................DLB-24

Barnes, A. S., and Company DLB-49

Barnes, Djuna 1892-1982........DLB-4, 9, 45

Barnes, Margaret Ayer 1886-1967.............DLB-9

Barnes, Peter 1931- DLB-13

Barnes, William 1801-1886 ....DLB-32

Barnes and Noble Books DLB-46

Barney, Natalie 1876-1972 ....DLB-4

Baron, Richard W., Publishing Company.......DLB-46

Barr, Robert 1850-1912 ....DLB-70, 92

Barrax, Gerald William 1933- DLB-41

Barrett, Eaton Stannard 1786-1820...........DLB-116

Barrie, James M. 1860-1937...................DLB-10

Barrie and Jenkins DLB-112

Barrio, Raymond 1921- DLB-82

Barry, Philip 1896-1949 ....DLB-7

Barry, Robertine (see Françoise)

Barse and Hopkins DLB-46

Barstow, Stan 1928- DLB-14

Barth, John 1930- DLB-2

Barthelme, Donald 1931-1989........DLB-2; Y-80, 89

Barthelme, Frederick 1943- Y-85

Bartlett, John 1820-1905 ....DLB-1

Bartol, Cyrus Augustus 1813-1900 ....DLB-1

Barton, Bernard 1784-1849 ....DLB-96

Bartram, John 1699-1777......................DLB-31

Bartram, William 1739-1823 ....DLB-37

Basic Books DLB-46

Bass, T. J. 1932- Y-81

Bassett, John Spencer 1867-1928..............DLB-17

Bassler, Thomas Joseph (see Bass, T. J.)

Bate, Walter Jackson 1918- DLB-67, 103

Bates, Katharine Lee 1859-1929 ....DLB-71

Batsford, B. T. [publishing house]...........DLB-106

Baum, L. Frank 1856-1919 ....DLB-22

Baum, Vicki 1888-1960 ....DLB-85

Baumbach, Jonathan 1933- Y-80

Bawden, Nina 1925- DLB-14

Bax, Clifford 1886-1962....................DLB-10, 100

Bayer, Eleanor (see Perry, Eleanor)

Bayer, Konrad 1932-1964 ....DLB-85

Bazin, Hervé 1911- DLB-83

Beach, Sylvia 1887-1962 ....DLB-4

Beacon Press.................................DLB-49

Beadle and Adams.............................DLB-49

Beagle, Peter S. 1939- Y-80

Beal, M. F. 1937- Y-81

Beale, Howard K. 1899-1959 ....DLB-17

Beard, Charles A. 1874-1948 ....DLB-17

A Beat Chronology: The First Twenty-five
    Years, 1944-1969...........................DLB-16

Beattie, Ann 1947- Y-82

Beattie, James 1735-1803 ....DLB-109

Beauchemin, Nérée 1850-1931 ....DLB-92

Beauchemin, Yves 1941- DLB-60

Beaugrand, Honoré 1848-1906 ....DLB-99

Beaulieu, Victor-Lévy 1945- DLB-53

Beaumont, Francis circa 1584-1616
    and Fletcher, John 1579-1625..............DLB-58

Beauvoir, Simone de 1908-1986.........DLB-72; Y-86

Becher, Ulrich 1910- DLB-69

Becker, Carl 1873-1945 ....DLB-17

Becker, Jurek 1937- DLB-75

Becker, Jürgen 1932- DLB-75

Beckett, Samuel 1906-1989..........DLB-13, 15, Y-90

Beckford, William 1760-1844..................DLB-39

Beckham, Barry 1944- DLB-33

Beddoes, Thomas Lovell 1803-1849.............DLB-96

Beecher, Catharine Esther 1800-1878..........DLB-1

Beecher, Henry Ward 1813-1887................DLB-3, 43

Beer, George L. 1872-1920 ....DLB-47

Beer, Patricia 1919- DLB-40

Beerbohm, Max 1872-1956....................DLB-34, 100

Beer-Hofmann, Richard 1866-1945..............DLB-81

Beers, Henry A. 1847-1926.....................................DLB-71

Beeton, S. O. [publishing house]..................DLB-106

Bégon, Elisabeth 1696-1755..........................DLB-99

Behan, Brendan 1923-1964...............................DLB-13

Behn, Aphra 1640?-1689 ....DLB-39, 80

Behn, Harry 1898-1973......................................DLB-61

Behrman, S. N. 1893-1973.........................DLB-7, 44

Belaney, Archibald Stansfeld (see Grey Owl)

Belasco, David 1853-1931.................................DLB-7

Belford, Clarke and Company DLB-49

Belitt, Ben 1911- DLB-5

Belknap, Jeremy 1744-1798 ....DLB-30, 37

Bell, James Madison 1826-1902 ....DLB-50

Bell, Marvin 1937- DLB-5

Bell, Millicent 1919- DLB-111

Bell, George, and Sons DLB-106

Bell, Robert [publishing house].....................DLB-49

Bellamy, Edward 1850-1898 ....DLB-12

Bellamy, Joseph 1719-1790 ....DLB-31

La Belle Assemblée 1806-1837 ....DLB-110

Belloc, Hilaire 1870-1953.........................DLB-19, 100

Bellow, Saul 1915- DLB-2, 28; Y-82; DS-3

Belmont Productions DLB-46

Bemelmans, Ludwig 1898-1962 ....DLB-22

Bemis, Samuel Flagg 1891-1973 ....DLB-17

Bemrose, William [publishing house] DLB-106

Benchley, Robert 1889-1945 ....DLB-11

Benedetti, Mario 1920- DLB-113

Benedictus, David 1938- DLB-14

Benedikt, Michael 1935- DLB-5

Benét, Stephen Vincent 1898-1943 .....DLB-4, 48, 102

Benét, William Rose 1886-1950 ....DLB-45

Benford, Gregory 1941- Y-82

Benjamin, Park 1809-1864.......................DLB-3, 59, 73

Benn, Gottfried 1886-1956...............................DLB-56

Benn Brothers Limited.....................................DLB-106

Bennett, Arnold 1867-1931 ....DLB-10, 34, 98

Bennett, Charles 1899- DLB-44

Bennett, Gwendolyn 1902- DLB-51

Bennett, Hal 1930- DLB-33

Bennett, James Gordon 1795-1872................DLB-43

Bennett, James Gordon, Jr. 1841-1918 ....DLB-23

Bennett, John 1865-1956..................................DLB-42

Bennett, Louise 1919- DLB-117

Benoit, Jacques 1941- DLB-60

Benson, A. C. 1862-1925..................................DLB-98

Benson, Jackson J. 1930- DLB-111

Benson, Stella 1892-1933 ....DLB-36

Bentham, Jeremy 1748-1832...........................DLB-107

Bentley, E. C. 1875-1956..................................DLB-70

Bentley, Richard [publishing house]............DLB-106

Benton, Robert 1932- and Newman,
    David 1937- DLB-44

Benziger Brothers DLB-49

Beresford, Anne 1929- DLB-40

Beresford-Howe, Constance 1922- DLB-88

Berford, R. G., Company DLB-49

Berg, Stephen 1934- DLB-5

Bergengruen, Werner 1892-1964....................DLB-56

Berger, John 1926- DLB-14

Berger, Meyer 1898-1959.................................DLB-29

Berger, Thomas 1924- DLB-2; Y-80

Berkeley, Anthony 1893-1971..........................DLB-77

Berkeley, George 1685-1753 ....DLB-31, 101

The Berkley Publishing Corporation.............DLB-46

Bernard of Chartres circa 1060-1124?........DLB-115

Bernal, Vicente J. 1888-1915 ....DLB-82

Bernanos, Georges 1888-1948.........................DLB-72

Bernard, Harry 1898-1979...............................DLB-92

Bernard, John 1756-1828..................................DLB-37

Bernhard, Thomas 1931-1989 ....DLB-85

Berrigan, Daniel 1921- DLB-5

Berrigan, Ted 1934-1983....................................DLB-5

Berry, Wendell 1934- DLB-5, 6

Berryman, John 1914-1972..............................DLB-48

Bersianik, Louky 1930- DLB-60

Berton, Pierre 1920- DLB-68

Bessette, Gerard 1920- DLB-53

Bessie, Alvah 1904-1985....................................DLB-26

Bester, Alfred 1913- DLB-8

The Bestseller Lists: An Assessment.................Y-84

Betjeman, John 1906-1984....................DLB-20; Y-84

Betts, Doris 1932- Y-82

Beveridge, Albert J. 1862-1927.......................DLB-17

Beverley, Robert circa 1673-1722 ....DLB-24, 30

Beyle, Marie-Henri (see Stendhal)

Bibaud, Adèle 1854-1941.................................DLB-92

Bibaud, Michel 1782-1857.....................................DLB-99

Bibliographical and Textual Scholarship
    Since World War II Y-89

The Bicentennial of James Fenimore Cooper:
    An International Celebration Y-89

Bichsel, Peter 1935- DLB-75

Bickerstaff, Isaac John 1733-circa 1808.............DLB-89

Biddle, Drexel [publishing house]...................DLB-49

Bidwell, Walter Hilliard 1798-1881 ....DLB-79

Bienek, Horst 1930- DLB-75

Bierbaum, Otto Julius 1865-1910 ....DLB-66

Bierce, Ambrose 1842-1914?...............DLB-11, 12, 23, 71, 74

Bigelow, William F. 1879-1966 ....DLB-91

Biggle, Lloyd, Jr. 1923- DLB-8

Biglow, Hosea (see Lowell, James Russell)

Billings, Josh (see Shaw, Henry Wheeler)

Binding, Rudolf G. 1867-1938 ....DLB-66

Bingham, Caleb 1757-1817 ....DLB-42

Binyon, Laurence 1869-1943 ....DLB-19

Biographical Documents I Y-84

Biographical Documents II Y-85

Bioren, John [publishing house] DLB-49

Bioy Casares, Adolfo 1914- DLB-113

Bird, William 1888-1963 ....DLB-4

Birney, Earle 1904- DLB-88

Birrell, Augustine 1850-1933............................DLB-98

Bishop, Elizabeth 1911-1979 ....DLB-5

Bishop, John Peale 1892-1944 ....DLB-4, 9, 45

Bissett, Bill 1939- DLB-53

Black, David (D. M.) 1941- DLB-40

Black, Walter J. [publishing house] DLB-46

Black, Winifred 1863-1936...............................DLB-25

The Black Aesthetic: Background DS-8

The Black Arts Movement, by Larry Neal DLB-38

Black Theaters and Theater Organizations in
    America, 1961-1982: A Research List DLB-38

Black Theatre: A Forum [excerpts] DLB-38

Blackamore, Arthur 1679-? DLB-24, 39

Blackburn, Alexander L. 1929- Y-85

Blackburn, Paul 1926-1971 ....DLB-16; Y-81

Blackburn, Thomas 1916-1977 ....DLB-27

Blackmore, R. D. 1825-1900 ....DLB-18

Blackmur, R. P. 1904-1965................................DLB-63

Blackwell, Basil, Publisher...............................DLB-106

Blackwood, Caroline 1931- DLB-14

Blackwood's Edinburgh Magazine 1817-1980 ....DLB-110

Blair, Eric Arthur (see Orwell, George)

Blair, Francis Preston 1791-1876......................DLB-43

Blair, James circa 1655-1743 ....DLB-24

Blair, John Durburrow 1759-1823....................DLB-37

Blais, Marie-Claire 1939- DLB-53

Blaise, Clark 1940- DLB-53

Blake, Nicholas 1904-1972 ....DLB-77
    (see Day Lewis, C.)

Blake, William 1757-1827..................................DLB-93

The Blakiston Company......................................DLB-49

Blanchot, Maurice 1907- DLB-72

Blanckenburg, Christian Friedrich von
    1744-1796...DLB-94

Bledsoe, Albert Taylor 1809-1877 ....DLB-3, 79

Blelock and Company...DLB-49

Blennerhassett, Margaret Agnew 1773-1842 ....DLB-99

Bles, Geoffrey [publishing house].....................DLB-112

Blish, James 1921-1975......................................DLB-8

Bliss, E., and E. White [publishing house].......DLB-49

Bloch, Robert 1917- DLB-44

Block, Rudolph (see Lessing, Bruno)

Blondal, Patricia 1926-1959..............................DLB-88

Bloom, Harold 1930- DLB-67

Bloomer, Amelia 1818-1894...............................DLB-79

Bloomfield, Robert 1766-1823 ....DLB-93

Blotner, Joseph 1923- DLB-111

Blume, Judy 1938- DLB-52

Blunck, Hans Friedrich 1888-1961 ....DLB-66

Blunden, Edmund 1896-1974...................DLB-20, 100

Blunt, Wilfrid Scawen 1840-1922 ....DLB-19

Bly, Nellie (see Cochrane, Elizabeth)

Bly, Robert 1926- DLB-5

Boaden, James 1762-1839..................................DLB-89

The Bobbs-Merrill Archive at the
    Lilly Library, Indiana University.................Y-90

The Bobbs-Merrill Company DLB-46

Bobrowski, Johannes 1917-1965 ....DLB-75

Bodenheim, Maxwell 1892-1954................DLB-9, 45

Bodkin, M. McDonnell 1850-1933...................DLB-70

Bodley Head DLB-112

Bodmer, Johann Jakob 1698-1783...................DLB-97

Bodmershof, Imma von 1895-1982..................DLB-85

Bodsworth, Fred 1918- DLB-68

Boehm, Sydney 1908- DLB-44

Boer, Charles 1939- DLB-5

Boethius circa 480-circa 524.......DLB-115

Boethius of Dacia circa 1240-? DLB-115

Bogan, Louise 1897-1970 ....DLB-45

Bogarde, Dirk 1921- DLB-14

Bogue, David [publishing house] DLB-106

Bohn, H. G. [publishing house] DLB-106

Boie, Heinrich Christian 1744-1806 ....DLB-94

Bok, Edward W. 1863-1930 ....DLB-91

Boland, Eavan 1944- DLB-40

Bolingbroke, Henry St. John, Viscount 1678-1751.......DLB-101

Böll, Heinrich 1917-1985 ....Y-85, DLB-69

Bolling, Robert 1738-1775 ....DLB-31

Bolt, Carol 1941- DLB-60

Bolt, Robert 1924- DLB-13

Bolton, Herbert E. 1870-1953.......DLB-17

Bonaventura.......DLB-90

Bonaventure circa 1217-1274.......DLB-115

Bond, Edward 1934- DLB-13

Boni, Albert and Charles [publishing house].......DLB-46

Boni and Liveright.......DLB-46

Robert Bonner's Sons DLB-49

Bontemps, Arna 1902-1973 ....DLB-48, 51

The Book League of America.......DLB-46

Book Reviewing in America: I Y-87

Book Reviewing in America: II.......Y-88

Book Reviewing in America: III Y-89

Book Reviewing in America: IV.......Y-90

Book Reviewing in America: V Y-91

Book Supply Company.......DLB-49

The Booker Prize
   Address by Anthony Thwaite, Chairman
      of the Booker Prize Judges
   Comments from Former Booker Prize
      Winners.......Y-86

Boorstin, Daniel J. 1914- DLB-17

Booth, Mary L. 1831-1889 ....DLB-79

Booth, Philip 1925- Y-82

Booth, Wayne C. 1921- DLB-67

Borchardt, Rudolf 1877-1945 ....DLB-66

Borchert, Wolfgang 1921-1947 ....DLB-69

Borel, Petrus 1809-1859 ....DLB-119

Borges, Jorge Luis 1899-1986.......DLB-113; Y-86

Börne, Ludwig 1786-1837.......DLB-90

Borrow, George 1803-1881 ....DLB-21, 55

Bosco, Henri 1888-1976.......DLB-72

Bosco, Monique 1927- DLB-53

Boswell, James 1740-1795 ....DLB-104

Botta, Anne C. Lynch 1815-1891.......DLB-3

Bottomley, Gordon 1874-1948.......DLB-10

Bottoms, David 1949- Y-83

Bottrall, Ronald 1906- DLB-20

Boucher, Anthony 1911-1968 ....DLB-8

Boucher, Jonathan 1738-1804.......DLB-31

Boucher de Boucherville, George 1814-1894 ....DLB-99

Boudreau, Daniel (see Coste, Donat)

Bourassa, Napoléon 1827-1916.......DLB-99

Bourinot, John George 1837-1902.......DLB-99

Bourjaily, Vance Nye 1922- DLB-2

Bourne, Edward Gaylord 1860-1908 ....DLB-47

Bourne, Randolph 1886-1918 ....DLB-63

Bousoño, Carlos 1923- DLB-108

Bousquet, Joë 1897-1950 ....DLB-72

Bova, Ben 1932- Y-81

Bove, Emmanuel 1898-1945.......DLB-72

Bovard, Oliver K. 1872-1945 ....DLB-25

Bowen, Elizabeth 1899-1973 ....DLB-15

Bowen, Francis 1811-1890 ....DLB-1, 59

Bowen, John 1924- DLB-13

Bowen-Merrill Company DLB-49

Bowering, George 1935- DLB-53

Bowers, Claude G. 1878-1958.......DLB-17

Bowers, Edgar 1924- DLB-5

Bowers, Fredson Thayer 1905-1991 ....Y-91

Bowles, Paul 1910- DLB-5, 6

Bowles, Samuel III 1826-1878 ....DLB-43

Bowles, William Lisles 1762-1850.......DLB-93

Bowman, Louise Morey 1882-1944.......DLB-68

Boyd, James 1888-1944 ....DLB-9

Boyd, John 1919- DLB-8

Boyd, Thomas 1898-1935.......DLB-9

Boyesen, Hjalmar Hjorth 1848-1895.......DLB-12, 71

Boyle, Kay 1902- DLB-4, 9, 48, 86

Boyle, Roger, Earl of Orrery 1621-1679.......DLB-80

Boyle, T. Coraghessan 1948- Y-86

Brackenbury, Alison 1953- DLB-40

Brackenridge, Hugh Henry 1748-1816 ....DLB-11, 37

Brackett, Charles 1892-1969............................DLB-26

Brackett, Leigh 1915-1978.............................DLB-8, 26

Bradburn, John [publishing house].............................DLB-49

Bradbury, Malcolm 1932- DLB-14

Bradbury, Ray 1920- DLB-2, 8

Bradbury and Evans DLB-106

Braddon, Mary Elizabeth 1835-1915 ....DLB-18, 70

Bradford, Andrew 1686-1742 ....DLB-43, 73

Bradford, Gamaliel 1863-1932 ....DLB-17

Bradford, John 1749-1830............................DLB-43

Bradford, Roark 1896-1948 ....DLB-86

Bradford, William 1590-1657 ....DLB-24, 30

Bradford, William III 1719-1791 ....DLB-43, 73

Bradlaugh, Charles 1833-1891 ....DLB-57

Bradley, David 1950- DLB-33

Bradley, Ira, and Company............................DLB-49

Bradley, J. W., and Company............................DLB-49

Bradley, Marion Zimmer 1930- DLB-8

Bradley, William Aspenwall 1878-1939.......................DLB-4

Bradstreet, Anne 1612 or 1613-1672............................DLB-24

Bradwardine, Thomas circa 1295-1349 ....DLB-115

Brady, Frank 1924-1986............................DLB-111

Brady, Frederic A. [publishing house]........................DLB-49

Bragg, Melvyn 1939- DLB-14

Brainard, Charles H. [publishing house]......................DLB-49

Braine, John 1922-1986......................DLB-15; Y-86

Braithwaite, William Stanley 1878-1962.................DLB-50, 54

Bräker, Ulrich 1735-1798 ....DLB-94

Bramah, Ernest 1868-1942 ....DLB-70

Branagan, Thomas 1774-1843 ....DLB-37

Branch, William Blackwell 1927- DLB-76

Branden Press DLB-46

Brault, Jacques 1933- DLB-53

Braun, Volker 1939- DLB-75

Brautigan, Richard 1935-1984....................DLB-2, 5; Y-80, 84

Braxton, Joanne M. 1950- DLB-41

Bray, Anne Eliza 1790-1883 ....DLB-116

Bray, Thomas 1656-1730............................DLB-24

Braziller, George [publishing house] DLB-46

The Bread Loaf Writers' Conference 1983 ....Y-84

The Break-Up of the Novel (1922),
    by John Middleton Murry......................DLB-36

Breasted, James Henry 1865-1935 ....DLB-47

Brecht, Bertolt 1898-1956 ....DLB-56

Bredel, Willi 1901-1964............................DLB-56

Breitinger, Johann Jakob 1701-1776............................DLB-97

Bremser, Bonnie 1939- DLB-16

Bremser, Ray 1934- DLB-16

Brentano, Bernard von 1901-1964 ....DLB-56

Brentano, Clemens 1778-1842 ....DLB-90

Brentano's DLB-49

Brenton, Howard 1942- DLB-13

Breton, André 1896-1966............................DLB-65

Brewer, Warren and Putnam DLB-46

Brewster, Elizabeth 1922- DLB-60

Bridgers, Sue Ellen 1942- DLB-52

Bridges, Robert 1844-1930............................DLB-19, 98

Bridie, James 1888-1951 ....DLB-10

Briggs, Charles Frederick 1804-1877............................DLB-3

Brighouse, Harold 1882-1958 ....DLB-10

Brimmer, B. J., Company............................DLB-46

Brinnin, John Malcolm 1916- DLB-48

Brisbane, Albert 1809-1890............................DLB-3

Brisbane, Arthur 1864-1936............................DLB-25

British Academy DLB-112

The British Library and the Regular Readers' Group.......Y-91

The British Critic 1793-1843............................DLB-110

*The British Review and London
    Critical Journal* 1811-1825 ....DLB-110

Broadway Publishing Company......................DLB-46

Broch, Hermann 1886-1951............................DLB-85

Brochu, André 1942- DLB-53

Brock, Edwin 1927- DLB-40

Brod, Max 1884-1968............................DLB-81

Brodhead, John R. 1814-1873............................DLB-30

Brome, Richard circa 1590-1652............................DLB-58

Bromfield, Louis 1896-1956............................DLB-4, 9, 86

Broner, E. M. 1930- DLB-28

Brontë, Anne 1820-1849 ....DLB-21

Brontë, Charlotte 1816-1855 ....DLB-21

Brontë, Emily 1818-1848............................DLB-21, 32

Brooke, Frances 1724-1789 ....DLB-39, 99

Brooke, Henry 1703?-1783............................DLB-39

Brooke, Rupert 1887-1915 ....DLB-19

Brooker, Bertram 1888-1955 ....DLB-88

Brooke-Rose, Christine 1926- DLB-14

Cumulative Index

Brookner, Anita 1928- Y-87

Brooks, Charles Timothy 1813-1883 ....DLB-1

Brooks, Cleanth 1906- DLB-63

Brooks, Gwendolyn 1917- DLB-5, 76

Brooks, Jeremy 1926- DLB-14

Brooks, Mel 1926- DLB-26

Brooks, Noah 1830-1903 ....DLB-42

Brooks, Richard 1912- DLB-44

Brooks, Van Wyck 1886-1963 ....DLB-45, 63, 103

Brophy, Brigid 1929- DLB-14

Brossard, Chandler 1922- DLB-16

Brossard, Nicole 1943- DLB-53

Brother Antoninus (see Everson, William)

Brougham and Vaux, Henry Peter
Brougham, Baron 1778-1868 ....DLB-110

Brougham, John 1810-1880 ....DLB-11

Broughton, James 1913- DLB-5

Broughton, Rhoda 1840-1920 ....DLB-18

Broun, Heywood 1888-1939 ....DLB-29

Brown, Alice 1856-1948 ....DLB-78

Brown, Bob 1886-1959 ....DLB-4, 45

Brown, Cecil 1943- DLB-33

Brown, Charles Brockden 1771-1810 ....DLB-37, 59, 73

Brown, Christy 1932-1981 ....DLB-14

Brown, Dee 1908- Y-80

Browne, Francis Fisher 1843-1913 ....DLB-79

Brown, Frank London 1927-1962 ....DLB-76

Brown, Fredric 1906-1972 ....DLB-8

Brown, George Mackay 1921- DLB-14, 27

Brown, Harry 1917-1986 ....DLB-26

Brown, Marcia 1918- DLB-61

Brown, Margaret Wise 1910-1952 ....DLB-22

Brown, Morna Doris (see Ferrars, Elizabeth)

Brown, Oliver Madox 1855-1874 ....DLB-21

Brown, Sterling 1901-1989 ....DLB-48, 51, 63

Brown, T. E. 1830-1897 ....DLB-35

Brown, William Hill 1765-1793 ....DLB-37

Brown, William Wells 1814-1884 ....DLB-3, 50

Browne, Charles Farrar 1834-1867 ....DLB-11

Browne, Michael Dennis 1940- DLB-40

Browne, Wynyard 1911-1964 ....DLB-13

Browne and Nolan DLB-106

Brownell, W. C. 1851-1928 ....DLB-71

Browning, Elizabeth Barrett 1806-1861 ....DLB-32

Browning, Robert 1812-1889 ....DLB-32

Brownjohn, Allan 1931- DLB-40

Brownson, Orestes Augustus 1803-1876 ....DLB-1, 59, 73

Bruccoli, Matthew J. 1931- DLB-103

Bruce, Charles 1906-1971 ....DLB-68

Bruce, Leo 1903-1979 ....DLB-77

Bruce, Philip Alexander 1856-1933 ....DLB-47

Bruce Humphries [publishing house] DLB-46

Bruce-Novoa, Juan 1944- DLB-82

Bruckman, Clyde 1894-1955 ....DLB-26

Bruckner, Ferdinand 1891-1958 ....DLB-118

Brundage, John Herbert (see Herbert, John)

Brutus, Dennis 1924- DLB-117

Bryant, William Cullen 1794-1878 ....DLB-3, 43, 59

Brydges, Sir Samuel Egerton 1762-1837 ....DLB-107

Buchan, John 1875-1940 ....DLB-34, 70

Buchanan, Robert 1841-1901 ....DLB-18, 35

Buchman, Sidney 1902-1975 ....DLB-26

Buck, Pearl S. 1892-1973 ....DLB-9, 102

Bucke, Charles 1781-1846 ....DLB-110

Bucke, Richard Maurice 1837-1902 ....DLB-99

Buckingham, Joseph Tinker 1779-1861 and
Buckingham, Edwin 1810-1833 ....DLB-73

Buckler, Ernest 1908-1984 ....DLB-68

Buckley, William F., Jr. 1925- Y-80

Buckminster, Joseph Stevens 1784-1812 ....DLB-37

Buckner, Robert 1906- DLB-26

Budd, Thomas ?-1698 ....DLB-24

Budrys, A. J. 1931- DLB-8

Buechner, Frederick 1926- Y-80

Buell, John 1927- DLB-53

Buffum, Job [publishing house] DLB-49

Bugnet, Georges 1879-1981 ....DLB-92

Buies, Arthur 1840-1901 ....DLB-99

Bukowski, Charles 1920- DLB-5

Bullins, Ed 1935- DLB-7, 38

Bulwer-Lytton, Edward (also Edward Bulwer)
1803-1873 ....DLB-21

Bumpus, Jerry 1937- Y-81

Bunce and Brother DLB-49

Bunner, H. C. 1855-1896 ....DLB-78, 79

Bunting, Basil 1900-1985 ....DLB-20

Bunyan, John 1628-1688 ....DLB-39

Burch, Robert 1925- DLB-52

Burciaga, José Antonio 1940- DLB-82

Bürger, Gottfried August 1747-1794..............DLB-94

Burgess, Anthony 1917- DLB-14

Burgess, Gelett 1866-1951.............DLB-11

Burgess, John W. 1844-1931.............DLB-47

Burgess, Thornton W. 1874-1965.............DLB-22

Burgess, Stringer and Company DLB-49

Burk, John Daly circa 1772-1808.............DLB-37

Burke, Edmund 1729?-1797.............DLB-104

Burke, Kenneth 1897- DLB-45, 63

Burlingame, Edward Livermore 1848-1922.............DLB-79

Burnet, Gilbert 1643-1715 ....DLB-101

Burnett, Frances Hodgson 1849-1924.............DLB-42

Burnett, W. R. 1899-1982 ....DLB-9

Burney, Fanny 1752-1840.............DLB-39

Burns, Alan 1929- DLB-14

Burns, John Horne 1916-1953.............Y-85

Burns, Robert 1759-1796 ....DLB-109

Burns and Oates DLB-106

Burnshaw, Stanley 1906- DLB-48

Burr, C. Chauncey 1815?-1883 ....DLB-79

Burroughs, Edgar Rice 1875-1950.............DLB-8

Burroughs, John 1837-1921 ....DLB-64

Burroughs, Margaret T. G. 1917- DLB-41

Burroughs, William S., Jr. 1947-1981 ....DLB-16

Burroughs, William Seward 1914-
.............DLB-2, 8, 16; Y-81

Burroway, Janet 1936- DLB-6

Burt, A. L., and Company.............DLB-49

Burt, Maxwell S. 1882-1954 ....DLB-86

Burton, Miles (see Rhode, John)

Burton, Richard F. 1821-1890 ....DLB-55

Burton, Virginia Lee 1909-1968 ....DLB-22

Burton, William Evans 1804-1860 ....DLB-73

Burwell, Adam Hood 1790-1849 ....DLB-99

Bury, Lady Charlotte 1775-1861.............DLB-116

Busch, Frederick 1941- DLB-6

Busch, Niven 1903-1991.............DLB-44

Bussières, Arthur de 1877-1913.............DLB-92

Butler, E. H., and Company DLB-49

Butler, Juan 1942-1981 ....DLB-53

Butler, Octavia E. 1947- DLB-33

Butler, Samuel 1613-1680 ....DLB-101

Butler, Samuel 1835-1902.............DLB-18, 57

Butor, Michel 1926- DLB-83

Butterworth, Hezekiah 1839-1905.............DLB-42

Buttitta, Ignazio 1899- DLB-114

B. V. (see Thomson, James)

Byars, Betsy 1928- DLB-52

Byatt, A. S. 1936- DLB-14

Byles, Mather 1707-1788 ....DLB-24

Bynner, Witter 1881-1968 ....DLB-54

Byrd, William II 1674-1744 ....DLB-24

Byrne, John Keyes (see Leonard, Hugh)

Byron, George Gordon, Lord 1788-1824 ....DLB-96, 110

C

Caballero Bonald, José Manuel 1926- DLB-108

Cabell, James Branch 1879-1958 ....DLB-9, 78

Cable, George Washington 1844-1925.............DLB-12, 74

Cabrera Infante, Guillermo 1929- DLB-113

Cady, Edwin H. 1917- DLB-103

Cahan, Abraham 1860-1951 ....DLB-9, 25, 28

Cain, George 1943- DLB-33

Calder, John (Publishers), Limited.............DLB-112

Caldwell, Ben 1937- DLB-38

Caldwell, Erskine 1903-1987.............DLB-9, 86

Caldwell, H. M., Company DLB-49

Calhoun, John C. 1782-1850.............DLB-3

Calisher, Hortense 1911- DLB-2

Callaghan, Morley 1903-1990 ....DLB-68

Callaloo.............Y-87

A Call to Letters and an Invitation
   to the Electric Chair,
   by Siegfried Mandel DLB-75

Calmer, Edgar 1907- DLB-4

Calverley, C. S. 1831-1884.............DLB-35

Calvert, George Henry 1803-1889.............DLB-1, 64

Cambridge Press DLB-49

Cameron, Eleanor 1912- DLB-52

Cameron, George Frederick
   1854-1885.............DLB-99

Cameron, William Bleasdell 1862-1951.............DLB-99

Camm, John 1718-1778.............DLB-31

Campana, Dino 1885-1932.............DLB-114

Campbell, Gabrielle Margaret Vere
   (see Shearing, Joseph)

Campbell, James Edwin 1867-1896 ....DLB-50

Campbell, John 1653-1728...............DLB-43

Campbell, John W., Jr. 1910-1971...............DLB-8

Campbell, Thomas 1777-1844 ....DLB-93

Campbell, William Wilfred 1858-1918 ....DLB-92

Campbell, Roy 1901-1957 ....DLB-20

Campion, Thomas 1567-1620 ....DLB-58

Camus, Albert 1913-1960 ....DLB-72

Canby, Henry Seidel 1878-1961...............DLB-91

Candelaria, Cordelia 1943- DLB-82

Candelaria, Nash 1928- DLB-82

Candour in English Fiction (1890),
    by Thomas Hardy...............DLB-18

Canetti, Elias 1905- DLB-85

Cannan, Gilbert 1884-1955 ....DLB-10

Cannell, Kathleen 1891-1974 ....DLB-4

Cannell, Skipwith 1887-1957 ....DLB-45

Cantwell, Robert 1908-1978 ....DLB-9

Cape, Jonathan, and Harrison Smith
    [publishing house]...............DLB-46

Cape, Jonathan, Limited...............DLB-112

Capen, Joseph 1658-1725...............DLB-24

Capote, Truman 1924-1984 ....DLB-2; Y-80, 84

Cardarelli, Vincenzo 1887-1959...............DLB-114

Cardinal, Marie 1929- DLB-83

Carey, Henry circa 1687-1689-1743 ....DLB-84

Carey, M., and Company...............DLB-49

Carey, Mathew 1760-1839...............DLB-37, 73

Carey and Hart...............DLB-49

Carlell, Lodowick 1602-1675...............DLB-58

Carleton, G. W. [publishing house]...............DLB-49

Carlile, Richard 1790-1843...............DLB-110

Carlyle, Jane Welsh 1801-1866...............DLB-55

Carlyle, Thomas 1795-1881...............DLB-55

Carman, Bliss 1861-1929...............DLB-92

Carnero, Guillermo 1947- DLB-108

Carossa, Hans 1878-1956...............DLB-66

Carpenter, Stephen Cullen ?-1820?...............DLB-73

Carpentier, Alejo 1904-1980...............DLB-113

Carr, Emily 1871-1945...............DLB-68

Carr, Virginia Spencer 1929- DLB-111

Carrier, Roch 1937- DLB-53

Carroll, Gladys Hasty 1904- DLB-9

Carroll, John 1735-1815...............DLB-37

Carroll, John 1809-1884...............DLB-99

Carroll, Lewis 1832-1898...............DLB-18

Carroll, Paul 1927- DLB-16

Carroll, Paul Vincent 1900-1968...............DLB-10

Carroll and Graf Publishers DLB-46

Carruth, Hayden 1921- DLB-5

Carryl, Charles E. 1841-1920 ....DLB-42

Carswell, Catherine 1879-1946 ....DLB-36

Carter, Angela 1940- DLB-14

Carter, Elizabeth 1717-1806...............DLB-109

Carter, Henry (see Leslie, Frank)

Carter, Landon 1710-1778...............DLB-31

Carter, Lin 1930- Y-81

Carter, Martin 1927- DLB-117

Carter, Robert, and Brothers DLB-49

Carter and Hendee...............DLB-49

Caruthers, William Alexander 1802-1846...............DLB-3

Carver, Jonathan 1710-1780 ....DLB-31

Carver, Raymond 1938-1988...............Y-84, 88

Cary, Joyce 1888-1957...............DLB-15, 100

Casey, Juanita 1925- DLB-14

Casey, Michael 1947- DLB-5

Cassady, Carolyn 1923- DLB-16

Cassady, Neal 1926-1968...............DLB-16

Cassell and Company...............DLB-106

Cassell Publishing Company...............DLB-49

Cassill, R. V. 1919- DLB-6

Cassity, Turner 1929- DLB-105

Castellanos, Rosario 1925-1974...............DLB-113

Castlemon, Harry (see Fosdick, Charles Austin)

Caswall, Edward 1814-1878 ....DLB-32

Cather, Willa 1873-1947...............DLB-9, 54, 78; DS-1

Catherwood, Mary Hartwell 1847-1902 ....DLB-78

Catton, Bruce 1899-1978...............DLB-17

Causley, Charles 1917- DLB-27

Caute, David 1936- DLB-14

Cawein, Madison 1865-1914...............DLB-54

The Caxton Printers, Limited DLB-46

Cayrol, Jean 1911- DLB-83

Celan, Paul 1920-1970...............DLB-69

Celaya, Gabriel 1911-1991...............DLB-108

Céline, Louis-Ferdinand 1894-1961 ....DLB-72

Center for Bibliographical Studies and
    Research at the University of
    California, Riverside Y-91

Center for the Book Research Y-84

Centlivre, Susanna 1669?-1723 ....DLB-84

The Century Company DLB-49

Cervantes, Lorna Dee 1954- DLB-82

Chacón, Eusebio 1869-1948 ....DLB-82

Chacón, Felipe Maximiliano 1873-? DLB-82

Challans, Eileen Mary (see Renault, Mary)

Chalmers, George 1742-1825 ....DLB-30

Chamberlain, Samuel S. 1851-1916 ....DLB-25

Chamberland, Paul 1939- DLB-60

Chamberlin, William Henry 1897-1969 ....DLB-29

Chambers, Charles Haddon 1860-1921 ....DLB-10

Chambers, W. and R. [publishing house] DLB-106

Chamisso, Albert von 1781-1838 ....DLB-90

Champfleury 1821-1889 ....DLB-119

Chandler, Harry 1864-1944 ....DLB-29

Chandler, Raymond 1888-1959 ....DS-6

Channing, Edward 1856-1931 ....DLB-17

Channing, Edward Tyrrell 1790-1856 ....DLB-1, 59

Channing, William Ellery 1780-1842 ....DLB-1, 59

Channing, William Ellery II 1817-1901 ....DLB-1

Channing, William Henry 1810-1884 ....DLB-1, 59

Chaplin, Charlie 1889-1977 ....DLB-44

Chapman, George 1559 or 1560-1634 ....DLB-62

Chapman, John DLB-106

Chapman, William 1850-1917 ....DLB-99

Chapman and Hall DLB-106

Chappell, Fred 1936- DLB-6, 105

Chappell, Fred, A Detail in a Poem DLB-105

Charbonneau, Jean 1875-1960 ....DLB-92

Charbonneau, Robert 1911-1967 ....DLB-68

Charles, Gerda 1914- DLB-14

Charles, William [publishing house] DLB-49

The Charles Wood Affair:
  A Playwright Revived Y-83

Charlotte Forten: Pages from her Diary DLB-50

Charteris, Leslie 1907- DLB-77

Charyn, Jerome 1937- Y-83

Chase, Borden 1900-1971 ....DLB-26

Chase, Edna Woolman 1877-1957 ....DLB-91

Chase-Riboud, Barbara 1936- DLB-33

Chateaubriand, François-René de 1768-1848 ....DLB-119

Chatterton, Thomas 1752-1770 ....DLB-109

Chatto and Windus DLB-106

Chauncy, Charles 1705-1787 ....DLB-24

Chauveau, Pierre-Joseph-Olivier 1820-1890 ....DLB-99

Chávez, Fray Angélico 1910- DLB-82

Chayefsky, Paddy 1923-1981 ....DLB-7, 44; Y-81

Cheever, Ezekiel 1615-1708 ....DLB-24

Cheever, George Barrell 1807-1890 ....DLB-59

Cheever, John 1912-1982 ....DLB-2, 102; Y-80, 82

Cheever, Susan 1943- Y-82

Chelsea House DLB-46

Cheney, Ednah Dow (Littlehale) 1824-1904 ....DLB-1

Cheney, Harriet Vaughn 1796-1889 ....DLB-99

Cherry, Kelly 1940 ....Y-83

Cherryh, C. J. 1942- Y-80

Chesnutt, Charles Waddell 1858-1932 ....DLB-12, 50, 78

Chester, George Randolph 1869-1924 ....DLB-78

Chesterfield, Philip Dormer Stanhope,
  Fourth Earl of 1694-1773 ....DLB-104

Chesterton, G. K. 1874-1936 ....DLB-10, 19, 34, 70, 98

Cheyney, Edward P. 1861-1947 ....DLB-47

Chicano History DLB-82

Chicano Language DLB-82

Child, Francis James 1825-1896 ....DLB-1, 64

Child, Lydia Maria 1802-1880 ....DLB-1, 74

Child, Philip 1898-1978 ....DLB-68

Childers, Erskine 1870-1922 ....DLB-70

Children's Book Awards and Prizes DLB-61

Childress, Alice 1920- DLB-7, 38

Childs, George W. 1829-1894 ....DLB-23

Chilton Book Company DLB-46

Chittenden, Hiram Martin 1858-1917 ....DLB-47

Chivers, Thomas Holley 1809-1858 ....DLB-3

Chopin, Kate 1850-1904 ....DLB-12, 78

Chopin, Rene 1885-1953 ....DLB-92

Choquette, Adrienne 1915-1973 ....DLB-68

Choquette, Robert 1905- DLB-68

The Christian Publishing Company DLB-49

Christie, Agatha 1890-1976 ....DLB-13, 77

Church, Benjamin 1734-1778 ....DLB-31

Church, Francis Pharcellus 1839-1906 ....DLB-79

Church, William Conant 1836-1917 ....DLB-79

Churchill, Caryl 1938- DLB-13

Churchill, Charles 1731-1764 ....DLB-109

Churchill, Sir Winston 1874-1965 ....DLB-100

Churton, E., and Company DLB-106

Chute, Marchette 1909- DLB-103

Ciardi, John 1916-1986 ....DLB-5; Y-86

Cibber, Colley 1671-1757 ....DLB-84

Cirese, Eugenio 1884-1955 ....DLB-114

City Lights Books DLB-46

Cixous, Hélène 1937- DLB-83

Clampitt, Amy 1920- DLB-105

Clapper, Raymond 1892-1944 ....DLB-29

Clare, John 1793-1864 ....DLB-55, 96

Clarendon, Edward Hyde, Earl of
    1609-1674 ....DLB-101

Clark, Alfred Alexander Gordon (see Hare, Cyril)

Clark, Ann Nolan 1896- DLB-52

Clark, C. M., Publishing Company DLB-46

Clark, Catherine Anthony 1892-1977 ....DLB-68

Clark, Charles Heber 1841-1915 ....DLB-11

Clark, Davis Wasgatt 1812-1871 ....DLB-79

Clark, Eleanor 1913- DLB-6

Clark, J. P. 1935- DLB-117

Clark, Lewis Gaylord 1808-1873 ....DLB-3, 64, 73

Clark, Walter Van Tilburg 1909-1971 ....DLB-9

Clarke, Austin 1896-1974 ....DLB-10, 20

Clarke, Austin C. 1934- DLB-53

Clarke, Gillian 1937- DLB-40

Clarke, James Freeman 1810-1888 ....DLB-1, 59

Clarke, Rebecca Sophia 1833-1906 ....DLB-42

Clarke, Robert, and Company.....................DLB-49

Claudius, Matthias 1740-1815 ....DLB-97

Clausen, Andy 1943- DLB-16

Claxton, Remsen and Haffelfinger DLB-49

Clay, Cassius Marcellus 1810-1903...............DLB-43

Cleary, Beverly 1916- DLB-52

Cleaver, Vera 1919- and
    Cleaver, Bill 1920-1981 ....DLB-52

Cleland, John 1710-1789 ....DLB-39

Clemens, Samuel Langhorne
    1835-1910 ....DLB-11, 12, 23, 64, 74

Clement, Hal 1922- DLB-8

Clemo, Jack 1916- DLB-27

Clifford, James L. 1901-1978 ....DLB-103

Clifton, Lucille 1936- DLB-5, 41

Clode, Edward J. [publishing house] DLB-46

Clough, Arthur Hugh 1819-1861 ....DLB-32

Cloutier, Cécile 1930- DLB-60

Clutton-Brock, Arthur 1868-1924.................DLB-98

Coates, Robert M. 1897-1973 ....DLB-4, 9, 102

Coatsworth, Elizabeth 1893- DLB-22

Cobb, Jr., Charles E. 1943- DLB-41

Cobb, Frank I. 1869-1923 ....DLB-25

Cobb, Irvin S. 1876-1944 ....DLB-11, 25, 86

Cobbett, William 1763-1835..................DLB-43, 107

Cochran, Thomas C. 1902- DLB-17

Cochrane, Elizabeth 1867-1922 ....DLB-25

Cockerill, John A. 1845-1896 ....DLB-23

Cocteau, Jean 1889-1963 ....DLB-65

Coderre, Emile (see Jean Narrache)

Coffee, Lenore J. 1900?-1984 ....DLB-44

Coffin, Robert P. Tristram 1892-1955 ....DLB-45

Cogswell, Fred 1917- DLB-60

Cogswell, Mason Fitch 1761-1830 ....DLB-37

Cohen, Arthur A. 1928-1986 ....DLB-28

Cohen, Leonard 1934- DLB-53

Cohen, Matt 1942- DLB-53

Colden, Cadwallader 1688-1776 ....DLB-24, 30

Cole, Barry 1936- DLB-14

Colegate, Isabel 1931- DLB-14

Coleman, Emily Holmes 1899-1974.................DLB-4

Coleridge, Hartley 1796-1849 ....DLB-96

Coleridge, Mary 1861-1907...................DLB-19, 98

Coleridge, Samuel Taylor 1772-1834..........DLB-93, 107

Colette 1873-1954 ....DLB-65

Colette, Sidonie Gabrielle (see Colette)

Collier, John 1901-1980.........................DLB-77

Collier, Mary 1690-1762.........................DLB-95

Collier, P. F. [publishing house]...............DLB-49

Collier, Robert J. 1876-1918 ....DLB-91

Collin and Small DLB-49

Collins, Isaac [publishing house]...............DLB-49

Collins, Mortimer 1827-1876 ....DLB-21, 35

Collins, Wilkie 1824-1889 ....DLB-18, 70

Collins, William 1721-1759 ....DLB-109

Collyer, Mary 1716?-1763? DLB-39

Colman, Benjamin 1673-1747 ....DLB-24

Colman, George, the Elder
    1732-1794 ....DLB-89

Colman, George, the Younger 1762-1836 ....DLB-89

Colman, S. [publishing house]...................DLB-49

Colombo, John Robert 1936- DLB-53

Colter, Cyrus 1910- DLB-33

Colum, Padraic 1881-1972 ....DLB-19

Colwin, Laurie 1944- Y-80

Comden, Betty 1919- and Green,
    Adolph 1918- DLB-44

Comi, Girolamo 1890-1968 ....DLB-114

The Comic Tradition Continued
    [in the British Novel] DLB-15

Commager, Henry Steele 1902- DLB-17

The Commercialization of the Image of
    Revolt, by Kenneth Rexroth...............DLB-16

Community and Commentators: Black
    Theatre and Its Critics DLB-38

Compton-Burnett, Ivy 1884?-1969 ....DLB-36

Conan, Laure 1845-1924 ....DLB-99

Conde, Carmen 1901- DLB-108

Conference on Modern Biography Y-85

Congreve, William 1670-1729..............DLB-39, 84

Conkey, W. B., Company DLB-49

Connell, Evan S., Jr. 1924- DLB-2; Y-81

Connelly, Marc 1890-1980 ....DLB-7; Y-80

Connolly, Cyril 1903-1974 ....DLB-98

Connolly, James B. 1868-1957 ....DLB-78

Connor, Ralph 1860-1937 ....DLB-92

Connor, Tony 1930- DLB-40

Conquest, Robert 1917- DLB-27

Conrad, John, and Company DLB-49

Conrad, Joseph 1857-1924................DLB-10, 34, 98

Conroy, Jack 1899-1990............................Y-81

Conroy, Pat 1945- DLB-6

The Consolidation of Opinion: Critical
    Responses to the Modernists...............DLB-36

Constable and Company Limited.................DLB-112

Constant, Benjamin 1767-1830 ....DLB-119

Constant de Rebecque, Henri-Benjamin de
    (see Constant, Benjamin)

Constantin-Weyer, Maurice 1881-1964 ....DLB-92

Constantine, David 1944- DLB-40

Contempo Caravan: Kites in a Windstorm.........Y-85

A Contemporary Flourescence of Chicano
    Literature...Y-84

The Continental Publishing Company............DLB-49

A Conversation with Chaim Potok Y-84

Conversations with Publishers I: An Interview

with Patrick O'Connor Y-84

Conversations with Rare Book Dealers I: An
    Interview with Glenn Horowitz.................Y-90

The Conversion of an Unpolitical Man,
    by W. H. Bruford DLB-66

Conway, Moncure Daniel 1832-1907 ....DLB-1

Cook, David C., Publishing Company DLB-49

Cook, Ebenezer circa 1667-circa 1732 ....DLB-24

Cook, Michael 1933- DLB-53

Cooke, George Willis 1848-1923................DLB-71

Cooke, Increase, and Company DLB-49

Cooke, John Esten 1830-1886 ....DLB-3

Cooke, Philip Pendleton 1816-1850...........DLB-3, 59

Cooke, Rose Terry 1827-1892................DLB-12, 74

Coolbrith, Ina 1841-1928 ....DLB-54

Cooley, Peter 1940- DLB-105

Cooley, Peter, Into the Mirror DLB-105

Coolidge, George [publishing house]............DLB-49

Coolidge, Susan (see Woolsey, Sarah Chauncy)

Cooper, Giles 1918-1966 ....DLB-13

Cooper, James Fenimore 1789-1851 ....DLB-3

Cooper, Kent 1880-1965 ....DLB-29

Coover, Robert 1932- DLB-2; Y-81

Copeland and Day DLB-49

Coppel, Alfred 1921- Y-83

Coppola, Francis Ford 1939- DLB-44

Corazzini, Sergio 1886-1907....................DLB-114

Corcoran, Barbara 1911- DLB-52

Corelli, Marie 1855-1924........................DLB-34

Corle, Edwin 1906-1956 ....Y-85

Corman, Cid 1924- DLB-5

Cormier, Robert 1925- DLB-52

Corn, Alfred 1943- Y-80

Cornish, Sam 1935- DLB-41

Cornwall, Barry (see Procter, Bryan Waller)

Cornwell, David John Moore (see le Carré, John)

Corpi, Lucha 1945- DLB-82

Corrington, John William 1932- DLB-6

Corrothers, James D. 1869-1917................DLB-50

Corso, Gregory 1930- DLB-5, 16

Cortázar, Julio 1914-1984.....................DLB-113

Cortez, Jayne 1936- DLB-41

Corvo, Baron (see Rolfe, Frederick William)

Cory, William Johnson 1823-1892...............DLB-35

Cosmopolitan Book Corporation DLB-46

Costain, Thomas B. 1885-1965 ....DLB-9

Coste, Donat 1912-1957...DLB-88

Cotter, Joseph Seamon, Sr. 1861-1949 ....DLB-50

Cotter, Joseph Seamon, Jr. 1895-1919 ....DLB-50

Cotton, John 1584-1652 ....DLB-24

Coulter, John 1888-1980 ....DLB-68

Cournos, John 1881-1966..DLB-54

Coventry, Francis 1725-1754...DLB-39

Coverly, N. [publishing house]......................................DLB-49

Covici-Friede DLB-46

Coward, Noel 1899-1973 ....DLB-10

Coward, McCann and Geoghegan DLB-46

Cowles, Gardner 1861-1946 ....DLB-29

Cowley, Hannah 1743-1809 ....DLB-89

Cowley, Malcolm 1898-1989 ....DLB-4, 48; Y-81, 89

Cowper, William 1731-1800...............................DLB-104, 109

Cox, A. B. (see Berkeley, Anthony)

Cox, Palmer 1840-1924 ....DLB-42

Coxe, Louis 1918- DLB-5

Coxe, Tench 1755-1824 ....DLB-37

Cozzens, James Gould 1903-1978................DLB-9; Y-84; DS-2

Crabbe, George 1754-1832...DLB-93

Craddock, Charles Egbert (see Murfree, Mary N.)

Cradock, Thomas 1718-1770 ....DLB-31

Craig, Daniel H. 1811-1895..DLB-43

Craik, Dinah Maria 1826-1887.....................................DLB-35

Cranch, Christopher Pearse 1813-1892....................DLB-1, 42

Crane, Hart 1899-1932..DLB-4, 48

Crane, R. S. 1886-1967..DLB-63

Crane, Stephen 1871-1900...................................DLB-12, 54, 78

Crapsey, Adelaide 1878-1914...DLB-54

Craven, Avery 1885-1980 ....DLB-17

Crawford, Charles 1752-circa 1815................................DLB-31

Crawford, F. Marion 1854-1909 ....DLB-71

Crawford, Isabel Valancy 1850-1887 ....DLB-92

Crawley, Alan 1887-1975..DLB-68

Crayon, Geoffrey (see Irving, Washington)

Creasey, John 1908-1973...DLB-77

Creative Age Press DLB-46

Creel, George 1876-1953...DLB-25

Creeley, Robert 1926- DLB-5, 16

Creelman, James 1859-1915...DLB-23

Cregan, David 1931- DLB-13

Creighton, Donald Grant 1902-1979 ....DLB-88

Cremazie, Octave 1827-1879...DLB-99

Crémer, Victoriano 1909?- DLB-108

Crescas, Hasdai circa 1340-1412?.................................DLB-115

Cresset Press...DLB-112

Crèvecoeur, Michel Guillaume Jean de
    1735-1813..DLB-37

Crews, Harry 1935- DLB-6

Crichton, Michael 1942- Y-81

A Crisis of Culture: The Changing Role
    of Religion in the New Republic...........................DLB-37

Crispin, Edmund 1921-1978 ....DLB-87

Cristofer, Michael 1946- DLB-7

"The Critic as Artist" (1891), by Oscar Wilde DLB-57

Criticism In Relation To Novels (1863),
    by G. H. Lewes...DLB-21

Crockett, David (Davy) 1786-1836...........................DLB-3, 11

Croft-Cooke, Rupert (see Bruce, Leo)

Crofts, Freeman Wills 1879-1957 ....DLB-77

Croker, John Wilson 1780-1857....................................DLB-110

Croly, Herbert 1869-1930 ....DLB-91

Croly, Jane Cunningham 1829-1901............................DLB-23

Crosby, Caresse 1892-1970 ....DLB-48

Crosby, Caresse 1892-1970 and Crosby,
    Harry 1898-1929...DLB-4

Crosby, Harry 1898-1929 ....DLB-48

Crossley-Holland, Kevin 1941- DLB-40

Crothers, Rachel 1878-1958 ....DLB-7

Crowell, Thomas Y., Company DLB-49

Crowley, John 1942- Y-82

Crowley, Mart 1935- DLB-7

Crown Publishers DLB-46

Crowne, John 1641-1712 ....DLB-80

Crowninshield, Frank 1872-1947 ....DLB-91

Croy, Homer 1883-1965..DLB-4

Crumley, James 1939- Y-84

Cruz, Victor Hernández 1949- DLB-41

Csokor, Franz Theodor 1885-1969...............................DLB-81

Cuala Press DLB-112

Cullen, Countee 1903-1946 ....DLB-4, 48, 51

Culler, Jonathan D. 1944- DLB-67

The Cult of Biography
    Excerpts from the Second Folio Debate:
        "Biographies are generally a disease of

English Literature"–Germaine Greer,
Victoria Glendinning, Auberon Waugh,
and Richard Holmes Y-86

Cumberland, Richard 1732-1811 ....DLB-89

Cummings, E. E. 1894-1962 ....DLB-4, 48

Cummings, Ray 1887-1957 ....DLB-8

Cummings and Hilliard..........................DLB-49

Cummins, Maria Susanna 1827-1866 ....DLB-42

Cundall, Joseph [publishing house] DLB-106

Cuney, Waring 1906-1976 ....DLB-51

Cuney-Hare, Maude 1874-1936 ....DLB-52

Cunningham, Allan 1784-1842 ....DLB-116

Cunningham, J. V. 1911- DLB-5

Cunningham, Peter F. [publishing house] DLB-49

Cuomo, George 1929- Y-80

Cupples and Leon..............................DLB-46

Cupples, Upham and Company.................DLB-49

Cuppy, Will 1884-1949 ....DLB-11

Currie, Mary Montgomerie Lamb Singleton,
Lady Currie (see Fane, Violet)

Curti, Merle E. 1897- DLB-17

Curtis, Cyrus H. K. 1850-1933.................DLB-91

Curtis, George William 1824-1892 ....DLB-1, 43

Curzon, Sarah Anne 1833-1898.................DLB-99

D

D. M. Thomas: The Plagiarism Controversy......Y-82

Dabit, Eugène 1898-1936 ....DLB-65

Daborne, Robert circa 1580-1628 ....DLB-58

Dacey, Philip 1939- DLB-105

Dacey, Philip, Eyes Across Centuries:
Contemporary Poetry and "That
Vision Thing".................................DLB-105

Daggett, Rollin M. 1831-1901 ....DLB-79

Dahlberg, Edward 1900-1977 ....DLB-48

Dale, Peter 1938- DLB-40

Dall, Caroline Wells (Healey) 1822-1912 ......DLB-1

Dallas, E. S. 1828-1879 ....DLB-55

The Dallas Theater Center DLB-7

D'Alton, Louis 1900-1951.......................DLB-10

Daly, T. A. 1871-1948 ....DLB-11

Damon, S. Foster 1893-1971....................DLB-45

Damrell, William S. [publishing house] DLB-49

Dana, Charles A. 1819-1897 ....DLB-3, 23

Dana, Richard Henry, Jr. 1815-1882.............DLB-1

Dandridge, Ray Garfield DLB-51

Dane, Clemence 1887-1965.....................DLB-10

Danforth, John 1660-1730......................DLB-24

Danforth, Samuel I 1626-1674..................DLB-24

Danforth, Samuel II 1666-1727.................DLB-24

Dangerous Years: London Theater,
1939-1945...................................DLB-10

Daniel, John M. 1825-1865 ....DLB-43

Daniel, Samuel 1562 or 1563-1619 ....DLB-62

Daniel Press..................................DLB-106

Daniells, Roy 1902-1979 ....DLB-68

Daniels, Josephus 1862-1948...................DLB-29

Danner, Margaret Esse 1915- DLB-41

Dantin, Louis 1865-1945 ....DLB-92

Darley, George 1795-1846.......................DLB-96

Darwin, Charles 1809-1882 ....DLB-57

Darwin, Erasmus 1731-1802.....................DLB-93

Daryush, Elizabeth 1887-1977...................DLB-20

Dashwood, Edmée Elizabeth Monica
de la Pasture (see Delafield, E. M.)

d'Aulaire, Edgar Parin 1898-   and
d'Aulaire, Ingri 1904- DLB-22

Davenant, Sir William 1606-1668 ....DLB-58

Davenport, Robert ?-?..........................DLB-58

Daves, Delmer 1904-1977.......................DLB-26

Davey, Frank 1940- DLB-53

Davies, Peter, Limited...........................DLB-112

Davidson, Avram 1923- DLB-8

Davidson, Donald 1893-1968 ....DLB-45

Davidson, John 1857-1909 ....DLB-19

Davidson, Lionel 1922- DLB-14

Davie, Donald 1922- DLB-27

Davies, Robertson 1913- DLB-68

Davies, Samuel 1723-1761 ....DLB-31

Davies, W. H. 1871-1940........................DLB-19

Daviot, Gordon 1896?-1952......................DLB-10
(see also Tey, Josephine)

Davis, Charles A. 1795-1867 ....DLB-11

Davis, Clyde Brion 1894-1962....................DLB-9

Davis, Dick 1945- DLB-40

Davis, Frank Marshall 1905-?....................DLB-51

Davis, H. L. 1894-1960..........................DLB-9

Davis, John 1774-1854..........................DLB-37

Davis, Margaret Thomson 1926- DLB-14

Davis, Ossie 1917- DLB-7, 38

Davis, Rebecca Harding 1831-1910 ....DLB-74

Davis, Richard Harding 1864-1916 ....DLB-12, 23, 78, 79

Davis, Samuel Cole 1764-1809 ....DLB-37

Davison, Peter 1928- DLB-5

Davys, Mary 1674-1732 ....DLB-39

DAW Books...............................DLB-46

Dawson, William 1704-1752 ....DLB-31

Day, Benjamin Henry 1810-1889...............................DLB-43

Day, Clarence 1874-1935...............................DLB-11

Day, Dorothy 1897-1980...............................DLB-29

Day, Frank Parker 1881-1950 ....DLB-92

Day, John circa 1574-circa 1640...............................DLB-62

Day, The John, Company...............................DLB-46

Day Lewis, C. 1904-1972 ....DLB-15, 20
(see also Blake, Nicholas)

Day, Mahlon [publishing house]...............................DLB-49

Day, Thomas 1748-1789 ....DLB-39

Deacon, William Arthur 1890-1977...............................DLB-68

Deal, Borden 1922-1985...............................DLB-6

de Angeli, Marguerite 1889-1987 ....DLB-22

De Bow, James Dunwoody Brownson 1820-1867...............................DLB-3, 79

de Bruyn, Günter 1926- DLB-75

de Camp, L. Sprague 1907- DLB-8

The Decay of Lying (1889), by Oscar Wilde [excerpt]...............................DLB-18

Dedication, *Ferdinand Count Fathom* (1753), by Tobias Smollett...............................DLB-39

Dedication, *Lasselia* (1723), by Eliza Haywood [excerpt]...............................DLB-39

Dedication, *The History of Pompey the Little* (1751), by Francis Coventry...............................DLB-39

Dedication, *The Wanderer* (1814), by Fanny Burney...............................DLB-39

Defense of *Amelia* (1752), by Henry Fielding...............................DLB-39

Defoe, Daniel 1660-1731...............................DLB-39, 95, 101

de Fontaine, Felix Gregory 1834-1896...............................DLB-43

De Forest, John William 1826-1906...............................DLB-12

DeFrees, Madeline 1919- DLB-105

DeFrees, Madeline, The Poet's Kaleidoscope: The Element of Surprise in the Making of the Poem...............................DLB-105

de Graff, Robert 1895-1981 ....Y-81

de Graft, Joe 1924-1978 ....DLB-117

Deighton, Len 1929- DLB-87

DeJong, Meindert 1906-1991 ....DLB-52

Dekker, Thomas circa 1572-1632 ....DLB-62

Delacorte, Jr., George T. 1894-1991...............................DLB-91

Delafield, E. M. 1890-1943...............................DLB-34

Delahaye, Guy 1888-1969...............................DLB-92

de la Mare, Walter 1873-1956...............................DLB-19

Deland, Margaret 1857-1945...............................DLB-78

Delaney, Shelagh 1939- DLB-13

Delany, Martin Robinson 1812-1885...............................DLB-50

Delany, Samuel R. 1942- DLB-8, 33

de la Roche, Mazo 1879-1961 ....DLB-68

Delbanco, Nicholas 1942- DLB-6

De León, Nephtalí 1945- DLB-82

Delgado, Abelardo Barrientos 1931- DLB-82

De Libero, Libero 1906-1981 ....DLB-114

DeLillo, Don 1936- DLB-6

de Lisser H. G. 1878-1944...............................DLB-117

Dell, Floyd 1887-1969...............................DLB-9

Dell Publishing Company...............................DLB-46

delle Grazie, Marie Eugene 1864-1931...............................DLB-81

del Rey, Lester 1915- DLB-8

Del Vecchio, John M. 1947- DS-9

de Man, Paul 1919-1983...............................DLB-67

Demby, William 1922- DLB-33

Deming, Philander 1829-1915...............................DLB-74

Demorest, William Jennings 1822-1895...............................DLB-79

Denham, Sir John 1615-1669...............................DLB-58

Denison, Merrill 1893-1975...............................DLB-92

Denison, T. S., and Company DLB-49

Dennie, Joseph 1768-1812...............................DLB-37, 43, 59, 73

Dennis, John 1658-1734 ....DLB-101

Dennis, Nigel 1912-1989...............................DLB-13, 15

Dent, Tom 1932- DLB-38

Dent, J. M., and Sons...............................DLB-112

Denton, Daniel circa 1626-1703 ....DLB-24

DePaola, Tomie 1934- DLB-61

De Quincey, Thomas 1785-1859...............................DLB-110

Derby, George Horatio 1823-1861...............................DLB-11

Derby, J. C., and Company DLB-49

Derby and Miller...............................DLB-49

Derleth, August 1909-1971 ....DLB-9

The Derrydale Press DLB-46

Desaulniers, Gonsalve 1863-1934.................DLB-92

Desbiens, Jean-Paul 1927- DLB-53

des Forêts, Louis-René 1918- DLB-83

DesRochers, Alfred 1901-1978 ....DLB-68

Desrosiers, Léo-Paul 1896-1967 ....DLB-68

Destouches, Louis-Ferdinand (see Céline,
    Louis-Ferdinand)

De Tabley, Lord 1835-1895.......................DLB-35

Deutsch, Babette 1895-1982......................DLB-45

Deutsch, André, Limited DLB-112

Deveaux, Alexis 1948- DLB-38

The Development of Lighting in the Staging
    of Drama, 1900-1945 [in Great Britain] DLB-10

de Vere, Aubrey 1814-1902.......................DLB-35

The Devin-Adair Company DLB-46

De Voto, Bernard 1897-1955 ....DLB-9

De Vries, Peter 1910- DLB-6; Y-82

Dewdney, Christopher 1951- DLB-60

Dewdney, Selwyn 1909-1979.......................DLB-68

DeWitt, Robert M., Publisher....................DLB-49

DeWolfe, Fiske and Company DLB-49

Dexter, Colin 1930- DLB-87

de Young, M. H. 1849-1925.......................DLB-25

The Dial Press..................................DLB-46

Diamond, I. A. L. 1920-1988 ....DLB-26

Di Cicco, Pier Giorgio 1949- DLB-60

Dick, Philip K. 1928- DLB-8

Dick and Fitzgerald DLB-49

Dickens, Charles 1812-1870 ....DLB-21, 55, 70

Dickey, James 1923- DLB-5; Y-82; DS-7

Dickey, William 1928- DLB-5

Dickinson, Emily 1830-1886......................DLB-1

Dickinson, John 1732-1808 ....DLB-31

Dickinson, Jonathan 1688-1747 ....DLB-24

Dickinson, Patric 1914- DLB-27

Dickinson, Peter 1927- DLB-87

Dicks, John [publishing house]..................DLB-106

Dickson, Gordon R. 1923- DLB-8

Didion, Joan 1934- DLB-2; Y-81, 86

Di Donato, Pietro 1911- DLB-9

Dillard, Annie 1945- Y-80

Dillard, R. H. W. 1937- DLB-5

Dillingham, Charles T., Company DLB-49

The G. W. Dillingham Company DLB-49

Dintenfass, Mark 1941- Y-84

Diogenes, Jr. (see Brougham, John)

DiPrima, Diane 1934- DLB-5, 16

Disch, Thomas M. 1940- DLB-8

Disney, Walt 1901-1966..........................DLB-22

Disraeli, Benjamin 1804-1881 ....DLB-21, 55

D'Israeli, Isaac 1766-1848......................DLB-107

Ditzen, Rudolf (see Fallada, Hans)

Dix, Dorothea Lynde 1802-1887...................DLB-1

Dix, Dorothy (see Gilmer, Elizabeth Meriwether)

Dix, Edwards and Company DLB-49

Dixon, Paige (see Corcoran, Barbara)

Dixon, Richard Watson 1833-1900 ....DLB-19

Dobell, Sydney 1824-1874........................DLB-32

Döblin, Alfred 1878-1957........................DLB-66

Dobson, Austin 1840-1921 ....DLB-35

Doctorow, E. L. 1931- DLB-2, 28; Y-80

Dodd, William E. 1869-1940......................DLB-17

Dodd, Mead and Company DLB-49

Doderer, Heimito von 1896-1968 ....DLB-85

Dodge, B. W., and Company DLB-46

Dodge, Mary Mapes 1831?-1905 ....DLB-42, 79

Dodge Publishing Company........................DLB-49

Dodgson, Charles Lutwidge (see Carroll, Lewis)

Dodsley, Robert 1703-1764 ....DLB-95

Dodson, Owen 1914-1983 ....DLB-76

Doesticks, Q. K. Philander, P. B. (see Thomson,
    Mortimer)

Donahoe, Patrick [publishing house].............DLB-49

Donald, David H. 1920- DLB-17

Donaldson, Scott 1928- DLB-111

Donleavy, J. P. 1926- DLB-6

Donnadieu, Marguerite (see Duras, Marguerite)

Donnelley, R. R., and Sons Company..............DLB-49

Donnelly, Ignatius 1831-1901 ....DLB-12

Donohue and Henneberry DLB-49

Donoso, José 1924- DLB-113

Doolady, M. [publishing house] DLB-49

Dooley, Ebon (see Ebon)

Doolittle, Hilda 1886-1961 ....DLB-4, 45

Dor, Milo 1923- DLB-85

Doran, George H., Company DLB-46

Dorgelès, Roland 1886-1973 ....DLB-65

Dorn, Edward 1929- DLB-5

Dorr, Rheta Childe 1866-1948....................................DLB-25

Dorst, Tankred 1925- DLB-75

Dos Passos, John 1896-1970 ....DLB-4, 9; DS-1

Doubleday and Company DLB-49

Dougall, Lily 1858-1923 ....DLB-92

Doughty, Charles M. 1843-1926 ....DLB-19, 57

Douglas, Keith 1920-1944 ....DLB-27

Douglas, Norman 1868-1952.....................................DLB-34

Douglass, Frederick 1817?-1895..................DLB-1, 43, 50, 79

Douglass, William circa 1691-1752 ....DLB-24

Dover Publications DLB-46

Doves Press DLB-112

Dowden, Edward 1843-1913 ....DLB-35

Downes, Gwladys 1915- DLB-88

Downing, J., Major (see Davis, Charles A.)

Downing, Major Jack (see Smith, Seba)

Dowson, Ernest 1867-1900 ....DLB-19

Doxey, William [publishing house] DLB-49

Doyle, Sir Arthur Conan 1859-1930........................DLB-18, 70

Doyle, Kirby 1932- DLB-16

Drabble, Margaret 1939- DLB-14

Drach, Albert 1902- DLB-85

The Dramatic Publishing Company...........................DLB-49

Dramatists Play Service...DLB-46

Draper, John W. 1811-1882 ....DLB-30

Draper, Lyman C. 1815-1891 ....DLB-30

Dreiser, Theodore 1871-1945 ....DLB-9, 12, 102; DS-1

Drewitz, Ingeborg 1923-1986.....................................DLB-75

Drieu La Rochelle, Pierre 1893-1945 ....DLB-72

Drinkwater, John 1882-1937......................................DLB-10, 19

The Drue Heinz Literature Prize
  Excerpt from "Excerpts from a Report
    of the Commission," in David
    Bosworth's *The Death of Descartes*
  An Interview with David Bosworth Y-82

Drummond, William Henry 1854-1907.......................DLB-92

Dryden, John 1631-1700......................................DLB-80, 101

Duane, William 1760-1835...DLB-43

Dubé, Marcel 1930- DLB-53

Dubé, Rodolphe (see Hertel, François)

Du Bois, W. E. B. 1868-1963 ....DLB-47, 50, 91

Du Bois, William Pène 1916- DLB-61

Ducharme, Réjean 1941- DLB-60

Duck, Stephen 1705?-1756..DLB-95

Duckworth, Gerald, and Company Limited DLB-112

Dudek, Louis 1918- DLB-88

Duell, Sloan and Pearce...DLB-46

Duffield and Green..DLB-46

Duffy, Maureen 1933- DLB-14

Dugan, Alan 1923- DLB-5

Dugas, Marcel 1883-1947 ....DLB-92

Dugdale, William [publishing house].........................DLB-106

Duhamel, Georges 1884-1966 ....DLB-65

Dukes, Ashley 1885-1959 ....DLB-10

Dumas, Alexandre, *père* 1802-1870.........................DLB-119

Dumas, Henry 1934-1968..DLB-41

Dunbar, Paul Laurence 1872-1906...................DLB-50, 54, 78

Duncan, Norman 1871-1916......................................DLB-92

Duncan, Robert 1919-1988 ....DLB-5, 16

Duncan, Ronald 1914-1982.......................................DLB-13

Duncan, Sara Jeannette 1861-1922...........................DLB-92

Dunigan, Edward, and Brother...................................DLB-49

Dunlap, John 1747-1812 ....DLB-43

Dunlap, William 1766-1839 ....DLB-30, 37, 59

Dunn, Douglas 1942- DLB-40

Dunn, Stephen 1939- DLB-105

Dunn, Stephen,
  The Good, The Not So Good DLB-105

Dunne, Finley Peter 1867-1936...........................DLB-11, 23

Dunne, John Gregory 1932- Y-80

Dunne, Philip 1908- DLB-26

Dunning, Ralph Cheever 1878-1930 ....DLB-4

Dunning, William A. 1857-1922 ....DLB-17

Duns Scotus, John circa 1266-1308...........................DLB-115

Dunsany, Edward John Moreton Drax
  Plunkett, Lord 1878-1957 ....DLB-10, 77

Dupin, Amantine-Aurore-Lucile (see Snad, George)

Durand, Lucile (see Bersianik, Louky)

Duranty, Walter 1884-1957 ....DLB-29

Duras, Marguerite 1914- DLB-83

Durfey, Thomas 1653-1723..DLB-80

Durrell, Lawrence 1912-1990 ....DLB-15, 27; Y-90

Durrell, William [publishing house] DLB-49

Dürrenmatt, Friedrich 1921- DLB-69

Dutton, E. P., and Company DLB-49

Duvoisin, Roger 1904-1980 ....DLB-61

Duyckinck, Evert Augustus 1816-1878....................DLB-3, 64

Duyckinck, George L. 1823-1863 ....DLB-3

Duyckinck and Company DLB-49

Dwight, John Sullivan 1813-1893 ....DLB-1

Dwight, Timothy 1752-1817 ....DLB-37

Dyer, Charles 1928- DLB-13

Dyer, George 1755-1841 ....DLB-93

Dyer, John 1699-1757 ....DLB-95

Dylan, Bob 1941- DLB-16

E

Eager, Edward 1911-1964 ....DLB-22

Earle, James H., and Company DLB-49

Early American Book Illustration,
    by Sinclair Hamilton DLB-49

Eastlake, William 1917- DLB-6

Eastman, Carol ?- DLB-44

Eastman, Max 1883-1969 ....DLB-91

Eberhart, Richard 1904- DLB-48

Ebner, Jeannie 1918- DLB-85

Ebner-Eschenbach, Marie von 1830-1916 .....DLB-81

Ebon 1942- DLB-41

Ecco Press DLB-46

Eckhart, Meister circa 1260-circa 1328 ....DLB-115

The Eclectic Review 1805-1868 ....DLB-110

Edel, Leon 1907- DLB-103

Edes, Benjamin 1732-1803 ....DLB-43

Edgar, David 1948- DLB-13

Edgeworth, Maria 1768-1849 ....DLB-116

The Edinburgh Review 1802-1929 ....DLB-110

Edinburgh University Press DLB-112

The Editor Publishing Company DLB-49

Edmonds, Randolph 1900- DLB-51

Edmonds, Walter D. 1903- DLB-9

Edschmid, Kasimir 1890-1966 ....DLB-56

Edwards, Jonathan 1703-1758 ....DLB-24

Edwards, Jonathan, Jr. 1745-1801 ....DLB-37

Edwards, Junius 1929- DLB-33

Edwards, Richard 1524-1566 ....DLB-62

Effinger, George Alec 1947- DLB-8

Eggleston, Edward 1837-1902 ....DLB-12

Eggleston, Wilfred 1901-1986 ....DLB-92

Ehrenstein, Albert 1886-1950 ....DLB-81

Ehrhart, W. D. 1948- DS-9

Eich, Günter 1907-1972 ....DLB-69

Eichendorff, Joseph Freiherr von
    1788-1857 ....DLB-90

1873 Publishers' Catalogues DLB-49

Eighteenth-Century Aesthetic Theories...........DLB-31

Eighteenth-Century Philosophical
    Background DLB-31

Eigner, Larry 1927- DLB-5

Eisenreich, Herbert 1925-1986 ....DLB-85

Eisner, Kurt 1867-1919 ....DLB-66

Eklund, Gordon 1945- Y-83

Ekwensi, Cyprian 1921- DLB-117

Elder, Lonne III 1931- DLB-7, 38, 44

Elder, Paul, and Company DLB-49

Elements of Rhetoric (1828; revised, 1846),
    by Richard Whately [excerpt]....................DLB-57

Elie, Robert 1915-1973 ....DLB-88

Eliot, George 1819-1880.................................DLB-21, 35, 55

Eliot, John 1604-1690 ....DLB-24

Eliot, T. S. 1888-1965 ....DLB-7, 10, 45, 63

Elizondo, Sergio 1930- DLB-82

Elkin, Stanley 1930- DLB-2, 28; Y-80

Elles, Dora Amy (see Wentworth, Patricia)

Ellet, Elizabeth F. 1818?-1877 ....DLB-30

Elliot, Ebenezer 1781-1849.............................DLB-96

Elliott, George 1923- DLB-68

Elliott, Janice 1931- DLB-14

Elliott, William 1788-1863 ....DLB-3

Elliott, Thomes and Talbot............................DLB-49

Ellis, Edward S. 1840-1916.............................DLB-42

Ellis, Frederick Staridge [publishing house]...DLB-106

The George H. Ellis Company.........................DLB-49

Ellison, Harlan 1934- DLB-8

Ellison, Ralph 1914- DLB-2, 76

Ellmann, Richard 1918-1987 ....DLB-103; Y-87

The Elmer Holmes Bobst Awards
    in Arts and Letters....................................Y-87

Emanuel, James Andrew 1921- DLB-41

Emecheta, Buchi 1944- DLB-117

The Emergence of Black Women Writers..........DS-8

Emerson, Ralph Waldo 1803-1882 ....DLB-1, 59, 73

Emerson, William 1769-1811 ....DLB-37

Empson, William 1906-1984 ....DLB-20

The End of English Stage Censorship,
    1945-1968..DLB-13

Ende, Michael 1929- DLB-75

Engel, Marian 1933-1985 ....DLB-53

Engle, Paul 1908- DLB-48

English Composition and Rhetoric (1866),
by Alexander Bain [excerpt] DLB-57

The English Renaissance of Art (1908),
by Oscar Wilde................DLB-35

Enright, D. J. 1920- DLB-27

Enright, Elizabeth 1909-1968................DLB-22

L'Envoi (1882), by Oscar Wilde DLB-35

Epps, Bernard 1936- DLB-53

Epstein, Julius 1909- and
Epstein, Philip 1909-1952 ....DLB-26

Equiano, Olaudah circa 1745-1797................DLB-37, 50

Eragny Press................DLB-112

Erichsen-Brown, Gwethalyn Graham
(see Graham, Gwethalyn)

Eriugena, John Scottus circa 810-877................DLB-115

Ernst, Paul 1866-1933 ....DLB-66, 118

Erskine, John 1879-1951 ....DLB-9, 102

Ervine, St. John Greer 1883-1971................DLB-10

Eschenburg, Johann Joachim 1743-1820................DLB-97

Eshleman, Clayton 1935- DLB-5

Ess Ess Publishing Company DLB-49

Essay on Chatterton (1842),
by Robert Browning................DLB-32

Essex House Press................DLB-112

Estes, Eleanor 1906-1988 ....DLB-22

Estes and Lauriat DLB-49

Etherege, George 1636-circa 1692................DLB-80

Ets, Marie Hall 1893- DLB-22

Etter, David 1928- DLB-105

Eudora Welty: Eye of the Storyteller Y-87

Eugene O'Neill Memorial Theater Center................DLB-7

Eugene O'Neill's Letters: A Review Y-88

Evans, Donald 1884-1921................DLB-54

Evans, George Henry 1805-1856 ....DLB-43

Evans, Hubert 1892-1986................DLB-92

Evans, M., and Company................DLB-46

Evans, Mari 1923- DLB-41

Evans, Mary Ann (see Eliot, George)

Evans, Nathaniel 1742-1767 ....DLB-31

Evans, Sebastian 1830-1909................DLB-35

Everett, Alexander Hill 1790-1847................DLB-59

Everett, Edward 1794-1865................DLB-1, 59

Everson, R. G. 1903- DLB-88

Everson, William 1912- DLB-5, 16

Every Man His Own Poet; or, The
Inspired Singer's Recipe Book (1877),
by W. H. Mallock................DLB-35

Ewart, Gavin 1916- DLB-40

Ewing, Juliana Horatia 1841-1885................DLB-21

The Examiner 1808-1881................DLB-110

Exley, Frederick 1929- Y-81

Experiment in the Novel (1929),
by John D. Beresford DLB-36

Eyre and Spottiswoode................DLB-106

F

"F. Scott Fitzgerald: St. Paul's Native Son
and Distinguished American Writer":
University of Minnesota Conference,
29-31 October 1982 ....Y-82

Faber, Frederick William 1814-1863................DLB-32

Faber and Faber Limited DLB-112

Faccio, Rena (see Aleramo, Sibilla)

Fair, Ronald L. 1932- DLB-33

Fairfax, Beatrice (see Manning, Marie)

Fairlie, Gerard 1899-1983................DLB-77

Fallada, Hans 1893-1947 ....DLB-56

Fancher, Betsy 1928- Y-83

Fane, Violet 1843-1905 ....DLB-35

Fanfrolico Press................DLB-112

Fantasy Press Publishers DLB-46

Fante, John 1909-1983 ....Y-83

Al-Farabi circa 870-950................DLB-115

Farber, Norma 1909-1984 ....DLB-61

Farigoule, Louis (see Romains, Jules)

Farley, Walter 1920-1989................DLB-22

Farmer, Philip José 1918- DLB-8

Farquhar, George circa 1677-1707................DLB-84

Farquharson, Martha (see Finley, Martha)

Farrar and Rinehart................DLB-46

Farrar, Straus and Giroux DLB-46

Farrell, James T. 1904-1979 ....DLB-4, 9, 86; DS-2

Farrell, J. G. 1935-1979................DLB-14

Fast, Howard 1914- DLB-9

Faulkner, William 1897-1962
................DLB-9, 11, 44, 102; DS-2; Y-86

Fauset, Jessie Redmon 1882-1961 ....DLB-51

Faust, Irvin 1924- DLB-2, 28; Y-80

Fawcett Books..DLB-46

Fearing, Kenneth 1902-1961 ....DLB-9

Federal Writers' Project DLB-46

Federman, Raymond 1928- Y-80

Feiffer, Jules 1929- DLB-7, 44

Feinberg, Charles E. 1899-1988 ....Y-88

Feinstein, Elaine 1930- DLB-14, 40

Felipe, León 1884-1968 ....DLB-108

Fell, Frederick, Publishers DLB-46

Fels, Ludwig 1946- DLB-75

Felton, Cornelius Conway 1807-1862............................DLB-1

Fennario, David 1947- DLB-60

Fenno, John 1751-1798..DLB-43

Fenno, R. F., and Company..DLB-49

Fenton, James 1949- DLB-40

Ferber, Edna 1885-1968......................................DLB-9, 28, 86

Ferdinand, Vallery III (see Salaam, Kalamu ya)

Ferguson, Sir Samuel 1810-1886...................................DLB-32

Ferguson, William Scott 1875-1954 ....DLB-47

Fergusson, Robert 1750-1774.......................................DLB-109

Ferland, Albert 1872-1943..DLB-92

Ferlinghetti, Lawrence 1919- DLB-5, 16

Fern, Fanny (see Parton, Sara Payson Willis)

Ferrars, Elizabeth 1907- DLB-87

Ferret, E., and Company DLB-49

Ferrier, Susan 1782-1854..DLB-116

Ferrini, Vincent 1913- DLB-48

Ferron, Jacques 1921-1985 ....DLB-60

Ferron, Madeleine 1922- DLB-53

Fetridge and Company DLB-49

Feuchtwanger, Lion 1884-1958 ....DLB-66

Fichte, Johann Gottlieb 1762-1814 ....DLB-90

Ficke, Arthur Davison 1883-1945 ....DLB-54

Fiction Best-Sellers, 1910-1945 ....DLB-9

Fiction into Film, 1928-1975: A List of Movies
  Based on the Works of Authors in
  British Novelists, 1930-1959....................................DLB-15

Fiedler, Leslie A. 1917- DLB-28, 67

Field, Edward 1924- DLB-105

Field, Edward, The Poetry File DLB-105

Field, Eugene 1850-1895...DLB-23, 42

Field, Nathan 1587-1619 or 1620 ....DLB-58

Field, Rachel 1894-1942 ....DLB-9, 22

A Field Guide to Recent Schools of
  American Poetry Y-86

Fielding, Henry 1707-1754 ....DLB-39, 84, 101

Fielding, Sarah 1710-1768..DLB-39

Fields, James Thomas 1817-1881..................................DLB-1

Fields, Julia 1938- DLB-41

Fields, W. C. 1880-1946..DLB-44

Fields, Osgood and Company DLB-49

Fifty Penguin Years Y-85

Figes, Eva 1932- DLB-14

Figuera, Angela 1902-1984 ....DLB-108

Filson, John circa 1753-1788..DLB-37

Finch, Anne, Countess of Winchilsea
  1661-1720..DLB-95

Finch, Robert 1900- DLB-88

Findley, Timothy 1930- DLB-53

Finlay, Ian Hamilton 1925- DLB-40

Finley, Martha 1828-1909..DLB-42

Finney, Jack 1911- DLB-8

Finney, Walter Braden (see Finney, Jack)

Firbank, Ronald 1886-1926..DLB-36

Firmin, Giles 1615-1697 ....DLB-24

First Edition Library/Collectors' Reprints, Inc. Y-91

First Strauss "Livings" Awarded to Cynthia
  Ozick and Raymond Carver
  An Interview with Cynthia Ozick
  An Interview with Raymond Carver.............................Y-83

Fischer, Karoline Auguste Fernandine
  1764-1842..DLB-94

Fish, Stanley 1938- DLB-67

Fishacre, Richard 1205-1248..DLB-115

Fisher, Clay (see Allen, Henry W.)

Fisher, Dorothy Canfield 1879-1958 ....DLB-9, 102

Fisher, Leonard Everett 1924- DLB-61

Fisher, Roy 1930- DLB-40

Fisher, Rudolph 1897-1934...................................DLB-51, 102

Fisher, Sydney George 1856-1927 ....DLB-47

Fisher, Vardis 1895-1968..DLB-9

Fiske, John 1608-1677 ....DLB-24

Fiske, John 1842-1901 ....DLB-47, 64

Fitch, Thomas circa 1700-1774.....................................DLB-31

Fitch, William Clyde 1865-1909....................................DLB-7

FitzGerald, Edward 1809-1883.....................................DLB-32

Fitzgerald, F. Scott 1896-1940

...................DLB-4, 9, 86; Y-81; DS-1

Fitzgerald, Penelope 1916- DLB-14

Fitzgerald, Robert 1910-1985 ....Y-80

Fitzgerald, Thomas 1819-1891 ....DLB-23

Fitzgerald, Zelda Sayre 1900-1948 ....Y-84

Fitzhugh, Louise 1928-1974 ....DLB-52

Fitzhugh, William circa 1651-1701 ....DLB-24

Flanagan, Thomas 1923- Y-80

Flanner, Hildegarde 1899-1987 ....DLB-48

Flanner, Janet 1892-1978 ....DLB-4

Flaubert, Gustave 1821-1880 ....DLB-119

Flavin, Martin 1883-1967 ....DLB-9

Flecker, James Elroy 1884-1915 ....DLB-10, 19

Fleeson, Doris 1901-1970 ....DLB-29

Fleißer, Marieluise 1901-1974 ....DLB-56

Fleming, Ian 1908-1964 ....DLB-87

The Fleshly School of Poetry and Other Phenomena of the Day (1872), by Robert Buchanan DLB-35

The Fleshly School of Poetry: Mr. D. G. Rossetti (1871), by Thomas Maitland (Robert Buchanan) DLB-35

Fletcher, J. S. 1863-1935 ....DLB-70

Fletcher, John (see Beaumont, Francis)

Fletcher, John Gould 1886-1950 ....DLB-4, 45

Flieg, Helmut (see Heym, Stefan)

Flint, F. S. 1885-1960 ....DLB-19

Flint, Timothy 1780-1840 ....DLB-734

Folio Society DLB-112

Follen, Eliza Lee (Cabot) 1787-1860 ....DLB-1

Follett, Ken 1949- Y-81, DLB-87

Follett Publishing Company DLB-46

Folsom, John West [publishing house] DLB-49

Foote, Horton 1916- DLB-26

Foote, Samuel 1721-1777 ....DLB-89

Foote, Shelby 1916- DLB-2, 17

Forbes, Calvin 1945- DLB-41

Forbes, Ester 1891-1967 ....DLB-22

Forbes and Company DLB-49

Force, Peter 1790-1868 ....DLB-30

Forché, Carolyn 1950- DLB-5

Ford, Charles Henri 1913- DLB-4, 48

Ford, Corey 1902-1969 ....DLB-11

Ford, Ford Madox 1873-1939 ....DLB-34, 98

Ford, J. B., and Company DLB-49

Ford, Jesse Hill 1928- DLB-6

Ford, John 1586-? DLB-58

Ford, R. A. D. 1915- DLB-88

Ford, Worthington C. 1858-1941 ....DLB-47

Fords, Howard, and Hulbert DLB-49

Foreman, Carl 1914-1984 ....DLB-26

Forester, Frank (see Herbert, Henry William)

Fornés, María Irene 1930- DLB-7

Forrest, Leon 1937- DLB-33

Forster, E. M. 1879-1970 ....DLB-34, 98

Forster, Georg 1754-1794 ....DLB-94

Forsyth, Frederick 1938- DLB-87

Forten, Charlotte L. 1837-1914 ....DLB-50

Fortune, T. Thomas 1856-1928 ....DLB-23

Fosdick, Charles Austin 1842-1915 ....DLB-42

Foster, Genevieve 1893-1979 ....DLB-61

Foster, Hannah Webster 1758-1840 ....DLB-37

Foster, John 1648-1681 ....DLB-24

Foster, Michael 1904-1956 ....DLB-9

Fouqué, Caroline de la Motte 1774-1831 ....DLB-90

Fouqué, Friedrich de la Motte 1777-1843 ....DLB-90

Four Essays on the Beat Generation, by John Clellon Holmes DLB-16

Four Seas Company DLB-46

Four Winds Press DLB-46

Fournier, Henri Alban (see Alain-Fournier)

Fowler and Wells Company DLB-49

Fowles, John 1926- DLB-14

Fox, John, Jr. 1862 or 1863-1919 ....DLB-9

Fox, Paula 1923- DLB-52

Fox, Richard K. [publishing house] DLB-49

Fox, Richard Kyle 1846-1922 ....DLB-79

Fox, William Price 1926- DLB-2; Y-81

Fraenkel, Michael 1896-1957 ....DLB-4

France, Richard 1938- DLB-7

Francis, C. S. [publishing house] DLB-49

Francis, Convers 1795-1863 ....DLB-1

Francis, Dick 1920- DLB-87

Francis, Jeffrey, Lord 1773-1850 ....DLB-107

François 1863-1910 ....DLB-92

Francke, Kuno 1855-1930 ....DLB-71

Frank, Bruno 1887-1945 ....DLB-118

Frank, Leonhard 1882-1961 ....DLB-56, 118

Frank, Melvin (see Panama, Norman)

Frank, Waldo 1889-1967 ....DLB-9, 63

Franken, Rose 1895?-1988 ....Y-84

Franklin, Benjamin 1706-1790 ....DLB-24, 43, 73

Franklin, James 1697-1735..DLB-43

Franklin Library...DLB-46

Frantz, Ralph Jules 1902-1979 ....DLB-4

Fraser, G. S. 1915-1980 ....DLB-27

Frayn, Michael 1933- DLB-13, 14

Frederic, Harold 1856-1898....................................DLB-12, 23

Freeling, Nicolas 1927- DLB-87

Freeman, Douglas Southall 1886-1953 ....DLB-17

Freeman, Legh Richmond 1842-1915 ....DLB-23

Freeman, Mary E. Wilkins 1852-1930...............DLB-12, 78

Freeman, R. Austin 1862-1943 ....DLB-70

French, Alice 1850-1934..DLB-74

French, David 1939- DLB-53

French, James [publishing house] DLB-49

French, Samuel [publishing house]............................DLB-49

Samuel French, Limited DLB-106

Freneau, Philip 1752-1832 ....DLB-37, 43

Fried, Erich 1921-1988...DLB-85

Friedman, Bruce Jay 1930- DLB-2, 28

Friel, Brian 1929- DLB-13

Friend, Krebs 1895?-1967?..DLB-4

Fries, Fritz Rudolf 1935- DLB-75

Fringe and Alternative Theater
    in Great Britain DLB-13

Frisch, Max 1911- DLB-69

Frischmuth, Barbara 1941- DLB-85

Fritz, Jean 1915- DLB-52

Frost, Robert 1874-1963 ....DLB-54; DS-7

Frothingham, Octavius Brooks 1822-1895 ....DLB-1

Froude, James Anthony 1818-1894 ....DLB-18, 57

Fry, Christopher 1907- DLB-13

Frye, Northrop 1912-1991 ....DLB-67, 68

Fuchs, Daniel 1909- DLB-9, 26, 28

Fuentes, Carlos 1928- DLB-113

Fuertas, Gloria 1918- DLB-108

The Fugitives and the Agrarians:
    The First Exhibition..Y-85

Fuller, Charles H., Jr. 1939- DLB-38

Fuller, Henry Blake 1857-1929................................DLB-12

Fuller, John 1937- DLB-40

Fuller, Roy 1912-1991 ....DLB-15, 20

Fuller, Samuel 1912- DLB-26

Fuller, Sarah Margaret, Marchesa
    D'Ossoli 1810-1850.......................................DLB-1, 59, 73

Fulton, Len 1934- Y-86

Fulton, Robin 1937- DLB-40

Furman, Laura 1945- Y-86

Furness, Horace Howard 1833-1912 ....DLB-64

Furness, William Henry 1802-1896 ....DLB-1

Furthman, Jules 1888-1966......................................DLB-26

The Future of the Novel (1899),
    by Henry James DLB-18

G

The G. Ross Roy Scottish Poetry
    Collection at the University of
    South Carolina Y-89

Gaddis, William 1922- DLB-2

Gág, Wanda 1893-1946..DLB-22

Gagnon, Madeleine 1938- DLB-60

Gaine, Hugh 1726-1807 ....DLB-43

Gaine, Hugh [publishing house] DLB-49

Gaines, Ernest J. 1933- DLB-2, 33; Y-80

Gaiser, Gerd 1908-1976..DLB-69

Galaxy Science Fiction Novels DLB-46

Gale, Zona 1874-1938..DLB-9, 78

Gallagher, William Davis 1808-1894......................DLB-73

Gallant, Mavis 1922- DLB-53

Gallico, Paul 1897-1976 ....DLB-9

Galsworthy, John 1867-1933 ....DLB-10, 34, 98

Galt, John 1779-1839..DLB-99, 116

Galvin, Brendan 1938- DLB-5

Gambit DLB-46

Gammer Gurton's Needle DLB-62

Gannett, Frank E. 1876-1957....................................DLB-29

García, Lionel G. 1935- DLB-82

García Lorca, Federico 1898-1936............................DLB-108

García Marquez, Gabriel 1928- DLB-113

Gardam, Jane 1928- DLB-14

Garden, Alexander circa 1685-1756 ....DLB-31

Gardner, John 1933-1982 ....DLB-2; Y-82

Garis, Howard R. 1873-1962......................................DLB-22

Garland, Hamlin 1860-1940 ....DLB-12, 71, 78

Garneau, Francis-Xavier 1809-1866............................DLB-99

Garneau, Hector de Saint-Denys 1912-1943 ....DLB-88

Garneau, Michel 1939- DLB-53

Garner, Hugh 1913-1979 ....DLB-68

Garnett, David 1892-1981 ....DLB-34

Garraty, John A. 1920- DLB-17

Garrett, George 1929- DLB-2, 5; Y-83

Garrick, David 1717-1779 ....DLB-84

Garrison, William Lloyd 1805-1879 ....DLB-1, 43

Garth, Samuel 1661-1719 ....DLB-95

Garve, Andrew 1908- DLB-87

Gary, Romain 1914-1980 ....DLB-83

Gascoyne, David 1916- DLB-20

Gaskell, Elizabeth Cleghorn 1810-1865 ....DLB-21

Gaspey, Thomas 1788-1871 ....DLB-116

Gass, William Howard 1924- DLB-2

Gates, Doris 1901- DLB-22

Gates, Henry Louis, Jr. 1950- DLB-67

Gates, Lewis E. 1860-1924 ....DLB-71

Gatto, Alfonso 1909-1976 ....DLB-114

Gautier, Théophile 1811-1872 ....DLB-119

Gauvreau, Claude 1925-1971 ....DLB-88

Gay, Ebenezer 1696-1787 ....DLB-24

Gay, John 1685-1732 ....DLB-84, 95

The Gay Science (1866),
by E. S. Dallas [excerpt] DLB-21

Gayarré, Charles E. A. 1805-1895 ....DLB-30

Gaylord, Charles [publishing house] DLB-49

Geddes, Gary 1940- DLB-60

Geddes, Virgil 1897- DLB-4

Geis, Bernard, Associates DLB-46

Geisel, Theodor Seuss 1904-1991 ....DLB-61; Y-91

Gelb, Arthur 1924- DLB-103

Gelb, Barbara 1926- DLB-103

Gelber, Jack 1932- DLB-7

Gélinas, Gratien 1909- DLB-88

Gellert, Christian Füerchtegott 1715-1769 ....DLB-97

Gellhorn, Martha 1908- Y-82

Gems, Pam 1925- DLB-13

A General Idea of the College of Mirania (1753),
by William Smith [excerpts] DLB-31

Genet, Jean 1910-1986 ....DLB-72; Y-86

Genevoix, Maurice 1890-1980 ....DLB-65

Genovese, Eugene D. 1930- DLB-17

Gent, Peter 1942- Y-82

George, Henry 1839-1897 ....DLB-23

George, Jean Craighead 1919- DLB-52

Gerhardie, William 1895-1977 ....DLB-36

Gérin-Lajoie, Antoine 1824-1882 ....DLB-99

German Drama from Naturalism
to Fascism: 1889-1933 ....DLB-118

German Transformation from the Baroque
to the Enlightenment, The DLB-97

Germanophilism, by Hans Kohn DLB-66

Gernsback, Hugo 1884-1967 ....DLB-8

Gerould, Katharine Fullerton 1879-1944 ....DLB-78

Gerrish, Samuel [publishing house] DLB-49

Gerrold, David 1944- DLB-8

Gersonides 1288-1344 ....DLB-115

Gerstenberg, Heinrich Wilhelm von
1737-1823 ....DLB-97

Geßner, Salomon 1730-1788 ....DLB-97

Geston, Mark S. 1946- DLB-8

Al-Ghazali 1058-1111 ....DLB-115

Gibbon, Edward 1737-1794 ....DLB-104

Gibbon, John Murray 1875-1952 ....DLB-92

Gibbon, Lewis Grassic (see Mitchell, James Leslie)

Gibbons, Floyd 1887-1939 ....DLB-25

Gibbons, William ?-? DLB-73

Gibson, Graeme 1934- DLB-53

Gibson, Wilfrid 1878-1962 ....DLB-19

Gibson, William 1914- DLB-7

Gide, André 1869-1951 ....DLB-65

Giguère, Diane 1937- DLB-53

Giguère, Roland 1929- DLB-60

Gil de Biedma, Jaime 1929-1990 ....DLB-108

Gilbert, Anthony 1899-1973 ....DLB-77

Gilbert, Michael 1912- DLB-87

Gilder, Jeannette L. 1849-1916 ....DLB-79

Gilder, Richard Watson 1844-1909 ....DLB-64, 79

Gildersleeve, Basil 1831-1924 ....DLB-71

Giles, Henry 1809-1882 ....DLB-64

Giles of Rome circa 1243-1316 ....DLB-115

Gill, Eric 1882-1940 ....DLB-98

Gill, William F., Company DLB-49

Gillespie, A. Lincoln, Jr. 1895-1950 ....DLB-4

Gilliam, Florence ?-? DLB-4

Gilliatt, Penelope 1932- DLB-14

Gillott, Jacky 1939-1980 ....DLB-14

Gilman, Caroline H. 1794-1888 ....DLB-3, 73

Gilman, W. and J. [publishing house] DLB-49

Gilmer, Elizabeth Meriwether 1861-1951 ....DLB-29

Gilmer, Francis Walker 1790-1826 ....DLB-37

Gilroy, Frank D. 1925- DLB-7

Ginsberg, Allen 1926- DLB-5, 16

Ginzkey, Franz Karl 1871-1963 ....DLB-81

Giono, Jean 1895-1970 ....DLB-72

Giotti, Virgilio 1885-1957 ....DLB-114

Giovanni, Nikki 1943- DLB-5, 41

Gipson, Lawrence Henry 1880-1971 ....DLB-17

Girard, Rodolphe 1879-1956 ....DLB-92

Giraudoux, Jean 1882-1944 ....DLB-65

Gissing, George 1857-1903 ....DLB-18

Gladstone, William Ewart 1809-1898 ....DLB-57

Glaeser, Ernst 1902-1963 ....DLB-69

Glanville, Brian 1931- DLB-15

Glapthorne, Henry 1610-1643? DLB-58

Glasgow, Ellen 1873-1945 ....DLB-9, 12

Glaspell, Susan 1876-1948 ....DLB-7, 9, 78

Glass, Montague 1877-1934 ....DLB-11

Glassco, John 1909-1981 ....DLB-68

Glauser, Friedrich 1896-1938 ....DLB-56

F. Gleason's Publishing Hall DLB-49

Gleim, Johann Wilhelm Ludwig 1719-1803 .....DLB-97

Glover, Richard 1712-1785 ....DLB-95

Glück, Louise 1943- DLB-5

Godbout, Jacques 1933- DLB-53

Goddard, Morrill 1865-1937 ....DLB-25

Goddard, William 1740-1817 ....DLB-43

Godey, Louis A. 1804-1878 ....DLB-73

Godey and McMichael DLB-49

Godfrey, Dave 1938- DLB-60

Godfrey, Thomas 1736-1763 ....DLB-31

Godine, David R., Publisher DLB-46

Godkin, E. L. 1831-1902 ....DLB-79

Godwin, Gail 1937- DLB-6

Godwin, Parke 1816-1904 ....DLB-3, 64

Godwin, William 1756-1836 ....DLB-39, 104

Goering, Reinhard 1887-1936 ....DLB-118

Goes, Albrecht 1908- DLB-69

Goethe, Johann Wolfgang von 1749-1832 ......DLB-94

Goffe, Thomas circa 1592-1629 ....DLB-58

Goffstein, M. B. 1940- DLB-61

Gogarty, Oliver St. John 1878-1957 ....DLB-15, 19

Goines, Donald 1937-1974 ....DLB-33

Gold, Herbert 1924- DLB-2; Y-81

Gold, Michael 1893-1967 ....DLB-9, 28

Goldberg, Dick 1947- DLB-7

Golden Cockerel Press DLB-112

Golding, William 1911- DLB-15, 100

Goldman, William 1931- DLB-44

Goldsmith, Oliver
 1730 or 1731-1774 ....DLB-39, 89, 104

Goldsmith, Oliver 1794-1861 ....DLB-99

Goldsmith Publishing Company DLB-46

Gollancz, Victor, Limited DLB-112

Gomme, Laurence James
 [publishing house] DLB-46

González-T., César A. 1931- DLB-82

González, Angel 1925- DLB-108

The Goodman Theatre DLB-7

Goodrich, Frances 1891-1984 and
 Hackett, Albert 1900- DLB-26

Goodrich, S. G. [publishing house] DLB-49

Goodrich, Samuel Griswold 1793-1860 ......DLB-1, 42, 73

Goodspeed, C. E., and Company DLB-49

Goodwin, Stephen 1943- Y-82

Gookin, Daniel 1612-1687 ....DLB-24

Gordon, Caroline 1895-1981 ....DLB-4, 9, 102; Y-81

Gordon, Giles 1940- DLB-14

Gordon, Mary 1949- DLB-6; Y-81

Gordone, Charles 1925- DLB-7

Gore, Catherine 1800-1861 ....DLB-116

Gorey, Edward 1925- DLB-61

Görres, Joseph 1776-1848 ....DLB-90

Gosse, Edmund 1849-1928 ....DLB-57

Gotlieb, Phyllis 1926- DLB-88

Gottsched, Johann Christoph 1700-1766 ....DLB-97

Götz, Johann Nikolaus 1721-1781 ....DLB-97

Gould, Wallace 1882-1940 ....DLB-54

Govoni, Corrado 1884-1965 ....DLB-114

Goyen, William 1915-1983 ....DLB-2; Y-83

Gozzano, Guido 1883-1916 ....DLB-114

Gracq, Julien 1910- DLB-83

Grady, Henry W. 1850-1889 ....DLB-23

Graf, Oskar Maria 1894-1967 ....DLB-56

Graham, George Rex 1813-1894................................DLB-73

Graham, Gwethalyn 1913-1965................................DLB-88

Graham, Lorenz 1902-1989...................................DLB-76

Graham, R. B. Cunninghame 1852-1936.......................DLB-98

Graham, Shirley 1896-1977..................................DLB-76

Graham, W. S. 1918-..DLB-20

Graham, William H. [publishing house].....................DLB-49

Graham, Winston 1910-......................................DLB-77

Grahame, Kenneth 1859-1932.................................DLB-34

Grainger, Martin Allerdale 1874-1941.......................DLB-92

Gramatky, Hardie 1907-1979.................................DLB-22

Grandbois, Alain 1900-1975.................................DLB-92

Granich, Irwin (see Gold, Michael)

Grant, George 1918-1988....................................DLB-88

Grant, George Monro 1835-1902..............................DLB-99

Grant, Harry J. 1881-1963..................................DLB-29

Grant, James Edward 1905-1966..............................DLB-26

Grass, Günter 1927-..DLB-75

Grasty, Charles H. 1863-1924...............................DLB-25

Grau, Shirley Ann 1929-....................................DLB-2

Graves, John 1920-...Y-83

Graves, Richard 1715-1804..................................DLB-39

Graves, Robert 1895-1985.........................DLB-20, 100; Y-85

Gray, Asa 1810-1888..DLB-1

Gray, David 1838-1861......................................DLB-32

Gray, Simon 1936-..DLB-13

Gray, Thomas 1716-1771.....................................DLB-109

Grayson, William J. 1788-1863..............................DLB-3, 64

The Great War and the Theater, 1914-1918
  [Great Britain]..DLB-10

Greeley, Horace 1811-1872..................................DLB-3, 43

Green, Adolph (see Comden, Betty)

Green, Duff 1791-1875......................................DLB-43

Green, Gerald 1922-..DLB-28

Green, Henry 1905-1973.....................................DLB-15

Green, Jonas 1712-1767.....................................DLB-31

Green, Joseph 1706-1780....................................DLB-31

Green, Julien 1900-..DLB-4, 72

Green, Paul 1894-1981..............................DLB-7, 9; Y-81

Green, T. and S. [publishing house]........................DLB-49

Green, Timothy [publishing house]..........................DLB-49

Greenberg: Publisher.......................................DLB-46

Green Tiger Press..DLB-46

Greene, Asa 1789-1838......................................DLB-11

Greene, Benjamin H. [publishing house].....................DLB-49

Greene, Graham 1904-1991
  ....DLB-13, 15, 77, 100; Y-85, Y-91

Greene, Robert 1558-1592...................................DLB-62

Greenhow, Robert 1800-1854.................................DLB-30

Greenough, Horatio 1805-1852...............................DLB-1

Greenwell, Dora 1821-1882..................................DLB-35

Greenwillow Books..DLB-46

Greenwood, Grace (see Lippincott, Sara Jane Clarke)

Greenwood, Walter 1903-1974................................DLB-10

Greer, Ben 1948-...DLB-6

Greg, W. R. 1809-1881......................................DLB-55

Gregg Press..DLB-46

Gregory, Isabella Augusta
  Persse, Lady 1852-1932...................................DLB-10

Gregory, Horace 1898-1982..................................DLB-48

Gregory of Rimini circa 1300-1358..........................DLB-115

Gregynog Press...DLB-112

Grenfell, Wilfred Thomason 1865-1940.......................DLB-92

Greve, Felix Paul (see Grove, Frederick Philip)

Greville, Fulke, First Lord Brooke
  1554-1628..DLB-62

Grey, Zane 1872-1939.......................................DLB-9

Grey Owl 1888-1938...DLB-92

Grey Walls Press...DLB-112

Grier, Eldon 1917-...DLB-88

Grieve, C. M. (see MacDiarmid, Hugh)

Griffith, Elizabeth 1727?-1793.............................DLB-39, 89

Griffiths, Trevor 1935-....................................DLB-13

Griggs, S. C., and Company.................................DLB-49

Griggs, Sutton Elbert 1872-1930............................DLB-50

Grignon, Claude-Henri 1894-1976............................DLB-68

Grigson, Geoffrey 1905-....................................DLB-27

Grimké, Angelina Weld 1880-1958............................DLB-50, 54

Grimm, Hans 1875-1959......................................DLB-66

Grimm, Jacob 1785-1863.....................................DLB-90

Grimm, Wilhelm 1786-1859...................................DLB-90

Griswold, Rufus Wilmot 1815-1857...........................DLB-3, 59

Gross, Milt 1895-1953......................................DLB-11

Grosset and Dunlap...DLB-49

Grossman Publishers..DLB-46

Grosseteste, Robert circa 1160-1253........................DLB-115

Grosvenor, Gilbert H. 1875-1966............................DLB-91

Groulx, Lionel 1878-1967...................................DLB-68

Grove, Frederick Philip 1879-1949 ....DLB-92

Grove Press DLB-46

Grubb, Davis 1919-1980 ....DLB-6

Gruelle, Johnny 1880-1938 ....DLB-22

Guare, John 1938- DLB-7

Guest, Barbara 1920- DLB-5

Guèvremont, Germaine 1893-1968 ....DLB-68

Guillén, Jorge 1893-1984 ....DLB-108

Guilloux, Louis 1899-1980 ....DLB-72

Guiney, Louise Imogen 1861-1920 ....DLB-54

Guiterman, Arthur 1871-1943 ....DLB-11

Günderrode, Caroline von 1780-1806 ......DLB-90

Gunn, Bill 1934-1989 ....DLB-38

Gunn, James E. 1923- DLB-8

Gunn, Neil M. 1891-1973 ....DLB-15

Gunn, Thom 1929- DLB-27

Gunnars, Kristjana 1948- DLB-60

Gurik, Robert 1932- DLB-60

Gustafson, Ralph 1909- DLB-88

Gütersloh, Albert Paris 1887-1973 ....DLB-81

Guthrie, A. B., Jr. 1901- DLB-6

Guthrie, Ramon 1896-1973 ....DLB-4

The Guthrie Theater DLB-7

Guy, Ray 1939- DLB-60

Guy, Rosa 1925- DLB-33

Gwynne, Erskine 1898-1948 ....DLB-4

Gyles, John 1680-1755 ....DLB-99

Gysin, Brion 1916- DLB-16

H

H. D. (see Doolittle, Hilda)

Hackett, Albert (see Goodrich, Frances)

Hadden, Briton 1898-1929 ....DLB-91

Hagelstange, Rudolf 1912-1984 ....DLB-69

Haggard, H. Rider 1856-1925 ....DLB-70

Haig-Brown, Roderick 1908-1976 ....DLB-88

Haight, Gordon S. 1901-1985 ....DLB-103

Hailey, Arthur 1920- DLB-88; Y-82

Haines, John 1924- DLB-5

Hake, Thomas Gordon 1809-1895 ....DLB-32

Halbe, Max 1865-1944 ....DLB-118

Haldeman, Joe 1943- DLB-8

Haldeman-Julius Company DLB-46

Hale, E. J., and Son DLB-49

Hale, Edward Everett 1822-1909 ......DLB-1, 42, 74

Hale, Leo Thomas (see Ebon)

Hale, Lucretia Peabody 1820-1900 ....DLB-42

Hale, Nancy 1908-1988 ....DLB-86; Y-80, 88

Hale, Sarah Josepha (Buell) 1788-1879 .....DLB-1, 42, 73

Haley, Alex 1921-1992 ....DLB-38

Haliburton, Thomas Chandler 1796-1865 .....DLB-11, 99

Hall, Donald 1928- DLB-5

Hall, James 1793-1868 ....DLB-73, 74

Hall, Samuel [publishing house] DLB-49

Hallam, Arthur Henry 1811-1833 ....DLB-32

Halleck, Fitz-Greene 1790-1867 ....DLB-3

Hallmark Editions DLB-46

Halper, Albert 1904-1984 ....DLB-9

Halperin, John William 1941- DLB-111

Halstead, Murat 1829-1908 ....DLB-23

Hamann, Johann Georg 1730-1788 ....DLB-97

Hamburger, Michael 1924- DLB-27

Hamilton, Alexander 1712-1756 ....DLB-31

Hamilton, Alexander 1755?-1804 ....DLB-37

Hamilton, Cicely 1872-1952 ....DLB-10

Hamilton, Edmond 1904-1977 ....DLB-8

Hamilton, Elizabeth 1758-1816 ....DLB-116

Hamilton, Gail (see Corcoran, Barbara)

Hamilton, Ian 1938- DLB-40

Hamilton, Patrick 1904-1962 ....DLB-10

Hamilton, Virginia 1936- DLB-33, 52

Hamilton, Hamish, Limited DLB-112

Hammett, Dashiell 1894-1961 ....DS-6

Dashiell Hammett: An Appeal in *TAC* Y-91

Hammon, Jupiter 1711-died between
    1790 and 1806 ....DLB-31, 50

Hammond, John ?-1663 ....DLB-24

Hamner, Earl 1923- DLB-6

Hampton, Christopher 1946- DLB-13

Handel-Mazzetti, Enrica von 1871-1955 ......DLB-81

Handke, Peter 1942- DLB-85

Handlin, Oscar 1915- DLB-17

Hankin, St. John 1869-1909 ....DLB-10

Hanley, Clifford 1922- DLB-14

Hannah, Barry 1942- DLB-6

Hannay, James 1827-1873 ....DLB-21

Hansberry, Lorraine 1930-1965 ....DLB-7, 38

Hapgood, Norman 1868-1937 ....DLB-91

Harcourt Brace Jovanovich.........................DLB-46

Hardenberg, Friedrich von (see Novalis)

Harding, Walter 1917- DLB-111

Hardwick, Elizabeth 1916- DLB-6

Hardy, Thomas 1840-1928 ....DLB-18, 19

Hare, Cyril 1900-1958 ....DLB-77

Hare, David 1947- DLB-13

Hargrove, Marion 1919- DLB-11

Harlow, Robert 1923- DLB-60

Harness, Charles L. 1915- DLB-8

Harper, Fletcher 1806-1877 ....DLB-79

Harper, Frances Ellen Watkins 1825-1911..........DLB-50

Harper, Michael S. 1938- DLB-41

Harper and Brothers DLB-49

Harrap, George G., and Company Limited

....DLB-112

Harris, Benjamin ?-circa 1720...................DLB-42, 43

Harris, Christie 1907- DLB-88

Harris, George Washington 1814-1869 ....DLB-3, 11

Harris, Joel Chandler 1848-1908

..............................DLB-11, 23, 42, 78, 91

Harris, Mark 1922- DLB-2; Y-80

Harris, Wilson 1921- DLB-117

Harrison, Charles Yale 1898-1954 ....DLB-68

Harrison, Frederic 1831-1923 ....DLB-57

Harrison, Harry 1925- DLB-8

Harrison, James P., Company DLB-49

Harrison, Jim 1937- Y-82

Harrison, Paul Carter 1936- DLB-38

Harrison, Susan Frances 1859-1935 ....DLB-99

Harrison, Tony 1937- DLB-40

Harrisse, Henry 1829-1910 ....DLB-47

Harsent, David 1942- DLB-40

Hart, Albert Bushnell 1854-1943.................DLB-17

Hart, Julia Catherine 1796-1867 ....DLB-99

Hart, Moss 1904-1961................................DLB-7

Hart, Oliver 1723-1795................................DLB-31

Hart-Davis, Rupert, Limited DLB-112

Harte, Bret 1836-1902 ....DLB-12, 64, 74, 79

Hartlaub, Felix 1913-1945 ....DLB-56

Hartlebon, Otto Erich 1864-1905 ....DLB-118

Hartley, L. P. 1895-1972 ....DLB-15

Hartley, Marsden 1877-1943........................DLB-54

Härtling, Peter 1933- DLB-75

Hartman, Geoffrey H. 1929- DLB-67

Hartmann, Sadakichi 1867-1944....................DLB-54

Harvey, Jean-Charles 1891-1967...................DLB-88

Harvill Press Limited...............................DLB-112

Harwood, Lee 1939- DLB-40

Harwood, Ronald 1934- DLB-13

Haskins, Charles Homer 1870-1937 ....DLB-47

Hass, Robert 1941- DLB-105

The Hatch-Billops Collection.......................DLB-76

Hauff, Wilhelm 1802-1827...........................DLB-90

A Haughty and Proud Generation (1922),
  by Ford Madox Hueffer DLB-36

Hauptmann, Carl 1858-1921 ....DLB-66, 118

Hauptmann, Gerhart 1862-1946 ....DLB-66, 118

Hauser, Marianne 1910- Y-83

Hawker, Robert Stephen 1803-1875...............DLB-32

Hawkes, John 1925- DLB-2, 7; Y-80

Hawkins, Sir John 1719 or 1721-1789.............DLB-104

Hawkins, Walter Everette 1883-? DLB-50

Hawthorne, Nathaniel 1804-1864...............DLB-1, 74

Hay, John 1838-1905...............................DLB-12, 47

Hayden, Robert 1913-1980 ....DLB-5, 76

Haydon, Benjamin Robert 1786-1846 ....DLB-110

Hayes, John Michael 1919- DLB-26

Hayley, William 1745-1820 ....DLB-93

Hayman, Robert 1575-1629 ....DLB-99

Hayne, Paul Hamilton 1830-1886 ....DLB-3, 64, 79

Haywood, Eliza 1693?-1756...........................DLB-39

Hazard, Willis P. [publishing house]................DLB-49

Hazlitt, William 1778-1830...........................DLB-110

Hazzard, Shirley 1931- Y-82

Head, Bessie 1937-1986................................DLB-117

Headley, Joel T. 1813-1897..........................DLB-30

Heaney, Seamus 1939- DLB-40

Heard, Nathan C. 1936- DLB-33

Hearn, Lafcadio 1850-1904........................DLB-12, 78

Hearne, John 1926- DLB-117

Hearne, Samuel 1745-1792 ....DLB-99

Hearst, William Randolph 1863-1951 ....DLB-25

Heath, Catherine 1924- DLB-14

Heath, Roy A. K. 1926- DLB-117

Heath-Stubbs, John 1918- DLB-27

Heavysege, Charles 1816-1876.................................DLB-99

Hebel, Johann Peter 1760-1826 ....DLB-90

Hébert, Anne 1916- DLB-68

Hébert, Jacques 1923- DLB-53

Hecht, Anthony 1923- DLB-5

Hecht, Ben 1894-1964 ....DLB-7, 9, 25, 26, 28, 86

Hecker, Isaac Thomas 1819-1888.............................DLB-1

Hedge, Frederic Henry 1805-1890.....................DLB-1, 59

Hegel, Georg Wilhelm Friedrich 1770-1831 ....DLB-90

Heidish, Marcy 1947- Y-82

Heidsenbüttel 1921- DLB-75

Heine, Heinrich 1797-1856.....................................DLB-90

Heinemann, Larry 1944- DS-9

Heinemann, William, Limited.................................DLB-112

Heinlein, Robert A. 1907- DLB-8

Heinrich, Willi 1920- DLB-75

Heinse, Wilhelm 1746-1803 ....DLB-94

Heller, Joseph 1923- DLB-2, 28; Y-80

Hellman, Lillian 1906-1984 ....DLB-7; Y-84

Helprin, Mark 1947- Y-85

Helwig, David 1938- DLB-60

Hemans, Felicia 1793-1835 ....DLB-96

Hemingway, Ernest 1899-1961
.................................DLB-4, 9, 102; Y-81, 87; DS-1

Hemingway: Twenty-Five Years Later.......................Y-85

Hémon, Louis 1880-1913 ....DLB-92

Hemphill, Paul 1936- Y-87

Hénault, Gilles 1920- DLB-88

Henchman, Daniel 1689-1761.................................DLB-24

Henderson, Alice Corbin 1881-1949 ....DLB-54

Henderson, Archibald 1877-1963 ....DLB-103

Henderson, David 1942- DLB-41

Henderson, George Wylie 1904- DLB-51

Henderson, Zenna 1917- DLB-8

Henisch, Peter 1943- DLB-85

Henley, Beth 1952- Y-86

Henley, William Ernest 1849-1903 ....DLB-19

Henry, Alexander 1739-1824....................................DLB-99

Henry, Buck 1930-..DLB-26

Henry, Marguerite 1902- DLB-22

Henry, Robert Selph 1889-1970 ....DLB-17

Henry, Will (see Allen, Henry W.)

Henschke, Alfred (see Klabund)

Henry of Ghent circa 1217-1229 - 1293.................DLB-115

Hensley, Sophie Almon 1866-1946...............................DLB-99

Henty, G. A. 1832-1902..DLB-18

Hentz, Caroline Lee 1800-1856 ....DLB-3

Herbert, Alan Patrick 1890-1971 ....DLB-10

Herbert, Frank 1920-1986 ....DLB-8

Herbert, Henry William 1807-1858 ....DLB-3, 73

Herbert, John 1926- DLB-53

Herbst, Josephine 1892-1969 ....DLB-9

Herburger, Günter 1932- DLB-75

Hercules, Frank E. M. 1917- DLB-33

Herder, B., Book Company DLB-49

Herder, Johann Gottfried 1744-1803 ....DLB-97

Hergesheimer, Joseph 1880-1954.....................DLB-9, 102

Heritage Press DLB-46

Hermes, Johann Timotheus 1738-1821...................DLB-97

Hermlin, Stephan 1915- DLB-69

Hernton, Calvin C. 1932- DLB-38

"The Hero as Man of Letters: Johnson,
Rousseau, Burns" (1841), by Thomas
Carlyle [excerpt]..DLB-57

The Hero as Poet. Dante; Shakspeare (1841),
by Thomas Carlyle..DLB-32

Herrick, E. R., and Company....................................DLB-49

Herrick, Robert 1868-1938 ....DLB-9, 12, 78

Herrick, William 1915- Y-83

Herrmann, John 1900-1959......................................DLB-4

Hersey, John 1914- DLB-6

Hertel, François 1905-1985 ....DLB-68

Hervé-Bazin, Jean Pierre Marie (see Bazin, Hervé)

Hervey, John, Lord 1696-1743 ....DLB-101

Herzog, Emile Salomon Wilhelm (see Maurois, André)

Hesse, Hermann 1877-1962......................................DLB-66

Hewat, Alexander circa 1743-circa 1824.................DLB-30

Hewitt, John 1907- DLB-27

Hewlett, Maurice 1861-1923 ....DLB-34

Heyen, William 1940- DLB-5

Heyer, Georgette 1902-1974 ....DLB-77

Heym, Stefan 1913- DLB-69

Heytesbury, William circa 1310-1372 or 1373 ....DLB-115

Heyward, Dorothy 1890-1961 and
Heyward, DuBose 1885-1940..................................DLB-7

Heyward, DuBose 1885-1940 ....DLB-7, 9, 45

Heywood, Thomas 1573 or 1574-1641 ....DLB-62

Hickman, William Albert 1877-1957 ....DLB-92

Hidalgo, José Luis 1919-1947 ....DLB-108

Hiebert, Paul 1892-1987....................................DLB-68

Hierro, José 1922- DLB-108

Higgins, Aidan 1927- DLB-14

Higgins, Colin 1941-1988 ....DLB-26

Higgins, George V. 1939- DLB-2; Y-81

Higginson, Thomas Wentworth
    1823-1911....................................DLB-1, 64

Highwater, Jamake 1942?- DLB-52; Y-85

Hildesheimer, Wolfgang 1916-1991....................................DLB-69

Hildreth, Richard 1807-1865....................................DLB-1, 30, 59

Hill, Aaron 1685-1750....................................DLB-84

Hill, Geoffrey 1932- DLB-40

Hill, George M., Company....................................DLB-49

Hill, "Sir" John 1714?-1775....................................DLB-39

Hill, Lawrence, and Company, Publishers DLB-46

Hill, Leslie 1880-1960....................................DLB-51

Hill, Susan 1942- DLB-14

Hill, Walter 1942- DLB-44

Hill and Wang....................................DLB-46

Hilliard, Gray and Company....................................DLB-49

Hillyer, Robert 1895-1961....................................DLB-54

Hilton, James 1900-1954....................................DLB-34, 77

Hilton and Company....................................DLB-49

Himes, Chester 1909-1984....................................DLB-2, 76

Hine, Daryl 1936- DLB-60

Hinojosa-Smith, Rolando 1929- DLB-82

Hippel, Theodor Gottlieb von 1741-1796....................DLB-97

The History of the Adventures of Joseph Andrews
    (1742), by Henry Fielding [excerpt] DLB-39

Hirsch, E. D., Jr. 1928- DLB-67

Hoagland, Edward 1932- DLB-6

Hoagland, Everett H. III 1942- DLB-41

Hoban, Russell 1925- DLB-52

Hobsbaum, Philip 1932- DLB-40

Hobson, Laura Z. 1900- DLB-28

Hochman, Sandra 1936- DLB-5

Hodder and Stoughton, Limited DLB-106

Hodgins, Jack 1938- DLB-60

Hodgman, Helen 1945- DLB-14

Hodgson, Ralph 1871-1962....................................DLB-19

Hodgson, William Hope 1877-1918....................................DLB-70

Hoffenstein, Samuel 1890-1947....................................DLB-11

Hoffman, Charles Fenno 1806-1884....................................DLB-3

Hoffman, Daniel 1923- DLB-5

Hoffmann, E. T. A. 1776-1822....................................DLB-90

Hofmann, Michael 1957- DLB-40

Hofmannsthal, Hugo von 1874-1929....................DLB-81, 118

Hofstadter, Richard 1916-1970....................................DLB-17

Hogan, Desmond 1950- DLB-14

Hogan and Thompson DLB-49

Hogarth Press....................................DLB-112

Hogg, James 1770-1835 ....DLB-93, 116

Hohl, Ludwig 1904-1980....................................DLB-56

Holbrook, David 1923- DLB-14, 40

Holcroft, Thomas 1745-1809....................................DLB-39, 89

Holden, Jonathan 1941- DLB-105

Holden, Jonathan, Contemporary
    Verse Story-telling....................................DLB-105

Holden, Molly 1927-1981....................................DLB-40

Hölderlin, Friedrich 1770-1843 ....DLB-90

Holiday House DLB-46

Holland, Norman N. 1927- DLB-67

Hollander, John 1929- DLB-5

Holley, Marietta 1836-1926....................................DLB-11

Hollingsworth, Margaret 1940- DLB-60

Hollo, Anselm 1934- DLB-40

Holloway, Emory 1885-1977....................................DLB-103

Holloway, John 1920- DLB-27

Holloway House Publishing Company....................................DLB-46

Holme, Constance 1880-1955....................................DLB-34

Holmes, Abraham S. 1821?-1908....................................DLB-99

Holmes, Oliver Wendell 1809-1894 ....DLB-1

Holmes, John Clellon 1926-1988 ....DLB-16

Holst, Hermann E. von 1841-1904....................................DLB-47

Holt, Henry, and Company....................................DLB-49

Holt, John 1721-1784 ....DLB-43

Holt, Rinehart and Winston....................................DLB-46

Holthusen, Hans Egon 1913- DLB-69

Hölty, Ludwig Christoph Heinrich
    1748-1776....................................DLB-94

Holz, Arno 1863-1929....................................DLB-118

Home, Henry, Lord Kames (see Kames, Henry Home, Lord)

Home, John 1722-1808 ....DLB-84

Home Publishing Company....................................DLB-49

Home, William Douglas 1912- DLB-13

Homes, Geoffrey (see Mainwaring, Daniel)

Honan, Park 1928- DLB-111

Hone, William 1780-1842...................................DLB-110

Honig, Edwin 1919- DLB-5

Hood, Hugh 1928- DLB-53

Hood, Thomas 1799-1845..................................DLB-96

Hook, Theodore 1788-1841................................DLB-116

Hooker, Jeremy 1941- DLB-40

Hooker, Thomas 1586-1647................................DLB-24

Hooper, Johnson Jones 1815-1862.........................DLB-3, 11

Hopkins, Gerard Manley 1844-1889 ....DLB-35, 57

Hopkins, John H., and Son...............................DLB-46

Hopkins, Lemuel 1750-1801...............................DLB-37

Hopkins, Pauline Elizabeth 1859-1930 ....DLB-50

Hopkins, Samuel 1721-1803 ....DLB-31

Hopkinson, Francis 1737-1791 ....DLB-31

Horgan, Paul 1903- DLB-102; Y-85

Horizon Press...DLB-46

Horne, Frank 1899-1974 ....DLB-51

Horne, Richard Henry (Hengist) 1802
       or 1803-1884.....................................DLB-32

Hornung, E. W. 1866-1921 ....DLB-70

Horovitz, Israel 1939- DLB-7

Horton, George Moses 1797?-1883?........................DLB-50

Horváth, Ödön von 1901-1938 ....DLB-85

Horwood, Harold 1923- DLB-60

Hosford, E. and E. [publishing house] DLB-49

Hotchkiss and Company...................................DLB-49

Hough, Emerson 1857-1923 ....DLB-9

Houghton Mifflin Company................................DLB-49

Houghton, Stanley 1881-1913.............................DLB-10

Household, Geoffrey 1900-1988...........................DLB-87

Housman, A. E. 1859-1936 ....DLB-19

Housman, Laurence 1865-1959 ....DLB-10

Houwald, Ernst von 1778-1845............................DLB-90

Hovey, Richard 1864-1900 ....DLB-54

Howard, Donald R. 1927-1987 ....DLB-111

Howard, Maureen 1930- Y-83

Howard, Richard 1929- DLB-5

Howard, Roy W. 1883-1964 ....DLB-29

Howard, Sidney 1891-1939 ....DLB-7, 26

Howe, E. W. 1853-1937...................................DLB-12, 25

Howe, Henry 1816-1893 ....DLB-30

Howe, Irving 1920- DLB-67

Howe, Joseph 1804-1873 ....DLB-99

Howe, Julia Ward 1819-1910 ....DLB-1

Howell, Clark, Sr. 1863-1936 ....DLB-25

Howell, Evan P. 1839-1905 ....DLB-23

Howell, Soskin and Company DLB-46

Howells, William Dean 1837-1920 ....DLB-12, 64, 74, 79

Howitt, William 1792-1879 and
       Howitt, Mary 1799-1888...........................DLB-110

Hoyem, Andrew 1935- DLB-5

de Hoyos, Angela 1940- DLB-82

Hoyt, Henry [publishing house]..........................DLB-49

Hubbard, Elbert 1856-1915 ....DLB-91

Hubbard, Kin 1868-1930..................................DLB-11

Hubbard, William circa 1621-1704........................DLB-24

Huber, Therese 1764-1829 ....DLB-90

Huch, Friedrich 1873-1913 ....DLB-66

Huch, Ricarda 1864-1947 ....DLB-66

Huck at 100: How Old Is
       Huckleberry Finn? Y-85

Hudson, Henry Norman 1814-1886..........................DLB-64

Hudson, W. H. 1841-1922 ....DLB-98

Hudson and Goodwin DLB-49

Huebsch, B. W. [publishing house].......................DLB-46

Hughes, David 1930- DLB-14

Hughes, John 1677-1720..................................DLB-84

Hughes, Langston 1902-1967................DLB-4, 7, 48, 51, 86

Hughes, Richard 1900-1976...............................DLB-15

Hughes, Ted 1930- DLB-40

Hughes, Thomas 1822-1896 ....DLB-18

Hugo, Richard 1923-1982 ....DLB-5

Hugo, Victor 1802-1885 ....DLB-119

Hugo Awards and Nebula Awards DLB-8

Hull, Richard 1896-1973 ....DLB-77

Hulme, T. E. 1883-1917..................................DLB-19

Humboldt, Alexander von 1769-1859 ....DLB-90

Humboldt, Wilhelm von 1767-1835 ....DLB-90

Hume, David 1711-1776...................................DLB-104

Hume, Fergus 1859-1932 ....DLB-70

Humorous Book Illustration DLB-11

Humphrey, William 1924- DLB-6

Humphreys, David 1752-1818 ....DLB-37

Humphreys, Emyr 1919- DLB-15

Huncke, Herbert 1915- DLB-16

Huneker, James Gibbons 1857-1921........................DLB-71

Hunt, Irene 1907- DLB-52

Hunt, Leigh 1784-1859 ....DLB-96, 110

Hunt, William Gibbes 1791-1833 ....DLB-73

Hunter, Evan 1926- Y-82

Hunter, Jim 1939- DLB-14

Hunter, Kristin 1931- DLB-33

Hunter, N. C. 1908-1971 ....DLB-10

Hunter-Duvar, John 1821-1899 ....DLB-99

Hurd and Houghton DLB-49

Hurst, Fannie 1889-1968 ....DLB-86

Hurst and Blackett DLB-106

Hurst and Company DLB-49

Hurston, Zora Neale 1901?-1960 ....DLB-51, 86

Husson, Jules-François-Félix (see Champfleury)

Huston, John 1906-1987 ....DLB-26

Hutcheson, Francis 1694-1746 ....DLB-31

Hutchinson, Thomas 1711-1780 ....DLB-30, 31

Hutchinson and Company (Publishers) Limited
....DLB-112

Hutton, Richard Holt 1826-1897 ....DLB-57

Huxley, Aldous 1894-1963 ....DLB-36, 100

Huxley, Elspeth Josceline 1907- DLB-77

Huxley, T. H. 1825-1895 ....DLB-57

Huyghue, Douglas Smith 1816-1891 ....DLB-99

Hyman, Trina Schart 1939- DLB-61

I

Ibn Bajja circa 1077-1138 ....DLB-115

Ibn Gabirol, Solomon
circa 1021-circa 1058 ....DLB-115

The Iconography of Science-Fiction Art DLB-8

Iffland, August Wilhelm 1759-1814 ....DLB-94

Ignatow, David 1914- DLB-5

Iles, Francis (see Berkeley, Anthony)

Imbs, Bravig 1904-1946 ....DLB-4

Inchbald, Elizabeth 1753-1821 ....DLB-39, 89

Inge, William 1913-1973 ....DLB-7

Ingelow, Jean 1820-1897 ....DLB-35

The Ingersoll Prizes Y-84

Ingraham, Joseph Holt 1809-1860 ....DLB-3

Inman, John 1805-1850 ....DLB-73

Innerhofer, Franz 1944- DLB-85

Innis, Harold Adams 1894-1952 ....DLB-88

Innis, Mary Quayle 1899-1972 ....DLB-88

International Publishers Company DLB-46

An Interview with James Ellroy Y-91

An Interview with George Greenfield, Literary Agent......Y-91

An Interview with Russell Hoban Y-90

An Interview with Tom Jenks Y-86

An Interview with Peter S. Prescott Y-86

An Interview with David Rabe Y-91

Introduction to Paul Laurence Dunbar,
Lyrics of Lowly Life (1896),
by William Dean Howells DLB-50

Introductory Essay: *Letters of Percy Bysshe
Shelley* (1852), by Robert Browning DLB-32

Introductory Letters from the Second Edition
of *Pamela* (1741), by Samuel Richardson ...DLB-39

Irving, John 1942- DLB-6; Y-82

Irving, Washington
1783-1859 ....DLB-3, 11, 30, 59, 73, 74

Irwin, Grace 1907- DLB-68

Irwin, Will 1873-1948 ....DLB-25

Isherwood, Christopher 1904-1986 ....DLB-15; Y-86

The Island Trees Case: A Symposium on School
Library Censorship
An Interview with Judith Krug
An Interview with Phyllis Schlafly
An Interview with Edward B. Jenkinson
An Interview with Lamarr Mooneyham
An Interview with Harriet Bernstein........Y-82

Ivers, M. J., and Company DLB-49

J

Jackmon, Marvin E. (see Marvin X)

Jackson, Angela 1951- DLB-41

Jackson, Helen Hunt 1830-1885 ....DLB-42, 47

Jackson, Holbrook 1874-1948 ....DLB-98

Jackson, Laura Riding 1901-1991 ....DLB-48

Jackson, Shirley 1919-1965 ....DLB-6

Jacob, Piers Anthony Dillingham (see Anthony, Piers)

Jacobi, Friedrich Heinrich 1743-1819 ....DLB-94

Jacobi, Johann Georg 1740-1841 ....DLB-97

Jacobs, George W., and Company DLB-49

Jacobson, Dan 1929- DLB-14

Jahier, Piero 1884-1966 ....DLB-114

Jahnn, Hans Henny 1894-1959 ....DLB-56

Jakes, John 1932- Y-83

James, George P. R. 1801-1860 ....DLB-116

James, Henry 1843-1916 ....DLB-12, 71, 74

James, John circa 1633-1729 ....DLB-24

James Joyce Centenary: Dublin, 1982 ....Y-82

James Joyce Conference.....................................Y-85

James, P. D. 1920- DLB-87

James, U. P. [publishing house] DLB-49

Jameson, Anna 1794-1860....................................DLB-99

Jameson, Fredric 1934- DLB-67

Jameson, J. Franklin 1859-1937.....................................DLB-17

Jameson, Storm 1891-1986..................................DLB-36

Jarrell, Randall 1914-1965 ....DLB-48, 52

Jarrold and Sons DLB-106

Jasmin, Claude 1930- DLB-60

Jay, John 1745-1829.................................DLB-31

Jefferies, Richard 1848-1887.................................DLB-98

Jeffers, Lance 1919-1985.................................DLB-41

Jeffers, Robinson 1887-1962 ....DLB-45

Jefferson, Thomas 1743-1826.................................DLB-31

Jelinek, Elfriede 1946- DLB-85

Jellicoe, Ann 1927- DLB-13

Jenkins, Robin 1912- DLB-14

Jenkins, William Fitzgerald (see Leinster, Murray)

Jenkins, Herbert, Limited.................................DLB-112

Jennings, Elizabeth 1926- DLB-27

Jens, Walter 1923- DLB-69

Jensen, Merrill 1905-1980.................................DLB-17

Jephson, Robert 1736-1803.................................DLB-89

Jerome, Jerome K. 1859-1927.................................DLB-10, 34

Jerome, Judson 1927-1991 ....DLB-105

Jerome, Judson, Reflections: After
    a Tornado.................................DLB-105

Jesse, F. Tennyson 1888-1958 ....DLB-77

Jewett, John P., and Company DLB-49

Jewett, Sarah Orne 1849-1909 ....DLB-12, 74

The Jewish Publication Society.................................DLB-49

Jewitt, John Rodgers 1783-1821.................................DLB-99

Jewsbury, Geraldine 1812-1880 ....DLB-21

Joans, Ted 1928- DLB-16, 41

John Edward Bruce: Three Documents DLB-50

John of Dumbleton circa 1310-circa 1349 ....DLB-115

John O'Hara's Pottsville Journalism Y-88

John Steinbeck Research Center Y-85

John Webster: The Melbourne Manuscript.................................Y-86

Johnson, B. S. 1933-1973 ....DLB-14, 40

Johnson, Benjamin [publishing house] DLB-49

Johnson, Benjamin, Jacob, and
    Robert [publishing house].................................DLB-49

Johnson, Charles 1679-1748.................................DLB-84

Johnson, Charles R. 1948- DLB-33

Johnson, Charles S. 1893-1956 ....DLB-51, 91

Johnson, Diane 1934- Y-80

Johnson, Edgar 1901- DLB-103

Johnson, Edward 1598-1672 ....DLB-24

Johnson, Fenton 1888-1958.................................DLB-45, 50

Johnson, Georgia Douglas 1886-1966.................................DLB-51

Johnson, Gerald W. 1890-1980 ....DLB-29

Johnson, Helene 1907- DLB-51

Johnson, Jacob, and Company DLB-49

Johnson, James Weldon 1871-1938.................................DLB-51

Johnson, Lionel 1867-1902.................................DLB-19

Johnson, Nunnally 1897-1977.................................DLB-26

Johnson, Owen 1878-1952.................................Y-87

Johnson, Pamela Hansford 1912- DLB-15

Johnson, Pauline 1861-1913.................................DLB-92

Johnson, Samuel 1696-1772.................................DLB-24

Johnson, Samuel 1709-1784.................................DLB-39, 95, 104

Johnson, Samuel 1822-1882.................................DLB-1

Johnson, Uwe 1934-1984.................................DLB-75

Johnston, Annie Fellows 1863-1931 ....DLB-42

Johnston, Basil H. 1929- DLB-60

Johnston, Denis 1901-1984.................................DLB-10

Johnston, George 1913- DLB-88

Johnston, Jennifer 1930- DLB-14

Johnston, Mary 1870-1936.................................DLB-9

Johnston, Richard Malcolm 1822-1898.................................DLB-74

Johnstone, Charles 1719?-1800? DLB-39

Jolas, Eugene 1894-1952.................................DLB-4, 45

Jones, Alice C. 1853-1933.................................DLB-92

Jones, Charles C., Jr. 1831-1893 ....DLB-30

Jones, D. G. 1929- DLB-53

Jones, David 1895-1974.................................DLB-20, 100

Jones, Ebenezer 1820-1860 ....DLB-32

Jones, Ernest 1819-1868 ....DLB-32

Jones, Gayl 1949- DLB-33

Jones, Glyn 1905- DLB-15

Jones, Gwyn 1907- DLB-15

Jones, Henry Arthur 1851-1929 ....DLB-10

Jones, Hugh circa 1692-1760 ....DLB-24

Jones, James 1921-1977.................................DLB-2

Cumulative Index

Jones, LeRoi (see Baraka, Amiri)

Jones, Lewis 1897-1939 ....DLB-15

Jones, Major Joseph (see Thompson, William Tappan)

Jones, Preston 1936-1979 ....DLB-7

Jones, Sir William 1746-1794 ....DLB-109

Jones, William Alfred 1817-1900....................DLB-59

Jones's Publishing House................................DLB-49

Jong, Erica 1942- DLB-2, 5, 28

Jonke, Gert F. 1946- DLB-85

Jonson, Ben 1572?-1637 ....DLB-62

Jordan, June 1936- DLB-38

Joseph, Jenny 1932- DLB-40

Joseph, Michael, Limited DLB-112

Josephson, Matthew 1899-1978........................DLB-4

Josiah Allen's Wife (see Holley, Marietta)

Josipovici, Gabriel 1940- DLB-14

Josselyn, John ?-1675 ....DLB-24

Joudry, Patricia 1921- DLB-88

Joyaux, Philippe (see Sollers, Philippe)

Joyce, Adrien (see Eastman, Carol)

Joyce, James 1882-1941 ....DLB-10, 19, 36

Judd, Orange, Publishing Company DLB-49

Judd, Sylvester 1813-1853............................DLB-1

June, Jennie (see Croly, Jane Cunningham)

Jung, Franz 1888-1963 ....DLB-118

Jünger, Ernst 1895- DLB-56

Jung-Stilling, Johann Heinrich
    1740-1817..DLB-94

Justice, Donald 1925- Y-83

K

Kacew, Romain (see Gary, Romain)

Kafka, Franz 1883-1924................................DLB-81

Kalechofsky, Roberta 1931- DLB-28

Kaler, James Otis 1848-1912.........................DLB-12

Kames, Henry Home, Lord 1696-1782.........DLB-31, 104

Kandel, Lenore 1932- DLB-16

Kanin, Garson 1912- DLB-7

Kant, Hermann 1926- DLB-75

Kant, Immanuel 1724-1804..........................DLB-94

Kantor, Mackinlay 1904-1977 ....DLB-9, 102

Kaplan, Fred 1937- DLB-111

Kaplan, Johanna 1942- DLB-28

Kaplan, Justin 1925- DLB-111

Karsch, Anna Louisa 1722-1791 ....DLB-97

Kasack, Hermann 1896-1966 ....DLB-69

Kaschnitz, Marie Luise 1901-1974 ....DLB-69

Kästner, Erich 1899-1974.............................DLB-56

Kattan, Naim 1928- DLB-53

Katz, Steve 1935- Y-83

Kauffman, Janet 1945- Y-86

Kaufman, Bob 1925- DLB-16, 41

Kaufman, George S. 1889-1961 ....DLB-7

Kavanagh, Patrick 1904-1967........................DLB-15, 20

Kavanagh, P. J. 1931- DLB-40

Kaye-Smith, Sheila 1887-1956.......................DLB-36

Kazin, Alfred 1915- DLB-67

Keane, John B. 1928- DLB-13

Keating, H. R. F. 1926- DLB-87

Keats, Ezra Jack 1916-1983 ....DLB-61

Keats, John 1795-1821 ....DLB-96, 110

Keble, John 1792-1866................................DLB-32, 55

Keeble, John 1944- Y-83

Keeffe, Barrie 1945- DLB-13

Keeley, James 1867-1934 ....DLB-25

W. B. Keen, Cooke and Company DLB-49

Keillor, Garrison 1942- Y-87

Keith, Marian 1874?-1961 ....DLB-92

Keller, Gary D. 1943- DLB-82

Kelley, Edith Summers 1884-1956....................DLB-9

Kelley, William Melvin 1937- DLB-33

Kellogg, Ansel Nash 1832-1886......................DLB-23

Kellogg, Steven 1941- DLB-61

Kelly, George 1887-1974...............................DLB-7

Kelly, Hugh 1739-1777 ....DLB-89

Kelly, Piet and Company..............................DLB-49

Kelly, Robert 1935- DLB-5

Kelmscott Press DLB-112

Kemble, Fanny 1809-1893 ....DLB-32

Kemelman, Harry 1908- DLB-28

Kempowski, Walter 1929- DLB-75

Kendall, Claude [publishing company]...............DLB-46

Kendell, George 1809-1867...........................DLB-43

Kenedy, P. J., and Sons DLB-49

Kennedy, Adrienne 1931- DLB-38

Kennedy, John Pendleton 1795-1870 ....DLB-3

Kennedy, Leo 1907- DLB-88

Kennedy, Margaret 1896-1967....................DLB-36

Kennedy, Richard S. 1920- DLB-111

Kennedy, William 1928- Y-85

Kennedy, X. J. 1929- DLB-5

Kennelly, Brendan 1936- DLB-40

Kenner, Hugh 1923- DLB-67

Kennerley, Mitchell [publishing house] DLB-46

Kent, Frank R. 1877-1958............................DLB-29

Keppler and Schwartzmann DLB-49

Kerner, Justinus 1776-1862...........................DLB-90

Kerouac, Jack 1922-1969 ....DLB-2, 16; DS-3

Kerouac, Jan 1952- DLB-16

Kerr, Charles H., and Company DLB-49

Kerr, Orpheus C. (see Newell, Robert Henry)

Kesey, Ken 1935- DLB-2, 16

Kessel, Joseph 1898-1979 ....DLB-72

Kessel, Martin 1901- DLB-56

Kesten, Hermann 1900- DLB-56

Keun, Irmgard 1905-1982............................DLB-69

Key and Biddle DLB-49

Keyserling, Eduard von 1855-1918...............DLB-66

Kidd, Adam 1802?-1831................................DLB-99

Kidd, William [publishing house] DLB-106

Kiely, Benedict 1919- DLB-15

Kiggins and Kellogg DLB-49

Kiley, Jed 1889-1962......................................DLB-4

Killens, John Oliver 1916- DLB-33

Killigrew, Thomas 1612-1683 ....DLB-58

Kilmer, Joyce 1886-1918 ....DLB-45

Kilwardby, Robert circa 1215-1279.............DLB-115

King, Clarence 1842-1901 ....DLB-12

King, Florence 1936......................................Y-85

King, Francis 1923- DLB-15

King, Grace 1852-1932...........................DLB-12, 78

King, Solomon [publishing house] DLB-49

King, Stephen 1947- Y-80

King, Woodie, Jr. 1937- DLB-38

Kinglake, Alexander William 1809-1891 .....DLB-55

Kingsley, Charles 1819-1875 ....DLB-21, 32

Kingsley, Henry 1830-1876 ....DLB-21

Kingsley, Sidney 1906- DLB-7

Kingston, Maxine Hong 1940- Y-80

Kinnell, Galway 1927- DLB-5; Y-87

Kinsella, Thomas 1928- DLB-27

Kipling, Rudyard 1865-1936....................DLB-19, 34

Kirby, William 1817-1906.............................DLB-99

Kirk, John Foster 1824-1904 ....DLB-79

Kirkconnell, Watson 1895-1977 ....DLB-68

Kirkland, Caroline M. 1801-1864 ....DLB-3, 73, 74

Kirkland, Joseph 1830-1893.........................DLB-12

Kirkup, James 1918- DLB-27

Kirouac, Conrad (see Marie-Victorin, Frère)

Kirsch, Sarah 1935- DLB-75

Kirst, Hans Hellmut 1914-1989 ....DLB-69

Kitchin, C. H. B. 1895-1967.........................DLB-77

Kizer, Carolyn 1925- DLB-5

Klabund 1890-1928.......................................DLB-66

Klappert, Peter 1942- DLB-5

Klass, Philip (see Tenn, William)

Klein, A. M. 1909-1972 ....DLB-68

Kleist, Ewald von 1715-1759 ....DLB-97

Kleist, Heinrich von 1777-1811....................DLB-90

Klinger, Friedrich Maximilian
    1752-1831 ....DLB-94

Klopstock, Friedrich Gottlieb 1724-1803 .....DLB-97

Klopstock, Meta 1728-1758 ....DLB-97

Kluge, Alexander 1932- DLB-75

Knapp, Joseph Palmer 1864-1951 ....DLB-91

Knapp, Samuel Lorenzo 1783-1838..............DLB-59

Knickerbocker, Diedrich (see Irving, Washington)

Knigge, Adolph Franz Friedrich Ludwig,
    Freiherr von 1752-1796............................DLB-94

Knight, Damon 1922- DLB-8

Knight, Etheridge 1931- DLB-41

Knight, John S. 1894-1981............................DLB-29

Knight, Sarah Kemble 1666-1727................DLB-24

Knight, Charles, and Company...................DLB-106

Knister, Raymond 1899-1932.......................DLB-68

Knoblock, Edward 1874-1945 ....DLB-10

Knopf, Alfred A. 1892-1984 ....Y-84

Knopf, Alfred A. [publishing house].............DLB-46

Knowles, John 1926- DLB-6

Knox, Frank 1874-1944.................................DLB-29

Knox, John Armoy 1850-1906 ....DLB-23

Knox, Ronald Arbuthnott 1888-1957 ....DLB-77

Kober, Arthur 1900-1975..............................DLB-11

Koch, Howard 1902- DLB-26

Koch, Kenneth 1925- DLB-5

Koenigsberg, Moses 1879-1945................DLB-25

Koeppen, Wolfgang 1906- DLB-69

Körner, Theodor 1791-1813................DLB-90

Koertge, Ronald 1940- DLB-105

Koestler, Arthur 1905-1983 ....Y-83

Kolb, Annette 1870-1967................DLB-66

Kolbenheyer, Erwin Guido 1878-1962 ....DLB-66

Kolleritsch, Alfred 1931- DLB-85

Kolodny, Annette 1941- DLB-67

Komroff, Manuel 1890-1974................DLB-4

Konigsburg, E. L. 1930- DLB-52

Kooser, Ted 1939- DLB-105

Kopit, Arthur 1937- DLB-7

Kops, Bernard 1926?- DLB-13

Kornbluth, C. M. 1923-1958 ....DLB-8

Kornfeld, Paul 1889-1942................DLB-118

Kosinski, Jerzy 1933-1991 ....DLB-2; Y-82

Kotzebue, August von 1761-1819................DLB-94

Kraf, Elaine 1946- Y-81

Krasna, Norman 1909-1984 ....DLB-26

Kraus, Karl 1874-1936................DLB-118

Krauss, Ruth 1911- DLB-52

Kreisel, Henry 1922- DLB-88

Kreuder, Ernst 1903-1972................DLB-69

Kreymborg, Alfred 1883-1966................DLB-4, 54

Krieger, Murray 1923- DLB-67

Krim, Seymour 1922-1989 ....DLB-16

Krock, Arthur 1886-1974................DLB-29

Kroetsch, Robert 1927- DLB-53

Krutch, Joseph Wood 1893-1970 ....DLB-63

Kubin, Alfred 1877-1959................DLB-81

Kubrick, Stanley 1928- DLB-26

Kumin, Maxine 1925- DLB-5

Kunene, Mazisi 1930- DLB-117

Kunnert, Günter 1929- DLB-75

Kunitz, Stanley 1905- DLB-48

Kunjufu, Johari M. (see Amini, Johari M.)

Kunze, Reiner 1933- DLB-75

Kupferberg, Tuli 1923- DLB-16

Kurz, Isolde 1853-1944 ....DLB-66

Kusenberg, Kurt 1904-1983................DLB-69

Kuttner, Henry 1915-1958................DLB-8

Kyd, Thomas 1558-1594 ....DLB-62

Kyger, Joanne 1934- DLB-16

Kyne, Peter B. 1880-1957 ....DLB-78

L

L. E. L. (see Landon, Letitia Elizabeth)

Laberge, Albert 1871-1960................DLB-68

Laberge, Marie 1950- DLB-60

Lacombe, Patrice (see Trullier-Lacombe, Joseph Patrice)

Lacretelle, Jacques de 1888-1985................DLB-65

Ladd, Joseph Brown 1764-1786................DLB-37

La Farge, Oliver 1901-1963................DLB-9

Lafferty, R. A. 1914- DLB-8

La Guma, Alex 1925-1985................DLB-117

Lahaise, Guillaume (see Delahaye, Guy)

Lahontan, Louis-Armand de Lom d'Arce, Baron de 1666-1715? DLB-99

Laird, Carobeth 1895- Y-82

Laird and Lee................DLB-49

Lalonde, Michèle 1937- DLB-60

Lamantia, Philip 1927- DLB-16

Lamb, Charles 1775-1834................DLB-93, 107

Lamb, Lady Caroline 1785-1828................DLB-116

Lambert, Betty 1933-1983................DLB-60

L'Amour, Louis 1908?- Y-80

Lampman, Archibald 1861-1899................DLB-92

Lamson, Wolffe and Company................DLB-49

Lancer Books DLB-46

Landesman, Jay 1919- and Landesman, Fran 1927- DLB-16

Landon, Letitia Elizabeth 1802-1838 ....DLB-96

Landor, William Savage 1775-1864................DLB-93, 107

Landry, Napoléon-P. 1884-1956 ....DLB-92

Lane, Charles 1800-1870................DLB-1

The John Lane Company................DLB-49

Lane, Laurence W. 1890-1967................DLB-91

Lane, M. Travis 1934- DLB-60

Lane, Patrick 1939- DLB-53

Lane, Pinkie Gordon 1923- DLB-41

Laney, Al 1896- DLB-4

Lang, Andrew 1844-1912 ....DLB-98

Langevin, André 1927- DLB-60

Langgässer, Elisabeth 1899-1950 ....DLB-69

Langhorne, John 1735-1779...........................DLB-109

Langton, Anna 1804-1893...............................DLB-99

Lanham, Edwin 1904-1979..............................DLB-4

Lanier, Sidney 1842-1881................................DLB-64

Lapointe, Gatien 1931-1983 ....DLB-88

Lapointe, Paul-Marie 1929- DLB-88

Lardner, Ring 1885-1933.....................DLB-11, 25, 86

Lardner, Ring, Jr. 1915- DLB-26

Lardner 100: Ring Lardner
     Centennial Symposium Y-85

Larkin, Philip 1922-1985..................................DLB-27

La Roche, Sophie von 1730-1807 ....DLB-94

La Rocque, Gilbert 1943-1984 ....DLB-60

Laroque de Roquebrune, Robert
     (see Roquebrune, Robert de)

Larrick, Nancy 1910- DLB-61

Larsen, Nella 1893-1964................................DLB-51

Lasker-Schüler, Else 1869-1945 ....DLB-66

Lasnier, Rina 1915- DLB-88

Lathrop, Dorothy P. 1891-1980 ....DLB-22

Lathrop, George Parsons 1851-1898 ....DLB-71

Lathrop, John, Jr. 1772-1820 ....DLB-37

Latimore, Jewel Christine McLawler (see Amini,
     Johari M.)

Laughlin, James 1914- DLB-48

Laumer, Keith 1925- DLB-8

Laurence, Margaret 1926-1987 ....DLB-53

Laurents, Arthur 1918- DLB-26

Laurie, Annie (see Black, Winifred)

Laut, Agnes Christiana 1871-1936..................DLB-92

Lavater, Johann Kaspar 1741-1801 ....DLB-97

Lavin, Mary 1912- DLB-15

Lawless, Anthony (see MacDonald, Philip)

Lawrence, David 1888-1973 ....DLB-29

Lawrence, D. H. 1885-1930.................DLB-10, 19, 36, 98

Lawson, John ?-1711.......................................DLB-24

Lawson, Robert 1892-1957 ....DLB-22

Lawson, Victor F. 1850-1925 ....DLB-25

Layton, Irving 1912- DLB-88

Lea, Henry Charles 1825-1909 ....DLB-47

Lea, Tom 1907- DLB-6

Leacock, John 1729-1802 ....DLB-31

Leacock, Stephen 1869-1944...........................DLB-92

Leadenhall Press DLB-106

Leapor, Mary 1722-1746 ....DLB-109

Lear, Edward 1812-1888 ....DLB-32

Leary, Timothy 1920- DLB-16

Leary, W. A., and Company............................DLB-49

Léautaud, Paul 1872-1956...............................DLB-65

Leavitt and Allen DLB-49

le Carré, John 1931- DLB-87

Lécavelé, Roland (see Dorgelès, Roland)

Lechlitner, Ruth 1901- DLB-48

Leclerc, Félix 1914- DLB-60

Le Clézio, J. M. G. 1940- DLB-83

Lectures on Rhetoric and Belles Lettres (1783),
     by Hugh Blair [excerpts]............................DLB-31

Leder, Rudolf (see Hermlin, Stephan)

Lederer, Charles 1910-1976.............................DLB-26

Ledwidge, Francis 1887-1917...........................DLB-20

Lee, Dennis 1939- DLB-53

Lee, Don L. (see Madhubuti, Haki R.)

Lee, George W. 1894-1976...............................DLB-51

Lee, Harper 1926- DLB-6

Lee, Harriet (1757-1851) and
     Lee, Sophia (1750-1824)..............................DLB-39

Lee, Laurie 1914- DLB-27

Lee, Nathaniel circa 1645 - 1692 ....DLB-80

Lee, Vernon 1856-1935 ....DLB-57

Lee and Shepard...DLB-49

Le Fanu, Joseph Sheridan 1814-1873.....................DLB-21, 70

Leffland, Ella 1931- Y-84

le Fort, Gertrud von 1876-1971 ....DLB-66

Le Gallienne, Richard 1866-1947 ....DLB-4

Legaré, Hugh Swinton 1797-1843.....................DLB-3, 59, 73

Legaré, James M. 1823-1859............................DLB-3

Léger, Antoine-J. 1880-1950...........................DLB-88

Le Guin, Ursula K. 1929- DLB-8, 52

Lehman, Ernest 1920- DLB-44

Lehmann, John 1907- DLB-27, 100

Lehmann, John, Limited DLB-112

Lehmann, Rosamond 1901-1990 ....DLB-15

Lehmann, Wilhelm 1882-1968.........................DLB-56

Leiber, Fritz 1910- DLB-8

Leicester University Press DLB-112

Leinster, Murray 1896-1975 ....DLB-8

Leisewitz, Johann Anton 1752-1806 ....DLB-94

Leitch, Maurice 1933- DLB-14

Leland, Charles G. 1824-1903 ....DLB 11

Lemay, Pamphile 1837-1918 ....DLB-99

Lemelin, Roger 1919- DLB-88

Le Moine, James MacPherson
  1825-1912 ....DLB-99

Le Moyne, Jean 1913- DLB-88

L'Engle, Madeleine 1918- DLB-52

Lennart, Isobel 1915-1971 ....DLB-44

Lennox, Charlotte 1729 or 1730-1804 ....DLB-39

Lenski, Lois 1893-1974 ....DLB-22

Lenz, Hermann 1913- DLB-69

Lenz, J. M. R. 1751-1792 ....DLB-94

Lenz, Siegfried 1926- DLB-75

Leonard, Hugh 1926- DLB-13

Leonard, William Ellery 1876-1944 ....DLB-54

Leonowens, Anna 1834-1914 ....DLB-99

LePan, Douglas 1914- DLB-88

Leprohon, Rosanna Eleanor 1829-1879 ....DLB-99

Le Queux, William 1864-1927 ....DLB-70

Lerner, Max 1902- DLB-29

Lernet-Holenia, Alexander 1897-1976 ....DLB-85

Le Rossignol, James 1866-1969 ....DLB-92

Lescarbot, Marc circa 1570-1642 ....DLB-99

LeSieg, Theo. (see Geisel, Theodor Seuss)

Leslie, Frank 1821-1880 ....DLB-43, 79

The Frank Leslie Publishing House DLB-49

Lesperance, John 1835?-1891 ....DLB-99

Lessing, Bruno 1870-1940 ....DLB-28

Lessing, Doris 1919- DLB-15; Y-85

Lessing, Gotthold Ephraim 1729-1781 ....DLB-97

LeSeur, William Dawson 1840-1917 ....DLB-92

Lettau, Reinhard 1929- DLB-75

Letter to [Samuel] Richardson on *Clarissa*
  (1748), by Henry Fielding DLB-39

Lever, Charles 1806-1872 ....DLB-21

Levertov, Denise 1923- DLB-5

Levi, Peter 1931- DLB-40

Levien, Sonya 1888-1960 ....DLB-44

Levin, Meyer 1905-1981 ....DLB-9, 28; Y-81

Levine, Norman 1923- DLB-88

Levine, Philip 1928- DLB-5

Levy, Benn Wolfe 1900-1973 ....DLB-13; Y-81

Lewes, George Henry 1817-1878 ....DLB-55

Lewis, Alfred H. 1857-1914 ....DLB-25

Lewis, Alun 1915-1944 ....DLB-20

Lewis, C. Day (see Day Lewis, C.)

Lewis, Charles B. 1842-1924 ....DLB-11

Lewis, C. S. 1898-1963 ....DLB-15, 100

Lewis, Henry Clay 1825-1850 ....DLB-3

Lewis, Janet 1899- Y-87

Lewis, Matthew Gregory 1775-1818 ....DLB-39

Lewis, R. W. B. 1917- DLB-111

Lewis, Richard circa 1700-1734 ....DLB-24

Lewis, Sinclair 1885-1951 ....DLB-9, 102; DS-1

Lewis, Wyndham 1882-1957 ....DLB-15

Lewisohn, Ludwig 1882-1955 ....DLB-4, 9, 28, 102

Lezama Lima, José 1910-1976 ....DLB-113

The Library of America DLB-46

The Licensing Act of 1737 ....DLB-84

Lichtenberg, Georg Christoph 1742-1799 .....DLB-94

Liebling, A. J. 1904-1963 ....DLB-4

Lieutenant Murray (see Ballou, Maturin Murray)

Lighthall, William Douw 1857-1954 ....DLB-92

Lilar, Françoise (see Mallet-Joris, Françoise)

Lillo, George 1691-1739 ....DLB-84

Lilly, Wait and Company DLB-49

Limited Editions Club DLB-46

Lincoln and Edmands DLB-49

Lindsay, Jack 1900- Y-84

Lindsay, Vachel 1879-1931 ....DLB-54

Linebarger, Paul Myron Anthony (see
  Smith, Cordwainer)

Link, Arthur S. 1920- DLB-17

Linn, John Blair 1777-1804 ....DLB-37

Linton, Eliza Lynn 1822-1898 ....DLB-18

Linton, William James 1812-1897 ....DLB-32

Lion Books DLB-46

Lionni, Leo 1910- DLB-61

Lippincott, J. B., Company DLB-49

Lippincott, Sara Jane Clarke 1823-1904 ....DLB-43

Lippmann, Walter 1889-1974 ....DLB-29

Lipton, Lawrence 1898-1975 ....DLB-16

Liscow, Christian Ludwig 1701-1760 ....DLB-97

Lispector, Clarice 1925-1977 ....DLB-113

The Literary Chronicle and Weekly Review 1819-1828 ....DLB-110

Literary Documents: William Faulkner and the People-to-People Program Y-86

Literary Documents II: *Library Journal*– Statements and Questionnaires from First Novelists...Y-87

Literary Effects of World War II [British novel]...DLB-15

Literary Prizes [British]......................................DLB-15

Literary Research Archives: The Humanities Research Center, University of Texas.........................Y-82

Literary Research Archives II: Berg Collection of English and American Literature of the New York Public Library Y-83

Literary Research Archives III: The Lilly Library Y-84

Literary Research Archives IV: The John Carter Brown Library Y-85

Literary Research Archives V: Kent State Special Collections Y-86

Literary Research Archives VI: The Modern Literary Manuscripts Collection in the Special Collections of the Washington University Libraries...Y-87

Literary Research Archives VII: The University of Virginia Libraries Y-91

"Literary Style" (1857), by William Forsyth [excerpt] DLB-57

Literatura Chicanesca: The View From Without.....................................DLB-82

Literature at Nurse, or Circulating Morals (1885), by George Moore......................................DLB-18

Littell, Eliakim 1797-1870................................DLB-79

Littell, Robert S. 1831-1896 ....DLB-79

Little, Brown and Company DLB-49

Littlewood, Joan 1914- DLB-13

Lively, Penelope 1933- DLB-14

Liverpool University Press.................................DLB-112

Livesay, Dorothy 1909- DLB-68

Livesay, Florence Randal 1874-1953.....................DLB-92

Livings, Henry 1929- DLB-13

Livingston, Anne Howe 1763-1841...........................DLB-37

Livingston, Myra Cohn 1926- DLB-61

Livingston, William 1723-1790...........................DLB-31

Lizárraga, Sylvia S. 1925- DLB-82

Llewellyn, Richard 1906-1983...........................DLB-15

Lloyd, Edward [publishing house] DLB-106

Lobel, Arnold 1933- DLB-61

Lochridge, Betsy Hopkins (see Fancher, Betsy)

Locke, David Ross 1833-1888 ....DLB-11, 23

Locke, John 1632-1704.......................................DLB-31, 101

Locke, Richard Adams 1800-1871 ....DLB-43

Locker-Lampson, Frederick 1821-1895......................DLB-35

Lockhart, John Gibson 1794-1854.....................DLB-110, 116

Lockridge, Ross, Jr. 1914-1948 ....Y-80

Locrine and *Selimus* DLB-62

Lodge, David 1935- DLB-14

Lodge, George Cabot 1873-1909 ....DLB-54

Lodge, Henry Cabot 1850-1924.............................DLB-47

Loeb, Harold 1891-1974 ....DLB-4

Logan, James 1674-1751.....................................DLB-24

Logan, John 1923- DLB-5

Logue, Christopher 1926- DLB-27

London, Jack 1876-1916 ....DLB-8, 12, 78

The London Magazine 1820-1829....................................DLB-110

Long, H., and Brother.......................................DLB-49

Long, Haniel 1888-1956 ....DLB-45

Longfellow, Henry Wadsworth 1807-1882................DLB-1, 59

Longfellow, Samuel 1819-1892.............................DLB-1

Longley, Michael 1939- DLB-40

Longmans, Green and Company DLB-49

Longmore, George 1793?-1867....................................DLB-99

Longstreet, Augustus Baldwin 1790-1870 ....DLB-3, 11, 74

Longworth, D. [publishing house] DLB-49

Lonsdale, Frederick 1881-1954.............................DLB-10

A Look at the Contemporary Black Theatre Movement...DLB-38

Loos, Anita 1893-1981 ....DLB-11, 26; Y-81

Lopate, Phillip 1943- Y-80

López, Diana (see Isabella, Ríos)

Loranger, Jean-Aubert 1896-1942 ....DLB-92

Lorca, Federico García 1898-1936.........................DLB-108

The Lord Chamberlain's Office and Stage Censorship in England DLB-10

Lord, John Keast 1818-1872 ....DLB-99

Lorde, Audre 1934- DLB-41

Lorimer, George Horace 1867-1939.......................DLB-91

Loring, A. K. [publishing house] DLB-49

Loring and Mussey DLB-46

Lossing, Benson J. 1813-1891 ....DLB-30

Lothar, Ernst 1890-1974......................................DLB-81

Lothrop, D., and Company DLB-49

Lothrop, Harriet M. 1844-1924 ....DLB-42

The Lounger, no. 20 (1785), by Henry
Mackenzie DLB-39

Lounsbury, Thomas R. 1838-1915................DLB-71

Lovell, John W., Company DLB-49

Lovell, Coryell and Company DLB-49

Lovesey, Peter 1936- DLB-87

Lovingood, Sut (see Harris, George Washington)

Low, Samuel 1765-? DLB-37

Lowell, Amy 1874-1925 ....DLB-54

Lowell, James Russell 1819-1891...............DLB-1, 11, 64, 79

Lowell, Robert 1917-1977 ....DLB-5

Lowenfels, Walter 1897-1976 ....DLB-4

Lowndes, Marie Belloc 1868-1947 ....DLB-70

Lowry, Lois 1937- DLB-52

Lowry, Malcolm 1909-1957 ....DLB-15

Lowther, Pat 1935-1975................................DLB-53

Loy, Mina 1882-1966....................................DLB-4, 54

Lozeau, Albert 1878-1924 ....DLB-92

Lucas, E. V. 1868-1938.................................DLB-98

Lucas, Fielding, Jr. [publishing house] DLB-49

Luce, Henry R. 1898-1967 ....DLB-91

Luce, John W., and Company......................DLB-46

Lucie-Smith, Edward 1933- DLB-40

Lucini, Gian Pietro 1867-1914 ....DLB-114

Ludlum, Robert 1927- Y-82

Ludwig, Jack 1922- DLB-60

Luke, Peter 1919- DLB-13

The F. M. Lupton Publishing Company........DLB-49

Lurie, Alison 1926- DLB-2

Lyall, Gavin 1932- DLB-87

Lyly, John circa 1554-1606............................DLB-62

Lynd, Robert 1879-1949................................DLB-98

Lyon, Matthew 1749-1822.............................DLB-43

Lytle, Andrew 1902- DLB-6

Lytton, Edward (see Bulwer-Lytton, Edward)

Lytton, Edward Robert Bulwer 1831-1891.................DLB-32

M

Maass, Joachim 1901-1972 ....DLB-69

Mabie, Hamilton Wright 1845-1916 ....DLB-71

Mac A'Ghobhainn, Iain (see Smith, Iain Crichton)

MacArthur, Charles 1895-1956 ....DLB-7, 25, 44

Macaulay, Catherine 1731-1791 ....DLB-104

Macaulay, David 1945- DLB-61

Macaulay, Rose 1881-1958 ....DLB-36

Macaulay, Thomas Babington 1800-1859................DLB-32, 55

Macaulay Company..DLB-46

MacBeth, George 1932- DLB-40

Macbeth, Madge 1880-1965 ....DLB-92

MacCaig, Norman 1910- DLB-27

MacDiarmid, Hugh 1892-1978.......................DLB-20

MacDonald, Cynthia 1928- DLB-105

MacDonald, George 1824-1905......................DLB-18

MacDonald, John D. 1916-1986...............DLB-8; Y-86

MacDonald, Philip 1899?-1980.......................DLB-77

Macdonald, Ross (see Millar, Kenneth)

MacDonald, Wilson 1880-1967.......................DLB-92

Macdonald and Company (Publishers) DLB-112

MacEwen, Gwendolyn 1941- DLB-53

Macfadden, Bernarr 1868-1955................DLB-25, 91

MacGregor, Mary Esther (see Keith, Marian)

Machado, Antonio 1875-1939 ....DLB-108

Machado, Manuel 1874-1947 ....DLB-108

Machar, Agnes Maule 1837-1927 ....DLB-92

Machen, Arthur Llewelyn Jones 1863-1947 ....DLB-36

MacInnes, Colin 1914-1976............................DLB-14

MacInnes, Helen 1907-1985...........................DLB-87

Mack, Maynard 1909- DLB-111

MacKaye, Percy 1875-1956............................DLB-54

Macken, Walter 1915-1967 ....DLB-13

Mackenzie, Alexander 1763-1820 ....DLB-99

Mackenzie, Compton 1883-1972................DLB-34, 100

Mackenzie, Henry 1745-1831 ....DLB-39

Mackey, William Wellington 1937- DLB-38

Mackintosh, Elizabeth (see Tey, Josephine)

Macklin, Charles 1699-1797 ....DLB-89

MacLean, Katherine Anne 1925- DLB-8

MacLeish, Archibald 1892-1982 ....DLB-4, 7, 45; Y-82

MacLennan, Hugh 1907-1990.........................DLB-68

MacLeod, Alistair 1936- DLB-60

Macleod, Norman 1906- DLB-4

Macmillan and Company................................DLB-106

The Macmillan Company................................DLB-49

MacNamara, Brinsley 1890-1963 ....DLB-10

MacNeice, Louis 1907-1963 ....DLB-10, 20

MacPhail, Andrew 1864-1938 ....DLB-92

Macpherson, James 1736-1796................DLB-109

Macpherson, Jay 1931- DLB-53

Macpherson, Jeanie 1884-1946 ....DLB-44

Macrae Smith Company DLB-46

Macrone, John [publishing house] DLB-106

MacShane, Frank 1927- DLB-111

Macy-Masius..DLB-46

Madden, David 1933- DLB-6

Maddow, Ben 1909- DLB-44

Madgett, Naomi Long 1923- DLB-76

Madhubuti, Haki R. 1942- DLB-5, 41; DS-8

Madison, James 1751-1836................................DLB-37

Maginn, William 1794-1842 ....DLB-110

Mahan, Alfred Thayer 1840-1914 ....DLB-47

Maheux-Forcier, Louise 1929- DLB-60

Mahin, John Lee 1902-1984............................DLB-44

Mahon, Derek 1941- DLB-40

Mailer, Norman 1923- DLB-2, 16, 28; Y-80, 83; DS-3

Maillet, Adrienne 1885-1963.............................DLB-68

Maimonides, Moses 1138-1204.......................DLB-115

Maillet, Antonine 1929- DLB-60

Main Selections of the Book-of-the-Month Club,
    1926-1945...DLB-9

Main Trends in Twentieth-Century
    Book Clubs...DLB-46

Mainwaring, Daniel 1902-1977 ....DLB-44

Mair, Charles 1838-1927 ....DLB-99

Major, André 1942- DLB-60

Major, Clarence 1936- DLB-33

Major, Kevin 1949- DLB-60

Major Books DLB-46

Makemie, Francis circa 1658-1708 ....DLB-24

The Making of a People,
    by J. M. Ritchie DLB-66

Malamud, Bernard 1914-1986................DLB-2, 28; Y-80, 86

Malleson, Lucy Beatrice (see Gilbert, Anthony)

Mallet-Joris, Françoise 1930- DLB-83

Mallock, W. H. 1849-1923 ....DLB-18, 57

Malone, Dumas 1892-1986................................DLB-17

Malraux, André 1901-1976...............................DLB-72

Malthus, Thomas Robert 1766-1834 ....DLB-107

Maltz, Albert 1908-1985................................DLB-102

Malzberg, Barry N. 1939- DLB-8

Mamet, David 1947- DLB-7

Manchester University Press............................DLB-112

Mandel, Eli 1922- DLB-53

Mandeville, Bernard 1670-1733....................DLB-101

Mandiargues, André Pieyre de 1909- DLB-83

Manfred, Frederick 1912- DLB-6

Mangan, Sherry 1904-1961 ....DLB-4

Mankiewicz, Herman 1897-1953....................DLB-26

Mankiewicz, Joseph L. 1909- DLB-44

Mankowitz, Wolf 1924- DLB-15

Manley, Delariviere 1672?-1724...............DLB-39, 80

Mann, Abby 1927- DLB-44

Mann, Heinrich 1871-1950 ....DLB-66, 118

Mann, Horace 1796-1859.....................................DLB-1

Mann, Klaus 1906-1949.....................................DLB-56

Mann, Thomas 1875-1955.................................DLB-66

Manning, Marie 1873?-1945.............................DLB-29

Manning and Loring..DLB-49

Mano, D. Keith 1942- DLB-6

Manor Books DLB-46

March, William 1893-1954 ....DLB-9, 86

Marchand, Leslie A. 1900- DLB-103

Marchessault, Jovette 1938- DLB-60

Marcus, Frank 1928- DLB-13

Marek, Richard, Books......................................DLB-46

Mariani, Paul 1940- DLB-111

Marie-Victorin, Frère 1885-1944 ....DLB-92

Marinetti, Filippo Tommaso 1876-1944 .....DLB-114

Marion, Frances 1886-1973...............................DLB-44

Marius, Richard C. 1933- Y-85

The Mark Taper Forum DLB-7

Markfield, Wallace 1926- DLB-2, 28

Markham, Edwin 1852-1940 ....DLB-54

Markle, Fletcher 1921-1991 ....DLB-68; Y-91

Marlatt, Daphne 1942- DLB-60

Marlowe, Christopher 1564-1593....................DLB-62

Marlyn, John 1912- DLB-88

Marmion, Shakerley 1603-1639 ....DLB-58

Marquand, John P. 1893-1960...................DLB-9, 102

Marqués, René 1919-1979...............................DLB-113

Marquis, Don 1878-1937..........................DLB-11, 25

Marriott, Anne 1913- DLB-68

Marryat, Frederick 1792-1848....................DLB-21
Marsh, George Perkins 1801-1882...........DLB-1, 64
Marsh, James 1794-1842 ....DLB-1, 59
Marsh, Capen, Lyon and Webb....................DLB-49
Marsh, Ngaio 1899-1982 ....DLB-77
Marshall, Edison 1894-1967 ....DLB-102
Marshall, Edward 1932- DLB-16
Marshall, James 1942- DLB-61
Marshall, Joyce 1913- DLB-88
Marshall, Paule 1929- DLB-33
Marshall, Tom 1938- DLB-60
Marsilius of Padua circa 1275-circa 1342 .....DLB-115
Marston, John 1576-1634 ....DLB-58
Marston, Philip Bourke 1850-1887..............DLB-35
Martens, Kurt 1870-1945 ....DLB-66
Martien, William S. [publishing house] DLB-49
Martin, Abe (see Hubbard, Kin)
Martin, Claire 1914- DLB-60
Martin, Jay 1935- DLB-111
Martin du Gard, Roger 1881-1958 ....DLB-65
Martineau, Harriet 1802-1876 ....DLB-21, 55
Martínez, Max 1943- DLB-82
Martyn, Edward 1859-1923 ....DLB-10
Marvin X 1944- DLB-38
Marzials, Theo 1850-1920 ....DLB-35
Masefield, John 1878-1967...........................DLB-10, 19
Mason, A. E. W. 1865-1948 ....DLB-70
Mason, Bobbie Ann 1940- Y-87
Mason Brothers...DLB-49
Massey, Gerald 1828-1907.............................DLB-32
Massinger, Philip 1583-1640 ....DLB-58
Masters, Edgar Lee 1868-1950.......................DLB-54
Mather, Cotton 1663-1728 ....DLB-24, 30
Mather, Increase 1639-1723...........................DLB-24
Mather, Richard 1596-1669............................DLB-24
Matheson, Richard 1926- DLB-8, 44
Matheus, John F. 1887- DLB-51
Mathews, Cornelius 1817?-1889..................DLB-3, 64
Mathews, Elkin [publishing house] DLB-112
Mathias, Roland 1915- DLB-27
Mathis, June 1892-1927.................................DLB-44
Mathis, Sharon Bell 1937- DLB-33
Matthews, Brander 1852-1929.....................DLB-71, 78

Matthews, Jack 1925- DLB-6
Matthews, William 1942- DLB-5
Matthiessen, F. O. 1902-1950........................DLB-63
Matthiessen, Peter 1927- DLB-6
Maugham, W. Somerset 1874-1965.........DLB-10, 36, 77, 100
Mauriac, Claude 1914- DLB-83
Mauriac, François 1885-1970 ....DLB-65
Maurice, Frederick Denison 1805-1872.........DLB-55
Maurois, André 1885-1967..............................DLB-65
Maury, James 1718-1769................................DLB-31
Mavor, Elizabeth 1927- DLB-14
Mavor, Osborne Henry (see Bridie, James)
Maxwell, H. [publishing house] DLB-49
Maxwell, John [publishing house]................DLB-106
Maxwell, William 1908- Y-80
May, Elaine 1932- DLB-44
May, Thomas 1595 or 1596-1650 ....DLB-58
Mayer, Mercer 1943- DLB-61
Mayer, O. B. 1818-1891 ....DLB-3
Mayes, Wendell 1919- DLB-26
Mayfield, Julian 1928-1984 ....DLB-33; Y-84
Mayhew, Henry 1812-1887 ....DLB-18, 55
Mayhew, Jonathan 1720-1766 ....DLB-31
Mayne, Seymour 1944- DLB-60
Mayor, Flora Macdonald 1872-1932............DLB-36
Mayröcker, Friederike 1924- DLB-85
Mazursky, Paul 1930- DLB-44
McAlmon, Robert 1896-1956.....................DLB-4, 45
McArthur, Peter 1866-1924...........................DLB-92
McBride, Robert M., and Company...............DLB-46
McCaffrey, Anne 1926- DLB-8
McCarthy, Cormac 1933- DLB-6
McCarthy, Mary 1912-1989................DLB-2; Y-81
McCay, Winsor 1871-1934.............................DLB-22
McClatchy, C. K. 1858-1936..........................DLB-25
McClellan, George Marion 1860-1934..........DLB-50
McCloskey, Robert 1914- DLB-22
McClung, Nellie Letitia 1873-1951 ....DLB-92
McClure, Joanna 1930- DLB-16
McClure, Michael 1932- DLB-16
McClure, Phillips and Company DLB-46
McClure, S. S. 1857-1949 ....DLB-91
McClurg, A. C., and Company.......................DLB-49

McCluskey, John A., Jr. 1944- DLB-33

McCollum, Michael A. 1946 ....Y-87

McConnell, William C. 1917- DLB-88

McCord, David 1897- DLB-61

McCorkle, Jill 1958- Y-87

McCorkle, Samuel Eusebius 1746-1811 ....DLB-37

McCormick, Anne O'Hare 1880-1954 ....DLB-29

McCormick, Robert R. 1880-1955 ....DLB-29

McCourt, Edward 1907-1972 ....DLB-88

McCoy, Horace 1897-1955 ....DLB-9

McCrae, John 1872-1918 ....DLB-92

McCullagh, Joseph B. 1842-1896...................DLB-23

McCullers, Carson 1917-1967 ....DLB-2, 7

McCulloch, Thomas 1776-1843 ....DLB-99

McDonald, Forrest 1927- DLB-17

McDonald, Walter 1934- DLB-105, DS-9

McDonald, Walter, Getting Started:
    Accepting the Regions You Own—
    or Which Own You DLB-105

McDougall, Colin 1917-1984........................DLB-68

McDowell, Obolensky DLB-46

McEwan, Ian 1948- DLB-14

McFadden, David 1940- DLB-60

McFarlane, Leslie 1902-1977 ....DLB-88

McGahern, John 1934- DLB-14

McGee, Thomas D'Arcy 1825-1868 ....DLB-99

McGeehan, W. O. 1879-1933 ....DLB-25

McGill, Ralph 1898-1969..............................DLB-29

McGinley, Phyllis 1905-1978 ....DLB-11, 48

McGirt, James E. 1874-1930.........................DLB-50

McGlashan and Gill DLB-106

McGough, Roger 1937- DLB-40

McGraw-Hill..DLB-46

McGuane, Thomas 1939- DLB-2; Y-80

McGuckian, Medbh 1950- DLB-40

McGuffey, William Holmes 1800-1873..........DLB-42

McIlvanney, William 1936- DLB-14

McIlwraith, Jean Newton 1859-1938 ....DLB-92

McIntyre, James 1827-1906..........................DLB-99

McIntyre, O. O. 1884-1938 ....DLB-25

McKay, Claude 1889-1948 ....DLB-4, 45, 51, 117

The David McKay Company DLB-49

McKean, William V. 1820-1903 ....DLB-23

McKinley, Robin 1952- DLB-52

McLachlan, Alexander 1818-1896 ....DLB-99

McLaren, Floris Clark 1904-1978 ....DLB-68

McLaverty, Michael 1907- DLB-15

McLean, John R. 1848-1916..........................DLB-23

McLean, William L. 1852-1931 ....DLB-25

McLennan, William 1856-1904 ....DLB-92

McLoughlin Brothers..................................DLB-49

McLuhan, Marshall 1911-1980 ....DLB-88

McMaster, John Bach 1852-1932....................DLB-47

McMurtry, Larry 1936- DLB-2; Y-80, 87

McNally, Terrence 1939- DLB-7

McNeil, Florence 1937- DLB-60

McNeile, Herman Cyril 1888-1937 ....DLB-77

McPherson, James Alan 1943- DLB-38

McPherson, Sandra 1943- Y-86

McWhirter, George 1939- DLB-60

Mead, Matthew 1924- DLB-40

Mead, Taylor ?- DLB-16

Medill, Joseph 1823-1899.............................DLB-43

Medoff, Mark 1940- DLB-7

Meek, Alexander Beaufort 1814-1865............DLB-3

Meeke, Mary ?-1816? DLB-116

Meinke, Peter 1932- DLB-5

Mejia Vallejo, Manuel 1923- DLB-113

Melançon, Robert 1947- DLB-60

Mell, Max 1882-1971 ....DLB-81

Mellow, James R. 1926- DLB-111

Meltzer, David 1937- DLB-16

Meltzer, Milton 1915- DLB-61

Melville, Herman 1819-1891........................DLB-3, 74

Memoirs of Life and Literature (1920),
    by W. H. Mallock [excerpt]....................DLB-57

Mencken, H. L. 1880-1956 ....DLB-11, 29, 63

Mendelssohn, Moses 1729-1786....................DLB-97

Méndez M., Miguel 1930- DLB-82

Mercer, Cecil William (see Yates, Dornford)

Mercer, David 1928-1980............................DLB-13

Mercer, John 1704-1768..............................DLB-31

Meredith, George 1828-1909.................DLB-18, 35, 57

Meredith, Owen (see Lytton, Edward Robert Bulwer)

Meredith, William 1919- DLB-5

Mérimée, Prosper 1803-1870......................DLB-119

Merivale, John Herman 1779-1844 ....DLB-96

Meriwether, Louise 1923- DLB-33

Merlin Press...DLB-112

Merriam, Eve 1916- DLB-61

The Merriam Company..............................DLB-49

Merrill, James 1926- DLB-5; Y-85

Merrill and Baker DLB-49

The Mershon Company..............................DLB-49

Merton, Thomas 1915-1968.................DLB-48; Y-81

Merwin, W. S. 1927- DLB-5

Messner, Julian [publishing house]...............DLB-46

Metcalf, J. [publishing house]....................DLB-49

Metcalf, John 1938- DLB-60

The Methodist Book Concern........................DLB-49

Methuen and Company...............................DLB-112

Mew, Charlotte 1869-1928 ....DLB-19

Mewshaw, Michael 1943- Y-80

Meyer, E. Y. 1946- DLB-75

Meyer, Eugene 1875-1959...........................DLB-29

Meyers, Jeffrey 1939- DLB-111

Meynell, Alice 1847-1922 ....DLB-19, 98

Meyrink, Gustav 1868-1932.........................DLB-81

Micheaux, Oscar 1884-1951.........................DLB-50

Micheline, Jack 1929- DLB-16

Michener, James A. 1907?- DLB-6

Micklejohn, George circa 1717-1818 ....DLB-31

Middle Hill Press DLB-106

Middleton, Christopher 1926- DLB-40

Middleton, Stanley 1919- DLB-14

Middleton, Thomas 1580-1627.......................DLB-58

Miegel, Agnes 1879-1964 ....DLB-56

Miles, Josephine 1911-1985 ....DLB-48

Milius, John 1944- DLB-44

Mill, James 1773-1836 ....DLB-107

Mill, John Stuart 1806-1873 ....DLB-55

Millar, Kenneth 1915-1983...............DLB-2; Y-83; DS-6

Millay, Edna St. Vincent 1892-1950 ....DLB-45

Miller, Arthur 1915- DLB-7

Miller, Caroline 1903- DLB-9

Miller, Eugene Ethelbert 1950- DLB-41

Miller, Henry 1891-1980................DLB-4, 9; Y-80

Miller, J. Hillis 1928- DLB-67

Miller, James [publishing house]..................DLB-49

Miller, Jason 1939- DLB-7

Miller, May 1899- DLB-41

Miller, Perry 1905-1963.......................DLB-17, 63

Miller, Walter M., Jr. 1923- DLB-8

Miller, Webb 1892-1940............................DLB-29

Millhauser, Steven 1943- DLB-2

Millican, Arthenia J. Bates 1920- DLB-38

Mills and Boon....................................DLB-112

Milman, Henry Hart 1796-1868 ....DLB-96

Milne, A. A. 1882-1956...................DLB-10, 77, 100

Milner, Ron 1938- DLB-38

Milner, William [publishing house]...............DLB-106

Milnes, Richard Monckton (Lord Houghton)
    1809-1885....................................DLB-32

Minton, Balch and Company DLB-46

Miron, Gaston 1928- DLB-60

Mitchel, Jonathan 1624-1668 ....DLB-24

Mitchell, Adrian 1932- DLB-40

Mitchell, Donald Grant 1822-1908 ....DLB-1

Mitchell, Gladys 1901-1983 ....DLB-77

Mitchell, James Leslie 1901-1935.................DLB-15

Mitchell, John (see Slater, Patrick)

Mitchell, John Ames 1845-1918....................DLB-79

Mitchell, Julian 1935- DLB-14

Mitchell, Ken 1940- DLB-60

Mitchell, Langdon 1862-1935 ....DLB-7

Mitchell, Loften 1919- DLB-38

Mitchell, Margaret 1900-1949......................DLB-9

Mitchell, W. O. 1914- DLB-88

Mitford, Mary Russell 1787-1855 ....DLB-110, 116

Mittelholzer, Edgar 1909-1965....................DLB-117

Mitterer, Erika 1906- DLB-85

Mizener, Arthur 1907-1988........................DLB-103

Modern Age Books..................................DLB-46

"Modern English Prose" (1876),
    by George Saintsbury..........................DLB-57

The Modern Language Association of America
    Celebrates Its Centennial......................Y-84

The Modern Library DLB-46

Modern Novelists—Great and Small (1855), by
    Margaret Oliphant.............................DLB-21

"Modern Style" (1857), by Cockburn
    Thomson [excerpt] DLB-57

The Modernists (1932), by Joseph Warren
    Beach...DLB-36

Modiano, Patrick 1945- DLB-83

Moffat, Yard and Company..........................DLB-46

Monkhouse, Allan 1858-1936 ....DLB-10

Monro, Harold 1879-1932..............................DLB-19

Monroe, Harriet 1860-1936 ....DLB-54, 91

Monsarrat, Nicholas 1910-1979....................DLB-15

Montale, Eugenio 1896-1981......................DLB-114

Montagu, Lady Mary Wortley
　　1689-1762..................................DLB-95, 101

Montague, John 1929- DLB-40

Montgomery, James 1771-1854....................DLB-93

Montgomery, John 1919- DLB-16

Montgomery, Lucy Maud 1874-1942 ....DLB-92

Montgomery, Marion 1925- DLB-6

Montgomery, Robert Bruce (see Crispin, Edmund)

Montherlant, Henry de 1896-1972 ....DLB-72

The Monthly Review 1749-1844 ....DLB-110

Montigny, Louvigny de 1876-1955 ....DLB-92

Moodie, John Wedderburn Dunbar
　　1797-1869...DLB-99

Moodie, Susanna 1803-1885 ....DLB-99

Moody, Joshua circa 1633-1697 ....DLB-24

Moody, William Vaughn 1869-1910 ....DLB-7, 54

Moorcock, Michael 1939- DLB-14

Moore, Catherine L. 1911- DLB-8

Moore, Clement Clarke 1779-1863 ....DLB-42

Moore, Dora Mavor 1888-1979......................DLB-92

Moore, George 1852-1933 ....DLB-10, 18, 57

Moore, Marianne 1887-1972 ....DLB-45; DS-7

Moore, Mavor 1919- DLB-88

Moore, Richard 1927- DLB-105

Moore, Richard, The No Self, the Little Self, and
　　the Poets..DLB-105

Moore, T. Sturge 1870-1944 ....DLB-19

Moore, Thomas 1779-1852 ....DLB-96

Moore, Ward 1903-1978.................................DLB-8

Moore, Wilstach, Keys and Company............DLB-49

The Moorland-Spingarn
　　Research Center.....................................DLB-76

Moraga, Cherríe 1952- DLB-82

Morales, Alejandro 1944- DLB-82

Morales, Rafael 1919- DLB-108

More, Hannah 1745-1833 ....DLB-107, 109, 116

Morency, Pierre 1942- DLB-60

Moretti, Marino 1885-1979 ....DLB-114

Morgan, Berry 1919- DLB-6

Morgan, Charles 1894-1958.....................DLB-34, 100

Morgan, Edmund S. 1916- DLB-17

Morgan, Edwin 1920- DLB-27

Morgan, Sydney Owenson, Lady
　　1776?-1859 ....DLB-116

Morgner, Irmtraud 1933- DLB-75

Morier, James Justinian
　　1782 or 1783?-1849 ....DLB-116

Morin, Paul 1889-1963 ....DLB-92

Morison, Samuel Eliot 1887-1976 ....DLB-17

Moritz, Karl Philipp 1756-1793 ....DLB-94

Morley, Christopher 1890-1957......................DLB-9

Morley, John 1838-1923 ....DLB-57

Morris, George Pope 1802-1864 ....DLB-73

Morris, Lewis 1833-1907 ....DLB-35

Morris, Richard B. 1904-1989.......................DLB-17

Morris, William 1834-1896 ....DLB-18, 35, 57

Morris, Willie 1934- Y-80

Morris, Wright 1910- DLB-2; Y-81

Morrison, Arthur 1863-1945.........................DLB-70

Morrison, Charles Clayton 1874-1966 ....DLB-91

Morrison, Toni 1931- DLB-6, 33; Y-81

Morrow, William, and Company....................DLB-46

Morse, James Herbert 1841-1923 ....DLB-71

Morse, Jedidiah 1761-1826...........................DLB-37

Morse, John T., Jr. 1840-1937 ....DLB-47

Mortimer, John 1923- DLB-13

Morton, John P., and Company.....................DLB-49

Morton, Nathaniel 1613-1685 ....DLB-24

Morton, Sarah Wentworth 1759-1846...........DLB-37

Morton, Thomas circa 1579-circa 1647 ....DLB-24

Möser, Justus 1720-1794 ....DLB-97

Mosley, Nicholas 1923- DLB-14

Moss, Arthur 1889-1969................................DLB-4

Moss, Howard 1922- DLB-5

The Most Powerful Book Review in America
　　[*New York Times Book Review*]........................Y-82

Motion, Andrew 1952- DLB-40

Motley, John Lothrop 1814-1877 ....DLB-1, 30, 59

Motley, Willard 1909-1965 ....DLB-76

Motteux, Peter Anthony 1663-1718 ....DLB-80

Mottram, R. H. 1883-1971 ....DLB-36

Mouré, Erin 1955- DLB-60

Movies from Books, 1920-1974......................DLB-9

Mowat, Farley 1921- DLB-68

Mowbray, A. R., and Company, Limited...................DLB-106

Mowrer, Edgar Ansel 1892-1977 ....DLB-29

Mowrer, Paul Scott 1887-1971 ....DLB-29

Moxon, Edward [publishing house] DLB-106

Mucedorus..DLB-62

Mueller, Lisel 1924- DLB-105

Muhajir, El (see Marvin X)

Muhajir, Nazzam Al Fitnah (see Marvin X)

Muir, Edwin 1887-1959.........................DLB-20, 100

Muir, Helen 1937- DLB-14

Mukherjee, Bharati 1940- DLB-60

Muldoon, Paul 1951- DLB-40

Müller, Friedrich (see Müller, Maler)

Müller, Maler 1749-1825 ....DLB-94

Müller, Wilhelm 1794-1827 ....DLB-90

Mumford, Lewis 1895-1990 ....DLB-63

Munby, Arthur Joseph 1828-1910 ....DLB-35

Munday, Anthony 1560-1633.........................DLB-62

Munford, Robert circa 1737-1783 ....DLB-31

Munonye, John 1929- DLB-117

Munro, Alice 1931- DLB-53

Munro, George [publishing house] DLB-49

Munro, H. H. 1870-1916...............................DLB-34

Munro, Norman L. [publishing house]...............................DLB-49

Munroe, James, and Company...............................DLB-49

Munroe, Kirk 1850-1930 ....DLB-42

Munroe and Francis DLB-49

Munsell, Joel [publishing house]...............................DLB-49

Munsey, Frank A. 1854-1925...............................DLB-25, 91

Munsey, Frank A., and Company DLB-49

Murdoch, Iris 1919- DLB-14

Murfree, Mary N. 1850-1922...............................DLB-12, 74

Murger, Henry 1822-1861 ....DLB-119

Murger, Louis-Henri (see Murger, Henry)

Muro, Amado 1915-1971 ....DLB-82

Murphy, Arthur 1727-1805...............................DLB-89

Murphy, Beatrice M. 1908- DLB-76

Murphy, Emily 1868-1933...............................DLB-99

Murphy, John, and Company DLB-49

Murphy, Richard 1927- DLB-40

Murray, Albert L. 1916- DLB-38

Murray, Gilbert 1866-1957...............................DLB-10

Murray, Judith Sargent 1751-1820 ....DLB-37

Murray, Pauli 1910-1985 ....DLB-41

Musäus, Johann Karl August 1735-1787...............................DLB-97

Muschg, Adolf 1934- DLB-75

Musil, Robert 1880-1942 ....DLB-81

Mussey, Benjamin B., and Company DLB-49

Myers, Gustavus 1872-1942...............................DLB-47

Myers, L. H. 1881-1944...............................DLB-15

Myers, Walter Dean 1937- DLB-33

N

Nabbes, Thomas circa 1605-1641 ....DLB-58

Nabl, Franz 1883-1974 ....DLB-81

Nabokov, Vladimir 1899-1977...........DLB-2; Y-80, Y-91; DS-3

Nabokov Festival at Cornell...............................Y-83

The Vladimir Nabokov Archive
    in the Berg Collection...............................Y-91

Nafis and Cornish...............................DLB-49

Naipaul, Shiva 1945-1985 ....Y-85

Naipaul, V. S. 1932- Y-85

Nancrede, Joseph [publishing house] DLB-49

Narrache, Jean 1893-1970...............................DLB-92

Nasby, Petroleum Vesuvius (see Locke, David Ross)

Nash, Ogden 1902-1971 ....DLB-11

Nash, Eveleigh [publishing house]...............................DLB-112

Nast, Condé 1873-1942 ....DLB-91

Nathan, Robert 1894-1985 ....DLB-9

The National Jewish Book Awards Y-85

The National Theatre and the Royal Shakespeare
    Company: The National Companies DLB-13

Naughton, Bill 1910- DLB-13

Neagoe, Peter 1881-1960...............................DLB-4

Neal, John 1793-1876...............................DLB-1, 59

Neal, Joseph C. 1807-1847 ....DLB-11

Neal, Larry 1937-1981...............................DLB-38

The Neale Publishing Company DLB-49

Neely, F. Tennyson [publishing house]...............................DLB-49

Negri, Ada 1870-1945 ....DLB-114

"The Negro as a Writer," by
    G. M. McClellan...............................DLB-50

"Negro Poets and Their Poetry," by
    Wallace Thurman DLB-50

Neihardt, John G. 1881-1973...............................DLB-9, 54

Nelligan, Emile 1879-1941 ....DLB-92

Nelson, Alice Moore Dunbar 1875-1935 ....DLB-50

Nelson, Thomas, and Sons [U.S.] DLB-49

Nelson, Thomas, and Sons [U.K.]...............................DLB-106

Nelson, William 1908-1978 ....DLB-103

Nelson, William Rockhill 1841-1915 ....DLB-23

Nemerov, Howard 1920-1991...........................DLB-5, 6; Y-83

Ness, Evaline 1911-1986..DLB-61

Neugeboren, Jay 1938- DLB-28

Neumann, Alfred 1895-1952 ....DLB-56

Nevins, Allan 1890-1971 ....DLB-17

The New American Library DLB-46

New Approaches to Biography: Challenges
    from Critical Theory, USC Conference
    on Literary Studies, 1990 ....Y-90

New Directions Publishing Corporation DLB-46

A New Edition of *Huck Finn*......................................Y-85

New Forces at Work in the American Theatre:
    1915-1925 ....DLB-7

New Literary Periodicals: A Report
    for 1987 ....Y-87

New Literary Periodicals: A Report
    for 1988 ....Y-88

New Literary Periodicals: A Report
    for 1989 ....Y-89

New Literary Periodicals: A Report
    for 1990 ....Y-90

New Literary Periodicals: A Report
    for 1991 ....Y-91

The New Monthly Magazine 1814-1884 ....DLB-110

The New *Ulysses*...Y-84

The New Variorum Shakespeare Y-85

A New Voice: The Center for the Book's First
    Five Years Y-83

The New Wave [Science Fiction].................................DLB-8

Newbolt, Henry 1862-1938 ....DLB-19

Newbound, Bernard Slade (see Slade, Bernard)

Newby, P. H. 1918- DLB-15

Newby, Thomas Cautley [publishing house] DLB-106

Newcomb, Charles King 1820-1894 ....DLB-1

Newell, Peter 1862-1924..DLB-42

Newell, Robert Henry 1836-1901 ....DLB-11

Newman, David (see Benton, Robert)

Newman, Frances 1883-1928.......................................Y-80

Newman, John Henry 1801-1890....................DLB-18, 32, 55

Newman, Mark [publishing house] DLB-49

Newnes, George, Limited DLB-112

Newsome, Effie Lee 1885-1979....................................DLB-76

Newspaper Syndication of American Humor DLB-11

Nichol, B. P. 1944- DLB-53

Nicholas of Cusa 1401-1464.......................................DLB-115

Nichols, Dudley 1895-1960..DLB-26

Nichols, John 1940- Y-82

Nichols, Mary Sargeant (Neal) Gove
    1810-1884...DLB-1

Nichols, Peter 1927- DLB-13

Nichols, Roy F. 1896-1973..DLB-17

Nichols, Ruth 1948- DLB-60

Nicolson, Harold 1886-1968.......................................DLB-100

Nicholson, Norman 1914- DLB-27

Ní Chuilleanáin, Eiléan 1942- DLB-40

Nicol, Eric 1919- DLB-68

Nicolai, Friedrich 1733-1811 ....DLB-97

Nicolay, John G. 1832-1901 and
    Hay, John 1838-1905 ....DLB-47

Niebuhr, Reinhold 1892-1971....................................DLB-17

Niedecker, Lorine 1903-1970......................................DLB-48

Nieman, Lucius W. 1857-1935 ....DLB-25

Niggli, Josefina 1910- Y-80

Niles, Hezekiah 1777-1839...DLB-43

Nims, John Frederick 1913- DLB-5

Nin, Anaïs 1903-1977...DLB-2, 4

1985: The Year of the Mystery:
    A Symposium Y-85

Nissenson, Hugh 1933- DLB-28

Niven, Frederick John 1878-1944...............................DLB-92

Niven, Larry 1938- DLB-8

Nizan, Paul 1905-1940..DLB-72

Nobel Peace Prize
    The 1986 Nobel Peace Prize
        Nobel Lecture 1986: Hope, Despair
        and Memory
        Tributes from Abraham Bernstein,
        Norman Lamm, and John R. Silber.................Y-86

The Nobel Prize and Literary
    Politics..Y-88

Nobel Prize in Literature
    The 1982 Nobel Prize in Literature
        Announcement by the Swedish Academy
        of the Nobel Prize
        Nobel Lecture 1982: The Solitude of Latin
        America
        Excerpt from *One Hundred Years*
        of Solitude

The Magical World of Macondo A Tribute to Gabriel García Márquez..................Y-82

The 1983 Nobel Prize in Literature
Announcement by the Swedish
Academy
Nobel Lecture 1983
The Stature of William Golding..........................Y-83

The 1984 Nobel Prize in Literature
Announcement by the Swedish
Academy
Jaroslav Seifert Through the Eyes of the
English-Speaking Reader
Three Poems by Jaroslav Seifert......................Y-84

The 1985 Nobel Prize in Literature
Announcement by the Swedish
Academy
Nobel Lecture 1985...Y-85

The 1986 Nobel Prize in Literature
Nobel Lecture 1986: This Past Must
Address Its Present.......................................Y-86

The 1987 Nobel Prize in Literature
Nobel Lecture 1987...Y-87

The 1988 Nobel Prize in Literature
Nobel Lecture 1988...Y-88

The 1989 Nobel Prize in Literature
Nobel Lecture 1989...Y-89

The 1990 Nobel Prize in Literature
Nobel Lecture 1990...Y-90

The 1991 Nobel Prize in Literature
Nobel Lecture 1991...Y-91

Noel, Roden 1834-1894..DLB-35

Nodier, Charles 1780-1844 ....DLB-119

Nolan, William F. 1928- DLB-8

Noland, C. F. M. 1810?-1858 ....DLB-11

Nonesuch Press DLB-112

Noonday Press...DLB-46

Noone, John 1936- DLB-14

Nordhoff, Charles 1887-1947 ....DLB-9

Norman, Charles 1904- DLB-111

Norman, Marsha 1947- Y-84

Norris, Charles G. 1881-1945..............................DLB-9

Norris, Frank 1870-1902 ....DLB-12

Norris, Leslie 1921- DLB-27

Norse, Harold 1916- DLB-16

North Point Press...DLB-46

Norton, Alice Mary (see Norton, Andre)

Norton, Andre 1912- DLB-8, 52

Norton, Andrews 1786-1853 ....DLB-1

Norton, Caroline 1808-1877.................................DLB-21

Norton, Charles Eliot 1827-1908 ....DLB-1, 64

Norton, John 1606-1663..DLB-24

Norton, Thomas (see Sackville, Thomas)

Norton, W. W., and Company DLB-46

Norwood, Robert 1874-1932.................................DLB-92

Nossack, Hans Erich 1901-1977.........................DLB-69

A Note on Technique (1926), by Elizabeth
A. Drew [excerpts]...DLB-36

Nourse, Alan E. 1928- DLB-8

Novalis 1772-1801..DLB-90

Novaro, Mario 1868-1944......................................DLB-114

The Novel in [Robert Browning's] "The Ring
and the Book" (1912), by Henry James.................DLB-32

The Novel of Impressionism,
by Jethro Bithell...DLB-66

Novel-Reading: *The Works of Charles Dickens,
The Works of W. Makepeace Thackeray* (1879),
by Anthony Trollope DLB-21

The Novels of Dorothy Richardson (1918), by
May Sinclair...DLB-36

Novels with a Purpose (1864),
by Justin M'Carthy..DLB-21

Noventa, Giacomo 1898-1960 ....DLB-114

Nowlan, Alden 1933-1983.....................................DLB-53

Noyes, Alfred 1880-1958......................................DLB-20

Noyes, Crosby S. 1825-1908 ....DLB-23

Noyes, Nicholas 1647-1717...................................DLB-24

Noyes, Theodore W. 1858-1946 ....DLB-29

Nugent, Frank 1908-1965 ....DLB-44

Nutt, David [publishing house] DLB-106

Nye, Edgar Wilson (Bill) 1850-1896.....................DLB-11, 23

Nye, Robert 1939- DLB-14

O

Oakes, Urian circa 1631-1681 ....DLB-24

Oates, Joyce Carol 1938- DLB-2, 5; Y-81

Oberholtzer, Ellis Paxson 1868-1936..........................DLB-47

O'Brien, Edna 1932- DLB-14

O'Brien, Fitz-James 1828-1862.............................DLB-74

O'Brien, Kate 1897-1974..DLB-15

O'Brien, Tim 1946- Y-80, DS-9

O'Casey, Sean 1880-1964......................................DLB-10

Ochs, Adolph S. 1858-1935...................................DLB-25

O'Connor, Flannery 1925-1964 ....DLB-2; Y-80

Octopus Publishing Group DLB-112

Odell, Jonathan 1737-1818 ....DLB-31, 99

O'Dell, Scott 1903-1989 ....DLB-52

Odets, Clifford 1906-1963 ....DLB-7, 26

Odhams Press Limited DLB-112

O'Donnell, Peter 1920- DLB-87

O'Faolain, Julia 1932- DLB-14

O'Faolain, Sean 1900- DLB-15

Off Broadway and Off-Off-Broadway DLB-7

Off-Loop Theatres DLB-7

Offord, Carl Ruthven 1910- DLB-76

O'Flaherty, Liam 1896-1984 ....DLB-36; Y-84

Ogilvie, J. S., and Company DLB-49

O'Grady, Desmond 1935- DLB-40

O'Hagan, Howard 1902-1982 ....DLB-68

O'Hara, Frank 1926-1966 ....DLB-5, 16

O'Hara, John 1905-1970 ....DLB-9, 86; DS-2

O. Henry (see Porter, William Sydney)

O'Keeffe, John 1747-1833 ....DLB-89

Olaudah Equiano and Unfinished Journeys:
    The Slave-Narrative Tradition and
    Twentieth-Century Continuities, by
    Paul Edwards and Pauline T. Wangman DLB-117

Old Franklin Publishing House DLB-49

Older, Fremont 1856-1935 ....DLB-25

Oliphant, Laurence 1829?-1888 ....DLB-18

Oliphant, Margaret 1828-1897 ....DLB-18

Oliver, Chad 1928- DLB-8

Oliver, Mary 1935- DLB-5

Ollier, Claude 1922- DLB-83

Olsen, Tillie 1913?- DLB-28; Y-80

Olson, Charles 1910-1970 ....DLB-5, 16

Olson, Elder 1909- DLB-48, 63

On Art in Fiction (1838), by
    Edward Bulwer DLB-21

On Learning to Write Y-88

On Some of the Characteristics of Modern
    Poetry and On the Lyrical Poems of Alfred
    Tennyson (1831), by Arthur Henry
    Hallam DLB-32

"On Style in English Prose" (1898), by Frederic
    Harrison DLB-57

"On Style in Literature: Its Technical Elements"
    (1885), by Robert Louis Stevenson DLB-57

"On the Writing of Essays" (1862),
    by Alexander Smith DLB-57

Ondaatje, Michael 1943- DLB-60

O'Neill, Eugene 1888-1953 ....DLB-7

Onetti, Juan Carlos 1909- DLB-113

Onofri, Arturo 1885-1928 ....DLB-114

Opie, Amelia 1769-1853 ....DLB-116

Oppen, George 1908-1984 ....DLB-5

Oppenheim, E. Phillips 1866-1946 ....DLB-70

Oppenheim, James 1882-1932 ....DLB-28

Oppenheimer, Joel 1930- DLB-5

Optic, Oliver (see Adams, William Taylor)

Orczy, Emma, Baroness 1865-1947 ....DLB-70

Orlovitz, Gil 1918-1973 ....DLB-2, 5

Orlovsky, Peter 1933- DLB-16

Ormond, John 1923- DLB-27

Ornitz, Samuel 1890-1957 ....DLB-28, 44

Orton, Joe 1933-1967 ....DLB-13

Orwell, George 1903-1950 ....DLB-15, 98

The Orwell Year Y-84

Osbon, B. S. 1827-1912 ....DLB-43

Osborne, John 1929- DLB-13

Osgood, Herbert L. 1855-1918 ....DLB-47

Osgood, James R., and Company DLB-49

Osgood, McIlvaine and Company DLB-112

O'Shaughnessy, Arthur 1844-1881 ....DLB-35

O'Shea, Patrick [publishing house] DLB-49

Oswald, Eleazer 1755-1795 ....DLB-43

Ostenso, Martha 1900-1963 ....DLB-92

Otero, Miguel Antonio 1859-1944 ....DLB-82

Otis, James (see Kaler, James Otis)

Otis, James, Jr. 1725-1783 ....DLB-31

Otis, Broaders and Company DLB-49

Ottendorfer, Oswald 1826-1900 ....DLB-23

Otway, Thomas 1652-1685 ....DLB-80

Ouellette, Fernand 1930- DLB-60

Ouida 1839-1908 ....DLB-18

Outing Publishing Company DLB-46

Outlaw Days, by Joyce Johnson DLB-16

The Overlook Press DLB-46

Overview of U.S. Book Publishing, 1910-1945 ....DLB-9

Owen, Guy 1925- DLB-5

Owen, John [publishing house] DLB-49

Owen, Robert 1771-1858 ....DLB-107

Owen, Wilfred 1893-1918 ....DLB-20

Owen, Peter, Limited DLB-112

Owsley, Frank L. 1890-1956 ....DLB-17

Ozick, Cynthia 1928- DLB-28; Y-82

P

Pacey, Desmond 1917-1975...........................DLB-88

Pack, Robert 1929- DLB-5

Packaging Papa: *The Garden of Eden*...................Y-86

Padell Publishing Company...........................DLB-46

Padgett, Ron 1942- DLB-5

Page, L. C., and Company...........................DLB-49

Page, P. K. 1916- DLB-68

Page, Thomas Nelson 1853-1922..............DLB-12, 78

Page, Walter Hines 1855-1918...................DLB-71, 91

Paget, Violet (see Lee, Vernon)

Pain, Philip ?-circa 1666 ....DLB-24

Paine, Robert Treat, Jr. 1773-1811 ....DLB-37

Paine, Thomas 1737-1809................DLB-31, 43, 73

Palazzeschi, Aldo 1885-1974...........................DLB-114

Paley, Grace 1922- DLB-28

Palfrey, John Gorham 1796-1881 ....DLB-1, 30

Palgrave, Francis Turner 1824-1897.................DLB-35

Paltock, Robert 1697-1767 ....DLB-39

Pan Books Limited...........................DLB-112

Panamaa, Norman 1914-   and
    Frank, Melvin 1913-1988   ....DLB-26

Panero, Leopoldo 1909-1962 ....DLB-108

Pangborn, Edgar 1909-1976...........................DLB-8

"Panic Among the Philistines": A Postscript,
    An Interview with Bryan Griffin.................Y-81

Panneton, Philippe (see Ringuet)

Panshin, Alexei 1940- DLB-8

Pansy (see Alden, Isabella)

Pantheon Books DLB-46

Paperback Library...........................DLB-46

Paperback Science Fiction DLB-8

Paquet, Alfons 1881-1944...........................DLB-66

Paradis, Suzanne 1936- DLB-53

Parents' Magazine Press...........................DLB-46

Parisian Theater, Fall 1984: Toward
    A New Baroque...........................Y-85

Parizeau, Alice 1930- DLB-60

Parke, John 1754-1789 ....DLB-31

Parker, Dorothy 1893-1967..............DLB-11, 45, 86

Parker, Gilbert 1860-1932 ....DLB-99

Parker, James 1714-1770...........................DLB-43

Parker, Theodore 1810-1860 ....DLB-1

Parker, William Riley 1906-1968 ....DLB-103

Parker, J. H. [publishing house]...................DLB-106

Parker, John [publishing house]...................DLB-106

Parkman, Francis, Jr. 1823-1893 ....DLB-1, 30

Parks, Gordon 1912- DLB-33

Parks, William 1698-1750...........................DLB-43

Parks, William [publishing house]...................DLB-49

Parley, Peter (see Goodrich, Samuel Griswold)

Parnell, Thomas 1679-1718 ....DLB-95

Parrington, Vernon L. 1871-1929...............DLB-17, 63

Partridge, S. W., and Company DLB-106

Parton, James 1822-1891...........................DLB-30

Parton, Sara Payson Willis 1811-1872 ....DLB-43, 74

Pastan, Linda 1932- DLB-5

Pastorius, Francis Daniel 1651-circa 1720 ....DLB-24

Patchen, Kenneth 1911-1972 ....DLB-16, 48

Pater, Walter 1839-1894 ....DLB-57

Paterson, Katherine 1932- DLB-52

Patmore, Coventry 1823-1896..............DLB-35, 98

Paton, Joseph Noel 1821-1901 ....DLB-35

Patrick, John 1906- DLB-7

Pattee, Fred Lewis 1863-1950 ....DLB-71

Pattern and Paradigm: History as
    Design, by Judith Ryan DLB-75

Patterson, Eleanor Medill 1881-1948...........................DLB-29

Patterson, Joseph Medill 1879-1946 ....DLB-29

Pattillo, Henry 1726-1801 ....DLB-37

Paul, Elliot 1891-1958...........................DLB-4

Paul, Jean (see Richter, Johann Paul Friedrich)

Paul, Kegan, Trench, Trübner and Company
    Limited DLB-106

Paul, Peter, Book Company DLB-49

Paul, Stanley, and Company Limited...................DLB-112

Paulding, James Kirke 1778-1860................DLB-3, 59, 74

Paulin, Tom 1949- DLB-40

Pauper, Peter, Press DLB-46

Paxton, John 1911-1985...........................DLB-44

Payn, James 1830-1898...........................DLB-18

Payne, John 1842-1916...........................DLB-35

Payne, John Howard 1791-1852 ....DLB-37

Payson and Clarke...........................DLB-46

Peabody, Elizabeth Palmer 1804-1894...................DLB-1

Peabody, Elizabeth Palmer [publishing
house]..DLB-49

Peabody, Oliver William Bourn 1799-1848...............DLB-59

Peachtree Publishers, Limited DLB-46

Peacock, Thomas Love 1785-1866......................DLB-96, 116

Pead, Deuel ?-1727.................................DLB-24

Peake, Mervyn 1911-1968............................DLB-15

Pear Tree Press....................................DLB-112

Pearson, H. B. [publishing house]...................DLB-49

Peck, George W. 1840-1916.........................DLB-23, 42

Peck, H. C., and Theo. Bliss [publishing
house]..DLB-49

Peck, Harry Thurston 1856-1914 ....DLB-71, 91

Peele, George 1556-1596 ....DLB-62

Pellegrini and Cudahy DLB-46

Pelletier, Aimé (see Vac, Bertrand)

Pemberton, Sir Max 1863-1950......................DLB-70

Penguin Books [U.S.]...............................DLB-46

Penguin Books [U.K.]...............................DLB-112

Penn Publishing Company...........................DLB-49

Penn, William 1644-1718............................DLB-24

Penna, Sandro 1906-1977............................DLB-114

Penner, Jonathan 1940- Y-83

Pennington, Lee 1939- Y-82

Pepys, Samuel 1633-1703 ....DLB-101

Percy, Thomas 1729-1811 ....DLB-104

Percy, Walker 1916-1990...............DLB-2; Y-80, 90

Perec, Georges 1936-1982 ....DLB-83

Perelman, S. J. 1904-1979 ....DLB-11, 44

Periodicals of the Beat Generation DLB-16

Perkins, Eugene 1932- DLB-41

Perkoff, Stuart Z. 1930-1974 ....DLB-16

Perley, Moses Henry 1804-1862 ....DLB-99

Permabooks DLB-46

Perry, Bliss 1860-1954 ....DLB-71

Perry, Eleanor 1915-1981 ....DLB-44

"Personal Style" (1890), by John Addington
Symonds DLB-57

Perutz, Leo 1882-1957..............................DLB-81

Pestalozzi, Johann Heinrich 1746-1827 ....DLB-94

Peter, Laurence J. 1919-1990........................DLB-53

Peter of Spain circa 1205-1277......................DLB-115

Peterkin, Julia 1880-1961 ....DLB-9

Peters, Lenrie 1932- DLB-117

Peters, Robert 1924- DLB-105

Peters, Robert, Foreword to
Ludwig of Bavaria..............................DLB-105

Petersham, Maud 1889-1971 and
Petersham, Miska 1888-1960.....................DLB-22

Peterson, Charles Jacobs 1819-1887.................DLB-79

Peterson, Len 1917-...............................DLB-88

Peterson, Louis 1922- DLB-76

Peterson, T. B., and Brothers.....................DLB-49

Petitclair, Pierre 1813-1860 ....DLB-99

Petry, Ann 1908- DLB-76

Phaidon Press Limited DLB-112

Pharr, Robert Deane 1916-1989 ....DLB-33

Phelps, Elizabeth Stuart 1844-1911 ....DLB-74

Philippe, Charles-Louis 1874-1909 ....DLB-65

Philips, John 1676-1708.............................DLB-95

Phillips, David Graham 1867-1911 ....DLB-9, 12

Phillips, Jayne Anne 1952- Y-80

Phillips, Robert 1938- DLB-105

Phillips, Robert, Finding, Losing,
Reclaiming: A Note on My Poems.................DLB-105

Phillips, Stephen 1864-1915.........................DLB-10

Phillips, Ulrich B. 1877-1934 ....DLB-17

Phillips, Willard 1784-1873.........................DLB-59

Phillips, Sampson and Company....................DLB-49

Phillpotts, Eden 1862-1960 ....DLB-10, 70

Philosophical Library DLB-46

"The Philosophy of Style" (1852), by
Herbert Spencer DLB-57

Phinney, Elihu [publishing house] DLB-49

Phoenix, John (see Derby, George Horatio)

PHYLON (Fourth Quarter, 1950),
The Negro in Literature:
The Current Scene DLB-76

Piccolo, Lucio 1903-1969............................DLB-114

Pickard, Tom 1946- DLB-40

Pickering, William [publishing house] DLB-106

Pickthall, Marjorie 1883-1922 ....DLB-92

Pictorial Printing Company DLB-49

Pike, Albert 1809-1891 ....DLB-74

Pilon, Jean-Guy 1930- DLB-60

Pinckney, Josephine 1895-1957......................DLB-6

Pindar, Peter (see Wolcot, John)

Pinero, Arthur Wing 1855-1934 ....DLB-10

Pinget, Robert 1919- DLB-83

Pinnacle Books DLB-46

Pinsky, Robert 1940- Y-82

Pinter, Harold 1930- DLB-13

Piontek, Heinz 1925- DLB-75

Piozzi, Hester Lynch [Thrale] 1741-1821 ....DLB-104

Piper, H. Beam 1904-1964 ....DLB-8

Piper, Watty DLB-22

Pisar, Samuel 1929- Y-83

Pitkin, Timothy 1766-1847 ....DLB-30

The Pitt Poetry Series: Poetry
    Publishing Today Y-85

Pitter, Ruth 1897- DLB-20

Pix, Mary 1666-1709 ....DLB-80

The Place of Realism in Fiction (1895), by
    George Gissing DLB-18

Plante, David 1940- Y-83

Platen, August von 1796-1835 ....DLB-90

Plath, Sylvia 1932-1963 ....DLB-5, 6

Platt and Munk Company DLB-46

Playboy Press DLB-46

Plays, Playwrights, and Playgoers DLB-84

Playwrights and Professors, by Tom
    Stoppard DLB-13

Playwrights on the Theater DLB-80

Plenzdorf, Ulrich 1934- DLB-75

Plessen, Elizabeth 1944- DLB-75

Plievier, Theodor 1892-1955 ....DLB-69

Plomer, William 1903-1973 ....DLB-20

Plumly, Stanley 1939- DLB-5

Plumpp, Sterling D. 1940- DLB-41

Plunkett, James 1920- DLB-14

Plymell, Charles 1935- DLB-16

Pocket Books DLB-46

Poe, Edgar Allan 1809-1849 ....DLB-3, 59, 73, 74

Poe, James 1921-1980 ....DLB-44

The Poet Laureate of the United States
    Statements from Former Consultants
    in Poetry Y-86

Pohl, Frederik 1919- DLB-8

Poirier, Louis (see Gracq, Julien)

Polanyi, Michael 1891-1976 ....DLB-100

Poliakoff, Stephen 1952- DLB-13

Polidori, John William 1795-1821 ....DLB-116

Polite, Carlene Hatcher 1932- DLB-33

Pollard, Edward A. 1832-1872 ....DLB-30

Pollard, Percival 1869-1911 ....DLB-71

Pollard and Moss DLB-49

Pollock, Sharon 1936- DLB-60

Polonsky, Abraham 1910- DLB-26

Poniatowski, Elena 1933- DLB-113

Poole, Ernest 1880-1950 ....DLB-9

Poore, Benjamin Perley 1820-1887 ....DLB-23

Pope, Alexander 1688-1744 ....DLB-95, 101

Popular Library DLB-46

Porlock, Martin (see MacDonald, Philip)

Porpoise Press DLB-112

Porter, Anna Maria 1780-1832 ....DLB-116

Porter, Eleanor H. 1868-1920 ....DLB-9

Porter, Henry ?-? DLB-62

Porter, Jane 1776-1850 ....DLB-116

Porter, Katherine Anne 1890-1980 ....DLB-4, 9, 102; Y-80

Porter, Peter 1929- DLB-40

Porter, William Sydney 1862-1910 ....DLB-12, 78, 79

Porter, William T. 1809-1858 ....DLB-3, 43

Porter and Coates DLB-49

Portis, Charles 1933- DLB-6

Poston, Ted 1906-1974 ....DLB-51

Postscript to [the Third Edition of] Clarissa
    (1751), by Samuel Richardson DLB-39

Potok, Chaim 1929- DLB-28; Y-84

Potter, David M. 1910-1971 ....DLB-17

Potter, John E., and Company DLB-49

Pottle, Frederick A. 1897-1987 ....DLB-103; Y-87

Poulin, Jacques 1937- DLB-60

Pound, Ezra 1885-1972 ....DLB-4, 45, 63

Powell, Anthony 1905- DLB-15

Pownall, David 1938- DLB-14

Powys, John Cowper 1872-1963 ....DLB-15

Powys, Llewelyn 1884-1939 ....DLB-98

Powys, T. F. 1875-1953 ....DLB-36

The Practice of Biography: An Interview with
    Stanley Weintraub Y-82

The Practice of Biography II: An Interview with
    B. L. Reid Y-83

The Practice of Biography III: An Interview with
    Humphrey Carpenter Y-84

The Practice of Biography IV: An Interview with
    William Manchester Y-85

The Practice of Biography V: An Interview with
    Justin Kaplan Y-86

The Practice of Biography VI: An Interview with
    David Herbert Donald Y-87

Praed, Winthrop Mackworth 1802-1839 ....DLB-96

Praeger Publishers DLB-46

Pratt, E. J. 1882-1964 ....DLB-92

Pratt, Samuel Jackson 1749-1814 ....DLB-39

Preface to *Alwyn* (1780), by Thomas
    Holcroft DLB-39

Preface to *Colonel Jack* (1722), by Daniel
    Defoe DLB-39

Preface to *Evelina* (1778), by Fanny Burney DLB-39

Preface to *Ferdinand Count Fathom* (1753), by
    Tobias Smollett DLB-39

Preface to *Incognita* (1692), by William
    Congreve DLB-39

Preface to *Joseph Andrews* (1742), by
    Henry Fielding DLB-39

Preface to *Moll Flanders* (1722), by Daniel
    Defoe DLB-39

Preface to *Poems* (1853), by Matthew
    Arnold DLB-32

Preface to *Robinson Crusoe* (1719), by Daniel
    Defoe DLB-39

Preface to *Roderick Random* (1748), by Tobias
    Smollett DLB-39

Preface to *Roxana* (1724), by Daniel Defoe DLB-39

Preface to *St. Leon* (1799),
    by William Godwin DLB-39

Preface to Sarah Fielding's *Familiar Letters*
    (1747), by Henry Fielding [excerpt] DLB-39

Preface to Sarah Fielding's *The Adventures of
    David Simple* (1744), by Henry Fielding DLB-39

Preface to *The Cry* (1754), by Sarah Fielding DLB-39

Preface to *The Delicate Distress* (1769), by
    Elizabeth Griffin DLB-39

Preface to *The Disguis'd Prince* (1733), by Eliza
    Haywood [excerpt] DLB-39

Preface to *The Farther Adventures of Robinson
    Crusoe* (1719), by Daniel Defoe DLB-39

Preface to the First Edition of *Pamela* (1740), by
    Samuel Richardson DLB-39

Preface to the First Edition of *The Castle of
    Otranto* (1764), by Horace Walpole DLB-39

Preface to *The History of Romances* (1715), by
    Pierre Daniel Huet [excerpts] DLB-39

Preface to *The Life of Charlotta du Pont* (1723),
    by Penelope Aubin DLB-39

Preface to *The Old English Baron* (1778), by
    Clara Reeve DLB-39

Preface to the Second Edition of *The Castle of
    Otranto* (1765), by Horace Walpole DLB-39

Preface to *The Secret History, of Queen Zarah, and
    the Zarazians* (1705), by Delarivière
    Manley DLB-39

Preface to the Third Edition of *Clarissa* (1751),
    by Samuel Richardson [excerpt] DLB-39

Preface to *The Works of Mrs. Davys* (1725), by
    Mary Davys DLB-39

Preface to Volume 1 of *Clarissa* (1747), by
    Samuel Richardson DLB-39

Preface to Volume 3 of *Clarissa* (1748), by
    Samuel Richardson DLB-39

Préfontaine, Yves 1937- DLB-53

Prelutsky, Jack 1940- DLB-61

Premises, by Michael Hamburger DLB-66

Prentice, George D. 1802-1870 ....DLB-43

Prentice-Hall DLB-46

Prescott, William Hickling 1796-1859 ....DLB-1, 30, 59

The Present State of the English Novel (1892),
    by George Saintsbury......................................DLB-18

Preston, Thomas 1537-1598...................................DLB-62

Price, Reynolds 1933- DLB-2

Price, Richard 1949- Y-81

Priest, Christopher 1943- DLB-14

Priestley, J. B. 1894-1984................DLB-10, 34, 77, 100; Y-84

Prime, Benjamin Young 1733-1791 ....DLB-31

Prince, F. T. 1912- DLB-20

Prince, Thomas 1687-1758....................................DLB-24

The Principles of Success in Literature (1865), by
    George Henry Lewes [excerpt] DLB-57

Prior, Matthew 1664-1721 ....DLB-95

Pritchard, William H. 1932- DLB-111

Pritchett, V. S. 1900- DLB-15

Procter, Adelaide Anne 1825-1864............................DLB-32

Procter, Bryan Waller 1787-1874.............................DLB-96

The Profession of Authorship:
    Scribblers for Bread Y-89

The Progress of Romance (1785), by Clara Reeve
    [excerpt] DLB-39

Prokosch, Frederic 1906-1989................................DLB-48

The Proletarian Novel DLB-9

Propper, Dan 1937- DLB-16

The Prospect of Peace (1778), by Joel Barlow.............DLB-37

Proud, Robert 1728-1813 ....DLB-30

Proust, Marcel 1871-1922....................................DLB-65

Prynne, J. H. 1936- DLB-40

Przybyszewski, Stanislaw 1868-1927.............................DLB-66

Pseudo-Dionysius the Areopagite floruit circa 500.....DLB-115

The Public Lending Right in America
    Statement by Sen. Charles McC. Mathias, Jr.
    PLR and the Meaning of Literary Property
    Statements on PLR by American Writers...................Y-83

The Public Lending Right in the United Kingdom
    Public Lending Right: The First Year in the
       United Kingdom......................................Y-83

The Publication of English Renaissance
    Plays..DLB-62

Publications and Social Movements
    [Transcendentalism].....................................DLB-1

Publishers and Agents: The Columbia
    Connection Y-87

Publishing Fiction at LSU Press Y-87

Pugin, A. Welby 1812-1852 ....DLB-55

Puig, Manuel 1932-1990...............................DLB-113

Pulitzer, Joseph 1847-1911...........................DLB-23

Pulitzer, Joseph, Jr. 1885-1955 ....DLB-29

Pulitzer Prizes for the Novel, 1917-1945.........................DLB-9

Purdy, Al 1918- DLB-88

Purdy, James 1923- DLB-2

Pusey, Edward Bouverie 1800-1882 ....DLB-55

Putnam, George Palmer 1814-1872...................DLB-3, 79

Putnam, Samuel 1892-1950................................DLB-4

G. P. Putnam's Sons [U.S.] DLB-49

G. P. Putnam's Sons [U.K.] DLB-106

Puzo, Mario 1920- DLB-6

Pyle, Ernie 1900-1945...................................DLB-29

Pyle, Howard 1853-1911 ....DLB-42

Pym, Barbara 1913-1980.....................DLB-14; Y-87

Pynchon, Thomas 1937- DLB-2

Pyramid Books...DLB-46

Pyrnelle, Louise-Clarke 1850-1907 ....DLB-42

Q

Quad, M. (see Lewis, Charles B.)

The Quarterly Review 1809-1967 ....DLB-110

Quasimodo, Salvatore 1901-1968....................DLB-114

The Queen City Publishing House DLB-49

Queneau, Raymond 1903-1976.......................DLB-72

Quesnel, Joseph 1746-1809............................DLB-99

The Question of American Copyright
    in the Nineteenth Century
      Headnote
      Preface, by George Haven Putnam
      The Evolution of Copyright, by Brander
        Matthews
      Summary of Copyright Legislation in the
        United States, by R. R. Bowker
      Analysis of the Provisions of the Copyright
        Law of 1891, by George Haven Putnam
      The Contest for International Copyright,
        by George Haven Putnam
      Cheap Books and Good Books,
        by Brander Matthews...........................DLB-49

Quin, Ann 1936-1973....................................DLB-14

Quincy, Samuel, of Georgia ?-?......................DLB-31

Quincy, Samuel, of Massachusetts 1734-1789 ....DLB-31

Quintana, Leroy V. 1944- DLB-82

Quist, Harlin, Books.......................................DLB-46

Quoirez, Françoise (see Sagan, Françoise)

R

Rabe, David 1940- DLB-7

Radcliffe, Ann 1764-1823...............................DLB-39

Raddall, Thomas 1903- DLB-68

Radiguet, Raymond 1903-1923 ....DLB-65

Radványi, Netty Reiling (see Seghers, Anna)

Raimund, Ferdinand Jakob 1790-1836 ....DLB-90

Raine, Craig 1944- DLB-40

Raine, Kathleen 1908- DLB-20

Ralph, Julian 1853-1903.................................DLB-23

Ralph Waldo Emerson in 1982........................Y-82

Rambler, no. 4 (1750), by Samuel Johnson
    [excerpt] DLB-39

Ramée, Marie Louise de la (see Ouida)

Ramler, Karl Wilhelm 1725-1798 ....DLB-97

Rampersad, Arnold 1941- DLB-111

Ramsay, Allan 1684 or 1685-1758 ....DLB-95

Ramsay, David 1749-1815 ....DLB-30

Rand, Avery and Company.............................DLB-49

Rand McNally and Company.........................DLB-49

Randall, Dudley 1914- DLB-41

Randall, Henry S. 1811-1876.........................DLB-30

Randall, James G. 1881-1953 ....DLB-17

The Randall Jarrell Symposium: A Small
    Collection of Randall Jarrells
      Excerpts From Papers Delivered at

the Randall Jarrell Symposium...............................Y-86

Randolph, A. Philip 1889-1979................................DLB-91

Randolph, Anson D. F. [publishing house] DLB-49

Randolph, Thomas 1605-1635.................................DLB-58

Random House DLB-46

Ranlet, Henry [publishing house] DLB-49

Ransom, John Crowe 1888-1974.........................DLB-45, 63

Raphael, Frederic 1931- DLB-14

Raphaelson, Samson 1896-1983 ....DLB-44

Raskin, Ellen 1928-1984.......................................DLB-52

Rattigan, Terence 1911-1977.................................DLB-13

Rawlings, Marjorie Kinnan
    1896-1953 ....DLB-9, 22, 102

Raworth, Tom 1938- DLB-40

Ray, David 1932- DLB-5

Ray, Gordon N. 1915-1986 ....DLB-103

Ray, Henrietta Cordelia 1849-1916 ....DLB-50

Raymond, Henry J. 1820-1869 ....DLB-43, 79

Raymond Chandler Centenary Tributes
    from Michael Avallone, James Elroy, Joe Gores,
    and William F. Nolan Y-88

Reach, Angus 1821-1856......................................DLB-70

Read, Herbert 1893-1968......................................DLB-20

Read, Opie 1852-1939..DLB-23

Read, Piers Paul 1941- DLB-14

Reade, Charles 1814-1884.....................................DLB-21

Reader's Digest Condensed Books............................DLB-46

Reading, Peter 1946- DLB-40

Reaney, James 1926- DLB-68

Rèbora, Clemente 1885-1957 ....DLB-114

Rechy, John 1934- Y-82

The Recovery of Literature:
    Criticism in the 1990s:
    A Symposium Y-91

Redding, J. Saunders 1906-1988 ....DLB-63, 76

Redfield, J. S. [publishing house]..........................DLB-49

Redgrove, Peter 1932- DLB-40

Redmon, Anne 1943- Y-86

Redmond, Eugene B. 1937- DLB-41

Redpath, James [publishing house].........................DLB-49

Reed, Henry 1808-1854...DLB-59

Reed, Henry 1914- DLB-27

Reed, Ishmael 1938- DLB-2, 5, 33; DS-8

Reed, Sampson 1800-1880 ....DLB-1

Reedy, William Marion 1862-1920..........................DLB-91

Reese, Lizette Woodworth 1856-1935............................DLB-54

Reese, Thomas 1742-1796......................................DLB-37

Reeve, Clara 1729-1807 ....DLB-39

Reeves, John 1926- DLB-88

Regnery, Henry, Company DLB-46

Reid, Alastair 1926- DLB-27

Reid, B. L. 1918-1990...DLB-111

Reid, Christopher 1949- DLB-40

Reid, Helen Rogers 1882-1970 ....DLB-29

Reid, James ?-? DLB-31

Reid, Mayne 1818-1883 ....DLB-21

Reid, Thomas 1710-1796..DLB-31

Reid, Whitelaw 1837-1912......................................DLB-23

Reilly and Lee Publishing Company.........................DLB-46

Reimann, Brigitte 1933-1973...................................DLB-75

Reisch, Walter 1903-1983 ....DLB-44

Remarque, Erich Maria 1898-1970 ....DLB-56

"Re-meeting of Old Friends": The Jack Kerouac
    Conference Y-82

Remington, Frederic 1861-1909...............................DLB-12

Renaud, Jacques 1943- DLB-60

Renault, Mary 1905-1983 ....Y-83

Rendell, Ruth 1930- DLB-87

Representative Men and Women: A Historical
    Perspective on the British Novel,
    1930-1960..DLB-15

(Re-)Publishing Orwell...Y-86

Reuter, Gabriele 1859-1941.....................................DLB-66

Revell, Fleming H., Company DLB-49

Reventlow, Franziska Gräfin zu
    1871-1918..DLB-66

Review of Reviews Office DLB-112

Review of [Samuel Richardson's] *Clarissa* (1748),
    by Henry Fielding..DLB-39

The Revolt (1937), by Mary
    Colum [excerpts]...DLB-36

Rexroth, Kenneth 1905-1982.....................DLB-16, 48; Y-82

Rey, H. A. 1898-1977 ....DLB-22

Reynal and Hitchcock..DLB-46

Reynolds, G. W. M. 1814-1879 ....DLB-21

Reynolds, John Hamilton 1794-1852.........................DLB-96

Reynolds, Mack 1917- DLB-8

Reynolds, Sir Joshua 1723-1792...............................DLB-104

Reznikoff, Charles 1894-1976.............................DLB-28, 45

"Rhetoric" (1828; revised, 1859), by

Thomas de Quincey [excerpt]................DLB-57

Rhett, Robert Barnwell 1800-1876 ....DLB-43

Rhode, John 1884-1964................DLB-77

Rhodes, James Ford 1848-1927................DLB-47

Rhys, Jean 1890-1979................DLB-36, 117

Ricardo, David 1772-1823................DLB-107

Ricardou, Jean 1932-................DLB-83

Rice, Elmer 1892-1967................DLB-4, 7

Rice, Grantland 1880-1954................DLB-29

Rich, Adrienne 1929-................DLB-5, 67

Richards, David Adams 1950-................DLB-53

Richards, George circa 1760-1814................DLB-37

Richards, I. A. 1893-1979................DLB-27

Richards, Laura E. 1850-1943................DLB-42

Richards, William Carey 1818-1892................DLB-73

Richards, Grant [publishing house]................DLB-112

Richardson, Charles F. 1851-1913................DLB-71

Richardson, Dorothy M. 1873-1957................DLB-36

Richardson, Jack 1935-................DLB-7

Richardson, John 1796-1852................DLB-99

Richardson, Samuel 1689-1761................DLB 39

Richardson, Willis 1889-1977................DLB-51

Richler, Mordecai 1931-................DLB-53

Richter, Conrad 1890-1968................DLB-9

Richter, Hans Werner 1908-................DLB-69

Richter, Johann Paul Friedrich 1763-1825................DLB-94

Rickerby, Joseph [publishing house]................DLB-106

Rickword, Edgell 1898-1982................DLB-20

Riddell, John (see Ford, Corey)

Ridge, Lola 1873-1941................DLB-54

Riding, Laura (see Jackson, Laura Riding)

Ridler, Anne 1912-................DLB-27

Ridruego, Dionisio 1912-1975................DLB-108

Riel, Louis 1844-1885................DLB-99

Riffaterre, Michael 1924-................DLB-67

Riis, Jacob 1849-1914................DLB-23

Riker, John C. [publishing house]................DLB-49

Riley, John 1938-1978................DLB-40

Rilke, Rainer Maria 1875-1926................DLB-81

Rinehart and Company................DLB-46

Ringuet 1895-1960................DLB-68

Ringwood, Gwen Pharis 1910-1984................DLB-88

Rinser, Luise 1911-................DLB-69

Ríos, Isabella 1948-................DLB-82

Ripley, Arthur 1895-1961................DLB-44

Ripley, George 1802-1880................DLB-1, 64, 73

The Rising Glory of America: Three Poems................DLB-37

The Rising Glory of America: Written in 1771 (1786), by Hugh Henry Brackenridge and Philip Freneau................DLB-37

Riskin, Robert 1897-1955................DLB-26

Risse, Heinz 1898-................DLB-69

Ritchie, Anna Mowatt 1819-1870................DLB-3

Ritchie, Anne Thackeray 1837-1919................DLB-18

Ritchie, Thomas 1778-1854................DLB-43

Rites of Passage [on William Saroyan]................Y-83

The Ritz Paris Hemingway Award................Y-85

Rivard, Adjutor 1868-1945................DLB-92

Rivera, Tomás 1935-1984................DLB-82

Rivers, Conrad Kent 1933-1968................DLB-41

Riverside Press................DLB-49

Rivington, James circa 1724-1802................DLB-43

Rivkin, Allen 1903-1990................DLB-26

Roa Bastos, Augusto 1917-................DLB-113

Robbe-Grillet, Alain 1922-................DLB-83

Robbins, Tom 1936-................Y-80

Roberts, Charles G. D. 1860-1943................DLB-92

Roberts, Dorothy 1906-................DLB-88

Roberts, Elizabeth Madox 1881-1941................DLB-9, 54, 102

Roberts, Kenneth 1885-1957................DLB-9

Roberts Brothers................DLB-49

Robertson, A. M., and Company................DLB-49

Robertson, William 1721-1793................DLB-104

Robinson, Casey 1903-1979................DLB-44

Robinson, Edwin Arlington 1869-1935................DLB-54

Robinson, Henry Crabb 1775-1867................DLB-107

Robinson, James Harvey 1863-1936................DLB-47

Robinson, Lennox 1886-1958................DLB-10

Robinson, Mabel Louise 1874-1962................DLB-22

Robinson, Therese 1797-1870................DLB-59

Roblès, Emmanuel 1914-................DLB-83

Roccatagliata Ceccardi, Ceccardo 1871-1919................DLB-114

Rodgers, Carolyn M. 1945-................DLB-41

Rodgers, W. R. 1909-1969................DLB-20

Rodriguez, Richard 1944-................DLB-82

Roethke, Theodore 1908-1963................DLB-5

Rogers, Pattiann 1940- DLB-105

Rogers, Samuel 1763-1855 ....DLB-93

Rogers, Will 1879-1935 ....DLB-11

Rohmer, Sax 1883-1959 ....DLB-70

Roiphe, Anne 1935- Y-80

Rojas, Arnold R. 1896-1988 ....DLB-82

Rolfe, Frederick William 1860-1913 ....DLB-34

Rolland, Romain 1866-1944 ....DLB-65

Rolvaag, O. E. 1876-1931 ....DLB-9

Romains, Jules 1885-1972 ....DLB-65

Roman, A., and Company DLB-49

Romero, Orlando 1945- DLB-82

Roosevelt, Theodore 1858-1919 ....DLB-47

Root, Waverley 1903-1982...............................DLB-4

Roquebrune, Robert de 1889-1978................DLB-68

Rosa, João Guimarãres 1908-1967 ....DLB-113

Rose, Reginald 1920- DLB-26

Rosei, Peter 1946- DLB-85

Rosen, Norma 1925- DLB-28

Rosenberg, Isaac 1890-1918..........................DLB-20

Rosenfeld, Isaac 1918-1956...........................DLB-28

Rosenthal, M. L. 1917- DLB-5

Ross, Leonard Q. (see Rosten, Leo)

Ross, Sinclair 1908- DLB-88

Ross, W. W. E. 1894-1966 ....DLB-88

Rossen, Robert 1908-1966.............................DLB-26

Rossetti, Christina 1830-1894.......................DLB-35

Rossetti, Dante Gabriel 1828-1882................DLB-35

Rossner, Judith 1935- DLB-6

Rosten, Leo 1908- DLB-11

Bertram Rota and His Bookshop........................Y-91

Roth, Gerhard 1942- DLB-85

Roth, Henry 1906?- DLB-28

Roth, Joseph 1894-1939 ....DLB-85

Roth, Philip 1933- DLB-2, 28; Y-82

Rothenberg, Jerome 1931- DLB-5

Routhier, Adolphe-Basile 1839-1920.............DLB-99

Routier, Simone 1901-1987 ....DLB-88

Routledge, George, and Sons DLB-106

Rowe, Elizabeth Singer 1674-1737............DLB-39, 95

Rowe, Nicholas 1674-1718.............................DLB-84

Rowlandson, Mary circa 1635-circa 1678 .....DLB-24

Rowley, William circa 1585-1626 ....DLB-58

Rowson, Susanna Haswell circa 1762-1824 ....DLB-37

Roy, Camille 1870-1943.................................DLB-92

Roy, Gabrielle 1909-1983 ....DLB-68

Roy, Jules 1907- DLB-83

The Royal Court Theatre and the English
Stage Company DLB-13

The Royal Court Theatre and the New
Drama...DLB-10

The Royal Shakespeare Company
at the Swan Y-88

Royall, Anne 1769-1854 ....DLB-43

The Roycroft Printing Shop..........................DLB-49

Rubens, Bernice 1928- DLB-14

Rudd and Carleton DLB-49

Rudkin, David 1936- DLB-13

Ruffin, Josephine St. Pierre 1842-1924 ....DLB-79

Ruggles, Henry Joseph 1813-1906................DLB-64

Rukeyser, Muriel 1913-1980 ....DLB-48

Rule, Jane 1931- DLB-60

Rulfo, Juan 1918-1986.................................DLB-113

Rumaker, Michael 1932- DLB-16

Rumens, Carol 1944- DLB-40

Runyon, Damon 1880-1946 ....DLB-11, 86

Rush, Benjamin 1746-1813 ....DLB-37

Rusk, Ralph L. 1888-1962 ....DLB-103

Ruskin, John 1819-1900 ....DLB-55

Russ, Joanna 1937- DLB-8

Russell, B. B., and Company.........................DLB-49

Russell, Benjamin 1761-1845 ....DLB-43

Russell, Bertrand 1872-1970......................DLB-100

Russell, Charles Edward 1860-1941.............DLB-25

Russell, George William (see AE)

Russell, R. H., and Son.................................DLB-49

Rutherford, Mark 1831-1913........................DLB-18

Ryan, Michael 1946- Y-82

Ryan, Oscar 1904- DLB-68

Ryga, George 1932- DLB-60

Rymer, Thomas 1643?-1713.........................DLB-101

Ryskind, Morrie 1895-1985...........................DLB-26

S

The Saalfield Publishing Company................DLB-46

Saba, Umberto 1883-1957 ....DLB-114

Saberhagen, Fred 1930- DLB-8

Sackler, Howard 1929-1982 ....DLB-7

Sackville, Thomas 1536-1608
    and Norton, Thomas 1532-1584...........DLB-62

Sackville-West, V. 1892-1962.....................DLB-34

Sadlier, D. and J., and Company DLB-49

Sadlier, Mary Anne 1820-1903 ....DLB-99

Saffin, John circa 1626-1710 ....DLB-24

Sagan, Françoise 1935- DLB-83

Sage, Robert 1899-1962................................DLB-4

Sagel, Jim 1947- DLB-82

Sahagún, Carlos 1938- DLB-108

Sahkomaapii, Piitai (see Highwater, Jamake)

Sahl, Hans 1902- DLB-69

Said, Edward W. 1935- DLB-67

Saiko, George 1892-1962............................DLB-85

St. Dominic's Press DLB-112

Saint-Exupéry, Antoine de 1900-1944.........DLB-72

St. Johns, Adela Rogers 1894-1988 ....DLB-29

St. Martin's Press..DLB-46

St. Omer, Garth 1931- DLB-117

Saint Pierre, Michel de 1916-1987 ....DLB-83

Saintsbury, George 1845-1933 ....DLB-57

Saki (see Munro, H. H.)

Salaam, Kalamu ya 1947- DLB-38

Salas, Floyd 1931- DLB-82

Salemson, Harold J. 1910-1988...................DLB-4

Salinas, Luis Omar 1937- DLB-82

Salinger, J. D. 1919-.............................DLB-2, 102

Salt, Waldo 1914- DLB-44

Salustri, Carlo Alberto (see Trilussa)

Salverson, Laura Goodman 1890-1970........DLB-92

Sampson, Richard Henry (see Hull, Richard)

Samuels, Ernest 1903- DLB-111

Sanborn, Franklin Benjamin 1831-1917.......DLB-1

Sánchez, Ricardo 1941- DLB-82

Sanchez, Sonia 1934- DLB-41; DS-8

Sand, George 1804-1876 ....DLB-119

Sandburg, Carl 1878-1967 ....DLB-17, 54

Sanders, Ed 1939- DLB-16

Sandoz, Mari 1896-1966.............................DLB-9

Sandwell, B. K. 1876-1954 ....DLB-92

Sandys, George 1578-1644 ....DLB-24

Sangster, Charles 1822-1893 ....DLB-99

Santayana, George 1863-1952................DLB-54, 71

Santmyer, Helen Hooven 1895-1986................Y-84

Sapir, Edward 1884-1939 ....DLB-92

Sapper (see McNeile, Herman Cyril)

Sarduy, Severo 1937- DLB-113

Sargent, Pamela 1948- DLB-8

Saroyan, William 1908-1981 ....DLB-7, 9, 86; Y-81

Sarraute, Nathalie 1900- DLB-83

Sarrazin, Albertine 1937-1967 ....DLB-83

Sarton, May 1912- DLB-48; Y-81

Sartre, Jean-Paul 1905-1980.......................DLB-72

Sassoon, Siegfried 1886-1967.....................DLB-20

Saturday Review Press DLB-46

Saunders, James 1925- DLB-13

Saunders, John Monk 1897-1940................DLB-26

Saunders, Margaret Marshall 1861-1947.......DLB-92

Saunders and Otley.....................................DLB-106

Savage, James 1784-1873...........................DLB-30

Savage, Marmion W. 1803?-1872...............DLB-21

Savage, Richard 1697?-1743.......................DLB-95

Savard, Félix-Antoine 1896-1982 ....DLB-68

Sawyer, Ruth 1880-1970.............................DLB-22

Sayers, Dorothy L. 1893-1957.........DLB-10, 36, 77, 100

Sayles, John Thomas 1950- DLB-44

Sbarbaro, Camillo 1888-1967.....................DLB-114

Scannell, Vernon 1922- DLB-27

Scarry, Richard 1919- DLB-61

Schaeffer, Albrecht 1885-1950....................DLB-66

Schaeffer, Susan Fromberg 1941- DLB-28

Schaper, Edzard 1908-1984 ....DLB-69

Scharf, J. Thomas 1843-1898......................DLB-47

Schelling, Friedrich Wilhelm Joseph von
    1775-1854...DLB-90

Schickele, René 1883-1940 ....DLB-66

Schiller, Friedrich 1759-1805 ....DLB-94

Schlaf, Johannes 1862-1941 ....DLB-118

Schlegel, August Wilhelm 1767-1845 ....DLB-94

Schlegel, Dorothea 1763-1839....................DLB-90

Schlegel, Friedrich 1772-1829....................DLB-90

Schleiermacher, Friedrich 1768-1834 ....DLB-90

Schlesinger, Arthur M., Jr. 1917- DLB-17

Schlumberger, Jean 1877-1968 ....DLB-65

Schmid, Eduard Hermann Wilhelm
    (see Edschmid, Kasimir)

Schmidt, Arno 1914-1979........................DLB-69

Schmidt, Michael 1947- DLB-40

Schmidtbonn, Wilhelm August 1876-1952.................DLB-118

Schmitz, James H. 1911- DLB-8

Schnitzler, Arthur 1862-1931........................DLB-81, 118

Schnurre, Wolfdietrich 1920- DLB-69

Schocken Books........................DLB-46

Schönbeck, Virgilio (see Giotti, Virgilio)

Schönherr, Karl 1867-1943 ....DLB-118

Scholartis Press........................DLB-112

The Schomburg Center for Research
  in Black Culture........................DLB-76

Schopenhauer, Arthur 1788-1860 ....DLB-90

Schopenhauer, Johanna 1766-1838 ....DLB-90

Schorer, Mark 1908-1977........................DLB-103

Schouler, James 1839-1920 ....DLB-47

Schrader, Paul 1946- DLB-44

Schreiner, Olive 1855-1920 ....DLB-18

Schroeder, Andreas 1946- DLB-53

Schubart, Christian Friedrich Daniel
  1739-1791........................DLB-97

Schubert, Gotthilf Heinrich 1780-1860 ....DLB-90

Schulberg, Budd 1914- DLB-6, 26, 28; Y-81

Schulte, F. J., and Company........................DLB-49

Schurz, Carl 1829-1906 ....DLB-23

Schuyler, George S. 1895-1977........................DLB-29, 51

Schuyler, James 1923-1991........................DLB-5

Schwartz, Delmore 1913-1966........................DLB-28, 48

Schwartz, Jonathan 1938- Y-82

Science Fantasy........................DLB-8

Science-Fiction Fandom and Conventions DLB-8

Science-Fiction Fanzines: The Time Binders........................DLB-8

Science-Fiction Films........................DLB-8

Science Fiction Writers of America and the
  Nebula Awards........................DLB-8

Scott, Dixon 1881-1915........................DLB-98

Scott, Duncan Campbell 1862-1947........................DLB-92

Scott, Evelyn 1893-1963 ....DLB-9, 48

Scott, F. R. 1899-1985........................DLB-88

Scott, Frederick George 1861-1944........................DLB-92

Scott, Harvey W. 1838-1910........................DLB-23

Scott, Paul 1920-1978........................DLB-14

Scott, Sarah 1723-1795........................DLB-39

Scott, Tom 1918- DLB-27

Scott, Sir Walter 1771-1832........................DLB-93, 107, 116

Scott, William Bell 1811-1890........................DLB-32

Scott, Walter, Publishing Company Limited........................DLB-112

Scott, William R. [publishing house]........................DLB-46

Scott-Heron, Gil 1949- DLB-41

Charles Scribner's Sons........................DLB-49

Scripps, E. W. 1854-1926 ....DLB-25

Scudder, Horace Elisha 1838-1902........................DLB-42, 71

Scudder, Vida Dutton 1861-1954 ....DLB-71

Scupham, Peter 1933- DLB-40

Seabrook, William 1886-1945 ....DLB-4

Seabury, Samuel 1729-1796 ....DLB-31

Sears, Edward I. 1819?-1876........................DLB-79

Sears Publishing Company DLB-46

Seaton, George 1911-1979........................DLB-44

Seaton, William Winston 1785-1866........................DLB-43

Secker, Martin, and Warburg Limited........................DLB-112

Secker, Martin [publishing house]........................DLB-112

Sedgwick, Arthur George 1844-1915........................DLB-64

Sedgwick, Catharine Maria 1789-1867 ....DLB-1, 74

Sedgwick, Ellery 1872-1930........................DLB-91

Seeger, Alan 1888-1916........................DLB-45

Seers, Eugene (see Dantin, Louis)

Segal, Erich 1937- Y-86

Seghers, Anna 1900-1983........................DLB-69

Seid, Ruth (see Sinclair, Jo)

Seidel, Frederick Lewis 1936- Y-84

Seidel, Ina 1885-1974........................DLB-56

Seizin Press........................DLB-112

Séjour, Victor 1817-1874........................DLB-50

Séjour Marcou et Ferrand,
  Juan Victor (see Séjour, Victor)

Selby, Hubert, Jr. 1928- DLB-2

Selden, George 1929-1989........................DLB-52

Selected English-Language Little Magazines and
  Newspapers [France, 1920-1939]........................DLB-4

Selected Humorous Magazines (1820-1950)........................DLB-11

Selected Science-Fiction Magazines and
  Anthologies DLB-8

Seligman, Edwin R. A. 1861-1939 ....DLB-47

Seltzer, Chester E. (see Muro, Amado)

Seltzer, Thomas [publishing house]........................DLB-46

Senancour, Etienne de 1770-1846 ....DLB-119

Sendak, Maurice 1928- DLB-61

Senécal, Eva 1905- DLB-92

Sensation Novels (1863), by H. L. Manse DLB-21

Seredy, Kate 1899-1975..................................DLB-22

Serling, Rod 1924-1975 ....DLB-26

Service, Robert 1874-1958..................................DLB-92

Seton, Ernest Thompson 1860-1942..........................DLB-92

Settle, Mary Lee 1918- DLB-6

Seume, Johann Gottfried 1763-1810 ....DLB-94

Seuss, Dr. (see Geisel, Theodor Seuss)

Sewall, Joseph 1688-1769 ....DLB-24

Sewall, Richard B. 1908- DLB-111

Sewell, Samuel 1652-1730 ....DLB-24

Sex, Class, Politics, and Religion [in the British
    Novel, 1930-1959]..................................DLB-15

Sexton, Anne 1928-1974 ....DLB-5

Shaara, Michael 1929-1988 ....Y-83

Shadwell, Thomas 1641?-1692..................................DLB-80

Shaffer, Anthony 1926- DLB-13

Shaffer, Peter 1926- DLB-13

Shaftesbury, Anthony Ashley Cooper,
    Third Earl of 1671-1713 ....DLB-101

Shairp, Mordaunt 1887-1939..................................DLB-10

Shakespeare, William 1564-1616 ....DLB-62

Shakespeare Head Press..................................DLB-112

Shange, Ntozake 1948- DLB-38

Shapiro, Karl 1913- DLB-48

Sharon Publications DLB-46

Sharpe, Tom 1928- DLB-14

Shaw, Albert 1857-1947 ....DLB-91

Shaw, Bernard 1856-1950..................................DLB-10, 57

Shaw, Henry Wheeler 1818-1885 ....DLB-11

Shaw, Irwin 1913-1984..................................DLB-6, 102; Y-84

Shaw, Robert 1927-1978 ....DLB-13, 14

Shay, Frank [publishing house]..................................DLB-46

Shea, John Gilmary 1824-1892 ....DLB-30

Sheaffer, Louis 1912- DLB-103

Shearing, Joseph 1886-1952..................................DLB-70

Shebbeare, John 1709-1788..................................DLB-39

Sheckley, Robert 1928- DLB-8

Shedd, William G. T. 1820-1894 ....DLB-64

Sheed, Wilfred 1930- DLB-6

Sheed and Ward [U.S.]..................................DLB-46

Sheed and Ward Limited [U.K.] DLB-112

Sheldon, Alice B. (see Tiptree, James, Jr.)

Sheldon, Edward 1886-1946 ....DLB-7

Sheldon and Company DLB-49

Shelley, Mary Wollstonecraft 1797-1851 ....DLB-110, 116

Shelley, Percy Bysshe 1792-1822 ....DLB-96, 110

Shenstone, William 1714-1763..................................DLB-95

Shepard, Sam 1943- DLB-7

Shepard, Thomas I 1604 or 1605-1649..........................DLB-24

Shepard, Thomas II 1635-1677..................................DLB-24

Shepard, Clark and Brown..................................DLB-49

Sheridan, Frances 1724-1766..................................DLB-39, 84

Sheridan, Richard Brinsley 1751-1816 ....DLB-89

Sherman, Francis 1871-1926..................................DLB-92

Sherriff, R. C. 1896-1975 ....DLB-10

Sherwood, Robert 1896-1955..................................DLB-7, 26

Shiels, George 1886-1949 ....DLB-10

Shillaber, B.[enjamin] P.[enhallow]
    1814-1890..................................DLB-1, 11

Shine, Ted 1931- DLB-38

Ship, Reuben 1915-1975 ....DLB-88

Shirer, William L. 1904- DLB-4

Shirley, James 1596-1666 ....DLB-58

Shockley, Ann Allen 1927- DLB-33

Shorthouse, Joseph Henry 1834-1903 ....DLB-18

Showalter, Elaine 1941- DLB-67

Shulevitz, Uri 1935- DLB-61

Shulman, Max 1919-1988 ....DLB-11

Shute, Henry A. 1856-1943..................................DLB-9

Shuttle, Penelope 1947- DLB-14, 40

Sidgwick and Jackson Limited..................................DLB-112

Sidney, Margaret (see Lothrop, Harriet M.)

Sidney's Press DLB-49

Siegfried Loraine Sassoon: A Centenary Essay
    Tributes from Vivien F. Clarke and
        Michael Thorpe..................................Y-86

Sierra Club Books..................................DLB-49

Siger of Brabant circa 1240-circa 1284..................DLB-115

Sigourney, Lydia Howard (Huntley)
    1791-1865 ....DLB-1, 42, 73

Silkin, Jon 1930- DLB-27

Silliphant, Stirling 1918- DLB-26

Sillitoe, Alan 1928- DLB-14

Silman, Roberta 1934- DLB-28

Silverberg, Robert 1935- DLB-8

Silverman, Kenneth 1936- DLB-111

Simak, Clifford D. 1904-1988 ....DLB-8

Simcoe, Elizabeth 1762-1850..DLB-99

Simcox, George Augustus 1841-1905 ....DLB-35

Sime, Jessie Georgina 1868-1958 ....DLB-92

Simenon, Georges 1903-1989...........................DLB-72; Y-89

Simic, Charles 1938- DLB-105

Simic, Charles, Images and "Images" DLB-105

Simmel, Johannes Mario 1924- DLB-69

Simmons, Ernest J. 1903-1972 ....DLB-103

Simmons, Herbert Alfred 1930- DLB-33

Simmons, James 1933- DLB-40

Simms, William Gilmore 1806-1870

....DLB-3, 30, 59, 73

Simms and M'Intyre DLB-106

Simon, Claude 1913- DLB-83

Simon, Neil 1927- DLB-7

Simon and Schuster DLB-46

Simons, Katherine Drayton Mayrant 1890-1969 ....Y-83

Simpson, Helen 1897-1940...DLB-77

Simpson, Louis 1923- DLB-5

Simpson, N. F. 1919- DLB-13

Sims, George 1923- DLB-87

Sims, George R. 1847-1922 ....DLB-35, 70

Sinclair, Andrew 1935- DLB-14

Sinclair, Bertrand William 1881-1972 ....DLB-92

Sinclair, Jo 1913- DLB-28

Sinclair Lewis Centennial Conference................................Y-85

Sinclair, Lister 1921- DLB-88

Sinclair, May 1863-1946 ....DLB-36

Sinclair, Upton 1878-1968...DLB-9

Sinclair, Upton [publishing house]...............................DLB-46

Singer, Isaac Bashevis 1904-1991 ....DLB-6, 28, 52; Y-91

Singmaster, Elsie 1879-1958 ....DLB-9

Sinisgalli, Leonardo 1908-1981 ....DLB-114

Siodmak, Curt 1902- DLB-44

Sissman, L. E. 1928-1976 ....DLB-5

Sisson, C. H. 1914- DLB-27

Sitwell, Edith 1887-1964..DLB-20

Sitwell, Osbert 1892-1969..DLB-100

Skeffington, William [publishing house]......................DLB-106

Skelton, Robin 1925- DLB-27, 53

Skinner, Constance Lindsay 1877-1939 ....DLB-92

Skinner, John Stuart 1788-1851....................................DLB-73

Skipsey, Joseph 1832-1903 ....DLB-35

Slade, Bernard 1930- DLB-53

Slater, Patrick 1880-1951..DLB-68

Slavitt, David 1935- DLB-5, 6

Sleigh, Burrows Willcocks Arthur
          1821-1869 ....DLB-99

A Slender Thread of Hope: The Kennedy
          Center Black Theatre Project...............................DLB-38

Slesinger, Tess 1905-1945..DLB-102

Slick, Sam (see Haliburton, Thomas Chandler)

Sloane, William, Associates..DLB-46

Small, Maynard and Company.....................................DLB-49

Small Presses in Great Britain and Ireland,
          1960-1985 ....DLB-40

Small Presses I: Jargon Society Y-84

Small Presses II: The Spirit That
          Moves Us Press...Y-85

Small Presses III: Pushcart Press Y-87

Smart, Christopher 1722-1771 ....DLB-109

Smart, Elizabeth 1913-1986...DLB-88

Smiles, Samuel 1812-1904 ....DLB-55

Smith, A. J. M. 1902-1980..DLB-88

Smith, Adam 1723-1790...DLB-104

Smith, Alexander 1829-1867....................................DLB-32, 55

Smith, Betty 1896-1972..Y-82

Smith, Carol Sturm 1938- Y-81

Smith, Charles Henry 1826-1903.................................DLB-11

Smith, Charlotte 1749-1806 ....DLB-39, 109

Smith, Cordwainer 1913-1966.....................................DLB-8

Smith, Dave 1942- DLB-5

Smith, Dodie 1896- DLB-10

Smith, Doris Buchanan 1934- DLB-52

Smith, E. E. 1890-1965...DLB-8

Smith, Elihu Hubbard 1771-1798................................DLB-37

Smith, Elizabeth Oakes (Prince) 1806-1893.................DLB-1

Smith, George O. 1911-1981..DLB-8

Smith, Goldwin 1823-1910 ....DLB-99

Smith, H. Allen 1907-1976 ....DLB-11, 29

Smith, Harrison, and Robert Haas
          [publishing house]...DLB-46

Smith, Horatio (Horace) 1779-1849............................DLB-116

Smith, Horatio (Horace) 1779-1849 and
          James Smith 1775-1839..DLB-96

Smith, Iain Chrichton 1928- DLB-40

Smith, J. Allen 1860-1924 ....DLB-47

Smith, J. Stilman, and Company...................................DLB-49

Smith, John 1580-1631 ....DLB-24, 30

Smith, Josiah 1704-1781 ....DLB-24

Smith, Ken 1938- DLB-40

Smith, Lee 1944- Y-83

Smith, Logan Pearsall 1865-1946....................DLB-98

Smith, Mark 1935- Y-82

Smith, Michael 1698-circa 1771 ....DLB-31

Smith, Red 1905-1982 ....DLB-29

Smith, Roswell 1829-1892 ....DLB-79

Smith, Samuel Harrison 1772-1845....................DLB-43

Smith, Samuel Stanhope 1751-1819 ....DLB-37

Smith, Seba 1792-1868 ....DLB-1, 11

Smith, Stevie 1902-1971 ....DLB-20

Smith, Sydney 1771-1845 ....DLB-107

Smith, Sydney Goodsir 1915-1975....................DLB-27

Smith, W. B., and Company....................DLB-49

Smith, W. H., and Son....................DLB-106

Smith, William 1727-1803 ....DLB-31

Smith, William 1728-1793 ....DLB-30

Smith, William Gardner 1927-1974....................DLB-76

Smith, William Jay 1918- DLB-5

Smithers, Leonard [publishing house]....................DLB-112

Smollett, Tobias 1721-1771 ....DLB-39, 104

Snellings, Rolland (see Touré, Askia Muhammad)

Snodgrass, W. D. 1926- DLB-5

Snow, C. P. 1905-1980....................DLB-15, 77

Snyder, Gary 1930- DLB-5, 16

Sobiloff, Hy 1912-1970....................DLB-48

The Society for Textual Scholarship
    and *TEXT* Y-87

Soffici, Ardengo 1879-1964....................DLB-114

Solano, Solita 1888-1975....................DLB-4

Sollers, Philippe 1936- DLB-83

Solmi, Sergio 1899-1981....................DLB-114

Solomon, Carl 1928- DLB-16

Solway, David 1941- DLB-53

Solzhenitsyn and America....................Y-85

Sontag, Susan 1933- DLB-2, 67

Sorrentino, Gilbert 1929- DLB-5; Y-80

Sorge, Reinhard Johannes 1892-1916 ....DLB-118

Sotheby, William 1757-1833....................DLB-93

Soto, Gary 1952- DLB-82

Sources for the Study of Tudor
    and Stuart Drama....................DLB-62

Souster, Raymond 1921- DLB-88

Southerland, Ellease 1943- DLB-33

Southern, Terry 1924- DLB-2

Southern Writers Between the Wars....................DLB-9

Southerne, Thomas 1659-1746....................DLB-80

Southey, Caroline Anne Bowles 1786-1854....................DLB-116

Southey, Robert 1774-1843....................DLB-93, 107

Spacks, Barry 1931- DLB-105

Spark, Muriel 1918- DLB-15

Sparks, Jared 1789-1866 ....DLB-1, 30

Sparshott, Francis 1926- DLB-60

Späth, Gerold 1939- DLB-75

The Spectator 1828- DLB-110

Spellman, A. B. 1935- DLB-41

Spencer, Anne 1882-1975....................DLB-51, 54

Spencer, Elizabeth 1921- DLB-6

Spencer, Herbert 1820-1903....................DLB-57

Spencer, Scott 1945- Y-86

Spender, J. A. 1862-1942....................DLB-98

Spender, Stephen 1909- DLB-20

Spicer, Jack 1925-1965....................DLB-5, 16

Spielberg, Peter 1929- Y-81

Spier, Peter 1927- DLB-61

Spinrad, Norman 1940- DLB-8

Spofford, Harriet Prescott 1835-1921 ....DLB-74

Squibob (see Derby, George Horatio)

Staël, Germaine de 1766-1817 ....DLB-119

Staël-Holstein, Anne-Louise Germaine de
    (see Staël, Germaine de)

Stafford, Jean 1915-1979....................DLB-2

Stafford, William 1914- DLB-5

Stage Censorship: "The Rejected Statement"
    (1911), by Bernard Shaw [excerpts]....................DLB-10

Stallings, Laurence 1894-1968 ....DLB-7, 44

Stallworthy, Jon 1935- DLB-40

Stampp, Kenneth M. 1912- DLB-17

Stanford, Ann 1916- DLB-5

Stanton, Elizabeth Cady 1815-1902 ....DLB-79

Stanton, Frank L. 1857-1927....................DLB-25

Stapledon, Olaf 1886-1950....................DLB-15

Star Spangled Banner Office DLB-49

Starkweather, David 1935- DLB-7

Statements on the Art of Poetry DLB-54

Stead, Robert J. C. 1880-1959....................DLB-92

Steadman, Mark 1930- DLB-6

The Stealthy School of Criticism (1871), by
Dante Gabriel Rossetti DLB-35

Stearns, Harold E. 1891-1943 ....DLB-4

Stedman, Edmund Clarence 1833-1908 ....DLB-64

Steegmuller, Francis 1906- DLB-111

Steele, Max 1922- Y-80

Steele, Richard 1672-1729.....................DLB-84, 101

Steele, Wilbur Daniel 1886-1970.....................DLB-86

Steere, Richard circa 1643-1721........................DLB-24

Stegner, Wallace 1909- DLB-9

Stehr, Hermann 1864-1940..............................DLB-66

Steig, William 1907- DLB-61

Stein, Gertrude 1874-1946..................DLB-4, 54, 86

Stein, Leo 1872-1947 ....DLB-4

Stein and Day Publishers....................................DLB-46

Steinbeck, John 1902-1968 ....DLB-7, 9; DS-2

Steiner, George 1929- DLB-67

Stendhal 1783-1842 ....DLB-119

Stephen Crane: A Revaluation Virginia
Tech Conference, 1989.....................................Y-89

Stephen, Leslie 1832-1904.................................DLB-57

Stephens, Alexander H. 1812-1883 ....DLB-47

Stephens, Ann 1810-1886 ....DLB-3, 73

Stephens, Charles Asbury 1844?-1931................DLB-42

Stephens, James 1882?-1950 ....DLB-19

Sterling, George 1869-1926.............................DLB-54

Sterling, James 1701-1763 ....DLB-24

Sterling, John 1806-1844 ....DLB-116

Stern, Gerald 1925- DLB-105

Stern, Madeleine B. 1912- DLB-111

Stern, Gerald, Living in Ruin.........................DLB-105

Stern, Richard 1928- Y-87

Stern, Stewart 1922- DLB-26

Sterne, Laurence 1713-1768.............................DLB-39

Sternheim, Carl 1878-1942 ....DLB-56, 118

Stevens, Wallace 1879-1955.............................DLB-54

Stevenson, Anne 1933- DLB-40

Stevenson, Robert Louis 1850-1894 ....DLB-18, 57

Stewart, Donald Ogden 1894-1980..........DLB-4, 11, 26

Stewart, Dugald 1753-1828 ....DLB-31

Stewart, George, Jr. 1848-1906 ....DLB-99

Stewart, George R. 1895-1980...........................DLB-8

Stewart and Kidd Company DLB-46

Stewart, Randall 1896-1964.............................DLB-103

Stickney, Trumbull 1874-1904 ....DLB-54

Stiles, Ezra 1727-1795.....................................DLB-31

Still, James 1906- DLB-9

Stith, William 1707-1755 ....DLB-31

Stock, Elliot [publishing house]......................DLB-106

Stockton, Frank R. 1834-1902 ....DLB-42, 74

Stoddard, Ashbel [publishing house]................DLB-49

Stoddard, Richard Henry 1825-1903 ....DLB-3, 64

Stoddard, Solomon 1643-1729.........................DLB-24

Stoker, Bram 1847-1912.............................DLB-36, 70

Stokes, Frederick A., Company.........................DLB-49

Stokes, Thomas L. 1898-1958 ....DLB-29

Stolberg, Christian Graf zu 1748-1821 ....DLB-94

Stolberg, Friedrich Leopold Graf zu
1750-1819 ....DLB-94

Stone, Herbert S., and Company DLB-49

Stone, Lucy 1818-1893 ....DLB-79

Stone, Melville 1848-1929 ....DLB-25

Stone, Ruth 1915- DLB-105

Stone, Samuel 1602-1663 ....DLB-24

Stone and Kimball DLB-49

Stoppard, Tom 1937- DLB-13; Y-85

Storey, Anthony 1928- DLB-14

Storey, David 1933- DLB-13, 14

Story, Thomas circa 1670-1742........................DLB-31

Story, William Wetmore 1819-1895 ....DLB-1

Storytelling: A Contemporary Renaissance Y-84

Stoughton, William 1631-1701........................DLB-24

Stowe, Harriet Beecher 1811-1896.......DLB-1, 12, 42, 74

Stowe, Leland 1899- DLB-29

Strand, Mark 1934- DLB-5

Strahan and Company......................................DLB-106

Stratemeyer, Edward 1862-1930 ....DLB-42

Stratton and Barnard..DLB-49

Straub, Peter 1943- Y-84

Street, Cecil John Charles (see Rhode, John)

Street and Smith DLB-49

Streeter, Edward 1891-1976..............................DLB-11

Stribling, T. S. 1881-1965.................................DLB-9

Strickland, Samuel 1804-1867...........................DLB-99

Stringer and Townsend DLB-49

Stringer, Arthur 1874-1950.............................DLB-92

Strittmatter, Erwin 1912- DLB-69

Strother, David Hunter 1816-1888....................DLB-3

Strouse, Jean 1945- DLB-111

Stuart, Dabney 1937- DLB-105

Stuart, Dabney, Knots into Webs:
    Some Autobiographical Sources DLB-105

Stuart, Jesse 1906-1984 ....DLB-9, 48, 102; Y-84

Stuart, Lyle [publishing house] DLB-46

Stubbs, Harry Clement (see Clement, Hal)

Studio...DLB-112

The Study of Poetry (1880), by Matthew
    Arnold DLB-35

Sturgeon, Theodore 1918-1985 ....DLB-8; Y-85

Sturges, Preston 1898-1959........................DLB-26

"Style" (1840; revised, 1859), by Thomas
    de Quincey [excerpt] DLB-57

"Style" (1888), by Walter Pater.....................DLB-57

Style (1897), by Walter Raleigh [excerpt] DLB-57

"Style" (1877), by T. H. Wright [excerpt].........DLB-57

"Le Style c'est l'homme" (1892),
    by W. H. Mallock............................DLB-57

Styron, William 1925- DLB-2; Y-80

Suárez, Mario 1925- DLB-82

Such, Peter 1939- DLB-60

Suckling, Sir John 1609-1642 ....DLB-58

Suckow, Ruth 1892-1960.........................DLB-9, 102

Sudermann, Hermann 1857-1928 ....DLB-118

Sue, Eugène 1804-1857 ....DLB-119

Sue, Marie-Joseph (see Sue, Eugène)

Suggs, Simon (see Hooper, Johnson Jones)

Sukenick, Ronald 1932- Y-81

Suknaski, Andrew 1942- DLB-53

Sullivan, Alan 1868-1947...........................DLB-92

Sullivan, C. Gardner 1886-1965 ....DLB-26

Sullivan, Frank 1892-1976.........................DLB-11

Sulte, Benjamin 1841-1923.........................DLB-99

Sulzer, Johann Georg 1720-1779 ....DLB-97

Summers, Hollis 1916- DLB-6

Sumner, Henry A. [publishing house].............DLB-49

Surtees, Robert Smith 1803-1864 ....DLB-21

A Survey of Poetry
    Anthologies, 1879-1960........................DLB-54

Surveys of the Year's Biography
    A Transit of Poets and Others: American
        Biography in 1982.........................Y-82
    The Year in Literary Biography.................Y-83
    The Year in Literary Biography.................Y-84
    The Year in Literary Biography.................Y-85

The Year in Literary Biography.....................Y-86
The Year in Literary Biography.....................Y-87
The Year in Literary Biography.....................Y-88
The Year in Literary Biography...........Y-89, Y-90, Y-91

Surveys of the Year's Book Publishing
    The Year in Book Publishing Y-86

Surveys of the Year's Drama
    The Year in Drama............................Y-82
    The Year in Drama............................Y-83
    The Year in Drama............................Y-84
    The Year in Drama............................Y-85
    The Year in Drama............................Y-87
    The Year in Drama............................Y-88
    The Year in Drama..................Y-89, Y-90, Y-91

Surveys of the Year's Fiction
    The Year's Work in Fiction: A Survey Y-82
    The Year in Fiction: A Biased View Y-83
    The Year in Fiction Y-84
    The Year in Fiction Y-85
    The Year in Fiction Y-86
    The Year in the Novel Y-87
    The Year in Short Stories Y-87
    The Year in the Novel Y-88, Y-90, Y-91
    The Year in Short Stories Y-88, Y-90, Y-91
    The Year in Fiction Y-89

Surveys of the Year's Poetry
    The Year's Work in American Poetry Y-82
    The Year in Poetry............................Y-83
    The Year in Poetry............................Y-84
    The Year in Poetry............................Y-85
    The Year in Poetry............................Y-86
    The Year in Poetry............................Y-87
    The Year in Poetry............................Y-88
    The Year in Poetry............................Y-89

Sutherland, Efua Theodora 1924- DLB-117

Sutherland, John 1919-1956 ....DLB-68

Sutro, Alfred 1863-1933...........................DLB-10

Swados, Harvey 1920-1972 ....DLB-2

Swain, Charles 1801-1874..........................DLB-32

Swallow Press DLB-46

Swan Sonnenschein Limited........................DLB-106

Swanberg, W. A. 1907- DLB-103

Swenson, May 1919-1989...........................DLB-5

Swerling, Jo 1897- DLB-44

Swift, Jonathan 1667-1745 ....DLB-39, 95, 101

Swinburne, A. C. 1837-1909 ....DLB-35, 57

Swineshead, Richard floruit circa 1350 ....DLB-115

Swinnerton, Frank 1884-1982.....................DLB-34

Swisshelm, Jane Grey 1815-1884 ....DLB-43

Swope, Herbert Bayard 1882-1958.................DLB-25

Swords, T. and J., and Company....................DLB-49

Swords, Thomas 1763-1843 and
  Swords, James ?-1844 ....DLB-73

Symonds, John Addington 1840-1893 ....DLB-57

Symons, Arthur 1865-1945 ....DLB-19, 57

Symons, Julian 1912- DLB-87

Symons, Scott 1933- DLB-53

Synge, John Millington 1871-1909 ....DLB-10, 19

T

Taché, Joseph-Charles 1820-1894 ....DLB-99

Tafolla, Carmen 1951- DLB-82

Taggard, Genevieve 1894-1948 ....DLB-45

Tagger, Theodor (see Bruckner, Ferdinand)

Tait, J. Selwin, and Sons DLB-49

Tait's Edinburgh Magazine 1832-1861 ....DLB-110

The Takarazaka Revue Company Y-91

Talvj or Talvi (see Robinson, Therese)

Taradash, Daniel 1913- DLB-44

Tarbell, Ida M. 1857-1944.....................................DLB-47

Tardivel, Jules-Paul 1851-1905.....................................DLB-99

Tarkington, Booth 1869-1946.....................................DLB-9, 102

Tashlin, Frank 1913-1972.....................................DLB-44

Tate, Allen 1899-1979 ....DLB-4, 45, 63

Tate, James 1943- DLB-5

Tate, Nahum circa 1652-1715.....................................DLB-80

Taylor, Bayard 1825-1878 ....DLB-3

Taylor, Bert Leston 1866-1921.....................................DLB-25

Taylor, Charles H. 1846-1921 ....DLB-25

Taylor, Edward circa 1642-1729 ....DLB-24

Taylor, Henry 1942- DLB-5

Taylor, Sir Henry 1800-1886.....................................DLB-32

Taylor, Mildred D. ?- DLB-52

Taylor, Peter 1917- Y-81

Taylor, William, and Company DLB-49

Taylor-Made Shakespeare? Or Is
  "Shall I Die?" the Long-Lost Text
  of Bottom's Dream? Y-85

Teasdale, Sara 1884-1933 ....DLB-45

The Tea-Table (1725), by Eliza Haywood
  [excerpt] DLB-39

Telles, Lygia Fagundes 1924- DLB-113

Temple, Sir William 1628-1699.....................................DLB-101

Tenn, William 1919- DLB-8

Tennant, Emma 1937- DLB-14

Tenney, Tabitha Gilman 1762-1837.....................................DLB-37

Tennyson, Alfred 1809-1892.....................................DLB-32

Tennyson, Frederick 1807-1898.....................................DLB-32

Terhune, Albert Payson 1872-1942 ....DLB-9

Terry, Megan 1932- DLB-7

Terson, Peter 1932- DLB-13

Tesich, Steve 1943- Y-83

Tessa, Delio 1886-1939 ....DLB-114

Tey, Josephine 1896?-1952 ....DLB-77

Thacher, James 1754-1844.....................................DLB-37

Thackeray, William Makepeace
  1811-1863.....................................DLB-21, 55

Thames and Hudson Limited DLB-112

Thanet, Octave (see French, Alice)

The Theater in Shakespeare's Time.....................................DLB-62

The Theatre Guild DLB-7

Thelwall, John 1764-1834 ....DLB-93

Theriault, Yves 1915-1983 ....DLB-88

Thério, Adrien 1925- DLB-53

Theroux, Paul 1941- DLB-2

Thibaudeau, Colleen 1925- DLB-88

Thielen, Benedict 1903-1965 ....DLB-102

Thoma, Ludwig 1867-1921 ....DLB-66

Thoma, Richard 1902- DLB-4

Thomas, Audrey 1935- DLB-60

Thomas, D. M. 1935- DLB-40

Thomas, Dylan 1914-1953 ....DLB-13, 20

Thomas, Edward 1878-1917.....................................DLB-19, 98

Thomas, Gwyn 1913-1981.....................................DLB-15

Thomas, Isaiah 1750-1831.....................................DLB-43, 73

Thomas, Isaiah [publishing house] DLB-49

Thomas, John 1900-1932 ....DLB-4

Thomas, Joyce Carol 1938- DLB-33

Thomas, Lorenzo 1944- DLB-41

Thomas, R. S. 1915- DLB-27

Thompson, David 1770-1857.....................................DLB-99

Thompson, Dorothy 1893-1961 ....DLB-29

Thompson, Francis 1859-1907.....................................DLB-19

Thompson, George Selden (see Selden, George)

Thompson, John 1938-1976.....................................DLB-60

Thompson, John R. 1823-1873.....................................DLB-3, 73

Thompson, Lawrance 1906-1973.....................................DLB-103

Thompson, Maurice 1844-1901 ....DLB-71, 74

Thompson, Ruth Plumly 1891-1976..............................DLB-22

Thompson, Thomas Phillips 1843-1933.....................DLB-99

Thompson, William Tappan 1812-1882..................DLB-3, 11

Thomson, Edward William 1849-1924......................DLB-92

Thomson, James 1700-1748 ....DLB-95

Thomson, James 1834-1882 ....DLB-35

Thomson, Mortimer 1831-1875 ....DLB-11

Thoreau, Henry David 1817-1862................................DLB-1

Thorpe, Thomas Bangs 1815-1878 ....DLB-3, 11

Thoughts on Poetry and Its Varieties (1833),
by John Stuart Mill DLB-32

Thrale, Hester Lynch (see Piozzi,
Hester Lynch [Thrale])

Thümmel, Moritz August von
1738-1817..DLB-97

Thurber, James 1894-1961 ....DLB-4, 11, 22, 102

Thurman, Wallace 1902-1934 ....DLB-51

Thwaite, Anthony 1930- DLB-40

Thwaites, Reuben Gold 1853-1913.............................DLB-47

Ticknor, George 1791-1871 ....DLB-1, 59

Ticknor and Fields DLB-49

Ticknor and Fields (revived) DLB-46

Tieck, Ludwig 1773-1853 ....DLB-90

Tietjens, Eunice 1884-1944 ....DLB-54

Tilt, Charles [publishing house]...............................DLB-106

Tilton, J. E., and Company DLB-49

Time and Western Man (1927), by Wyndham
Lewis [excerpts]...DLB-36

Time-Life Books DLB-46

Times Books...DLB-46

Timothy, Peter circa 1725-1782 ....DLB-43

Timrod, Henry 1828-1867 ....DLB-3

Tinsley Brothers...DLB-106

Tiptree, James, Jr. 1915- DLB-8

Titus, Edward William 1870-1952..............................DLB-4

Toklas, Alice B. 1877-1967 ....DLB-4

Tolkien, J. R. R. 1892-1973..DLB-15

Tollet, Elizabeth 1694-1754 ....DLB-95

Tolson, Melvin B. 1898-1966 ....DLB-48, 76

Tom Jones (1749), by Henry
Fielding [excerpt]..DLB-39

Tomlinson, Charles 1927- DLB-40

Tomlinson, H. M. 1873-1958 ....DLB-36, 100

Tompkins, Abel [publishing house] DLB-49

Tompson, Benjamin 1642-1714 ....DLB-24

Tonks, Rosemary 1932- DLB-14

Toole, John Kennedy 1937-1969..................................Y-81

Toomer, Jean 1894-1967 ....DLB-45, 51

Tor Books..DLB-46

Torberg, Friedrich 1908-1979....................................DLB-85

Torrence, Ridgely 1874-1950 ....DLB-54

Toth, Susan Allen 1940- Y-86

Tough-Guy Literature..DLB-9

Touré, Askia Muhammad 1938- DLB-41

Tourgée, Albion W. 1838-1905..................................DLB-79

Tourneur, Cyril circa 1580-1626................................DLB-58

Tournier, Michel 1924- DLB-83

Tousey, Frank [publishing house] DLB-49

Tower Publications..DLB-46

Towne, Benjamin circa 1740-1793.............................DLB-43

Towne, Robert 1936- DLB-44

Tracy, Honor 1913- DLB-15

Traill, Catharine Parr 1802-1899...............................DLB-99

Train, Arthur 1875-1945..DLB-86

The Transatlantic Publishing Company......................DLB-49

Transcendentalists, American...DS-5

Translators of the Twelfth Century: Literary Issues
Raised and Impact Created................................DLB-115

Traven, B. 1882? or 1890?-1969? DLB-9, 56

Travers, Ben 1886-1980..DLB-10

Trelawny, Edward John 1792-1881 ....DLB-110, 116

Tremain, Rose 1943- DLB-14

Tremblay, Michel 1942- DLB-60

Trends in Twentieth-Century
Mass Market Publishing....................................DLB-46

Trent, William P. 1862-1939 ....DLB-47

Trescot, William Henry 1822-1898............................DLB-30

Trevor, William 1928- DLB-14

Trilling, Lionel 1905-1975....................................DLB-28, 63

Trilussa 1871-1950..DLB-114

Triolet, Elsa 1896-1970..DLB-72

Tripp, John 1927- DLB-40

Trocchi, Alexander 1925- DLB-15

Trollope, Anthony 1815-1882................................DLB-21, 57

Trollope, Frances 1779-1863......................................DLB-21

Troop, Elizabeth 1931- DLB-14

Trotter, Catharine 1679-1749.....................................DLB-84

Trotti, Lamar 1898-1952 ....DLB-44

Trottier, Pierre 1925- DLB-60

Troupe, Quincy Thomas, Jr. 1943- DLB-41

Trow, John F., and Company......................DLB-49

Truillier-Lacombe, Joseph-Patrice
    1807-1863................................DLB-99

Trumbo, Dalton 1905-1976 ....DLB-26

Trumbull, Benjamin 1735-1820 ....DLB-30

Trumbull, John 1750-1831 ....DLB-31

T. S. Eliot Centennial...............................Y-88

Tucholsky, Kurt 1890-1935 ....DLB-56

Tucker, George 1775-1861 ....DLB-3, 30

Tucker, Nathaniel Beverley 1784-1851.........DLB-3

Tucker, St. George 1752-1827..................DLB-37

Tuckerman, Henry Theodore 1813-1871.......DLB-64

Tunis, John R. 1889-1975 ....DLB-22

Tuohy, Frank 1925- DLB-14

Tupper, Martin F. 1810-1889 ....DLB-32

Turbyfill, Mark 1896- DLB-45

Turco, Lewis 1934- Y-84

Turnbull, Andrew 1921-1970...................DLB-103

Turnbull, Gael 1928- DLB-40

Turner, Arlin 1909-1980 ....DLB-103

Turner, Charles (Tennyson) 1808-1879.........DLB-32

Turner, Frederick 1943- DLB-40

Turner, Frederick Jackson 1861-1932 ....DLB-17

Turner, Joseph Addison 1826-1868..............DLB-79

Turpin, Waters Edward 1910-1968..............DLB-51

Twain, Mark (see Clemens, Samuel Langhorne)

The 'Twenties and Berlin,
    by Alex Natan DLB-66

Tyler, Anne 1941- DLB-6; Y-82

Tyler, Moses Coit 1835-1900..................DLB-47, 64

Tyler, Royall 1757-1826.........................DLB-37

Tylor, Edward Burnett 1832-1917 ....DLB-57

U

Udall, Nicholas 1504-1556 ....DLB-62

Uhland, Ludwig 1787-1862.......................DLB-90

Uhse, Bodo 1904-1963 ....DLB-69

Ulibarrí, Sabine R. 1919- DLB-82

Ulica, Jorge 1870-1926 ....DLB-82

Unamuno, Miguel de 1864-1936 ....DLB-108

Under the Microscope (1872), by A. C.
    Swinburne DLB-35

Unger, Friederike Helene 1741-1813 ....DLB-94

Ungaretti, Giuseppe 1888-1970..................DLB-114

United States Book Company DLB-49

Universal Publishing and Distributing
    Corporation..............................DLB-46

The University of Iowa Writers'
    Workshop Golden Jubilee......................Y-86

University of Wales Press.........................DLB-112

"The Unknown Public" (1858), by
    Wilkie Collins [excerpt] DLB-57

Unruh, Fritz von 1885-1970..................DLB-56, 118

Unwin, T. Fisher [publishing house] DLB-106

Upchurch, Boyd B. (see Boyd, John)

Updike, John 1932- DLB-2, 5; Y-80, 82; DS-3

Upton, Charles 1948- DLB-16

Upward, Allen 1863-1926 ....DLB-36

Urista, Alberto Baltazar (see Alurista)

Urzidil, Johannes 1896-1976 ....DLB-85

The Uses of Facsimile Y-90

Uslar Pietri, Arturo 1906- DLB-113

Ustinov, Peter 1921- DLB-13

Uz, Johann Peter 1720-1796 ....DLB-97

V

Vac, Bertrand 1914- DLB-88

Vail, Laurence 1891-1968.........................DLB-4

Vailland, Roger 1907-1965 ....DLB-83

Vajda, Ernest 1887-1954..........................DLB-44

Valente, José Angel 1929- DLB-108

Valenzuela, Luisa 1938- DLB-113

Valgardson, W. D. 1939- DLB-60

Valverde, José María 1926- DLB-108

Van Allsburg, Chris 1949- DLB-61

Van Anda, Carr 1864-1945 ....DLB-25

Vanbrugh, Sir John 1664-1726 ....DLB-80

Vance, Jack 1916?- DLB-8

Van Doren, Mark 1894-1972....................DLB-45

van Druten, John 1901-1957.....................DLB-10

Van Duyn, Mona 1921- DLB-5

Van Dyke, Henry 1852-1933 ....DLB-71

Van Dyke, Henry 1928- DLB-33

Vane, Sutton 1888-1963.........................DLB-10

Vanguard Press DLB-46

van Itallie, Jean-Claude 1936- DLB-7

Vann, Robert L. 1879-1940 ....DLB-29

Van Rensselaer, Mariana Griswold
   1851-1934 ....DLB-47

Van Rensselaer, Mrs. Schuyler (see Van
   Rensselaer, Mariana Griswold)

Van Vechten, Carl 1880-1964 ....DLB-4, 9

van Vogt, A. E. 1912- DLB-8

Varley, John 1947- Y-81

Varnhagen von Ense, Karl August
   1785-1858 ....DLB-90

Varnhagen von Ense, Rahel 1771-1833 ......DLB-90

Vassa, Gustavus (see Equiano, Olaudah)

Vega, Janine Pommy 1942- DLB-16

Veiller, Anthony 1903-1965 ....DLB-44

Venegas, Daniel ?-? DLB-82

Verplanck, Gulian C. 1786-1870 ....DLB-59

Very, Jones 1813-1880 ....DLB-1

Vian, Boris 1920-1959 ....DLB-72

Vickers, Roy 1888?-1965 ....DLB-77

Victoria 1819-1901 ....DLB-55

Victoria Press DLB-106

Vidal, Gore 1925- DLB-6

Viebig, Clara 1860-1952 ....DLB-66

Viereck, George Sylvester 1884-1962 ....DLB-54

Viereck, Peter 1916- DLB-5

Viets, Roger 1738-1811 ....DLB-99

Viewpoint: Politics and Performance, by David
   Edgar DLB-13

Vigneault, Gilles 1928- DLB-60

Vigny, Albert de 1797-1863 ....DLB-119

Vigolo, Giorgio 1894-1983 ....DLB-114

The Viking Press DLB-46

Villanueva, Tino 1941- DLB-82

Villard, Henry 1835-1900 ....DLB-23

Villard, Oswald Garrison 1872-1949 ....DLB-25, 91

Villarreal, José Antonio 1924- DLB-82

Villemaire, Yolande 1949- DLB-60

Villiers, George, Second Duke
   of Buckingham 1628-1687 ....DLB-80

Vine Press DLB-112

Viorst, Judith ?- DLB-52

Vivanco, Luis Felipe 1907-1975 ....DLB-108

Vizetelly and Company DLB-106

Voaden, Herman 1903- DLB-88

Volkoff, Vladimir 1932- DLB-83

Volland, P. F., Company DLB-46

von der Grün, Max 1926- DLB-75

Vonnegut, Kurt 1922- ....DLB-2, 8; Y-80; DS 3

Voß, Johann Heinrich 1751-1826 ....DLB-90

Vroman, Mary Elizabeth circa 1924-1967 ...DLB-33

W

Wackenroder, Wilhelm Heinrich
   1773-1798 ....DLB-90

Waddington, Miriam 1917- DLB-68

Wade, Henry 1887-1969 ....DLB-77

Wagenknecht, Edward 1900- DLB-103

Wagner, Heinrich Leopold 1747-1779 ....DLB-94

Wagoner, David 1926- DLB-5

Wah, Fred 1939- DLB-60

Waiblinger, Wilhelm 1804-1830 ....DLB-90

Wain, John 1925- DLB-15, 27

Wainwright, Jeffrey 1944- DLB-40

Waite, Peirce and Company DLB-49

Wakoski, Diane 1937- DLB-5

Walck, Henry Z. DLB-46

Walcott, Derek 1930- DLB-117; Y-81

Waldman, Anne 1945- DLB-16

Walker, Alice 1944- DLB-6, 33

Walker, George F. 1947- DLB-60

Walker, Joseph A. 1935- DLB-38

Walker, Margaret 1915- DLB-76

Walker, Ted 1934- DLB-40

Walker and Company DLB-49

Walker, Evans and Cogswell Company DLB-49

Walker, John Brisben 1847-1931 ....DLB-79

Wallace, Edgar 1875-1932 ....DLB-70

Wallant, Edward Lewis 1926-1962 ....DLB-2, 28

Walpole, Horace 1717-1797 ....DLB-39, 104

Walpole, Hugh 1884-1941 ....DLB-34

Walrond, Eric 1898-1966 ....DLB-51

Walser, Martin 1927- DLB-75

Walser, Robert 1878-1956 ....DLB-66

Walsh, Ernest 1895-1926 ....DLB-4, 45

Walsh, Robert 1784-1859 ....DLB-59

Wambaugh, Joseph 1937- DLB-6; Y-83

Warburton, William 1698-1779 ....DLB-104

Ward, Aileen 1919- DLB-111

Ward, Artemus (see Browne, Charles Farrar)

Ward, Arthur Henry Sarsfield (see Rohmer, Sax)

Ward, Douglas Turner 1930- DLB-7, 38

Ward, Lynd 1905-1985..............................DLB-22

Ward, Lock and Company DLB-106

Ward, Mrs. Humphry 1851-1920...................DLB-18

Ward, Nathaniel circa 1578-1652..................DLB-24

Ward, Theodore 1902-1983 ....DLB-76

Wardle, Ralph 1909-1988 ....DLB-103

Ware, William 1797-1852 ....DLB-1

Warne, Frederick, and Company [U.S.] DLB-49

Warne, Frederick, and Company [U.K.].........DLB-106

Warner, Charles Dudley 1829-1900..............DLB-64

Warner, Rex 1905- DLB-15

Warner, Susan Bogert 1819-1885.............DLB-3, 42

Warner, Sylvia Townsend 1893-1978................DLB-34

Warner Books DLB-46

Warr, Bertram 1917-1943 ....DLB-88

Warren, John Byrne Leicester (see De Tabley, Lord)

Warren, Lella 1899-1982 ....Y-83

Warren, Mercy Otis 1728-1814 ....DLB-31

Warren, Robert Penn 1905-1989.............DLB-2, 48; Y-80, 89

Warton, Joseph 1722-1800 ....DLB-104, 109

Warton, Thomas 1728-1790................DLB-104, 109

Washington, George 1732-1799 ....DLB-31

Wassermann, Jakob 1873-1934....................DLB-66

Wasson, David Atwood 1823-1887...................DLB-1

Waterhouse, Keith 1929- DLB-13, 15

Waterman, Andrew 1940- DLB-40

Waters, Frank 1902- Y-86

Watkins, Tobias 1780-1855 ....DLB-73

Watkins, Vernon 1906-1967 ....DLB-20

Watmough, David 1926- DLB-53

Watson, James Wreford (see Wreford, James)

Watson, Sheila 1909- DLB-60

Watson, Wilfred 1911- DLB-60

Watt, W. J., and Company...........................DLB-46

Watterson, Henry 1840-1921 ....DLB-25

Watts, Alan 1915-1973................................DLB-16

Watts, Franklin [publishing house] DLB-46

Watts, Isaac 1674-1748 ....DLB-95

Waugh, Auberon 1939- DLB-14

Waugh, Evelyn 1903-1966..............................DLB-15

Way and Williams DLB-49

Wayman, Tom 1945- DLB-53

Weatherly, Tom 1942- DLB-41

Weaver, Robert 1921- DLB-88

Webb, Frank J. ?-?.....................................DLB-50

Webb, James Watson 1802-1884....................DLB-43

Webb, Mary 1881-1927................................DLB-34

Webb, Phyllis 1927- DLB-53

Webb, Walter Prescott 1888-1963...................DLB-17

Webster, Augusta 1837-1894.........................DLB-35

Webster, Charles L., and Company.................DLB-49

Webster, John 1579 or 1580-1634? DLB-58

Webster, Noah 1758-1843.................DLB-1, 37, 42, 43, 73

Wedekind, Frank 1864-1918 ....DLB-118

Weems, Mason Locke 1759-1825 ....DLB-30, 37, 42

Weidenfeld and Nicolson.............................DLB-112

Weidman, Jerome 1913- DLB-28

Weinbaum, Stanley Grauman 1902-1935..........DLB-8

Weintraub, Stanley 1929- DLB-111

Weisenborn, Günther 1902-1969 ....DLB-69

Weiß, Ernst 1882-1940.................................DLB-81

Weiss, John 1818-1879..................................DLB-1

Weiss, Peter 1916-1982 ....DLB-69

Weiss, Theodore 1916- DLB-5

Weisse, Christian Felix 1726-1804 ....DLB-97

Welch, Lew 1926-1971? DLB-16

Weldon, Fay 1931- DLB-14

Wellek, René 1903- DLB-63

Wells, Carolyn 1862-1942 ....DLB-11

Wells, Charles Jeremiah circa 1800-1879.........DLB-32

Wells, H. G. 1866-1946................................DLB-34, 70

Wells, Robert 1947- DLB-40

Wells-Barnett, Ida B. 1862-1931 ....DLB-23

Welty, Eudora 1909- DLB-2, 102; Y-87

Wendell, Barrett 1855-1921 ....DLB-71

Wentworth, Patricia 1878-1961 ....DLB-77

Werfel, Franz 1890-1945 ....DLB-81

The Werner Company..................................DLB-49

Werner, Zacharias 1768-1823 ....DLB-94

Wersba, Barbara 1932- DLB-52

Wescott, Glenway 1901- DLB-4, 9, 102

Wesker, Arnold 1932- DLB-13

Wesley, Charles 1707-1788 ....DLB-95

Wesley, John 1703-1791.................................DLB-104

Wesley, Richard 1945- DLB-38

Wessels, A., and Company................................DLB-46

West, Anthony 1914-1988 ....DLB-15

West, Dorothy 1907- DLB-76

West, Jessamyn 1902-1984.........................DLB-6; Y-84

West, Mae 1892-1980 ....DLB-44

West, Nathanael 1903-1940.....................DLB-4, 9, 28

West, Paul 1930- DLB-14

West, Rebecca 1892-1983 ....DLB-36; Y-83

West and Johnson DLB-49

Western Publishing Company............................DLB-46

The Westminster Review 1824-1914 ....DLB-110

Wetherald, Agnes Ethelwyn 1857-1940 ....DLB-99

Wetherell, Elizabeth (see Warner, Susan Bogert)

Wetzel, Friedrich Gottlob 1779-1819 ....DLB-90

Wezel, Johann Karl 1747-1819........................DLB-94

Whalen, Philip 1923- DLB-16

Whalley, George 1915-1983 ....DLB-88

Wharton, Edith 1862-1937 ....DLB-4, 9, 12, 78

Wharton, William 1920s?- Y-80

What's Really Wrong With Bestseller Lists..........Y-84

Wheatley, Dennis Yates 1897-1977 ....DLB-77

Wheatley, Phillis circa 1754-1784 ....DLB-31, 50

Wheeler, Charles Stearns 1816-1843 ....DLB-1

Wheeler, Monroe 1900-1988 ....DLB-4

Wheelock, John Hall 1886-1978 ....DLB-45

Wheelwright, John circa 1592-1679..................DLB-24

Wheelwright, J. B. 1897-1940 ....DLB-45

Whetstone, Colonel Pete (see Noland, C. F. M.)

Whicher, Stephen E. 1915-1961.......................DLB-111

Whipple, Edwin Percy 1819-1886.................DLB-1, 64

Whitaker, Alexander 1585-1617 ....DLB-24

Whitaker, Daniel K. 1801-1881........................DLB-73

Whitcher, Frances Miriam 1814-1852................DLB-11

White, Andrew 1579-1656................................DLB-24

White, Andrew Dickson 1832-1918 ....DLB-47

White, E. B. 1899-1985 ....DLB-11, 22

White, Edgar B. 1947- DLB-38

White, Ethel Lina 1887-1944............................DLB-77

White, Henry Kirke 1785-1806.........................DLB-96

White, Horace 1834-1916................................DLB-23

White, Phyllis Dorothy James (see James, P. D.)

White, Richard Grant 1821-1885......................DLB-64

White, Walter 1893-1955.................................DLB-51

White, William, and Company...........................DLB-49

White, William Allen 1868-1944....................DLB-9, 25

White, William Anthony Parker (see Boucher, Anthony)

White, William Hale (see Rutherford, Mark)

Whitechurch, Victor L. 1868-1933...................DLB-70

Whitehead, Alfred North 1861-1947..............DLB-100

Whitehead, James 1936- Y-81

Whitehead, William 1715-1785.................DLB-84, 109

Whitfield, James Monroe 1822-1871 ....DLB-50

Whiting, John 1917-1963.................................DLB-13

Whiting, Samuel 1597-1679.............................DLB-24

Whitlock, Brand 1869-1934.............................DLB-12

Whitman, Albert, and Company.......................DLB-46

Whitman, Albery Allson 1851-1901..................DLB-50

Whitman, Alden 1913-1990..............................Y-91

Whitman, Sarah Helen (Power) 1803-1878 ....DLB-1

Whitman, Walt 1819-1892........................DLB-3, 64

Whitman Publishing Company..........................DLB-46

Whittemore, Reed 1919- DLB-5

Whittier, John Greenleaf 1807-1892.................DLB-1

Whittlesey House DLB-46

Wideman, John Edgar 1941- DLB-33

Wiebe, Rudy 1934- DLB-60

Wiechert, Ernst 1887-1950..............................DLB-56

Wied, Martina 1882-1957................................DLB-85

Wieland, Christoph Martin 1733-1813 ....DLB-97

Wieners, John 1934- DLB-16

Wier, Ester 1910- DLB-52

Wiesel, Elie 1928- DLB-83; Y-87

Wiggin, Kate Douglas 1856-1923....................DLB-42

Wigglesworth, Michael 1631-1705 ....DLB-24

Wilbur, Richard 1921- DLB-5

Wild, Peter 1940- DLB-5

Wilde, Oscar 1854-1900....................DLB-10, 19, 34, 57

Wilde, Richard Henry 1789-1847.................DLB-3, 59

Wilde, W. A., Company....................................DLB-49

Wilder, Billy 1906- DLB-26

Wilder, Laura Ingalls 1867-1957 ....DLB-22

Wilder, Thornton 1897-1975...................DLB-4, 7, 9

Wildgans, Anton 1881-1932............................DLB-118

Wiley, Bell Irvin 1906-1980 ....DLB-17

Wiley, John, and Sons...DLB-49

Wilhelm, Kate 1928- DLB-8

Wilkes, George 1817-1885...DLB-79

Wilkinson, Anne 1910-1961...DLB-88

Wilkinson, Sylvia 1940- Y-86

Wilkinson, William Cleaver 1833-1920.........................DLB-71

Willard, L. [publishing house]....................................DLB-49

Willard, Nancy 1936- DLB-5, 52

Willard, Samuel 1640-1707 ....DLB-24

William of Auvergne 1190-1249.................................DLB-115

William of Conches circa 1090-circa 1154...................DLB-115

William of Ockham circa 1285-1347...........................DLB-115

William of Ockham 1200/1205-1266/1271 ....DLB-115

Williams, A., and Company...DLB-49

Williams, Ben Ames 1889-1953 ....DLB-102

Williams, C. K. 1936- DLB-5

Williams, Chancellor 1905- DLB-76

Williams, Charles 1886-1945......................................DLB-100

Williams, Denis 1923- DLB-117

Williams, Emlyn 1905- DLB-10, 77

Williams, Garth 1912- DLB-22

Williams, George Washington 1849-1891.....................DLB-47

Williams, Heathcote 1941- DLB-13

Williams, Hugo 1942- DLB-40

Williams, Isaac 1802-1865 ....DLB-32

Williams, Joan 1928- DLB-6

Williams, John A. 1925- DLB-2, 33

Williams, John E. 1922- DLB-6

Williams, Jonathan 1929- DLB-5

Williams, Miller 1930- DLB-105

Williams, Raymond 1921- DLB-14

Williams, Roger circa 1603-1683................................DLB-24

Williams, Samm-Art 1946- DLB-38

Williams, Sherley Anne 1944- DLB-41

Williams, T. Harry 1909-1979 ....DLB-17

Williams, Tennessee 1911-1983.................DLB-7; Y-83; DS-4

Williams, Valentine 1883-1946....................................DLB-77

Williams, William Appleman 1921- DLB-17

Williams, William Carlos 1883-1963
....DLB-4, 16, 54, 86

Williams, Wirt 1921- DLB-6

Williams Brothers..DLB-49

Williamson, Jack 1908- DLB-8

Willingham, Calder Baynard, Jr. 1922- DLB-2, 44

Willis, Nathaniel Parker 1806-1867..............DLB-3, 59, 73, 74

Wilmer, Clive 1945- DLB-40

Wilson, A. N. 1950- DLB-14

Wilson, Angus 1913-1991..DLB-15

Wilson, Arthur 1595-1652...DLB-58

Wilson, Augusta Jane Evans 1835-1909 ....DLB-42

Wilson, Colin 1931- DLB-14

Wilson, Edmund 1895-1972...DLB-63

Wilson, Ethel 1888-1980...DLB-68

Wilson, Harriet E. Adams 1828?-1863?.......................DLB-50

Wilson, Harry Leon 1867-1939......................................DLB-9

Wilson, John 1588-1667 ....DLB-24

Wilson, John 1785-1854..DLB-110

Wilson, Lanford 1937- DLB-7

Wilson, Margaret 1882-1973 ....DLB-9

Wilson, Michael 1914-1978 ....DLB-44

Wilson, Woodrow 1856-1924.......................................DLB-47

Wimsatt, William K., Jr. 1907-1975.............................DLB-63

Winchell, Walter 1897-1972 ....DLB-29

Winchester, J. [publishing house] DLB-49

Winckelmann, Johann Joachim 1717-1768...................DLB-97

Windham, Donald 1920- DLB-6

Wingate, Allan [publishing house]..............................DLB-112

Winsor, Justin 1831-1897 ....DLB-47

John C. Winston Company...DLB-49

Winters, Yvor 1900-1968...DLB-48

Winthrop, John 1588-1649 ....DLB-24, 30

Winthrop, John, Jr. 1606-1676 ....DLB-24

Wirt, William 1772-1834 ....DLB-37

Wise, John 1652-1725...DLB-24

Wiseman, Adele 1928- DLB-88

Wishart and Company..DLB-112

Wisner, George 1812-1849...DLB-43

Wister, Owen 1860-1938 ....DLB-9, 78

Witherspoon, John 1723-1794 ....DLB-31

Withrow, William Henry 1839-1908.............................DLB-99

Wittig, Monique 1935- DLB-83

Wodehouse, P. G. 1881-1975 ....DLB-34

Wohmann, Gabriele 1932- DLB-75

Woiwode, Larry 1941- DLB-6

Wolcot, John 1738-1819...DLB-109

Wolcott, Roger 1679-1767 ....DLB-24

Wolf, Christa 1929- DLB-75

Wolfe, Gene 1931- DLB-8

Wolfe, Thomas 1900-1938 ....DLB-9, 102; Y-85; DS-2

Wollstonecraft, Mary 1759-1797 ....DLB-39, 104

Wondratschek, Wolf 1943- DLB-75

Wood, Benjamin 1820-1900 ....DLB-23

Wood, Charles 1932- DLB-13

Wood, Mrs. Henry 1814-1887 ....DLB-18

Wood, Joanna E. 1867-1927 ....DLB-92

Wood, Samuel [publishing house] DLB-49

Wood, William ?-? DLB-24

Woodberry, George Edward 1855-1930 ....DLB-71, 103

Woodbridge, Benjamin 1622-1684 ....DLB-24

Woodcock, George 1912- DLB-88

Woodhull, Victoria C. 1838-1927 ....DLB-79

Woodmason, Charles circa 1720-? DLB-31

Woodress, Jr., James Leslie 1916- DLB-111

Woodson, Carter G. 1875-1950 ....DLB-17

Woodward, C. Vann 1908- DLB-17

Woolf, David (see Maddow, Ben)

Woolf, Leonard 1880-1969 ....DLB-100

Woolf, Virginia 1882-1941 ....DLB-36, 100

Woollcott, Alexander 1887-1943 ....DLB-29

Woolman, John 1720-1772 ....DLB-31

Woolner, Thomas 1825-1892 ....DLB-35

Woolsey, Sarah Chauncy 1835-1905 ....DLB-42

Woolson, Constance Fenimore 1840-1894 ....DLB-12, 74

Worcester, Joseph Emerson 1784-1865 ....DLB-1

Wordsworth, Dorothy 1771-1855 ....DLB-107

Wordsworth, Elizabeth 1840-1932 ....DLB-98

Wordsworth, William 1770-1850 ....DLB-93, 107

The Works of the Rev. John Witherspoon
    (1800-1801) [excerpts] DLB-31

A World Chronology of Important Science
    Fiction Works (1818-1979) DLB-8

World Publishing Company DLB-46

Worthington, R., and Company DLB-49

Wouk, Herman 1915- Y-82

Wreford, James 1915- DLB-88

Wright, Charles 1935- Y-82

Wright, Charles Stevenson 1932- DLB-33

Wright, Frances 1795-1852 ....DLB-73

Wright, Harold Bell 1872-1944 ....DLB-9

Wright, James 1927-1980 ....DLB-5

Wright, Jay 1935- DLB-41

Wright, Louis B. 1899-1984 ....DLB-17

Wright, Richard 1908-1960 ....DLB-76, 102; DS-2

Wright, Richard B. 1937- DLB-53

Wright, Sarah Elizabeth 1928- DLB-33

Writers and Politics: 1871-1918,
    by Ronald Gray DLB-66

Writers' Forum Y-85

Writing for the Theatre, by Harold Pinter DLB-13

Wycherley, William 1641-1715 ....DLB-80

Wylie, Elinor 1885-1928 ....DLB-9, 45

Wylie, Philip 1902-1971 ....DLB-9

Y

Yates, Dornford 1885-1960 ....DLB-77

Yates, J. Michael 1938- DLB-60

Yates, Richard 1926- DLB-2; Y-81

Yearsley, Ann 1753-1806 ....DLB-109

Yeats, William Butler 1865-1939 ....DLB-10, 19, 98

Yep, Laurence 1948- DLB-52

Yerby, Frank 1916-1991 ....DLB-76

Yezierska, Anzia 1885-1970 ....DLB-28

Yolen, Jane 1939- DLB-52

Yonge, Charlotte Mary 1823-1901 ....DLB-18

A Yorkshire Tragedy DLB-58

Yoseloff, Thomas [publishing house] DLB-46

Young, Al 1939- DLB-33

Young, Edward 1683-1765 ....DLB-95

Young, Stark 1881-1963 ....DLB-9, 102

Young, Waldeman 1880-1938 ....DLB-26

Young, William [publishing house] DLB-49

Yourcenar, Marguerite 1903-1987 ....DLB-72; Y-88

"You've Never Had It So Good," Gusted by
    "Winds of Change": British Fiction in the
    1950s, 1960s, and After DLB-14

Z

Zachariä, Friedrich Wilhelm 1726-1777 ....DLB-97

Zamora, Bernice 1938- DLB-82

Zand, Herbert 1923-1970 ....DLB-85

Zangwill, Israel 1864-1926 ....DLB-10

Zapata Olivella, Manuel 1920- DLB-113

Zebra Books DLB-46

Zebrowski, George 1945- DLB-8

Zech, Paul 1881-1946.............DLB-56

Zelazny, Roger 1937- DLB-8

Zenger, John Peter 1697-1746 ....DLB-24, 43

Zieber, G. B., and Company DLB-49

Zieroth, Dale 1946- DLB-60

Zimmer, Paul 1934- DLB-5

Zindel, Paul 1936- DLB-7, 52

Zolotow, Charlotte 1915- DLB-52

Zschokke, Heinrich 1771-1848.............DLB-94

Zubly, John Joachim 1724-1781 ....DLB-31

Zu-Bolton II, Ahmos 1936- DLB-41

Zuckmayer, Carl 1896-1977 ....DLB-56

Zukofsky, Louis 1904-1978.............DLB-5

zur Mühlen, Hermynia 1883-1951.............DLB-56

Zweig, Arnold 1887-1968 ....DLB-66

Zweig, Stefan 1881-1942 ....DLB-81, 118

Cumulative Index

ISBN 0-8103-7596-6

(Continued from front endsheets)

80: *Restoration and Eighteenth-Century Dramatists,* First Series, edited by Paula R. Backscheider (1989)

81: *Austrian Fiction Writers, 1875-1913,* edited by James Hardin and Donald G. Daviau (1989)

82: *Chicano Writers,* First Series, edited by Francisco A. Lomelí and Carl R. Shirley (1989)

83: *French Novelists Since 1960,* edited by Catharine Savage Brosman (1989)

84: *Restoration and Eighteenth-Century Dramatists,* Second Series, edited by Paula R. Backscheider (1989)

85: *Austrian Fiction Writers After 1914,* edited by James Hardin and Donald G. Daviau (1989)

86: *American Short-Story Writers, 1910-1945,* First Series, edited by Bobby Ellen Kimbel (1989)

87: *British Mystery and Thriller Writers Since 1940,* First Series, edited by Bernard Benstock and Thomas F. Staley (1989)

88: *Canadian Writers, 1920-1959,* Second Series, edited by W. H. New (1989)

89: *Restoration and Eighteenth-Century Dramatists,* Third Series, edited by Paula R. Backscheider (1989)

90: *German Writers in the Age of Goethe, 1789-1832,* edited by James Hardin and Christoph E. Schweitzer (1989)

91: *American Magazine Journalists, 1900-1960,* First Series, edited by Sam G. Riley (1990)

92: *Canadian Writers, 1890-1920,* edited by W. H. New (1990)

93: *British Romantic Poets, 1789-1832,* First Series, edited by John R. Greenfield (1990)

94: *German Writers in the Age of Goethe: Sturm und Drang to Classicism,* edited by James Hardin and Christoph E. Schweitzer (1990)

95: *Eighteenth-Century British Poets,* First Series, edited by John Sitter (1990)

96: *British Romantic Poets, 1789-1832,* Second Series, edited by John R. Greenfield (1990)

97: *German Writers from the Enlightenment to Sturm und Drang, 1720-1764,* edited by James Hardin and Christoph E. Schweitzer (1990)

98: *Modern British Essayists,* First Series, edited by Robert Beum (1990)

99: *Canadian Writers Before 1890,* edited by W. H. New (1990)

100: *Modern British Essayists,* Second Series, edited by Robert Beum (1990)

101: *British Prose Writers, 1660-1800,* First Series, edited by Donald T. Siebert (1991)

102: *American Short-Story Writers, 1910-1945,* Second Series, edited by Bobby Ellen Kimbel (1991)

103: *American Literary Biographers,* First Series, edited by Steven Serafin (1991)

104: *British Prose Writers, 1660-1800,* Second Series, edited by Donald T. Siebert (1991)

105: *American Poets Since World War II,* Second Series, edited by R. S. Gwynn (1991)

106: *British Literary Publishing Houses, 1820-1880,* edited by Patricia J. Anderson and Jonathan Rose (1991)

107: *British Romantic Prose Writers, 1789-1832,* First Series, edited by John R. Greenfield (1991)

108: *Twentieth-Century Spanish Poets,* First Series, edited by Michael L. Perna (1991)

109: *Eighteenth-Century British Poets,* Second Series, edited by John Sitter (1991)

110: *British Romantic Prose Writers, 1789-1832,* Second Series, edited by John R. Greenfield (1991)

111: *American Literary Biographers,* Second Series, edited by Steven Serafin (1991)

112: *British Literary Publishing Houses, 1881-1965,* edited by Jonathan Rose and Patricia J. Anderson (1991)

113: *Modern Latin-American Fiction Writers,* First Series, edited by William Luis (1992)

114: *Twentieth-Century Italian Poets,* First Series, edited by Giovanna Wedel De Stasio, Glauco Cambon, and Antonio Illiano (1992)

115: *Medieval Philosophers,* edited by Jeremiah Hackett (1992)

116: *British Romantic Novelists, 1789-1832,* edited by Bradford K. Mudge (1992)

117: *Twentieth-Century Caribbean and Black African Writers,* First Series, edited by Bernth Lindfors and Reinhard Sander (1992)